# Privacy
# Volume I

# The International Library of Essays in Law and Legal Theory
*Series Editor: Tom D. Campbell*

## Schools

**Natural Law, Vols I & II**  *John Finnis*
**Justice**  *Thomas Morawetz*
**Law and Economics, Vols I & II**  *Jules Coleman and Jeffrey Lange*
**Critical Legal Studies**  *James Boyle*
**Marxian Legal Theory**  *Csaba Varga*
**Legal Reasoning, Vols I & II**  *Aulis Aarnio and Neil MacCormick*
**Legal Positivism**  *Mario Jori*
**American Legal Theory**  *Robert Summers*

**Law and Language**  *Fred Schauer*
**Sociological Theories of Law**  *Kahei Rokumoto*
**Rights**  *Carlos Nino*
**Law and Psychology**  *Martin Levine*
**Feminist Legal Theory, Vols I & II**  *Frances Olsen*
**Law and Society**  *Werner Krawietz*
**Contemporary Criminological Theory**  *Francis Cullen and Velmer Burton*

## Areas

**Criminal Law**  *Thomas Morawetz*
**Tort Law**  *Ernest Weinrib*
**Contract Law, Vols I & II**  *Larry Alexander*
**Anti-Discrimination Law**  *Christopher McCrudden*
**Consumer Law**  *Iain Ramsay*
**International Law**  *Martti Koskenniemi*
**Property Law, Vols I & II**  *Elizabeth Mensch and Alan Freeman*
**Constitutional Law**  *Mark Tushnet*
**Procedure**  *Denis Galligan*
**Evidence and Proof**  *William Twining and Alex Stein*
**Company Law**  *Sally Wheeler*
**Privacy, Vols I & II**  *Raymond Wacks*

**Administrative Law**  *Denis Galligan*
**Child Law**  *Harry Krause*
**Family Law, Vols I & II**  *Harry Krause*
**Welfare Law**  *Peter Robson*
**Medicine and the Law**  *Bernard Dickens*
**Commercial Law**  *Ross Cranston*
**Environmental Law**  *Michael Blumm*
**Conflict of Laws**  *Richard Fentiman*
**Law and Religion**  *Wojciech Sadurski*
**Human Rights Law**  *Philip Alston*
**European Community Law, Vols I & II**  *Francis Snyder*
**Tax Law, Vols I & II**  *Patricia White*
**Media Law**  *Eric Barendt*

## Legal Cultures

**Comparative Legal Cultures**  *Csaba Varga*
**Law and Anthropology**  *Peter Sack*
**Hindu Law and Legal Theory**  *Ved Nanda*
**Islamic Law and Legal Theory**  *Ian Edge*
**Chinese Law and Legal Theory**  *Michael Palmer*
**Socialist Law**  *W. Butler*

**Japanese Law and Legal Theory**  *Koichiro Fujikura*
**Law and Development**  *Anthony Carty*
**Jewish Law and Legal Theory**  *Martin Golding*
**Legal Education**  *Martin Levine*
**Civil Law**  *Ralf Rogowski*

## Future Volumes

Labour Law, African Law and Legal Theory, Postmodernism and Law, Law and History, Law and Ethics and Cumulative index.

# Privacy
# Volume I
The Concept of 'Privacy'

*Edited by*

# Raymond Wacks

*University of Hong Kong*

# Dartmouth
**Aldershot · Hong Kong · Singapore · Sydney**

Published by
Dartmouth Publishing Company Limited
Gower House
Croft Road
Aldershot
Hants GU11 3HR
England

**British Library Cataloguing in Publication Data**
Privacy. – (International Library of Essays in Law & Legal Theory)
 I. Wacks, Raymond  II. Series
  347.302858

ISBN 1 85521 315 X

Printed in Great Britain by Galliard (Printers) Ltd, Great Yarmouth

# Contents

## PART III  THE ECONOMICS OF 'PRIVACY'

# Acknowledgements

The editor and publishers wish to thank the following for permission to use copyright material.

Georgia Law Review for essays: Edward J. Bloustein (1978), 'Privacy Is Dear at Any Price: A Response to Professor Posner's Economic Theory', *Georgia Law Review*, **12**, pp. 429–53, and Richard A. Posner (1978), 'The Right of Privacy', *Georgia Law Review*, **12**, pp. 393–422.

Harvard Civil Rights – Civil Liberties Law Review for the essay: Tom Gerety (1977), 'Redefining Privacy', *Harvard Civil Rights – Civil Liberties Law Review*, **12**, pp. 233–96. Permission granted by the Harvard Civil Rights – Civil Liberties Law Review. Copyright © 1977 by the President and Fellows of Harvard College.

Kluwer Academic Publishers for essays: W.A. Parent (1983), 'A New Definition of Privacy for the Law', *Law and Philosophy*, **2**, pp. 305–38, and Judith Wagner DeCew (1986), 'The Scope of Privacy in Law and Ethics', *Law and Philosophy*, **5**, pp. 145–73. Reprinted by permission of Kluwer Academic Publishers.

H.J. McCloskey (1971), 'The Political Ideal of Privacy', *Philosophical Quarterly*, **21**, pp. 303–14. Copyright © H.J. McCloskey.

New York University Law Review for the essay: Hyman Gross (1967), 'The Concept of Privacy', *New York University Law Review*, **42**, pp. 34–54.

Robert C. Post (1989), 'The Social Foundations of Privacy: Community and Self in the Common Law Tort', *California Law Review*, **77**, pp. 957–1010. Copyright © Robert C. Post.

Princeton University Press for the essay: Judith Jarvis Thomson (1975), 'The Right to Privacy', *Philosophy & Public Affairs*, **4**, pp. 295–314. Copyright © 1975 by Princeton University Press. Reprinted by permission of Princeton University Press.

Sweet & Maxwell Limited for the essay: Raymond Wacks (1980), 'The Poverty of "Privacy"', *The Law Quarterly Review*, **96**, pp. 73–89.

University of Chicago Press for essays: Jack Hirshleifer (1980), 'Privacy: Its Origin, Function and Future', *The Journal of Legal Studies*, **9**, pp. 649–64, and Richard A. Epstein (1980), 'A Taste for Privacy? Evolution and the Emergence of a Naturalistic Ethic', *The Journal of Legal Studies*, **9**, pp. 665–81. Copyright © The University of Chicago Press.

# Series Preface

The International Library of Law and Legal Theory is designed to provide important research materials in an accessible form. Each volume contains essays of central theoretical importance in its subject area. The series as a whole makes available an extensive range of valuable material which will be of considerable interest to those involved in the research, teaching and study of law.

The series has been divided into three sections. The Schools section is intended to represent the main distinctive approaches and topics of special concern to groups of scholars. The Areas section takes in the main branches of law with an emphasis on essays which present analytical and theoretical insights of broad application. The section on Legal Cultures makes available the distinctive legal theories of different legal traditions and takes up topics of general comparative and developmental concern.

I have been delighted and impressed by the way in which the editors of the individual volumes have set about the difficult task of selecting, ordering and presenting essays from the immense quantity of academic legal writing published in journals throughout the world. Editors were asked to pick out those essays from law, philosophy and social science journals which they consider to be fundamental for the understanding of law, as seen from the perspective of a particular approach or sphere of legal interest. This is not an easy task and many difficult decisions have had to be made in order to ensure that a representative sample of the best journal essays available takes account of the scope of each topic or school.

I should like to express my thanks to all the volume editors for their willing participation and scholarly judgement. The interest and enthusiasm which the project has generated is well illustrated by the fact that an original projection of 12 volumes drawn up in 1989 has now become a list of some 60 volumes. I must also acknowledge the vision, persistence and constant cheerfulness of John Irwin of the Dartmouth Publishing Company and the marvellous work done in the Dartmouth office by Mrs Margaret O'Reilly and Sonia Hubbard.

TOM D. CAMPBELL
Series Editor
*The Faculty of Law*
*The Australian National University*

# Introduction

The discourse on 'privacy' is anything but coherent, though it is perhaps tendentious for one who has long regarded this development with unease so to characterize it.[1] Yet while it is undeniable that, at least in legal terms, 'privacy' has 'come a long way'[2] since its original formulation by Warren and Brandeis[3] as a right against embarrassing publicity, some may want to repudiate my position that the voluminous literature on the subject has failed to produce a lucid or consistent meaning of a concept which, particularly in the United States, continues to provide a forum for contesting, *inter alia*, the rights of women[4] (especially in respect of abortion),[5] the use of contraceptives,[6] the freedom of homosexuals and lesbians,[7] the right to obscene or pornographic publications,[8] and the problems generated by AIDS.[9] An important consequence of this harnessing of 'privacy' in the pursuit of so many disparate, sometimes competing, political ideals has been inevitable analytical turmoil.

The essays in Volume I represent, at least in my view, some of the best attempts to elucidate the concept of 'privacy', though they proceed from several different standpoints. I shall suggest a means by which some of this conceptual confusion might be avoided. In Volume II the principal features of the remarkable legal evolution of the 'right of privacy' in both constitutional and tort law are traced.

## The Concept of 'Privacy'

The concern to protect 'privacy' in its broadest, and least lucid, sense is founded upon a conception of the individual and his or her relationship with society. The idea of private and public spheres of activity assumes a community in which such a classification is possible, though this positive conception of 'privacy' is a modern one which grew out of a twin movement in political and legal thought. The emergence of the nation-state and theories of sovereignty in the 16th and 17th centuries produced the idea of a distinctly public realm.[10] On the other hand, a delineation of a private sphere free from the encroachment of the state emerged as a response to the claims of monarchs (and subsequently of parliaments) to untrammelled power to make law.[11] Thus the development of the modern state, the regulation of social and economic behaviour, the perception of a 'private' zone and so on are natural prerequisites to this form of demarcation.[12] But while there is ample historical evidence for this phenonomenon, it is best captured by sociological models in which it is shown to be expressive of the values of certain forms of society. In other words, there is an apparent relationship between the existence of a public/private dichotomy and other fundamental features of a society. One such model is the distinctive representation of societies as exhibiting the characteristics of *Gemeinschaft* (in which, broadly speaking, there is a community of internalized norms and traditions regulated according to status but mediated by love, duty and a shared understanding and purpose). Another is *Gesellschaft* (where self-interested individuals compete for personal material advantage in a so-called free market).[13]

The division between a public and private sphere is a central tenet of liberalism. Indeed, 'liberalism may be said largely to have been an argument about where the boundaries of [the] private sphere lie, according to what principles they are to be drawn, whence interference derives and how it is to be checked'.[14] The extent to which the law might legitimately intrude upon the 'private' is a recurring theme, especially in 19th-century liberal doctrine: 'One of the central goals of nineteenth century legal thought was to create a clear separation between constitutional, criminal and regulatory law – public law – and the law of private transactions – torts, contracts, property and commercial law.'[15] The question of the limits of the criminal law in enforcing 'private morality' also continues to vex legal and moral philosophers.[16]

## Problems of Definition

While the drawing of the public/private boundary is logically anterior to any conception of the role of law, it is also constituted by law. This circularity is compounded by the fact that non-legal regulation of what is apparently 'private' may exercise significant controls over such behaviour. Moreover, it would be misleading to assume that, even in liberal thought, there is a consistent or definitive boundary between what is 'private' and what is 'public'. A vast literature devoted to the resolution of these difficulties inevitably raises complex methodological and epistemological questions which frequently obscure rather than illuminate. Without suggesting that sociological and philosophical enquiries of this kind be neglected, I suggest that a more constructive means of resolving some of the problems encountered in regulating the collection, storage and use of private facts about an individual might be found by seeking to identify what *specific interests* of the individual we think the law ought to protect. At the core of the preoccupation with the 'right to privacy' is protection against the misuse of personal, sensitive information.

This is not to deny the importance of rights or even their formulation in broad terms which facilitate their recognition by the common law; however, as one American commentator has recently acknowledged, 'a natural "right" to privacy is simply inconceivable as a legal right – sanctioned perhaps by society but clearly not enforceable by government ... Privacy itself is beyond the scope of law.'[17] By attempting to address the problem of 'privacy' as the protection of 'personal information', the pervasive difficulties that are generally (and, I believe, mistakenly) forced into the straitjacket of 'privacy' might find a less artificial and more effective legal resolution. The concept of 'privacy' has become too vague and unwieldy a concept to perform useful analytical work.[18] It has grown into as nebulous a notion as 'freedom' (with which it is not infrequently equated) or 'autonomy' (with which it is often confused).[19] This ambiguity has actually undermined the importance of the value of 'privacy' and impeded its effective legal protection.

An acceptable definition of 'privacy' remains elusive.[20] Thus, one particularly ubiquitous and influential conception (especially in the legal literature) conceives of 'privacy' as a *claim*: the 'claim of individuals, groups, or institutions to determine for themselves when, how, and to what extent information about them is communicated to others'.[21] To regard 'privacy' as a claim (or, *a fortiori*, a right) not only presumes the value of 'privacy', but fails to define its content[22] and is well described as a kind of 'logical synecdoche'[23] for it is defining the part by the whole. It would, moreover, include the use or disclosure of *any* information about an individual. A similar criticism may be levelled at those conceptions of 'privacy' as an 'area of life' or a psychological state.

Westin's definition has, however, exerted even greater influence in respect of its description of 'privacy' in terms of the extent to which an individual has *control* over information about himself or herself.[24] For control over information to be co-extensive with 'privacy', an individual would have to be said to have lost 'privacy' if he or she is prevented from exercising this control, even if he or she is *unable* to disclose personal information. This suggests a pre-emptive view of 'privacy'[25] by which its value is assumed. Similarly, if I knowingly and voluntarily disclose personal information, I do not thereby lose 'privacy' because I am exercising (rather than relinquishing) control. But this sense of control does not adequately describe 'privacy', for although I may have control over whether to disclose the information, it may be obtained by other means. And if control is meant in a stronger sense (namely that to disclose information, even voluntarily, constitutes a loss of control because I am no longer able to curtail the dissemination of the information by others), it describes the *potential* rather than the *actual* loss of 'privacy'. Hence, I may not attract any interest from others and therefore I will be accorded 'privacy' whether I want it or not. There is a distinction between my controlling the flow of information about myself and my being known about in fact. In order to establish whether such control actually protects my 'privacy', according to this argument, it is also necessary to know, for instance, whether the recipient of the information is bound by restrictive norms. Furthermore, if 'privacy' is regarded as an aspect of control (or autonomy), it is assumed that what is at issue is my freedom to choose 'privacy'. But, as suggested above, I may choose to *abandon* my 'privacy'; the control-based definition therefore relates to the question of *which* choices I exercise rather than the *manner* in which I exercise them. It is, in other words, a definition which *assumes* the value of 'privacy'.

## The Features of 'Privacy'

As will be apparent from the readings in both Volumes I and II, considerable disagreement and confusion exist in respect of the features of 'privacy'. Thus, Gavison,[26] for example, conceives of 'privacy' as 'limited accessibility' – a cluster of three related but independent components:

(a)  *secrecy*: information known about an individual;
(b)  *anonymity*: attention paid to an individual;
(c)  *solitude*: physical access to an individual.

A loss of 'privacy' (as distinct from an infringement of a 'right' of 'privacy') occurs, in this account, where others obtain information about an individual, pay attention to him or her, or gain access to him or her. The claimed virtues of this approach are, first, that it is neutral, facilitating an objective identification of a loss of 'privacy'; secondly, it demonstrates the coherence of 'privacy' as a value; thirdly, it suggests the utility of the concept in legal contexts (for it identifies those occasions calling for legal protection); fourthly, it includes 'typical' invasions of 'privacy' and excludes those issues mentioned above which, though often thought to be 'privacy' questions, are best regarded as moral or legal issues in their own right (noise, odours, prohibition of abortion, contraception, homosexuality, and so on).

Yet even this analysis presents certain difficulties. In particular, in her effort to define 'privacy' in such a way as to avoid pre-empting questions as to its desirability, Gavison is driven to rejecting definitions which limit themselves to the *quality* of the information divulged. She therefore dismisses the view that, to constitute a part of 'privacy', the information concerned must be 'private' in the sense of being intimate or related to the individual's identity. If a loss of 'privacy' occurs whenever *any* information about an individual becomes known (the secrecy component), the concept loses its intuitive meaning.

It would appear to be a distortion to describe *every* instance of the dissemination of information about an individual as a loss of 'privacy', yet the requirement of a value-free definition of 'privacy' dictates that to confine the ambit of 'privacy'-invading conduct to the transfer or communication of *'private'* information is to invoke a value judgment in respect of the desirability of 'privacy'. To the extent, however, that 'privacy' is a function of information or knowledge about the individual, this seems to be inevitable. In other words, in so far as the question of information about an individual is concerned, a limiting or controlling factor is required; it is submitted that the most acceptable limiting factor is that the information be 'personal'. To claim that whenever an individual is the subject of attention or when access to him is gained he necessarily loses 'privacy' is again to divest our concern for 'privacy' of much of its intuitive meaning. Having attention focused upon us or being subjected to uninvited intrusions upon our solitude are objectionable in their own right, but our concern for the individual's 'privacy' in these circumstances is strongest when he or she is engaged in activities which we would normally consider 'private'. The Peeping Tom is more likely to affront our conception of what is 'private' than someone who follows an individual in public.

## The Coherence of 'Privacy'

Apart from its utility or application as a *legal* concept (see Volume II), the coherence of the very idea of 'privacy' is suspect. This is evident in two respects. First, it is sometimes argued that by protecting the values underpinning 'privacy' (property rights, human dignity, preventing or compensating the infliction of emotional distress, etc.), moral and legal discourse concerning 'privacy' may be dispensed with. This essentially reductionist argument obviously has its major purchase in relation to the need for the *legal* protection of 'privacy'. But if it can be demonstrated that the concept is largely parasitic, that its protection may be secured by safeguarding other (primary) interests, its conceptual distinctiveness is thrown into considerable doubt. Secondly, even among those who deny the parasitical character of 'privacy', there is little agreement concerning its principal defining features. Again, these concerns are especially important in the context of arguments concerning the *legal* protection of 'privacy'. But it is clear that unless a concept is sufficiently distinctive to facilitate coherent analytical identification and description, the prospects for its satisfactory legal recognition and application are bound to be poor.

Such problems are not, of course, peculiar to the notion of 'privacy'. 'Freedom', 'security', 'liberty' and other values are, to a greater or lesser extent, vulnerable to similar criticism. But unless it is to be argued that subscribing to generalized values exhibits our commitment to them, it seems perverse not to attempt to refine the nature and scope of the problem, especially if this might actually engender more effective protection.

## 'Privacy' as the Protection of 'Personal Information'

Without undermining the significance of 'privacy' as a value, a less problematic and more direct method of attempting to resolve the difficulties associated with its protection is to isolate the essential issues that give rise to such claims. Indeed, in view of the confusion that generally afflicts discussions of the concept, there is an overwhelming case for seeking to liberate the subject from the presumptive force of its value-laden starting-point concerning the desirability of 'privacy'. If it is replied that it is possible to arrive at a *neutral* definition of 'privacy', it must be said that such attempts inevitably strip the concept of much of its intuitive meaning and explanatory power. Thus to conceive of 'privacy' as 'limited accessibility' avoids loading the concept with a positive value, but it also results in *any* loss of solitude by or information about an individual having to be counted as a loss of 'privacy'.

There are, moreover, a number of associated problems that might be obviated by adopting the alternative approach proposed here. In particular, three specific analytical difficulties might be briefly mentioned. First, arguments about the meaning of 'privacy' frequently proceed from fundamentally different premises. Thus, for instance, where 'privacy' is described as a 'right'[27] issue is not seriously joined with those who conceive it to be a 'condition'.[28] The former is usually a normative statement about the need for 'privacy' (however defined); the latter merely makes a descriptive statement about 'privacy'.

Secondly, claims about the desirability of 'privacy' confuse its instrumental and inherent value; 'privacy' is regarded by some as an end in itself,[29] while others view it as instrumental in the securing of other social ends such as creativity,[30] love[31] or emotional release.[32] Thirdly, there is, among discussions of 'privacy', a confusion between descriptive accounts especially of the law[33] on the one hand, and normative accounts on the other. A considerable effort has been made in an ultimately futile attempt to reconcile these two fundamentally antagonistic perspectives.

There is little doubt that originally the 'archetypal' complaints in the 'privacy' field related to what, in legal terms, have come to be described as 'public disclosure of private facts' and 'intrusion upon an individual's seclusion, solitude or private affairs'. (These categories are considered in Volume II.) More recently the subject of the collection and use of computerized personal data has become an important aspect of the discussions of 'privacy'.[34] It is clear that, at bottom, these three questions share a concern to limit the extent to which 'private facts' about the individual are respectively published, intruded upon or misused. My own view is therefore that a more rational, direct and effective method of seeking to address the central questions of 'privacy' is to avoid the conceptual labyrinth that has so far impaired their satisfactory resolution. This is not to suggest that certain conditions (for instance, being alone) or certain activities (such as telephone-tapping) ought not to be characterized as 'privacy' or 'invasions of privacy' respectively. But, except to describe the underlying value, the term 'privacy' ought to be resisted – especially as a legal term of art. It adds little to our understanding either of the interest that it seeks to protect or of the conduct that it is designed to regulate. But, more importantly, eschewing the concept facilitates a clearer analysis of the problems and their possible solution.

In locating the problems of privacy at the level of personal information, two obvious questions arise. First, what is to be understood by 'personal' and, secondly, under what circumstances is a matter to be regarded as 'personal'? Is something 'personal' by virtue simply of the claim by an individual that it is so, or are certain matters *intrinsically* personal? The assertion, in other words, that something is 'personal' may be norm-dependent or norm-invoking. To claim that my political views are personal must depend on certain norms which prohibit or curtail inquiries into, or unauthorized reports of, such views. It may, however, suffice for me to invoke the norm that I am entitled to keep my views to myself.

These norms are clearly culture-relative as well as changing. Anthropological evidence suggests that primitive societies have differential 'privacy' attitudes. And it can hardly be doubted that in modern societies, conceptions of what is 'private' will differ and change. There is certainly less diffidence in most modern communities with regard to several aspects of private life than characterized societies of even 50 years ago. Is there not a class of information that may plausibly be described as 'personal'? Normally it is objected that 'privateness' is *not* an attribute of the information itself; that the *same* information may be regarded as very private in one context and not so private or not private at all in another. Naturally X may be more inclined to divulge intimate facts to his psychiatrist or to a close friend than to his employer or his wife. And his objection to the disclosure of the information by a newspaper might be expected to be even stronger. But the information remains 'personal' in all three contexts. What changes is the extent to which he is prepared to permit the information to become known or to be used. It is counter-intuitive to describe the information in the first context (the psychiatrist) as 'not private at all' or even 'not so private'. We should surely want to say that the psychiatrist is listening to *personal* facts being discussed. Were the conversation to be surreptitiously recorded or the psychiatrist called upon to testify in court as to his patient's homosexuality or infidelity, we should want to say that *personal information* was being recorded or disclosed. The context has manifestly changed, but it affects the degree to which it would be reasonable to expect the individual to object to the information being used or spread abroad, not the *quality* of the information itself.

Any definition of 'personal information' must therefore include *both* elements. It should refer both to the *quality* of the information and to the *reasonable expectations of the individual concerning its use*. The one is, in large part, a function of the other. In other words, the concept of 'personal information' postulated here functions both descriptively as well as normatively. Since 'personal' relates to social norms, to so describe something implies that it satisfies certain of the conditions specified in the norms, without which the normative implications would have no validity. Thus if a letter is marked 'personal' or if its contents clearly indicate that it is personal, the implication is that it satisfies one or more of the conditions necessary for its being conceived as 'personal'; this is a descriptive account.

'Personal information' includes those facts, communications or opinions which relate to the individual and which it would be reasonable to expect him to regard as intimate or sensitive and therefore to want to withhold, or at least to restrict their collection, use or circulation. It might immediately be objected that, by resting the notion of 'personal information' on an *objective* determination of an individual's expectations, the definition is actually an exclusively normative one and therefore pre-empts enquiries concerning the desirability or otherwise of protecting 'personal information'. But any attempt to classify information as 'personal', 'sensitive' or 'intimate' proceeds on the assumption that such information warrants special treatment. To the extent that it is necessary to define the information by reference to some objective criterion (since a subjective test would clearly be unacceptable), it is inevitable that the classification depends on what may legitimately be claimed to be 'personal'. Only information which it is reasonable to wish to withhold is likely, under any test, to be the focus of our concern. An individual who regards information concerning say, his car, as personal and therefore seeks to withhold details of the size of its engine will find it difficult to convince anyone that his vehicle's registration document constitutes a disclosure of 'personal information'. An objective test of what is 'personal' will operate to exclude such species of information.

But this becomes more difficult where the individual's claim relates to information which affects his 'private life'. It would not be unreasonable, for instance, for an individual to wish to prevent the disclosure of facts concerning his trial and conviction for theft. Applying the proposed definition of 'personal information' as a first-order test of whether such information is 'personal' may suggest that the claim is a legitimate one. But such a claim is likely to be defeated on the ground that the administration of justice is an open and public process. The passage of time may, however, alter the nature of such events and what was once a *public* matter may, several years later, be reasonably considered as private.

Similarly, the publication of what was once 'public' information garnered from old newspapers may several years later be considered an offensive disclosure of personal information. It does not therefore follow that the objective test pre-empts the 'balancing' of the individual's right or claim to withhold 'personal information' on the one hand, and the competing interests of the community in, say, freedom of expression on the other. By voluntarily disclosing or acceding to the use or dissemination of personal information, the individual does not relinquish his claim that he retain certain control over it. He may, for instance, allow the information to be used for one purpose (such as medical diagnosis), but object when it is used for another (such as employment). With regard to opinions about an individual expressed by a third party, the existence of which the individual is *aware* (such as references sought by him for a job application), it would be reasonable to expect him to permit access to such material only by those who are directly concerned in the decision whether or not to employ him. Where he does *not* know that assessments have been made about him (where, for example, he is described as a 'bad risk' on the computerized files of a credit reference agency) or that his communications have been intercepted or recorded, he may reasonably be expected to object to the use or disclosure (and in the case of surreptitious surveillance, to the actual acquisition) of the information, particularly if it is (actually or potentially) misleading or inaccurate *were he aware* of its existence. There is naturally a whole range of 'items' of 'personal information' the use or disclosure of which one might expect individuals to wish to resist. A complete catalogue of such information would be impossible (and probably pointless).

In seeking to withhold or limit the circulation of 'personal information', is the individual not engaged in a form of deception, especially where the information depicts him in an unfavourable light? This is the burden of Posner's application of his 'economic analysis of law' to the subject of personal information.[35] As he asserts, 'To the extent that people conceal personal information in order to mislead, the economic case for according legal protection to such information is no better than that for permitting fraud in the sale of goods.'[36]

But even if one were to accept the 'economic' perspective, it does not follow that one would accept the assessment of the economic 'value' of withholding personal information; individuals may be willing to trade off their interest in restricting the circulation of such information against their 'societal' interest in its free flow. In other words Posner has not shown, and may be unable to show, that his calculation of 'competing' interests is necessarily the correct, or even the most likely, one. This analysis cannot be pursued here, but it is worth noting that Posner's claim that his economic theory 'explains' the operation of law produces a certain dissonance if one compares the protection of 'privacy' in the US with that prevailing in England.

Posner also argues that transaction-cost considerations may militate against the legal protection of personal information. Where the information is discrediting and accurate, there is a social incentive to make it generally available: accurate information facilitates reliance on the individual to whom the information relates. It is therefore socially efficient to allow a society a right of access to such information rather than to permit the individual to conceal it. In the case of nondiscrediting or false information, the value to the individual of concealment exceeds the value of access to it by the community. Information which is false does not advance rational decision-making and is therefore of little use.

## Notes

1. See R. Wacks (1989), *Personal Information: Privacy and the Law*, Oxford: Clarendon Press, upon which I have drawn extensively here; R. Wacks (1980), *The Protection of Privacy*, London: Sweet & Maxwell; 'The Right to Privacy' in R. Wacks (ed.) (1992), *Human Rights in Hong Kong*, Hong Kong: Oxford University Press. Also see Chapter 7 in this volume.
2. The present Chief Justice of the US Supreme Court acknowledged this almost two decades ago: see W. Rhenquist (1974), 'Is an Expanded Right of Privacy Consistent with Fair and Consistent Law Enforcement? Or Privacy, You've Come a Long Way, Baby', *Kansas Law Review*, **23**, 1.
3. S.D. Warren and L.D. Brandeis (1890), 'The Right to Privacy', *Harvard Law Review*, **4**, 193. For recent examinations of the development of their (fairly limited) tort, see R.C. Post (1991), 'Rereading Warren and Brandeis: Privacy, Property, and Appropriation', *Case Western Reserve Law Review*, **41**, 647; S.W. Halpern (1990), 'The "Inviolate Personality" – Warren and Brandeis After One Hundred Years', *Northern Illinois University Law Review*, **10**, 387.
4. See M.A. Fineman (1991), 'Intimacy Outside of the Natural Family', *Connecticut Law Review*, **23**, 955; E.M. Schneider (1991), 'The Violence of Privacy', *Connecticut Law Review*, **23**, 973; A.L. Allen and E. Mack (1990), 'How Privacy Got Its Gender', *Northern Illinois University Law Review*, **10**, 441. See generally, C. Mackinnon (1989), *Towards a Feminist Theory of the State*.
5. The Supreme Court's recent decision in *Planned Parenthood v. Casey* 112 S.Ct. 2791 (1992) to affirm its judgment in *Roe v. Wade* 410 US 113 (1973) plainly reflects a fundamental division in American society on the question of abortion. Justice Scalia's scathing assault on the majority judgment bears ample testimony to the strength of feelings on the issue. See Ely (1973; Chapter 6 of Volume II); R.G. Morgan (1979), '*Roe v. Wade* and the Lesson of the *Pre-Roe* Case Law; *Michigan Law Review*, **77**, 1724; T. Huff (1980), 'Thinking Clearly about Privacy', *Washington Law Review*, **55**, 777.
6. Following the Supreme Court's decision in *Griswold v. Connecticut* 381 US 479 (1965). See S.J. Schnably (1991), 'Beyond Griswold: Foucauldian and Republican Approaches to Privacy', *Connecticut Law Review*, **23**, 861.
7. The Supreme Court's decision in *Bowers v. Hardwick* 468 US 186 (1986) generated considerable criticism. For a vigorous attack on the majority's reasoning in this case and in *Thornburgh v. American College of Obstetricians and Gynecologists* (invalidating certain provisions relating to abortion on the ground that they burdened the constitutional right of privacy) see D.A.J. Richards (1986), 'Constitutional Legitimacy and Constitutional Privacy', *New York University Law Review*, **61**, 800; A.T. Sheppard (1988), 'Private Passion, Public Outrage: Thoughts on *Bowers v. Hardwick*', *Rutgers Law Journal*, **40**, 521. See too K. Thomas (1992), 'Beyond Privacy', *Columbia*

Law Review, 1431, and Sheppard (1988; Chapter 7 of Volume II). Michelman (1988; Chapter 8 of Volume II) develops a 'republican, anti-authoritarian' case and Rubenfeld (1989; Chapter 9 of Volume II) constructs an 'anti-totalitarian' argument to refute the majority's judgment. For Thomas neither of these positions is able to 'yield a sufficiently concrete understanding of the political practices that intersect the law of homosexuality' (1498). Thomas acknowledges that the concept of 'privacy' provides an inadequate basis on which to protect the rights of the homosexual and lesbian community against homophobic violence. See Volume II.

8.  See *Stanley v. Georgia* 394 US 557 (1969).
9.  See E. Campbell (1990), 'Mandatory AIDS Testing and Privacy: A Psycholegal Perspective', *North Dakota Law Review*, **66**, 449; R. Turkington (1989), 'Confidentiality Policy for HIV-Related Information: An Analytic Framework for Sorting Out Hard and Easy Cases', *Villanova Law Review*, **34**, 871; R. Wacks (1988), 'Controlling AIDS: Some Legal Issues', *NLJ*, **138**, 254, 283.
10. See A.H. Saxonhouse, 'Classical Greek Conceptions of Public and Private' in S.I. Benn and G.F. Gaus (eds) (1983), *Public and Private in Social Life*, London: Croom Helm and St Martin's Press, 380; D. Hanson (1970), *From Kingdom to Commonwealth: The Development of Civic Consciousness in English Political Thought*, Cambridge, Mass: Harvard University Press, 1–19, quoted by M.J. Horwitz (1982), 'The History of the Public/Private Distinction', *University of Pennsylvania Law Review*, **130**, 1423; H. Arendt (1958), *The Human Condition*, Chicago: University of Chicago Press, 38ff.
11. J. Appleby (1978), *Economic Thought and Ideology in Seventeenth Century England*, Princeton, NJ: Princeton University Press, 62–3, quoted by Horwitz, 'The History of the Public/Private Distinction', see note 10 above.
12. See R.H. Mnookin (1982), 'The Public/Private Dichotomy: Political Disagreement and Academic Reputation', *University of Pennsylvania Law Review*, **130**, 1429.
13. F. Tönnies (1887), *Gemeinschaft und Gesellschaft*, trans. C.P. Loomis (1955), *Community and Association*, East Lansing, Mich.: Michigan State University Press.
14. S. Lukes (1973), *Individualism*, Oxford: Basil Blackwell, 62. See too E. Kamenka, 'Public/Private in Marxist Theory and Marxist Practice' in Benn and Gaus, *Public and Private in Social Life*, 267, 273–4 (note 10 above).
15. Horwitz, 'The History of the Public/Private Distinction', 1423, 1424 (note 10 above).
16. This is illustrated by the Hart/Devlin debate concerning, in particular, the issue of homosexual acts between consenting adults. The liberal position is, of course, exemplified by the Wolfenden Report (*Report of the Committee on Homosexual Offences and Prostitution*, Cmnd. 247, 1957), which based itself on J.S. Mill's 'harm principle' expressed in *On Liberty* (1859). See too the *Report of the Committee on Obscenity and Film Censorship* (chairman: Bernard Williams) Cmnd. 7772, 1979.
17. R.F. Hixson (1987), *Privacy in a Public Society: Human Rights in Conflict*, New York, Oxford: Oxford University Press, 98.
18. For an early expression of these difficulties, see F. Davis (1959), 'What Do We Mean by "Right to Privacy"?', *South Dakota Law Review*, **4**, 1.
19. For an attempt to derive the right to privacy from the 'moral principle ... of respect for individual liberty' see R.B. Hallborg (1986), 'Principles of Liberty and the Right to Privacy', *Law and Philosophy*, **5**, 175. See Volume II.
20. '[A]s a descriptive or analytic term, "right to privacy" is virtually meaningless.' Zimmerman (1983; Chapter 12 in Volume II), 299.
21. A. Westin, *Privacy and Freedom*, London: Bodley Head, 7.
22. See D.N. McCormick (1974), 'Privacy: A Problem of Definition', *British Journal of Law & Society*, **1**, 75.
23. T. Gerety (1977; Chapter 8).
24. See, for instance, Fried (1968; Chapter 3), 482; R. Parker (1974), 'A Definition of Privacy', *Rutgers Law Review*, **27**, 275, 280–81; A. Miller (1971), *The Assault on Privacy*, Ann Arbor: The University of Michigan Press, 25; E.L. Beardsley, 'Privacy: Autonomy and Selective Disclosure' in J.R. Pennock and J.W. Chapman (eds) (1971), *Privacy, Nomos*, **XIII** 56, 70; E. Shils (1966), 'Privacy: Its Constitution and Vicissitudes', *Law & Contemporary Problems*, **31**, 281; H. Gross (1967; Chapter 4); T. Gerety (1977; Chapter 8).

25.  Gavison (1980; Chapter 6).
26.  Ibid.
27.  The *Report of the Committee on Privacy* (chairman: K. Younger) Cmnd. 5012, 1972, confused
     'rights' and 'liberties': D.N. McCormick (1973), 'Right of Privacy', *Law Quarterly Review*, **89**,
     23; *id.* 'Privacy: A Problem of Definition'. Cf. N. Marsh (1973), 'Hohfeld and Privacy', *Law
     Quarterly Review*, **89**, 183.
28.  L. Lusky (1972), 'Invasion of Privacy: A Clarification of Concepts', *Columbia Law Review*, **72**,
     693, 709; M.A. Weinstein (1971; Chapter 13).
29.  Beardsley, note 24 above; S.I. Benn, 'Privacy, Freedom and Respect for Persons', *Nomos*, **XIII**, 1.
30.  M.A. Weinstein (1971; Chapter 13).
31.  C. Fried, *An Anatomy of Values: Problems of Personal and Social Choice*, Cambridge, Mass.:
     Harvard University Press.
32.  Westin, note 21 above, 33.
33.  See the essays in Volume II by Prosser (1960; Chapter 3) and Bloustein (1964; Chapter 4).
34.  See D.H. Flaherty (1991), 'On the Utility of Constitutional Rights to Privacy and Data Protection',
     *Case Western Reserve Law Review*, **41**, 831; S. Simitis (1987), 'Reviewing Privacy in an
     Information Society', *University of Pennsylvania Law Review*, **135**, 707.
35.  Though he employs (with little clarity) the term 'privacy', Posner (rightly, it is submitted)
     concentrates his attention on the question of personal information. See R. Posner (1978; Chapter
     15); 'An Economic Theory of Privacy' in Schoeman (ed.), *Philosophical Dimensions of Privacy*;
     R.A. Epstein (1980; Chapter 16). Cf. C.E. Baker (1978), 'Posner's Privacy Mystery and the
     Failure of the Economic Analysis of Law, *Georgia Law Review*, **12**, 475; E.J. Bloustein (1978;
     Chapter 17).
36.  Posner (1978; Chapter 15), 401.

# Part I
# Defining 'Privacy'

# [1]

JUDITH JARVIS THOMSON          The Right to Privacy

## I

Perhaps the most striking thing about the right to privacy is that nobody seems to have any very clear idea what it is. Consider, for example, the familiar proposal that the right to privacy is the right "to be let alone." On the one hand, this doesn't seem to take in enough. The police might say, "We grant we used a special X-ray device on Smith, so as to be able to watch him through the walls of his house; we grant we trained an amplifying device on him so as to be able to hear everything he said; but we let him strictly alone: we didn't touch him, we didn't even go near him—our devices operate at a distance." Anyone who believes there is a right to privacy would presumably believe that it has been violated in Smith's case; yet he would be hard put to explain precisely how, if the right to privacy is the right to be let alone. And on the other hand, this account of the right to privacy lets in far too much. If I hit Jones on the head with a brick I have not let him alone. Yet, while hitting Jones on the head with a brick is surely violating some right of Jones', doing it should surely not turn out to violate his right to privacy. Else, where is this to end? Is *every* violation of a right a violation of the right to privacy?

It seems best to be less ambitious, to begin with at least. I suggest,

I am grateful to the members of the Society for Ethical and Legal Philosophy for criticisms of the first draft of the following paper. Alan Sparer made helpful criticisms of a later draft.

then, that we look at some specific, imaginary cases in which people
would say, "There, in that case, the right to privacy has been violated,"
and ask ourselves precisely why this would be said, and what, if anything, would justify saying it.

II

But there is a difficulty to be taken note of first. What I have in mind
is that there may not be so much agreement on the cases as I implied.
Suppose that my husband and I are having a fight, shouting at each
other as loud as we can; and suppose that we have not thought to
close the windows, so that we can easily be heard from the street
outside. It seems to me that anyone who stops to listen violates no
right of ours; stopping to listen is at worst bad, Not Nice, not done by
the best people. But now suppose, by contrast, that we are having a
quiet fight, behind closed windows, and cannot be heard by the
normal person who passes by; and suppose that someone across the
street trains an amplifier on our house, by means of which he can hear
what we say; and suppose that he does this in order to hear what we
say. It seems to me that anyone who does this does violate a right of
ours, the right to privacy, I should have thought.

But there is room for disagreement. It might be said that in neither
case is there a violation of a right, that both are cases of mere bad
behavior—though no doubt worse behavior in the second case than in
the first, it being very much naughtier to train amplifiers on people's
houses than merely to stop in the street to listen.

Or, alternatively, it might be said that in both cases there is a violation of a right, the right to privacy in fact, but that the violation is less
serious in the first case than in the second.

I think that these would both be wrong. I think that we have in
these two cases, not merely a difference in degree, but a difference
in quality: that the passerby who stops to listen in the first case may
act badly, but violates no one's rights, whereas the neighbor who uses
an amplifier in the second case does not merely act badly but violates
a right, the right to privacy. But I have no argument for this. I take
it rather as a datum in this sense: it seems to me there would be a
mark against an account of the right to privacy if it did not yield the

*The Right to Privacy*

conclusion that these two cases do differ in the way I say they do, and moreover explain why they do.

But there is one thing perhaps worth drawing attention to here: doing so may perhaps diminish the inclination to think that a right is violated in both cases. What I mean is this. There is a familiar account of rights—I speak now of rights generally, and not just of the right to privacy—according to which a man's having a right that something shall not be done to him just itself consists in its being the case that anyone who does it to him acts badly or wrongly or does what he ought not do. Thus, for example, it is said that to have a right that you shall not be killed or imprisoned just itself consists in its being the case that if anyone does kill or imprison you, he acts badly, wrongly, does what he ought not do. If this account of rights were correct, then my husband and I would have a right that nobody shall stop in the street and listen to our loud fight, since anyone who does stop in the street and listen acts badly, wrongly, does what he ought not do. Just as we have a right that people shall not train amplifiers on the house to listen to our quiet fights.

But this account of rights is just plain wrong. There are many, many things we ought not do to people, things such that if we do them to a person, we act badly, but which are not such that to do them is to violate a right of his. It is bad behavior, for example to be ungenerous and unkind. Suppose that you dearly love chocolate ice cream but that, for my part, I find that a little of it goes a long way. I have been given some and have eaten a little, enough really, since I don't care for it very much. You then, looking on, ask, "May I have the rest of your ice cream?" It would be bad indeed if I were to reply, "No, I've decided to bury the rest of it in the garden." I ought not do that; I ought to give it to you. But you have no right that I give it to you, and I violate no right of yours if I do bury the stuff.

Indeed, it is possible that an act which is not a violation of a right should be a far worse act than an act which is. If you did not merely want that ice cream but needed it, for your health perhaps, then my burying it would be monstrous, indecent, though still, of course, no violation of a right. By contrast, if you snatch it away, steal it, before I can bury it, then while you violate a right (the ice cream is mine,

*Privacy I*

*Philosophy & Public Affairs*

after all), your act is neither monstrous nor indecent—if it's bad at all, it's anyway not very bad.

From the point of view of conduct, of course, this doesn't really matter: bad behavior is bad behavior, whether it is a violation of a right or not. But if we want to be clear about *why* this or that bit of bad behavior is bad, then these distinctions do have to get made and looked into.

## III

To return, then, to the two cases I drew attention to, and which I suggest we take to differ in this way: in one of them a right is violated, in the other not. It isn't, I think, the fact that an amplifying device is used in the one case, and not in the other, that is responsible for this difference. On the one hand, consider someone who is deaf: if he passes by while my husband and I are having a loud fight at an open window and turns up his hearing-aid so as to be able to hear us, it seems to me he no more violates our right to privacy than does one who stops to listen and can hear well enough without a hearing-aid. And on the other hand, suppose that you and I have to talk over some personal matters. It is most convenient to meet in the park, and we do so, taking a bench far from the path since we don't want to be overheard. It strikes a man to want to know what we are saying to each other in that heated fashion, so he creeps around in the bushes behind us and crouches back of the bench to listen. He thereby violates the right to privacy—fully as much as if he had stayed a hundred yards away and used an amplifying device to listen to us.

## IV

The cases I drew attention to are actually rather difficult to deal with, and I suggest we back away from them for a while and look at something simpler.

Consider a man who owns a pornographic picture. He wants that nobody but him shall ever see that picture—perhaps because he wants that nobody shall know that he owns it, perhaps because he feels that someone else's seeing it would drain it of power to please. So he keeps it locked in his wall-safe, and takes it out to look at only at night or after pulling down the shades and closing the curtains. We have

*The Right to Privacy*

heard about his picture, and we want to see it, so we train our X-ray device on the wall-safe and look in. To do this is, I think, to violate a right of his—the right to privacy, I should think.

No doubt people who worry about violations of the right to privacy are not worried about the possibility that others will look at their *possessions*. At any rate, this doesn't worry them very much. That it is not nothing, however, comes out when one thinks on the special source of discomfort there is if a burglar doesn't go straight for the TV set and the silver, and then leave, but if he stops for a while just to look at things—e.g. at your love letters or at the mound of torn socks on the floor of your closet. The trespass and the theft *might* swamp everything else; but they might not: the burglar's merely looking around in that way might make the episode feel worse than it otherwise would have done.

So I shall suppose that we do violate this man's right to privacy if we use an X-ray device to look at the picture in his wall-safe. And now let us ask how and why.

To own a picture is to have a cluster of rights in respect of it. The cluster includes, for example, the right to sell it to whomever you like, the right to give it away, the right to tear it, the right to look at it. These rights are all "positive rights": rights to do certain things to or in respect of the picture. To own a picture is also to have certain "negative rights" in respect of it, that is, rights that others shall not do certain things to it—thus, for example, the right that others shall not sell it or give it away or tear it.

Does owning a picture also include having the negative right that others shall not look at it? I think it does. If our man's picture is good pornography, it would be pretty mingy of him to keep it permanently hidden so that nobody but him shall ever see it—a nicer person would let his friends have a look at it too. But he is within his rights to hide it. If someone is about to tear his picture, he can snatch it away: it's his, so he has a right that nobody but him shall tear it. If someone is about to look at his picture, he can snatch it away or cover it up: it's his, so he has a right that nobody but him shall look at it.

It is important to stress that he has not merely the right to snatch the picture away in order that nobody shall tear it, he has not merely

the right to do everything he can (within limits) to prevent people
from tearing it, he has also the right that nobody *shall* tear it. What
I have in mind is this. Suppose we desperately want to tear his picture. He locks it in his wall-safe to prevent us from doing so. And
suppose we are so eager that we buy a penetrating long-distance
picture-tearer: we sit quietly in our apartment across the street, train
the device on the picture in the wall-safe, press the button—and lo!
we have torn the picture. The fact that he couldn't protect his picture
against the action of the device doesn't make it all right that we use it.

Again, suppose that there was a way in which he could have protected his picture against the action of the device: the rays won't pass
through platinum, and he could have encased the picture in platinum.
But he would have had to sell everything else he owns in order to pay
for the platinum. The fact he didn't do this does not make it all right
for us to have used the device.

We all have a right to do what we can (within limits) to secure
our belongings against theft. I gather, however, that it's practically
impossible to secure them against a determined burglar. Perhaps only
hiring armed guards or sealing the house in solid steel will guarantee
that our possessions cannot be stolen; and perhaps even these things
won't work. The fact (if it's a fact) that we can't guarantee our belongings against theft; the fact (if it's a fact) that though we can,
the cost of doing so is wildly out of proportion to the value of the
things, and therefore we don't; neither of these makes it all right for
the determined burglar to walk off with them.

Now I said that if a man owns a picture he can snatch it away or
he can cover it up to prevent anyone else from *looking* at it. He can
also hide it in his wall-safe. But I think he has a right, not merely to
do what he can (within limits) to prevent it from being looked at: he
has a right that it shall not be looked at—just as he has a right that
it shall not be torn or taken away from him. That he has a right that
it shall not be looked at comes out, I think, in this way: if he hides
it in his wall-safe, and we train our X-ray device on the wall-safe and
look in, we have violated a right of his in respect of it, and the right
is surely the right that it shall not be looked at. The fact that he
couldn't protect his picture against the action of an X-ray device which
enables us to look at it doesn't make it all right that we use the X-ray

*The Right to Privacy*

device to look at it—just as the fact that he can't protect his picture
against the action of a long-distance picture-tearing device which
enables us to tear his picture doesn't make it all right that we use the
device to tear it.

Compare, by contrast, a subway map. You have no right to take it
off the wall or cover it up: you haven't a right to do whatever you
can to prevent it from being looked at. And if you do cover it up, and
if anyone looks through the covering with an X-ray device, he violates
no right of yours: you do not have a right that nobody but you shall
look at it—it's not *yours*, after all.

Looking at a picture doesn't harm it, of course, whereas tearing a
picture does. But this doesn't matter. If I use your toothbrush I don't
harm it; but you, all the same, have a right that I shall not use it.

However, to have a right isn't always to claim it. Thus, on any
view to own a picture is to have (among other rights) the right that
others shall not tear it. Yet you might want someone else to do this and
therefore (1) invite him to, or (2) get him to whether he wants to or
not—e.g. by carefully placing it where he'll put his foot through it when
he gets out of bed in the morning. Or again, while not positively
wanting anyone else to tear the picture, you might not care whether
or not it is torn, and therefore you might simply (3) let someone tear
it—e.g. when, out of laziness, you leave it where it fell amongst the
things the children are in process of wrecking. Or again still, you
might positively want that nobody shall tear the picture and yet in a
fit of absent-mindedness (4) leave it in some place such that another
person would have to go to some trouble if he is to avoid tearing it,
or (5) leave it in some place such that another person could not reasonably be expected to know that it still belonged to anybody.

Similarly, you might want someone else to look at your picture
and therefore (1) invite him to, or (2) get him to whether he wants
to or not. Or again, while not positively wanting anyone else to look
at the picture, you might not care whether or not it is looked at, and
therefore you might simply (3) let it be looked at. Or again still, you
might positively want that nobody shall look at the picture, and yet
in a fit of absent-mindedness (4) leave it in some place such that
another person would have to go to some trouble if he is to avoid
looking at it (at least, avert his eyes) or (5) leave it in some place

such that another person could not reasonably be expected to know that it still belonged to anybody.

In all of these cases, it is permissible for another person on the one hand to tear the picture, on the other to look at it: no right of the owner's is violated. I think it fair to describe them as cases in which, though the owner had a right that the things not be done, he *waived* the right: in cases (1), (2), and (3) intentionally, in cases (4) and (5) unintentionally. It is not at all easy to say under what conditions a man has waived a right—by what acts of commission or omission and in what circumstances. The conditions vary, according as the right is more or less important; and while custom and convention, on the one hand, and the cost of securing the right, on the other hand, play very important roles, it is not clear precisely what roles. Nevertheless there plainly is such a thing as waiving a right; and given a man has waived his right to a thing, we violate no right of his if we do not accord it to him.

There are other things which may bring about that although a man had a right to a thing, we violate no right of his if we do not accord it to him: he may have transferred the right to another or he may have forfeited the right or he may still have the right, though it is overridden by some other, more stringent right. (This is not meant to be an exhaustive list.) And there are also some circumstances in which it is not clear what should be said. Suppose someone steals your picture and invites some third party (who doesn't know it's yours) to tear it or look at it; or suppose someone takes your picture by mistake, thinking it's his, and invites some third party (who doesn't know it's yours) to tear it or look at it; does the *third* party violate a right of yours if he accepts the invitation? A general theory of rights should provide an account of all of these things.

It suffices here, however, to stress one thing about rights: a man may have had a right that we shall not do a thing, he may even still have a right that we shall not do it, consistently with its being the case that we violate no right of his if we go ahead.

If this is correct, we are on the way to what we want. I said earlier that when we trained our X-ray device on that man's wall-safe in order to have a look at his pornographic picture, we violated a right

**The Right to Privacy**

of his, the right to privacy, in fact. It now turns out (if I am right) that we violated a property right of his, specifically the negative right that others shall not look at the picture, this being one of the (many) rights which his owning the picture consists of. I shall come back a little later to the way in which these rights interconnect.

V

We do not, of course, care nearly as much about our possessions as we care about ourselves. We do not want people looking at our torn socks; but it would be much worse to have people watch us make faces at ourselves in the mirror when we thought no one was looking or listen to us while we fight with our families. So you might think I have spent far too much time on that pornographic picture.

But in fact, if what I said about pornographic pictures was correct, then the point about ourselves comes through easily enough. For if we have fairly stringent rights over our property, we have very much more stringent rights over our own persons. None of you came to possess your knee in axactly the way in which you came to possess your shoes or your pornographic pictures: I take it you neither bought nor inherited your left knee. And I suppose you could not very well sell your left knee. But that isn't because it isn't yours to sell—some women used to sell their hair, and some people nowadays sell their blood—but only because who'd buy a used left knee? For if anyone wanted to, you are the only one with a right to sell yours. Again, it's a nasty business to damage a knee; but you've a right to damage yours, and certainly nobody else has—its being your left knee includes your having the right that nobody else but you shall damage it. And, as I think, it also includes your having the right that nobody else shall touch it or look at it. Of course you might invite somebody to touch or look at your left knee; or you might let someone touch or look at it; or again still, you might in a fit of absent-mindedness leave it in some place such that another person would have to go to some trouble if he is to avoid touching or looking at it. In short, you might waive your right that your left knee not be touched or looked at. But that is what doing these things would be: waiving a right.

I suppose there are people who would be deeply distressed to learn

that they had absent-mindedly left a knee uncovered, and that somebody was looking at it. Fewer people would be deeply distressed to
learn that they had absent-mindedly left their faces uncovered. Most
of us wouldn't, but Moslem women would; and so might a man whose
face had been badly disfigured, in a fire, say. Suppose you woke up
one morning and found that you had grown fangs or that you no
longer had a nose; you might well want to claim a right which most
of us so contentedly waive: the right that your face not be looked at.
That we have such a right comes out when we notice that if a man
comes for some reason or another to want his face not to be looked at,
and if he therefore keeps it covered, and if we then use an X-ray
device in order to be able to look at it through the covering, we
violate a right of his in respect of it, and the right we violate is surely
the right that his face shall not be looked at. Compare again, by contrast, a subway map. No matter how much you may want a subway
map to not be looked at, if we use an X-ray device in order to be able
to look at it through the covering you place over it, we violate no
right of yours: you do not have a right that nobody but you shall look
at it—it is not *yours*, after all.

Listening, I think, works in the same way as looking. Suppose you
are an opera singer, a great one, so that lots of people want to listen
to you. You might sell them the right to listen. Or you might invite
them to listen or let them listen or absent-mindedly sing where they
cannot help but listen. But if you have decided you are no longer
willing to be listened to; if you now sing only quietly, behind closed
windows and carefully sound-proofed walls; and if somebody trains
an amplifier on your house so as to be able to listen, he violates a
right, the right to not be listened to.

These rights—the right to not be looked at and the right to not be
listened to[1]—are analogous to rights we have over our property. It

1. In "A Definition of Privacy," *Rutgers Law Review*, 1974, p. 281, Richard
B. Parker writes:

The definition of privacy defended in this article is that *privacy is control
over when and by whom the various parts of us can be sensed by others*. By
"sensed," is meant simply seen, heard, touched, smelled, or tasted. By "parts
of us," is meant the parts of our bodies, our voices, and the products of our
bodies. "Parts of us" also includes objects very closely associated with us. By
"closely associated" is meant primarily what is spatially associated. The ob-

*The Right to Privacy*

sounds funny to say we have such rights. They are not mentioned
when we give lists of rights. When we talk of rights, those that come
to mind are the grand ones: the right to life, the right to liberty, the
right to not be hurt or harmed, and property rights. Looking at and
listening to a man do not harm him, but neither does stroking his left
knee harm him, and yet he has a right that it shall not be stroked
without permission. Cutting off all a man's hair while he's asleep will
not harm him, nor will painting his elbows green; yet he plainly has
a right that these things too shall not be done to him. These un-grand
rights seem to be closely enough akin to be worth grouping together
under one heading. For lack of a better term, I shall simply speak
of "the right over the person," a right which I shall take to consist of
the un-grand rights I mentioned, and others as well.

When I began, I said that if my husband and I are having a quiet
fight behind closed windows and cannot be heard by the normal person who passes by, then if anyone trains an amplifier on us in order
to listen he violates a right, the right to privacy, in fact. It now turns
out (if I am right) that he violates our right to not be listened to,
which is one of the rights included in the right over the person.

I had said earlier that if we use an X-ray device to look at the
pornographic picture in a man's wall-safe, we violate his right to
privacy. And it then turned out (if I was right) that we violated the

---

jects which are "parts of us" are objects we usually keep with us or locked up
in a place accessible only to us.

The right to privacy, then, is presumably the right to this control. But I find
this puzzling, on a number of counts. First, why *control*? If my neighbor invents
an X-ray device which enables him to look through walls, then I should imagine
I thereby lose control over who can look at me: going home and closing the
doors no longer suffices to prevent others from doing so. But my right to privacy
is not violated until my neighbor actually does train the device on the wall of my
house. It is the actual looking that violates it, not the acquisition of power to
look. Second, there *are* other cases. Suppose a more efficient bugging device is invented: instead of tapes, it produces neatly typed transcripts (thereby eliminating the middlemen). One who reads those transcripts does not *hear* you, but
your right to privacy is violated just as if he does.

On the other hand, this article is the first I have seen which may be taken
to imply (correctly, as I think) that there are such rights as the right to not be
looked at and the right to not be listened to. And in any case, Professor Parker's
interest is legal rather than moral: he is concerned to find a definition which
will be useful in legal contexts. (I am incompetent to estimate how successful
he is in doing this.)

I am grateful to Charles Fried for drawing my attention to this article.

right that others shall not look at the picture, which is one of the rights which his owning the picture consists in.

It begins to suggest itself, then, as a simplifying hypothesis, that the right to privacy is itself a cluster of rights, and that it is not a distinct cluster of rights but itself intersects with the cluster of rights which the right over the person consists in and also with the cluster of rights which owning property consists in. That is, to use an X-ray device to look at the picture is to violate a right (the right that others shall not look at the picture) which is both one of the rights which the right to privacy consists in and also one of the rights which property-ownership consists in. Again, that to use an amplifying device to listen to us is to violate a right (the right to not be listened to) which is both one of the rights which the right to privacy consists in and also one of the rights which the right over the person consists in.

Some small confirmation for this hypothesis comes from the other listening case. I had said that if my husband and I are having a loud fight, behind open windows, so that we can easily be heard by the normal person who passes by, then if a passerby stops to listen, he violates no right of ours, and so in particular does not violate our right to privacy. Why doesn't he? I think it is because, though he listens to us, we have *let* him listen (whether intentionally or not), we have waived our right to not be listened to—for we took none of the conventional and easily available steps (such as closing the windows and lowering our voices) to prevent listening. But this would only be an explanation if waiving the right to not be listened to were waiving the right to privacy, or if it were at least waiving the only one among the rights which the right to privacy consists in which might plausibly be taken to have been violated by the passerby.

But for further confirmation, we shall have to examine some further violations of the right to privacy.

VI

The following cases are similar to the ones we have just been looking at. (a) A deaf spy trains on your house a bugging device which produces, not sounds on tape, but a typed transcript, which he then reads. (Cf. footnote 1.) (b) A blind spy trains on your house an X-ray device

*The Right to Privacy*

which produces, not views of you, but a series of bas-relief panels, which he then feels. The deaf spy doesn't listen to you, the blind spy doesn't look at you, but both violate your right to privacy just as if they did.

It seems to me that in both these cases there is a violation of that same right over the person which is violated by looking at or listening to a person. You have a right, not merely that you not be looked at or listened to but also that you not have your words transcribed, and that you not be modeled in bas-relief. These are rights that the spies violate, and it is these rights in virtue of the violation of which they violate your right to privacy. Of course, one may waive these rights: a teacher presumably waives the former when he enters the class-room, and a model waives the latter when he enters the studio. So these cases seem to present no new problem.

## VII

A great many cases turn up in connection with information.

I should say straightaway that it seems to me none of us has a right over any fact to the effect that that fact shall not be known by others. You may violate a man's right to privacy by looking at him or listening to him; there is no such thing as violating a man's right to privacy by simply knowing something about him.

Where our rights in this area do lie is, I think, here: we have a right that certain steps shall not be taken to find out facts, and we have a right that certain uses shall not be made of facts. I shall briefly say a word about each of these.

If we use an X-ray device to look at a man in order to get personal information about him, then we violate his right to privacy. Indeed, we violate his right to privacy whether the information we want is personal or impersonal. We might be spying on him in order to find out what he does all alone in his kitchen at midnight; or we might be spying on him in order to find out how to make puff pastry, which we already know he does in the kitchen all alone at midnight; either way his right to privacy is violated. But in both cases, the simplifying hypothesis seems to hold: in both cases we violate a right (the right to not be looked at) which is both one of the rights which the right to privacy consists in and one of the rights which the right over the person consists in.

What about torturing a man in order to get information? I suppose that if we torture a man in order to find out how to make puff pastry, then though we violate his right to not be hurt or harmed, we do not violate his right to privacy. But what if we torture him to find out what he does in the kitchen all alone at midnight? Presumably in that case we violate both his right to not be hurt or harmed and his right to privacy—the latter, presumably, because it was personal information we tortured him to get. But here too we can maintain the simplifying hypothesis: we can take it that to torture a man in order to find out personal information is to violate a right (the right to not be tortured to get personal information) which is both one of the rights which the right to privacy consists in and one of the rights which the right to not be hurt or harmed consists in.

And so also for extorting information by threat: if the information is not personal, we violate only the victim's right to not be coerced by threat; if it is personal, we presumably also violate his right to privacy —in that we violate his right to not be coerced by threat to give personal information, which is both one of the rights which the right to privacy consists in and one of the rights which the right to not be coerced by threat consists in.

I think it a plausible idea, in fact, that doing something to a man to get personal information from him is violating his right to privacy only if doing that to him is violating some right of his not identical with or included in the right to privacy. Thus writing a man a letter asking him where he was born is no violation of his right to privacy: writing a man a letter is no violation of any right of his. By contrast, spying on a man to get personal information is a violation of the right to privacy, and spying on a man for any reason is a violation of the right over the person, which is not identical with or included in (though it overlaps) the right to privacy. Again, torturing a man to get personal information is presumably a violation of the right to privacy, and torturing a man for any reason is a violation of the right to not be hurt or harmed, which is not identical with or included in (though it overlaps) the right to privacy. If the idea is right, the sim-

# The Right to Privacy

plifying hypothesis is trivially true for this range of cases. If a man has a right that we shall not do such and such to him, then he has a right that we shall not do it to him in order to get personal information from him. And his right that we shall not do it to him in order to get personal information from him is included in both his right that we shall not do it to him, and (if doing it to him for this reason is violating his right to privacy) his right to privacy.

I suspect the situation is the same in respect of uses of information. If a man gives us information on the condition we shall not spread it, and we then spread it, we violate his right to confidentiality, whether the information is personal or impersonal. If the information is personal, I suppose we also violate his right to privacy—by virtue of violating a right (the right to confidentiality in respect of personal information) which is both one of the rights which the right to privacy consists in and one of the rights which the right to confidentiality consists in. The point holds whether our motive for spreading the information is malice or profit or anything else.

Again, suppose I find out by entirely legitimate means (e.g. from a third party who breaks no confidence in telling me) that you keep a pornographic picture in your wall-safe; and suppose that, though I know it will cause you distress, I print the information in a box on the front page of my newspaper, thinking it newsworthy: Professor Jones of State U. Keeps Pornographic Picture in Wall-Safe! Do I violate your right to privacy? I am, myself, inclined to think not. But if anyone thinks I do, he can still have the simplifying hypothesis: he need only take a stand on our having a right that others shall not cause us distress, and then add that what is violated here is the right to not be caused distress by the publication of personal information, which is one of the rights which the right to privacy consists in, and one of the rights which the right to not be caused distress consists in. Distress, after all, is the heart of the wrong (if there is a wrong in such a case): a man who positively wants personal information about himself printed in newspapers, and therefore makes plain he wants it printed, is plainly not wronged when newspapers cater to his want.

(My reluctance to go along with this is not due to a feeling that we have no such right as the right to not be caused distress: that we have such a right seems to me a plausible idea. So far as I can see, there is nothing special about physical hurts and harms; mental hurts and harms are hurts and harms too. Indeed, they may be more grave and long-lasting than the physical ones, and it is hard to see why we should be thought to have rights against the one and not against the other. My objection is, rather, that even if there is a right to not be caused distress by the publication of personal information, it is mostly, if not always, overridden by what seems to me a more stringent right, namely the public's right to a press which prints any and all information, personal or impersonal, which it deems newsworthy; and thus that in the case I mentioned no right is violated, and hence, a fortiori, the right to privacy is not violated.[2]

## VIII

The question arises, then, whether or not there are *any* rights in the right to privacy cluster which aren't also in some other right cluster. I suspect there aren't any, and that the right to privacy is everywhere overlapped by other rights. But it's a difficult question. Part of the difficulty is due to its being (to put the best face on it) unclear just what is in this right to privacy cluster. I mentioned at the outset that there is disagreement on cases; and the disagreement becomes even more stark as we move away from the kinds of cases I've so far been drawing attention to which seem to me to be the central, core cases.

What should be said, for example, of the following?

(a) The neighbors make a terrible racket every night. Or they cook foul-smelling stews. Do they violate my right to privacy? Some think yes, I think not. But even if they do violate my right to privacy, perhaps all would be well for the simplifying hypothesis since their doing this is presumably a violation of another right of mine, roughly, the right to be free of annoyance in my house.

(b) The city, after a city-wide referendum favoring it, installs

2. It was Warren and Brandeis, in their now classic article, "The Right to Privacy," *Harvard Law Review*, 1890, who first argued that the law ought to recognize wrongs that are (they thought) committed in cases such as these. For a superb discussion of this article, see Harry Kalven, Jr., "Privacy in Tort Law—Were Warren and Brandeis Wrong?" *Law and Contemporary Problems*, Spring 1966.

*The Right to Privacy*

loudspeakers to play music in all the buses and subways. Do they violate
my right to privacy? Some think yes, I think not. But again perhaps
all is well: it is if those of us in the minority have a right to be free of
what we (though not the majority) regard as an annoyance in public
places.

(c) You are famous, and photographers follow you around, everywhere you go, taking pictures of you. Crowds collect and stare at you.
Do they violate your right to privacy? Some think yes, I think not: it
seems to me that if you do go out in public, you waive your right to not
be photographed and looked at. But of course you, like the rest of us,
have a right to be free of (what anyone would grant was) annoyance
in public places; so in particular, you have a right that the photographers and crowds not press in too closely.

(d) A stranger stops you on the street and asks, "How much do you
weigh?" Or an acquaintance, who has heard of the tragedy, says, "How
terrible you must have felt when your child was run over by that
delivery truck!"[3] Or a cab driver turns around and announces, "My
wife is having an affair with my psychoanalyst." Some think that your
right to privacy is violated here; I think not. There is an element of
coercion in such cases: the speaker is trying to force you into a
relationship you do not want, the threat being your own embarrassment at having been impolite if you refuse. But I find it hard to see
how we can be thought to have a right against such attempts. Of
course the attempt may be an annoyance. Or a sustained series of such
attempts may become an annoyance. (Consider, for example, an
acquaintance who takes to stopping at your office *every morning* to
ask if you slept well.) If so, I suppose a right *is* violated, namely, the
right against annoyances.

(e) Some acquaintances of yours indulge in some very personal
gossip about you.[4] Let us imagine that all of the information they
share was arrived at without violation of any right of yours, and that
none of the participants violates a confidence in telling what he tells.
Do they violate a right of yours in sharing the information? If they
do, there is trouble for the simplifying hypothesis, for it seems to me
there is no right not identical with, or included in, the right to privacy

3. Example from Thomas Nagel.        4. Example from Gilbert Harman.

cluster which they could be thought to violate. On the other hand, it seems to me they *don't* violate any right of yours. It seems to me we simply do not have rights against others that they shall not gossip about us.

(f) A state legislature makes it illegal to use contraceptives. Do they violate the right to privacy of the citizens of that state? No doubt certain techniques for enforcing the statute (e.g., peering into bedroom windows) would be obvious violations of the right to privacy; but is there a violation of the right to privacy in the mere enacting of the statute—in addition to the violations which may be involved in enforcing it? I think not. But it doesn't matter for the simplifying hypothesis if it is: making a kind of conduct illegal is infringing on a liberty, and we all of us have a right that our liberties not be infringed in the absence of compelling need to do so.

## IX

The fact, supposing it a fact, that every right in the right to privacy cluster is also in some other right cluster does not by itself show that the right to privacy is in any plausible sense a "derivative" right. A more important point seems to me to be this: the fact that we have a right to privacy does not explain our having any of the rights in the right to privacy cluster. What I have in mind is this. We have a right to not be tortured. Why? Because we have a right to not be hurt or harmed. I have a right that my pornographic picture shall not be torn. Why? Because it's mine, because I own it. I have a right to do a somersault now. Why? Because I have a right to liberty. I have a right to try to preserve my life. Why? Because I have a right to life. In these cases we explain the having of one right by appeal to the having of another which includes it. But I don't have a right to not be looked at because I have a right to privacy; I don't have a right that no one shall torture me in order to get personal information about me because I have a right to privacy; one is inclined, rather, to say that it is because I have *these* rights that I have a right to privacy.

This point, supposing it correct, connects with what I mentioned at the outset: that nobody seems to have any very clear idea what the right to privacy is. We are confronted with a cluster of rights—a cluster

# The Right to Privacy

with disputed boundaries—such that most people think that to violate at least any of the rights in the core of the cluster is to violate the right to privacy; but what have they in common other than their being rights such that to violate them is to violate the right to privacy? To violate these rights is to not let someone alone? To violate these rights is to visit indignity on someone? There are too many acts in the course of which we do not let someone alone, in the course of which we give affront to dignity, but in the performing of which we do not violate anyone's right to privacy. That we feel the need to find something in common to all of the rights in the cluster and, moreover, feel we haven't yet got it in the very fact that they *are* all in the cluster, is a consequence of our feeling that one cannot explain our having any of the rights in the cluster in the words: "Because we have a right to privacy."

But then if, as I take it, every right in the right to privacy cluster is also in some other right cluster, there is no need to find the that-which-is-in-common to all rights in the right to privacy cluster and no need to settle disputes about its boundaries. For if I am right, the right to privacy is "derivative" in this sense: it is possible to explain in the case of each right in the cluster how come we have it without ever once mentioning the right to privacy. Indeed, the wrongness of every violation of the right to privacy can be explained without ever once mentioning it. Someone tortures you to get personal information from you? He violates your right to not be tortured to get personal information from you, and you have that right because you have the right to not be hurt or harmed—and it is because you have this right that what he does is wrong. Someone looks at your pornographic picture in your wall-safe? He violates your right that your belongings not be looked at, and you have that right because you have ownership rights—and it is because you have them that what he does is wrong. Someone uses an X-ray device to look at you through the walls of your house? He violates your right to not be looked at, and you have that right because you have rights over your person analogous to the rights you have over your property—and it is because you have these rights that what he does is wrong.

In any case, I suggest it is a useful heuristic device in the case of

any purported violation of the right to privacy to ask whether or not
the act is a violation of any other right, and if not whether the act
*really* violates a right at all. We are still in such deep dark in respect
of rights that any simplification at all would be well worth having.[5]

5. Frederick Davis' article, "What Do We Mean by 'Right to Privacy'?" *South
Dakota Law Review*, Spring 1959, concludes, in respect of tort law, that

> If truly fundamental interests are accorded the protection they deserve, no
> need to champion a right to privacy arises. Invasion of privacy is, in reality, a
> complex of more fundamental wrongs. Similarly, the individual's interest in
> privacy itself, however real, is derivative and a state better vouchsafed by
> protecting more immediate rights [p. 20]. . . . Indeed, one can logically argue
> that the concept of a right to privacy was never required in the first place,
> and that its whole history is an illustration of how well-meaning but im-
> patient academicians can upset the normal development of the law by pushing
> it too hard [p. 230].

I am incompetent to assess this article's claims about the law, but I take the
liberty of warmly recommending it to philosophers who have an interest in
looking further into the status and nature of the right to privacy.

# [2]

W. A. PARENT

# A NEW DEFINITION OF PRIVACY FOR THE LAW

ABSTRACT. The paper begins with a defence of a new definition of privacy as the absence of undocumented personal knowledge. In the middle section, I criticise alternative accounts of privacy. Finally, I show how my definition can be worked into contemporary American Law.

## I. THE NEW DEFINITION

### 1. *Introduction*

American privacy jurisprudence is in conceptual shambles. Our courts have yet to defend a credible conception of privacy. Instead they continue to work with spurious and sometimes even irreconcilable definitions.[1] Law journal articles on privacy have only managed to contribute to the general confusion by advancing analyses that are equally impoverished. The absence of a clear, precise, and persuasive definition of privacy is particularly shocking and inexcusable when we consider the large, significant workload that the judiciary has assigned to this concept over the past twenty years: landmark cases ranging from the right to use contraceptives to abortion and euthanasia have become integral privacy doctrine.

My principal aim here is to trace the development of the present privacy quagmire and to suggest what might be done to straighten

---

[1] This fact hasn't escaped all legal scholars. See, for example, Raymond Wacks's 'The Poverty of Privacy,' *The Law Quarterly Review* 96 (1980): 73–90; Harry Wellington's 'Common Law Rules and Constitutional Double Standards: Some Notes on Adjudication,' *Yale Law Journal* 83 (1973): 221–311 and Louis Henkin's 'Privacy and Autonomy,' *Columbia Law Review* 74 (1974): pp. 1410–33.

*Law and Philosophy* 2 (1983) 305–338.   0167–5249/83/0023–0305 $03.40.
© 1983 by D. Reidel Publishing Company.

out this "haystack in a hurricane."[2] Specifically, I will offer a new
definition of privacy that captures its essential, core meaning and
consequently enables us to differentiate it from other related but
distinct ideals. I then discuss the judicial mishandling of the concept and suggest some of its causes. Finally, I indicate how privacy
properly conceived can be integrated into contemporary American
law.

## 2. *The Definition*

I propose that privacy be defined as the condition of not having
undocumented personal information about oneself known by
others. To clarify this definition the notion of undocumented
personal information must be explained. Very few legal scholars
have attempted such an explication, but it is of crucial importance
if we are to present a conception of privacy that will lend itself to
ready application by the courts.

Several accounts of personal information can be dismissed
straightaway. To claim, for example, that whether a piece of information about *A* is personal depends entirely upon *A*'s own
attitude and sensitivity towards it cannot be reconciled with the
incontrovertible fact that when a person willingly discloses
intimate truths about himself, not caring how much of himself is
known to others, he is indeed disclosing personal information
about himself. Nor should we identify personal information with
facts about a person that are no one else's business. After all, we
do often and with warrant argue that investigative agencies
charged with the responsibility of law enforcement are entitled to
obtain personal information about citizens. Just because the information is someone else's business doesn't alter its sensitive and
sometimes intimate nature.

My suggestion is that personal information be understood to
consist of facts about a person which most individuals in a given

---

[2] This memorable expression was coined by a Judge Biggs in the case of
Ettore v. Philco Television Broadcasting Corp., 229 F. 2d 481 (3rd Cir.,
1956), at 485.

time do not want widely known about themselves. They may not mind if a few close friends, relatives, or professional associates know these facts, but they would mind very much if the information passed beyond this limited circle of acquaintances.[3] In contemporary America, facts about a person's sexual habits, drinking habits, income, the state of his marriage, and his health belong to the class of personal information. Ten years from now some of these facts may be a part of everyday conversation; if so their disclosure would not diminish individual privacy.

This account of personal information, which makes it a function of existing cultural norms and social practices, needs to be broadened a bit to accommodate a particular and unusual class of cases of the following sort. Most of us don't care if our height, say, is widely known. But there are a few persons who are extremely sensitive about their height (or weight or voice pitch, etc.). They might take extreme measures to ensure that other people not find it out. For such individuals height is a very personal matter. Were someone to find it out by ingenious snooping we should not hesitate to talk about an invasion of privacy.

Let us, then, say that personal information consists of facts that most persons in a given society choose not to reveal about themselves (except to close friends, family,...) or of facts about which a particular individual is acutely sensitive and therefore does not choose to reveal about himself — even though most persons don't care if these same facts about themselves are widely known.

At this point someone might raise a question about the status of information belonging to the public record, that is, in newspapers, court proceedings, title offices, government archives, etc. Such information is available to the public; any one of us can look it up. It is, then, a kind of public property. Should it be excluded from

---

[3] Thus I venture the belief that most people consider information concerning the condition of their homes, particularly their bedrooms and bathrooms, as being personal. A hostess might well show some guests her "private quarters," but she almost certainly will not invite just anyone in for a grand tour.

the category of personal information? I believe it should not. There is, after all, nothing odd or misleading about the proposition that public documents contain some very personal information about persons. We might discover, for example, that Jones and Smith were arrested many years ago for engaging in homosexual activities. I will henceforth refer to personal facts belonging to the public record as documented.

My definition of privacy excludes knowledge of documented personal information. I do this for a simple reason. Suppose that *A* is browsing through some old newspapers and happens to see *B*'s name in a story about child prodigies who unaccountably fail to succeed as adults. *B* had become an obsessive gambler who committed suicide. Should we accuse *A* of invading *B*'s privacy? An affirmative answer needlessly blurs the distinction between the public and the private. What belongs to the public domain cannot without glaring paradox be called private and consequently should not be incorporated within a viable conception of privacy.

Thus I agree with the opinion, expressed in the well-known and much respected Second Restatement of Torts, that 'there is no liability (under invasion of privacy) for giving publicity to facts about the plaintiff's life which are matters of public record...'[4] And this is simply because the concept of privacy cannot reasonably be understood as embracing such facts. The U.S. Supreme Court has also recognized this point. In *Cox Broadcasting Corp.* v. *Cohn* Mr. Justice White, writing for the majority, affirmed that "the interests in privacy fade when the information involved already appears on the public record."[5]

No one will plausibly object that my definition is too broad. But is it too narrow? For instance, must not an adequate conception of privacy take into consideration the impressions we form of each other as well as the information we acquire about each other?

---

[4] Restatement of Torts (Second), Tentative Draft No. 13, section 652D, Comment C, at 114. The parenthetical addition is mine. See also Prosser's *Handbook of the Law of Torts*, 4th ed. (1971), section 116, pp. 810–11.
[5] Cox Broadcasting Corp. v. Cohn, 420 U.S. 469 (1975), at 19.

*Privacy for the Law* 309

Well, impressions are beliefs that are acquired from brief or casual encounters with a person or thing. Impressions can turn out to be either true or false. If they are true and concern personal facts about a person then they comprise personal information whose acquisition and disclosure does implicate bonafide privacy interests. If false, their acquisition and disclosure falls under the concept of libel or slander.

I believe, and have argued at length elsewhere[6] that privacy is an ideal distinct from values like secrecy, solitude, and autonomy. One very important virtue of my proposed definition is that it permits these distinctions and requires that they be respected in our moral-legal reasoning instead of being ignored or buried behind inflationary analyses. The search for adequate definitions is, as Plato averred, the search for essential ideas[7] or distinguishing characteristics. Those who charge me with narrowness should ask themselves whether the ideas, over and above that of undocumented personal information, which they would like to see incorporated under privacy cannot be more clearly and perspicuously articulated through other concepts.

## 3. The Right to Privacy

The concept of a right to privacy is quite different from and should not be confused with the concept of privacy simpliciter. The former is designed for the purpose of enabling us to discuss, classify, and condemn wrongful or unjustified invasions of privacy. To say that we possess a right to privacy means essentially that we are entitled not to be victimized by gratuitous or indiscriminate snooping, prying, spying, etc. It is one thing for me voluntarily to disclose undocumented personal facts about myself, or to have such facts responsibly gathered as a necessary part of important law-enforcement activities, for example. It is quite another matter

---

6 'Recent Work on the Concept of Privacy,' *The American Philosophical Quarterly*, forthcoming.
7 See *Theaetetus*, 206c–207a, and 208c, where Plato makes it clear he is seeking some mark by which knowledge differs from all other things.

if newspapers, the government, or private persons obtain and/or disseminate undocumented personal information about me without any compelling reasons or if in the pursuit of legitimate objectives they deploy irresponsible prying techniques. To argue against the latter we need the concept of a right to privacy.

Let me elaborate a bit on wrongful invasions of privacy. I think we can usefully classify them into three categories. There are first of all *gratuitous* or *wanton* intrusions, which can be broken down into the following kinds:

(1)     those that serve no legitimate purpose, being simply products of idle curiosity or malicious prankstering;

(2)     those that are unnecessary in that less intrusive means of obtaining the needed information are available — e.g., sending questionnaires instead of wiretapping;

(3)     those that are arbitrary and capricious — e.g., a government official orders surveillance on a group of citizens chosen at random on the grounds one of them might be involved in criminal activity.

The second category consists of *indiscriminate* invasions, and these can be broken down into two broad classes:

(1)     those that acquire information that is not relevant to the justifying purpose involved, as when the police secretly observe a restroom trying to apprehend homosexuals and in the process watch hundreds of innocent persons partake of the facility;

(2)     those that are carried out in such a way that persons with no business knowing the personal facts acquired are permitted cognitive access to them, as when a welfare officer discloses highly sensitive information about a recipient to his family and neighbors.

The third category of wrongful invasions of privacy includes failures to institute or enforce suitable safeguards for the procured information, thus allowing it to fall into the wrong hands. In view of the huge amounts of undocumented personal information

*Privacy for the Law* 311

generated today — perhaps this is the single most important consequence of living with computer technology — it is imperative that the storage facilities for the collected data be made secure against unwanted break-ins.

To guard against violations of the right to privacy I propose five requirements that must be met by anyone advocating the acquisition disclosure of undocumented personal knowledge.

A. *The need requirement.* There must be a valid or legitimate need for invading privacy.

B. *The probable cause requirement.* There must be probable cause to believe that the information sought is relevant to the justifying need. And there must be probable cause to believe that this information (and not some other, irrelevant information) can be obtained by the techniques recommended.

C. *The alternative means requirement.* There mustn't be any alternative, less intrusive means available for obtaining the desired information.

D. *The warrant requirement.* An impartial judicial officer must issue a warrant particularly describing the place to be searched and the information sought. The Fourth Amendment to the U.S. Constitution usually imposes this requirement on law enforcement officers.

E. *The security requirement.* There must be restrictions on cognitive access to the information during the times of its acquisition, disclosure, and storage, so that only persons entitled to know the facts have them.

The above is, of course, very sketchy, more an adumbration than a complete theory of the right to privacy. Still it does isolate most of the crucial questions that must be addressed when asking whether a particular program or activity does violate the right. To be sure reasonable persons will occasionally disagree over whether uses of physical, psychological, and data surveillance are gratuitous or indiscriminate.

Hence arguments concerning alleged violations of the right to privacy will continue to occupy us, and their resolutions will shape the contour of the right. But at least we will be arguing about

312                                                    *W. A. Parent*

privacy and not some other value. Our reasoning will be correctly
focused. Unhappily this cannot be said of our courts' recent
efforts.


## II. THE JUDICIAL MISHANDLING OF PRIVACY

### 4. *The Griswold Opinion*

The trouble all began in 1965 with the Supreme Court decision
*Griswold* v. *Connecticut*. The appellant Griswold was Director of
Connecticut's Planned Parenthood League. In that capacity he was
giving out information, instruction, and medical advice to married
persons regarding the use of contraceptives. Connecticut law forbade such activity. It also prohibited married couples from using
contraceptive devices. Griswold was arrested and convicted for
violating this law. He appealed and his case went all the way to the
Supreme Court.

   Mr. Justice Douglas wrote the majority opinion for the Court.
Refusing to judge the issue on liberty grounds, Douglas argued for
the existence of a constitutionally protected right to privacy. This
was not an easy task since the Constitution nowhere mentions a
right to privacy. Douglas's ingenious strategy involved the claim
that the specific guarantees of the Bill of Rights have penumbras
formed by emanations from these guarantees. These penumbras,
which breathe life and substance into our constitutional entitlements, create zones of privacy. These in turn form a general right
to privacy. *Griswold*, according to Douglas, concerns the kind of
intimate relationship between husband and wife that lies safely
within the privacy penumbra. The Connecticut contraceptive law
had a maximum destructive impact on this relationship. Accordingly it must be struck down.[8]

   Douglas's argument raises a number of vexing questions. We can
ask, as Mr. Justice Black did in dissent, whether any penumbral
analysis purporting to establish the existence of rights not express-

---

[8]  Griswold v. Connecticut, 381 U.S. 479 (1965), at 482–487.

ly enumerated in the constitutional text is legitimate. After all, if the founding fathers had intended to include privacy among the rights to be granted constitutional protection why didn't they explicitly say so? Black mordantly summed up the point this way: "I like my privacy as well as the next one, but I am nevertheless compelled to admit that government has a right to invade it unless prohibited by some specific constitutional provision."[9]

To my mind an even more urgent question to ask in light of Douglas's opinion is, how exactly are we to understand the meaning of the privacy that we are now told constitutes a fundamental right of the people? Douglas does not offer a definition of it, but without some attempt at conceptual elucidation one is hard pressed to assess his claim that privacy is indeed presupposed by several constitutional articles. It also becomes difficult to know what kinds of conduct the Court will subsequently declare to be in violation of the right to privacy.

The omission of a privacy definition is especially frustrating and disappointing in view of the fact, forcefully underscored in the Harlan and White dissents, that the Connecticut law under challenge in *Griswold* seemed most offensive to liberty interests, not privacy interests. For it prohibited an activity, hence constrained choice, hence limited the freedom, in a paradigmatic sense of the word, to pursue what many citizens probably regarded as a prudent, responsible objective. The way in which the law directly imperiled privacy was much less evident and only tangentially relevant to the Court's principal argument.

## 5. *The Eisenstadt Definition and Its Applications*

It took seven years before the U.S. Supreme Court told us how it conceived of the newly created privacy right. In *Eisenstadt v. Baird*, a case involving the validity of a Massachusetts statute that prohibited the use of contraceptives by unmarried couples, Mr. Justice Brennan writing for the majority declared:

---

[9]  Ibid., p. 510.

314                                                        *W. A. Parent*

It is true that in *Griswold* the right to privacy in question inhered in the
marital relationship. Yet the marital couple is not an independent entity with
a mind and heart of its own, but an association of two individuals each with
a separate intellectual and emotional makeup. If the right of privacy means
anything, it is the right of the *individual*, married or single, to be free from
unwarranted government intrusion into matters so fundamentally affecting a
person as the decision whether to bear or beget a child.[10]

The Massachusetts law was found by Brennan and three other Justices to be a violation of this right.

The following year we were told that the right to privacy,
understood as a species of the right to make fundamentally important decisions, is broad enough to encompass a woman's decision
whether or not to have an abortion, provided this decision concerns a nonviable fetus (the Court identified viability with the
capacity to lead a meaningful life outside the womb and placed it
at between 24–28 weeks of gestation) and is made in consultation
with a licensed physician.[11] During the next five years the
Supreme Court issued several more abortion decisions in which
they dealt with questions ranging from the rights of the husbands
and parents of women seeking abortions[12] to the responsibility
for funding the abortions of poor women.[13] For our purposes what
is most significant about these cases is that they (or at least the
majority opinions) treat the *Eisenstadt* definition as an established
part of Constitutional Law.

This fact of judicial usage received further confirmation in the
1977 case of *Whalen* v. *Roe*. The issue here was whether the state
of New York could record, in a centralized computer file, the
names and addresses of everyone who pursuant to a doctor's prescription obtains a Schedule II drug — e.g., cocaine, amphetamine,

---

[10]  Eisenstadt v. Baird, 405 U.S. 438 (1972), at 453.
[11]  Roe v. Wade, 410 U.S. 113 (1973), at 153.
[12]  See, for example, Planned Parenthood of Central Missouri v. Danforth,
428 U.S. 52 (1976); and Bellotti v. Baird, 428 U.S. 132 (1977).
[13]  See, for example, Maher v. Roe, 432 U.S. 464 (1977); and Beal v. Doe,
432 U.S. 438 (1977).

or other substance for which there is both a lawful and an unlawful market. In the course of upholding the validity of this practice the Court, in an opinion by Mr. Justice Stevens, singled out the interest in independence in making certain kinds of important decisions as a defining element in many of the privacy cases they had decided.[14]

In developing the contours of the right of privacy the Supreme Court has been faced with the difficult task of ranking different kinds of personal choices in terms of their importance to human well-being. The abortion and contraception choices have been classified as fundamentally important and hence as subsumable under the right of privacy. Other kinds of personal decisions have been refused this status. For example, in *Village of Belle Terre* v. *Boraas*, the Court ruled, over the vigorous dissent of Mr. Justice Marshall, that local communities may set limits on the number of single, unrelated adults living together in one household.[15] And the Court has refused to afford constitutional protection to the decision by homosexuals to have sexual intercourse with consenting adults in private.[16]

Several state courts have followed the U.S. Supreme Court in identifying the right of privacy with the right of individuals to make fundamentally important decisions. The New Jersey Supreme Court, for instance, in the famous *Quinlan* case, declared that the constitutional right to privacy "...is broad enough to encompass a patient's decision to decline medical treatment under certain circumstances, in much the same way as it is broad enough to encompass a woman's decision to terminate pregnancy under certain conditions."[17] The California Appeal Court asserted, in *People* v. *Privitera*, that the right to privacy explicitly set forth in the California Constitution "encompasses a fundamental and

---

[14] Whalen v. Roe 429 U.S. 589 (1977), at 599.
[15] Village of Belle Terre v. Boraas 416 U.S. 1 (1974).
[16] Doe v. Commonwealth's Attorney, 425 U.S. 901 (1976), affirming the decision in 403 F. Supp. 1199 (E.D. Va.).
[17] *In the Matter of Quinlan*, 355 A. 2d 647 (1976), at 663.

compelling interest of the cancer patient to choose or reject his or her own medical treatment on the advice of a licensed medical doctor."[18] And the Alaska Supreme Court ruled that the state and federal right to privacy is broad enough to protect the decision of adults to use marijuana in their homes.[19]

## 6. *A Respectful Dissent*

The above summary clearly shows that the right to privacy has come a long way in American law and has done so in a relatively short time. But has the journey been misguided from the outset? I believe that it has, and for the following reason. The *Eisenstadt* definition confuses the values of privacy and liberty. A person who makes and executes his own decisions without government interference can quite properly be described as acting in the absence of officially imposed (external) constraints. The commonly accepted and philosophically justified conception of liberty is precisely the absence of external constraints. Laws that effectively prevent citizens from pursuing various activities infringe (sometimes justifiably, sometimes not) on personal liberty. The laws in *Griswold, Eisenstadt, Roe, Privitera,* and *Ravin* all infringed liberty and were challenged for this reason.[20]

---

[18] People v. Privitera, 74 C.A. 3d 936 (1977), at 959. The Court of Appeal accordingly ruled that cancer patients do have the right to try leatrile as a treatment. The California Supreme Court disagreed, however. It accepted the privacy conceptualization of the issue, but argued that the right to privacy does not encompass the cancer patient's decision whether or not to use laetrile. See, People v. Privitera, 23 Cal. 3d. 697 (1979).

[19] Ravin v. State, 537 P. 2d. 494 (1975).

[20] Of course the enforcement of a law forbidding the use of contraceptives would raise serious and legitimate privacy questions, for doubtless all kinds of sensitive, undocumented personal information could be discovered in police raids. Douglas recognized this fact when he asked, "Would we allow the police to search the sacred precincts of marital bedrooms for telltale signs of the use of contraceptives? The very idea is repulsive to the notion of privacy surrounding the marital relationship." See *Griswold*, p. 516. But this difficulty is not the gravamen of petitioners' complaint. Nor is it addressed by the *Eisenstadt* definition.

At least two of the Supreme Court Justices recognized this. Writing separate concurring opinions in *Griswold*, Harlan and White argued that, in Harlan's words, "the proper constitutional inquiry in this case is whether the Connecticut statute infringes the Due Process Clause of the Fourteenth Amendment because the enactment violates basic values 'implicit in the concept of ordered liberty.' "[21] Both men thought that it did.[22]

A few law professors have taken note of this confusion between privacy and liberty. Henkin points it out as does Wellington, who goes on to urge the Supreme Court to develop a coherent and systematic theory of the right to liberty embodied in the Fifth and Fourteenth Amendments to the Constitution.[23] I enthusiastically endorse Wellington's suggestion. And I suggest that the Court might well want to incorporate the *Eisenstadt* definition in such a theory. For part of what the right to liberty means is that citizens ought not to be subject to unwarranted government coercion in matters which fundamentally affect their lives. Mr. Justice Harlan deserves credit for recognizing just this point and giving clear expression to it well before *Griswold:*

The full scope of the liberty guaranteed by the Due Process Clause cannot be found in or limited by the precise terms of the specific guarantees elsewhere presented in the Constitution. This 'liberty' is not a series of isolated points picked out in terms of the taking of property; the freedom of speech, press, and religion, the right to keep and bear arms; the freedom from unreasonable searches and seizures; and so on. It is a rational continuum which, broadly

---

[21] Ibid., p. 500.

[22] Justice Rehnquist makes a similar point about the Texas statute under challenge in Roe v. Wade. See his dissenting opinion, p. 172.

[23] See the Henkin and Wellington essays cited in note 1. For readers who may not be familiar with the constitutional amendments, the Fifth provides in part that no person "shall be compelled in any criminal case to be a witness against himself, not be deprived of life, liberty, or property without due process of law." This amendment constrains the federal government. The Fourteenth Amendment constrains state governments. It provides in part that no state shall "deprive any person of life, liberty, or property, without due process of law...."

speaking, includes freedom from all substantial arbitrary impositions and purposeless restraints ... and which also recognizes what a reasonable and sensitive judgment must, that certain interests require particularly careful scrutiny of the state needs asserted to justify their abridgement.[24]

Doubtless many of the Court's judgments about the arbitrariness or reasonableness of particular statutory or administrative restraints will be contested. A preponderance of legal opinion now believes, for instance, that the decision reached in the infamous *Lochner* decision, striking down a law that forbade employees in biscuit, bread, or confectionary establishments from contracting to work more than 60 hours per week or 10 hours per day, was mistaken.[25] Few constitutional scholars now accept the thesis, defended at length in *Lochner*, that laws designed to guard employees from unsafe or hazardous working conditions constitute arbitrary restrictions on liberty. But the remedy for *Lochner* does not consist either in judicial retreat from substantive due process, where judges assess the justification for laws which abridge basic liberties, or in feats of conceptual legerdemain. Instead it demands rigorous disciplined reasoning aimed at constructing credible criteria for distinguishing justifiable from unjustifiable forms of government coercion.

### 7. *The Brandeis Definition and Its Influence*

There is a second conception of privacy that several former members of the U.S. Supreme Court, including William Douglas,[26] Potter Stewart,[27] and Abe Fortas have embraced. According to it, privacy consists simply of being let alone. Fortas provides a more embellished formulation. The right to privacy, he says, "is, simply stated, the right to be let alone; to live one's life as one chooses, free from assault, intrusion, or invasion except as they can be justi-

---

[24]  Poe v. Ullman, 367 U.S. 497 (1962), at 543.
[25]  Lochner v. U.S., 198 U.S. 45 (1905).
[26]  See Douglas's *The Rights of the People* (Westport: Greenwood, 1958).
[27]  See, for example, Stewart's opinions in Katz v. U.S., 389 U.S. 347 (1967), at 350, and in Whalen v. Roe, 429 U.S. 589 (1977), at 608.

*Privacy for the Law* 319

fied by the clear needs of the community living under a government of law."[28]

A number of distinguished law professors think of privacy in essentially this way. Paul Freund, for example, argues that the right to privacy conceived of as the right to be left alone can serve a useful role as a principle of law.[29] Bloustein distinguishes individual privacy from group privacy and equates the former with the right to be let alone.[30] Posner, Monagham, and Konvitz share this view of privacy.[31] Shattuck, writing as a spokesman for the ACLU, gives his support to it.[32]

The definition owes its origin and much of its popularity to the writings of Louis Brandeis. In the classic essay 'The Right to Privacy,' written almost 100 years ago, Brandeis and Samuel Warren argued that American common law must respond to the growing threat to individual privacy posed by technological innovations like instantaneous photography as well as by irresponsible "newspaper enterprise" — i.e., gossip. The two young lawyers were especially worried about a press that in their opinion was

> overstepping in every direction the obvious bounds of propriety and of decency. Gossip is no longer the resource of the idle and of the vicious, but

[28] Time v. Hill, 385 U.S. 374 (1967), at 412. See also Fortas' opinion in Gertz v. Robert Welch, Inc., 418 U.S. 323 U.S. 323 (1974), at 412–13.
[29] Paul Freund, 'Privacy: One Concept or Many?' in *Nomos XIII: Privacy*, ed. J. Pennock and J. Chapman (New York: Atherton Press, 1971), pp. 182–98.
[30] Edward Bloustein, 'Group Privacy: The Right to Huddle,' in his *Individual and Group Privacy* (New Brunswick: Transaction Books, 1978), pp. 123–86.
[31] Henry Paul Monagham, 'Of "Liberty" and "Property,"' *Cornell Law Review* 62 (1977): 405–44; Milton Konvitz; 'Privacy and the Law: A Philosophical Prelude,' *Law and Contemporary Problems* 31 (1966): 272–80; Richard Posner, *The Economics of Justice* (Cambridge: Harvard U. Press, 1981), p. 272. Posner differentiates two bona fide senses of "privacy," those of secrecy and seclusion, and maintains that the latter protects our interest in being let alone.
[32] John Shattuck ed., *Rights of Privacy* (Skokie: National Textbook Co., 1977), in his introductory comments.

has become a trade, which is pursued with industry as well as effrontery. To satisfy a prurient task the details of sexual relations are spread broadcast in the columns of the daily papers. To occupy the indolent, column upon column is filled with idle gossip, which can only be secured by intrusion upon the domestic circle. The intensity and complexity of life, attendant upon advancing civilization, have rendered necessary some retreat from the world, and man, under the refining influence of culture, has become more sensitive to publicity so that solitude and privacy have become more essential to the individual; but modern enterprise and invention have, through invasion upon his privacy, subjected him to mental pain and distress far greater than could be inflicted by mere bodily injury.[33]

Warren and Brandeis thought that the law should respond to this most troublesome situation by granting formal recognition to the general right to be let alone, a right more basic than because presupposed by the venerable common-law right to intellectual and artistic property.[34] And they clearly identified the right to be let alone with the right to privacy.[35] Their argument, in short, was that the right to privacy is an integral and indispensible part of American common law whose enforcement had become necessary in order to forestall a way of life where "what is whispered in the closet shall be proclaimed from the housetops."[36]

Almost 40 years after the publication of 'The Right to Privacy' Brandeis reiterated his advocacy of the right to be let alone in a new famous dissent to the Supreme Court's decision, in *Olmstead v. N.Y.*, that wiretapping private telephone conversations did not violate the Fourth Amendment's prohibition against unreasonable searches and seizures.[37] The majority of the Court emphasized

---

[33] Samuel Warren and Louis Brandeis, 'The Right to Privacy,' *Harvard Law Review* 4 (1980): 196.
[34] In Warren's and Brandeis's words "no basis is discerned upon which the right to restrain publication and reproduction of such so-called literary and artistic works can be rested, except the right to privacy... ." Ibid., p. 207.
[35] Ibid., pp. 205–7.
[36] Ibid., p. 195.
[37] The Fourth Amendmend reads: "The right of the people to be secure in their persons, houses, papers, and effects, against unreasonable searches and seizures, shall not be violated, and no warrants shall issue, but upon probable

that wiretapping does not involve an actual physical trespass, but Brandeis did not see this as a reason for worrying less about invasion of privacy. On the contrary, he saw it as a reason for more concern and for more judicial diligence. In his words: "Whenever a telephone line is tapped, the privacy of the persons at both ends of of the line is invaded, and all conversations between them upon any subject, and although proper, confidential, and privileged, may be overheard."[38] Brandeis went on to proffer his well-known analysis of the Fourth Amendment:

The makers of our Constitution undertook to secure conditions favorable to the pursuit of happiness. They recognized the significance of man's spiritual nature, of his feelings and of his intellect. They knew that only a part of the pain, pleasure, and satisfactions of life are to be found in material things. They sought to protect Americans in their beliefs, their thoughts, their emotions, and their sensations. They conferred, as against the Government, the right to be let alone — the most comprehensive of rights and the right most valued by civilized men. To protect this right, every unjustifiable intrusion by the Government upon the privacy of the individual, whatever the means employed, must be deemed a violation of the Fourth Amendment.[39]

The right to privacy has never been so eloquently and passionately praised!

## 8. *A Second Respectful Dissent*

Unfortunately neither has the right been so badly misunderstood! Think about some of the ways in which *A* can fail to leave *B* alone: by hitting him, interrupting his conversation, shouting at him, repeatedly calling him, joining him for lunch. There is no compelling reason of logic or law to describe any of these actions as an invasion of privacy. To do so engenders a needlessly inflationary conception that manages to accomplish the nearly impossible feat of hopelessly obscuring the central, paradigmatic

---

cause, supported by Oath or affirmation, and particularly describing the place to be searched, and the person or things to be seized."

[38] Olmstead v. U.S., 277 U.S. 439 (1928), at 475–76.

[39] Ibid., p. 478.

meaning of privacy, viz., the condition of not having undocumented personal facts about oneself known by others. Of course privacy can be invaded through certain forms of human interaction. For example, if *A* interrupts *B*'s conversation with *C* and in the process finds out something very personal about *B* it would probably be entirely appropriate to talk about an invasion of privacy. But it is a serious mistake to insist that all instances of not letting a person alone are so similar to this one that we can call them all infringements of privacy.

## III. PROSSER, AND RECENT RESCUE ATTEMPTS

### 9. *The Failure of Prosser's Analysis*

One of the most influential essays on privacy, arguably the most important essay after Warren's and Brandeis's, is William Prosser's.[40] Prosser was an expert in the law of torts. His purpose in proffering an analysis of privacy cannot be understood as an attempt to rectify the judicial mishandling of the concept — the essay 'Privacy' was published in 1960 before this terrible quagmire began. Rather, Prosser wanted to bring some order and coherence to the tort law of privacy by classifying the huge number (over 300) of cases that the courts had until then decided on privacy grounds into distinct categories. His conclusion was that "the law of privacy comprises four distinct kinds of invasion of four different interests of the plaintiff — which interests have almost nothing in common except that each represents an interference with the right of the plaintiff 'to be let alone.' "[41]

Let us briefly examine Prosser's four privacy torts, to see whether he did fulfill his estimable purpose. The first form of privacy invasion is intrusion upon the plaintiff's seclusion or solitude, or into his private affairs. Typical of the cases falling under this category is *DeMay* v. *Roberts*, in which a young man in-

---

[40] William Prosser, 'Privacy,' *California Law Review* 48 (1960): 383–423.
[41] Ibid., p. 389.

truded upon a woman giving birth.[42] The woman didn't know the intruder, was very disturbed that he should be present at at time like this, and sued him for invasion of privacy.

Should the law endorse this conceptualization? The difficulty is that there are many ways to intrude upon a person's seclusion or solitude and it isn't at all obvious why we need to describe each in terms of privacy. In the *DeMay* case a cause of action for invasion of privacy would have been legally feasible and conceptually appropriate. But individuals complaining of environmental intrusions upon their solitude — e.g., loud noises, offensive odors — should seek a legal remedy under the law of nuisance. (They might also claim a violation of their right to property.) The intrusions of burglars definitely involves physical trespass; whether they also implicate privacy interests depends on what the burglars find out about their victims. Only intrusions that result in the acquisition of undocumented personal knowledge should be decided under privacy law.

Prosser's second privacy tort is public disclosure of embarrassing private facts. Typical of cases falling under this category is *Sidis* v. *F-R Publishing Corp.*[43] Sidis was a child prodigy who in his adult years became a recluse seeking anonymity, solitude, and privacy. The New Yorker magazine published a story on him which focused on his abandonment of intellectual pursuits for a life of simple, eccentric pleasures. He sued for invasion of privacy. *Melvin* v. *Reid*[44] is another common kind of disclosure case. The plaintiff was a former prostitute and defendant in a sensational murder trial. She was acquitted, left her life of shame, married, and began to lead a respectable life. Seven years later the defendant made and exhibited a motion picture which reenacted her true story using her past name. She sued for invasion of privacy.

I believe that *Sidis* is a genuine privacy case. (I also believe that he should have won the case.) But cases like *Melvin* are not

[42] DeMay v. Roberts, 9 N.W. 146 (1881).
[43] Sidis v. F-R Publishing Corp., 113 F. 2d 806 (1940).
[44] Melvin v. Reid, 112 Cal. App. 283 (1931).

because the facts revealed in them are undocumented. Anyone could easily — i.e., without resort to snooping or prying — have found out about the plaintiff's past life.

Prosser's third privacy tort is publicity that places the plaintiff in a false light in the public eye. Belonging to this category are cases like *Gill* v. *Curtis Publishing Co.*,[45] where the face of an innocent person was used to ornament an article on profane love, and *Peay* v. *Curtis Publishing Co.*,[46] where the face of an innocent cab driver was published in an article on the cheating propensities of cabbies.

False light grievances should be conceptualized and brought under the law of libel or slander. Invasion of privacy always involves the finding out of true information about persons. We must remember that persons can be injured badly by the disclosure of personal information about themselves. And when this information is no one else's business they can quite properly appeal to the right of privacy for legal protection.

The last privacy tort Prosser distinguishes is appropriation for the defendant's advantage of the plaintiff's name or likeness. Here we confront cases like *Roberson* v. *Rochester Folding Box Co.*,[47] where a beautiful young woman's picture was used without her consent to advertise flour, and *Pollard* v. *Photographic Co.*,[48] in which a photographer took plaintiff's picture and put it on sale.

It is a mistake to conceptualize these kinds of cases in terms of privacy. For they don't involve the finding out of personal facts about anyone. Most of them have essentially to do with the issue of financial renumeration and consequently should be handled as property cases. If the gravamen of petitioner's complaint is not financial but concerns the preemption of choice — she wasn't asked whether her name or likeness could be used — the right to liberty becomes the focus of attention. In neither situation does

---

[45] Gill v. Curtis Publishing Co., 38 Cal. 2d 273 (1952).

[46] Peay v. Curtis Publishing Co., 192 F. Supp. 395 (D.D.C., 1948).

[47] Roberson v. Rochester Folding Box Co., 64 N.E. 442 (1902).

[48] Pollard v. Photographic Co., 40 Ch. D. 345 (1888).

Privacy for the Law                                                          325

the concept of privacy have a useful role to play. Indeed it only
deflects attention away from the real issues at stake.

So Prosser's analysis is largely a failure. This should come as no
surprise, though, since he starts off on the wrong foot by accepting past judicial usage of the term "privacy" without blinking a
critical eye. Anyone who works from the naive assumption that
the courts have all along been working with an adequate conception of privacy is asking for trouble.

## 10. *The Failure of Recent Rescue Efforts*

A good number of legal scholars and philosophers have within the
past decade offered their own definitions of privacy. These can be
understood as attempts to clean up the disheveled haystack. Unfortunately they only contribute to the conceptual chaos.

Consider first Gerety's proposal that privacy be equated with
autonomy over the intimacies of personal identity.[49] What does he
have in mind by such intimacies? It turns out they consist of fundamental personal decisions that most of us would not want to be
regulated by law.[50] Decisions relating to sex receive most of
Gerety's attention. For him the paradigmatic form of privacy invasion is intrusion upon sexual autonomy.[51] Greenawalt[52] and
Richards[53] advance similar views of privacy. We can dispose of the
Gerety conception very quickly, for it is substantially equivalent
to the *Eisenstadt* definition and thus stands vulnerable to the
charge of conflating privacy with (one dimension of) liberty. If
anyone needs further convincing, there are two compelling counter-

---

[49] Tom Gerety, 'Redefining Privacy,' *Harvard Civil Rights – Civil Liberties
Law Review* 12 (1977): 236.
[50] Ibid., p. 273.
[51] Ibid., p. 296.
[52] Kent Greenawalt, 'Privacy and Its Legal Protections,' *Hastings Center
Studies* 2 (1974): 45–68.
[53] David A. J. Richards, 'Sexual Autonomy and the Constitutional Right to
Privacy: A Case Study in Human Rights and the Unwritten Constitution,'
*Hastings Law Journal* 30 (1979): 957–1018.

examples to the definition. Consider the case of a comatose patient who lacks any kind of autonomy. Efforts to safeguard his privacy still make perfectly good sense, and can be entirely successful. So the claim that autonomy over the intimacies of personal identity is a necessary condition of a person's privacy should be rejected. That such autonomy is not a sufficient condition either is shown by the fact that we can keep a suspected criminal under constant surveillance, thereby diminishing his privacy, without necessarily jeopardizing his sexual life.

One of the most popular recent conceptions of privacy identifies it with control over information about oneself. Elizabeth Beardsley, for example, equates the right to privacy with the right to selective disclosure and explicates the latter as the right to decide when and how much information about ourselves we will make known to others.[54] Fried[55] at times speaks of privacy in this way, as does Wasserstrom.[56] Alan Westin is perhaps its best-known advocate: privacy, he avers, is the claim of individuals, groups, or institutions to determine for themselves when, how, and to what extent information about them is communicated to others.[57]

This definition is far too broad. It implies, contrary to common sense and common usage, that whenever I go out in public my privacy is compromised since by doing so I lose considerable control over information that others can acquire about me. What jeopardizes privacy is the acquisition of personal facts about me and these are not imperiled by public activities.

An amended Westin conception, identifying privacy with

---

[54]. Elizabeth Beardsley, 'Privacy: Autonomy and Selective Disclosure,' in *Nomos XIII*, p. 65.

[55] Charles Fried, 'Privacy,' *Yale Law Journal* 77 (1968): 483.

[56] Richard Wasserstrom, 'The Legal and Philosophical Foundations of the Right to Privacy,' in *Biomedical Ethics* ed. Thomas Mappes and Jane Zembaty (New York, McGrawhill, 1981), p. 110.

[57] Alan Westin, *Privacy and Freedom* (New York: Atheneum, 1967), pp. 7 and 42.

control over personal information, has a few adherents, including Gross[58] and Wasserstrom[59] (the latter as well as Fried vacillate between these two definitions). But it too is unsatisfactory. For one thing it is subject to the comatose counterexample. It is also vulnerable to what might be called the voluntary self-disclosure counterexample. Suppose that *A* freely divulges all of the most intimate, personal facts about himself to *B*. Has *A* exercised control over this information? Well in one basic sense of "control" he certainly has, since it was within his power either to disclose or not to disclose and he chose to do the former. Yet in telling all to *B*, *A* has lost privacy. Here is a paradigm case where liberty is exercised at the expense of privacy.

Nor is control over personal information a necessary condition of privacy, if by "control" we mean the power to prevent disclosure of such information to individuals other than those to whom we have chosen to reveal it. Suppose that *B* has the technological prowess and the political authority to obtain all sorts of personal information about citizen *A*. And further suppose that *A* can do nothing to stop *B* from doing so and from disclosing the acquired facts to anyone he pleases. Under these circumstances *A* lacks control over these facts: he is without the power to prevent their disclosure by *B*. But is *A* without privacy? No, not unless *B* actually proceeds to initiate a prying and dissemination campaign against him. That *A*'s privacy is threatened doesn't mean it is actually diminished.

Still another control conception of privacy that has gained increasing support during the last decade, especially among social scientists, identifies it with control over access to the self. Irwin Altman is its most persuasive advocate. In two influential essays he attempts to defend the idea that privacy consists of a boundary control process whereby people can make themselves accessible

---

[58] Hyman Gross, 'Privacy and Autonomy,' in *Nomos XIII*, p. 170.
[59] Richard Wasserstrom, 'Privacy: Some Assumptions and Arguments,' in *Philosophical Law*, ed. Richard Bronaugh (Westport: Greenwood, 1978), pp. 157 and 162.

to others or close themselves off.[60] Van Den Haag[61] and Parker[62] offer similar conceptions.

This definition is no more plausible than any of the previous control species. It falls prey to the threatened loss and comatose counterexamples. In addition, it indulges the utterly fantastic assumption that we can and should exercise complete sovereignty over personal relationships. Plausible moral principles dictate that such relationships be founded on mutual accord and respect.

Something is radically wrong with the effort to conceive of privacy as a form of control. The right to control, whether it be over sexual matters, personal information, or access to oneself should be seen not as constitutive of the right to privacy but as an integral element of the right to liberty. Whenever one person or group of persons tries to deprive another of control over some aspect of his life, we should recognize this as attempted coercion and should evaluate it as such, under the general concept of freedom-limiting action.

One final definition of privacy should be mentioned. It equates privacy with the limitation of access to the self. Gavison[63] and Garrett[64] defend it. This definition is in one way broader than Altman's, since exercising autonomy is only one way to ensure distance from oneself. Unfortunately, it is no more convincing than the control conception. If "access" is taken to designate something like physical proximity to a person then this definition succumbs to the threatened loss counterexample. If "access" is

---

[60] Irwin Altman, 'Privacy — A Conceptual Analysis,' *Environment and Behavior* 8 (1976): 7–29; and Altman, 'Privacy Regulation: Culturally Universal or Culturally Specific?' *The Journal of Social Issues* 33 (1977): 66–84.

[61] Ernest Van Den Haag, 'On Privacy,' in *Nomos XIII*, p. 149.

[62] Richard Parker, 'A Definition of Privacy,' *Rutger's Law Review* 27 (1974). 286.

[63] Ruth Gavison, 'Privacy and the Limits of Law,' *Yale Law Journal* 89 (1980): 428.

[64] Roland Garrett, 'The Nature of Privacy,' *Philosophy Today* 18 (1974): 274.

*Privacy for the Law* 329

taken to designate knowledge of the self[65] then another problem emerges. Suppose that *A* taps *B*'s phone and overhears many of *B*'s intimate conversations. But there have been limits set on *A*'s snooping. He can only listen when there is in the opinion of a designated court probable cause to believe that *B* is planning a crime. Here we have a case of limited cognitive access *with* invasion of privacy.

The above survey does, I hope, strengthen the case for my own definition. Privacy ought to be conceived as the condition of not having undocumented personal information about oneself known. This account captures the essential meaning or, if you will, the form of privacy. Our courts should embrace it but they haven't thus far. So what can be done? One would be naive to suggest that the judiciary simply dismiss the *Griswold-Eisenstadt* line of cases and begin anew. The place of precedent in legal reasoning is firmly established and quite indispensable. In Part IV, I offer some more realistic suggestions.

## IV. FASHIONING A CREDIBLE PRIVACY JURISPRUDENCE

### 11. *Privacy and the Fourth Amendment*

I have argued that it is a mistake to interpret the Fifth and Fourteenth Amendments to the U.S. Constitution as safeguarding individual privacy. Rather their express purpose is to protect life, *liberty*, and property against unwarranted governmental intrusions. Are there any constitutional provisions that do safeguard privacy as I have defined it?

The Fourth Amendment, which condemns unreasonable searches and seizures and requires for any search the issuance of a warrant "particularly describing the place to be searched, and the persons or things to be seized," clearly is designed, among other things, to ensure that the government not acquire sensitive personal knowledge about citizens via arbitrary investigative methods (it

---

[65] Hyman Gross proposed this amended definition in his 'The Concept of Privacy,' *The New York University Law Review*, 42 (1967): 34–35.

is also designed to ensure that the government not arbitrarily interfere with citizens' enjoyment of their property). The warrant requirement in particular reflects our founding fathers' concern for what I earlier called indiscriminate invasions of privacy. And the reasonableness requirement serves to condemn what I have called gratuitous invasions of privacy. So the Amendment as a whole can plausibly be interpreted to presuppose a right to privacy.

It is convincing to say, then, that while privacy is not among the explicitly enumerated Constitutional rights it is nonetheless a right protected by the Constitution. It follows that whenever the Supreme Court is presented with questions concerning the admissibility of evidence secured by wiretapping or by other forms of official prying, or with questions concerning the need to obtain a search warrant before conducting a search, it inevitably engages in the difficult task of defining the contours of the right to privacy presupposed by the Fourth Amendment.

Over the past fifteen years the Court has been busily engaged in just this task. Here is a brief sampling of its opinions. In *Katz* v. *U.S.* it ruled that the police may not attach electronic listening devices to the outside of a telephone booth in order to record the conversations of a person suspected of conveying information on bets and wages without first obtaining a search warrant.[66] In *Berger* v. *N.Y.* the Court invalidated a permissive eavesdropping statute authorizing the indiscriminate use of electronic surveillance devices.[67] In *Stanley* v. *Georgia* it ruled that allegedly pornographic movies seized without a search warrant from the defendant's home could not be introduced as evidence in his trial.[68] In *Lo-Ji Sales, Inc.* v. *N.Y.* the Court declared that a search of an adult bookstore resulting in the seizure of several films and magazines violated petitioner's Fourth Amendment rights because the warrant issued failed to particularly describe the things to be

---

[66] Katz v. U.S., 389 U.S. 347 (1967).
[67] Berger v. N.Y., 388 U.S. 41 (1967).
[68] Stanley v. Georgia, 394 U.S. 557 (1969).

## Privacy for the Law                                                331

seized.[69] Finally, in *Steagold* v. *U.S.* the Court ruled that the police may not search for the subject of an arrest warrant in the home of a third party without first obtaining a search warrant.[70]

A more controversial area of Fourth Amendment jurisprudence involves automobile searches by the police. In several recent cases the Court has held that law enforcement officers who have probable cause to believe that contraband is concealed somewhere within a moving vehicle may conduct a warrantless search of the vehicle and of any individual compartments and containers they happen to find there.[71] Justices Marshall and Brennan have vigorously dissented from this broad ruling. Marshall argued that it will have profound implications for the privacy of citizens riding in automobiles. In his words:

A closed paper bag, a tool box, a knapsack, a suitcase, an attache case can alike be searched without the protection of the judgement of a neutral magistrate, based only on the rarely disturbed decision of a police officer that he has probable cause to search for contraband in the vehicle. The Court derives satisfaction from the fact that its rule does not exalt the rights of the wealthy over the rights of the poor. A rule so broad that all citizens lose vital Fourth Amendment protection is no cause for celebration.[72]

Two points merit emphasis here. First, reasonable persons are going to disagree when applying the right of privacy to particular searches. The judgments of purpose and responsibility that have to be made are not self-evident.[73] Second, and more significantly, the

---

[69]  Lo-Ji Sales v. N.Y., 442 U.S. 319 (1979).

[70]  Steagold v. U.S., 101 S. Ct. 1642 (1981).

[71]  See, for example, Texas v. White, 423 U.S. 67 (1975), and U.S. v. Ross, 72 L. Ed. 2ed 572 (1982).

[72]  U.S. v. Ross, at 605.

[73]  However in a case just handed down the Court did unanimously agree that the Fourth Amendment does not forbid the police from placing a beeper (radio transmitter which emits periodic signals that can be picked up by a radio receiver) in a drum of chloroform for the purpose of monitoring the progress of a car that carried the drum. Law enforcement officers reasonably believed that the parties under surveillance were conspiring to manufacture controlled substances, including methamphetamine, in violation of federal law. See Knotts v. U.S., 51 LW 4232 (1983).

*Privacy I*

*W. A. Parent*

law should require that these judgements be made, whenever possible and feasible, by a judge after he has been provided with all of the relevant data pertaining to the need for a search and its required scope. Procedural restraints governing the origination and implementation of privacy-invading techniques are of indispensable importance in safeguarding our dignity.

## 12. *Privacy and the First Amendment*

The First Amendment to the Constitution provides in part that "Congress shall make no law...abridging and freedom of speech, or of the press...' At first glance it might seem that the right to privacy is seriously jeopardized by this provision. After all, speech and the press are two prominent vehicles through which undocumented personal knowledge is disclosed, so if there aren't any legal restrictions whatsoever on their operation then what's to stop gratuitous and indiscriminate invasions of privacy on a massive scale?

Of course one should be surprised if this were indeed a consequence of First Amendment jurisprudence since, as we have seen, the Fourth Amendment serves in part to protect against just such a possibility. Are we to assume that the two Amendments work against each other?[74] No, for the simple reason that the Supreme Court has never treated the First Amendment as an absolute. Justifiable exceptions for the "no law" rule have been recognized and in my view the safeguarding of individual privacy against wrongful assault can and should be included among them. Let me elaborate.

The Supreme Court has never taken the position that the publication of obscenity is guaranteed under the First Amendment.[75] Every state has laws forbidding the sale of child porno-

---

[74] Mr. Justice Powell is surely right when observing that "the framers of the Constitution certainly did not think these fundamental rights (those belonging to the Bill of Rights) of a free society are incompatible with each other." See his majority opinion in Lloyd Corp. v. Tanner, 407 U.S. 551, at 570.

[75] Roth v. U.S., 354 U.S. 476 (1957), and Miller v. Ca., 413 U.S. 15 (1973).

graphy, for example. Similarly, the Court has never defended the view that public speech, no matter how inflammatory, enjoys an absolute immunity from legal restrictions. It all depends on the nature of the words used and the circumstances under which they are uttered.[76] Nor has the Court taken a completely hands-off attitude towards the publication of false statements about individuals. Libelous utterances do not fall within the area of constitutionally protected speech.[77]

Privacy deserves to count as a First Amendment limiting principle as well. Whenever the press discloses undocumented personal information about an individual in an entirely gratuitous, arbitrary, or indiscriminate manner it should be subject to legal sanctions. After all, the hurt and damage caused by such disclosures can be as severe and traumatic as that brought about by defamatory publications, instigative language, or obscenity. In other words, we can be seriously wronged by invasions of privacy and there is no compelling reason why the right to freedom of speech and of the press should be interpreted to allow this wrong while forbidding other comparable offenses.

Unfortunately First Amendment privacy jurisprudence is not faring well. For one thing, the Courts have too often confused false-light defamation grievances with bona fide privacy issues, this due unquestionably to Prosser's influence (see Part III, section 9). In addition, the Courts have on occasion treated cases involving the disclosure of documented personal information as raising legitimate privacy interests.[78] This is unfortunate because, as I

---

[76] Schenck v. U.S., 249 U.S. 47 (1919) is the classic case here. The Court introduced the "clear and present danger" test for deciding whether inflammatory speech can be stopped.

[77] See Brauhainais v. Illinois, 343 U.S. 250 (1952).

[78] See, for example, Melvin v. Reid, and Briscoe v. Reader's Digest Association, Inc., 4 C. 3d 529 (1971), in which a former truck hijacker's identity, already a part of the public record, was divulged in Reader's Digest some eleven years after he had committed the crime. The California Supreme Court ruled that the publication of plaintiff's name was not newsworthy, interfered with his rehabilitative process, and therefore furnished him with a valid cause of action under privacy law.

have argued earlier, documented facts belong to the public sphere and therefore cannot without undue strain be brought under the concept of privacy. Finally, when the Courts have been presented with obviously gratuitous infringements of bona fide privacy interests they have not always given protection to these interests. A classic instance of this failure is *Sidis* v. *F-R Publishing Corp.*[79] Sidis was a child prodigy – he was lecturing to Harvard professors on the Fourth Dimension at 11. In his latter years he sought privacy and solitude, living a quiet and rather eccentric life. The New Yorker magazine interrupted his quest for anonymity by publishing two articles with pictures depicting his "decline" from scholarly preeminence. Sidis sued the magazine but, much to the chagrin of privacy lovers, lost resoundingly. We can only hope that the future will bring more promising results.

### 13. *Privacy and Whalen*

In my opinion *Whalen* v. *Roe* is the most significant privacy decision rendered by the supreme Court in the last decade. I say this for two reasons: for the first time the Justices explicitly endorse a conception of privacy that is nearly adequate; and they display some moral sensitivity to some of the conditions that must be satisfied if our right to privacy (in the sense defended in this paper) is to be taken seriously.

The facts of *Whalen* are as follows. The state of New York required that the names and addresses of all persons obtaining schedule II drugs – e.g., opium, cocaine, amphetamines and other drugs for which there is both a lawful and an unlawful use – be kept on record in a centralized computer file. This information was put on magnetic tapes that were then stored in a vault. After five years the tapes would be destroyed. A locked fence and alarm system provided security for the information-processing system. Public disclosure of the patient's identity was prohibited.

The Court unanimously agreed that this legislation did not

---

[79]  Sidis v. F-R Publishing Corp., 113 F. 2d 806 (2d Circ., 1940).

infringe the patient's right to privacy. But in reaching this (reasonable, I believe) conclusion, the judges exhibited a genuine concern for the privacy interests at stake. Thus Justice Stevens wrote:

We are not unaware of the threat to privacy implied in the accumulation of vast amounts of personal information in computerized data banks or other massive government files. The collecting of taxes, the distribution of welfare and social security benefits, the supervision of public health, the direction of our armed forces, and the enforcement of the criminal laws all require the orderly preservation of great quantities of information, much of which is personal in nature and potentially embarrassing or harmful if disclosed. The right to collect and use such data for public purposes is typically accompanied by a concomitant statutory or regulatory duty to avoid unwarranted disclosures.[80]

The Court has appropriately scrutinized the New York scheme to ensure that it does not allow gratuitous or indiscriminate invasions of privacy and that the personal facts accumulated and filed in the State Department of Health are secure against unjustified cognitive access. In so doing it has used the criteria I set forth (Part I, section 3) for identifying wrongful invasions of privacy. And it has appropriated, at last, a conception of privacy quite different from the *Griswold-Eisenstadt* definition, a conception that focuses essentially on the interest in avoiding disclosure of personal matters. Justice Stevens uses exactly these words[81] to describe it. If the Court were to combine this account with their observation in *Cohn* that facts belonging to the public record are not a part of the privacy interest then they would have the right definition. We might then see a new era of conceptually accurate, morally responsible privacy jurisprudence.

The recent case of *H. L.* v. *Matheson* reminds us, however, that even with the correct conception of privacy members of the Court will continue to disagree over the question of its wrongful invasion. Utah law requires that physicians notify, if possible, the

---

[80] Whalen v. Roe, 429 U.S. 589 (1976), at 605.
[81] Ibid., p. 599.

parents or guardians of a minor upon whom an abortion is to be performed. It also requires physicians to notify the husband of a woman seeking an abortion. A majority on the Court did not believe that this law violated women's right to privacy. Justice Marshall, joined by Brennan and Blackman, strongly disagreed. Marshall, utilizing the *Whalen* definition of privacy, expressed his dissent thus:

Many minors, like appellant, oppose parental notice and seek instead to preserve the fundamental, personal right to privacy. It is for these minors that the parental notification requirement creates a problem. In this context, involving the minor's parents against her wishes effectively cancels her right to avoid disclosure of her personal choice. Moreover, the notice requirement publicizes her private consultation with her doctor and interjects additional parties in the very conference held confidential in *Roe* v. *Wade*.[82]

Surely the crucial issue here is whether the disclosures of an intention to abort serves a valid purpose. The claim that it will bring about greater familial cohesion is problematic, given the emotional nature of the subject and the communications gap that characterizes so many parent-daughter relationships. The argument that notification will minimize the likelihood of rash, unwise decisions to abort is also problematic. It will more likely either preempt any decision at all on the part of the women — they will see themselves as having no choice but to have the baby — or drive them to defy the law, at possible risk to their own health, seeking any doctor willing to perform a secret abortion. If no persuasive arguments are forthcoming in defense of the notification requirement, we should declare it a gratuitous invasion of privacy and accordingly invalidate ıt as a violation of the right to privacy protected by though not explicitly mentioned in the Constitution.

## 14. *Privacy and the Ninth Amendment*

The Ninth Amendment reads: "The enumeration in the Constitution of certains rights, shall not be construed to deny or disparage

---

[82]   H. L. v. Matheson, 101 S. Ct. 1164 (1981), at 1186.
[83]   Griswold v. Connecticut, at 493.

## Privacy for the Law 337

others retained by the people." Justice Goldberg attempted to find the right of privacy in this Amendment thereby making it part of the Constitution. However, his argument, set out at great length in *Griswold*, rests on a fallacy. For he supposes that it is the responsibility of judges to decide which rights not named in the Constitution are retained by the people. Judges are to make such decisions looking to the traditions and collective conscience (whatever that is) of the people.[83] But there is nothing in the Ninth Amendment authorizing the judiciary to undertake this task. The only reasonable interpretation of the Amendment is that *the people* can and should decide which rights they want for themselves.

There are various means available for the people to exercise this right with respect to privacy. We can push for privacy legislation in Congress. We can urge our state representatives and governors to pass laws and regulations safeguarding privacy against wrongful invasion. Finally, we can demand that our State Constitutions give formal recognition to a basic right to privacy. California citizens did this in 1972. They passed a Legislative Constitutional Amendment adding privacy to the inalienable rights of the people set forth in Article 1, Section 1.[84] Some of the arguments deployed on behalf of this Amendment were badly confused — for example, the right to privacy is equated with the right to be let alone.[85] Nonetheless important points were made, particularly concerning the serious dangers posed by the proliferation of government snooping and data collection. Many were made painfully aware of the fact that, in the language of the Election Brochure, "computerization of records makes it possible to create cradle-to-grave profiles on every American."[86]

---

[84] Article 1, Section 1 of the California Constitution now begins: "All people are by nature free and independent and have inalienable rights. Among these are enjoying and defending life and liberty, acquiring, possessing, and protecting property, and pursuing and obtaining safety, happiness, *and privacy*." (Italics mine.)

[85] California Election Brochure, Proposition 11 (Nov., 1972), p. 27.

[86] Ibid., p. 26.

338 *W. A. Parent*

The right to privacy is uniquely qualified for use in arguments urging the responsible exercise of high technology information processing and management capabilities. These capabilities will become increasingly powerful during the last third of this century, so the need to demand our privacy properly conceived in terms of undocumented personal knowledge will become more urgent and more vital. It might also become more difficult given the predictable resistance of technology capitalists. The future role of privacy in the law hangs in the balance.

Dept. of Philosophy
University of Santa Clara
Santa Clara, CA 95053
U.S.A.

# [3]

## Privacy*

## Charles Fried†

Privacy has become the object of considerable concern. The purely fortuitous intrusions inherent in a compact and interrelated society have multiplied. The more insidious intrusions of increasingly sophisticated scientific devices into previously untouched areas, and the burgeoning claims of public and private agencies to personal information, have created a new sense of urgency in defense of privacy. The intensity of the debates about electronic eavesdropping and the privilege against self-incrimination are but two examples of this urgency.

The purpose of this essay is not to add yet another concrete proposal, nor even to call attention to yet another intrusion upon privacy. Rather I propose to examine the foundations of the right of privacy—the reasons why men feel that invasions of that right injure them in their very humanity.

### I.

To bring out the special quality of the concern over privacy I shall first put a not entirely hypothetical proposal, which should serve to isolate from restrictions and intrusions in general whatever is peculiar about invasions of privacy.

There are available today electronic devices to be worn on one's person which emit signals permitting one's exact location to be determined by a monitor some distance away.[1] These devices are so small as to be entirely unobtrusive: other persons cannot tell that a subject is "wired," and even the subject himself—if he could forget the initial installation—need be no more aware of the device than of a small bandage. Moreover, existing technology can produce devices capable of monitoring not only a person's location, but other significant facts about him: his temperature, pulse rate, blood pressure, the alcoholic content of his blood, the sounds in his immediate environment—e.g., what he

* The author wishes to express his thanks to the Editors of the Yale Law Journal for their very great understanding and skill in helping him to extricate the material for this article from a much longer work now in progress, of which the discussion of privacy is a small part.

† Professor of Law, Harvard Law School. A.B. 1956 Princeton University; LL.B. 1960 Columbia University; M.A. Oxon. 1961.

1. For a discussion of these devices and the legal issues to which they give rise, see Note, *Anthropotelemetry: Dr. Schwitzgebel's Machine* 80 HARV. L. REV. 403 (1966).

The Yale Law Journal                          Vol. 77: 475, 1968

says and what is said to him—and perhaps in the not too distant future even the pattern of his brain waves. The suggestion has been made, and is being actively investigated, that such devices might be employed in the surveillance of persons on probation or parole.

Probation leaves an offender at large in the community as an alternative to imprisonment, and parole is the release of an imprisoned person prior to the time that all justification for supervising him and limiting his liberty has expired. Typically, both probation and parole are granted subject to various restrictions. Most usually the probationer or parolee is not allowed to leave a prescribed area. Also common are restrictions on the kinds of places he may visit—bars, pool halls, brothels, and the like—or the persons he may associate with, and on the activities he may engage in. The most common restriction of the latter sort is a prohibition on drinking, but sometimes probation and parole have been revoked for "immorality"—that is, intercourse with a person other than a spouse. There are also affirmative conditions, such as a requirement that the subject work regularly in an approved employment, maintain an approved residence or report regularly to correctional, social, or psychiatric personnel. Failure to abide by such conditions is thought to endanger the rehabilitation of the subject and to identify him as a poor risk.

Now the application of personal monitoring to probation and parole is obvious. Violations of any one of the conditions and restrictions could be uncovered immediately by devices using present technology or developments of it; by the same token, a wired subject assured of detection would be much more likely to obey. Although monitoring is admitted to be unusually intrusive, it is argued that this particular use of monitoring is entirely proper, since it justifies the release of persons who would otherwise remain in prison, and since surely there is little that is more intrusive and unprivate than a prison regime. Moreover, no one is obliged to submit to monitoring: an offender may decline and wait in prison until his sentence has expired or until he is judged a proper risk for parole even without monitoring. Proponents of monitoring suggest that seen in this way monitoring of offenders subject to supervision is no more offensive than the monitoring on an entirely voluntary basis of epileptics, diabetics, cardiac patients and the like.

## II.

Much of the discussion about this and similar (though perhaps less futuristic) measures has proceeded in a fragmentary way to catalogue the

Privacy

disadvantages they entail: the danger of the information falling into the wrong hands, the opportunity presented for harassment, the inevitable involvement of persons as to whom no basis for supervision exists, the use of the material monitored by the government for unauthorized purposes, the danger to political expression and association, and so on.[2] Such arguments are often sufficiently compelling, but situations may be envisaged where they are overridden. The monitoring case in some of its aspects is such a situation. And yet one often wants to say the invasion of privacy is wrong, intolerable, although each discrete objection can be met. The reason for this, I submit, is that privacy is much more that just a possible social technique for assuring this or that substantive interest. Such analyses of the value of privacy often lead to the conclusion that the various substantive interests may after all be protected as well by some other means, or that if they cannot be protected quite as well, still those other means will do, given the importance of our reasons for violating privacy. It is just because this instrumental analysis makes privacy so vulnerable that we feel impelled to assign to privacy some intrinsic significance. But to translate privacy to the level of an intrinsic value might seem more a way of cutting off analysis than of carrying it forward. In this essay I hope to show that it is possible to discuss what it means to accord to privacy such a high status and to show why the value of privacy should be recognized.

It is my thesis that privacy is not just one possible means among others to insure some other value, but that it is necessarily related to ends and relations of the most fundamental sort: respect, love, friendship and trust. Privacy is not merely a good technique for furthering these fundamental relations; rather without privacy they are simply inconceivable. They require a context of privacy or the possibility of privacy for their existence. To make clear the necessity of privacy as a context for respect, love, friendship and trust is to bring out also why a threat to privacy seems to threaten our very integrity as persons. To respect, love, trust, feel affection for others and to regard ourselves as

2. The literature on privacy is enormous. A. WESTIN, PRIVACY AND FREEDOM (1967), provides an exhaustive bibliography as well as a critical review of the literature. In addition, Part One of that book presents a sensitive general theory of privacy much along the lines of the present article. Of particular interest also is the symposium on privacy in 31 LAW & CONTEMP. PROB. 251-435 (1966).

For an example of the fragmentary approach referred to in the text, as applied to one manifestation of privacy, the privilege against self-incrimination, see McNaughton, *The Privilege Against Self-Incrimination: Its Constitutional Affectation, Raison d'Etre and Miscellaneous Implications,* 51 J. CRIM. L.C. & P.S. 138 (1960). Dean Prosser takes this fragmentary approach to the right of privacy as recognized by tort law. *See* Prosser, *Privacy,* 48 CALIF. L. REV. 383 (1960). And he has been criticized for it. Bloustein, *Privacy as an Aspect of Human Dignity: An Answer to Dean Prosser,* 39 N.Y.U.L. REV. 962 (1964).

the objects of love, trust and affection is at the heart of our notion of ourselves as persons among persons, and privacy is the necessary atmosphere for these attitudes and actions, as oxygen is for combustion.

### III.

The conception of privacy as a necessary context for love, friendship and trust depends on a complex account of these concepts, and they in turn depend on the more general notions of morality, respect and personality. If my sketch of this underlying perspective leaves the reader full of doubts and queries, I draw comfort from the fact that a more elaborate presentation of this system is in progress.[3] I only hope that the sketch I give here has sufficient coherence to lay the basis for the discussion of privacy which is the primary concern of this essay.

Love, friendship and trust are not just vague feelings or emotions; they each comprise a system of dispositions, beliefs and attitudes which are organized according to identifiable principles. Though love, friendship and trust differ from each other, they each build on a common conception of personality and its entitlements. This conception is a moral conception of the basic entitlements and duties of persons in regard to each other, and the structure of that conception is articulated by what I call the principle of morality and the correlative attitude of respect.

The view of morality upon which my conception of privacy rests is one which recognizes basic rights in persons, rights to which all are entitled equally, by virtue of their status as persons. These rights are subject to qualification only in order to ensure equal protection of the same rights in others. In this sense, the view is Kantian; it requires recognition of persons as ends, and forbids the overriding of their most fundamental interests for the purpose of maximizing the happiness or welfare of all. It has received contemporary exposition in the work of John Rawls, who—summing up the fundamental interests of persons in the term "liberty"—has formulated the maxim that social institutions must be framed so as to entitle each person to the maximum liberty compatible with a like liberty for all.[4]

---

3. For a preliminary statement of the larger scheme, see Fried, *Reason and Action*, 11 NATURAL L.F. 13 (1966).

4. The ethical system I sketch here is essentially Kantian. Different aspects of it are expressed in I. KANT, FOUNDATIONS OF THE METAPHYSICS OF MORALS (L. Beck transl. 1959) and in I. KANT, METAPHYSICAL ELEMENTS OF JUSTICE (J. Ladd transl. 1965). For a discussion of the use of the term morality to apply primarily to the principles governing the relations of persons with each other see Falk, *Morality, Self and Others*, and Frankena, *Recent Conceptions of Morality*, in MORALITY AND THE LANGUAGE OF CONDUCT (H. Casta-

Privacy

The principle of morality does not purport to represent the highest value in a person's economy of values and interests. It necessarily assumes that persons have a variety of substantive values and interests and it is consistent with a large range of ethical systems which rank these values and interests in many different ways. It functions rather as a constraint upon systems and orderings of values and interests, demanding that whatever their content might be, they may be pursued only if and to the extent that they are consistent with an equal right of all persons to a similar liberty to pursue their interests, whatever they might be. Thus the principle of morality, far from representing a complete system of values, establishes only the equal liberty of each person to define and pursue his values free from undesired impingements by others. The principal of morality establishes not a complete value system but the basic entitlements of persons vis-à-vis each other.[5]

Correlative to this view of morality—and indeed to any view which recognizes moral entitlements in persons—is the concept of respect.[6] Respect is the attitude which is manifested when a person observes the constraints of the principle of morality in his dealings with another person, and thus respects the basic rights of the other. Respect is also an attitude which may be taken in part as defining the concept of a person: persons are those who are obliged to observe the constraints of the principle of morality in their dealings with each other,[7] and thus to show respect towards each other.[8] Self-respect is, then, the attitude by which a person believes himself to be entitled to be treated by other persons in accordance with the principle of morality.

The principle of morality and its correlative, respect, lie at the bottom of our conception of justice and fair play, as moral philosophers

ñeda & G. Nakhnikian eds. 1963). Much of what I say derives, however, not from Kant, but more directly from the writings of John Rawls, who in his published and unpublished work has developed a comprehensive system of concepts and principles. In addition to the published articles (*Legal Obligation and the Duty of Fair Play*, in LAW AND PHILOSOPHY 3 (S. Hook ed. 1964); *The Sense of Justice*, 72 PHIL. REV. 281 (1963); *Constitutional Liberty and the Concept of Justice*, in NOMOS VI, JUSTICE 98 (C. Friedrich & J. Chapman eds. 1963); *Justice as Fairness*, 67 PHIL. REV. 164 (1958)), I have profited greatly from an opportunity to read Professor Rawls' unpublished chapters on justice and his lectures on Kant and Hegel. *See also* Hart, *Are There Any Natural Rights?*, 64 PHIL. REV. 175 (1955).

5.  For a discussion see Fried, *Natural Law and the Concept of Justice*, 74 ETHICS 237, 250 (1964).

6.  The concept of respect is also Kantian. I. KANT, CRITIQUE OF PRACTICAL REASON 76-84 (L. Beck transl. 1956). The best recent discussion of this concept of respect and its relation to personality is J. PIAGET, THE MORAL JUDGMENT OF THE CHILD (M. Gabain transl. 1948). An excellent and fundamental illustration of the importance of respect in human relations is Hegel's dialectic of the master and the slave, discussed in 2 J. PLAMENATZ, MAN AND SOCIETY 154-56, 188-92 (1963).

7.  The condition is sufficient, not necessary, since children, lunatics, and some others are also to be considered persons. All persons are entitled to the respect of other persons.

8.  *See generally* PIAGET, *supra* note 6; Rawls, *The Sense of Justice*, *supra* note 4.

The Yale Law Journal                    Vol. 77: 475, 1968

have convincingly argued. Perhaps less obviously, they play an important part in our concepts of love, friendship and trust.[9] It is my thesis
that an essential part of the morality which underlies these relations is
the constraint of respect for the privacy of all, by state and citizen alike.

IV.

There can be no thought of counting on an accepted core of meaning
in developing the concept of love. What I say about love therefore cannot be taken as expressing a synthesis of all that has plausibly been
thought and said on the subject. Nevertheless an important tradition of
thought about love holds that it is a necessary feature of that emotion
that the beloved person be valued for his own sake, and not on account
of some attribute or product.[10] This aspect of love corresponds to the respect which we are obligated to accord each other. But morality requires
impartial respect; love, surely, is not so impartial. The respect required
by morality is a necessary condition for love; it is not sufficient. The further element in love is a spontaneous relinquishment of certain entitlements of one's own to the beloved, a free and generous relinquishment
inspired by a regard which goes beyond impartial respect. But a sense of
freedom and generosity depends—logically depends—on a sense of the
secure possession of the claims one renounces and the gifts one bestows.
I shall argue that the nature of the gifts of love and friendship is such
that privacy is necessary to provide one important aspect of security.

This account has emphasized the necessity to love of a voluntary relinquishment of rights. But love is not, of course, so negative nor so one-
sided. Persons love, hoping to be loved in return, and thus the fulfilled
form of the relationship is one of mutual relinquishment of entitlement, but not simply of relinquishment. The fulfilled form is the mutual relinquishment of rights in favor of new, shared interests which the
lovers create and value as the expression of their relationship.
Thus love is an active and creative relationship not only of reciprocal
relinquishment but reciprocal support as well. The structure of this reciprocal relationship is complex and elusive,[11] and I shall not analyze it
further here. For present purposes it is sufficient to see that the gift, the

---

9. For a discussion of the relationship between these concepts and the principle of
morality see Rawls, *The Sense of Justice, supra* note 4. Although my account differs from
Rawls' in some respects, it is based on his.

10. *Cf.* ARISTOTLE, NICOMACHEAN ETHICS bk. 8, chs. 2-3.

11. For an excellent discussion see M. SCHELER, THE NATURE OF SYMPATHY, especially
ch. 7 (P. Heath transl. 1954).

Privacy

relinquishment, is logically prior to the relationship which requires it; and if privacy is necessary to the first, it is necessary to the second.

Friendship differs from love largely in the degree of absorption in the relationship and of the significance which the relationship has in the total economy of a person's life and interests. Allowing for these differences of degree, love and friendship are close in that they have a similar relation to the more general concepts of morality and respect. And that similar relation is all that I propose here concerning friendship.

Intuitively, trust is an attitude of expectation about another person. But it would be a mistake to see it as simply a recognition of a disposition in another and a reliance that he will act in accordance with that disposition.[12] To be sure, we have expressions such as "trust him to do *that*," where "*that*" may be a vile deed which we know to be in character for that person, or perhaps a fit of sneezing during a grand evening at the opera on the part of a person given to sneezing when in close proximity to perfumed ladies. But these usages are ironical. Although trust has to do with reliance on a disposition of another person, it is reliance on a disposition of a special sort: the disposition to act morally, to deal fairly with others, to live up to one's undertakings, and so on. Thus to trust another is first of all to expect him to accept the principle of morality in his dealings with you, to respect your status as a person, your personality.

Trust, like love and friendship, is in its central sense a *relation*: it is reciprocal. Fairness does not require that we sacrifice our interests for the sake of those who are not willing to show us a similar forbearance. Thus as to those who do not accept morality, who are wicked and deceitful, the occasion for trust does not arise. We do not trust them, and they have no reason to trust us in the full sense of a relationship of mutual expectation, for our posture towards them is not one of cooperative mutual forbearance but of defensive watchfulness. Thus not only can a thoroughly untrustworthy person not be trusted; he cannot trust others, for he is disabled from entering into the relations of voluntary reciprocal forbearance for mutual advantage which trust consists of. At most an untrustworthy person can predict more or less accurately how another will behave, but the behavior he predicts will not arise out of a relation of mutual respect which each party has for the personality of the other

---

12. For a brilliant sociological analysis of trust, which seems perhaps to overemphasize this aspect of trust, see Garfinkel, *A Conception of, and Experiments with, "Trust" as a Condition of Stable Concerted Actions*, in MOTIVATION AND SOCIAL INTERACTION 187 (O. Harvey ed. 1963).

The Yale Law Journal                        Vol. 77: 475, 1968

and a reciprocal willingness to work together according to the constraints of morality.

Trust is like love and friendship in that it is a "free" relationship. Morality does not require that we enter into relations of trust with our fellow men. But trust differs from love or friendship in that it is not always a relation we seek simply for its own sake. It is more functional. Persons build relations on trust in part because such relations are useful to accomplish other ends. (In a sense love and friendship are needed for the pursuit of ends too, but they are ends that arise out of the relationship itself, and are shared in it.) However, the other ends never dominate entirely: they may be attainable without genuine trust, and the recourse to trust is then an independent and concurrent affirmation of respect for human personality. So, whether as individuals or as states, we conduct our business when we can on the basis of trust, not just because it is more efficient to do so—it may not be—but because we value the relations built on trust for their own sake. Finally, trust is also less intrusive than love or friendship. Trust can be limited to the particular matter at hand, and does not imply a disposition to seek more and more mutually shared ends. Thus, one can trust persons for whom one has neither love nor liking, although friendship and love imply, at least in the standard cases, trust as well.

## V.

Privacy is closely implicated in the notions of respect and self-respect, and of love, friendship and trust. Quite apart from any philosophical analysis this is intuitively obvious. In this section I shall try to make the connection explicit. In general it is my thesis that in developed social contexts love, friendship and trust are only possible if persons enjoy and accord to each other a certain measure of privacy.

It is necessary at the outset to sharpen the intuitive concept of privacy. As a first approximation, privacy seems to be related to secrecy, to limiting the knowledge of others about oneself. This notion must be refined. It is not true, for instance, that the less that is known about us the more privacy we have. Privacy is not simply an absence of information about us in the minds of others; rather it is the *control* we have over information about ourselves.

To refer for instance to the privacy of a lonely man on a desert island would be to engage in irony. The person who enjoys privacy is able to grant or deny access to others. Even when one considers private situa-

Privacy

tions into which outsiders could not possibly intrude, the context implies some alternative situation where the intrusion is possible. A man's house may be private, for instance, but that is because it is constructed —with doors, windows, window shades—to allow it to be made private, and because the law entitles a man to exclude unauthorized persons. And even the remote vacation hide-away is private just because one resorts to it in order—in part—to preclude access to unauthorized persons.

Privacy, thus, is control over knowledge about oneself. But it is not simply control over the quantity of information abroad; there are modulations in the quality of the knowledge as well. We may not mind that a person knows a general fact about us, and yet feel our privacy invaded if he knows the details. For instance, a casual acquaintance may comfortably know that I am sick, but it would violate my privacy if he knew the nature of the illness. Or a good friend may know what particular illness I am suffering from, but it would violate my privacy if he were actually to witness my suffering from some symptom which he must know is associated with the disease.[13]

VI.

There are reasons other than its relation to love, friendship and trust why we value privacy. Most obviously, privacy in its dimension of control over information is an aspect of personal liberty. Acts derive their meaning partly from their social context—from how many people know about them and what the knowledge consists of.[14] A reproof administered out of the hearing of third persons may be an act of kindness, but if administered in public it becomes cruel and degrading. Thus, for instance, if a man cannot be sure that third persons are not listening—if his privacy is not secure—he is denied the freedom to do what he regards as an act of kindness.

Besides giving us control over the context in which we act, privacy has a more defensive role in protecting our liberty. We may wish to do or say things not forbidden by the restraints of morality, but which are nevertheless unpopular or unconventional. If we thought that our every word and deed were public, fear of disapproval or more tangible retalia-

13. These modulations are explored with great subtlety and a wealth of concrete illustrations in E. GOFFMAN, BEHAVIOR IN PUBLIC PLACES (1963); E. GOFFMAN, ENCOUNTERS (1961); E. GOFFMAN, THE PRESENTATION OF SELF IN EVERYDAY LIFE (1959).
14. The writings of Erving Goffman, *supra* note 13, are replete with illustrations of the connections between context and relations among persons.

The Yale Law Journal                    Vol. 77: 475, 1968

tion might keep us from doing or saying things which we would do or say if we could be sure of keeping them to ourselves or within a circle of those who we know approve or tolerate our tastes.[15]

For these important reasons, among others, men would value privacy even if there were nothing in the world called love, friendship or trust. These reasons support the familiar arguments for the right of privacy. Yet they leave privacy with less security than we feel it deserves; they leave it vulnerable to arguments that a particular invasion of privacy will secure to us other kinds of liberty which more than compensate for what is lost. To present privacy then, only as an aspect of or an aid to general liberty, is to miss some of its most significant differentiating features. The value of title to control of some information about ourselves is more nearly absolute than that. For privacy is the necessary context for relationships which we would hardly be human if we had to do without—the relationships of love, friendship and trust.

Love and friendship, as analyzed here, involve the initial respect for the rights of others which morality requires of everyone. They further involve the voluntary and spontaneous relinquishment of *something* between friend and friend, lover and lover. The title to information about oneself conferred by privacy provides the necessary something. To be friends or lovers persons must be intimate to some degree with each other. But intimacy is the sharing of information about one's actions, beliefs, or emotions which one does not share with all, and which one has the right not to share with anyone. By conferring this right, privacy creates the moral capital which we spend in friendship and love.

The entitlements of privacy are not just one kind of entitlement among many which a lover can surrender to show his love. Love or friendship can be partially expressed by the gift of other rights—gifts of property or of service. But these gifts, without the intimacy of shared private information, cannot alone constitute love or friendship. The man who is generous with his possessions, but not with himself, can hardly be a friend, nor—and this more clearly shows the necessity of privacy for love—can the man who, voluntarily or involuntarily, shares everything about himself with the world indiscriminately.

Privacy is essential to friendship and love in another respect besides providing what I call "moral capital." The rights of privacy are among those basic entitlements which men must respect in each other; and mutual respect is the minimal precondition for love and friendship.

15. *Cf.* Schwartz, *On Current Proposals to Legalize Wire Tapping*, 103 U. PA. L. REV. 157, 157-58, 161-65 (1954).

Privacy

Privacy also provides the means for modulating those degrees of friendship which fall short of love. Few persons have the emotional resources to be on the most intimate terms with all their friends. Privacy grants the control over information which enables us to maintain degrees of intimacy. Thus even between friends the restraints of privacy apply; since friendship implies a *voluntary* relinquishment of private information, one will not wish to know what his friend or lover has not chosen to share with him. The rupture of this balance by a third party—the state perhaps—thrusting information concerning one friend upon another might well destroy the limited degree of intimacy the two have achieved.

Finally, there is a more extreme case where privacy serves not to save something which will be "spent" on a friend, but to keep it from all the world. There are thoughts whose expression to a friend or lover would be a hostile act, though the entertaining of them is completely consistent with friendship or love. That is because these thoughts, prior to being given expression, are mere unratified possibilities for action. Only by expressing them do we adopt them, choose them as part of ourselves, and draw them into our relations with others.[16] Now a sophisticated person knows that a friend or lover must entertain thoughts which if expressed would be wounding, and so—it might be objected—why should he attach any significance to their actual expression? In a sense the objection is well taken. If it were possible to give expression to these thoughts and yet make clear to ourselves and to others that we do not thereby ratify, adopt them as our own, it might be that in some relations at least another could be allowed complete access to us. But this possibility is not a very likely one.[17] Thus this most complete form of privacy is perhaps also the most basic, as it is necessary not only to our freedom to define our relations to others but also to our freedom to define ourselves.[18] To be deprived of this control not only over what we do but over who we are is the ultimate assault on liberty, personality, and self-respect.

Trust is the attitude of expectation that another will behave according to the constraints of morality. Insofar as trust is only instrumental to

16. *Compare* M. MONTAIGNE, *De la Solitude*, in ESSAIS, ch. 38, *with* J.-P. SARTRE, BEING AND NOTHINGNESS pt. 2 (H. Barnes transl. 1956).
17. Perhaps it is, after all, one of the functions of psychoanalysis to provide such a possibility.
18. Erving Goffman has suggested to me in conversation that new methods of data storage and retrieval pose a threat to privacy in that it is possible to make readily accessible information about a person's remote and forgotten past. This means a person is unable to change his own and other's definitions of him as readily as once may have been the case.

The Yale Law Journal                    Vol. 77: 475, 1968

the more convenient conduct of life, its purposes could be as well served by cheap and efficient surveillance of the person upon whom one depends. One does not trust machines or animals; one takes the fullest economically feasible precautions against their going wrong. Often, however, we choose to trust people where it would be safer to take precautions—to watch them or require a bond from them. This must be because, as I have already argued, we value the relation of trust for its own sake. It is one of those relations, less inspiring than love or friendship, but also less tiring, through which we express our humanity.

There can be no trust where there is no possibility of error. More specifically, a man cannot know that he is trusted unless he has a right to act without constant surveillance so that he knows he can betray the trust. Privacy confers that essential right. And since, as I have argued, trust in its fullest sense is reciprocal, the man who cannot be trusted cannot himself trust or learn to trust. Without privacy and the possibility of error which it protects that aspect of his humanity is denied to him.

## VII.

The previous sections have explored the meaning of the concept of privacy and the significance of privacy to the notion of personality and to the relations of love, trust and friendship which are inseparable from it. The conclusions have been abstract and entirely general. But the concrete expressions of privacy in particular societies and cultures differ enormously. It remains to be shown why such differences both are to be expected and are entirely consistent with the general conceptions I have put forward.

In concrete situations and actual societies, control over information about oneself, like control over one's bodily security or property, can only be relative and qualified. As is true for property or bodily security, the control over privacy must be limited by the rights of others. And as in the cases of property and bodily security, so too with privacy the more one ventures into the outside, the more one pursues one's other interests with the aid of, in competition with, or even in the presence of others, the more one must risk invasions of privacy. Moreover, as with property and personal security, it is the business of legal and social institutions to define and protect the right of privacy which emerges intact from the hurly-burly of social interactions. Now it would be absurd to argue that these concrete definitions and protections, differing as they do from society to society, are or should be strict derivations from general principles, the only legitimate variables being differing empirical

486

Privacy

circumstances (such as, for instance, differing technologies or climatic conditions). The delineation of standards must be left to a political and social process the results of which will accord with justice if two conditions are met: (1) the process itself is just, that is the interests of all are fairly represented; and (2) the outcome of the process protects basic dignity and provides moral capital for personal relations in the form of absolute title to at least some information about oneself.[19]

The particular areas of life which are protected by privacy will be conventional at least in part, not only because they are the products of political processes, but also because of one of the reasons we value privacy. Insofar as privacy is regarded as moral capital for relations of love, friendship and trust, there are situations where what kinds of information one is entitled to keep to oneself is not of the first importance. The important thing is that there be *some* information which is protected.[20] Convention may quite properly rule in determining the particular areas which are private.

Convention plays another more important role in fostering privacy and the respect and esteem which it protects; it designates certain areas, intrinsically no more private than other areas, as symbolic of the whole institution of privacy, and thus deserving of protection beyond their particular importance. This apparently exaggerated respect for conventionally protected areas compensates for the inevitable fact that privacy is gravely compromised in any concrete social system: it is compromised by the inevitably and utterly just exercise of rights by others, it is compromised by the questionable but politically sanctioned exercise of rights by others, it is compromised by conduct which society does not condone but which it is unable or unwilling to forbid, and it is compromised by plainly wrongful invasions and aggressions. In all this hurly-burly there is a real danger that privacy might be crushed altogether, or what would be as bad, that any venture outside the most limited area of activity would mean risking an almost total compromise of privacy.

Given these threats to privacy in general, social systems have given symbolic importance to certain conventionally designated areas of privacy. Thus in our culture the excretory functions are shielded by more or less absolute privacy, so much so that situations in which this privacy is violated are experienced as extremely distressing, as detracting from one's dignity and self-esteem.[21] But there does not seem to be any reason

19. *Cf.* Rawls, *Legal Obligation and the Duty of Fair Play, supra* note 4.
20. Thus, for instance, so long as the mails are still private, wire tapping may not be so severe an imposition, particularly if people do not in any case consider telephone conversations as necessarily private.
21. There is another form of mortification in total institutions; beginning with ad-

The Yale Law Journal                    Vol. 77: 475, 1968

connected with the principles of respect, esteem and the like why this would have to be so, and one can imagine other cultures in which it was not so, but where the same symbolic privacy was attached to, say, eating and drinking.[22] There are other more subtly modulated symbolic areas of privacy, some of which merge into what I call substantive privacy (that is, areas where privacy does protect substantial interests). The very complex norms of privacy about matters of sex and health are good examples.

An excellent, very different sort of example of a contingent, symbolic recognition of an area of privacy as an expression of respect for personal integrity is the privilege against self-incrimination and the associated doctrines denying officials the power to compel other kinds of information without some explicit warrant. By according the privilege as fully as it does, our society affirms the extreme value of the individual's control over information about himself. To be sure, prying into a man's personal affairs by asking questions of others or by observing him is not prevented by the privilege. Rather it is the point of the privilege that a man cannot be forced to make public information about himself. Thereby his sense of control over what others know of him is significantly enhanced, even if other sources of the same information exist. Without his cooperation, the other sources are necessarily incomplete, since he himself is the only ineluctable witness to his own present life, public or private, internal or manifest. And information about himself which others have to give out is in one sense information over which he has already relinquished control.

---

mission a kind of contaminative exposure occurs. On the outside, the individual can hold objects of self-feeling—such as his body, his immediate actions, his thoughts, and some of his possessions—clear of contact with alien and contaminating things. But in total institutions these territories of the self are violated; the boundary that the individual places between his being and the environment is invaded and the embodiments of self profaned.

. . . .

New audiences not only learn discreditable facts about oneself that are ordinarily concealed but are also in a position to perceive some of these facts directly. Prisoners and mental patients cannot prevent their visitors from seeing them in humiliating circumstances. Another example is the shoulder patch of ethnic identification worn by concentration-camp inmates. Medical and security examinations often expose the inmate physically, sometimes to persons of both sexes; a similar exposure follows from collective sleeping arrangements and doorless toilets. An extreme here, perhaps, is the situation of a self-destructive mental patient who is stripped naked for what is felt to be his own protection and placed in a constantly lit seclusion room, into whose Judas window any person passing on the ward can peer. In general, of course, the inmate is never fully alone; he is always within sight and often earshot of someone, if only his fellow inmates. Prison cages with bars for walls fully realize such exposure. E. GOFFMAN, ASYLUMS 23-25 (1961) (footnotes omitted).

22. *See generally* A. WESTIN, PRIVACY AND FREEDOM ch. 1 (1967). It is apparently traditional for the commanding officer of a naval vessel to eat alone.

Privacy

The privilege is contingent and symbolic. It is part of a whole structure of rules by which there is created an institution of privacy sufficient to the sense of respect, trust and intimacy. It is contingent in that it cannot, I believe, be shown that some particular set of rules is necessary to the existence of such an institution of privacy. It is symbolic because the exercise of the privilege provides a striking expression of society's willingness to accept constraints on the pursuit of valid, perhaps vital interests in order to recognize the right of privacy and the respect for the individual that privacy entails. Conversely, a proceeding in which compulsion is brought to bear on an individual to force him to make revelations about himself provides a striking and dramatic instance of a denial of title to control information about oneself, to control the picture we would have others have of us.[23] In this sense such a procedure quite rightly seems profoundly humiliating.[24] Nevertheless it is not clear to me that a system is unjust which sometimes allows such an imposition.

In calling attention to the symbolic aspect of some areas of privacy I do not mean to minimize their importance. On the contrary, they are highly significant as expressions of respect for others in a general situation where much of what we do to each other may signify a lack of respect or at least presents no occasion for expressing respect. That this is so is shown not so much in the occasions where these symbolic constraints are observed, for they are part of our system of expectations, but where they are violated.[25] Not only does a person feel his standing is gravely compromised by such symbolic violations, but also those who wish to degrade and humiliate others often choose just such symbolic aggressions and invasions on the assumed though conventional area of privacy.

## VIII.

Let us return now to the concrete problem of electronic monitoring to see whether the foregoing elucidation of the concept of privacy will

23. The struggle between Thomas More and King Henry VIII's officers to compel More to state his views on Henry's claims to ecclesiastical supremacy provides an example of how this aspect of privacy is linked to conceptions of personal integrity. *See* R. CHAMBERS, THOMAS MORE (1935).

24. It is just because the privilege bears this relation to the notion of personal integrity, at once intimate and symbolic, that criticisms which examine it as a tool for accomplishing this or that other purpose—*e.g.*, 6-7 J. BENTHAM, *Rationale of Judicial Evidence*, in THE WORKS OF JEREMY BENTHAM (J. Bowring ed. 1843); McNaughton, *supra* note 2—seem so unanswerable yet one feels they somehow miss the point.

25. Erving Goffman gives numerous examples of subtle, implicit norms, of whose pervasive and powerful hold on us we are quite unaware until they are violated. E. GOFFMAN, BEHAVIOR IN PUBLIC PLACES (1963).

The Yale Law Journal                        Vol. 77: 475, 1968

help to establish on firmer ground the intuitive objection that monitoring is an intolerable violation of privacy. Let us consider the more intrusive forms of monitoring where not only location but conversations and perhaps other data are monitored.

Obviously such a system of monitoring drastically curtails or eliminates altogether the power to control information about oneself. But, it might be said, this is not a significant objection if we assume the monitored data will go only to authorized persons—probation or parole officers—and cannot be prejudicial so long as the subject of the monitoring is not violating the conditions under which he is allowed to be at liberty. But this retort misses the importance of privacy as a context for all kinds of relations, from the most intense to the most casual. For all of these may require a context of some degree of intimacy, and intimacy is made impossible by monitoring.

It is worth being more precise about this notion of intimacy. Monitoring obviously presents vast opportunities for malice and misunderstanding on the part of authorized personnel. For that reason the subject has reason to be constantly apprehensive and inhibited in what he does. There is always an unseen audience, which is the more threatening because of the possibility that one may forget about it and let down his guard, as one would not with a visible audience. But even assuming the benevolence and understanding of the official audience, there are serious consequences to the fact that no degree of true intimacy is possible for the subject. Privacy is not, as we have seen, just a defensive right. It rather forms the necessary context for the intimate relations of love and friendship which give our lives much of whatever affirmative value they have. In the role of citizen or fellow worker, one need reveal himself to no greater extent than is necessary to display the attributes of competence and morality appropriate to those relations. In order to be a friend or lover one must reveal far more of himself. Yet where any intimate revelation may be heard by monitoring officials, it loses the quality of exclusive intimacy required of a gesture of love or friendship. Thus monitoring, in depriving one of privacy, destroys the possibility of bestowing the gift of intimacy, and makes impossible the essential dimension of love and friendship.

Monitoring similarly undermines the subject's capacity to enter into relations of trust. As I analyzed trust, it required the possibility of error on the part of the person trusted. The negation of trust is constant surveillance—such as monitoring—which minimizes the possibility of undetected default. The monitored parolee is denied the sense of self-respect inherent in being trusted by the government which has released

Privacy

him. More important, monitoring prevents the parolee from entering into true *relations* of trust with persons in the outside world. An employer, unaware of the monitoring, who entrusts a sum of money to the parolee cannot thereby grant him the sense of responsibility and autonomy which an unmonitored person in the same position would have. The parolee in a real—if special and ironical—sense, cannot be trusted.

Now let us consider the argument that however intrusive monitoring may seem, surely prison life is more so. In part, of course, this will be a matter of fact. It may be that even a reasonably secure and well-run prison will allow prisoners occasions for conversation among themselves, with guards, or with visitors, which are quite private. Such a prison regime would in this respect be less intrusive than monitoring. Often prison regimes do not allow even this, and go far toward depriving a prisoner of any sense of privacy: if the cells have doors, these may be equipped with peep-holes. But there is still an important difference between this kind of prison and monitoring: the prison environment is overtly, even punitively unprivate. The contexts for relations to others are obviously and drastically different from what they are on the "outside." This, it seems to me, itself protects the prisoner's human orientation where monitoring only assails it. If the prisoner has a reasonably developed capacity for love, trust and friendship and has in fact experienced ties of this sort, he is likely to be strongly aware (at least for a time) that prison life is a drastically different context from the one in which he enjoyed those relations, and this awareness will militate against his confusing the kinds of relations that can obtain in a "total institution" like a prison with those of freer social settings on the outside.

Monitoring, by contrast, alters only in a subtle and unobtrusive way —though a significant one—the context for relations. The subject *appears* free to perform the same actions as others and to enter the same relations, but in fact an important element of autonomy, of control over one's environment is missing: he cannot be private. A prisoner can adopt a stance of withdrawal, of hibernation as it were, and thus preserve his sense of privacy intact to a degree. A person subject to monitoring by virtue of being in a free environment, dealing with people who expect him to have certain responses, capacities and dispositions, is forced to make at least a show of intimacy to the persons he works closely with, those who would be his friends, and so on. They expect these things of him, because he is assumed to have the capacity and disposition to enter into ordinary relations with them. Yet if he does—if, for instance, he enters into light banter with slight sexual overtones with

The Yale Law Journal                    Vol. 77: 475, 1968

the waitress at the diner where he eats regularly[26]—he has been forced to violate his own integrity by being forced to reveal to his official monitors even so small an aspect of his private personality, the personality he wishes to reserve for persons towards whom he will make some gestures of intimacy and friendship. Theoretically, of course, a monitored parolee might adopt the same attitude of withdrawal that a prisoner does, but in fact that too would be a costly and degrading experience. He would be tempted, as in prison he would not be, to "give himself away" and to act like everyone else, since in every outward respect he seems like everyone else. Moreover, by withdrawing, the person subject to monitoring would risk seeming cold, unnatural, odd, inhuman to the very people whose esteem and affection he craves. In prison the circumstances dictating a reserved and tentative facade are so apparent to all that adopting such a facade is no reflection on the prisoner's humanity.

Finally, the insidiousness of a technique which forces a man to betray himself in this humiliating way or else seem inhuman is compounded when one considers that the subject is also forced to betray others who may become intimate with him. Even persons in the overt oppressiveness of a prison do not labor under the burden of this double betrayal.

As against all of these considerations, there remains the argument that so long as monitoring depends on the consent of the subject, who feels it is preferable to prison, to close off this alternative in the name of a morality so intimately concerned with liberty is absurd. This argument may be decisive; I am not at all confident that the alternative of monitored release should be closed off. My analysis does show, I think that it involves costs to the prisoner which are easily overlooked, that on inspection it is a less desirable alternative than might at first appear. Moreover, monitoring presents systematic dangers to potential subjects as a class. Its availability as a compromise between conditional release and continued imprisonment may lead officials who are in any doubt whether or not to trust a man on parole or probation to assuage their doubts by resorting to monitoring.

The seductions of monitored release disguise not only a cost to the subject but to society as well. The discussion of trust should make clear that unmonitored release is a very different experience from monitored release, and so the educational and rehabilitative effect of unmonitored release is also different. Unmonitored release affirms in a far more significant way the relations of trust between the convicted criminal and society which the criminal violated by his crime and which we should now

26. *Cf.* E. GOFFMAN, ENCOUNTERS 37-45 (1961).

Privacy

be seeking to reestablish. But trust can only arise, as any parent knows, through the experience of being trusted.

IX.

The discussion of privacy in this essay has explored the meaning and significance of the concept. It reveals privacy as that aspect of social order by which persons control access to information about themselves. How this control is granted to individuals and the means for bringing about the social structures which express the notion of privacy have not been of direct concern. Clearly many of the social structures by which persons express their respect for the privacy of others are informal and implicit. The sanctions for violating the expectations set up by these structures, if they exist at all, are often subtle and informal too. But legal rules also play a large part in establishing the social context of privacy. These rules guarantee to a person the claim to control certain areas, his home, perhaps his telephone communications, etc., and back this guarantee with enforceable sanctions. Now these legal norms are more or less incomprehensible without some understanding of what kind of a situation is sought to be established with their aid. Without this understanding we cannot sense the changing law they demand in changing circumstances.

What is less obvious is that law is not just an instrument for protecting privacy; it is an essential element, in our culture, of the institution itself. The concept of privacy requires, as we have seen, a sense of control and a justified, acknowledged power to control aspects of one's environment. But in most developed societies the only way to give a person the full measure of both the sense and the fact of control is to give him a legal title to control. A legal right to control is control which is the least open to question and argument; it is the kind of control we are most serious about. As we have seen, privacy is not just an absence of information abroad about ourselves; it is a feeling of security in control over that information. By using the public, impersonal and ultimate institution of law to grant persons this control, we at once put the right to control as far beyond question as we can and at the same time show how seriously we take that right.

# [4]

## THE CONCEPT OF PRIVACY

### HYMAN GROSS*

*With the Supreme Court's recent decision in* Griswold v. Connecticut, *the scope of the legal protection of privacy has achieved new significance. Mr. Gross contends that there is a conceptual muddle surrounding the legal right of privacy, and that development of a legally protected interest in privacy requires recognition of the particular condition of human life that is sought to be protected. To facilitate such conceptual clarification, he attempts to distinguish privacy from other conditions of human life by isolating its unique characteristics. Mr. Gross regards the* Griswold *case as unsatisfactory, reasoning that although the case was ostensibly based upon privacy, the decision was in fact reached by punning on the concept of privacy. He also concludes that in their articles on that subject Dean Prosser has failed to recognize, and Professor Bloustein to identify satisfactorily, the nature of privacy.*

CONCERN about privacy is concern about conditions of life, and it is so in the law as it is elsewhere. Unfortunately, failings in our use of language sometimes tend to distract or frustrate this concern, and we are forced to pursue detours of analysis in order to make legal argument on the subject sound. The predicament seems the sort for which we might invoke Professor H. L. A. Hart's observation that "in law as elsewhere, we can know and yet not understand."[1] Without difficulty we regularly recognize those situations in which a violation of privacy is threatened or accomplished, yet stumble when trying to make clear what privacy is. In such a quandary we feel that we know how to use a word but have difficulty setting straight those (including ourselves) who misuse it. As a result, our ability to articulate and apply *principles* of legal protection diminishes, for we become uncertain about precisely what it is that compels us toward protective measures and wherein it differs from what has already been recognized or refused recognition under established legal theory.

To make good the claim that privacy is indeed noticed and protected, a preliminary indication of the range of legal protection is in order. A synoptic view discloses at one end privacy of personality: First the very attributes by which a person is recognized—name, likeness, perhaps voice; then the intimate facts of one's life. At the other end, in the direction of less immediately personal matters, one finds protection of confidential information —income tax information, census information, financial affairs, and the like. In between is legal protection for spoken communi-

---

\* Teaching Fellow, New York University School of Law.
[1] Hart, Definition and Theory in Jurisprudence 3 (1953).

cations by laws against wiretapping and an assortment of on- and off-premises eavesdropping and recording techniques; protection for written communication by laws prohibiting prying into mail, telegrams, and other communications in public and private channels; protection against surveillance in private and, to a lesser extent, public places; privileges to withhold from public disclosure communications made within certain confidential relationships; and constitutional and statutory rights to be secure against unwarranted intrusions into the physical person, into papers and possessions, and into private places by curious agencies of the public authority.

To substantiate my further claim that the concept of privacy is infected with pernicious ambiguities, I shall offer an account of the uses of the word "privacy" which is intended to disclose the nature of the confusion, and then go on to consider three ventures in legal theory which in different ways incorporate this confusion. The first is the Supreme Court's opinion in *Griswold v. Connecticut*,[2] which seems to me a notable and regrettable exercise in the use of this ambiguity, and indeed a malformation of constitutional law which thrives because of the conceptual vacuum surrounding the legal notion of privacy. Following this I shall consider a widely noted article by Dean Prosser,[3] and Professor Bloustein's criticism of it.[4] Dean Prosser, while contributing much to our understanding of the development of law in this area, pursues the thesis that what has been recognized as an interest in privacy may be reduced without remainder to one of several other interests protected in other areas of the law of torts. This thesis seems to me to rest squarely on a conceptual fault regarding privacy. Professor Bloustein's criticism of the view fails to make that clear. He argues that there is indeed a separate interest in privacy and indicates why privacy is valuable, but he does not tell us what privacy is. Thus, the true issue with Dean Prosser is never joined. And extending this omission to a larger context which would include the *Griswold* opinion, we are left unable to articulate principles which illuminate our concern because we are not clear what our concern is about.

# I

Privacy is a state of affairs, and before we speak of "rights of" or "interests in" or "invasions of" it, we ought to be acquainted with its distinguishing features. I suggest that *privacy is*

---

[2] 381 U.S. 479 (1965).

[3] Prosser, Privacy, 48 Calif. L. Rev. 383 (1960) [hereinafter Prosser].

[4] Bloustein, Privacy as an Aspect of Human Dignity: An Answer to Dean Prosser, 39 N.Y.U.L. Rev. 962 (1964) [hereinafter Bloustein].

*the condition of human life in which acquaintance with a person or with affairs of his life which are personal to him is limited.* It seems quite clear that a great many practices in our society are designed to create or preserve such a condition. Such mundane examples as clothes, window blinds, bedroom doors, and filing-cabinet locks begin an indefinitely long list of objects whose use is motivated at least in part by concern for privacy. All the areas of legal protection of privacy indicated previously involve concern for such a condition of life, and it is to be particularly emphasized that tort law in this area, from Warren and Brandeis on, as well as constitutional law, are sensitive precisely to this concern.[5]

An interest in privacy exists when preservation of privacy might concern someone affected by such privacy, and a legal interest exists when there is legal recognition of that concern. A legal right of privacy exists to the extent that such legal interest *may be* (not *could be*) accorded protection by legal procedures. But privacy in these contexts does not exist because of such legal recognition. It exists—like secrecy, security, or tranquility—by virtue of habits of life appropriate to its existence.

It is true that in some instances the law itself is the social practice used to create privacy—for example, restrictions upon further disclosure of personal information obtained by the Government. More often, the law is only a back-up protection for privacy, resorted to when other means to insure privacy have been frustrated. In neither case, however, is privacy just whatever the law says it is. The law does not determine what privacy is, but only what situations of privacy will be afforded legal protection, or will be made private by virtue of legal protection. Privacy, no less than good reputation or physical safety, is a creature of life in a human community and not the contrivance of a legal system concerned with its protection. We should not be misled, therefore, in speaking of a legally recognized interest in privacy or the rights attending it. Privacy in these contexts does not exist because of such recognition, but depends only upon habits of life. I confess that these notions seem embarrassingly obvious and trivial when read apart from passages in legal literature which disregard them.[6]

---

[5] For an indication of an historical connection between torts and constitutional law see McKay, The Right of Privacy: Emanations and Intimations, 64 Mich. L. Rev. 259–61 (1965).

[6] For an illustration of such a passage close at hand see the metaphor constructed in Griswold v. Connecticut, 381 U.S. 479, 484 (1965), and text accompanying note 9 infra where the analysis is disoriented by the apparent suggestion that states of affairs (privacy) are created by the legal rights which preserve them. To rehabilitate the Court's statement, "zones of privacy" would have to have read into it a meaning of zones in which government interference with privacy is restricted.

Interference with privacy may be accomplished by acts of two different sorts. The transgressor may himself become acquainted with a private matter; or he may acquaint others with something which is still private even though it is known to him. The first sort of interference we describe as an intrusion; while the second kind we speak of as disclosure or publicity, depending upon whether or not the intended recipients of the communication are individually identifiable.

Now to more troubling matters.

There are at least four different sorts of states other than those with which we have so far been concerned, which are sometimes designated by "privacy." For reasons which I shall attempt to make clear, the word when used for any such other designation is best viewed as a derivative or *weak* sense of the word, while the sense in which we have here defined "privacy" is the primary or strong sense.[7] The weak senses become clear by illustration.

When the telephone rings at home and we are solicited for dancing lessons or a magazine subscription we might speak of our privacy being disturbed. We might say the same if we hear what is going on in the next apartment. In these cases privacy is conceived as *mental repose*. And interestingly, in the last example, it is not our privacy (in the strong sense of "privacy") which is compromised by what we hear, but rather our neighbor's; for it is we who are learning something about him.

Again, suppose that a man lives deep in a wilderness of a thousand acres, nine hundred acres of which are then taken for homestead settlement. Although he is still sheltered on his remaining hundred not only from the public gaze but from even a public glimpse, we might speak loosely of a loss of privacy. Here "privacy" is used to designate *physical solitude*.

With reference to another variety of situations, we inexactly use the word "privacy" to speak of *physical exclusiveness*. Privacy, we might say, is compromised by the janitor's passkey or by another's license to enter upon our land.

---

[7] The matter of a criterion for distinguishing senses of a word is not a simple one. Perplexing issues of modern philosophy and linguistic theory bear heavily on this. For our present purposes we may adopt as practically adequate the following naïve test: In any sentence which uses "privacy" in a characteristic way and which expresses a statement of fact or a statement whose truth depends upon the meaning of "privacy," does a different interpretation of "privacy" (1) require that a different procedure be pursued for verification of the statement, or (2) require an appeal to different rules of word-use to verify the statement? If either (1) or (2) is the case, the different interpretation of "privacy" is an interpretation *in a different sense*, but not otherwise. For an illuminating technical discussion see J. L. Austin, The Meaning of a Word, in Philosophical Papers 37 (Urmson & Warnock eds. 1961).

Last, and of greatest significance for present purposes, we sometimes speak of such things as planning a family, deciding about our children's education or about church affiliation or where to live, as private matters. Anyone who would venture to determine the conduct of these affairs for us would, we might say, be encroaching upon our privacy. "Privacy" in this sense refers to our *autonomy*.[8]

Injury to what is designated by "privacy" in these weak senses is met in the law with remedies for wrongs other than offense to privacy. Most notable are those for trespass and nuisance, and there are of course further statutory and constitutional sources of remedy apart from traditional common-law classifications.

In speaking of *weak* senses of "privacy" we should notice that "privacy" is used in such a sense only as a synonym for another term which more nicely makes reference to one of the states of affairs described above. For "privacy" in the *strong* sense, however, there is no exact synonym. Regarding uses in the weak sense, correctness of use is a question of permissible substitution of terms according to prevailing rules of usage. In the case of uses in the strong sense, correctness depends upon an appropriate reference to something in the world. Thus, if the use of "privacy" in a weak sense is questioned, the proper response is to point to a rule of synonymity which permits such use. A further question, about appropriate reference, might then be raised, but only if the term said to be synonymous with "privacy" is there itself being used in a strong sense. In practice we tend to telescope these two steps and this obscures the very important difference between a question of permissible choice of a word and a question of proper reference by the word chosen.

Since language is used to manage in the world it might fairly be expected to develop to serve best that end rather than to create interesting challenges for games of linguistic analysis. While this expectation is on the whole justified there is present in the development of natural languages the persistent influence of the mental processes of those who use the language. From a strictly logical point of view this contributes impurity to language. To bolster my account of logical confusion I offer a suggestion of how weak senses are produced by such processes.

---

[8] As we shall see, it is in this sense that "privacy" is at issue in Griswold. For an interesting suggestion that the concern for privacy is ultimately a concern for a species of autonomy—namely the privilege of keeping things to oneself—see Rossiter, The Free Man in the Free Society, in The Essentials of Freedom 89 (English ed. 1960). This should be carefully distinguished from what obtains in contexts in which "privacy" is used to designate autonomy.

First there is an elementary matter of the quest for a noun to correspond to an adjective. "Private" is opposed to "public" in the political-community sense, for example. We want a word to designate the thing which private matters partake of, and what is more natural than "privacy"? (In a corresponding sense, "the public" names that to which public matters appertain.) The use of "privacy" to designate autonomy seems largely, though not entirely, a result of this process.

More important than this species of grammatical convenience are phenomena of psychological association. There are here four kinds of situations in which psychological associations on occasions of word-use affect usage. *First*, privacy, in a given situation, may depend upon physical solitude, or mental repose, or physical exclusiveness, or autonomy. When, for example, we observe that the Marquis de Sade secured his privacy by occupying a castle we are noticing physical solitude and physical exclusiveness as necessary for privacy. *Second*, these other states of affairs may depend upon privacy for their existence. Thus, privacy is said to be a requirement for autonomy when we remark that success in a criminal enterprise requires avoidance of police surveillance. *Third*, privacy and the pseudonymous states may both depend for their existence upon the presence of the same thing. In this regard a closed door may be the *sine qua non* of privacy or of any of the others. The situation would be defined by a sign on the door—"Private," "Do Not Enter," "No Trespassing," "Do Not Disturb," "Authorized Personnel Only." Permissible conduct—eavesdropping, knocking, entering, occupying, and so on—would vary with the different signs, and so would indicate the states sought to be protected by the sign. But without such a sign the door confronts us as a common physical requirement for all of them. *Fourth*, although not related one as a requirement for the other, or by a requirement common to both, privacy and the others may often accompany one another. For example, privacy is taken to be concomitant with autonomy when we reflect that people are more likely to indulge eccentric whims in their own homes than elsewhere.

All of these grounds of association conspire to confuse us about privacy, and the confusion is often not innocent when insinuated into legal theory. Having fudged the concept of privacy we have put ourselves in a position where we cannot discern the interest we seek to protect, but only the situation which involves it. Considerations are advanced which are appropriate to the vindication of an interest in privacy for the purpose of vindicating an interest in something else bearing its name. Since the interests are different the arguments are inadequate or irrelevant to the purposes at hand. The word has been mistaken for the substance, and good reasons for protecting privacy are proffered in a context in which they cannot serve as reasons at all.

This faulty device is the hinge on which the decision of *Griswold v. Connecticut* turns most heavily.

## II

Mrs. Griswold and Dr. Buxton were convicted as accessories under a Connecticut statute making the use of contraceptive devices illegal. They gave advice, provided examinations, and prescribed the use of various contraceptive devices to married persons. The constitutionality of the statute was put in question before the Supreme Court.

The opinion of the Court, delivered by Justice Douglas, relies principally upon a right of privacy which married persons are said to enjoy, and which is found to be violated by the Connecticut law. The creation of a principle of constitutional protection for this right provides a display of prodigious powers of metaphor. The specific guarantees of the Bill of Rights are said to have "penumbras, formed by emanations from those guarantees . . . . Various guarantees create zones of privacy."[9] The scheme of argument, which is diffused through the opinion, is sufficiently remarkable to warrant a marshaling and examination of its details.

Directed to the conclusion that a law purporting to regulate certain intimate matters of marriage is a violation of a constitutionally protected right of privacy, the course of reasoning runs as follows. (1) Some things not expressly protected in the Bill of Rights have been recognized by the Court as forms of what is expressly mentioned, and therefore accorded protection—for example, the right of association, which has been held to be the right to express opinions and so within the first amendment guaranty of free speech.[10] (2) Privacy with regard to one's associations has been recognized as a right protected by the first amendment because required disclosure would act as a restraint on the free exercise of the protected activity.[11] (3) Hence a first amendment right of privacy has been recognized though it does not appear in terms in the Bill of Rights.[12] (4) In addition to the first amendment, we may look to the third amendment's qualified

[9] 381 U.S. 479, 484 (1965).
[10] Id. at 483.
[11] See ibid.
[12] See id. at 482-84.

protection against the quartering of soldiers; the fifth amendment's protection against involuntary self-incrimination; the ninth amendment's reassurance regarding unenumerated rights of the people; and particularly the fourth amendment's guaranty of security for persons, private places, and private things—all of these give privacy a place in the scheme of constitutional protection.[13] (5) The Court has previously considered constitutional protection of privacy in a variety of contexts,[14] including a local ordinance prohibiting as a nuisance door-to-door solicitations without the householder's invitation;[15] the loudspeaker broadcast of radio programs in public conveyances;[16] unreasonable search and seizure by police;[17] police eavesdropping on a conversation in the visitors room of a jail;[18] inspection of a home for rat infestation by a health department inspector without a search warrant;[19] and a statute providing for the sterilization of certain classes of recidivists.[20] (6) "The Fourth and Fifth Amendments were described in *Boyd v. United States* . . . as protection against all governmental invasions 'of the sanctity of a man's home and the privacies of life.' "[21] (7) Marriage is a relationship within the zone of privacy created by constitutional guaranties.[22] (8) Marriage is an *association* of the most intimate sort, and for an even nobler purpose than any protected in the freedom of association cases cited above.[23] (9) The prohibition against the use of contraceptives in that relationship (*i.e.*, association) is destructive of it.[24] (10) Hence such a law destroys something which the Constitution protects, and is therefore unconstitutional.[25]

A complete critique of the opinion as a rational procedure is outside the present undertaking. What is important is the element of punning on which the decision is made to turn. Puns on "privacy" are twice employed.[26]

---

[13] See id. at 484, 485.

[14] Id. at 485.

[15] See Breard v. City of Alexandria, 341 U.S. 622, 626, 644–45 (1951).

[16] See Public Util. Comm'n v. Pollak, 343 U.S. 451 (1952).

[17] See Monroe v. Pape, 365 U.S. 167 (1961).

[18] See Lanza v. New York, 370 U.S. 139 (1962).

[19] See Frank v. Maryland, 359 U.S. 360 (1959).

[20] See Skinner v. Oklahoma, 316 U.S. 535, 541 (1942).

[21] 381 U.S. at 484.

[22] Id. at 485.

[23] See id. at 486.

[24] See id. at 485.

[25] See ibid.

[26] It is interesting to observe that this opinion is not the first in which Justice Douglas has discerned an issue of "privacy" which departs from the conventional legal notion. In Public Util. Comm'n v. Pollak, 343 U.S. 451, 467–69 (1952), the dissenting opinion of Justice Douglas found privacy jeopardized when audiences of bus riders were subjected to uninvited broadcasts (1) because their mental re-

To create the right frame of mind preliminarily, a kaleido-
scopic right of privacy is made to appear. This is done by projecting dissimilar senses of "privacy" to create the illusion of a
single referent for "privacy." It is accomplished in those portions
of the opinion referred to above in (4), (5), and (6). Just as a
kaleidoscope presents an image for which there is no corresponding object, the *Griswold* opinion presents a word "privacy" for
which there is no referent. Here the pun does not consist in moving from one sense to another, but in contriving a composite term
whose sense is illusory.

In this setting of verbal mystery the Court performs the
major trick—a pun on "privacy of association." Nondisclosure of
organization records has been constitutionally protected,[27] and
this represents protection of privacy of association; therefore

---

pose was disturbed and (2) because a potential instrument for control over men's
minds was in operation. In his dissent in Poe v. Ullman, 367 U.S. 497, 509 (1961),
an earlier case in which the Connecticut anticontraceptive statute was in question,
privacy was again seen as the issue (1) because the state was undertaking to control marital intimacies, and (more conventionally) (2) because if the state can
make a law it can enforce it, and so police could investigate the intimacies of the
marriage relation. The concurring opinion of Justice Goldberg in Griswold also
speaks of a right of marital privacy, 381 U.S. at 486, 487, and this theme is sounded
in various briefs in the case, perhaps on cue from the previous dissenting opinion
in Poe. Of particular interest is Brief for Appellants, pp. 79–89, Griswold v. Connecticut, 381 U.S. 479 (1965), citing 1 Harper & James, Torts 678–79 (1956), in
which the constitutional right of privacy asserted here is said to parallel the right
of privacy recognized in tort law. Evidently sensing that the tort cases all have
something which this case does not have, the argument is then shifted to hypothetical invasions of true privacy—the kind recognized in tort law—which would
indeed occur if the Connecticut statute were to be enforced by police searches of
a kind that are normally made when a serious crime has occurred. The dissenting
opinion in Poe makes the same analogy to tort law, 367 U.S. 497, 521 & n.12, citing
Cooley, Torts 29 (2d ed. 1888), and Warren & Brandeis, The Right to Privacy, 4
Harv. L. Rev. 192 (1890), and then proceeds to shift to the situation which, though
not existing here or in any other case, is posed as a frightful spectre—police investigation of the intimacies of the marriage relation. See 367 U.S. at 522.

This gambit is repeated in the Court's opinion in Griswold. The Court asks:
"Would we allow the police to search the sacred precincts of marital bedrooms
for telltale signs of the use of contraceptives? The very idea is repulsive to the
notions of privacy surrounding the marriage relationship." 381 U.S. at 485–86.
There is a return here to the concept of privacy that has been recognized in
constitutional law, albeit to a situation utterly foreign to the facts of this case.
What the Court fails to distinguish is the loss of marital autonomy constituted by
any enforcement of the statute, on the one hand, and the violation of marital
privacy constituted by the particular means of enforcement which it poses hypo-
thetically, on the other. It is axiomatic that a fundamentally offensive intrusion is
a subject of constitutional prohibition without regard to the law whose enforcement
it serves. Such intrusion has been held violative of the due process clause of the
fourteenth amendment when it fails to "respect certain decencies of civilized conduct." Rochin v. California, 342 U.S. 165, 173 (1952). Search for contraceptives in
the marital bedroom may well be found to constitute such a failure, if and when
such a search takes place.

[27] 381 U.S. at 483, citing NAACP v. Alabama, 357 U.S. 449 (1958).

activities which are part of marital privacy (and so within the privacy of an association) have grounds for constitutional protection against legislative regulation. The decoy in the argument is "privacy," used in the strong sense in the nondisclosure case, but used in the weak sense of *autonomy* in the present case of statutory prohibition. (It should be noted further that the cases extending first amendment protection to include freedom of association[28] relate to the kind of associations that exist at least in part for the purpose of formulating and expressing opinions— clearly an activity within the free speech guaranty. But a marriage conceived as a species of association does not have such a purpose and therefore does not entail the issue of freedom of expression. It therefore has no claim to be an association protected under the first amendment guaranty. In short, "association" has been used for a bit of subsidiary word-play.)

By this technique of verbal deception the meaning of constitutional provisions as clarified and elaborated through a history of interpretation is in fact ignored, and a heterologous growth in common speech substituted. Thus, regard for interests in privacy which do in some measure underlie the interdictions of the third, fourth, and fifth amendments are obscured by an illogical association with interests of a quite different sort. The word "privacy" is put to torture until it confesses a constitutional guaranty for everything it designates in household parlance. The encroachment upon solitude and disturbance of repose occasioned by the salesman at the front door is said to involve the matter of privacy, as does the disruption of repose by a loudspeaker on a bus, and loss of autonomy through application of a sterilization law.[29] In this way a verbal groundwork is provided for deciding that something called "privacy" is offended by a state law regulating marital intimacies, an area of accustomed autonomy.

Though we may counsel the avoidance of ambiguity, we cannot question that the Supreme Court may fashion whatever words it chooses to comprehend what it has in mind to protect; and that therefore the word "privacy" may be used to designate particular things said to be protected by the Constitution—including freedom from legislative regulation of marital intimacies. But what the Supreme Court cannot do is make an eccentricity in common word usage do the job of legal reasoning in constitutional inter-

---

28 NAACP v. Button, 371 U.S. 415 (1963); NAACP v. Alabama, 357 U.S. 449 (1958); Schware v. Board of Bar Examiners, 353 U.S. 232 (1957); DeJonge v. Oregon, 299 U.S. 353 (1937), cited in Griswold v. Connecticut, 381 U.S. 479, 483 (1965).

29 See notes 15, 16, 20 supra.

pretation. It cannot give autonomy protection under constitutional rights of privacy simply because the word "privacy" is sometimes loosely used to designate autonomy. That is what has been attempted in *Griswold*.

Indeed, following the procedure of *Griswold* it is not hard to imagine most of the scheme of constitutional civil rights being set out as details of the one true civil right, the right of privacy. All interdicted restraints and coercions and all prohibited interferences and intrusions would certainly enjoy its patronage (though deprivations might be included less easily). By exhausting the concept of privacy through such diffuse usage the interest in privacy which the law has increasingly recognized may be expected then to resume its former inarticulate condition.

It would be a mistake to leave an impression that the issue here is merely verbal. It is a matter of the use of language, but one that bears upon rudimentary concepts of constitutional law. Specifically, to conceive governmental regulation of this kind of activity as interference with privacy is to lose sight of the fact that privacy is not a matter of restraints or coercions, but rather of security. The third,[30] fourth, and fifth amendments, which are rightly said to protect interests in privacy, are guarantees of security, not freedom. They are not designed to prevent repression of the activities of the people, as the logic of *Griswold* would have it, but rather to set limits upon certain specified governmental activities which are in themselves obnoxious, though necessary. There is no need to stress here the difference between interests in security and interests in freedom—considerable attention has always been given to the question of their conflict and when one must yield to the other, particularly in the areas of criminal law enforcement and national security.[31]

In this regard, a source of confusion is perhaps avoided if we speak of security as "freedom from," distinguishing it from "freedom to." At any rate both notions seem to have been subsumed in the parlance of constitutional law under the term "liberty";[32] thus, for example, "the right of the people to be

---

[30] Although protection of privacy is clearly involved in the prohibition against quartering of soldiers, it is not only protection of seclusion but of a power of exclusion and of freedom from molestation (and perhaps avoidance of upset to the domestic economy) which the third amendment typically aims at. Some weak senses of "privacy" are thus involved here.

[31] A balancing of such countervailing interests is the approach taken by the Court in Breard v. City of Alexandria, 341 U.S. 622 (1951), where freedom to solicit is weighed against the householder's domestic repose.

[32] It is interesting to note that Justice Bradley distinguishes "liberty" and "security" in speaking of the fifth and fourth amendments in Boyd v. United States, 116 U.S. 616, 630 (1886), cited and quoted in Griswold, 381 U.S. at 484.

secure" enunciated in the fourth amendment is said to be part of the concept of ordered liberty and so to be protected under the fourteenth amendment.[33] That privacy is a matter of security, not freedom, is clear even in the cases of "penumbral" protection under the first amendment,[34] which by its terms protects a "freedom to" rather than a "freedom from." The paradox is only apparent, for the Bill of Rights is addressed to broad courses of governmental conduct, not isolated single interests of the people.[35] Within these broad courses many interests are affected, and respect for a security interest in privacy has been found in some cases to be necessary for protection of the interest in free expression. And before leaving this area of conceptual confusion it is important to notice that the phrase "right to be let alone," which is widely offered as an illuminating synonym for "right of privacy," promotes by its gloss the very obscurity which we seek at this point to dispel.[36]

*Griswold*, in short, stands on a word which is disembodied from the constitutional provisions that give it meaning and which is used in accordance with some loose habits of everyday speech rather than the logic of constitutional law. If the legislature is

---

[33] Wolf v. Colorado, 338 U.S. 25, 27–28 (1949).

[34] See note 28 supra.

[35] The dissenting opinion of Justice Black in Griswold makes this clear. "There are, of course, guarantees in certain specific constitutional provisions which are designed in part to protect privacy at certain times and places with respect to certain activities." 381 U.S. at 508.

> One of the most effective ways of diluting or expanding a constitutionally guaranteed right is to substitute for the crucial word or words of a constitutional guarantee another word or words, more or less flexible and more or less restricted in meaning. This fact is well illustrated by the use of the term 'right of privacy' as a comprehensive substitute for the Fourth Amendment's guarantee against "unreasonable searches and seizures." "Privacy" is a broad, abstract, and ambiguous concept which can easily be shrunken in meaning but which can also, on the other hand, easily be interpreted as a constitutional ban against many things other than searches and seizures.

Id. at 509.

Further, Justice Black notes the Court's attempt to exalt to a constitutional rule a putative right of privacy preventing the state legislature from "passing any law deemed by this Court to interfere with 'privacy.'" Id. at 510 n.1. Quotation marks are the sign of a pun recognized: By only mentioning a word we can signal that its intended referent is anything it is in fact used to designate, rather than what it *normally* designates when used, i.e., the job it does when it appears without quotation marks; and when it is *used* rather than *mentioned* the reference is governed by the rules controlling the proper use of the word. In short, it appears that the existence of a language trick in the Court's opinion has not passed unnoticed in Justice Black's opinion.

[36] The phrase seems to have its origin in this context in Cooley, Torts 29 (2d ed. 1888). After long and frequently inspiring service it may now be ready for retirement in the interest of clarity, for unfortunately it is often understood as a description of the right of privacy rather than as simply a synonym for "right of privacy."

indeed to be excluded from the marital bedroom by the Supreme
Court, the grounds might well amount to something better than
linguistic confusion.

## III

It is clear from a reading of the cases which Dean Prosser
and Professor Bloustein examine that what is at stake in all of
them is an interest in the state of affairs we have described as
privacy. All involve improperly getting to know something personal or making it known to others. Dean Prosser concludes, however, that an assortment of different interests have been improperly packaged together in one tort box labelled "invasion of
privacy." Professor Bloustein's answer is that only one interest
is involved in all—human dignity. Both notions lead, though by
different paths, to a conceptual indeterminacy regarding privacy.
The result is an impairment of ability to discriminate exactly
what it is for which legal intervention is being solicited. Under
Dean Prosser's analysis this means losing sight of the specific
interest at stake, while under Professor Bloustein's approach it
means making a valuation of privacy but omitting what must
be apprehended to justify the valuation.

### A. Dean Prosser's "Several Torts" Thesis

Dean Prosser's position is that what is called "invasion of
privacy" may be any one of four distinct torts, each wrongful
conduct with respect to one of three distinct interests.[37]

One tort is constituted by intrusion upon the plaintiff's solitude or seclusion or by prying, and the interest said to be jeopardized is an interest in mental tranquility. Typical cases are of
uninvited entry into sequestered places; listening to or looking
at or recording what goes on in such a place (although not present
there); prying into personal papers and records; or even invading
the physical person to search out facts.[38]

The second variety of tort distinguished by Dean Prosser is
constituted by public disclosure of embarrassing facts. The interest which is found compromised is in reputation. Cases of this
sort typically involve publication of facts about a person which
are cause for shame.[39]

The third tort identified occurs when a person is placed

---

[37] See Prosser 389. Although Dean Prosser states that there are "four different interests," he subsequently distinguishes only three, as Professor Bloustein
points out. Bloustein 965 n.14.

[38] See Prosser 389–92.

[39] See Prosser 392–98.

in a false light before the public. Again, offense to an interest in reputation is said to be the gravamen. Situations of this sort are those in which a person is represented as having done something generally regarded unfavorably, though basis in fact is lacking for such depiction.[40]

The fourth tort distinguished is appropriation of a name or image—the very attributes of personality—for the benefit of the one who appropriates them. The victim here, it is asserted, has his proprietary interest in his personality violated. The range of cases of such commercial usage extends from advertising to works of literary and graphic art.[41]

Prosser concludes:

> Taking them in order—intrusion, disclosure, false light, and appropriation—the first and second require the invasion of something secret, secluded or private pertaining to a plaintiff; the third and fourth do not. The second and third depend upon publicity, while the first does not, nor does the fourth, although it usually involves it. The third requires falsity or fiction; the other three do not. The fourth involves a use for the defendant's advantage, which is not true of the rest.[42]

I shall consider separately each of the contentions which are here advanced to obliterate invasion of privacy as a distinct tort.

1. *False light cases do not require invasion of something private pertaining to the plaintiff.*—This statement calls for support by cases in which there is representation in a false light but in which nothing private has been invaded. No such case is offered by Dean Prosser. In fact there are cases exactly to the opposite effect, as, for example, where admittedly the public images of Hollywood personages were falsified by local publicity but relief was denied because rights of publicity accompanied distribution of the film and so nullified rights of privacy, deemed necessary for the action, which would otherwise exist.[43] To the same point is the case of the Koussevitzky biography which included numerous questionable anecdotes relating to the conductor's career in a work claiming the privilege of public interest in information, and where the court, while acknowledging the stories to be fabrications, nevertheless resolved the issue for defendants on the ground that no right of privacy existed with respect to the career of this public figure.[44] And again to the same point, there is the

---

[40] See Prosser 398–401.

[41] See Prosser 401–07.

[42] Prosser 407.

[43] Paramount Pictures, Inc. v. Leader Press, Inc., 24 F. Supp. 1004 (W.D. Okla. 1938), rev'd on other grounds, 106 F.2d 229 (10th Cir. 1939).

[44] Koussevitzky v. Allen, Towne & Heath, Inc., 188 Misc. 479, 68 N.Y.S.2d

case of the socially prominent couple who objected to the misleading impressions of scandalous goings-on in their life as portrayed in a scandal magazine, but who were held by the court to have lost their right of privacy in this regard by virtue of their social prominence and so to be without a cause of action for invasion of privacy.[45]

2. *Appropriation cases do not require invasion of something private pertaining to the plaintiff.*—Again no case is offered which bears this out. What we do find, however, are cases in which the action was precluded because no invasion of something private occurred, although the appropriation of a personality was unquestionably present. Examples are the case of a mother who objected to the use of her name in an insurance policy on her life, issued to her son as beneficiary, where the court found no invasion of the mother's privacy because no public communication of her name was involved and, therefore, no cause of action constituted, although clearly her name was appropriated by the insurance company for its commercial purposes;[46] cases where the name of a dress designer was used when the original creation displaying the name was copied,[47] and where world-renowned composers were mentioned as the composers of music used in a film,[48] both decided for defendant on the theory that no cause of action could lie regardless of the appropriation because privacy had been previously abandoned or was simply not being threatened by this sort of use of a name.

3. *Disclosure and false light cases depend upon publicity, while intrusion and appropriation cases do not, although the latter usually involve publicity.*—What we have here is an *ad hoc* principle of classification seeking to pass muster as a condition that must be met if there is to be a cause of action. It is hardly remarkable that disclosure and false light cases all *involve* publicity, for Dean Prosser has insured this by so defining these categories.[49] Since the wrongful act in all these cases is, by definition, an act of publicity, it is again hardly remarkable that in such cases the cause of action should *depend* upon publicity.

---

779 (Sup. Ct.), aff'd, 272 App. Div. 759, 69 N.Y.S.2d 432 (1st Dep't 1947). It is difficult to concur in the view that the fact here was that errors were "minor and unimportant . . . in an otherwise accurate biography . . . ." Prosser 400.

[45] Goelet v. Confidential, Inc., 5 App. Div. 2d 226, 171 N.Y.S.2d 223 (1st Dep't 1958).

[46] Holloman v. Life Ins. Co., 192 S.C. 454, 7 S.E.2d 169 (1940).

[47] Jaccard v. R. H. Macy & Co., 265 App. Div. 15, 37 N.Y.S.2d 570 (1st Dep't 1942).

[48] Shostakovich v. Twentieth Century-Fox Film Corp., 196 Misc. 67, 80 N.Y.S.2d 575 (Sup. Ct. 1948).

[49] See Prosser 392, 398.

But it need hardly be pointed out that the presence of publicity in these cases does not indicate that a particular interest is at stake in each which is not at stake in cases where there is no publicity. As soon as one is clear that the harm is in something being known, it becomes apparent that getting acquainted and acquainting others equally compromise a single interest, which is in privacy.

4. *False light cases require falsity or fiction, while the other kinds do not.*—Again it appears that a shared feature is used as a principle of classification, and so the feature is indeed a requirement for admission to the class. But a bolder assertion is intended —that the cases so classified take the wrong to be in the falsity or fiction rather than in the violation of privacy. Three groups of false light cases are distinguished by Dean Prosser, and his contention must be appraised for each.

The first group[50] is comprised of cases of false association— falsely attributing work or opinions to a person, or falsely placing him in some situation. But determining whether an action will lie (quite apart from an action for defamation) does not at all involve a consideration of the truth or falsity of what is represented, and most of these cases exhibit no important concern with plaintiff's allegations of falsity or defendant's allegations of truth or accuracy. What is of central concern in all is the fact that the representation was not *authorized*,[51] which is to say that privacy was not abandoned.

Cases of the second group[52] under this head involve some element of fictitious portrayal in a publication. In these cases the issue has uniformly been whether there is such a distorted use as to bar the claim of privilege for publication in the public interest: Is there only entertainment or some other frivolous thing at stake; or, rather, matters of public information which are paramount in importance to privacy and to which, therefore, it may be sacrificed? The fictitious character of what is published is regarded only as a weighing factor in this balancing of interests.

The third group[53] is the "rogues' gallery" cases, in which plaintiff has had his picture and other means of identification placed in a police file. The cases here do not appear to focus on the issue of a notorious association of the plaintiff before his conviction with persons already convicted, as Dean Prosser suggests,[54] but rather on the propriety of including a person in public police files before his conviction, quite apart from any implication

---

[50] See Prosser 398–99.
[51] See cases cited in Prosser 398 nn.130–31, 399 nn.132–35.
[52] See Prosser 399.
[53] Prosser 399–400.
[54] See Prosser 399–400.

that he is a convicted criminal. The issue developed in these cases is whether arrest alone is sufficient to justify the violation of privacy constituted by such general dissemination through an extensive network of police files.[55] The objection raised to such a procedure is the sort that might meet a suggestion that everyone be fingerprinted and indexed for possible future police reference —a blow to privacy, not reputation.

In all three varieties of "false light" cases, then, some interest in not being known or thought of is at stake, rather than an interest in not being known or thought of *falsely*. One must be careful in these cases to observe the difference between what motivates the lawsuit and what is necessary for the cause of action. Facts in whose absence an action would likely not have been brought are not necessarily facts in whose absence the cause of action will be found deficient.

5. *Appropriation cases involve a use for the defendant's advantage, while the other types do not.*—It is true, of course, that the "appropriation" cases all involve a use for the defendant's advantage, for (as before) if they did not they would not be so classified by Dean Prosser. But is the use of plaintiff's name or likeness for defendant's advantage in derogation of a *proprietary* right of plaintiff in his identity, as Dean Prosser indicates?[56] I suggest that this is a serious mislocation of the gravamen of the wrong. The offense is to sensibility; and, more particularly, to those sensibilities of a person which are offended by another's use of his personality *regardless of any advantage*. Qualifications requiring a use for defendant's advantage do indeed exist. But when there is this requirement for a cause of action it is only to insure that a particular offense to privacy is unredeemed by a paramount public interest in unhindered communication—that the assault on privacy has been perpetrated merely to promote some selfish interest. The requirement represents a balance struck between a public interest and an interest in privacy, not an element of definition of the interest in privacy. Pursuing the inessential character of "appropriation" further, we might consider the New York statute which makes invasion of privacy in that jurisdiction a classic variety of "appropriation" in Dean Prosser's sense—uses "for advertising purposes, or for the pur-

---

[55] See McGovern v. Van Riper, 137 N.J. Eq. 24, 43 A.2d 514 (Ch. 1945), aff'd in part, 137 N.J. Eq. 548, 45 A.2d 842 (Ct. Err. & App. 1946), and cases cited in Prosser 399 n.143.

[56] "The interest protected is not so much a mental as a proprietary one, in the exclusive use of the plaintiff's name and likeness as an aspect of his identity." Prosser 406.

poses of trade."[57] There are a number of cases under this statute
in which there is no value ascribable to the particular name or
picture used—an appropriate name or picture selected at random
could have been substituted and it would have made no difference
to the user. Nor was any loss of value in his name suffered by the
plaintiff. Yet a good prima facie case was made under the statute.[58]
Clearly, then, it is not the value of the name to user or to bearer
which matters here, but the unauthorized use itself. "Appropriation," then, is nothing more than unauthorized use, and this
species of invasion of privacy is nothing more than unauthorized
publicity given to a person's name or image.

It appears, then, that Dean Prosser's four elements may be
regarded as merely incidental to the single interest whose presence
in all privacy cases is necessary for recognition of a legal wrong.

## B. *Professor Bloustein's "Human Dignity" Approach*

Professor Bloustein's article is an attempt "to propose a
general theory of individual privacy which will reconcile the divergent strands of legal development—which will put the straws back
into the haystack."[59] What I wish to suggest is that he has added
them to the already massive haystack of "human dignity" concerns instead of collecting them into a stack of their own. He
objects to Dean Prosser's four haystacks but fails to compose the
straws of privacy law as a single *distinctive* haystack. His position
is that there is a single interest in privacy involved in all the
cases separately classed by Dean Prosser and that this interest is
at stake in many areas of the law—among them torts—where a
right of privacy is recognized. His avowed aim is to discover
"in the welter of cases and statutes the interest or social value
which is sought to be vindicated in the name of individual pri-

---

[57] N.Y. Civ. Rights Law §§ 50, 51. The law developed here is typical of
"appropriation" cases in other jurisdictions.

[58] See, e.g., Nebb v. Bell Syndicate, 41 F. Supp. 929 (S.D.N.Y. 1941);
Swacker v. Wright, 154 Misc. 822, 277 N.Y. Supp. 296 (Sup. Ct. 1935); People v.
Charles Scribner's Sons, 205 Misc. 818, 130 N.Y.S.2d 514 (Magis. Ct. 1954) (all dismissed on the different ground that a use of the *plaintiff's* name was not constituted
merely by the use of a name which was the same as his). Further indication that
privacy of personality, rather than its value, is the protected thing is provided in
the assumed name cases. When the assumed name has in fact become the personality's identification it is protected. See Gardella v. Log Cabin Prods. Co., 89
F.2d 891 (2d Cir. 1937). But when the assumed name is merely a pseudonymous
stage or business device, though of unquestionable value, it is not an attribute of
personality and hence its unauthorized use is not an invasion of privacy. See Davis
v. R. K. O. Radio Pictures, Inc., 16 F. Supp. 195 (S.D.N.Y. 1936); Jaccard v.
R. H. Macy & Co., 176 Misc. 88, 26 N.Y.S.2d 829 (Sup. Ct. 1941), aff'd, 265 App.
Div. 15, 37 N.Y.S.2d 570 (1st Dep't 1942).

[59] Bloustein 963.

vacy."[60] This seems exactly right, but what follows misses by overshooting the mark.

We are told that the unitary interest involved in privacy cases is a dignitary interest. Speaking of the intrusion cases, Professor Bloustein discriminates the real nature of the complaint as something "demeaning to individuality, . . . an affront to personal dignity."[61] Individuality, we are told, depends upon "the right to be free from certain types of intrusions."[62] With regard to the public disclosure cases, "the invasion of privacy is founded on an insult to individuality" when there is "massive disclosure," "degrading a person by laying his life open to public view. . . . [I]n the public disclosure cases it is his individuality which is lost."[63] Of the cases involving appropriation of personality the comment is made that "every man has a right to prevent the commercial exploitation of his personality, not because of its commercial worth, but because it would be demeaning to human dignity to fail to enforce such a right"[64] (though I take it Professor Bloustein would find such a demeaning result only if a man were not *able* to enforce such a right, or did not have such a right at all). The false light cases he takes to be concerned with conduct which uses "a person's name or likeness so as to offend his dignity as an individual."[65] And in speaking of the celebrated article of Warren and Brandeis, Professor Bloustein speaks of the right to privacy as "a right to be let alone."[66] Commenting on a phrase of those distinguished authors he says "I take the principle of 'inviolate personality' to posit the individual's independence, dignity and integrity; it defines man's essence as a unique and self-determining being."[67] The theme of self-determination is repeated in rationalizing the uniformity of interest involved in the case of witnessed childbirth[68] and the case of electronic eavesdropping in a home:[69] "[T]he underlying wrong in both instances was the

---

[60] Bloustein 963.

[61] Bloustein 973.

[62] Bloustein 973.

[63] Bloustein 981.

[64] Bloustein 989.

Professor Bloustein generally rejects the notion of proprietary interest and substitutes the rationale of degradation through commercialization, Bloustein 988, and "wrongful exercise of dominion over another" or "the objective diminution of personal freedom . . . ." Bloustein 990. Such an ample view of the matter seems to go considerably beyond what the cases stand for. See note 58 supra.

[65] Bloustein 993.

[66] Bloustein 970, referring to Warren & Brandeis, The Right to Privacy, 4 Harv. L. Rev. 193 (1890). See note 36 supra.

[67] Bloustein 971.

[68] Bloustein 972 & n.58, citing DeMay v. Roberts, 46 Mich. 160, 9 N.W. 146 (1881).

[69] Bloustein 974 & n.72, citing Silverman v. United States, 365 U.S. 505 (1961).

same; the act complained of was an affront to the individual's independence and freedom."[70]

Lifting these bits of abstract characterization from a work which is mostly careful analysis of concrete cases is necessary because they are all that Professor Bloustein gives us by way of identifying "privacy." There is a reliance on intuitive apprehension for more. We have seen in *Griswold* that intuition may lead us astray, particularly with regard to the suggestion that the interest in privacy is to be understood in terms of an interest in self-determination.[71]

What Professor Bloustein has done toward clarifying the legal concept of privacy may be summarized in this way. He has argued, quite correctly, that Dean Prosser's discernment of four separate interests receiving legal protection as "privacy" fails to distinguish the single interest which is harmed or threatened whenever an invasion of privacy occurs. However, in proceeding to characterize the omnipresent interest as an interest relating in some essential fashion to individual dignity, he has told us why it is important enough to merit legal protection, but not what it is. This leaves the way open for claims of violation of privacy on a number of occasions when some other interest is affected to the detriment of human dignity, some interest which the law has seen fit to disregard or treat as a wrong of another sort.

* * * * *

My principal concern has been to combat a case of what Ludwig Wittgenstein called "the bewitchment of our intelligence by means of language."[72] The result (or means) of such bewitchment in *Griswold* is legal theory in support of the decision which seems literally nonsensical. Dean Prosser, far from succumbing to bewitching verbal sham, has instead rejected as a product of such shamming the notion of a separate interest in privacy in our tort law. Professor Bloustein has argued against this rejection, but not in a way which disposes of its grounds.

---

[70] Bloustein 994.

[71] Professor Bloustein, in speaking of privacy as an aspect of the pursuit of happiness, Bloustein 1001 n.222, cites among the authorities the dissenting opinion of Justice Harlan in Poe v. Ullman, 367 U.S. 497, 522 (1961), and the dissenting opinion of Justice Douglas in Public Util. Comm'n v. Pollak, 343 U.S. 451, 467 (1952). Poe preceded Griswold as an attempt to have the Connecticut anti-contraceptive statute declared unconstitutional, while Pollak raised the issue of first and fifth amendment protection against loudspeaker broadcasts on federally operated public conveyances. These two cases stand alone in the Bloustein article as conceptual deviations, and serve as an illustration of what may happen to the concept of privacy when one takes an overly large view and adopts a human dignity criterion to certify a misused word.

[72] Wittgenstein, Philosophical Investigations I § 109 (Anscombe transl. 1953).

It is not the nicety of legal theory for its own sake that is of concern, but rather the interest which it serves. By determining the bearings of privacy a valuable condition of life becomes amenable to principles of legal navigation, and a course may be set with reference to currents of rational argument in an otherwise chaotic sea. For it is not running free in the swiftest tide that augurs a continuing voyage, though (as in *Griswold*) it may be the quickest way to shore.

# [5]

JUDITH WAGNER DeCEW

# THE SCOPE OF PRIVACY IN LAW AND ETHICS

## 1. INTRODUCTION

In both laws and ethics, "privacy" is an umbrella term for a wide variety of interests.[1] Due to the growth of computer technology and capacities for electronic surveillance, data collection and storage, concern has increased over protection from unwarranted observations and exploitation of personal communications and information including academic, medical, and employment records. In these areas privacy is most obviously at stake, and has traditionally been protected in tort law as an interest in "having control over information about oneself." In addition, privacy has been associated in recent constitutional law with such issues as possession of obscene matter in one's home, interracial marriage, attendance at public schools, sterilization, contraception, abortion, and other medical treatment.

---

[1] Part of this paper was delivered at the December 1985 Eastern Division American Philosophical Association Meetings. William Parent was commentator. Some of his replies are from those comments. Much of the research for this paper was completed while I was a Liberal Arts Fellow in Law and Philosophy at Harvard Law School. Subsequent work was supported by a fellowship from the American Council of Learned Societies under a grant from the National Endowment for the Humanities. I am grateful for that support. Earlier versions were presented to the School for Urban and Public Administration at Carnegie-Mellon University, and the philosophy departments at the University of Massachusetts at Amherst, Wellesley College, and Tufts University. I thank members of those audiences for their comments and thank Sissela Bok, Peggy Carter, Joshua Cohen, Fred Feldman, Michael Jubien, and Lewis Sargentich for helpful suggestions. I am especially indebted to Jonathan Adler, Leslie Burkholder, Catherine Elgin, Jean Hampton, Jonathan Pressler, Elizabeth Prevett, Thomas Scanlon, and Ferdinand Schoeman for criticisms of earlier drafts.

*Law and Philosophy* 5 (1986) 145–173.
© 1986 by D. Reidel Publishing Company.

146                                              *Judith Wagner DeCew*

We might agree that information such as the content of one's fantasies is private. There is also consensus that action such as wife-battering, even if done in the confines of one's home, is not wholly private. Nevertheless, there are troubling borderline cases. For example, should threats on another's life, made in confidence to a lawyer or psychiatrist, be protected in the name of privacy?[2] Complexities concerning the relationship between privacy and harm or the risk of harm, and the conflict between privacy and social good, have yet to be sorted out to determine the scope of privacy in law and ethics.

Much of the discussion of privacy has evolved from a constellation of legal judgments. Philosophers then entered the debate, attempting to illuminate just what a right to privacy can and should mean. In two recent articles William Parent has attempted to clarify confusion surrounding the concept of privacy.[3] He defends a definition of privacy focusing on personal knowledge not part of any public record. Subsequently he discredits alternate accounts of privacy, explains the importance of privacy as a moral value, and assesses recent privacy decisions in the law. Parent also claims that the constitutional cases since *Griswold v. Connecticut*[4] (banning disbursement of contraceptive information, instruction, and medical advice to married persons) invoking a right to privacy are "spurious" privacy cases because attempts to explain them in terms of privacy conflate privacy and liberty. My central goal is to show that we may dispute this claim about the constitutional privacy cases. I begin by presenting Parent's definition of privacy and highlighting strengths as well as serious difficulties of his approach. I then show why we must reject Parent's as well as other

---

[2] In a controversial decision the California Supreme Court answered negatively. Tarasoff v. Regents of University of California, 131 Cal. Rptr. 14 (1976).

[3] William A. Parent, "A New Definition of Privacy for the Law," *Law and Philosophy* 2 (1983) 305–338; "Privacy, Morality, and the Law," *Philosophy and Public Affairs* 12 (1983), 269–288. Page references to these articles will be given in parentheses using "LP" and "PPA" respectively.

[4] 381 U.S. 479 (1965).

narrow definitions, thus leaving it open to us to adopt a broader concept of privacy. After arguing that a notion of privacy relevant to the constitutional privacy cases need not merely confuse privacy and liberty, I discuss alternative conceptual bases for an account of privacy relevant to both tort and constitutional privacy claims.

Let me make two preliminary points. First, in this paper I shall not place special weight on privacy as a right, as opposed to a claim or interest. A claim is often described as an argument that someone deserves something. A right is then a justified claim; justified by laws or judicial decisions if it is a legal right, by moral principles if it is a moral right.[5] However I am making moral and legal points which are significant independently of whether we can ultimately make sense of rights, explain when they are binding, or show they are reducible to utilitarian claims. Since the literature on privacy uses rights terminology I must accommodate that. But because I am making no claim about a theory of rights, whenever possible I shall refer to privacy as an interest (which can be invaded), by which I mean something it would be a good thing to have, leaving open how extensively it ought to be protected.

Second, nothing in my discussion requires assuming that one endorse all the decisions in cases I cite. One need not accept the actual rulings to inquire whether there is a common notion of privacy at stake. Indeed, disagreement over some decisions is likely for at least two reasons. (i) The notion of privacy has been so poorly articulated that it is not clear what is protected and what is not. (ii) Even if we develop a clearer concept of privacy, that will not dictate how it should be balanced against other individual rights or public concerns. One may have an important interest in privacy that for legal or social reasons cannot be protected.

## 2. PRIVACY AND THE PUBLIC RECORD

Understanding Parent's reasonable but inadequate position on

---

[5] Joel Feinberg, *Social Philosophy*, Prentice-Hall (1973), 64—67.

privacy will provide a helpful way of addressing more general
issues about the scope and meaning of "privacy." Motivated by a
concern to provide a definition of privacy that a) "is by and large
consistent with ordinary language" and b) does "not usurp or
encroach upon the basic meanings and functions" of other related
concepts (PPA 269), Parent defines privacy as

(P) the condition of not having undocumented personal information [knowl-
edge] about oneself known [possessed] by others (LP 306, PPA 269).

He stresses that he is defining the "condition" of privacy as
opposed to the right to privacy. The difference, he explains, is that
the condition of privacy is a moral value for persons who also
prize freedom and individuality which should be protected against
unwarranted invasion in part by advocating a moral right to
privacy. This moral right is in turn protected by law, and on
Parent's view should be guaranteed more fully than it is at present.
The distinction is important because it allows us to acknowledge
that diminishing privacy need not violate a moral or legal right to
privacy, and vice versa.

Let us get clearer on the significance of (P). "Personal" knowledge is, according to Parent, knowledge of personal information.
Such information must be factual, he believes, because publicity
of falsehoods or subjective opinions does not constitute an
invasion of privacy; it is appropriately characterized as slander,
libel, or defamation. Furthermore, information which is personal
consists either a) of facts which most persons in a given society
choose not to reveal about themselves (except to close friends,
family...) or b) of facts about which a particular individual is
acutely sensitive and which he therefore does not choose to reveal
about himself, even though most people do not care if similar facts
are widely known about themselves (LP 307, PPA 270). Thus in
our culture facts about sexual preferences, salaries, physical or
mental health, etc. are examples of personal information. While
most of us do not consider our height or marital status to be
instances of personal information, they will be for those sensitive
about it.

## The Scope of Privacy 149

Finally, personal information is "documented" just in case it belongs to the public record, that is, just in case it can be found in newspapers, court proceedings, and other official documents available to the public (LP 307, PPA 270). This characterization is meant to exclude information about individuals kept on file for a particular purpose, such as medical or employment records, which are not available for public perusal.

A valuable feature of Parent's account is that he not only sees privacy as a coherent concept but also takes the view that there is something unique, fundamental, and of special value in privacy. In contrast, "reductionists"[6] such as Judith Thomson[7] have argued that the right to privacy is not an independent right but is "derivative" from other rights, most notably property rights and rights to bodily security. According to this hypothesis there is no such thing as *the* right to privacy, for any violation of a right to privacy violates some right not identical with or included in the right to privacy. Privacy is "derivative" in the sense that it is possible to explain each right in the cluster of privacy rights without ever mentioning the right to privacy. Hence there is no need to find whatever might be in common in the rights in the privacy cluster. Commentators taking this approach differ of course, yet all agree that talk of privacy as an independent notion will not be illuminating.[8] By considering Thomson's examples in detail Parent shows that it is surely *as* plausible that the reverse of reductionism is true, that other rights such as those of ownership or rights over

---

[6] I borrow this term from Ruth Gavison, "Privacy and the Limits of Law," 89 *The Yale Law Journal* 421 (1980).

[7] Judith Jarvis Thomson, "The Right to Privacy," *Philosophy and Public Affairs* 4 (1975), 295–314, especially 308–313.

[8] Others include Frederick Davis, "What Do We Mean By 'Right to Privacy'?," 4 *South Dakota Law Review* 1 (1959); Henry Kalven, "Privacy in Tort Law-Were Warren and Brandeis Wrong?," 31 *Law and Contemporary Problems* 326 (1966), who argues that tort protection from emotional harm first defended by Warren and Brandeis (see note 11) protects hypersensitivity; and Richard Posner, "The Right to Privacy," 12 *Georgia Law Review* 3 (1978), who suggests privacy claims indicate an unjustified wish to manipulate and defraud.

one's person, are "derivative" from privacy rights.[9] Indeed this is likely if there is a distinctive and important value designated by the term "privacy".

A second strength of Parent's approach is the extent to which he recognizes and accommodates the fact that privacy is a conventional or relative notion. Because what counts as personal information may vary from group to group or individual to individual, and may change over time, there is no fixed realm of the private. This relative feature of privacy is well known but not often emphasized. Nevertheless, it must be allowed for by an adequate account of privacy.[10]

## 3. BEYOND INFORMATION

In attempting to isolate the conceptual core of privacy, Parent is surely correct to abandon Judge Cooley's famous, but overbroad, characterization of privacy as a right "to be let alone."[11] Yet he

---

[9] For similar criticisms of Thomson's account, see Thomas Scanlon, "Thomson on Privacy," *Philosophy and Public Affairs* 4 (1975), 315–322; and Jeffrey Reimann, "Privacy, Intimacy, and Personhood," *Philosophy and Public Affairs* 6 (1976), 26–44.

[10] See Benn and Gaus, *Public and Private in Social Life,* St. Martin's Press (1983), and *Journal of Social Issues* 33 (1977), a special issue on "Privacy as a Behavioral Phenomenon," especially Irwin Altman, "Privacy Regulation: Culturally Specific?", 66–84, and Herbert Kelman, "Privacy and Research with Human Beings," 169–195, for descriptions of the variability of privacy protection in other societies.

[11] "The right to one's person may be said to be a right of complete immunity: to be let alone." T. Cooley, *Law of Torts,* 2nd ed., (1888), 29. Contrary to Parent's claim that Warren and Brandeis were the first to advocate this definition, they relied on Cooley's phrase as well as cases they felt were already precedents to argue that the law should "protect the privacies of private life" by securing for an individual the right of determining the extent to which his written work, thoughts, sentiments, or likeness could be given to the public, a right they viewed as only part of the right to be let alone. Samuel Warren and Louis Brandeis, "The Right to Privacy," 4 *Harvard Law Review* 193 (1890), especially 215 note.

overreacts in the opposite direction and defends a definition of privacy that is much too narrow. To see this, consider first Parent's emphasis on *undocumented* personal knowledge. Imagine a case in which personal information about some individual has become part of the public record through a violation of privacy. A news agency, for example, surreptitiously taps an entertainer's telephone and subsequently publishes revealing information about that person's sex life or drug use habits. Given Parent's definition of privacy, once that information becomes part of the public record there is no violation of privacy in repeated publication of the information. The entertainer has no recourse for future protection; the information is no longer private even if the original disclosure was an error or a moral wrong.

In defense of his view, Parent says "[w]hat belongs to the public domain cannot without glaring paradox be called private and consequently should not be incorporated within a viable conception of privacy" (LP 308). If the original publication surfaced in a nationally syndicated daily, subsequent publication might seem only mildly invasive. But if the first disclosure occurred in publicly accessible but obscure documents, it is difficult to deny that a widely distributed reprint would be a further intrusion on the individual's privacy. The general point is that we are not likely to view perpetrating a violation as any less of a violation just because the agent is not the first one to invade the other's privacy. Thus, for example, during Margaret Heckler's divorce proceedings her husband claimed they had not had sexual relations in 20 years. Although this information was publicly available to reporters in the courtroom, it seems clear that the subsequent media coverage not only diminished Heckler's privacy but also violated her right to privacy.

Parent replies that similar publicity about a rape victim, for example, cannot be condemned on privacy grounds but should be criticized because it abridges her anonymity. It is far from clear that his account reflects our ordinary linguistic usage or is even applicable to Heckler's case. And even if we did talk of a "right to anonymity" in certain instances, surely it would be accorded to the victim so that her privacy would not be invaded. Indeed, there are legal counterexamples to Parent's position.[12] Yet on Parent's account, once information becomes part of the public record, whether legitimately or not, further release of it is never a privacy invasion.

Moreover, if any personal information is part of the public record, then even the most insidious snooping to attain the information, by someone unaware that it is already documented, for example, does not constitute a privacy intrusion on Parent's account. There is no invasion of privacy as long as "the information revealed was publicly available and could have been found out by anyone, without resort to snooping or prying" (PPA 271). Parent's test depends on whether or not the personal information is part of the public domain. Yet most of us would find the snooping diminishes our privacy, even if it were based on error and unnecessary to learn the facts. Snooping, spying, and other methods of acquisition are not always determinative of a privacy invasion. For example, I may intrude on another's privacy by over-hearing a quiet conversation on a subway. Nevertheless, the mode of acquisition cannot be said to be irrelevant, as it apparently may be given Parent's account of privacy.

These considerations introduce a more general concern. Because Parent has identified privacy invasions with possession of un-documented personal information, there is no way on his account to judge what should or should not be a part of the public record. His descriptive emphasis on what is *as a matter of fact* part of the public record leaves no room for a normative sense of privacy encompassing interests *worthy* of protection.

Thus, for example, Blue Cross/Blue Shield guidelines have recently been revised so that for psychological/psychiatric as well as physical treatment, specific descriptions of the ailment being treated are required in order for patients to receive reimbursement.

---

[12] Briscoe v. Reader's Digest Association, 4 Cal. 3d 529 (1971); Melvin v. Reid, 112 Cal. App. 283 (1931).

## The Scope of Privacy                                                    153

While the Privacy Act of 1974 protects the content of medical and other records, if the detailed descriptions required by Blue Cross/ Blue Shield should be deemed necessary as public verification of the legitimacy of any payments, they will not be private given Parent's definition. The point is that even very personal information can, through legislative action or decisions by agencies requiring its release, become nonprivate according to his definition, by virtue of its becoming documented. That account gives no normative standard for what it is legitimate for the public to know.

A second question we can ask is why Parent characterizes privacy as the condition of not having undocumented personal *knowledge* about one possessed by others. One problem is that it may be difficult to determine the truth of some statements. Setting aside such cases, however, we may still ask why knowledge must be disseminated for there to be a loss of privacy. Parent says, "[i]nvasion of privacy must consist of truthful disclosures about a person ... privacy is invaded by certain kinds of intrusions, namely those of a cognitive nature that *result in the acquisition* of undocumented personal facts" (PPA 285, emphasis mine). It is never clear whether it is the acquisition or the disclosure of information that troubles Parent most deeply. But what if there is neither? If one secretly trains a telescope on another but discovers nothing that is not already public information, has there been no privacy invasion? Consider Parent's discussion of an example of Thomson's: a great opera singer, who no longer wants to be listened to, only sings quietly behind soundproof walls. If she is nonetheless heard through an ingenious and strategically placed amplifier, what knowledge about her is gained? Even if none, most of us would agree there has been a privacy invasion. Parent himself seems confused on such cases. In assessing this example he writes, "[i]f B's snooping is without justification it should be condemned as a violation of A's right to privacy" (PPA 280), indicating the unjustified spying itself, independently of any knowledge acquired, is determinative of a privacy violation. The problem then reduces to when such snooping is justified and when it is not. Yet according to Parent's definition we must agree that there have been no privacy invasions in cases where no undocumented personal facts become known.

We might make sense of his remarks by requiring information acquisition only for a loss of privacy, not for a violation of a right. Yet Parent does not give this reply, and he invites us to use his definition concerning when privacy is diminished as a legal standard presumably relevant for determining rights violations as well. He does suggest an alternative response, however, namely that knowledge *is* gained in many such cases. The snooper learns the person's posture and attire, for example, and learns of the opera singer what she sings, how often, etc. Nevertheless, with repeated observations it is less clear that *new* knowledge is gained. And when the information is trivial we have good reason to doubt that the knowledge gained helps explain *why* we consider privacy the issue. Parent concedes, moreover, that if one snoops and fails to gather information, then there is no privacy invasion although the action is condemnable as unwarranted trespass. But then the most he can say if the singer is practicing in a building owned by a third party is that the snooper committed a wrong against the owner, not the singer! If he tries to say there is a sense in which the listener does trespass against the singer, then "trespass" is merely standing in for a certain kind of privacy invasion, whether he admits it or not.

Third, even if we weaken Parent's definition so that we do not always require that knowledge be gained for privacy to be invaded, we may wonder why it is reasonable to focus on possession of *information* as central to privacy.[13] If privacy is merely the condition of not having others possess certain information, it appears that privacy is tantamount to *secrecy*, though Parent hopes to deny such an identification. Nearly every dictionary includes a

---

[13] Others who have characterized privacy almost exclusively in terms of the amount of information known about an individual include Charles Fried, *An Anatomy of Values*, Harvard (1970), 140; Arthur Miller, *The Assault on Privacy*, Harvard (1971), 25; A. Westin, *Privacy and Freedom* (1967), 7; and E. Beardsley, "Privacy, Autonomy, and Selective Disclosure," Nomos XIII: *Privacy*, R. Pennock, and J. Chapman, eds., New York (1971).

definition of privacy as secrecy or concealment. According to the *Oxford English Dictionary,* that which is private is "removed from public view or knowledge; not within the cognizance of people generally."[14] Private information is often that which conceals, and interests in not being seen or overheard seem central to many privacy cases. However, this merely shows that the concepts overlap. Privacy and secrecy are not coextensional. First, whatever is secret is concealed or withheld from others, and it may not always be private. Thus a secret treaty or military plans kept from the public are not private transactions or information. Second, privacy does not always imply secrecy. For private information about one's debts or odd behavior may be publicized. Although it is no longer concealed, it is no less private.[15] Characterizing privacy as what is *intended* to be concealed is no help. Similar counter-examples follow. Military secrets are intended to be concealed; it does not follow that they are private. Information or intimate caresses may be private even if there is no intention to conceal them.

Historically, protection of information has been prominent but not exhaustive in the development of privacy law. Warren and Brandeis first sought protection from publication, without consent or adequate justification, not only of personal information, but also of one's name or likeness. The Fourth and Fifth Amendment protection against unreasonable search and seizures and self-incrimination protect potentially oppressive governmental surveillance as well as information gathering. They now limit wiretapping and other forms of electronic eavesdropping in addition to the physical intrusions on privacy that were once their primary target.[16]

---

[14] *Oxford English Dictionary,* Oxford, Clarendon Press (1961), p. 1388.

[15] In *Secrets: On the Ethics of Concealment and Revelation,* Random House (1983), Sissela Bok discusses the complex relationships between privacy and secrecy. She suggests that often secrecy is used to guard what is private. See especially 10–14.

[16] Paul Bender, "Privacy," "*Our Endangered Rights: The ACLU Report on Civil Liberties Today,*" Norman Dorsen, ed., Pantheon (1984).

Moreover, it is widely recognized that others' physical access to one can limit one's privacy in other ways as well. Ruth Gavison has argued that one can lose privacy merely by becoming the object of attention, even if no new information becomes known and whether the attention is conscious and purposeful, or inadvertant.[17] More obviously, one's privacy is diminished when others gain physical proximity to them, as Peeping Toms for example, through observation of their bodies, behavior, or interactions, through entry into a home under false pretenses, or even by a move from a single-person office to a shared one. In none of these cases is it necessary for new information to be acquired for there to be a privacy intrusion. Scanlon makes the point graphically.

> If you press personal questions on me in a situation in which this is conventionally forbidden, I can always refuse to answer. But the *fact that no information is revealed* does not remove the violation, which remains just as does the analogous violation when you peek through my bathroom window but fail to see me because I have taken some mildly inconvenient evasive action.[18]

Parent responds that privacy is irrelevant here. At best there is harassment (and possibly trespass). Parent's general strategy, then, in cases where no new information is acquired, is to urge that while there *is* a violation, it is unrelated to privacy – either anonymity (rape victim), trespass (insidious snooping, opera singer), or harassment (Scanlon's case). But as an argument for a conclusion about privacy, this hardly suffices. That an act involves harassment, trespass, or infringes one's anonymity implies nothing about whether it also diminishes or violates one's privacy.

It might seem that the above cases compel characterization of privacy as *seclusion* or the state or condition of being withdrawn from others, the observations of others, or the public interest.[19] This definition may come closest to Judge Cooley's characteriza-

---

[17] Gavison, "Privacy and the Limits of Law," 429ff.

[18] Scanlon, "Thomson on Privacy," 317. Scanlon has suggested that Parent might argue that this is a violation of a right to privacy even if it is not a case when privacy is diminished. Yet Parent denies privacy is relevant at all.

[19] Davis, "What Do We Mean by 'Right to Privacy'?," 6.

tion of the right as "the right to be let alone." But even if a conversation or activity is private, it will fail to be secluded if it is in public view or if it is overheard, seen or otherwise observed by others. Discussion or activity intended to be private, such as child abuse or consenting sadomasochism, may be observed or may be of public concern. Analogously, even if a conversation or action is not in view of others, it may not be a private one in any sense except that it happens not to be observed or known about even if it is of great public interest.

Some aspect of seclusion is clearly protected by privacy law. The American Law Institute's *Restatement of the Law of Torts, Second* (1976) includes a section titled "Intrusion on Seclusion" (§ 652B), which reads:

> One who intentionally intrudes, physically or otherwise, upon the solitude or seclusion of another, or his private affairs or concerns, is subject to liability to the other for invasion of his privacy, if the invasion would be highly offensive to a reasonable person.

But this legal protection can be limited. What would ordinarily be considered privacy interests are not always protected if the individual involved is a public figure or if the information is not confidential. A clandestine search (without a warrant) through office files was not considered an invasion of privacy, despite a loss of privacy, since the information gathered and publicized was needed to judge the individual as a candidate for the U.S. Senate.[20] And when Ralph Nader complained that prior to his publication of *Unsafe at Any Speed*, General Motors agents interviewed acquaintances about his political, racial and sexual views, kept him under surveillance in public places, attempted to entrap him with women, made threatening, harassing, and obnoxious telephone calls to him, tapped his telephone, and eavesdropped on private conversations by means of mechanical and electronic equipment, the court asserted that

...mere gathering of information about a particular individual does not give

---

[20] Pearson v. Dodd, 410 F. 2d 701 (D.C. Cir. 1969).

rise to a cause of action under this theory. Privacy is invaded only if the information sought is of a confidential nature and the defendent's conduct was unreasonably intrusive.[21]

According to the opinion in Nader's case, *confidential content* is crucial to privacy. Yet other tort privacy claims are upheld because of the intrusiveness of the behavior, even if the information or photographs obtained are not at all confidential. For example, in *Dietemann v. Time Inc.*, two *Life* magazine reporters entered a disabled veteran's home under false pretenses and took clandestine photographs and recordings to learn about and publicize the quackery being practiced.[22] It was held and affirmed on appeal that this was an invasion of privacy even though the content was not confidential and whether or not the material was published.

The courts are clearly puzzled over the relationship between privacy and confidential content, publicity, and intrusiveness. Secrecy, seclusion, and confidential content alone cannot give an adequate picture of the realm of the private, although each may be a crucial aspect of some subset of privacy invasions. Unfortunately, Parent has neither acknowledged nor addressed this confusion. I wish to suggest that most of us find the *Nader* decision outrageous, the *Dietemann* result reasonable, and believe the opera singer's privacy has been invaded. If so, then we can agree that acquisition of undocumented personal knowledge is not always relevant to a privacy intrusion.[23] Our privacy interests are both more extensive and deeper than Parent's definition allows. He can at best capture much of the legal extension of the concept of privacy, not the nature of our moral notion of privacy.

---

[21] Nader v. General Motors Corporation, 25 N.R. 2d 560 (1970).

[22] 449 F. 2d 246 (1971).

[23] Compare Thomson, "The Right to Privacy," "...it seems to me none of us has a right over any fact to the effect that that fact shall not be known to others." Yet "...we have a right that certain steps shall not be taken to find out facts, and we have a right that certain uses shall not be made of facts" (307).

## 4. PRIVACY AND LIBERTY

I have argued that we must reject information acquisition and publication as solely determinative of privacy invasions. If we do so, and acknowledge that privacy concerns encompass not only information but activity and physical access as well, then we have good reason to consider whether the realm of the private can properly be taken to include the sort of privacy interests protected in constitutional law as well as those associated with tort law. Tort privacy, developed over the past 90 years, covers interests individuals have in protection not only from publication of information but also from unwarranted observations of themselves, their activities, materials, and conversations, whether those observations occur in person or through electronic surveillance. There has also been increased protection from having one's communications reproduced or misused without authorization and from having information about oneself appropriated or exploited.

The constitutional right to privacy, first announced by the Supreme Court twenty years ago in the *Griswold* case, has continued to be elusive. It has been used not only to guard rights to use and distribute contraceptives,[24] but also to protect abortion rights and to defend subsequent decisions concerning funding, father's rights, third party consent for minors, and protection of the fetus. Furthermore, the right to privacy was cited as one major reason for allowing "possession of obscene matter" in one's home[25] and it has been associated with cases on sterilization laws,[26] interracial marriage,[27] and attendance at public schools.[28]

Paradigmatically, tort privacy cases involve concerns with information, either conveyed by or about an individual. The more diverse constitutional privacy cases involve issues related to one's

---

[24] Eisenstadt v. Baird, 405 U.S. 438 (1972).
[25] Stanley v. Georgia, 394 U.S. 557 (1969).
[26] Skinner v. Oklahoma, 316 U.S. 535 (1942).
[27] Loving v. Virginia, 388 U.S. 1 (1967).
[28] Pierce v. Society of Sisters, 268 U.S. 510 (1925).

160                                            *Judith Wagner DeCew*

body, family relations, life style, or child rearing. In 1977, in
*Whalen v. Roe*, the Court made its most comprehensive effort thus
far to define the right to privacy, embracing both (i) an "individual interest in avoiding disclosure of personal matters" and (ii)
an "interest in independence in making certain kinds of important
decisions."[29] (The case was deemed to involve both aspects of
privacy, yet the Court upheld New York statutes for maintaining
computerized records of prescriptions for certain dangerous but
lawful drugs, even though the records included the patients'
names.)

Since its inception the constitutional right to privacy has been
severely criticized. It has been called "pernicious," "a malformation of constitutional law which thrives because of the conceptual
vacuum surrounding the legal notions of privacy," and "a composite term whose sense is illusory."[30] There is general worry that
the right flagrantly expresses subjective judicial ideology and is a
form of legislative policy-making not properly a function of the
courts, because there is no explicit passage in the Constitution or
Bill of Rights justifying the right as described by the Court. Worse
still, while other legal rights (such as the right to travel from state
to state) are not mentioned in the Constitution, they are plausibly
inferable in some way. But the constitutional right to privacy, it is
claimed, cannot be inferred from the intent of the framers or from
the governmental system depicted by the Constitution.

There is also a philosophically more important concern which I
wish to address, namely that the line of constitutional cases since
*Griswold* involve rights which have "no basis in any meaningful
conception of privacy."[31] Parent objects specifically to an account of privacy relevant to the constitutional cases which he describes as "control over significant personal matters" on the

---

[29] Whalen v. Roe, 429 U.S. 598–600 (1977).
[30] Hyman Gross, "The Concept of Privacy," 42 *New York Law Review* 34,
35, 42 (1967).
[31] Richard Posner, "Uncertain Protection of Privacy By the Supreme Court,"
*Supreme Court Review*, (1979) 173–216.

## The Scope of Privacy 161

grounds that it is based on a conceptual error: confusing privacy and liberty. He argues,

The defining idea of liberty is the absence of external restraints or coercion. A person who is behind bars or locked in a room or physically pinned to the ground is unfree to do many things. Similarly, a person who is prohibited by law from making certain choices should be described as having been denied the liberty or freedom to make them. The loss of liberty in these cases takes the form of a deprivation of autonomy. Hence we can meaningfully say that the right to liberty embraces in part the right of persons to make fundamentally important choices about their lives and therewith to exercise significant control over different aspects of their behavior. It is clearly distinguishable from the right to privacy, which condemns the unwarranted acquisition of undocumented personal knowledge. (PPA 274–5) ... All of these [constitutional privacy] cases conflate the right to privacy with the right to liberty (PPA 284, LP 316).

We can readily concur with Parent that an adequate account of privacy should not confuse it with other related concepts such as liberty or autonomy. And of course his concept of liberty is distinguishable from privacy as he has described it. But it is not at all clear that Parent has shown that the constitutional privacy cases involve no "genuine" privacy interests. His argument is not new,[32] yet it has often been accepted with little comment.

There is a practical reason why the Court avoided using liberty as the defense of the *Griswold* line of cases, although it does not provide a rationale for why privacy was used. According to the Fourteenth Amendment no state shall deprive any person of life, liberty or property, without due process of law. It was the "liberty" of this due process clause that was most commonly cited in a sequence of cases in the early 1900's striking down nearly 200 economic regulations, such as those fixing minimum wages for women.[33] But the Court was not in those cases merely addressing

---

[32] See, for example, Hyman Gross, "Privacy and Autonomy," Nomos XIII: *Privacy*, 180–81, and Louis Henkin, "Privacy and Autonomy," 74 *Columbia Law Review* 1410 (1974).

[33] Adkins v. Children's Hospital, 261 U.S. 525 (1925). The cases are often referred to as the Lochner era after the first case, Lochner v. New York, 191 U.S. 45 (1905), which limited work hours in a bakery.

fair procedures, and critics (led by Justice Oliver Wendell Holmes) felt that the due process clause was there being used in a substantive way to scrutinize economic regulation carefully and to hold laws unconstitutional if the Court believed they were unwise. This substantive due process doctrine, allowing courts to intrude on legislative value judgments, was widely discredited and discarded by the late 1930's.[34]

Given early association of a legal right to privacy as a right to be let alone and the well-known explanation of a concept of negative liberty in terms of freedom from interference, it is hardly surprising that privacy and liberty should often be equated. But our intuitive notion of privacy can be shown to be distinct from liberty. For example, one's privacy may constantly be invaded by surreptitious surveillance without affecting one's liberty, and one's liberty may be invaded by assault, by conferring undesired benefits, or by limiting one's choices (such as to burn one's draft card) without violating privacy interests. There are all sorts of liberties we do not have. I cannot leave the country without a passport nor is George Carlin free to parody dirty words on the airwaves during daytime hours. In neither case are we inclined to believe a privacy interest is at stake. While the word "privacy" could be used to mean freedom to live one's life without governmental interference, the Supreme Court cannot so use it since such a right is at stake in *every* case. Our lives are continuously limited, ofter seriously, by governmental regulation.[35] Privacy may not always be well-protected either, but it is not understood by the Court or in our

---

[34] Some commentators and a few Supreme Court Justices believe that under the name "privacy" the Court protected fundamental rights using substantive due process, even if they did not admit it. See Gerald Gunther, *Cases and Materials on Constitutional Law*, The Foundation Press (1980), 502–503 and 570ff; Justice Stewart in his comments on *Griswold* and his concurrence in *Roe*; William Rhenquist, "Is an Expanded Right of Privacy Consistent with Fair and Consistent Law Enforcement? or Privacy, You've Come a Long Way, Baby," 23 *Kansas Law Review* 1 (1974).

[35] John Hart Ely, "The Wages of Crying Wolf: A Comment on *Roe v. Wade*," 82 *Yale Law Journal* 920 (1973).

*The Scope of Privacy*                                                  163

ordinary language to be as comprehensive an interest as freedom from governmental regulation.

Perhaps concern about the relation between privacy and liberty in the *Griswold* line of cases can be understood as the view that the constitutional right of privacy protects certain liberties, namely freedom to perform acts that do not affect the interests of others, what J. S. Mill in *On Liberty* called "self-regarding" actions. With his juxtaposition of terms, Mill himself gave the impression that both "liberty" and "privacy" characterize the realm of action he was most concerned to protect. He first described

...a sphere of action in which society, as distinguished from the individual, has, if any, only an indirect interest: comprehending all that portion of a person's life and conduct which affects only himself, or, if it also affects others, only with their free, voluntary, and undeceived consent and participation. When I say only himself, I mean directly and in the first instance; for whatever affects himself may affect others through himself; ...This, then, is the appropriate region of human *liberty*.[36] (my emphasis)

Yet only two paragraphs later, while defending the necessity of maintaining such liberty, he cautioned that while modern states have prevented great "interference by law in the details of *private* life," traditional tendencies have been just the opposite. "The ancient Commonwealths thought themselves entitled to practise, and the ancient philosophers countenanced, the regulation of every part of *private* conduct by public authority."[37] (my emphasis)

However, in *Paris Adult Theatre*[38] the Court clearly and effec-

---

[36] John Stuart Mill, *On Liberty*, Penguin (1976), 71. Compare the ambiguous uses of the terms "private morality," "liberty," and "freedom of choice and action," in the Hart-Devlin debate over legislation of consenting homosexuality and prostitution. Lord Patrick Devlin, "Morals and the Criminal Law," *The Enforcement of Morals*, Oxford (1965); H. L. A. Hart, "Immorality and Treason," *The Listener*, (July 1959).

[37] Mill, *On Liberty*, 72.

[38] Paris Adult Theatre I et al. v. Slaton, District Attorney, et al. 413 U.S. 49. I thank Leslie Burkholder for reminding me of this argument. There is also no evidence that the *Griswold* court viewed the privacy right as equivalent to a Mill-type right.

tively rejects the idea that constitutional privacy is just freedom
with respect to self-regarding acts. It says, first, that the Constitution does not incorporate the proposition that conduct involving
consenting adults is always beyond regulation, whereas the Constitution does provide a right of privacy. Hence the latter is not
just a Mill-like right to freedom from legislative or other governmental interference in behavior that does not harm nonconsenting
others. Second, the Court lays out the sort of things it takes the
constitutional privacy right to protect. Some of the activities
protected, such as child-rearing, are not protected by a Mill-like
right. It also appears from the Court's reasoning that some things
protected by the Mill-like right, eating what one pleases, for
example, or watching obscene movies in a public cinema in
*Paris,* are not protected by the privacy right. Thus the constitutional right to privacy as it has developed is not even coextensional
with a Mill-type right to freedom from governmental interference
with behavior that does not prejudicially affect the welfare of
others.

The constitutional privacy cases generally involve an interest in
independence in making certain fundamental or personal decisions, and in virtue of that they do concern, as Parent recognizes,
autonomy to determine for oneself what to do.[39] But because
privacy does *not* just consist in possession of undocumented personal knowledge, and because an intuitive notion of privacy
invoked in the constitutional privacy cases does *not* conflate
privacy and liberty, we need not deny that there is a sense of
privacy relevant to those cases. To the contrary, I wish to show
that it is more intuitive to agree that privacy is related to liberty in
the following way. Many privacy issues, such as protection from
electronic surveillance, have no connection with autonomous
decision-making. Also, many self-determined choices, to drive a
loudspeaker through a quiet neighborhood, for example, can be

---

[39] See the familiar account of moral autonomy sketched by Robert Paul
Wolff in *In Defense of Anarchism,* Harper and Row (1970), 12–18.

made by an individual but are not in any further sense private decisions. A subset of autonomy cases, however, certain personal decisions regarding one's basic lifestyle, can plausibly be said to involve privacy interests as well. They should be viewed as liberty cases in virtue of their concern over decision-making *power*, whereas privacy is at stake because of the *nature* of the decision. More needs to be said about which decisions and activities are private ones, but it is no criticism or conflation of concepts to say that an act can be both a theft and a trespass. Similarly, acknowledging that in some cases there is both an invasion of privacy and a violation of liberty need not confuse those concepts.

Parent has not shown that a notion of privacy encompassing the constitutional cases must conflate privacy and liberty. If one already accepts his definition of privacy, the conclusion that privacy is irrelevant to the constitutional cases follows trivially. That conclusion, though, is unhelpful at best and question-begging at worst. It would be more productive to determine whether there is a broader sense of privacy which is relevant to the full range of cases where privacy is claimed to be at stake.

## 5. TOWARD A BROAD CONCEPTION OF PRIVACY

If we agree to reject the claim that the constitutional privacy cases cannot be said to be "genuine" privacy cases without conflating privacy and liberty, we have (at least) these two options: (i) We might draw on similarities between tort and constitutional privacy claims in order to develop a notion of privacy fundamental to informational and Fourth Amendment privacy concerns as well as the constitutional cases. Certain examples indicate this will be promising. Consider consenting homosexuality in one's home, for instance. We view it as a private matter whether the state is seeking to regulate the behavior, or if others are attempting to gain or exploit information about it. (ii) We could concede that whatever "privacy" means in the tort and Fourth Amendment cases, it means something different in the constitutional cases. Nevertheless, we might take that "something else" seriously as a distinct but legitimate use of the term which is not "spurious" but is reflected in our ordinary language.

Alternative (ii) may seem more fruitful since the wide diversity of privacy claims enumerated, as well as the use of the term in such varied aspects of social life including information, property, parts, decisions, activity, and enterprise, indicate why it is so difficult to isolate common elements in the full range of cases where privacy is central. Note, however, that even in tort law there is no fixed way of using "privacy" which we then proceed to analyze; yet the term has not in those cases been taken to be meaningless or empty. Hence I shall conclude this paper by exploring (i).

In an effort to distinguish privacy as a descriptive term from a normative use of the word encompassing interests *worthy* of protection (some subset of which, depending on the circumstances, actually are protected), it has sometimes been suggested that privacy concerns not merely the absence of others having information, but individual *control* over knowledge others have about one. While the interest was first discussed as control over *information* others have about oneself, it has been extended to include control over *actions* as well. On this view, privacy is a power to deny or grant access. But surely not every loss or gain of control over information about us, or what we do or have done to us, is a loss or gain of privacy. Consider a writer whose research unexpectedly reveals his shabby or inaccurate scholarship. Information about him has become known to others without his consent. He loses control of it, yet we would not say he has suffered a loss of privacy.[40] Similarly, if a policeman pushes me out of the way of an ambulance, I have lost control of what has been done to me, but we would not say that my privacy has been invaded. Not just any touching is a privacy intrusion. Characterization of a privacy interest as an ability to control is thus much too broad.

Nevertheless, it may be that control of some aspect of ourselves is a necessary condition for a loss of privacy. Perhaps for every

---

[40] Richard B. Parker, "A Definition of Privacy," 27 *Rutgers Law Review* 275 (1974).

*The Scope of Privacy*                                        167

privacy invasion the individual loses control over what is seen, heard, or read about him, over what is done with information, recordings, or photographs of him, over what is done to him (e.g., he is wired, or operated on without consent), or over what he does (e.g., uses contraceptives, reads pornography).

If this is so, then we might extend a traditional notion of property to include whatever one has control over. On this account every privacy invasion would also be a property invasion, but not the reverse, so that privacy interests would form a subset of property interests. We would be claiming not only that our bodies and minds and written work, but our reputations, information about us, and so on, are our property, stretching considerably our common notion of property. This is apparently Van den Haag's view. "Privacy is best treated as a property right," he says, and he focuses on exclusivity as the core of privacy when he defines privacy as exclusive access of a person to a realm of his own.[41]

I am concerned, however, that our intuitive sense of property rights breaks down in privacy contexts. Do we own behavior we do not want observed, or all information we want or have a right to suppress? Do we own our bodies in as straightforward and uncomplicated a sense as we own letters or land, or as the wealthy once owned slaves? It is more worrisome that even if this thesis could be defended adequately, focus on control or property ownership may not offer a *full explanation* of privacy issues. It

---

[41] Ernst Van den Haag, "On Privacy," *Nomos* XIII, *Privacy*. Scanlon claims that Thomson overstates the importance of ownership. Her examples, however, suggest that privacy rights are not always explainable in terms of property rights, but a variety of other rights as well. It has been argued that many of the Fourth and Fifth Amendment cases, such as Boyd v. U.S., 116 U.S. 616 (1886), Weeks v. U.S., 232 U.S. 383 (1914), and Gould v. U.S., 255 U.S. 298 (1921), putting private papers beyond the reach of governmental agents, requiring warrants, and reaffirming the protection against self-incrimination, rest on traditional property concepts. See "Formalism, Legal Realism, and Constitutionally Protected Privacy Under the Fourth and Fifth Amendments," 90 *Harvard Law Review* 945–91 (March 1977).

may fail to capture what is distinctive and most fundamental in the diverse privacy cases.

Noting that mention of "personal" rights is prominent in the Court's explanation of constitutional privacy, one might think that whether a privacy invasion involves information about oneself, bodily security, or choices about one's lifestyle, it always intrudes on a special zone close to oneself, something very personal. According to the *Oxford English Dictionary*, what is private affects "a person, or a small intimate body or group of persons apart from the general community; [it is] individual, personal."[42] One feature of Parent's definition which we have not yet rejected is his focus on "personal" information. While information is personal in this sense, we might attempt to extend his characterization of what is personal to cover activities as well as information, in order to generate a broader notion of privacy. Recall, however, that for Parent what is personal is relativized to individuals, and includes not only what most would choose to share, but also what that individual is "acutely sensitive" about. There are of course well-known difficulties with legal protection of peculiar sensitivities, and we might do better to adopt a "reasonable person" standard of what is personal.

There are still problems with this latter suggestion. If you tap my phone, but merely hear me placing an order for pizza, it seems reasonable to agree you violated my privacy although you heard no personal information and had no physical access to me. A decision to merge one's business with another may be a private but not a personal one. Such cases indicate that focus on what is personal to an individual will either be vacuous or will not adequately circumscribe what we understand as the scope of privacy.[43]

---

[42] 1389.

[43] Similar problems confront recent accounts of privacy in terms of the requirements for friendship or intimacy. Information about my salary, for example, is private but not intimate. See Fried, *An Anatomy of Values*, and Robert Gerstein's "Intimacy and Privacy," and Ferdinand Schoeman's "Privacy and Intimate Information," in Schoeman, ed., *Philosophical Dimensions of Privacy*, Cambridge (1984).

*The Scope of Privacy* 169

We do, however, have a crude intuition that what is private is that which is nobody else's business. In view of this, we might take the realm of the private to be whatever is not the legitimate con-concern of others, where those others may be private individuals in tort cases, the government for constitutional claims.[44] Despite the vagueness of this characterization, we can agree that information as well as activities and decisions can be private in this sense, allowing a basic conceptual relationship between tort and con-stitutional privacy interests. On this account privacy claims can be made by individuals, couples or small groups. Because some trivial claims can on this interpretation be private, there will be a broad spectrum of more and less important privacy interests. Moreover, what is legitimately the concern of others can vary according to circumstances and culture. Thus we might agree that in this coun-try a couple's decision about whether or not to use contraceptives is beyond the legitimate concern of others. Whereas it is at least arguable that governmental intrusion in such a decision could be legitimate in overpopulated countries such as China or India.

The obvious worry is that this account is overbroad. Consider, for example, Locke's principle that religious ends are not a legit-imate state concern.[45] If we wish to differentiate privacy and religious claims, among others, we must seek an explanation of which subclass of issues beyond the legitimate concern of others comprise the private ones. This is a very difficult task and not one that can be completed in this article. Yet I believe we can make progress if we attend to the various reasons people have for wanting privacy. Moreover, the similarity of reasons for protect-ing tort and constitutional privacy claims gives further evidence

---

[44] This is reminiscent of Joel Feinberg's suggestion that "it may be stretch-ing things a bit to use one label, 'the right to privacy,' for such a diversity of rights, except to indicate that there is a realm (or a number of realms) of human conduct that are simply nobody's business except the actor's, and a fortiori are beyond the legitimate attention of the criminal law." "Pornog-raphy and the Criminal Law," 40 *Pittsburgh Law Review* 115 (1979).

[45] Statement of this principle is the subject of the first *Letter Concerning Toleration, Works of John Locke*, 5–58.

that those claims are related in an important way, and strengthens
my position that an important interest in privacy is at stake in the
constitutional privacy cases.

People have many different reasons for wanting to control
information about themselves, ranging from freedom from
defamation to commercial gain. When freedom from scrutiny,
embarrassment, judgment, even ridicule, are at stake, as well as
protection from pressure to conform, prejudice, emotional distress,
and loss in self-esteem, opportunities, or finances arising from
them, we are more inclined to view the claim to control information as a privacy claim. A tort privacy action is one mechanism
society has created to accomplish such protection. By itself it is
not wholly adequate, however, because the interests that provide
the reasons for the screen on information include the interest in
being free to decide free of the threat of the same problems
which accompany an information leak. In other words, it is
plausible to maintain that worries about what information others
have are often *due* to worries about social control. What you can
do to me or what I can do free of the threat of scrutiny, judgment, etc. may often depend on what information, personal
or not, you, the state, or others have about me. Since my behavior is also affected by the extent to which I can make my own
choices, both the threat of an information leak and the threat of
decreased control over decision-making can have a chilling effect
on my behavior. Thus protecting a sanctuary for ourselves, a
refuge within which we can shape and carry on our lives and
relationships with others — intimacies as well as other activities —
without the threat of scrutiny, embarrassment, judgment, and the
deleterious consequences they might bring, is a major underlying
reason for protecting *both* information control and control over
decision-making. Furthermore, since people want control over
many things, and freedom is far broader than privacy, this similarity of reasons for protecting tort and constitutional privacy is
more fundamental than the idea that both involve freedom or control.

While this examination of reasons for protecting privacy does

*The Scope of Privacy* 171

not give a unified definition of privacy, it does indicate that privacy claims can be identified by looking at the justifications for such claims. An interest in privacy is at stake when intrusion by others is not legitimate *because* it jeopardizes or prohibits protection of a realm free from scrutiny, judgment, and the pressure, distress, or losses they can cause. While I have not given an exhaustive list of reasons for protecting privacy, I believe I have said enough to show there is a certain range of similar reasons for guarding tort and constitutional privacy claims which can be used to demarcate which intrusions are privacy invasions.

Of course if this characterization of the private is to be useful we need further explanation of the notion of legitimacy. Many cases will be clear. Thus, for example, neither my bathroom behavior nor information about it can be justified as the legitimate concern of others, given that I have no communicable disease or dangerous tendencies. In contrast, there is wide disagreement over whether a decision to have an abortion is a proper concern of anyone except the mother. Even if we believe details about one's sex life do not comprise the kind of information that is the legitimate concern of the state, we might have great difficulty determining whether or not, for an individual with AIDS, the danger of the disease and our lack of knowledge about its transmission justify viewing detailed information about that individual's sex life as legitimately of public concern.

Unfortunately there is a more serious difficulty with this proposal.[46] As presented, it does not allow us to account for the existence of *justifiable* invasions of privacy. If, for example, we determine that when an individual has AIDS, details about his sex life are legitimately the concern of state health officials, then according to the explanation given we must agree that there is no privacy invasion when they inquire about those intimacies. But this seems incorrect. What we want to say in such a case is that seeking such information *is* an invasion of the AIDS victim's

---

[46] I am grateful to Jonathan Pressler for emphasizing the importance of this problem.

172                                                    *Judith Wagner DeCew*

privacy, but that the intrusion is justified because of the serious-
ness of the health threat.

Perhaps the best way to handle this difficulty is to characterize
the realm of the private as whatever is not generally, that is,
according to a reasonable person under normal circumstances, or
according to certain social conventions, a legitimate concern of
others because of the threat of scrutiny or judgment and the
potential problems following from them. Privacy would thus be a
property of *types* of information and activities, and we could say
that any interference with them would be a privacy invasion,
although particular interferences could be justified. Much more
needs to be said, however, about determining relevant circumstances, conventions, and descriptions of types of acts, to fill out
this more general description.

This sort of account does have the advantage of allowing us to
clarify an important relationship between privacy and liberty. As
we have seen, loss of privacy can diminish freedom. Nevertheless,
defending privacy cannot always protect liberty. It cannot guard
against public assault, for example. If, however, privacy protects
against intrusions of others for a certain set of reasons, and if one
has liberty when one is free of external restraints and interferences,
then protection of privacy can preserve some liberty. We can in
this way make sense of Parent's claim "that privacy is a moral
value for persons who also prize freedom and individuality" (PPA
278).

An additional consequence is worth noting. Parent objects that
currently informational privacy is less well protected than the constitutional right to privacy. If a reasonable person would not be
troubled by publicity about a family wedding of the sort Warren
and Brandeis sought to protect, then in such cases privacy may
well be a petty tort.[47] And if in the balance it is more important

---

[47] Harry Kalven, "Privacy in Tort Law: Were Warren and Brandeis Wrong?"
Richard Epstein has argued that privacy is the least important tort in "Privacy,
Property Rights, and Misrepresentations," *Georgia Law Review* (1978). But
expanded protection of privacy in tort law is not as trivial as the original
Warren and Brandeis protection.

to exclude the state from decisions about whether or not to have a vasectomy, or to acquire contraceptive information and devices, than to have security against embarrassment arising from the use of one's name, correspondence, or photograph, then we may be able to support this recent trend over complaints against it.[48]

### 6. CONCLUSION

I have not provided a constitutional defense for citing privacy as one right at stake in the *Griswold* line of cases.[49] Nor have I attempted to enter the debate about how strictly to interpret the Constitution. Yet I have urged that it is reasonable for us to agree that there is an interest in privacy at issue in the constitutional cases because (1) privacy does *not* just consist in possession and acquisition of undocumented personal knowledge, (2) taking privacy to be relevant in the constitutional cases need *not* conflate the concepts privacy and liberty, and (3) similar interests provide reasons for protecting *both* tort privacy over information and constitutional privacy over decision-making. The implications of this view are significant. Current constitutional standards, controversial though they may be, require "strict scrutiny" for cases concerning "fundamental values," and privacy has been judged one such value. Thus these privacy claims have a *greater* chance of being protected when they conflict with other rights or general interests than they would have if only liberty, or freedom from governmental interference, were involved.

Department of Linguistics and Philosophy,
Massachusetts Institute of Technology,
Cambridge, MA 02139,
U.S.A.

---

[48] Richard Posner, "Uncertain Protection of Privacy by the Supreme Court."
[49] Others are working on this task. See, for example, David A. J. Richards, "Constitutional Privacy, Religious Disestablishment, and the Abortion Decisions," *Abortion: Moral and Legal Perspectives*, University of Massachusetts Press (1984), 148–174.

# [6]

# The Yale Law Journal

Volume 89, Number 3, January 1980

## Privacy and the Limits of Law

**Ruth Gavison†**

Anyone who studies the law of privacy today may well feel a sense of uneasiness. On one hand, there are popular demands for increased protection of privacy, discussions of new threats to privacy, and an intensified interest in the relationship between privacy and other values, such as liberty, autonomy, and mental health.[1] These demands have generated a variety of legal responses. Most states recognize a cause of action for invasions of privacy.[2] The Supreme Court has declared a constitutional right to privacy, a right broad enough to protect abortion and the use of contraceptives.[3] Congress enacted the Privacy Act of 1974[4] after long hearings and debate. These activities[5]

---

† Visiting Associate Professor of Law, Yale Law School. This Article develops some of the themes of my doctoral thesis, Privacy and Its Legal Protection, written under the supervision of Professor H.L.A. Hart. Much of the inspiration of this piece is still his. I am grateful to Bruce Ackerman, Bob Cover, Owen Fiss, George Fletcher, Harry Frankfurt, Jack Getman, Tony Kronman, Arthur Leff, Michael Moore, and Barbara Underwood, who read previous drafts and made many useful comments.

1. The best general treatment of privacy is still A. WESTIN, PRIVACY AND FREEDOM (1967). For treatment of a variety of privacy aspects, see NOMOS XIII, PRIVACY (R. Pennock & J. Chapman eds. 1971) (Yearbook of the American Society for Political and Legal Philosophy) [hereinafter cited as NOMOS].

2. W. PROSSER, THE LAW OF TORTS 804 (4th ed. 1971).

3. Roe v. Wade, 410 U.S. 113, 152-55 (1973) (right to privacy cited to strike down abortion statute); Eisenstadt v. Baird, 405 U.S. 438, 453 (1972) (right to privacy includes right of unmarried individual to use contraceptives); Griswold v. Connecticut, 381 U.S. 479, 484-86 (1965) (right to privacy includes right of married couple to use contraceptives). See generally Richards, Unnatural Acts and the Constitutional Right to Privacy: A Moral Theory, 45 FORDHAM L. REV. 1281 (1977); Comment, A Taxonomy of Privacy: Repose, Sanctuary, and Intimate Decision, 64 CALIF. L. REV. 1447 (1976) (developing constitutional right to privacy).

4. 5 U.S.C. § 552a (1976). For a discussion of the privacy exception to the Freedom of Information Act, 5 U.S.C. § 552(b)(7)(C) (1976), see J. O'REILLY, FEDERAL INFORMATION DISCLOSURE: PROCEDURES, FORMS AND THE LAW §§ 20.01-21.10 (1977); Cox, A Walk Through Section 552 of the Administrative Procedure Act: The Freedom of Information Act; The Privacy Act; and the Government in the Sunshine Act, 46 U. CIN. L. REV. 969 (1978).

5. Several constitutional and statutory provisions explicitly recognize the right to privacy. See, e.g., CAL. CONST. art. I, § 1 (1974 amendment recognizing, inter alia, right to privacy); PRIVACY PROTECTION STUDY COMM'N, PERSONAL PRIVACY IN AN INFORMATION SOCIETY (1977) (report on various aspects of privacy in U.S. with recommendations for additional protection of privacy).

The Yale Law Journal                                    Vol. 89: 421, 1980

seem to imply a wide consensus concerning the distinctness and importance of privacy.

On the other hand, much of the scholarly literature on privacy is
written in quite a different spirit. Commentators have argued that
privacy rhetoric is misleading: when we study the cases in which the
law (or our moral intuitions) suggest that a "right to privacy" has been
violated, we always find that some other interest has been involved.[6]
Consequently, they argue, our understanding of privacy will be improved if we disregard the rhetoric, look behind the decisions, and
identify the real interests protected. When we do so, they continue, we
can readily see why privacy itself is never protected: to the extent that
there is something distinct about claims for privacy, they are either
indications of hypersensitivity[7] or an unjustified wish to manipulate
and defraud.[8] Although these commentators disagree on many points,
they are united in denying the utility of thinking and talking about
privacy as a legal right, and suggest some form of reductionism.[9]

This Article is an attempt to vindicate the way most of us think and
talk about privacy issues: unlike the reductionists, most of us consider
privacy to be a useful concept. To be useful, however, the concept must
denote something that is distinct and coherent. Only then can it help
us in thinking about problems. Moreover, privacy must have a coher-

6. For studies of legal protection in this vein, see, *e.g.*, Davis, *What Do We Mean by
"Right to Privacy"?* 4 S.D. L. REV. 1 (1959); Dickler, *The Right of Privacy*, 70 U.S. L.
REV. 435 (1936); Kalven, *Privacy in Tort Law—Were Warren and Brandeis Wrong?* 31
LAW & CONTEMP. PROB. 326 (1966); Prosser, *Privacy*, 48 CALIF. L. REV. 383 (1960). For a
similar study of moral intuitions, see Thomson, *The Right to Privacy*, 4 PHILOSOPHY &
PUB. AFF. 295 (1975).

7. *See, e.g.*, Kalven, *supra* note 6, at 329 & n.22.

8. This aspect of privacy has been emphasized by Richard Posner. *See, e.g.*, Posner,
*Privacy, Secrecy, and Reputation*, 28 BUFFALO L. REV. 1 (1979) [hereinafter cited as
*Secrecy*]; Posner, *The Right to Privacy*, 12 GA. L. REV. 393 (1978) [hereinafter cited as
*Privacy*]. Other commentators have followed his lead. *See, e.g.*, Epstein, *Privacy, Property
Rights, and Misrepresentations*, 12 GA. L. REV. 455 (1978).

9. All reductionists claim that the concept of privacy does not illuminate thoughts
about legal protection. Professor Posner's version is the most extreme: he denies the
utility of all "intermediate" values, and advocates assessing acts and rules by the single,
ultimate principle of wealth maximization. *E.g.*, *Secrecy*, *supra* note 8, at 7-9; *Privacy*,
*supra* note 8, at 394.

The commentators cited in note 6 *supra* accept the utility of some differentiating concepts to denote different interests, such as property, reputation, and freedom from mental
distress, but claim that privacy should be reduced to these "same-level" concepts. This
form of reductionism is consistent with an acknowledgment that people want privacy,
and that satisfaction of this wish does denote an important human aspiration. The essence
of this reductionism is the claim that description and evaluation of the law or moral
intuitions are clarified by pointing out that we do not have an independent "right to
privacy." *See, e.g.*, Davis, *supra* note 6, at 18-24; Kalven, *supra* note 6, at 333-41. This
position is frequently found in the literature on privacy. *See, e.g.*, Epstein, *supra* note 8,
at 474; Freund, *Privacy: One Concept or Many*, in NOMOS, *supra* note 1, at 182, 190-93.

Privacy

ence in three different contexts. First, we must have a neutral concept of privacy that will enable us to identify when a loss of privacy has occurred so that discussions of privacy and claims of privacy can be intelligible. Second, privacy must have coherence as a value, for claims of legal protection of privacy are compelling only if losses of privacy are sometimes undesirable and if those losses are undesirable for similar reasons. Third, privacy must be a concept useful in legal contexts, a concept that enables us to identify those occasions calling for legal protection, because the law does not interfere to protect against every undesirable event.

Our everyday speech suggests that we believe the concept of privacy is indeed coherent and useful in the three contexts, and that losses of privacy (identified by the first), invasions of privacy (identified by the second), and actionable violations of privacy (identified by the third) are related in that each is a subset of the previous category. Using the same word in all three contexts reinforces the belief that they are linked. Reductionist analyses of privacy—that is, analyses denying the utility of privacy as a separate concept—sever these conceptual and linguistic links. This Article is an invitation to maintain those links, because an awareness of the relationships and the larger picture suggested by them may contribute to our understanding both of legal claims for protection, and of the extent to which those claims have been met.[10]

I begin by suggesting that privacy is indeed a distinct and coherent concept in all these contexts. Our interest in privacy, I argue, is related to our concern over our accessibility to others: the extent to which we are known to others, the extent to which others have physical access to us, and the extent to which we are the subject of others' attention. This concept of privacy as a concern for limited accessibility enables us to identify when losses of privacy occur. Furthermore, the reasons for which we claim privacy in different situations are similar. They are related to the functions privacy has in our lives: the promotion of liberty, autonomy, selfhood, and human relations, and furthering the existence of a free society.[11] The coherence of privacy as a concept and

10. This approach may also enhance our understanding and evaluation of the reductionist thesis. *See* pp. 460-67 *infra*.

11. The fact that my analysis demonstrates the value of privacy by showing its contribution to other goals does not make this just another type of reductionism. These instrumental justifications explain why we consider privacy a value but do not mean that we only protect privacy because of these other values. Complex instrumental arguments justify all values save ultimate ones, and perhaps we have no ultimate values in this sense at all. This does not mean that all values are reducible.

The Yale Law Journal                          Vol. 89: 421, 1980

the similarity of the reasons for regarding losses of privacy as undesirable support the notion that the legal system should make an explicit commitment to privacy as a value that should be considered in reaching legal results. This analysis does not require that privacy be protected in all cases; that result would require consideration of many factors not discussed here. I argue only that privacy refers to a unique concern that should be given weight in balancing values.

My analysis of privacy yields a better description of the law and a deeper understanding of both the appeal of the reductionist approach and its peril. The appeal lies in the fact that it highlights an important fact about the state of the law—privacy is seldom protected in the absence of some other interest. The danger is that we might conclude from this fact that privacy is not an important value and that losses of it should not feature as considerations for legal protection. In view of the prevalence of the reductionist view, the case for an affirmative and explicit commitment to privacy—vindicating the antireductionist perspective—becomes compelling.

## I.  The Meaning and Functions of Privacy

"Privacy" is a term used with many meanings. For my purposes, two types of questions about privacy are important. The first relates to the *status* of the term: is privacy a situation, a right, a claim, a form of control, a value? The second relates to the *characteristics* of privacy: is it related to information, to autonomy, to personal identity, to physical access? Support for all of these possible answers, in almost any combination, can be found in the literature.[12]

The two types of question involve different choices. Before resolving these issues, however, a general distinction must be drawn between the concept and the value of privacy. The concept of privacy identifies losses of privacy. As such, it should be neutral and descriptive only, so as not to preempt questions we might want to ask about such losses. Is the loser aware of the loss? Has he consented to it? Is the loss desirable? Should the law do something to prevent or punish such losses?

This is not to imply that the neutral concept of privacy is the most important, or that it is only legitimate to use "privacy" in this sense. Indeed, in the context of legal protection, privacy should also indicate a value. The coherence and usefulness of privacy as a value is due to a similarity one finds in the reasons advanced for its protection, a simi-

12.  *See* pp. 425-28 & pp. 437-40 *infra.*

Privacy

larity that enables us to draw principles of liability for invasions.[13] These reasons identify those aspects of privacy that are considered desirable. When we claim legal protection for privacy, we mean that only those aspects should be protected, and we no longer refer to the "neutral" concept of privacy. In order to see which aspects of privacy are desirable and thus merit protection as a value, however, we must begin our inquiry in a nonpreemptive way by starting with a concept that does not make desirability, or any of the elements that may preempt the question of desirability, part of the notion of privacy. The value of privacy can be determined only at the conclusion of discussion about what privacy is, and when—and why—losses of privacy are undesirable.[14]

In this section I argue that it is possible to advance a neutral concept of privacy, and that it can be shown to serve important functions that entitle it to prima facie legal protection. The coherence of privacy in the third context—as a legal concept—relies on our understanding of the functions and value of privacy; discussion of the way in which the legal system should consider privacy is therefore deferred until later sections.[15]

## A. *The Neutral Concept of Privacy*

### 1. *The Status of Privacy*

The desire not to preempt our inquiry about the value of privacy by adopting a value-laden concept at the outset is sufficient to justify viewing privacy as a situation of an individual vis-à-vis others, or as a condition of life. It also requires that we reject attempts to describe

13. Any appearance of circularity here is misleading. To say that the coherence of the descriptive concept of privacy follows from the reasons we have for protecting it does not mean that the privacy we wish to protect is coextensive with the situation identified by the descriptive concept. *See* note 14 *infra*. We must start with a descriptive concept, however, in order to analyze the reasons to value some aspects of privacy.

14. Typical elements that may preempt discussion of desirability are the wishes or choices of the individuals concerned, the nature of the information, or the way in which the information is acquired. One important example is the statement that invasions of privacy are undesirable when the information disseminated is "private." It is clear that the statement must mean that it is undesirable because the information should be seen as entitled to be kept private, that is, to not become known to the public. For clarity of thought, all of these elements should be excluded from the concept designed to identify the losses themselves. The best discussion of the need for a conceptual scheme that does not preempt questions is Parker, *A Definition of Privacy*, 27 RUTGERS L. REV. 275 (1974). *See generally* R. Gavison, Privacy and Its Legal Protection (1975) (unpublished D. Phil. thesis on file in Oxford, Harvard Law School, and Yale Law School libraries) (discussion of Parker).

15. *See* pp. 456-59 & pp. 467-71 *infra*.

The Yale Law Journal                        Vol. 89: 421, 1980

privacy as a claim,[16] a psychological state,[17] or an area that should not be invaded.[18] For the same reasons, another description that should be rejected is that of privacy as a form of control.[19]

This last point requires some elaboration, because it may appear that describing privacy as a form of control does not preempt important questions. Were privacy described in terms of control, for example, we could still ask whether X has lost control, and whether such loss is desirable. The appearance of a nonpreemptive concept is misleading, however, and is due to an ambiguity in the notion of control. Hyman Gross, for example, defines privacy as "control over acquaintance with one's personal affairs."[20] According to one sense of this definition,

16. Alan Westin has defined privacy as the "claim of individuals, groups, or institutions to determine for themselves when, how, and to what extent information about them is communicated to others." A. WESTIN, *supra* note 1, at 7. For a discussion of the influence of this definition on the study of privacy, see Lusky, *Invasion of Privacy: A Clarification of Concepts*, 72 COLUM. L. REV. 693, 693-95 (1972). It is interesting to note that Professor Westin also gives a second and quite different description of privacy: "Viewed in terms of the relation of the individual to social participation, privacy is the voluntary and temporary withdrawal of a person from the general society through physical or psychological means . . . ." A. WESTIN, *supra* note 1, at 7.

17. If we define privacy as a state of mind, we shall not be able to discuss losses of privacy that are unknown to the individual or whether such awareness is relevant to the desirability of such losses.

18. PRIVACY AND THE LAW, A REPORT BY THE BRITISH SECTION OF THE INTERNATIONAL COMM'N OF JUSTICE ¶ 19 (1970):

Accordingly, we shall use the word "privacy" in this report in the sense of that area of a man's life which, in any given circumstances, a reasonable man with an understanding of the legitimate needs of the community would think it wrong to invade.

This definition is simply a conclusion, not a tool to analyze whether a certain invasion should be considered wrong in the first place. Gerety, *Redefining Privacy*, 12 HARV. C.R.-C.L. L. REV. 233 (1977), makes a similar move when he invokes the description proposed in J. STEPHEN, LIBERTY, EQUALITY, FRATERNITY 160 (1967; 1st ed. 1873): "Conduct which can be described as indecent is always in one way or another a violation of privacy." *Id.* at 242. Professor Gerety is quite conscious, however, of the difference between descriptive and normative intuitions. His own definition of privacy invokes descriptive intuitions: "Privacy will be defined here as an autonomy or control over the intimacies of personal identity." *Id.* at 236. He adds, however, that it "carries with it a set of at least preliminary conclusions about rights and wrongs." *Id.*

19. Richard Parker, who is aware of the danger that conclusory definitions may preempt important questions, defines privacy as control over who senses us. Parker, *supra* note 14, at 280-81. Similarly, Professor Fried defines privacy as control over information. C. FRIED, AN ANATOMY OF VALUES 140 (1970) [hereinafter cited as VALUES]; Fried, *Privacy*, 77 YALE L.J. 475, 482 (1968) [hereinafter cited as *Privacy*]. Other writers whose definitions of privacy can be understood in these terms are A. MILLER, THE ASSAULT ON PRIVACY 25 (1971); A. WESTIN, *supra* note 1, at 7; Beardsley, *Privacy: Autonomy and Selective Disclosure*, in NOMOS, *supra* note 1, at 56, 70; Gerety, *supra* note 18, at 236; and Shils, *Privacy: Its Constitution and Vicissitudes*, 31 LAW & CONTEMP. PROB. 281, 282 (1966).

20. Gross, *Privacy and Autonomy*, in NOMOS, *supra* note 1, at 169, 169 [hereinafter cited as *Autonomy*]. *But see* Gross, *The Concept of Privacy*, 42 N.Y.U. L. REV. 34, 35-36 (1967) (defining privacy as "the condition of human life in which acquaintance with a person or with affairs of his life which are personal to him is limited") [hereinafter cited as *Concept*]. Gross does not even refer to his earlier contribution in his 1971 article in NOMOS.

Privacy

a voluntary, knowing disclosure does not involve loss of privacy because it is an exercise of control, not a loss of it.[21] In another, stronger sense of control, however, voluntary disclosure is a loss of control because the person who discloses loses the power to prevent others from further disseminating the information.

There are two problems here. The weak sense of control is not sufficient as a description of privacy, for X can have control over whether to disclose information about himself, yet others may have information and access to him through other means. The strong sense of control, on the other hand, may indicate loss of privacy when there is only a threat of such loss.[22] More important, "control" suggests that the important aspect of privacy is the ability to choose it and see that the choice is respected. All possible choices are consistent with enjoyment of control, however, so that defining privacy in terms of control relates it to the power to make certain choices rather than to the way in which we choose to exercise this power. But individuals may choose to have privacy or to give it up.[23] To be nonpreemptive, privacy must not depend on choice. We need a framework within which privacy may be the result of a specific exercise of control, as when X decides not to disclose certain information about himself, or the result of something imposed on an individual against his wish, as when the law prohibits the performance of sexual intercourse in a public place. Furthermore,

21. It will clearly not be a loss in Edward Shils's definition:
[P]rivacy exists where the persons whose actions engender or become the objects of information retain possession of that information, and any flow outward of that information from the persons to whom it refers (and who share it where more than one person is involved) occurs on the initiative of its possessors.
Shils, *supra* note 19, at 282. The control necessary here is over the outward flow of information, not control over those who receive the information. Hyman Gross has a more complex picture. He suggests that whether voluntary disclosure involves loss of privacy depends on whether the recipient is bound by restrictive norms. *Autonomy, supra* note 20, at 171.
22. People may simply be uninterested in an individual, and thus not care to acquire information about him. Such an individual will have "privacy" even if he resents it. To say that an individual controls the flow of information about himself is thus not enough to tell us whether he is known in fact. We also must know whether there are restrictive norms, whether these are obeyed, how the individual has chosen to exercise his control, and whether others have acquired information about him in other ways or at all. The view of privacy presented by Alan Westin is not vulnerable to this difficulty. *See* A. WESTIN, *supra* note 1.
23. For example, an individual may voluntarily choose to disclose everything about himself to the public. This disclosure obviously leads to a loss of privacy despite the fact that it involved an exercise of control. This much is conceded even by Professor Gross. *Autonomy, supra* note 20, at 171. Moreover, to prohibit the individual from making disclosures is a limitation of his control that would seem to increase his privacy. A similar problem confronts those who seek to promote liberty of action when they are asked whether an individual should be allowed to sell himself into slavery. The sale may be a free exercise of liberty, but the result is a restriction on liberty.

The Yale Law Journal                              Vol. 89: 421, 1980

the reasons we value privacy may have nothing to do with whether an individual has in fact chosen it. Sometimes we may be inclined to criticize an individual for not choosing privacy, and other times for choosing it. This criticism cannot be made if privacy is defined as a form of control.

Insisting that we start with a neutral concept of privacy does not mean that wishes, exercises of choice, or claims are not important elements in the determination of the aspects of privacy that are to be deemed desirable or of value. This insistence does mean, however, that we are saying something meaningful, and not merely repeating the implications of our concept, if we conclude that only choices of privacy should be protected by law.

Resolving the status of privacy is easier than resolving questions concerning the characteristics of privacy. Is privacy related to secrecy, freedom of action, sense of self, anonymity, or any specific combination of these elements? The answers here are not constrained by methodological concerns. The crucial test is the utility of the proposed concept in capturing the tenor of most privacy claims, and in presenting coherent reasons for legal protection that will justify grouping these claims together. My conception of privacy as related to secrecy, anonymity, and solitude is defended in these terms.

### 2. *The Characteristics of Privacy*

In its most suggestive sense, privacy is a limitation of others' access to an individual. As a methodological starting point, I suggest that an individual enjoys *perfect* privacy when he is completely inaccessible to others.[24] This may be broken into three independent components: in perfect privacy no one has any information about $X$, no one pays any attention to $X$, and no one has physical access to $X$. Perfect privacy is, of course, impossible in any society. The possession or enjoyment of privacy is not an all or nothing concept, however, and the total loss of privacy is as impossible as perfect privacy. A more important concept, then, is *loss* of privacy. A loss of privacy occurs as others obtain information about an individual, pay attention to him, or gain access to him. These three elements of secrecy, anonymity, and solitude are distinct and independent, but interrelated, and the complex concept of privacy is richer than any definition centered around

---

24. I use "enjoys" although individuals would doubtless suffer if exposed to "perfect privacy," and may resent privacy that is imposed on them against their will. "Perfect" privacy is used here only as a methodological starting point. There is no implication that such situations exist or that they are desirable.

Privacy

only one of them. The complex concept better explains our intuitions as to when privacy is lost, and captures more of the suggestive meaning of privacy. At the same time, it remains sufficiently distinctive to exclude situations that are sometimes labeled "privacy," but that are more related to notions of accountability and interference than to accessibility.

### a.  *Information Known About an Individual*

It is not novel to claim that privacy is related to the amount of information known about an individual. Indeed, many scholars have defined privacy exclusively in these terms,[25] and the most lively privacy issue now discussed is that related to information-gathering. Nevertheless, at least two scholars have argued that there is no inherent loss of privacy as information about an individual becomes known.[26] I believe these critics are wrong. If secrecy is not treated as an independent element of privacy, then the following are only some of the situations that will not be considered losses of privacy: (a) an estranged wife who publishes her husband's love letters to her, without his consent; (b) a single data-bank containing all census information and government files that is used by all government officials;[27] and (c) an employer who asks every conceivable question of his employees and yet has no obligation to keep the answers confidential. In none of these cases is there any intrusion, trespass, falsification, appropriation, or exposure of the individual to direct observation. Thus, unless the amount of information others have about an individual is considered at least partly determinative of the degree of privacy he has, these cases cannot be described as involving losses of privacy.

To talk of the "amount of information" known about an individual is to imply that it is possible to individuate items or pieces of information, to determine the number of people who know each item of in-

25. *E.g.*, Professor Fried in Values, *supra* note 19, at 140; A. Miller, *supra* note 19, at 25; A. Westin, *supra* note 1, at 7; Beardsley, *supra* note 19, at 56; Professor Gross in *Autonomy*, *supra* note 20, at 172-74; Shils, *supra* note 19, at 282.

26. Professor Gerety argues that information is part of privacy only if it is "private"—related to intimacy, identity, and autonomy. Gerety, *supra* note 18, at 281-95. Professor Parker suggests that there are times when loss of control over information does not mean loss of privacy, *e.g.*, examinations in which it is revealed the student did not study. Parker, *supra* note 14, at 282.

27. *See* Benn, *Privacy, Freedom, and Respect for Persons*, in Nomos, *supra* note 1, at 1, 11-12 (data banks as paradigmatic privacy issue). Unused data banks do not cause a loss of privacy, of course, because the mere existence of information on file does not make it known to anyone. Access to such data banks does create a threat that losses of privacy may occur. *See generally* Farhi, *Computers, Data Banks and the Individual: Is the Problem Privacy?* 5 Israel L. Rev. 542 (1970).

formation about $X$, and thus to quantify the information known about $X$. In fact, this is impossible, and the notion requires greater theoretical elaboration than it has received until now. It is nevertheless used here because in most cases its application is relatively clear. Only a few of the many problems involved need to be mentioned.

The first problem is whether we should distinguish between different kinds of knowledge about an individual, such as verbal as opposed to sensory knowledge, or among different types of sensory knowledge. For example, assume $Y$ learns that $X$ is bald because he reads a verbal description of $X$. At a later time, $Y$ sees $X$ and, naturally, observes that $X$ is bald. Has $Y$ acquired any further information about $X$, and if so, what is it? It might be argued that even a rereading of a verbal description may reveal to $Y$ further information about $X$, even though $Y$ has no additional source of information.[28]

A related set of problems arises when we attempt to compare different "amounts" of knowledge about the same individual. Who has more information about $X$, his wife after fifteen years of marriage, his psychiatrist after seven years of analysis, or the biographer who spends four years doing research and unearths details about $X$ that are not known either to the wife or to the analyst?[29]

A third set of problems is suggested by the requirement that for a loss of privacy to occur, the information must be "about" the individual. First, how specific must this relationship be? We know that most people have sexual fantasies and sexual relationships with others. Thus, we almost certainly "know" that our new acquaintances have sexual fantasies, yet they do not thereby suffer a loss of privacy. On the other hand, if we have detailed information about the sexual lives of a small number of people, and we are then introduced to one of them, does the translation of the general information into personal information about this person involve a loss of privacy? Consider the famous anecdote about the priest who was asked, at a party, whether he had heard any exceptional stories during confessionals. "In fact,"

28. Professor Parker suggests the example of an astronaut whose actions in a spaceship are thoroughly monitored by electrodes that feed data to a control desk. In addition, people at the control desk can observe the astronaut through a television camera. Parker argues that a prohibition against switching off the camera would result in further loss of privacy for the astronaut even though the camera provides no additional information. Parker, *supra* note 14, at 281. Parker seems correct, but not necessarily because loss of control over sensing is involved. The camera may provide people at the control desk with an additional, qualitatively different way to obtain the "same" information, and this may be equivalent to additional information.

29. The "amount" of information may not be as important as the quality and extent of the information. There is a difference between knowing a person, and knowing about him.

Privacy

the priest replied, "my first confessor is a good example, since he confessed to a murder." A few minutes later, an elegant man joined the
group, saw the priest, and greeted him warmly. When asked how he
knew the priest, the man replied: "Why, I had the honor of being his
first confessor."

The priest gave an "anonymous" piece of information, which became information "about" someone through the combination of the
anonymous statement with the "innocent" one made by the confessor.
Only the later statement was "about" a specific individual, but it
turned what was previously an anonymous piece of information into
further information "about" the individual. The translation here from
anonymous information to information about $X$ is immediate and un-
mistakable, but the process is similar to the combination of general
knowledge about a group of people and the realization that a certain
individual is a member of that group.[30]

Problems of the relationship between an individual and pieces of
information exist on another level as well. Is information about $X$'s
wife, car, house, parents, or dog information about $X$? Clearly, this is
information about the other people, animals, or things involved, but
can $X$ claim that disclosure of such information is a loss of his privacy?
Such claims have often been made.[31] Their plausibility in at least some
of the cases suggests that people's notions of themselves may extend
beyond their physical limits.[32]

A final set of problems concerns the importance of the truth of the
information that becomes known about an individual. Does dissemination of false information about $X$ mean that he has lost privacy? The
usual understanding of "knowledge" presupposes that the information
is true, but is this sense of "knowledge" relevant here? In one sense, $X$
has indeed lost privacy. People now believe they know more about him.
If the information is sufficiently spectacular, $X$ may lose his anonymity

30. Another example might be cross-cultural. If we know something about the psychological make-up of a certain class, does a person whom we meet lose further privacy
when we learn that he is a member of that class? We certainly may know more "about"
him than he might suspect, depending on the probability that he is typical of the class.

31. *See, e.g.,* Cox Broadcasting Corp. v. Cohn, 420 U.S. 469 (1975) (parent alleged that
his right to privacy was invaded by identification of daughter as victim of rape-murder);
Corliss v. E.W. Walker Co., 57 F. 434 (C.C.D. Mass. 1893), *injunction dissolved,* 64 F. 280
(C.C.D. Mass. 1894) (plaintiffs alleged publication of biography and picture of dead husband and father constituted injury to their feelings).

32. This "extension of self" is a complex phenomenon, and seems highly culture-
dependent. In some cases, it may be based on the idea that a person's choices reflect on
him; my spouse, my car, and my clothes are part of me in this sense. In cases in which
no choice is involved, such as those involving disclosures about parents, children, or
siblings, the "extension of self" may be based on a feeling of responsibility for or identification with the other person. *See* Benn, *supra* note 27, at 12.

and become the subject of other people's attention.[33] In another sense, however, X is not actually "known" any better. In fact, he may even be known less, because the false information may lead people to disregard some correct information about X that they already had.[34] Another difficulty is revealed when we consider statements whose truth is not easily determinable, such as "X is beautiful" or "X is dumb and irresponsible." Publication of such statements clearly leads to some loss of privacy: listeners now know what the speaker thinks about X, and this itself is information about X (as well as about the speaker). But does the listener also know that X is indeed beautiful? This is hard to tell.[35]

### b. *Attention Paid to an Individual*

An individual always loses privacy when he becomes the subject of attention. This will be true whether the attention is conscious and purposeful, or inadvertent. Attention is a primary way of acquiring information, and sometimes is essential to such acquisition, but attention alone will cause a loss of privacy even if no new information becomes known. This becomes clear when we consider the effect of calling, "Here is the President," should he attempt to walk the streets incognito. No further information is given, but none is necessary. The President loses whatever privacy his temporary anonymity could give him. He loses it because attention has focused on him.

Here too, however, some elaboration is needed. X may be the subject of Y's attention in two typical ways.[36] First, Y may follow X, stare at him, listen to him, or observe him in any other way. Alternatively, Y may concentrate his thoughts on X. Only the first way of paying attention is directly related to loss of privacy. Discussing, imagining, or thinking about another person is related to privacy in a more indirect way, if at all. Discussions may involve losses of privacy by communicat-

33. This explains the way in which defamation involves loss of privacy, or at least the threat of such a loss. Even if the defamatory information is false, it attracts attention to the person in ways that may involve loss of privacy.

34. *See* Roberts & Gregor, *Privacy: A Cultural View*, in NOMOS, *supra* note 1, at 199, 214 (promotion of privacy through systematic denial of truth).

35. The answer depends on our theories about evaluations. To the extent that some evaluations are susceptible to interpersonal assessment, we may say that such evaluations transmit "objective knowledge." To the extent we consider evaluations subjective only, any informational content is much more complex and limited. The distinction between fact and opinion is important in defamation law's doctrine of "fair comment." Fair comment is privileged, but the facts on which it is based must be accurate. The distinction is notoriously difficult to draw. *See, e.g.*, Titus, *Statement of Fact versus Statement of Opinion—A Spurious Dispute in Fair Comment*, 15 VAND. L. REV. 1203 (1962).

36. *See generally* THE SOCIAL STRUCTURE OF ATTENTION (M. Chance & R. Larsen eds. 1976) (theories of attention).

Privacy

ing information about a person or by creating an interest in the person under discussion that may itself lead to more attention. Thinking about a person may also produce an intensified effort to recall or obtain information about him. This mental activity may in turn produce a loss of privacy if new information is obtained. For the most part, however, thinking about another person, even in the most intense way, will involve no loss of privacy to the subject of this mental activity. The favorite subject of one's sexual fantasies may have causes for complaint, but it is unlikely that these will be related to loss of privacy.[37]

c.  *Physical Access to an Individual*

Individuals lose privacy when others gain physical access to them. Physical access here means physical proximity—that $Y$ is close enough to touch or observe $X$ through normal use of his senses. The ability to watch and listen, however, is not in itself an indication of physical access, because $Y$ can watch $X$ from a distance or wiretap $X$'s telephone. This explains why it is much easier for $X$ to know when $Y$ has physical access to him than when $Y$ observes him.

The following situations involving loss of privacy can best be understood in terms of physical access: (a) a stranger who gains entrance to a woman's home on false pretenses in order to watch her giving birth;[38] (b) Peeping Toms; (c) a stranger who chooses to sit on "our" bench, even though the park is full of empty benches; and (d) a move from a single-person office to a much larger one that must be shared with a colleague. In each of these cases, the essence of the complaint is not that more information about us has been acquired, nor that more attention has been drawn to us, but that our spatial aloneness has been diminished.[39]

d.  *Relations Among the Three Elements*

The concept of privacy suggested here is a complex of these three independent and irreducible elements: secrecy, anonymity, and solitude.[40]

37. It could be argued that the individual who fantasizes about another person is really thinking about a fictional entity, because the subject of the fantasies has been created by the fantasizer. *But cf.* Van den Haag, *On Privacy*, in NOMOS, *supra* note 1, at 149, 152 (arguing that publication of fantasies should be considered invasion of privacy).

38. *See* De May v. Roberts, 46 Mich. 160, 9 N.W. 146 (1881) (finding for plaintiff on these facts). Note that *De May* preceded what is considered the seminal article on privacy, Warren & Brandeis, *The Right to Privacy*, 4 HARV. L. REV. 193 (1890), by almost a decade.

39. For a comparative study of "spacing" and ways of maintaining physical distances, see E. HALL, THE HIDDEN DIMENSION (1966).

40. "Secrecy, anonymity, and solitude" are shorthand for "the extent to which an individual is known, the extent to which an individual is the subject of attention, and

The Yale Law Journal                    Vol. 89: 421, 1980

Each is independent in the sense that a loss of privacy may occur through a change in any one of the three, without a necessary loss in either of the other two. The concept is nevertheless coherent because the three elements are all part of the same notion of accessibility, and are related in many important ways. The three elements may coexist in the same situation. For example, the psychiatrist who sits next to his patient and listens to him acquires information about the patient,[41] pays attention to him, and has physical access to him. At the same time, none of the three elements is the necessary companion of the other two.

Information about X may of course be acquired by making X the subject of Y's attention. When Y follows, watches, or observes X in any way, he increases the likelihood of acquiring information about X. Similarly, when Y is in physical proximity to X, he has an opportunity to observe and thus obtain information about X. Nevertheless, information about X may be obtained when Y has no physical access to X, and when X is not the subject of Y's attention. It is possible to learn information about an individual by questioning his friends and neighbors, and thus without observing the individual or being in his physical proximity. It is also possible to learn information about an individual entirely by accident, when the individual is not even the subject of attention.[42]

the extent to which others have physical access to an individual." The fit between these phrases is close but not perfect, and some comments about the different connotations should be noted. "Secrecy" has an unpleasant sense, and "solitude" conjures up an image that may be quite different from the one connoted by "physical access to an individual." For the most part, however, these are small differences. The difference is much greater between "anonymity" and "being the subject of attention." I may stare hard, focusing all my attention on an individual, without knowing who he is. The subject of my attention is therefore anonymous. On the other hand, even the President has times when he is not the subject of anyone's attention, but we would not call him an anonymous individual. Nevertheless, the aspect of anonymity that relates to attention and privacy is that of being lost in a crowd. If the President could ever be lost in a crowd, he would be anonymous in this context. To draw attention to him in such a case will cost him his anonymity—and his privacy.

41. The psychiatrist acquires information that the patient tells him, and information that the patient furnishes through his gestures, tone of voice, facial expressions, and demeanor. *See* E. GOFFMAN, THE PRESENTATION OF SELF IN EVERYDAY LIFE 2 (1959) (distinguishing between "giving" and "giving off" information). Observation is a key source of information because we always transmit information about ourselves, even in situations in which no verbal communication occurs.

42. This suggests that it may be possible to compare the relative intrusiveness of ways to obtain certain information, *A*, about an individual, *X*. The least intrusive way to acquire the information is to have *X* volunteer it without being asked. A slightly more intrusive way to acquire the information is to ask *X* to provide it. *X* then has control over which questions to answer, and can challenge any that he feels are not necessary or appropriate. Observation of *X* is more likely to generate an amount of information greater than *A*, and thus to create loss of more privacy in this sense. It is also likely to

Privacy

Attention may be paid to $X$ without learning new information about him. The mother who follows her child in order to make sure the child does not harm himself is not interested in gaining new information about the child, nor will she necessarily obtain any new information. Pointing $X$ out in a crowd will increase the attention paid to $X$, even in the absence of any physical proximity.

Finally, an individual can be in physical proximity to others without their paying attention or learning any new information about him. Two people may sit in the same room without paying any attention to each other, and yet each will experience some loss of privacy.

The interrelations between the three elements may be seen when we consider the different aspects of privacy that may be involved in one situation. For instance, police attempt to learn of plans to commit crimes. Potential criminals may raise a privacy claim concerning this information, but are unlikely to gain much support. The criminal's desire that information about his plans not be known creates a privacy claim, but not a very convincing one. We might be more receptive, however, to another privacy claim that criminals might make concerning attention and observation, or the opportunity to be alone. If constant surveillance were the price of efficient law enforcement, we might feel the need to rethink the criminal law. The fact that these are two independent claims suggests that concern for the opportunity to have solitude and anonymity is related not only to the wish to conceal some kinds of information, but also to needs such as relaxation, concentration, and freedom from inhibition.[43]

Yet another privacy concern emerges when we talk about the right against self-incrimination. Again, the essence of the concern is not simply the information itself; we do not protect the suspect against police learning the information from other sources. Our concern relates to the way the information is acquired: it is an implication of privacy that individuals should not be forced to give evidence against

---

involve physical access, and both observation and physical access may have costs to the individual's concentration, relaxation, and intimacy. *See* p. 447 *infra*. Questioning other individuals about $X$ may also elicit an amount of information greater than $A$, and may attract attention to $X$ that leads to further loss of privacy. This explains the intrusiveness of "rough shadowing," which is public surveillance that draws attention to the fact that the individual is being followed. *See* Schultz v. Frankfort Marine, Accident & Plate Glass Ins. Co., 151 Wis. 537, 139 N.W. 386 (1913). It is not surprising that courts have found "rough shadowing" actionable as an invasion of privacy. *E.g.*, Pinkerton Nat'l Detective Agency, Inc. v. Stevens, 108 Ga. App. 159, 132 S.E.2d 119 (1963). In contrast, courts have permitted less obvious forms of following and watching for purposes of investigation. *E.g.*, Nader v. General Motors Corp., 25 N.Y.2d 560, 255 N.E.2d 765, 307 N.Y.S.2d 647 (1970); Forster v. Manchester, 410 Pa. 192, 189 A.2d 147 (1963).

43. For a detailed examination of these reasons, see p. 447 *infra*.

The Yale Law Journal                    Vol. 89: 421, 1980

themselves. Similarly, evidentiary privileges that may also be defended in terms of privacy do not reflect concern about the information itself. The concern here is the existence of relationships in which confidentiality should be protected, so that the parties know that confidences shared in these relationships will not be forced out. In some cases, disclosure will not be sought, and in others the law may even impose a duty against disclosure.

The irreducibility of the three elements may suggest that the complex concept of privacy lacks precision, and that we would do better to isolate each of the different concerns and discuss separately what the law should do to protect secrecy, anonymity, and solitude. Such isolation may indeed be fruitful for some purposes.[44] At present, however, the proposed concept suggests a coherent concern that is generally discussed in extra-legal contexts as "privacy." It therefore seems justified to prefer the complex notion of accessibility to the loss of richness in description that would result from any more particularistic analysis.

### e.  *What Privacy Is Not*

The neutral concept of privacy presented here covers such "typical" invasions of privacy as the collection, storage, and computerization of information; the dissemination of information about individuals; peeping, following, watching, and photographing individuals; intruding or entering "private" places; eavesdropping, wiretapping, reading of letters; drawing attention to individuals; required testing of individuals; and forced disclosure of information. At the same time, a number of situations sometimes said to constitute invasions of privacy will be seen not to involve losses of privacy per se under this concept. These include exposure to unpleasant noises, smells, and sights; prohibitions of such conduct as abortions, use of contraceptives, and "unnatural" sexual intercourse; insulting, harassing, or persecuting behavior; presenting individuals in a "false light"; unsolicited mail and unwanted phone calls; regulation of the way familial obligations should be discharged; and commercial exploitation.[45] These situations are all described as

---

44. In a general sense, the similarity of the reasons for protecting all three elements of privacy is sufficient to justify the coherence of the unitary concept. This coherence does not dictate treating all privacy cases the same way, however. It is plausible that legal protection of privacy may emphasize certain aspects more than others. *See* pp. 456-59 *infra* (limits of law) & pp. 465-67 *infra* (rise of new privacy claims). Treatment of the privacy issues raised by data systems, for example, may require specific legislation and regulation that is not universally applicable.

45. *See, e.g.*, COMMITTEE ON PRIVACY, REPORT 17-22, 327-28 (1972) (compiling definitions of privacy) [hereinafter cited as YOUNGER COMMITTEE].

Privacy

"invasions of privacy" in the literature, presumably indicating some felt usefulness in grouping them under the label of "privacy," and thus an explanation of the reasons for excluding these cases from my argument seems appropriate. Such an explanation may also clarify the proposed analysis and its methodological presuppositions.

The initial intuition is that privacy has to do with accessibility to an individual, as expressed by the three elements of information-gathering, attention, and physical access, and that this concept is distinct. It is part of this initial intuition that we want and deem desirable many things, and that we lose more than we gain by treating all of them as the same thing.[46] If the concepts we use give the appearance of differentiating concerns without in fact isolating something distinct, we are likely to fall victims to this false appearance and our chosen language will be a hindrance rather than a help. The reason for excluding the situations mentioned above, as well as those not positively identified by the proposed analysis, is that they present precisely such a danger.[47]

There is one obvious way to include all the so-called invasions of privacy under the term. Privacy can be defined as "being let alone," using the phrase often attributed—incorrectly—to Samuel Warren and Louis Brandeis.[48] The great simplicity of this definition gives it rhetorical force and attractiveness, but also denies it the distinctiveness that is necessary for the phrase to be useful in more than a conclusory sense. This description gives an appearance of differentiation while

46. I do not question the value of analyzing legal decisions and rules with a single measure, such as maximizing utility or wealth. *See, e.g., Privacy, supra* note 8, at 394. The price we pay for this illumination is high, however. First, it leads us to assume that we may reach the correct decision by maximizing only one value. Second, it wrongly suggests that we should never create "exclusionary reasons"—concepts, rights, rules, and principles that incorporate some kind of calculus in order to limit the need to consider certain questions in detail. *See, e.g.,* Rawls, *Two Concepts of Rules*, 64 PHILOSOPHICAL REV. 3 (1955).

47. Adjudicative techniques may cause the coherence of legal concepts to blur. For example, an early case may establish a "right to privacy." This "right" will be invoked in later cases, and as long as the situations are analogous the invocation is proper and illuminating. If a court relies on this right in situations that are significantly different from the early ones, however, it will be for different reasons than those that impelled the original court to grant recovery. The court may be encouraged to do so if it sees this as a way to rationalize a just result that cannot be reached in another way. Even with a just outcome, however, the concept loses its coherence, perhaps irrevocably, because we can no longer know what set of considerations is relevant for invoking it. This loss of coherence has already affected the development of privacy law. *See* pp. 438-40 *infra.*

48. Warren & Brandeis, *supra* note 38, never equated the right to privacy with the right to be let alone; the article implied that the right to privacy is a special case of the latter. *Id.* at 195. The notion of a right "to be let alone" was first advanced in T. COOLEY, LAW OF TORTS 29 (2d ed. 1888).

The Yale Law Journal                    Vol. 89: 421, 1980

covering almost any conceivable complaint anyone could ever make.[49]
A great many instances of "not letting people alone" cannot readily
be described as invasions of privacy. Requiring that people pay their
taxes or go into the army, or punishing them for murder, are just a few
of the obvious examples.

For similar reasons, we must reject Edward Bloustein's suggestion
that the coherence of privacy lies in the fact that all invasions are
violations of human dignity.[50] We may well be concerned with invasions of privacy, at least in part, because they are violations of
dignity.[51] But there are ways to offend dignity and personality that
have nothing to do with privacy. Having to beg or sell one's body in
order to survive are serious affronts to dignity, but do not appear to
involve loss of privacy.[52]

To speak in privacy terms about claims for noninterference by the
state in personal decisions is similar to identifying privacy with "being
let alone." There are two problems with this tendency. The first is that
the typical privacy claim is not a claim for noninterference by the state
at all. It is a claim *for* state interference in the form of legal protection
against other individuals, and this is obscured when privacy is discussed in terms of noninterference with personal decisions.[53] The
second problem is that this conception excludes from the realm of
privacy all claims that have nothing to do with highly personal decisions, such as an individual's unwillingness to have a file in a central
data-bank.[54] Moreover, identifying privacy as noninterference with
private action, often in order to avoid an explicit return to "substantive due process,"[55] may obscure the nature of the legal decision and

49. *See* W. PROSSER, *supra* note 2, at 804 (only characteristic all privacy cases share is
right to be let alone). This is not true of only explicit privacy cases, however. Actions for
assault, tort recovery, or challenges to business regulation can all be considered assertions
of the "right to be let alone." *See* Thomson, *supra* note 6, at 295. Requests for the government to take positive action may be the only claims that cannot be covered under this
label; in a contract action, for example, the claim in effect is that the plaintiff should
*not* be left alone to his own devices.

50. *See* Bloustein, *Privacy as an Aspect of Human Dignity: An Answer to Dean Prosser*,
39 N.Y.U. L. REV. 962, 971 (1964).

51. *See* pp. 444-56 *infra* (reasons to protect against losses of privacy).

52. For a similar critique of Bloustein, see *Concept, supra* note 20, at 51-53.

53. *See* MacCormick, *A Note Upon Privacy*, 89 LAW Q. REV. 23, 25-26 (1973).

54. *But cf.* Gerety, *supra* note 18, at 286-88 (effort to explain why files in data banks
are related to intimacy, in order to justify seeing them as involving privacy, defined as
control over intimate decisions). In fact, this conception of privacy has already created
problems in the interpretation of the privacy exception to the Freedom of Information
Act, 5 U.S.C. § 552(b)(7)(C) (1976). *See* Emerson, *The Right of Privacy and Freedom of
the Press*, 14 HARV. C.R.-C.L. L. REV. 329, 351-56 (1979); Kronman, *The Privacy Exemption to the Freedom of Information Act* (forthcoming in J. LEGAL STUD. (1980)).

55. *See, e.g.*, Emerson, *Nine Justices in Search of a Doctrine*, 64 MICH. L. REV. 219
(1965) (reasons that led Court to base Griswold v. Connecticut, 381 U.S. 479 (1965), on

Privacy

draw attention away from important considerations.[56] The limit of
state interference with individual action is an important question that
has been with us for centuries. The usual terminology for dealing with
this question is that of "liberty of action." It may well be that some
cases pose a stronger claim for noninterference than others, and that
the intimate nature of certain decisions affects these limits. This does
not justify naming this set of concerns "privacy," however. A better
way to deal with these issues may be to treat them as involving questions of liberty, in which enforcement may raise difficult privacy
issues.[57]

Noxious smells and other nuisances are described as problems of
privacy because of an analogy with intrusion. Outside forces that enter
private zones seem similar to invasions of privacy. There are no good
reasons, however, to expect any similarity between intrusive smells or
noises and modes of acquiring information about or access to an individual.[58]

Finally, some types of commercial exploitation are grouped under
privacy primarily because of legal history: the first cases giving a
remedy for unauthorized use of a name or picture, sometimes described

right to privacy); Ely, *The Wages of Crying Wolf: A Comment on* Roe v. Wade, 82 YALE
L.J. 920, 937-43 (1973) (criticizing use of privacy doctrine in abortion cases as misguided
effort to avoid discredited "substantive due process" doctrine).

56. *See, e.g., Autonomy, supra* note 20, at 180-81 (danger that corruption of concepts
of privacy will have dire consequences); Henkin, *Privacy and Autonomy*, 74 COLUM. L.
REV. 1410, 1426-32 (1974). The prediction that privacy would be used to obscure questions
of liberty came true in People v. Privitera, 23 Cal. 3d 697, 591 P.2d 919, 153 Cal. Rptr. 431
(1979) (prohibition of laetrile treatments does not violate privacy rights of cancer patients
or doctors). The *Privitera* court's conclusion seems correct as far as it goes, but it is arguable that privacy issues were not involved in the case at all. The question was not
whether decisions to use laetrile were "personal," but whether the state had a sufficient
interest to justify prohibition of a drug that was not proven dangerous. The court's conclusion that privacy was not involved made it oblivious to the liberty and paternalism
issues of the case.

57. *See, e.g.,* Griswold v. Connecticut, 381 U.S. 479, 484-85 (1965); P. DEVLIN, THE
ENFORCEMENT OF MORALS 1-25 (1968).

58. *See, e.g.,* Van den Haag, *supra* note 37, at 152-53, 166-67 (privacy includes "intrusion" by mail, noise, and smells); Public Utils. Comm'n v. Pollak, 343 U.S. 451, 469
(1952) (Douglas, J., dissenting) (music, news, and propaganda played in transit system
buses violated privacy rights of "captive audience"). It seems likely, however, that Justice
Douglas's notion of privacy relates more closely to liberty of choice; the Court's opinion
held that privacy was not involved because buses are public places. *Id.* at 464-65.

The problem of unsolicited mail also raises few if any privacy issues. The sender has
acquired the name and address of the recipient, but this may be done through the telephone directory and thus the loss of privacy appears negligible. The sale of mailing lists
is more troublesome. Professor Posner in *Privacy, supra* note 8, at 411, concludes that the
economics of the situation justifies such sales without compensation for the recipients, but
ignores the possible desire of individuals to be removed from mailing lists. *But see*
PRIVACY PROTECTION STUDY COMM'N, *supra* note 5, at 125-54.

as invasions of privacy,[59] usually involved commercial exploitation.[60] The essence of privacy is not freedom from commercial exploitation, however. Privacy can be invaded in ways that have nothing to do with such exploitation, and there are many forms of exploitation that do not involve privacy even under the broadest conception.[61] The use of privacy as a label for protection against some forms of commercial exploitation is another unfortunate illustration of the confusions that will inevitably arise if care is not taken to follow an orderly conceptual scheme.[62]

## B.  *The Functions of Privacy*

In any attempt to define the scope of desirable legal protection of privacy, we move beyond the neutral concept of "loss of privacy," and seek to describe the positive concept that identifies those aspects of privacy that are of value. Identifying the positive functions of privacy is not an easy task. We start from the obvious fact that both perfect privacy and total loss of privacy are undesirable. Individuals must be in some intermediate state—a balance between privacy and interaction—in order to maintain human relations, develop their capacities and sensibilities, create and grow, and even to survive. Privacy thus cannot be said to be a value in the sense that the more people have of it, the better. In fact, the opposite may be true.[63] In any event, my purpose

59. *See, e.g.,* Prosser, *supra* note 6, at 401-07. For the development of the right to privacy and the nature of the first cases, see W. PROSSER, *supra* note 2, at 802-04; Dickler, *supra* note 6, at 448-52. Dickler's article was the first scholarly attempt to "redefine" the right to privacy, noting that the cases could be grouped under three labels (trespass, defamation, unfair trade practices). *Id.* at 435.

60. *See, e.g.,* Pavesich v. New England Life Ins. Co., 122 Ga. 190, 50 S.E. 68 (1905). As Edward Bloustein argues, there is an element of loss of privacy in at least some of these cases. Advertisements may attract attention even when the subjects are anonymous. *See* Bloustein, *supra* note 50, at 985-91.

61. For example, individuals may be commercially exploited if they are compensated for their services at rates below the market price, but this does not seem to involve loss of privacy. Similarly, governmental wiretapping is an obvious example of an invasion of privacy that has not a hint of commercial exploitation.

62. A number of these cases have no relation to privacy whatsoever; the essence of the complaint is not that the plaintiff wants to prevent the use of his identifying features, but simply that he wants to be paid for such use. *See, e.g.,* Zacchini v. Scripps-Howard Broadcasting Co., 433 U.S. 562 (1977); Gautier v. Pro-Football, Inc., 278 A.D. 431, 106 N.Y.S.2d 553 (1951), *aff'd,* 304 N.Y. 354, 107 N.E.2d 485 (1952). In such cases, the doctrine of privacy is completely inappropriate, as noted in Nimmer, *The Right of Publicity,* 19 LAW & CONTEMP. PROB. 203 (1954).

63. Some critics of contemporary society frequently complain that we suffer from too much privacy, that we exalt the "private realm" and neglect the public aspects of life, and that as a result individuals are alienated, lonely, and scared. *See, e.g.,* H. ARENDT, THE HUMAN CONDITION 23-73 (1958); Arndt, *The Cult of Privacy,* 21 AUSTL. Q., Sept. 1979, at 68, 70-71 (1949). Other social critics emphasize the threat to privacy posed by modern society. *See, e.g.,* V. PACKARD, THE NAKED SOCIETY (1964). Indeed, much of the privacy

Privacy

here is not to determine the proper balance between privacy and interaction; I want only to identify the positive functions that privacy has in our lives. From them we can derive the limits of the value of privacy, and then this value can be balanced against others.

The best way in which to understand the value of privacy is to examine its functions. This approach is fraught with difficulties, however. These justifications for privacy are instrumental, in the sense that they point out how privacy relates to other goals. The strength of instrumental justifications depends on the extent to which other goals promoted by privacy are considered important, and on the extent to which the relationship between the two is established. In most cases, the link between the enjoyment of privacy and other goals is at least partly empirical, and thus this approach raises all the familiar problems of social science methodology.

Two possible ways to avoid these difficulties should be discussed before I proceed further. One approach rests the desirability of privacy on a want-satisfaction basis, and the other argues that privacy is an ultimate value. The want-satisfaction argument posits the desirability of satisfying wishes and thus provides a reason to protect all wishes to have privacy.[64] It does not require empirical links between privacy and other goals. Moreover, the notion that choice should be respected is almost universally accepted as a starting point for practical reasoning.[65] The want-satisfaction argument cannot carry us very far, however. It does not explain why we should prefer $X$'s wish to maintain his privacy against $Y$'s wish to pry or acquire information. Without explaining why wishes for privacy are more important than wishes to invade it, the want-satisfaction principle alone cannot support the desirability of privacy. Indeed, some wishes to have privacy do not enjoy even prima facie validity. The criminal needs privacy to complete his offense undetected, the con artist needs it to manipulate his victim; we would not find the mere fact that they wish to have privacy a good reason for

literature seems to share the assumption that additional legal protection is needed. Taken together, these two sets of complaints suggest that something is wrong with the contemporary balance between privacy and interaction. Contributions remain to be made to this critical literature.

64. *See, e.g.,* Beardsley, *supra* note 19, at 58 (principle that invasions of privacy are wrong derived from general principle that choice should be respected); Benn, *supra* note 27, at 8-9 (general principle of respect for persons, including principle of respect for their choices, explains our objection to invasions of privacy). To some extent, Benn's discussion goes beyond the want-satisfaction argument when he suggests that there is something especially disrespectful in certain invasions of privacy. *Id.* at 10-12. For a general discussion of want-satisfaction arguments, see Gavison, *supra* note 14.

65. *See, e.g.,* B. BARRY, POLITICAL ARGUMENT 38-43 (1965) (nature of want-regarding justifications and their importance in politics).

The Yale Law Journal                              Vol. 89: 421, 1980

protecting it. The want-satisfaction principle needs a supplement that will identify legitimate reasons for which people want and need privacy. This is the task undertaken by an instrumental inquiry. These reasons will identify the cases in which wishes to have privacy should override wishes to invade it. They will also explain why in some cases we say that people need privacy even though they have not chosen it.[66] Thus, these instrumentalist reasons will explain the distinctiveness of privacy.

The attractiveness of the argument that privacy is an ultimate value lies in the intuitive feeling that only ultimate values are truly important, and in the fact that claims that a value is ultimate are not vulnerable to the empirical challenges that can be made to functional analyses.[67] But these claims also obscure the specific functions of privacy. They prevent any discussion with people who do not share the intuitive belief in the importance of privacy. Given the current amount of skeptical commentary, such claims are bound to raise more doubts than convictions about the importance and distinctiveness of privacy.

Thus it appears that we cannot avoid a functional analysis. Such an analysis presents an enormous task, for the values served by privacy are many and diverse. They include a healthy, liberal, democratic, and pluralistic society; individual autonomy; mental health; creativity; and the capacity to form and maintain meaningful relations with others. These goals suffer from the same conceptual ambiguities that we have described for privacy, which makes it difficult to formulate questions for empirical research and very easy to miss the relevant questions. More important, the empirical data is not only scant, it is often double-edged. The evaluation of links between privacy and other values must therefore be extremely tentative. Nevertheless, much can be gained by identifying and examining instrumental arguments for privacy; this is

---

66. This is true because we can judge some of the effects of loss of privacy as bad, even if the individual has chosen that loss. An obvious example is the cheapening effect of life in the limelight. Public life, especially in a publication-oriented culture, involves a serious risk that individuals will receive almost constant publicity. Even though a person is insensitive to his own need for privacy, he may nonetheless need it.

67. *See, e.g.,* Bloustein, *Privacy is Dear at Any Price: A Response to Professor Posner's Economic Theory,* 12 GA. L. REV. 429, 442 (1978); Professor Fried in *Privacy, supra* note 19, at 476-78. Both writers stress that the claim of ultimacy strengthens the case for privacy by freeing it from links to other values. At the same time, both conclude by providing justifications that are at least partly instrumental. *Id.* at 478 (trust, love, friendship); Bloustein, *Privacy, Tort Law, and the Constitution: Is Warren and Brandeis' Tort Petty and Unconstitutional as Well?* 46 TEX. L. REV. 611, 618-19 (1968) (dignity, individuality, inviolate personality). Professor Fried's current position is unclear, however. *See* Fried, *Privacy: Economics and Ethics—A Comment on Posner,* 12 GA. L. REV. 423, 426 (1978) ("I am prepared to grant both Posner's and Thomson's attack upon the view which I stated earlier.")

Privacy

the indispensable starting point for any attempt to make sense of our concern with privacy, and to expose this concern to critical examination and evaluation.

It is helpful to start by seeking to identify those features of human life that would be impossible—or highly unlikely—without some privacy. Total lack of privacy is full and immediate access, full and immediate knowledge, and constant observation of an individual. In such a state, there would be no private thoughts, no private places, no private parts. Everything an individual did and thought would immediately become known to others.

There is something comforting and efficient about total absence of privacy for all.[68] A person could identify his enemies, anticipate dangers stemming from other people, and make sure he was not cheated or manipulated. Criminality would cease, for detection would be certain, frustration probable, and punishment sure. The world would be safer, and as a result, the time and resources now spent on trying to protect ourselves against human dangers and misrepresentations could be directed to other things.

This comfort is fundamentally misleading, however. Some human activities only make sense if there is some privacy. Plots and intrigues may disappear, but with them would go our private diaries, intimate confessions, and surprises. We would probably try hard to suppress our daydreams and fantasies once others had access to them. We would try to erase from our minds everything we would not be willing to publish, and we would try not to do anything that would make us likely to be feared, ridiculed, or harmed. There is a terrible flatness in the person who could succeed in these attempts. We do not choose against total lack of privacy only because we cannot attain it, but because its price seems much too high.[69]

In any event, total lack of privacy is unrealistic. Current levels of privacy are better in some ways, because we all have some privacy that

68. The notion of an ever-present, omniscient God exhibits to some extent a willingness to accept, in some context, life with a total lack of privacy. These features of God explain both the comfort and the regulatory force of religious belief.

69. *See, e.g.,* Bloustein, *supra* note 50, at 1003:

The man who is compelled to live every minute of his life among others and whose every need, thought, desire, fancy or gratification is subject to public scrutiny, has been deprived of his individuality and human dignity. Such an individual merges with the mass. His opinions, being public, tend never to be different; his aspirations, being known, tend always to be conventionally accepted ones; his feelings, being openly exhibited, tend to lose their quality of unique personal warmth and to become the feelings of every man. Such a being, although sentient, is fungible; he is not an individual.

For a similar analysis, see Bazelon, *Probing Privacy*, 12 GONZ. L. REV. 587, 592 (1977).

The Yale Law Journal                          Vol. 89: 421, 1980

cannot easily be taken from us.[70] The current state is also worse in some ways, because enjoyment of privacy is not equally distributed and some people have more security and power as a result. The need to protect privacy thus stems from two kinds of concern. First, in some areas we all tend to have insufficient amounts of privacy. Second, unequal distribution of privacy may lead to manipulation, deception, and threats to autonomy and democracy.[71]

Two clusters of concerns are relevant here. The first relates to our notion of the individual, and the kinds of actions we think people should be allowed to take in order to become fully realized. To this cluster belong the arguments linking privacy to mental health, autonomy, growth, creativity, and the capacity to form and create meaningful human relations. The second cluster relates to the type of society we want. First, we want a society that will not hinder individual attainment of the goals mentioned above. For this, society has to be liberal and pluralistic. In addition, we link a concern for privacy to our concept of democracy.

Inevitably, the discussion of functions that follows is sketchy and schematic. My purpose is to point out the many contexts in which privacy may operate, not to present full and conclusive arguments.

### 1. *Privacy and the Individual*

Functional arguments depend on a showing that privacy is linked to the promotion of something else that is accepted as desirable. In order to speak about individual goals, we must have a sense of what individuals are, and what they can and should strive to become. We do not have any one such picture, of course, and certainly none that is universally accepted. Nonetheless, privacy may be linked to goals such as creativity, growth, autonomy, and mental health that are accepted

---

70. The contents of our thoughts and consciousness, now relatively immune from observation and forced disclosure, may not always be free from discovery. Lie detectors are only one kind of technological development that could threaten this privacy. *See, e.g.,* Note, People v. Barbara: *The Admissibility of Polygraph Test Results in Support of a Motion for New Trial,* 1978 DET. C. L. REV. 347; Note, *The Polygraph and Pre-Employment Screening,* 13 HOUS. L. REV. 551 (1976). It is this sense of privacy that George Fletcher uses when he argues that the rule that people cannot be punished for thoughts alone serves to protect privacy. Fletcher, *Legality as Privacy,* in LIBERTY AND THE RULE OF LAW 182-207 (R. Cunningham ed. 1979).

71. It is arguable that only the first concern necessitates legal protection of privacy, whereas the second will be satisfied by any equalization of privacy no matter where the balance is drawn. It is possible, however, that very low levels of privacy are inconsistent with an autonomous and democratic society, even assuming that privacy is equally distributed. *See* pp. 451-56 *infra.* The dangers of unequal distribution of knowledge are dramatically described in G. ORWELL, 1984 (1949).

Privacy

as desirable by almost all such theories, yet in ways that are not dictated by any single theory. This may give functional arguments for privacy an eclectic appearance, but it may also indicate the strength of these arguments. It appears that privacy is central to the attainment of individual goals under *every* theory of the individual that has ever captured man's imagination.[72] It also seems that concern about privacy is evidenced in all societies, even those with few opportunities for physical privacy.[73] Because we have no single theory about the nature of the individual and the way in which individuals relate to others, however, it should be recognized that the way in which we perceive privacy contributing to individual goals will itself depend on the theory of the individual that we select.

In the following discussion, I will note where a difference in perspective may dictate different approaches or conclusions. These different perspectives relate to theories of human growth, development, and personality. It is easy to see that different answers to questions such as the following may yield different arguments for privacy: Is there a "real self" that can be known?[74] If there is, is it coherent and always consistent? If not, can we identify one that is better, and that we should strive to realize? Are human relations something essential, or a mere luxury? Should they ideally be based on full disclosure and total frankness? Or is this a misguided ideal, not only a practical impossibility?[75]

a. *Contextual Arguments*

Some arguments for privacy do not link it empirically with other goals. These arguments contend that privacy, by limiting access, creates the necessary context for other activities that we deem essential. Typical of these contextual arguments is the one advanced by Jeffrey Reiman that privacy is what enables development of individuality by allowing individuals to distinguish between their own thoughts and

72. There are advantages to working within a single such theory; the conceptual scheme is clear, and may provide a richness of association. On the other hand, because such theories are so different in conceptual scheme and coverage of the human condition, it would require enormous efforts to translate between them. Moreover, adherents of different theories tend to resist other theories as inadequate. It thus seems preferable not to choose a single framework of discussion.

73. *See, e.g.*, Roberts & Gregor, *supra* note 34, at 199-225.

74. Many therapeutic techniques stress the identification of the "real self," explaining deviations from it as inhibitions or repressions. It only makes sense to speak of self-realization and identification if there is a way to separate this self from behavior, which is affected by rationalizations, sublimations, and social controls.

75. The ideal of frankness as the only basis for human relations has been practiced by some participants in the encounter-group movement. *See, e.g.*, W. SCHUTZ, JOY (1969). For a criticism of this ideal of total frankness, see E. SCHUR, THE AWARENESS TRAP (1976); J. Silber, *Masks and Fig Leaves*, in NOMOS, *supra* note 1, at 226, 228-31.

The Yale Law Journal                                      Vol. 89: 421, 1980

feelings and those of others.[76] Similarly, Charles Fried advanced a contextual argument that privacy is necessary for the development of trust, love, and friendship.[77] Contextual arguments are instrumental, in that they relate privacy to another goal. They are strengthened by the fact that the link between privacy and the other goal is also conceptual.

A similar argument can be made about the relationship between privacy and intimacy. Here too, it is not simply the case that intimacy is more likely with increasing amounts of privacy. Being intimate in public is almost a contradiction in terms.[78] Such contextual arguments highlight an important goal for privacy, similar to that indicated by examining the possible consequences of a total loss of privacy. We can now move to a detailed examination of more specific functions of privacy.[79]

b.  *Freedom from Physical Access*

By restricting physical access to an individual, privacy insulates that individual from distraction and from the inhibitive effects that arise

76.  Reiman, *Privacy, Intimacy, and Personhood*, 6 PHILOSOPHY & PUB. AFF. 26, 31-36 (1977).

77.  *Privacy, supra* note 19, at 484. Fried suggests that human relations are determined by personal information shared with a partner but no one else. Privacy, which permits individual control over this information, provides the "moral capital" we spend in love and friendship. *Id.* at 484-85. It is not clear from Fried's analysis, however, whether it is useful in assessing the importance of a relationship to examine the amount of personal information shared by the parties. For example, two chess players preparing for a world championship may spend a great deal of time and money in order to acquire a vast amount of information about each other, but we would not say that they had an intimate relationship. Moreover, Fried's argument invokes the weak sense of "control" over information—control over the decision to disclose it, rather than control over the amount of information others actually have. *See* pp. 426-28 *supra* (distinction between two notions of control). Fried's argument at best supports only the right not to disclose personal information, which is usually not threatened anyway. It does not support arguments against gossip, for example. *See id.* at 490. Finally, it may be misleading to suggest that information about ourselves is capital that we spend to create love and friendship, because such information is always being generated and is thus inexhaustible. *See* Reiman, *supra* note 76, at 31-36 (critique of Fried's argument); Rachels, *Why Privacy is Important*, 4 PHILOSOPHY & PUB. AFF. 323, 325 (1975).

78.  The need for privacy is sufficiently strong, however, that even individuals in "total institutions" develop ways to achieve some intimacy despite near-constant surveillance. *See* E. GOFFMAN, ASYLUMS 173, 223-38 (1961).

79.  There are several ways that one can organize functional arguments for privacy. One obvious approach is to focus on the goals to which privacy is allegedly linked. Despite the clear attractions of this approach, the functional analysis I employ is structured around the ways in which privacy functions to promote goals, rather than on the goals themselves. Thus the contribution of privacy to autonomy or human relations, which is achieved in various ways, is mentioned in a number of different places. This organization is illuminating in identifying the ways in which privacy operates, which in turn suggests both the possibilities and the limits of regulation. The repetition in goals is a cost of this approach, but it saves repetition of functions. Furthermore, this structure points out clearly one of the important aspects of privacy: the way in which arguments for privacy are related to its function as a promoter of liberty.

Privacy

from close physical proximity with another individual. Freedom from distraction is essential for all human activities that require concentration, such as learning, writing, and all forms of creativity. Although writing and creativity may be considered luxuries, learning—which includes not only acquiring information and basic skills but also the development of mental capacities and moral judgment—is something that we all must do.[80] Learning, in turn, affects human growth, autonomy, and mental health.

Restricting physical access also permits an individual to relax. Even casual observation has an inhibitive effect on most individuals that makes them more formal and uneasy.[81] Is relaxation important? The answer depends partially upon one's theory of the individual. If we believe in one coherent "core" personality, we may feel that people should reflect that personality at all times. It could be argued that relaxation is unimportant—or undesirable—because it signals a discrepancy between the person in public and in private. The importance that all of us place on relaxation suggests that this theory is wrong, however, or at least overstated. Whatever the theory, people seem to need opportunities to relax, and this may link privacy to the ability of individuals to maintain their mental health. Furthermore, freedom from access contributes to the individual by permitting intimacy. Not all relationships are intimate, but those that are tend to be the most valued. Relaxation and intimacy together are essential for many kinds of human relations, including sexual ones. Privacy in the sense of freedom from physical access is thus not only important for individuals by themselves, but also as a necessary shield for intimate relations.[82]

Because physical access is a major way to acquire information, the power to limit it is also the power to limit such knowledge. Knowledge and access are not necessarily related, however. Knowledge is only one of the possible consequences of access, a subject to which we now turn.

---

80. The role of privacy in learning is underscored by the fact that one of the features of underprivileged families considered responsible for their children's failures in school is that most cannot provide the opportunity for privacy. *See* J. COLEMAN, EQUALITY OF EDUCATIONAL OPPORTUNITY 298-302 (1966) (influence of student's background on educational achievement).

81. Relaxed behavior does not necessarily include undesirable conduct; most kinds of relaxation are not prohibited even though they are unlikely in public. *See, e.g.,* J. BARTH, THE END OF THE ROAD 57-58 (1960) (character who thinks he is alone is observed behaving in ridiculous but not objectionable manner); Rachels, *supra* note 77, at 323-24 (analyzing this scene in privacy terms).

82. *See, e.g.,* Bloustein, *Group Privacy: The Right to Huddle,* 8 RUT.-CAM. L.J. 219, 224-46 (1977).

c. *Promoting Liberty of Action*

An important cluster of arguments for privacy builds on the way in which it severs the individual's conduct from knowledge of that conduct by others. Privacy thus prevents interference, pressures to conform, ridicule, punishment, unfavorable decisions, and other forms of hostile reaction. To the extent that privacy does this, it functions to promote liberty of action, removing the unpleasant consequences of certain actions and thus increasing the liberty to perform them.

This promotion of liberty of action links privacy to a variety of individual goals. It also raises a number of serious problems, both as to the causal link between privacy and other goals, and as to the desirability of this function.

*Freedom from censure and ridicule.* In addition to providing freedom from distractions and opportunities to concentrate, privacy also contributes to learning, creativity, and autonomy by insulating the individual against ridicule and censure at early stages of groping and experimentation. No one likes to fail, and learning requires trial and error, some practice of skills, some abortive first attempts before we are sufficiently pleased with our creation to subject it to public scrutiny. In the absence of privacy we would dare less, because all our early failures would be on record. We would only do what we thought we could do well. Public failures make us unlikely to try again.[83]

*Promoting mental health.* One argument linking privacy and mental health, made by Sidney Jourard,[84] suggests that individuals may become victims of mental illness because of pressures to conform to society's expectations. Strict obedience to all social standards is said inevitably to lead to inhibition, repression, alienation, symptoms of disease, and possible mental breakdown. On the other hand, disobedience may lead to sanctions. Ironically, the sanction for at least some deviations is a social declaration of insanity. By providing a refuge, privacy enables individuals to disobey in private and thus acquire the strength to obey in public.

Mental health is one of the least well-defined concepts in the litera-

---

83. For example, many pianists refuse to practice in the presence of others, and not simply to avoid distraction, inhibition, or self-consciousness. They practice alone so that they are the ones to decide when they are ready for an audience. It could be argued that privacy thus has its costs in terms of what the world learns about human achievement; some perfectionists are never sufficiently pleased with their creations, yet their work may be superior to much that is made public by others. Even if this were true, it does not prove that the lost masterpieces would have been created in the absence of privacy. Perfectionists are just as vulnerable to criticism as anybody else, perhaps even more so.

84. Jourard, *Some Psychological Aspects of Privacy*, 31 LAW & CONTEMP. PROB. 307, 309-11 (1966). A similar argument is made by Benn, *supra* note 27, at 24-25.

Privacy

ture.[85] It appears that Professor Jourard's argument for privacy uses the term in a minimalistic sense: avoiding mental breakdown. Whether mental breakdown is always undesirable is questionable.[86] More serious problems are raised when we examine the link between mental health and privacy. Must chronic obedience always lead to mental breakdown? This is plausible if individuals obey social norms only because of social pressures and fear of sanctions, but this is not the case. Professor Jourard identifies a need for privacy that applies only to those who do not accept the social norms. The strength of his argument thus depends on the likelihood that people reject some norms of their society, and may be adequate only for extremely totalitarian societies. It will probably also depend on the nature of the norms and expectations that are not accepted. Moreover, even if pressures to conform to social norms contribute to mental breakdown, the opposite may also be true. It could be argued that too much permissiveness is at least as dangerous to mental health as too much conformity. One of the important functions of social norms is to give people the sense of belonging to a group defined by shared values. People are likely to lose their sanity in the absence of such norms and the sense of security they provide.[87] Nevertheless, some individuals in institutions do complain that the absence of privacy affects their mental state, and these complaints support Jourard's argument.[88]

*Promoting autonomy.* Autonomy is another value that is linked to the function of privacy in promoting liberty. Moral autonomy is the reflective and critical acceptance of social norms, with obedience based on an independent moral evaluation of their worth.[89] Autonomy requires the capacity to make an independent moral judgment, the willingness to exercise it, and the courage to act on the results of this exercise even when the judgment is not a popular one.

85. *See* B. Wooton, Social Science and Social Pathology 210-21 (1959) (definitions of "mental health"). It is notable that this concept has been used in ways that include all the other individual goals mentioned above. For example, some see autonomy as a sign of mental health; others see the incapacity to form and maintain human relations as a sign of mental illness.

86. For privacy's contribution to be desirable, we must value X. Is the avoidance of mental breakdown always desirable? Would we prefer a person who could adjust to any society, or one who would break down if he had to cope with the requirements of life in a Nazi regime?

87. *See* E. Durkheim, Suicide: A Study in Sociology (1951) (mental breakdown may be affected by absence of social cohesiveness).

88. *See* E. Goffman, *supra* note 78, at 4, 23-25 (individuals are "mortified" and "violated" in mental hospitals).

89. *See* D. Riesman, Faces in the Crowd 736-41 (1952) (relationship between autonomy and nature of society); Benn, *supra* note 27, at 24-26 (argument for privacy in terms of autonomy).

We do not know what makes individuals autonomous, but it is probably easier to be autonomous in an open society committed to pluralism, toleration, and encouragement of independent judgment rather than blind submissiveness. No matter how open a society may be, however, there is a danger that behavior that deviates from norms will result in harsh sanctions. The prospect of this hostile reaction has an inhibitive effect. Privacy is needed to enable the individual to deliberate and establish his opinions. If public reaction seems likely to be unfavorable, privacy may permit an individual to express his judgments to a group of like-minded people. After a period of germination, such individuals may be more willing to declare their unpopular views in public.

It might be argued that history belies this argument for privacy in terms of autonomy: societies much more totalitarian than ours have always had some autonomous individuals, so that the lack of privacy does not mean the end of autonomy. Even if we grant that privacy may not be a necessary condition for autonomy for all, however, it is enough to justify it as a value that most people may require it. We are not all giants, and societies should enable all, not only the exceptional, to seek moral autonomy.[90]

*Promoting human relations.* Privacy also functions to promote liberty in ways that enhance the capacity of individuals to create and maintain human relations of different intensities. Privacy enables individuals to establish a plurality of roles and presentations to the world. This control over "editing" one's self is crucial, for it is through the images of others that human relations are created and maintained.

Privacy is also helpful in enabling individuals to continue relationships, especially those highest in one's emotional hierarchy, without denying one's inner thoughts, doubts, or wishes that the other partner cannot accept. This argument for privacy is true irrespective of whether we deem total disclosure to be an ideal in such relations. It is built on the belief that individuals, for reasons that they themselves do not justify, cannot emotionally accept conditions that seem threatening to them. Privacy enables partners to such a relationship to continue it, while feeling free to endorse those feelings in private.[91]

---

90. Professor Posner suggests an argument of this sort in *Privacy, supra* note 8, at 407. Such an argument could be made about creativity and human relations as well as autonomy. *See* Bloustein, *supra* note 50, at 1006.

91. *See Privacy, supra* note 19, at 485; Sheehy, *Can Couples Survive?* NEW YORK MAGAZINE, Feb. 19, 1973, at 35 ("Privacy is disallowed as being disloyal. But if the couple wants intimacy, both partners need to refresh themselves with privacy. That implies also being allowed to withdraw without guilt.")

Privacy

Each of these arguments based on privacy's promotion of liberty shares a common ground: privacy permits individuals to do what they would not do without it for fear of an unpleasant or hostile reaction from others. This reaction may be anything from legal punishment or compulsory commitment to threats to dissolve an important relationship. The question arises, then, whether it is appropriate for privacy to permit individuals to escape responsibility for their actions, wishes, and opinions.

It may be argued that we have rules because we believe that breaches of them are undesirable, and we impose social sanctions to discourage undesirable conduct. People are entitled to a truthful presentation and a reasonable consideration of their expectations by those with whom they interact. Privacy frustrates these mechanisms for regulation and education; to let it do so calls for some justification. In general, privacy will only be desirable when the liberty of action that it promotes is itself desirable, or at least permissible. It is illuminating to see when we seek to promote liberty directly, by changing social norms, and when we are willing to let privacy do the task.

Privacy is derived from liberty in the sense that we tend to allow privacy to the extent that its promotion of liberty is considered desirable. Learning, practicing, and creating require privacy, and this function is not problematic.[92] Similarly, because we usually believe that it is good for individuals to relax and to enjoy intimacy, we have no difficulty allowing the privacy necessary for these goals.

The liberty promoted by privacy also is not problematic in contexts in which we believe we should have few or no norms; privacy will be needed in such cases because some individuals will not share this belief, will lack the strength of their convictions, or be emotionally unable to accept what they would like to do. Good examples of such cases are ones involving freedom of expression, racial tolerance, and the functioning of close and intimate relations. The existence of official rules granting immunity from regulation, or even imposing duties of nondiscrimination, does not guarantee the absence of social forces calling for conformity or prejudice.[93] A spouse may understand and even support a partner's need to fantasize or to have other close relations, but may still find knowing about them difficult to accept. In such situations, respect for privacy is a way to force ourselves to be as tolerant as we

92. We may, however, question privacy that promotes the learning of skills we consider dangerous, or the development of opinions we consider outrageous, such as opinions favoring bigotry or genocide.

93. *See* G. ALLPORT, THE NATURE OF PREJUDICE 326-39 (1954) (difficulty of making ourselves disregard known prejudices).

The Yale Law Journal                              Vol. 89: 421, 1980

know we should be. We accept the need for privacy as an indication of the limits of human nature.

A related but distinct situation in which privacy is permitted is that in which we doubt the desirability of norms or expectations, or in which there is an obvious absence of consensus as to such desirability.[94] Treatment of homosexual conduct between consenting adults in private seems to be a typical case of this sort.[95] Another context in which we sometimes allow privacy to function in this way is when privacy would promote the liberty of individuals not to disclose some parts of their past, in the interest of rehabilitation or as a necessary protection against prejudice and irrationality.[96]

Privacy works in all these cases to ameliorate tensions between personal preferences and social norms by leading to nonenforcement of some standards.[97] But is this function desirable? When the liberty promoted is desirable, why not attack the norms directly? When it is not, why allow individuals to do in private what we would have good reasons for not wanting them to do at all?

Conceptually, this is a strong argument against privacy, especially because privacy perpetuates the very problems it helps to ease. With mental health, autonomy, and human relations, the mitigation of surface tensions may reduce incentives to face the difficulty and deal with it directly. When privacy lets people act privately in ways that would have unpleasant consequences if done in public, this may obscure the urgency of the need to question the public regulation itself. If homosexuals are not prosecuted, there is no need to decide whether such conduct between consenting adults in private can constitutionally be

94.  The distinction between the two types of cases may be illusory, however, if our incapacity to act on our convictions simply indicates doubt in our judgment.

95.  Some states still have laws against homosexual relations between consenting adults, *see* Note, *The Constitutionality of Laws Forbidding Private Homosexual Conduct*, 72 MICH. L. REV. 1613, 1613-14 (1974), and the Supreme Court has refused to declare them unconstitutional, *e.g.*, Doe v. Commonwealth, 403 F. Supp. 1199 (E.D. Va. 1975), *aff'd mem.*, 425 U.S. 901 (1976); *see* Richards, *supra* note 3, at 1319-20. These laws, however, are rarely if ever enforced against consenting adults; the decision not to enforce these laws is thus a decision to let the privacy of the relationship protect the participants from legal sanctions.

96.  *See* Melvin v. Reid, 112 Cal. App. 285, 297 P. 91 (1931) (revelation that woman was former prostitute and defendant in murder trial); Briscoe v. Reader's Digest Ass'n, 4 Cal. 3d 529, 483 P.2d 34, 93 Cal. Rptr. 866 (1971) (publication of prior record); *cf. Privacy, supra* note 8, at 415-16 (criticizing *Melvin*); Epstein, *supra* note 8, at 466-74 (deliberate concealment of information as misrepresentation).

97.  Alan Westin sees this as one of the major functions of privacy. A. WESTIN, *supra* note 1, at 23-51. It is important to note that this function would not be as strong in cases in which the level of legal enforcement was high. *See* note 98 *infra.*

Privacy

prohibited.[98] If people can keep their independent judgments known
only to a group of like-minded individuals, there is no need to deal
with the problem of regulating hostile reactions by others. It is easier,
at least in the shortrun and certainly for the person making the decision, to conceal actions and thoughts that may threaten an important
relationship. Thus, privacy reduces our incentive to deal with our
problems.

The situation is usually much more complex, however, and then the
use of privacy is justified. First, there are important limits on our
capacity to change positive morality,[99] and thus to affect social pressures
to conform. This may even cause an inability to change institutional
norms. When this is the case, the absence of privacy may mean total
destruction of the lives of individuals condemned by norms with only
questionable benefit to society. If the chance to achieve change in a
particular case is small, it seems heartless and naive to argue against
the use of privacy.[100] Although legal and social changes are unlikely
until individuals are willing to put themselves on the line, this course
of action should not be forced on any one. If an individual decides that
the only way he can maintain his sanity is to choose private deviance
rather than public disobedience, that should be his decision. Similarly,
if an individual prefers to present a public conformity rather than
unconventional autonomy, that is his choice. The least society can do
in such cases is respect such a choice.

Ultimately, our willingness to allow privacy to operate in this way
must be the outcome of our judgment as to the proper scope of liberty
individuals should have, and our assessment of the need to help ourselves and others against the limited altruism and rationality of individuals. Assume that an individual has a feature he knows others may
find objectionable—that he is a homosexual, for instance, or a communist, or committed a long-past criminal offense—but that feature is

98. The fact that such laws are not enforced, *see* note 95 *infra*, may explain why the
Supreme Court intervened in the more morally complicated issue of abortion, Roe v.
Wade, 410 U.S. 113, 116 (1973), but not in that of consensual homosexual conduct. A
ruling on homosexuality would have purely symbolic effect, whereas judicial noninterference in abortion issues would have perpetuated a situation in which safe abortions were
difficult to obtain. *Cf.* Poe v. Ullman, 367 U.S. 497, 508 (1961) (refusing to strike down
statute prohibiting sale of contraceptives because state did not enforce law).

99. *See* H.L.A. HART, THE CONCEPT OF LAW 171-73 (1961) (distinction between law and
morality is that law may be deliberately and consciously changed, whereas morality can
not).

100. To take a famous historical example, Socrates' trial did not make the case for
the principle of academic freedom to the Athenians. Thus, his public declaration that he
would continue teaching was heroic but could not have been demanded of him.

irrelevant in the context of a particular situation.[101] Should we support his wish to conceal these facts? Richard Posner[102] and Richard Epstein[103] argue that we should not. This is an understandable argument, but an extremely harsh one. Ideally, it would be preferable if we could all disregard prejudices and irrelevancies. It is clear, however, that we cannot. Given this fact, it may be best to let one's ignorance mitigate one's prejudice. There is even more to it than this. Posner and Epstein imply that what is behind the wish to have privacy in such situations is the wish to manipulate and cheat, and to deprive another of the opportunity to make an informed decision. But we always give only partial descriptions of ourselves, and no one expects anything else. The question is not whether we should edit, but how and by whom the editing should be done.[104] Here, I assert, there should be a presumption in favor of the individual concerned.

It is here that we return to contextual arguments and to the specter of a total lack of privacy. To have different individuals we must have a commitment to some liberty—the liberty to be different. But differences are known to be threatening, to cause hate and fear and prejudice.[105] These aspects of social life should not be overlooked, and oversimplified claims of manipulation should not be allowed to obscure them.

The only case in which this is less true is that of human relationships, where the equality between the parties is stronger and the essence of the relationship is voluntary and intimate. A unilateral decision by one of the parties not to disclose in order to maintain the relationship is of questionable merit. The individual is likely to choose what is easier for him, rather than for both. His decision denies the other

101. The notion of relevance is crucial, of course. There may be a number of borderline cases, but some will fall neatly in one of the categories. The fact that X is sterile is clearly relevant for Y, who wants children and considers marrying X. The fact that X prefers to have sex with people of his own gender does not seem relevant, however, to his qualifications as a clerk or even as a teacher.

102. *Privacy, supra* note 8, at 394-403; *Secrecy, supra* note 8, at 11-17.

103. Epstein, *supra* note 8, at 466-74.

104. For example, we would have less sympathy for an employer who demanded a "yes or no" answer from his employee to the question of whether the employee had a criminal record or was a member of the Communist Party. Such an employer may draw unwarranted inferences if the employee has no opportunity to explain his answer. Professor Posner has suggested that any such "irrational" conduct by prejudiced employers will ultimately be corrected by the market, because the victimized employees will command below-average wages, and the unprejudiced employers who hire them will obtain a competitive advantage. *Secrecy, supra* note 8, at 12 (example of ex-convicts). This is beside the point, however, because in the interim the employee suffers from high emotional and economic costs (in the form of irrational stigma and lower wage rates).

105. *See generally* G. ALLPORT, *supra* note 93 (nature of prejudice).

Privacy

party an understanding of the true relationship and the opportunity to decide whether to forgive, accommodate, or leave. Although we cannot rely on the altruism and willingness to forgive of employers or casual acquaintances, to deny a life partner the opportunity to make informed decisions may undermine the value of the relationship. This is another point at which our theories about human relations become relevant. The extent to which paternalistic protection should be a part of relationships between adults, and the forms such concern may appropriately take, are relevant in deciding this issue.

*Limiting exposure.* A further and distinct function of privacy is to enhance an individual's dignity, at least to the extent that dignity requires nonexposure. There is something undignified in exposure beyond the fact that the individual's choice of privacy has been frustrated.[106] A choice of privacy is in this sense distinct from a choice to interact. Rejection of the latter frustrates $X$'s wish, but there is no additional necessary loss of dignity and selfhood. In exposure, there is. It is hard to know what kind of exposures are undignified, and the effect such unwanted exposures have on individuals. The answer probably depends on the culture and the individual concerned,[107] but this is nonetheless an important function of privacy.

## 2. *Privacy and Society*

We desire a society in which individuals can grow, maintain their mental health and autonomy, create and maintain human relations, and lead meaningful lives. The analysis above suggests that some privacy is necessary to enable the individual to do these things, and privacy may therefore both indicate the existence of and contribute to a more pluralistic, tolerant society. In the absence of consensus concerning many limitations of liberty, and in view of the limits on our capacity to encourage tolerance and acceptance and to overcome prejudice, privacy must be part of our commitment to individual freedom and to a society that is committed to the protection of such freedom.

Privacy is also essential to democratic government because it fosters and encourages the moral autonomy of the citizen, a central requirement of a democracy. Part of the justification for majority rule and the right to vote is the assumption that individuals should participate in political decisions by forming judgments and expressing preferences. Thus, to the extent that privacy is important for autonomy, it is important for democracy as well.

---

106. *See, e.g.,* Benn, *supra* note 27, at 6-7; Reiman, *supra* note 76, at 38-39.
107. *See generally* H. LYND, ON SHAME AND THE SEARCH FOR IDENTITY (1958).

The Yale Law Journal                              Vol. 89: 421, 1980

This is true even though democracies are not necessarily liberal. A country might restrict certain activities, but it must allow some liberty of political action if it is to remain a democracy. This liberty requires privacy, for individuals must have the right to keep private their votes, their political discussions, and their associations if they are to be able to exercise their liberty to the fullest extent. Privacy is crucial to democracy in providing the opportunity for parties to work out their political positions, and to compromise with opposing factions, before subjecting their positions to public scrutiny. Denying the privacy necessary for these interactions would undermine the democratic process.[108]

Finally, it can be argued that respect for privacy will help a society attract talented individuals to public life. Persons interested in government service must consider the loss of virtually all claims and expectations of privacy in calculating the costs of running for public office. Respect for privacy might reduce those costs.[109]

## II. The Limits of Law

One of the advantages of this analysis is that it draws attention to—and explains—the fact that legal protection of privacy has always had, and will always have, serious limitations. In many cases, the law can-

---

108. *Cf.* NAACP v. Alabama *ex rel.* Patterson, 357 U.S. 449 (1958) (First Amendment freedom of association includes privacy of political association in order to guarantee effective expression of political views). *See generally* A. WESTIN, *supra* note 1, at 23-51 (relation between privacy and democracy); Bazelon, *supra* note 69, at 591-94 (same).

109. *See, e.g.*, Galella v. Onassis, 353 F. Supp. 196, 207-10 (S.D.N.Y. 1972), *aff'd and modified in part*, 487 F.2d 986 (2d Cir. 1973) (plaintiff was photographed at restaurants, clubs, theater, schools, funeral, and while shopping, walking down street, and riding bicycle); B. WOODWARD & S. ARMSTRONG, THE BRETHREN: INSIDE THE SUPREME COURT (1979) (detailed account of working relationships of Supreme Court Justices). At the same time, it is important to note that restrictions on invasions of public figures' privacy may conflict with the First Amendment. *See, e.g.*, T. EMERSON, THE SYSTEM OF FREEDOM OF EXPRESSION 6-7 (1970); Friedrich, *Secrecy versus Privacy: The Democratic Dilemma*, in NOMOS, *supra* note 1, at 105.

The constitutional right to privacy suffers from a split personality. On one hand, the Supreme Court has established a right that covers at least some tort actions. *See* note 3 *supra*. The right may include "the individual interest in avoiding disclosure of personal matters." Whalen v. Roe, 429 U.S. 589, 599 (1977). *But see* Paul v. Davis, 424 U.S. 693, 712-14 (1976) (state circulation of flyer publicizing plaintiff's arrest on shoplifting charges did not violate plaintiff's constitutional right to privacy). On the other hand, it has been suggested that First Amendment developments indicate that those aspects of privacy that conflict with the right to publish true information may be unconstitutional. The issue is far from closed. *See* Emerson, *supra* note 54, at 334-37; Comment, *First Amendment Limitations on Public Disclosure Actions*, 45 U. CHI. L. REV. 180 (1977). Some have gone so far as to suggest that the conflict between privacy and the First Amendment is illusory, because "privacy" is simply a conclusory word used by the courts. *See* Felcher & Rubin, *Privacy, Publicity, and the Portrayal of Real People by the Media*, 88 YALE L.J. 1577, 1585-88 (1979).

Privacy

not compensate for losses of privacy, and it has strong commitments to other ideals that must sometimes override the concern for privacy. Consequently, one cannot assume that court decisions protecting privacy reflect fully or adequately the perceived need for privacy in our lives.

Part of the reason for this inadequate reflection is that in many cases actions for such invasions are not initiated. The relative rarity of legal actions might be explained by expectations that such injuries are not covered by law, by the fact that many invasions of privacy are not perceived by victims, and by the feeling that legal remedies are inappropriate, in part because the initiation of legal action itself involves the additional loss of privacy. When these factors are forgotten, it is easy to conclude that privacy is not such an important value after all. This conclusion is mistaken, however, as the proposed analysis stresses. Understanding the difficulty of legal protection of privacy will help us resist the tendency to fall victim to this misperception.

It is obvious that privacy will have to give way, at times, to important interests in law enforcement, freedom of expression, research, and verification of data. The result is limits on the scope of legal protection of privacy. I shall concentrate on less obvious reasons why the scope of legal protection is an inadequate reflection of the importance of privacy.

To begin, there are many ways to invade an individual's privacy without his being aware of it. People usually know when they have been physically injured, when their belongings have been stolen, or when a contractual obligation has not been honored. It is more difficult to know when one's communications have been intercepted, when one is being observed or followed, or when others are reading one's dossier.[110] This absence of awareness is a serious problem in a legal system that relies primarily on complaints initiated by victims.[111] In

110. An interesting problem of this sort arises in the context of the disclosure exception to the Privacy Act of 1974, 5 U.S.C. § 552a(b) (1976), under which the guarantor of third parties' privacy interests is the government. If people request information about others, the individuals concerned are not notified, and information from files may be disclosed without their permission if the government does not decide to withhold it. *See,* *e.g.,* Boyer, *Computerized Medical Records and the Right to Privacy: The Emerging Federal Response,* 25 BUFFALO L. REV. 37 (1975) (medical files). The courts are now beginning to examine these problems. *E.g.,* Providence Journal Co. v. FBI, 460 F. Supp. 762, 767 (D.R.I. 1978) (standing under Privacy Act given to individual whose file was sought under Freedom of Information Act); Tax Reform Research Group v. IRS, 419 F. Supp. 415 (D.D.C. 1976) (ordering disclosure of officials involved in White House harassment of "enemies," but keeping targets' identities secret unless they express consent).

111. The problem may be aggravated by the fact that a major invader of privacy is the government, whose interest in exposing its own misconduct is always uncertain. *See,* *e.g.,* Weidner, *Discovery Techniques and Police Surveillance,* 7 UCLA-ALASKA L. REV. 190 (1978).

The Yale Law Journal                              Vol. 89: 421, 1980

some cases, victims learn of invasions of their privacy when information acquired about them is used in a public trial, as was the case with Daniel Ellsberg.[112] In most situations, however, there is no need to use the information publicly, and the victim will not be able to complain about the invasion simply because of his ignorance. The absence of complaints is thus no indication that invasions of privacy do not exist, or do not have undesirable consequences. Indeed, because deterrence depends at least partly on the probability of detection,[113] these problems of awareness may encourage such invasions.

Ironically, those invasions of privacy that pose no problem of detection, such as invasions through publication, have different features that make legal proceedings unattractive and thus unlikely for the prospective complainant. Legal actions are lengthy, expensive, and involve additional losses of privacy. In the usual case, plaintiffs do not wish to keep the essence of their action private. In a breach of contract suit, for example, the plaintiff may not seek publicity, but usually does not mind it. This is not true, however, for the victim of a loss of privacy. For him, a legal action will further publicize the very information he once sought to keep private, and will thus diminish the point of seeking vindication for the original loss.[114]

Moreover, for the genuine victim of a loss of privacy, damages and even injunctions are remedies of despair.[115] A broken relationship, exposure of a long-forgotten breach of standards, acute feelings of shame and degradation, cannot be undone through money damages. The only benefit may be a sense of vindication, and not all victims of invasions of privacy feel sufficiently strongly to seek such redress.

The limits of law in protecting privacy stem also from the law's commitment to interests that sometimes *require* losses of privacy, such as freedom of expression, interests in research, and the needs of law enforcement. In some of these cases, we would not even feel sympathy for

112. *See* N.Y. Times, April 28, 1973, at 1, col. 4 (reporting break-in to Ellsberg's psychiatrist's office).

113. *See, e.g.,* Andenaes, *The General Preventive Effects of Punishment,* 114 U. PA. L. REV. 949, 960-64 (1966) (risk of detection, apprehension, and conviction is of paramount importance to preventive effects of penal law).

114. A similar problem exists in defamation cases. In such cases, however, the plaintiff seeks a declaration that the publication was not true. Even the successful plaintiff in a privacy action has no guarantee of similar satisfaction. The trend in defamation law has reduced this difference. *See* Gertz v. Robert Welch, Inc., 418 U.S. 323, 377 (1974) (White, J., dissenting) (trend began with N.Y. Times Co. v. Sullivan, 376 U.S. 254 (1964)).

115. *See* Kalven, *supra* note 6, at 338-39 (suggesting that "privacy will recruit claimants inversely to the magnitude of the offense to privacy involved," and thus that law does not need a cause of action that exerts chilling effect on media but does not help worthy plaintiffs). Kalven also draws an analogy between actions for invasion of privacy and actions for breach of promise to marry. *Id.*

Privacy

the complainant: the criminal does not need privacy for his autonomy, mental health, or human relations. In other situations, however, the injury is real but legal vindication is considered too costly. Victims realize these facts, and this in turn reduces the tendency to seek vindication through law.

Finally, perhaps the most serious limit of legal protection is suggested by the instrumentalist analysis of privacy above. Privacy is important in those areas in which we want a refuge from pressures to conform, where we seek freedom from inhibition, the freedom to explore, dare, and grope. Invasions of privacy are hurtful because they expose us; they may cause us to lose our self-respect, and thus our capacity to have meaningful relations with others. The law, as one of the most public mechanisms society has developed, is completely out of place in most of the contexts in which privacy is deemed valuable.

These factors indicate that it is neither an accident nor a deliberate denial of its value that the law at present does not protect privacy in many instances. There are simply limits to the law's effectiveness. On the other hand, this does not indicate that there is nothing distinct behind claims for privacy. Emphasis of this point is important, for we must resist the temptation to see privacy as adequately reflected in the law or in reductive accounts. This is also an important reason to seek an explicit commitment to privacy as part of the law.

## III. Privacy as a Legal Concept

My analysis has shown that privacy is a coherent and useful concept in the first two contexts: losses of privacy may be identified by reference to the central notion of accessibility, and the reasons for considering it desirable are sufficiently similar to justify adopting it as a value. Most reductionists do not deny these facts;[116] they assert, however, that privacy is not a useful *legal* concept because analysis of actual legal protection, and claims for protection, suggests that it is not and is not likely to be protected simply for its own sake. I believe this denial of the utility of privacy as a legal concept is misleading and has some unfortunate results. To counteract that view, I therefore argue that the law should make an explicit commitment to privacy.

116. *See* note 6 *supra*. Richard Posner, however, does not consider privacy a value per se, and this is what makes his version of reductionism extreme. *See* note 8 *supra*. Although some of the points made here apply to Professor Posner's analysis as well, I deal only with moderate reductionists. For a criticism of Posner's approach, see Bloustein, *supra* note 67, at 429-42; Baker, *Posner's Privacy Mystery and the Failure of Economic Analysis of Law*, 12 GA. L. REV. 475 (1978).

The Yale Law Journal                                    Vol. 89: 421, 1980

## A.  *The Poverty of Reductionism*

One way to think about "the law of privacy" is to start by asking what privacy is, and proceed to question to what extent the law protects it. This approach raises questions as to why people want privacy, why it is that although they want it they do not make claims for legal protection, and, if they do, why the law is reluctant to respond. Answering these questions gives us a fuller understanding of the scope of actual legal protection and the way the law reflects social needs, the limits of the law in protecting human aspirations, and the need for further legal protection created by changes in social and technological conditions. In contrast, another approach to privacy starts from the legal decisions—or moral intuitions[117]—that define the scope of legal protection for privacy. The practical benefit of this approach is obvious: by reducing decisions to a small number of principles of liability, lawyers and judges are able to rely on legal tradition without having to consult all the cases anew each time a privacy claim is made.

In principle, the starting point should not affect the results of our attempt to find an adequate description of the scope of actual legal protection of privacy. It should not be surprising, however, that those starting from judicial decisions tend to conclude with a reductionist account. First, despite the common use of the term "privacy," the two starting points define different data to be explained. Those scholars who start from decisions, without an external concept of privacy, are led to rely on the concept that may be derived from the decisions themselves. One of the advantages of their enterprise is that their account seeks to explain *all* those cases in which the courts have explicitly invoked the concept of privacy.[118] There is no guarantee that the con-

---

117. Starting from legal decisions or moral intuitions about the scope of the right to privacy, or the scope of legal protection of privacy, is similar: in both cases what we study is the *conclusion* of a discussion of whether some action is actionable or a violation of a moral right. Thus Thomson's analysis, *see* Thomson, *supra* note 6, shares most of the weaknesses of legal analysis mentioned here. It also shares a similarity of purpose—to give a coherent description of what we have been doing under a single label.

118. Thus, Dean Prosser, the most influential of the reductionists, could offer as a strength of his description that analysis of more than 400 cases of privacy showed that they could all be neatly grouped under four categories of recovery, none of which primarily protects privacy. *See* W. PROSSER, *supra* note 2, at 804-14 (setting out four privacy categories of intrusion, disclosure, false light, and appropriation). But in fact, reductionist analyses fail in even their limited attempt to explain precedents. Some cases, frequently discussed in privacy terms, cannot be included under these categories without straining them and weakening their power of description and guidance. For example, Prosser's categories do not encompass claims by individuals under the Privacy Act, 5 U.S.C. § 552a(d)(2)(B) (1976), that some information about them should be deleted or corrected. Moreover, it is unclear whether Prosser could accommodate the "constitutional" right to privacy decisions because he does not have a category for noninterference in his account. Other accounts do provide such a category, however. *See* Gerety, *supra* note 18, at 261-81; Comment, *supra* note 3, at 1447.

460

Privacy

cepts arising from adjudication will be coherent,[119] however, especially
when the theoretical basis for the concept is not settled.[120] An attempt
to impose coherence on the use of a single concept in judicial decisions
is bound to be misleading when such a coherence does not in fact exist.
The reductionists have perceived this lack of coherence in the case of
privacy, and have concluded that the best way to describe existing law
is with several separate categories of recovery, all designed to protect
interests other than privacy and having little else in common.

It is here that the reductionists' starting point has blinded them to
other ways to deal with the lack of coherence in judicial decisions. In
some cases, the label of privacy has indeed been used to protect interests other than privacy because of the promise and limits of legal
categories. In most cases in which a claim of privacy has been made,
however, a loss of privacy has been involved. It is for this reason that
there are many common features to liability in privacy cases despite
the disparate principles that are used as an adequate account of the
law. The reductionists cannot explain this unity, and their account
obscures it.[121] On the other hand, dealing only with explicit privacy
decisions blinds the reductionists to those cases in which the law is in
fact used to protect privacy, albeit under a different label.

A second problem with reliance on actual decisions is that the data
base is narrow. We deal only with claims that have actually been
made, and primarily with cases in which the court has granted recovery. This may be misleading, particularly in areas such as privacy,
because there are numerous disincentives for invoking legal protection.[122] Finally, seeking to explain the scope of legal protection in order
to identify when courts are likely to give a remedy can obscure the
reasons why a remedy is not given, which may be crucial for understanding the larger issues.[123]

119.  The reasons for this are well known by any student of adjudication. Judges tend
(and are encouraged) to prefer a just result based on weak doctrine to an admission that
current law does not provide a way to justify an otherwise deserved recovery. The price
of justice is thus often the coherence of the concepts involved. Privacy is an example of
this, as I argue below. Similarly, I suspect that any concept of liberty derived from the
constitutional adjudication of the last 100 years will not have much coherence either.

120.  Warren & Brandeis, *supra* note 38, is notoriously vague on the conceptual question. For example, the authors never explicitly defined or described what they meant by
"privacy." *Compare* Prosser, *supra* note 6, at 392 (Warren and Brandeis meant freedom
from publicity) *with* Bloustein, *supra* note 50, at 971 (Warren and Brandeis meant
freedom from affronts to human dignity).

121.  Dean Prosser himself acknowledges the existence of these "common features," W.
PROSSER, *supra* note 2, at 814-15, but does not explain why there should be four different
torts, dealing with different invasions, and designed to protect interests as distinct as
those in reputation, property, and mental tranquility.

122.  *See* pp. 456-59 *supra.*

123.  One major difficulty is that the cases relied upon by the reductionist in order to
derive his concept of privacy will not accurately reflect all the fact situations in which a

The Yale Law Journal                          Vol. 89: 421, 1980

Starting from the extra-legal concept of privacy enables us to avoid these pitfalls. The account of legal protection resulting from this approach is at least as helpful to practitioners, and also has additional advantages over the reductionist account: it brings to the fore many important observations about privacy and its legal protection, and helps to draw attention to privacy costs.

The primary advantage the approach advocated here exhibits over even the best reductionist account[124] is that it will include within it all legal protection of one coherent value—privacy—in all branches of the law,[125] and under any label. Limited disclosures about individuals,

valid privacy claim could be advanced. This is true because there are many ways to defeat a possibly valid claim based on an alleged invasion of privacy. For instance, conduct may be actionable, but not constitute an invasion of privacy. *See, e.g.,* Peterson v. Idaho First Nat'l Bank, 83 Idaho 578, 367 P.2d 284 (1961). A loss of privacy may have occurred, but not as the result of conduct considered undesirable, as in the case of a loss of privacy resulting from certain research activity and from investigations to verify plaintiff's statements or damage claims. *See, e.g.,* FED. R. CIV. P. 35 (court may order parties to submit to mental or physical examination by physician). Even when the conduct is undesirable, it may not be actionable because it has not passed a certain threshold. *See, e.g.,* Virgil v. Sports Illustrated, Inc., 424 F. Supp. 1286, 1289 (S.D. Cal. 1976) (publication of fact plaintiff extinguished cigarettes in his mouth, dove off stairs to impress women, hurt himself in order to collect unemployment benefits, spent his time body-surfing, ate insects, and participated in gang fights as youngster, was "not sufficiently offensive" even to create jury question). Finally, courts may deny recovery even when the conduct is prima facie actionable because the defendant can establish a defense, which usually means that some competing interest is judged to be more important in the circumstances. The most important such defense raises the First Amendment, claiming that publication is of sufficient public interest to override individual privacy. *See, e.g.,* Time, Inc. v. Hill, 385 U.S. 374, 388-91 (1967) (First Amendment bar to invasion of privacy claim).

124.  Dean Prosser's account has been incorporated into the RESTATEMENT (SECOND) OF TORTS § 652A (1976), but it is not the best of the reductionist works. For example, there are explicit privacy cases that do not fit neatly into any of his categories, and Prosser's attempt to accommodate them strains the categories and deprives them of much force. One such group of privacy cases is that in which the plaintiff has attention attracted to him against his will. Prosser does not have such a category and must squeeze these cases into "intrusion." W. PROSSER, *supra* note 2, at 808-09. Another group of cases is that in which the plaintiff must answer certain questions as a condition of employment. Prosser groups one such case, Reed v. Orleans Parish School Bd., 21 So. 2d 895 (La. App. 1945), under "public disclosure of private facts," W. PROSSER, *supra* note 2, at 810 n.89, although no public disclosure was involved. Similarly, he groups Fifth Amendment cases of impelled self-incrimination under "intrusion." *Id.* at 807. For a detailed exposition of his account and its shortcomings, see R. Gavison, *supra* note 14.

125.  One of Prosser's problems is that he deals only with the law of torts, and cannot adequately discuss protection of privacy in other contexts. There is nothing illegitimate about dealing with one branch of the law for practical purposes, of course. For an example of the broader perspective gained through a synoptic view, however, see Bloustein, *supra* note 50.

There is no doubt that the only way to defeat the dangerous hegemony of Dean Prosser's account of legal thinking is by actually working out the description of the law of privacy that would follow from the proposed analysis, including sufficient detail so that practitioners and judges could rely on this description. I have tried to outline such a description in R. Gavison, *supra* note 14. For the gains of this analysis in the much simpler context of Israeli law, see R. Gavison, *The Minimum Area of Privacy—Israel,* in ISRAELI REPORTS TO THE TENTH INTERNATIONAL CONGRESS OF COMPARATIVE LAW 176 (1978).

Privacy

breaches of confidence, the reasons behind testimonial privileges, the right against self-incrimination, and privacy legislation—which have all been discussed in privacy terms but excluded by Prosser's reductionism —will be included.[126] So will be the exclusionary rule and rules of trespass and defamation to the extent they have been used to protect privacy. At the same time, this approach excludes those cases that explicitly refer to privacy in which the concept is invoked misleadingly. Some claims of appropriation,[127] and some claims of immunity from interference,[128] will be excluded. This description thus provides a better picture of current legal protection than does the reductionist account.

The reductionist approach fails even on its strongest claim to adequacy—the exposure of the limits of legal protection of privacy. The primary insight of these accounts is that the law never protects privacy per se, as is indicated by the fact that whenever a remedy for invasion of privacy is given, there is another interest such as property or reputation that is invaded as well. This insight, in general,[129] is quite true, and is certainly important. It reflects the limits of law discussed above. It is nonetheless misleading. It may be true that the law tends to protect privacy only when another interest is also invaded, whereas invasions of other interests may compel protection on their own. It does not follow from this that the presence of privacy in a situation does not serve as an additional reason for protection. Privacy, property, and reputation are all interests worthy of protection. The law grants none of them absolute protection. When two of them are invaded in one situation, recovery may be compelled even though neither alone would suffice. In such cases, the plaintiff would not have recovered had not his privacy been invaded. This operation of privacy is completely obscured by the reductionists.[130]

---

126. *See, e.g.,* Note, *Formalism, Legal Realism, and Constitutionally Protected Privacy Under the Fourth and Fifth Amendments,* 90 HARV. L. REV. 945 (1977); Note, *Medical Practice and the Right to Privacy,* 43 MINN. L. REV. 943 (1959). Dean Prosser excludes cases of limited disclosure because he insists that one element of the "genuine" privacy tort is publicity, and that limited disclosure is not enough. W. PROSSER, *supra* note 2, at 809-12.

127. *See* p. 440 *supra.*

128. *See* p. 439 *supra.*

129. There are at least some cases in which recovery for invasion of privacy has been given in which no other interest was involved (unless we take "freedom from mental distress" to be a distinct interest, which would engulf all privacy claims and many others as well). *See, e.g.,* Melvin v. Reid, 112 Cal. App. 285, 297 P. 91 (1931) (motion picture disclosed current identity of former prostitute who had been acquitted in murder trial seven years earlier).

130. De May v. Roberts, 46 Mich. 160, 9 N.W. 146 (1881), is probably best explained in such terms. Such a combination of motives appears in many of the appropriation

The Yale Law Journal                           Vol. 89: 421, 1980

Besides obscuring the extent of current legal protection, reductionist accounts obscure the continuity of legal protection over time. They give the erroneous impression that the concern with privacy is modern, whereas in fact both the wish to invade privacy and the need to control such wishes have been features of the human condition from antiquity. The common-law maxim that a person's home is his castle; early restrictions on the power of government officials to search, detain, or enter; strict norms of confidence; and prohibition of Peeping Toms or eavesdropping all attest to this early concern.[131] Even when the explicit label of privacy has not been invoked, the law has been used to protect privacy in a variety of ways. Warren and Brandeis, in their famous plea for explicit legal protection of privacy, traced much of this earlier protection by the law of contract, trespass, defamation, and breach of confidence.[132] They offered this tradition of protection as a ground for arguing that the courts could provide remedies for invasion of privacy without legislating a new cause of action in tort.[133] Awareness of this continuity helps us to understand the functions of

cases. *See, e.g.*, Pavesich v. New England Life Ins. Co., 122 Ga. 190, 50 S.E. 68 (1905). For the relevance of privacy rhetoric in explaining decisions, and as an argument against Posner's reductionism, see Epstein, *supra* note 8, at 461-65.

131. A certain sphere of privacy has been protected from the earliest times. Anglo-Saxon law and German tribal law protected the peace that attached to every freeman's dwelling, and offered compensation for damage to property, insulting words, and the mere act of intrusion. 1 DIE GESETZE DER ANGELSACHSEN Abt. 8, 15, 17, Hl. 11, Af. 40, Ine 6-6.3 (F. Liebermann ed. 1903); 1 F. POLLOCK & F. MAITLAND, THE HISTORY OF ENGLISH LAW 45 (2d ed. 1968).

The notion that one's home is protected from arbitrary intrusions by government officials finds little support in the polemics of reformers until the late 16th century and no support in case law until the 18th century. Medieval kings did not make available writs *de cursu* against lawless royal officials, though periodically they did permit inquiry into such official misconduct. *See* H. CAM, THE HUNDRED AND THE HUNDRED ROLLS, AN OUTLINE OF LOCAL GOVERNMENT IN MEDIEVAL ENGLAND (1930). Manorial bailiffs, subject to local custom, the sheriff, tax collectors, and creditors, subject to the limits on distraint proceedings, could enter a freeman's home restrained more by trespass liability than by any requirement of a warrant. 2 F. POLLOCK & F. MAITLAND, *supra*, at 575-78.

We know less about entry into the home to gather evidence for criminal law enforcement. The procedure for neighbors, jurors, and later magistrates to conduct such investigations is hidden by the use of the general issue, the rudimentary law of evidence, and the informality and local context of the criminal law. *See* S. MILSOM, HISTORICAL FOUNDATIONS OF THE COMMON LAW 357, 360 (1969); Baker, *Criminal Courts and Procedure at Common Law 1550-1800*, in CRIME IN ENGLAND 1550-1800 at 15, 16-17, 38-39 (J. Cockburn ed. 1977). It is unlikely that there were any real checks on evidence-gathering other than general tort liability. *But see* Samaha, *Hanging for Felony: the Rule of Law in Elizabethan Colchester*, 21 HIST. J. 763, 768-71, 774-75 (1978) (claiming early notions of rule of law and evidence procedure).

132. Warren & Brandeis, *supra* note 38, at 197-214.

133. This reliance on the history of legal protection makes Warren and Brandeis's article one that "does model better than anything in the literature the emergence of a common law principle." Wellington, *Common Law Rules and Constitutional Double Standards: Some Notes on Adjudication*, 83 YALE L.J. 221, 251 (1973).

Privacy

privacy in our lives, and the changes in circumstances that have led to new claims for protection.

There is nothing in reductionist accounts to suggest insights into why new claims for privacy arise. Nevertheless, understanding what has caused these new claims may be helpful in deciding what to do about them. Despite the tradition of legal protection, it is true that growing concern with losses of privacy is a modern phenomenon. This need not be because of any change in people's awareness, sensitivity, or conception of the essential components of the good life, as Warren and Brandeis implied.[134] Indeed, my analysis of privacy suggests that the functions of privacy are too basic to human life to be so sensitive to changes in perception,[135] and it is in any event doubtful whether modern man is more sensitive or morally sophisticated than his predecessors. Moreover, most individuals today have more opportunities for privacy than our ancestors ever did, as well as a greater ability to regain anonymity after any loss of privacy occurs.

The main reason for this modern concern appears to be a change in the nature and magnitude of threats to privacy, due at least in part to technological change. The legal protection of the past is inadequate not because the level of privacy it once secured is no longer sufficient, but because that level can no longer be secured. Advances in the technology of surveillance and the recording, storage, and retrieval of information[136] have made it either impossible or extremely costly for individuals to protect the same level of privacy that was once enjoyed.[137] "Overstepping" by the press, cited by Warren and Brandeis,[138] gives the old invasions of privacy via publication and gossip a new dimension through the speed and scope of the modern mass media. We can dramatize this point by noting that the loss of anonymity of public figures is of a new order of magnitude. Many old stories could not plausibly be written today: Victor Hugo's rehabilitated mayor, Shakespeare's disguised dukes, the benevolent great people who do charity in disguise, are all extremely unlikely in our modern culture.

---

134. Warren & Brandeis, *supra* note 38, at 193 ("Thus, in very early times, the law gave a remedy only for physical interference with life and property . . . . Later, there came a recognition of man's spiritual nature, of his feelings and his intellect.")

135. In this sense, privacy may indeed be related to defamation, which is one of the oldest concerns of law. *See* S. MILSOM, *supra* note 131, at 332-43; N. RAKOVER, DEFAMATION IN JEWISH LAW (1964).

136. *See, e.g.,* P. HEWITT, PRIVACY: THE INFORMATION GATHERERS (1977); A. MILLER, *supra* note 19; J. RULE, PRIVATE LIVES AND PUBLIC SURVEILLANCE (1973); A. WESTIN, *supra* note 1, at 158-68.

137. *See, e.g.,* YOUNGER COMMITTEE, *supra* note 45, at 153-76.

138. Warren & Brandeis, *supra* note 38, at 196.

The Yale Law Journal                                      Vol. 89: 421, 1980

The identification of technological developments as a major source of new concern may be supported by the fact that modern claims concerning the secrecy and anonymity aspects of privacy have not been accompanied by new claims concerning physical access: technological advances have affected the acquisition, storage, and dissemination of information, but gaining physical access is a process that has not changed much.[139] On the other hand, the increase in the number of people whose profession it is to observe and report, the intensified activity in search of publishable information, and the changes in the equipment that enables such enterprises, make it more likely that events and information will in fact be recorded and published.

Technology is not the whole story, however. The privacy concerns created by the mass media go beyond the fact that the development of scandal magazines and investigative journalism lets more people acquire more information more quickly. An additional problem is that journalism is crude, and may not do justice to the situation exposed. Partial truths are unsettling because they present a one-dimensional image of the subject, often without compassion or benevolence. This may be not unlike scandal journalism's old sister, gossip. The most important difference is that gossip usually concerns people who are already known in their other facets, and thus partial truths are less misleading. In contrast, there is no way that most readers of newspapers can correct for the one-dimensional images they receive through print.[140]

The new concern with privacy may also be explained, at least in part, as a tendency to put old claims in new terms.[141] From this perspective, part of the new interest in privacy is not caused by new needs, but rather by new doctrinal moves or hopes for legal change. Privacy has been used to overcome the limitations of defamation;[142] it has been used to avoid such historically loaded legal terms as "substantive due process" and "liberty";[143] and it has been used to avoid basing all

---

139. Not only has this process remained the same, but this is the area in which rising standards of living and safety have brought the most dramatic increases in privacy. *See Privacy, supra* note 8, at 396-97 (privacy increases with wealth of society).

140. A powerful literary illustration is provided by H. Böll, The Lost Honor of Katharina Blum (1975).

141. *See* notes 47, 119 *supra.*

142. Once it became established that truth was an absolute defense to a defamation claim, *see* Harnett & Thornton, *The Truth Hurts: A Critique of a Defense to Defamation,* 35 Va. L. Rev. 425 (1949), the only way to make truthful publications actionable was to develop new privacy doctrine. *See* Wade, *Defamation and the Right to Privacy,* 15 Vand. L. Rev. 1093, 1109, 1120 (1962) (approving use of privacy to overcome limitations of defamation).

143. *Compare* Lochner v. New York, 198 U.S. 45 (1905) (liberty of contract) *and* Gris-

Privacy

entitlements, without differentiation, on the notion of property.[144]

Finally, and perhaps most importantly, reductive accounts reinforce the tendency to overlook the privacy costs that may be involved in a case. Because these accounts suggest that privacy is only a label used to protect other interests, logic would dictate that whenever a privacy question is discussed, the balancing should be among the "real" interests involved. Consequently, privacy is made redundant despite its usage. Although we talk in terms of privacy, the reductionist suggests, what we actually take into consideration are the interests to which privacy is reducible.[145] It is this quality of reductionism that threatens to undermine our belief in the distinctness and importance of privacy, and to have an adverse effect on our policy decisions. The proposed analysis, by clarifying the distinctness and importance of privacy through a functional analysis, enables us to challenge such reductionism.

## B.  *The Case for an Explicit Commitment to Privacy*

There is much to be said for making an explicit legal commitment to privacy. Such a commitment would affirm that privacy is not just a convenient label, but a central value. An explicit commitment would put reductionist accounts in their correct perspective, as attempts to give lawyers and judges a guide to identify cases in which recovery is likely under a given heading. The legal protection of privacy is more than a mere by-product of the protection of other, more "respectable" values. An explicit commitment to privacy would recognize that losses of privacy are undesirable, at least in the circumstances in which such losses frustrate the functions and goals described above. It would recognize that such losses should be taken into account by the legal system, and that we should strive to minimize them.

Clearly, an explicit commitment to privacy does not mean that

wold v. Connecticut, 381 U.S. 479, 481-82 (1965) (refusing to apply substantive due process) *with id.* at 485-86 (right to privacy). For a critical discussion of this move, see Ely, *supra* note 55, at 937-43.

144. Warren & Brandeis, *supra* note 38, had this in mind when they insisted that privacy be protected as "personality," not as a property interest. *Id.* at 205-08. Privacy has been used to protect property, however. *See* pp. 439-40 *supra.* Professor Posner in *Privacy, supra* note 8, at 393-404, argues for an undifferentiated conception of privacy as a kind of property, and Thomson, *supra* note 6, at 303-06, notes that much of the privacy rhetoric is based on "ownership" grounds.

145. The most extreme example of such an analysis is Posner's. *See Privacy, supra* note 8; *Secrecy, supra* note 8. But the price that may be exacted by such an approach if it is used to make policy decisions about the scope of desirable legal protection becomes clear in works such as Kronman, *supra* note 54, and Felcher & Rubin, *supra* note 109, because these commentators actually conclude that privacy should not be considered an independent and distinct value.

The Yale Law Journal                              Vol. 89: 421, 1980

privacy deserves absolute protection. It does not mean that privacy is the one value we seek to promote, or even the most important among a number of values to which we are committed. This is true for all our values, however. None is protected absolutely, not even those to which a commitment is made in unequivocal terms in the Constitution. Nor would making such a commitment suggest that invasions of privacy would generally be actionable. I have indicated many of the reasons why it is unlikely to expect the law to protect privacy extensively. Making an explicit commitment could not be understood to deny the need for balancing; it would simply identify the factors that should be considered by the legal system.

In positive terms, the case for an explicit commitment to privacy is made by pointing out the distinctive functions of privacy in our lives. Privacy has as much coherence and attractiveness as other values to which we have made a clear commitment, such as liberty. Arguments for liberty, when examined carefully, are vulnerable to objections similar to the arguments we have examined for privacy, yet this vulnerability has never been considered a reason not to acknowledge the importance of liberty, or not to express this importance by an explicit commitment so that any loss will be more likely to be noticed and taken into consideration. Privacy deserves no less.

Further insight about the need for an explicit commitment to privacy comes from study of the arguments made against this approach. First, it may be argued that the American legal system has already made this commitment, and that we should concentrate on answering questions of the scope of legal protection rather than spend time arguing for commitments that have already been made. Questions of scope are no doubt important, and had a commitment to privacy been made and its implications internalized, there would indeed be no further need for an explicit affirmation. But the reductionist literature is at least as influential as that which affirms the distinctness and importance of privacy, and although it is true that some parts of the legal system are informed by an affirmation of privacy, it is equally clear that others are not. For the latter, an explicit commitment to privacy could make an important difference.[146]

A more substantive argument, and one inconsistent with the first, is that we should not make a commitment to privacy because there is no need for further legal protection: we already have all the privacy we could possibly want or need. In those areas in which invasions of

---

146. *See* note 109 *supra* (conflict between privacy and freedom of expression).

Privacy

privacy are undesirable, the law already provides a remedy. If anything, this argument goes, we need less legal protection today because
rising standards of living mean that individuals enjoy more privacy
than ever before. Critics emphasize the relatively small number of
difficult cases in which we sympathize with the person complaining
about invasion of his privacy. In the hundred years of the tort
remedy's existence, there has been only one Sidis,[147] one Melvin,[148]
one Barber.[149]

It is here that understanding the reasons for the new concern with
privacy becomes crucial. It is true that individuals today enjoy more
opportunities for privacy in some areas, but this observation, taken
alone, is misleading. The rarity of actions is not a good indication of
the need for privacy, or of the extent to which invasions are undesirable. We enjoy our privacy not because of new opportunities for
seclusion or because of greater control over our interactions, but because of our anonymity, because no one is interested in us. The
moment someone becomes sufficiently interested, he may find it quite
easy to take all that privacy away. He may follow us all the time, obtain information about us from a host of data systems, record our conversations, and intrude into our bedrooms. What protects privacy is
not the difficulty of invading it, but the lack of motive and interest of
others to do so. The important point, however, is that if our privacy is
invaded, it may be invaded today in more serious and more permanent
ways than ever before. Thus, although most of us are unlikely to
experience a substantial loss of privacy, we have an obligation to protect
those who lose their anonymity. In this sense, privacy is no different
from other basic entitlements. We are not primarily concerned with
the rights of criminal suspects because we have been exposed to police
brutality ourselves. We know that we may be exposed to it in the
future, but, more generally, we want to be part of a society that is
committed to minimizing violations of due process.

Even if the law had already dealt with all the situations in which
privacy should be legally protected, however, an explicit commitment
to privacy would still be significant. It is significant in ways that no
specific, localized legal protection can be. It would serve to remind us

147. Sidis v. F-R Publishing Corp., 34 F. Supp. 19 (S.D.N.Y. 1938), *aff'd*, 113 F.2d 806
(2d Cir.), *cert. denied*, 311 U.S. 711 (1940) (magazine story about former child prodigy
describing his current activities).

148. Melvin v. Reid, 112 Cal. App. 285, 297 P. 91 (1931) (movie about former prostitute
acquitted of murder seven years earlier).

149. Barber v. Time, Inc., 348 Mo. 1199, 159 S.W.2d 291 (1942) (picture taken of "insatiable eater" in hospital bed).

The Yale Law Journal                      Vol. 89: 421, 1980

of the importance of privacy, and thus to color our understanding of protection in specific contexts.

The result of this awareness would not necessarily or even primarily be more legal rules to protect privacy. For example, such an explicit commitment to privacy might focus attention on ways to ameliorate the difficulties resulting from the inappropriateness of current legal remedies and legal proceedings. Some thought could go into whether limits on the publicity of judicial proceedings that involve privacy claims could be established without paying too high a price in terms of freedom of expression or fair trials.[150] Moreover, an explicit commitment could increase individual sensitivity to losses of privacy and thus encourage people to prevent invasions of privacy without reliance on law at all. It may lead to increased efforts to make it possible to minimize losses of privacy without invoking the law, through such efforts as development of technological devices to make leaks from data systems more difficult. It would also draw the attention of those whose occupations involve systematic breaches of others' privacy, such as journalists, doctors, detectives, policemen, and therapists, to the fact that although some invasions of privacy are inevitable, a loss of sensitivity about such losses may corrupt the invader as well as harm the victim.

An explicit commitment to privacy is not vulnerable to the charge that the law should not protect privacy because its efficacy in doing so is limited. It might be argued that the contexts within which privacy has functional value are those in which the law is traditionally reluctant to interfere. This reluctance stems, at least in part, from an awareness that some questions cannot and should not be dealt with by the law. It is unlikely, for example, that the law will ever impose an obligation on parents to give their children some privacy in order to grow, develop autonomy, and explore others. We would probably find such a law an unpalatable interference with liberty. An explicit legal commitment to privacy might make such specific protection of privacy

---

150. Limits on the publicity of judicial proceedings, for various reasons, are not unknown. *See, e.g.*, Gannett Co., Inc. v. DePasquale, 99 S. Ct. 2898 (1979) (pretrial criminal hearings may be closed to press). In most situations, the imposition of criminal sanctions for truthful disclosures would probably not be upheld. *See* Landmark Communications, Inc. v. Virginia, 435 U.S. 829 (1978) (First Amendment does not permit criminal sanctions of third persons who publish truthful information about confidential proceedings before state judicial review commission). Other measures limiting the possibility of publication may be constitutional, however. *See, e.g.*, Cox Broadcasting Corp. v. Cohn, 420 U.S. 469, 491 (1975) (although First Amendment does not permit sanctions for accurate publication of rape victim's name obtained from public records, Court reserves "broader question" whether state may "protect an area of privacy free from unwanted publicity"); N.Y. Civ. Rights Law §§ 50, 51 (McKinney Supp. 1976) (recent amendment to privacy statute in response to *Cox Broadcasting*).

Privacy

unnecessary, however. Parents might then realize more fully that
privacy is important for their children, and this would lead them to
respect their children's privacy without any direct legal obligation to
do so.

The general commitment would also help in administering the laws.
It could serve as a principle of interpretation, pointing out the need
to balance losses of privacy, perhaps with a presumption in favor of
protecting privacy. It might also supplement existing privacy laws by
identifying improper conduct and invoking the general sense of obligation to obey the laws. A general commitment may thus lead to a reduction of invasions of privacy even in situations in which the victims
would not have sued had the invasions occurred, either because of
ignorance or for other reasons discussed above.

The functions of a general commitment to the value of privacy as a
part of the law are varied, and cannot be reduced to the amount of
protection actually given to that value in the legal system. Here again,
the commitment to privacy is no different than the commitment to
other values, such as freedom of expression or liberty. As I have argued
before, a commitment to privacy as a legal value may help to raise
awareness of its importance and thus deter reckless invasions. Most
importantly, however, an explicit commitment to privacy will have an
educational impact. This function is of special importance, because
most of us enjoy privacy without the need for legal protection. For the
most part, what we should learn is how to appreciate our available
privacy and use it well. A clear statement in the law that privacy is a
central value could make us more aware of the valuable functions
privacy can serve. Ultimately, the wish to have privacy must be in our
hearts, not only in our laws. But this does not mean that a commitment
to the value of privacy should not be in our laws as well.

# [7]

## THE POVERTY OF " PRIVACY "

NEARLY a century after Warren and Brandeis [1] identified " privacy " as a common law right to which individuals could lay claim, the concept remains problematic. But though the transatlantic debate has rarefied into controversies surrounding the meaning of " privacy " and the content of the " right to " privacy," the United Kingdom, despite the modest proposals for legislation made by the Younger Committee in 1972,[2] remains among the few jurisdictions in which " privacy " receives no explicit legal recognition.[3]

The judicial disinclination to acknowledge any immanent " right to privacy " in our law [4] (such as occurred most spectacularly in

---

[1] S. D. Warren and L. D. Brandeis, " The Right to Privacy " (1890) 4 Harv. Law Rev. 193, hereafter referred to as *Warren & Brandeis*.

[2] *Report of the Committee on Privacy*, Cmnd. 5012, 1972, Chairman: Kenneth Younger, hereafter referred to as *Younger Committee*. The Committee rejected by a majority the need for a " general right of privacy " (para. 659) and proposed the creation of a new crime and a new tort of unlawful surveillance (paras. 560–565), a new tort of disclosure or other use of information unlawfully acquired (para. 632) and, based on its view (discussed below) that the action for breach of confidence offered " the most effective protection of privacy in the whole of our existing law, civil and criminal " (para. 87) referred the question of this action to the Law Commissions with a view to its clarification and statement in legislative form. The Law Commissions in a Working Paper (No. 58, " Breach of Confidence," 1974), saw it as beyond the scope of their duty to question the assumption that the action for breach of confidence answered the needs of a remedy for invasion of privacy, and merely drafted the new torts proposed by the *Younger Committee*.

[3] " Privacy " in its various forms is recognised and protected in statutes enacted by most of the states of the United States and by Federal legislation (in particular the Privacy Act of 1974). Canada has both state and Federal statutes (in particular, the Protection of Privacy Act of 1974). The Australian Law Reform Commission has proposed a draft bill on " publication privacy " (See The Law Reform Commission, Discussion Paper No. 3, 1977). The French courts have recognised a general right to " privacy," which includes " *le droit au respect de la vie priveé* " and, are further able to accommodate most " privacy " claims within the broad provisions of Article 1382 of the Civil Code. Similarly, the German courts have ample scope for the protection of " privacy " within the rubric of *persönlichkeitsrechte* and the provisions of Article 823 (1) of the Civil Code. Legislation to control the collection and use of computer data (which, it is argued below, ought not to be conceived as a " privacy " issue) such as the American Privacy Act, has its counterpart in Canada, Scandinavia, and most European countries; they are summarised in the *Report of the Committee on Data Protection*, Cmnd. 7341, 1978, Chairman: Sir Norman Lindop (hereafter referred to as *Lindop Committee*), paras. 4.01—4.42, which proposed similar legislation for the United Kingdom.

[4] The opportunity has not really arisen and even if it did, it is difficult to adopt Winfield's sanguine view expressed in 1931 that the House of Lords might recognise a new tort of invasion of personal privacy in the light of the " social exigencies at the present day." P. Winfield, " Privacy " (1931) 47 L.Q.R. 23, 34. Nevertheless in *Malone* v. *Commissioner of Police of the Metropolis (No. 2)* [1979] 2 All E.R. 620, Sir Robert Megarry V.-C. declared that he would not shrink, in the proper circumstances, from enunciating a right to privacy on the telephone (when the defendant was a private person): " I am not unduly troubled by the absence of English authority: there has to be a first time for everything, and, if the principles of English law, and not least analogies from the existing rules, together with the requirements of justice and common sense, pointed firmly to such a right existing, then I think the court should not be deterred from recognising the right." (At 642).

the United States) coupled with the unlikelihood of the statutory
creation of such a right [5] suggest that the catalyst for change may,
once again, be the European Convention on Human Rights and
Fundamental Freedoms. [6] Whether the Convention is adopted as the
text for a British Bill of Rights [7] or an adverse ruling is given by
the European Court of Human Rights pointing to the lacunae in
our law, [8] the concept of " privacy " will inevitably insinuate itself
into the law as a means of describing the " interest," [9] " claim " [10]
power [11] or " right " [12] which is infringed. It is the purpose of this
article to suggest that this be resisted and that, whatever, its value
to the social sciences [13] or political theory, [14] the concept of
" privacy " be refused admission to English law.

---

[5] Six attempts at legislation by Private Members have sought, to a greater
or lesser extent to protect rights to " privacy." The most comprehensive Bill was
drafted by Justice and proposed by Brian Walden M.P. in 1969. (See *Younger
Committee*, Chap. 22).
 [6] Article 8 provides: "1. Everyone has the right to respect for his private
and family life, his home and his correspondence. 2. There shall be no interference
by a public authority with the exercise of this right except such as is in accordance
with the law . . ." The reference to " public authority " has been interpreted
though apparently not definitively) by the Consultative Assembly of the Council
of Europe in a way that does not restrict the right contained in paragraph
1 as availing against state invasions of privacy only, " but also against interference
by private persons or institutions, including the mass media." (Resolution 428,
January 23, 1970.)
 [7] This is what a House of Lords Select Committee regarded (by 6 to 5) as
the most acceptable proposal, *Report of the Select Committee on a Bill of Rights*
(1978) H.L. 176. See J. Jaconelli, " The European Convention on Human Rights
—The Text of a British Bill of Rights " [1976] *Public Law* 226.
 [8] The inadequacy of the law in controlling the use of telephone tapping by the
police was revealed in *Malone* v. *Commissioner of Police of the Metropolis (No. 2)
supra*. The Vice-Chancellor was in no doubt that such activities were in breach
of the European Convention on Human Rights, and the plaintiff is reported as
being anxious to prove Sir Robert correct, see *The Guardian* February 1, 1979.
 [9] L. Lusky, " Invasion of Privacy: A Clarification of Concepts " (1972) 72
Colum. Law Rev. 693.
 [10] A. F. Westin, *Privacy and Freedom* (1970) 7.
 [11] E. L. Beardsley, " Privacy: Autonomy and Selective Disclosure " in
*Privacy, Nomos XIII* (1971) edited by J. R. Pennock and J. W. Chapman (hereafter referred to as *Nomos XIII*) 56; R. B. Parker " A Definition of Privacy "
(1974) 27 Rutgers Law Rev. 275, 280; A. Miller, *The Assault on Privacy* (1971)
25; C. Fried, *An Anatomy of Values* (1970) 140; H. Gross, " Privacy and Autonomy," *Nomos XIII*, 169. The defects in conceiving of " privacy " in terms of
power or control are examined below.
 [12] See note 16.
 [13] It is used in anthropology (See Westin, *op. cit.* 11–18, J. M. Roberts and
T. Gregor, " Privacy: A Cultural View," *Nomos XIII* 199); sociology (See
P. Halmos, *Solitude and Privacy* (1953), E. Shils, " Privacy: Its Constitution and
Vicissitudes " (1966) 31 Law & Contemp. Problems 289; E. Goffman, *Relations
in Public* (1972); and psychology (See S. M. Jourard, " Some Psychological
Aspects of Privacy " (1966) 31 Law & Contemp. Problems 307, O. M. Ruebhausen
and O. G. Brim, " Privacy and Behavioral Research " (1965) 65 Colum.Law
Rev. 1184). There is, however, as one might expect, very little common ground
or consistency in what is considered to be " privacy " and the forms its infringement might assume.
 [14] See H. J. McCloskey, " The Political Ideal of Privacy " (1971) 21 Philosophical Quarterly 303; S. Lukes, *Individualism* (1973) Chap. 9, " Privacy ";
M. A. Weinstein, " The Uses of Privacy in the Good Life," *Nomos XIII* 88;
W. L. Weinstein, " The Private and the Free: A Conceptual Inquiry," *Nomos*

It would be folly to argue that certain conditions (such as being alone) or certain activities (such as the practices of the eavesdropper or Peeping Tom) will not or ought not to be intuitively characterised as "privacy" or "invasions of privacy" respectively, but it will be shown that the currency of "privacy" has been so devalued that it no longer warrants—if it ever did [15]—serious consideration as a legal term of art.

The long search for a "definition" of "privacy" has produced a continuing debate that is often sterile and, ultimately, futile. The debate is sterile for four main reasons. First, the premises upon which the proposed "definitions" are based are materially different. Thus, for example, those who assume "privacy" to be a "right" [16] have not really joined issue with those who conceive it to be a "condition," [17] "state," [18] "area of life" [19] and so on. The former are asserting a normative statement about the desirability of whatever it is that the particular writer regards as "privacy," while the latter are merely proffering a descriptive statement about "privacy."

Secondly, the objectives of the arguments tend to differ. For example, Prosser's famous essay [20] which marshalled several hundred "privacy" cases was a (successful) [21] attempt to demonstrate that the American law recognised four distinct torts [22] under the umbrella of "privacy." In his equally famous rejoinder, Bloustein [23] seized upon Prosser's atomisation of "privacy" and insisted that there is a single interest at the heart of the law's protection, namely "human

---

*XIII* 27. Again there is little shared ground concerning precisely what "privacy" means. See the discussion of the use of the "right to privacy" as a central tenet of democratic theory, below.

[15] See F. Davis. "What Do We Mean by 'Right to Privacy'?" (1959) 4 S. Dakota Law Rev. 1.

[16] See the criticism levelled at the Younger Committee for its failure to distinguish between "rights" and "liberties" by D. N. MacCormick (1973) 89 L.Q.R. 23 and the rejoinder by a member of the Committee, N. Marsh in (1973) 89 L.Q.R 183. See, too, D. N. MacCormick, "Privacy: A Problem of Definition" (1974) 1 Brit. J. of Law & Soc. 75.

[17] L. Lusky, *op. cit.* 709.

[18] A. F. Westin, *op. cit.* 31–32 describes "the four basic states of individual privacy" as solitude, small-group intimacy, anonymity and reserve.

[19] Justice, *Privacy and the Law* (1970), para. 19.

[20] W. L. Prosser, "Privacy" (1960) 48 Calif. Law Rev. 383 (hereafter referred to as Prosser). The article is almost exactly reproduced as the chapter on privacy in Prosser's work *The Law of Torts*, 4th ed. (1971).

[21] Prosser's fourfold classification "is alluded to in almost every decided privacy case in the last ten years or so," E. J. Bloustein "Privacy as an Aspect of Human Dignity: An Answer to Dean Prosser" (1964) 39 N.Y.U. Law Rev. 962. This comment relates to the period 1952 to 1962, but it is just as accurate when applied to the period since then.

[22] The four torts are: (i) intrusion upon the plaintiff's seclusion or solitude or into his private affairs: (ii) public disclosure of embarrassing private facts about the plaintiff; (iii) publicity which places the plaintiff in a false light in the public eye; (iv) appropriation, for the defendant's advantage, of the plaintiff's name or likeness.

[23] E. J. Bloustein, *op. cit.*

dignity." But in exposing the disparate interests [24] protected Prosser is merely describing the law; in his reply Bloustein, whatever the strength of his arguments, is engaged in seeking, at a higher level of abstraction, a wider explanation for the law's concern to protect "privacy."

Thirdly, the arguments as to the desirability of "privacy" frequently proceed from different standpoints. Some see "privacy" as an end in itself,[25] while others regard it as instrumental in the securing of other desirable social ends such as creativity,[26] love,[27] or emotional release.[28] The former position, though it is central to any argument in favour of "privacy" (however defined), does not adequately explain why it should prevail over competing interests such as free speech. The latter position is based on unproven empirical speculation. If they are to have any force, the two arguments must be seen together rather than in opposition.

Fourthly, the "definitions" usually beg more questions than they are designed to answer. For example, "privacy" is widely defined in terms of "control" over who has information about or access to the individual.[29] But in order to evaluate such "definitions" we need to know, for instance, what purpose, if any, is served by the exercise of this control. Normally the answers point to arguments in favour of the individual's right or claim to or interest in limiting the exposure to which he is subject, or the circulation of facts about him. These, however, are arguments for a specific exercise of choice, not for mere control. Another defect of the "control" definition is that it fails to account for the fact that if I want you to know a fact about me and I am unable to communicate it to you then, according to the definition of "privacy" in terms of control, I should have *lost* privacy for I have lost control over the circulation of information about myself. Equally, if I succeed in total disclosure of my private life to you I should *not* have lost privacy. Neither of these can be correct.[30]

The debate is ultimately futile for, in those legal systems which recognise a common law right to privacy (or its equivalent),

---

[24] Prosser claims that there are four different interests of the plaintiff protected, but, in fact, he identifies only three: mental feelings (intrusion), reputation (public disclosure and false light) and property (appropriation).

[25] E. L. Beardsley, *op. cit.* S. I. Benn, "Privacy, Freedom, and Respect for Persons," *Nomos XIII* 1.

[26] M. A. Weinstein, *op. cit.*

[27] C. Fried, *op. cit.*

[28] Westin, *op. cit.* 33. See, too, R. Ingham "Privacy and Psychology" in *Privacy* (1978) edited by J. B. Young; Jourard, *op. cit.*

[29] See note 11 above.

[30] This point is made by R. E. Gavison, "Privacy and its Legal Protection" (1975) Unpublished D.Phil. Thesis, University of Oxford. Other "definitions" might be attacked on different grounds; that is not, however, the chief object of this article.

" privacy " is entrenched in the vocabulary of the courts,[31] and where it is accorded statutory protection then " privacy " is simply what the legislature says it is.[32] And in this country where neither situation obtains, the controversy serves even less purpose: since the notion of " privacy " has not won a place in our jurisprudence, it is hard to see, particularly in the light of the abuse the concept has already suffered, what conceivable advantage could accrue from its reception now. Indeed, the recent occasions upon which the term has been employed by our courts inspire little confidence in the belief that it may escape similar abuse.[33]

The " right to privacy " has come a long way since its original formulation as a protection against gossip.[34] It has grown so large that it now threatens to devour itself. Denying an individual an

---

[31] See the discussion of " false light " and the American constitutional protection of the " right to privacy " below.

[32] Or, more correctly (since no country appears to have a statute which formulates in detail what " privacy " actually is or the precise circumstances in which it is invaded), the legislature declares in very specific terms that " privacy " is in issue in a particular context such as computer data, or in very general terms that, say, private lives are legally " protected."

[33] In *Bernstein of Leigh (Baron)* v. *Skyviews & General Ltd.* [1978] Q.B. 479 the plaintiff's country estate was photographed from an aeroplane by the defendant who then offered the photograph to the plaintiff for sale. The plaintiff declined the offer and instead sued for damages for trespass and injunctions to restrain the defendant from entering his air space and from invading his " right to privacy." The court held there had been neither a trespass nor an invasion of " privacy." The issue of trespass aside, Griffiths J. declared that were the plaintiff subjected to constant surveillance from the air, such conduct might well constitute " a monstrous invasion of his privacy " for which the court might give relief as an actionable nuisance. (At 143.) Whatever else it may be, it is hard to see how the aerial photography of a stately home invades its owner's " privacy." Indeed, the fact that the remedy, if any, for the bizarre example of aerial intrusion would lie in nuisance illustrates that in such circumstances it would be the impairment of the use and enjoyment of his property to which the victim objected rather than the assault on his personality implicit in the " privacy " doctrine. See R. Wacks, ' No Castles in the Air " (1977) 93 L.Q.R. 491 where the decision is more fully discussed. In *Woodward* v. *Hutchins* [1977] 1 W.L.R. 760 three pop stars and their manager sought an injunction to prevent an ex-employee from further disclosing intimate details about their lives to a newspaper. The cause of action was breach of confidence. The Court of Appeal held, however, that there was a pubic interest in the " truth " about the stars being told and their action failed. Though the Court (in particular Lord Denning M.R.) appear to have confused the " privacy " issue with the " confidence " issue (see below), Bridge L.J. made explicit reference to the " invasion of privacy " occasioned by the publicity and then went on to declare that if the defendant's disclosures were truthful the plaintiffs would recover no damages in libel, " and I think that they could only recover nominal damages for the breach of confidentiality, if there was one." (At 6.) The assumption here appears to be that the essence of the plaintiffs' complaint is the *falsity* of the disclosures, and thus that only " nominal damages " would be exigible for the truth. This undermines the central idea that underlies the whole Warren and Brandeis thesis *viz.* that the truth or falsity of an embarrassing public disclosure is irrelevant. (See below.) This case is examined in more detail in R. Wacks, " Pop Goes Privacy " (1978) 41 M.L.R. 67.

[34] The Warren and Brandeis essay is concerned exclusively with the misdemeanours of the press which was regarded as " overstepping in every direction " the obvious bounds of propriety and of decency, *Warren & Brandeis,* 196.

abortion [35] or long hair, [36] or subjecting him to advertising [37] or surveillance [38] are merely some of the activities which the American law happily accommodates under the wing of " privacy." In at least seven instances " privacy " has become almost irretrievably confused with other issues.

## 1. " PRIVACY " IS EQUATED WITH AUTONOMY

The pervasive tendency to treat " privacy " as synonymous with individual autonomy or, indeed, with freedom itself, is especially manifest in recent Supreme Court decisions on sexual freedom [39] and obscene material, [40] but this by no means exhausts the application of the concept [41] which, most recently, has been invoked to vindicate the " right to die." [42]

This alarming development may be attributable to two factors. The first harks back to the Warren and Brandeis thesis and the proposition that the essence of the " right to privacy " is the " right to be let alone "—a sweeping phrase which is as comprehensive as it is vague. If " privacy " consists in being " let alone " then every physical assault would constitute an invasion of privacy. [43]

Secondly, since the Constitution is silent on the subject of " privacy," the Supreme Court has, in its determination to protect this " fundamental personal right " [44] discovered in the provisions of the Bill of Rights [45] or even outside them [46] ample flexibility and scope for the development of implied " rights to privacy." Once this right is declared to emanate " from the totality of the constitutional

---

[35] *Roe* v. *Wade,* 410 U.S. 113 (1973); *Doe* v. *Bolton,* 410 U.S. 179 (1973).

[36] *Kelley* v. *Johnson,* 425 U.S. 238 (1976).

[37] *Lehman* v. *Shaker Heights,* 418 U.S. 298 (1974).

[38] *United States* v. *United States District Court,* 407 U.S. 297 (1972).

[39] *Roe* v. *Wade, supra; Griswold* v. *Connecticut,* 381 U.S. 479 (1965); *Doe* v. *Commonwealth's Attorney,* 403 F.Supp. 1199 (1976).

[40] See 2 (c) below.

[41] It has, for example, been applied to the issue of the compulsory wearing of motorcycle crash helmets: *State of Idaho* v. *Albertson,* 470 P. 2d 300 (1970); noise: see E. Van Den Haag, " On Privacy," *Nomos XIII* 149; and the zoning of homes: *Village of Belle Terre* v. *Boraas,* 416 U.S. 1 (1974).

[42] *In the Matter of Karen Quinlan,* 355 A. 2d 647 (1976).

[43] This was, in fact, the context (" the right to immunity from attacks and injuries ") in which the phrase " the right to be let alone " was first used, T. M. Cooley, *A Treatise on the Law of Torts,* 2nd ed. (1888), 24, 29.

[44] *Griswold* v. *Connecticut, supra* at 488, *per* Goldberg J. See *Poe* v. *Ullman,* 367 U.S. 497, 521 (1960), *per* Douglas J.

[45] The " right to privacy " has been extrapolated from the following Amendments: The First (freedom of speech), Fourth (protection against unreasonable searches and seizures), Fifth (right against self-incrimination), Ninth (enumerated rights do not deny or disparage other rights), and the Fourteenth ("due process ").

[46] " We deal with a right of privacy older than the Bill of Rights—older than our political parties, older than our school system." *Griswold* v. *Connecticut, supra* at 486, *per* Douglas J.

scheme under which we live," [47] it is not surprising that it has come to approximate what Mill in *On Liberty* understood by "privacy" in the widest possible sense when he said: "Over himself, over his own body and mind, the individual is sovereign." [48] But what is in issue here is not "privacy" but the limits of the law in regulating the individual's freedom of action. [49] This principle—that there is a sphere of thought and action that should be free from public interference—may well constitute "the central idea of liberalism," [50] but for the purposes of the legal recognition of a "right to privacy" it is only an ultimate norm which underpins the narrower and more specific right. [51] My autonomy is not necessarily affected by an invasion of "privacy" (*e.g.* my telephone is tapped) nor is my "privacy" necessarily invaded when my autonomy is curtailed (*e.g.* the provisions of the Theft Act do not invade my "privacy"). But if "privacy" is assigned an independent meaning (say, as my right to decide what information about me is circulated) then to curtail my autonomy may well invade my "privacy," for it restricts my freedom to choose "privacy."

## 2. "PRIVACY" HAS COLONISED OTHER LIBERTIES

Though more explicit legal protection is afforded to certain liberties, the appeal of "privacy" has resulted in a tendency, particularly by the Supreme Court, to characterise as invasions of "privacy" activities that could more accurately be described as infringements of those specific liberties. [52] This has occurred in three principal areas:

### (a) Freedom from unreasonable search

The Fourth Amendment establishes "the right of the people to be secure . . . against unreasonable searches and seizures," and sets out the conditions under which search warrants may be issued. In a long line of decisions [53] the court has sought to apply the Fourth

---

[47] *Poe* v. *Ullman, ibid.*, quoted by Goldberg J. in *Griswold* v. *Connecticut, ibid.*

[48] *On Liberty and Considerations on Representative Government*, edited by R. B. McCallum, Oxford: Blackwell (1946) 9.

[49] This is the stuff of the well ventilated Hart/Devlin debate. See H. L. A. Hart, *Law, Liberty and Morality* (1963); P. Devlin, *The Enforcement of Morals* (1965). See, too, S. I. Benn, "The Protection and Limitation of Privacy" (1978) 52 Austr.L.J. 601 and 688, 610; H. Gross, *op. cit.* 181.

[50] S. Lukes, *op. cit.* 62.

[51] E. Beardsley, *op. cit.*

[52] This might be regarded as the other side of the "autonomy" coin described above.

[53] In particular *Olmstead* v. *United States*, 277 U.S. 438 (1928); *On Lee* v. *United States*, 343 U.S 747 (1952); *Silverman* v. *United States*, 365 U.S. 505 (1961); *Wong Sun* v. *United States*, 371 U.S. 411 (1963); *Katz* v. *United States*, 389 U.S. 347, (1967); *United States* v. *United States District Court, supra;* *Brewer* v. *Williams*, 97 Sp.Ct. 1232 (1977); *Rakas* v. *Illinois*, 99 Sp.Ct. 421 (1979).

Amendment to "searches" conducted by means of electronic devices unimagined by its framers. In so doing the court has couched the liberty in terms of the "reasonable expectation of privacy" to which, say, the user of a telephone is entitled.[54]

That privacy is violated when a telephone conversation is tapped is undeniable, but the determination of the proper bounds of police power to search person and property is a much broader problem. It is easy to see why (with the help of a powerful dissenting judgment—which looks at the subject the other way round—by Brandeis J. himself [55]) the language of "privacy" has been used in these decisions—though English courts have managed perfectly well without it [56]—but it can only obscure the issues involved and, in consequence, diminish the force of the argument against excessive police power.[57]

### (b) *Freedom of association*

A similar development has taken place in what the Supreme Court has termed "associational privacy"[58] which consists in the right of an individual not to disclose details of groups or organisations with which he associates. In the leading case,[59] for example, the attorney general of Alabama failed to compel a civil rights group to produce a list of its members. It is, again, not hard to see why "privacy" interests have been called in aid, but this freedom is better safeguarded in its own name and is protected, in any event, by the First Amendment.[60]

---

[54] *Katz.* v. *United States, supra.*

[55] "Whenever a telephone line is tapped, the privacy of the persons at both ends of the line is invaded . . . To protect that right, every unjustifiable intrusion by the Government upon the privacy of the individual, whatever the means employed, must be deemed a violation of the fourth Amendment . . ." *Olmstead* v. *United States, supra,* 476–477, *per* Brandeis J. (dissenting).

[56] See for example *Ghani* v. *Jones* [1970] 1 Q.B. 693; *Elias* v. *Pasmore* [1934] 2 K.B. 164; *Truman (Frank) Export Ltd.* v. *Metropolitan Police Commissioner* [1977] Q.B. 952. But see the judgment of Sir Robert Megarry V.-C. in *Malone* v. *Commisstoner of the Police of the Metropolis (No. 2), supra,* where, in response to the plaintiff's brave contention that English law recognised the limited right to privacy on the telephone, the Vice-Chancellor, though rejecting the argument, implicitly acknowledged its appropriateness in such circumstances.

[57] "The Fourth Amendment, then, is a grand charter for privacy which rarely lives up to its promise because of the powerful exigencies of the criminal law. Most governmental searches occur when the Government is looking for evidence of wrongdoing. Under these circumstances it is unfortunate but not surprising that claims of privacy often run into heavy weather, and that as a practical and political matter competing claims of law enforcement are difficult to overcome," J. H. F. Shattuck, *Rights of Privacy* (1977) 43–44. See *Rakas* v. *Illinois,* 99 S.Ct. 421 (1979).

[58] *Uphaus* v. *Wyman,* 360 U.S. 516 (1959).

[59] *N.A.A.C.P.* v. *Alabama,* 357 U.S. 449 (1958).

[60] *United States* v. *Robel,* 389 U.S. 258 (1967). See too, *Talley* v. *California,* 362 U.S. 60 (1960), in which the court proclaimed the importance of "anonymous speech," *i.e.* the right to issue leaflets etc. without the identity of the author being disclosed.

### (c) *Freedom of expression*

In general, the question of the extent to which the law ought to control the distribution and use of obscene matter in a democratic society is resolved by reference to the competing claims of morality and free speech. Those who seek to abridge that freedom normally claim that the majority is entitled to impose its moral standards on the community, while the opponents of such a view reject the proposition that the majority has such a right and demand evidence of the " harm " which obscene matter is alleged to cause. Recently, however, the Supreme Court has used the " right to privacy ": to invalidate legislation proscribing the possession of obscene matter, ruling that in the privacy of his home an individual had the right to enjoy the materials of his choice.[61]

Whatever the present status of this view,[62] it seems to amount to looking at the problem from the wrong end of a telescope. Free speech requires a stronger justification than that its limitation will (as it must) infringe the freedom to read salacious books in one's home. Such a liberty is an indirect consequence of freedom of expression, not its rationale.[63] Moreover, the privacy-based argument implies that such a right is forfeited when one reads such material on a park bench. Indeed, without this right and the ancillary right to obtain such material, the freedom would exist " . . . only if one wrote or designed a tract in his attic and printed or processed it in his basement, so as to be able to read it in his study." [64]

### 3. " Privacy " is Confused with Confidentiality

The recipient of confidential information who breaches the confidence reposed in him by his confidant may, in addition, invade the latter's " privacy." In order for this to happen the information divulged would have to be " private " or " intimate," and this is rarely the case. Confidential relationships in which the parties agree

---

[61] *Stanley* v. *Georgia*, 394 U.S. 557 (1969).

[62] The court appears to have narrowed down its ruling in *Stanley* and to have held that state legislatures may enact prohibitions on the possession of obscene material; see *Paris Adult Theatre I* v. *Slaton*, 413 U.S. 49 (1973); *United States* v. *12 200-Foot Reels*, 413 U.S. 123 (1973); *Erznoznik* v. *City of Jacksonville*, 422 U.S. 205 (1975).

[63] *Cf.* D. N. MacCormick, " Privacy and Obscenity " in *Censorship and Obscenity* edited by R. Dhavan and C. Davies (1978). Professor MacCormick, in taking the position that the " protection of privacy is essentially an aspect of the protection of individual freedom of choice, of choice what kind of person to be," (92) equates " privacy " and autonomy. (See the discussion in (1) above.) He examines also the proposition that " privacy " is invaded by the public display of obscene matter, and finds such a view (which is, in any event, given short shrift by the Supreme Court in the *Erznoznik* case, *supra*) untenable. It must be so.     [64] *United States* v. *12 200-Foot Reels*, *supra*, 137, *per* Douglas J.

to impart the information communicated to no one or only to
authorised third parties, generally arise in the commercial world.
The facts shared are trade secrets or business confidences.
Occasionally, however, truly "private" facts may be the subject
of a confidential relationship; this may occur in the case of
marriage [65] or possibly employment,[66] and equity may enjoin disclosure.[67] Indeed, it was upon the foundation of this equitable
remedy that Warren and Brandeis built their argument that the
common law recognised a "right to privacy." [68]

Yet, despite the view of the Younger Committee to the contrary,[69] the action for breach of confidence is neither adequate nor
appropriate to deal with "many complaints in the privacy field." [70]
It is inadequate because the requirement of a "confidential relationship" effectively precludes the action from having any utility in
two crucial "privacy" areas—intrusion by physical or electronic
means and the public disclosure of private facts. In neither case is
there likely to be such a relationship between the victim and the
wrongdoer. The action is inappropriate because it is founded on
principles which have little to do with "privacy." And when it is
argued otherwise, there is generally a failure to distinguish between
the *disclosure* of information confidentially imparted (the major
breach of confidence issue), on the one hand, and the *publicity* given
to such information (the major "privacy" issue), on the other.
It is assumed that since the former may be restrained on, say,
the basis of the duty of good faith, the latter is based on the same
(inappropriate) principle.

### 4. "PRIVACY" IS CONFUSED WITH SECRECY

The perennial demand for greater openness in government and the
recognition of the public's "right to know" [71] sometimes becomes
enmeshed with the question of "privacy." [72] Either it asserted that

---

[65] *Duchess of Argyll* v. *Duke of Argyll* [1967] Ch. 302.

[66] *Woodward* v. *Hutchins, supra.* See note 33, *supra.*

[67] See G. Jones, "Restitution of Benefits Obtained in Breach of Another's Confidence" (1970) 86 L.Q.R. 463; A. Turner, *The Law of Trade Secrets* (1962) and
Supplement (1968); P. M. North, "Breach of Confidence: Is There a New Tort? "
(1972) 12 J.S.P.T.L. 149.

[68] *Warren & Brandeis,* 210–211.                    [69] See note 2, *supra.*

[70] *Younger Committee,* para. 657. See R. Wacks, "Breach of Confidence and
the Protection of Privacy" (1977) 127 New L.J. 328. A more fertile field of application might be the problems associated with computerised data banks, but even
here there are significant limitations: See *Lindop Committee,* Chap. 34. It is,
moreover, argued below that this ought not to be viewed as a "privacy" issue.

[71] The prospect of a Freedom of Information Act or at least an Official
Information Act (as proposed by the *Departmental Committee on Section 2 of the
Official Secrets Act 1911,* Cmnd. 5104, 1972, Chairman: Lord Franks) has, since the
Blunt affair. somewhat receded.

[72] See C. J. Friedrich, "Secrecy versus Privacy: The Democratic Dilemma,"
*Nomos XIII* 105.

the legal protection of privacy is inimical to the responsibility of a newspaper to inform its readers on important matters of government,[73] or the inscrutability of Whitehall and the provisions of the Official Secrets Acts are denounced as excessive "privacy of the government." [74]

The latter argument confuses " privacy " and " secrecy." " Secret " matters are not necessarily " private "; for a matter to be private it is not sufficient that it should be kept secret and so not publicised. It must not be public in the further sense that the person in question is not, in principle, liable to answer for the matter he wishes to keep private.[75]

## 5. " PRIVACY " IS CONFUSED WITH DEFAMATION

When " private " facts about an individual are gratuitously published the truth or falsity of those facts ought to be irrelevant. Should they be untrue *and* affect his reputation he may have a cause of action for defamation. But, of course, if the facts disclosed are true he will, in most common law jurisdictions, be met with the defence of justification—whatever the effect upon his reputation. An action for invasion of privacy may then be brought provided that the ingredients of the tort [76] are satisfied. In such circumstances it is often said [77] that it is the plaintiff's *reputation* which is the principal interest protected. This seems wrong for two reasons. First, the gravamen of the plaintiff's complaint is the publicity given to his " private " life; he seeks not merely " to prevent inaccurate portrayal of his private life, but to prevent its being depicted at all." [78] Secondly, the plaintiff ought not to be barred from recovery when the disclosure does not affect the esteem in which he is held or even enhances it.[79]

---

[73] See D. McQuail, " The Mass Media and Privacy " in J. B. Young (ed), *op. cit.* The American Freedom of Information Act of 1967 contains a " privacy exemption " which excludes from disclosure " personnel and medical files and similar files, the disclosure of which would constitute a clearly unwarranted invasion of personal privacy." (5 U.S.C. para. 552 (b) (6) ). See *Department of the Air Force* v. *Rose*, 425 U.S. 352 (1976).

[74] Friedrich, *op. cit.* 112. Secrecy and confidentiality were (since the action was perforce pleaded as a breach of confidence) interlocked in the so-called Crossman Diaries Case: *Attorney-General* v. *Jonathan Cape Ltd.* [1976] Q.B. 752. The equitable remedy was extended to " the completely new sphere of the citizen-State relationship," H. Street, *Freedom, the Individual and the Law,* 4th ed. (1977) 235.

[75] S. I. Benn, " The Protection and Limitation of Privacy " (1978) 52 Austr.L.J. 601, 603. See Lusky, *op. cit.* 707.

[76] Prosser indicates three elements of the tort: there must be publicity, the facts disclosed must be private facts and they must be offensive to a reasonable man. (Prosser 810.)

[77] Prosser 393. *Cf.* E. J. Bloustein, *op. cit.* 980–981. F. Davis, *op. cit.*

[78] *Warren & Brandeis,* 218.

[79] See *Sidis* v. *F. R. Publishing Corporation,* 113 F. 2d 806 (1940).

Yet the area of overlap between defamation and the action for invasion of privacy has become so great in the United States [80] that it is suggested that "the great majority of defamation cases can now be brought for invasion of the right to "privacy" and that the latter "may come to supplant the action for defamation." [81] A similar development appears to be at work in the constitutional protection of privacy where the Supreme Court has applied the standard it set for wrongfulness in actions for defamation [82] to a case which it regarded as "privacy" litigation. [83]

Another confusion between the two actions is the inclusion as one of the four "privacy" torts of the activity which consists in "publicity which places the plaintiff in a false light in the public eye." [84] Though the "false light need not necessarily be a defamatory one," [85] it invariably is, and the category may well be redundant [86] or a threat to the developed rules of defamation. [87] But the principal objection against its being grafted on to the notion of privacy is, quite simply, that the two have little in common. The interest affected by publicity which creates a false impression of an individual, more closely approximates the interest protected by the law of defamation than the law of privacy. [88]

Consequently, though the right under the Rehabilitation of Offenders Act 1974 not to have divulged a "spent conviction" [89] and

---

[80] A similar development has occurred in Germany; see *Younger Committee*, para. 71. But there, in view of the wide conception of "rights of the personality" (See note 3 above) this is not surprising.

[81] J. W. Wade, "Defamation and the Right of Privacy" (1962) 15 Vand. Law Rev. 1109; H. Kalven, "Privacy in Tort Law—Were Warren and Brandeis Wrong?" (1966) 31 Law & Contemp. Probs. 326, 341.

[82] *New York Times* v. *Sullivan*, 376 U.S. 254 (1964)

[83] *Time, Inc.* v. *Hill*, 385 U.S. 374 (1967). Perhaps this was an inevitable confusion for the thrust of the plaintiff's complaint in *Time* was not that private facts were disclosed, but that the article was "false and untrue." The application of the *Sullivan* test of proof of malice becomes less perplexing. Only Harlan J. declared: "To me this is not 'privacy' litigation in its truest sense." (At 476).

[84] Prosser 812. Though the Younger Committee believed that "no useful purpose would be served" by formulating a comprehensive definition of "privacy" (para. 58), it nevertheless opined that "placing someone in a false light is an aspect of defamation rather than of privacy," (para. 70) thereby providing a "definition" of "privacy" however rough. The Walden Bill expressly includes "false light" as an aspect of "privacy."

[85] Prosser 813.

[86] G. Dworkin, "The Common Law Protection of Privacy" (1967) 2 U.Tasm. Law Rev. 418, 426.

[87] Prosser 813–814; H. Kalven, *op. cit.* 341.

[88] This was the view of the *Younger Committee*, see note 84. F. Davis, *op. cit.* 9, regards both actions as turning on the "mental suffering" caused to the plaintiff.

[89] The Act's main objective is to mitigate the difficulties encountered by a convicted offender when he returns to society and, in particular, seeks employment. The prejudice against such a person, even though he may have "gone straight" has required the law to permit him, after the passage of a specified number of

a rape defendant's right to anonymity under the Sexual Offences (Amendent) Act 1976,[90] are often treated as "privacy" issues, they are not. They both protect reputation rather than "privacy"; the former by permitting the victim of disclosure to sue for defamation if his conviction is maliciously disclosed, the latter by protecting the defendant against the stigma of a charge as yet unproven.[91] Similarly, the suggestion that "privacy" might be protected by amending the defence of justification to require, in addition to proof of the truth of the statement, evidence that its publication is in the public interest,[92] presupposes that invasions of privacy by public disclosure are necessarily defamatory.

### 6. "PRIVACY" IS REGARDED AS A PROPRIETARY INTEREST

Another of the "privacy" torts which is widely accepted[93] is the "appropriation, for the defendant's benefit, of the plaintiff's

---

years, to deny that he was ever convicted. Moreover, should his conviction be disclosed, thereby diminishing the esteem in which he is held by right thinking members of society, he may sue for defamation and, provided the publisher acted with malice, recover damages for this truthful account. Strictly speaking, therefore, the protection of "privacy" is not involved. It is also arguable that the commission of an offence and the subsequent trial and conviction (or acquittal) of the defendant are anyway matters of public record and public interest. Thus not only does the question of rehabilitation of offenders relate to protecting the reputation of the victim of the disclosure, but the disclosure is of a public rather than a "private" fact. In addition, the plaintiff (as in the law of defamation generally) may base his complaint on publication to a single person; the interest in "privacy" appears to reside in the objection to wide publicity given to "private" facts.

[90] S. 6 confers anonymity on both the defendant and the victim in cases of rape. As far as the victim is concerned, the purpose of this provision has less to do with "privacy" or even reputation than the administration of justice which might otherwise be hampered by the reluctance of victims to report their experience. But the anonymity accorded to the defendant is premised on the theory that until he is convicted, he ought not (except in certain circumstances) to be identified because the public, wedded to the notion that there is no smoke without fire, may well convict him in their minds and even his eventual acquittal may fail to heal his fractured reputation. The same argument could, of course, be applied to other charges which carry a moral stigma (*e.g.* indecent assaults on children or even theft). In *Cox Broadcasting Corporation* v. *Cohn*, 420 U.S. 469 (1975), the Supreme Court held that the disclosure of the name of a rape victim (who died in the attack) constituted a *prima facie* case of invasion of her father's privacy. The court nevertheless found for the defendant on the ground that the criminal proceedings were matters of legitimate concern to the public. Again, it is misleading to conceive of the publication of facts of this kind as a "privacy" issue in the sense in which the "public disclosure" cases are normally described.

[91] *Hansard*, cols. 1922–1945 (20 May 1976) H.C.

[92] Both Committees on the Law of Defamation (The Porter Committee Cmnd. 7536, 1948, paras. 76–78 and the Faulks Committee, Cmnd. 5909, paras 137–140) rejected this proposal.

[93] Apart from its acceptance by the American law (See *Restatement of Torts* (Second) (1971), para. 652A, Prosser 804, and *Zacchini* v. *Scripps-Howard Broadcasting Co.* (1977) Sp.Ct. 2849) including statutory provisions such as the New

name or likeness." In fact it was this wrong that was first recognised by the American courts as sounding in "privacy."[94] Since the Warren and Brandeis thesis turns ultimately on decisions in which relief was founded upon some interest in "property,"[95] the alacrity with which the American law has accepted this form of commercial exploitation as an aspect of privacy[96] is hardly surprising. Yet Warren and Brandeis sought in these decisions a wider footing than property on which to base their new-fledged principle of an "inviolate personality." But, writing at a time when the concept of property was considerably narrower than it now is,[97] they were compelled to look elsewhere for a theoretical foundation.[98]

It is today rather artificial to see in the unauthorised use of name or image for commercial (usually advertising) purposes, an invasion of the victim's "privacy."[99] Whether or not the interest affected is labelled "property,"[1] the rationale for protection "is the straight-forward one of preventing unjust enrichment by the theft of good will."[2]

## 7. "Privacy" is said to be Affected by Computerised Data Banks

Most recently the "privacy" doctrine has moved into the area of information collection and storage, especially by computers.[3] It

York legislation which has become a prototype for similar statutes in other states (N.Y. Civ. Rights Law para. 50) see Davis, *op. cit.* 13–17) this aspect of "privacy" appears to be recognised, to a greater or lesser extent, in Canada, Germany, France, and other European countries. The Walden Bill expressly includes "appropriation" as an aspect of "privacy."

[94] *Pavesich* v. *New England Life Insurance Co.,* 50 S.E. 68 (1905), following the dissenting judgment of Gray J. in *Roberson* v. *Rochester Folding Box Co.,* 64 N.E. 442 (1902).

[95] *Gee* v. *Pritchard* (1818) 2 Swanst. 402; *Prince Albert* v. *Strange* (1849) 1 H. & Tw. 1; 1 Mac. & G. 25; *Woolsey* v. *Judd* (1855) 4 Duer 379.

[96] "(T)his form of invasion has bulked rather large in the law of privacy," Prosser 805.

[97] See D. F. Libling, "The Concept of Property: Property in Intangibles" (1978) 94 L.Q.R. 103.

[98] F. Davis, *op. cit.* 10.

[99] See E. J. Bloustein, *op. cit.* 987. *Cf.* Prosser 406.

[1] "Whether it be labelled as a 'property' right is immaterial; for here, as often elsewhere, the tag 'property' simply symbolises the fact that the courts enforce a claim which has pecuniary worth," *Haelan Laboratories* v. *Topps Chewing Gum Co.,* F. 2d 866 (1953). See Prosser 807.

[2] H. Kalven, *op. cit.* 331. Indeed, this aspect of "privacy" shows signs of being reconstructed as a "right of publicity" enjoyed by the individual whose name or image have a commercial value which he may wish to exploit in his own way. See M. B. Nimmer, "The Right of Publicity" (1954) 19 Law & Contemp.Probs. 203; *Cf.* F. Davis, *op. cit.* 17–18.

[3] A. R. Miller, *The Assault on Privacy* (1971); A. F. Westin and M. Baker, *Databanks in a Free Society* (1972); M. Warner and M. Stone, *The Data Bank Society* (1970); P. Hewitt, Privacy: *The Information Gatherers, N.C.C.L. Privacy Report* (1977); F. Hondius, *Emerging Data Protection in Europe* (1975). There have also been several government and international reports on the "privacy" aspect of data collection; see the *Lindop Committee,* Chap. 4.

is assumed, and forcibly asserted in an astonishingly prodigious literature, that the acquisition and use of personal information are a threat to our " privacy." Statutory regulation of computers is invariably couched in the language of " privacy." [4]

There can be little doubt that the advances in computerised data banks and the alarming speed with which information may be retrieved by micro-processors pose new and potentially destructive challenges to freedom. But it is too easily presumed that " privacy " is invaded. Even if " privacy " is assigned the meaning most favourable to this view (namely that " privacy " consists in the individual's ability to control the circulation of information about himself)—a definition criticised above—the proposition is unconvincing. It fails to account for other objections raised against data banks (albeit again in the name of " privacy ") such as their security, the storing of " opinion " rather than " fact," and the relevance of the information garnered to the purpose of its storage. It is, moreover, unlikely that most people would consider the activities of, say, credit bureaux, as an invasion of their " privacy," [5] though they may well object to them on the ground that the information they hold is incorrect. [6]

It is too shallow a view to see even in the misuse of personal information held by computers an automatic invasion of " privacy." What is lost is not so much " privacy," as the value of " privacy," [7] and this value would be more effectively vouchsafed by attending to the specific problems generated by the growing use of data banks.

---

[4] See the *Lindop Committee, ibid.*

[5] In its " Survey of Public Attitudes to Privacy," the Younger Committee sought, *inter alia*, to establish how people defined " privacy." Yet this aspect of " privacy " was not put (as one of the possible means of defining the essence of the concept) to the 1,596 interviewed. The closest of the issues to misuse of information was " not telling government " which only 9 per cent. thought constituted an invasion of " privacy," *Younger Committee*, App. III.

[6] The Consumer Credit Act 1974 requires the grantor of credit to supply the consumer on request with the name and address of any credit reference agency which has supplied information about him; on payment of a fee of 25p, the consumer must be issued with a copy of all information about him held by the agency. The Lindop Committee preferred to see the right of subject access as part of the detailed rules rather than as a general principle to be declared in its proposed Data Protection Act. (*Lindop Committee*, paras. 21.10–21.11).

[7] Parker, *op. cit*, points to three respects in which this is the case: first when information about an individual is gathered his " privacy " loses value because one of the important uses made of " privacy " is to control the flow of information about oneself, secondly, such gathering of information reduces the value of " privacy " by making it less secure, thirdly, it devalues one's " privacy " by making one uncertain of whether one still has it. Parker's general proposition that " the collection of data by government and other institutions . . . is not a loss of privacy *per se*, but rather a threat to one's privacy " (285) may not be entirely in accord with the view presented here, but it at least serves to undermine the widely held assumption that such activities *are, per se*, an invasion of privacy.

To raise the cry of " invasion of privacy " obstructs the careful and rational solution these problems require.[8]

## CONCLUSIONS

" Privacy " has grown into a large and unwieldy concept. Synonymous with autonomy, it has colonised traditional liberties, become entangled with confidentiality, secrecy, defamation, property, and the storage of information. It would be unreasonable to expect a notion so complex as " privacy " not to spill into regions with which it is closely related, but this process has resulted in the dilution of " privacy " itself, diminishing the prospect of its own protection as well as the protection of the related interests.

In this attenuated, confused and overworked condition, " privacy " seems beyond redemption. Any attempt to restore it to what it quintessentially is—an interest of the personality—seems doomed to fail for it comes too late. " Privacy " has become as nebulous a concept as " happiness " or " security." Except as a general abstraction of an underlying value, it should not be used as a means to describe a legal right or cause of action.

It is submitted that a more honest, effective and rational course is to approach the subject from the standpoint of the protection of " personal information." The problems of " privacy " are essentially threefold: the first concerns those activities which intrude, physically or electronically, into home or office and are best regulated by legislation of the kind advanced by the Younger Committee [9] without recourse to " privacy." The other two problems really concern " personal information ": publicity given to " personal information " and the use and potential misuse of " personal information " by data banks. These are more readily susceptible to analysis and, where necessary, legal (or even extra-legal) control in the context of protecting " personal information " than by the doctrinal application of " privacy " language and theory.

" Personal information " may be defined as those facts, commu-

---

[8] " (T)he exaggerated and hysterical approach of some commentators has done immense harm. By whipping up fear and suspicion of the computer they have themselves created the evil they have blamed on the machine . . . The clue to a successful approach lies, as it usually does, in drawing distinctions, and in adopting a flexible approach which treats each different problem in the light of its own special difficulties and complexities," C. Tapper, *Computer Law* (1978) 130.

[9] *Younger Committee*, paras. 562–563. Though the Lindop Committee perceived the need to deal with the problems of data protection as problems in their own right, it nevertheless succumbed to the temptation of " privacy " by offering a definition merely because, it would seem, " corresponding terms are used in the data protection statutes which have been enacted in Sweden, France, the U.S.A. and Canada and the term is still current here (indeed the White Paper (Cmnd. 6353, 1975) itself bears the title Computers and Privacy." *Lindop Committee*, para. 21.26.

nications or opinions which relate to the individual and which it would be reasonable to expect him to regard as intimate or confidential and therefore to want to withhold or at least to restrict their circulation. Other definitions may be sought and no attempt will be made here to defend the one proposed which is offered only as the starting point for a new method of analysis. What should be stressed, however, is the objectivity of the test which is central to this approach.[10]

Analysed from this perspective, most of the problems presently cast in a " privacy " mould are more likely to find effective resolution. By locating, as the core of the issue, the regulation of " personal information," the subject is liberated from a tendentiously predetermined general theory,[11] and specific answers may more easily be sought to specific, and frequently disparate, questions. Such progress is possible only if the law eschews the ambiguity, the abstractions and the poverty of " privacy."

RAYMOND WACKS.*

---

[10] *Cf. Lindop Committee*, para. 2.07. Westin, *op. cit.* 322–323, suggests " a new information theory " in which information would be classified to identify what is private and " non-circulating "; what is confidential, with limited circulation; and what is public or freely circulating.

[11] This is the single most persuasive argument for a new approach; the dissenting voice of Brown J. in the leading American decision on " privacy " has not been heard: " One of the most effective ways of diluting or expanding a constitutionally guaranteed right is to substitute for the crucial word or words of a constitutional guarantee another word or words more or less flexible and more or less restricted in meaning . . . ' Privacy ' is a broad, abstract and ambiguous concept which can easily be shrunken in meaning but which can also, on the other hand, easily be interpreted as a constitutional ban against many things . . ." *Griswold* v. *Connecticut, supra*, at 508.

* Senior Lecturer in Law, Oxford Polytechnic.

# [8]

# Harvard Civil Rights-Civil Liberties Law Review

Volume 12, Number 2                                      Spring, 1977

## REDEFINING PRIVACY*

*Tom Gerety***

Before I built a wall I'd ask to know
What I was walling in or walling out. . .
      Robert Frost, "Mending Wall"

Privacy is a legal wall badly in need of mending. It was thrown up in great haste, from a miscellany of legal rock and stone, on two occasions and so in two parts: the first was the great Warren and Brandeis article of 1890 on the right to privacy at common law;[1] the second was the *Griswold* decision[2] in 1965 on the same (or a corresponding)[3] right in constitutional law. Plainly the latter was built upon the former, if of different stones and by different masons — but not altogether different, for the Brandeis dissent in *Olmstead v. United States*,[4] speaking of "the most comprehensive of rights and the right most valued by civilized men,"[5] stands all but midway in time and conception between the two occasions.

---

*I want to thank Thomas I. Emerson for his help with the early drafts of this article and also Trudi Kiebala for her extensive research assistance.

**B.A. 1969, M.Phil. 1974, J.D. and Ph.D. 1976, Yale University. Fellow, Center for the Study of Ethics in the Professions, and Assistant Professor, Chicago-Kent College of Law, Illinois Institute of Technology.

[1] Warren & Brandeis, *The Right to Privacy*, 4 HARV. L. REV. 193 (1890).

[2] Griswold v. Connecticut, 381 U.S. 479 (1965).

[3] In just what sense the tort law right of privacy corresponds to the constitutional right is a question almost entirely neglected in discussions (and decisions) on privacy. Reviewing the federal constitutional usage up to and including *Griswold*, Prosser remarked upon an aspect of this ambiguity: "The Court never has made any attempt to define this right [to privacy guaranteed by the Constitution], or to indicate its limitations, if any; and nothing in the decisions has referred to tort liability. They suggested none the less that the Constitutional right, thus declared to exist, must have some application to tort liability; and that the decisions in four states denying any recognition of the right are to be overruled, as well as the limitation to commercial appropriation contained in the statutes of four other jurisdictions." W. PROSSER, HANDBOOK OF THE LAW OF TORTS 816-17 (1971). Few besides Prosser have even recognized this difficulty. Some have recognized implicitly that *at least as to remedies* there are significant distinctions between constitutional, statutory, and common law rights to privacy. *See, e.g.,* A. WESTIN, PRIVACY AND FREEDOM 384-99 (1967); T. EMERSON, THE SYSTEM OF FREEDOM OF EXPRESSION 547-48 (1970).

[4] 277 U.S. 438 (1928).

[5] *Id.* at 478.

By all accounts the concept of privacy has had an expansive, some would say an invasive,[6] history in American law and, more than law, in the American consciousness, in American culture, and in American institutions. Its very expansiveness, however, gives us reason to pause over the question of its continued usefulness and its ultimate viability in the various settings in which law is made and applied. Some have wondered "whether privacy, however great a value, can function as a constitutional concept: Can, that is, the protection of privacy provide a base from which to reason, a clue for policy?"[7]

The doubt in this regard comes not from the concept's meagerness but from its amplitude, for it has a protean capacity to be all things to all lawyers, and, as often defined and defended, it lacks readily apparent limitations of its own. The very language Brandeis used in *Olmstead* illustrates this nicely:[8] if privacy is indeed the most comprehensive of rights, is it not then too vast and weighty a thing to invoke in specific legal settings for specific and narrowly defined purposes?

A legal concept will do us little good if it expands like a gas to fill up the available space.[9] Take the example of justice: One cannot draw the line where it stops, or starts, in law courts, and with good reason, since such comprehensive and philosophical concepts ought to be everywhere felt but nowhere fixed in our imperfect legal institutions. A properly legal concept must be a principle that translates into a rule;[10] and the rule, in turn, must translate into a set of applications. But no such translations are feasible unless we impose some definite conceptual limits.

Privacy needs a definition; we want a general statement or set of

---

[6] Kalven, *Privacy in Tort Law — Were Warren and Brandeis Wrong?*, 31 LAW & CONTEMP. PROB. 326 (1966).

[7] *Id.* at 327. For a philosopher's doubts in this connection, see Thomson, *The Right to Privacy*, 4 PHIL. & PUB. AFF. 295 (1975): "[P]erhaps the most striking thing about the right to privacy is that nobody seems to have any very clear idea what it is."

[8] *See* p. 233 *supra*.

[9] It may be that any legal rule will grow like a beanstalk unless vigorously pruned. "The seductive plausibility of single steps in a chain of evolutionary development of a legal rule is often not perceived until a third, fourth, or fifth 'logical' extension occurs. Each step, when taken, appeared a reasonable step in relation to that which preceded it, although the aggregate or end result is one that would never have been seriously considered in the first instance. This kind of gestative propensity calls for the 'line drawing' familiar in the judicial, as in the legislative process: 'thus far but not beyond.' " United States v. Twelve 200-Foot Reels, 413 U.S. 123, 127 (1972) (Burger, C.J.).

[10] A legal principle is more abstract than a rule and provides guidance to changes in and expansion of the particular legal rules that apply to particular contexts. *See* Freund, *Privacy: One Concept or Many*, XIII NOMOS 182, 190-92 (1971).

general statements of the contents of an idea.[11] Such a statement ought above all to limit the valid applications of that idea. At its weakest, of course, a limiting definition need be no more than a limited list: the Smith family consists of x, y, and z.[12] But a more powerful definition, of the sort we want for privacy, identifies the necessary and sufficient conditions for any application of the concept defined. Where, and only where, these conditions obtain will the concept apply.[13] No doubt these limiting

---

[11] The chronic philosophical difficulties with definition — chiefly as to the ontological situation of what is defined — need not concern us here. The fact that definition is normative or prescriptive does not make it any the less a definition. The one to be offered here is admittedly a definition of what privacy *ought* to come to in law. But all legal definitions are in this sense normative.

[12] Even this definition is in one sense, as Richard Kraut has reminded me, strong and even too strong: it limits the Smith family to x, y, and z without telling us how to cope with the birth of w. Privacy, too, can be defined in this way to include several disparate rules of legal protection. *See, e.g.,* Beardsley, *Privacy: Autonomy and Selective Disclosure,* XIII NOMOS 56 (1971) (defining "two kinds of *violations* of the norm of privacy" without defining the norm). *See also* Bostwick, *The Taxonomy of Privacy: Repose, Sanctuary, and Intimate Decision,* 64 CAL. L. REV. 1447 (1976); Note, *Roe and Paris: Does Privacy Have a Principle?* 26 STAN. L. REV. 1161 (1974). Operational rules of this sort can explain more or less well the precedents that fall under them. They cannot tell us, though, how to handle other precedents, or more important, other rules. In fact, they cannot tell us why any given operational rules — or intuitions — belong to the concept of privacy. Thus, they are of little or no help in extending or restricting the legal protections of privacy.

A more moderate form of definition by a list is Wittgenstein's now classic concept of "family resemblance." Games, to take his instance, have certain typical characteristics by which we recognize them *as games.* Whether explicit or implicit, these characteristics form a kind of check-list definition — but now one flexible enough to include new members of the conceptual family. *See* L. WITTGENSTEIN, PHILOSOPHICAL INVESTIGATIONS §§ 66-67 (1st ed. 1953). The discursive portions of this article attempt something of the sort for privacy.

[13] In certain instances, we will have to make exception to the sufficiency (but not the necessity) of these conditions: there are always cases where the concept applies prima facie — because the necessary and normally sufficient conditions are met — but not upon further analysis. Legal concepts are notoriously "defeasible" in this sense: they are subject to rules of excuse or exception. *See* Hart, *The Ascription of Responsibility and Rights,* 49 PROC. OF THE ARISTOTELIAN SOC'Y 171, 175 (1948/49). *But see* Pitcher, *Hart on Action and Responsibility,* 69 PHIL. REV. 226 (1960); Feinberg, *Action and Responsibility,* in J. FEINBERG, DOING AND DESERVING 119-51 (1970). Hart argued that legal concepts, because defeasible, were largely indefinable. *See* Hart, *Definition and Theory in Jurisprudence,* 70 L.Q. REV. 37 (1954). But obviously some definition of a prima facie case is indispensable in adjudication. Hart himself acknowledged this in H.L.A. HART, THE CONCEPT OF LAW 13-17 (1961) ("Definition").

Note that Hart's discussion centers upon definition *per genus et differentiam, i.e.,* by giving a general class or kind *plus* a distinguishing attribute within that class. In this sense, the definition of privacy given here may be understood as locating privacy within the *genus* autonomy with the *differentiae* being identity and intimacy. But the distinction is only one of emphasis or approach.

conditions may themselves be concepts in need of further definition. And since we cannot build castles in the air, we will sooner or later have to rest all of our concepts on intuitions. So long as we can validate both our concepts and our intuitions, we need not apologize for building the former on the latter.[14]

Privacy will be defined here as an autonomy or control over the intimacies of personal identity. Autonomy, identity, and intimacy are all necessary (and together normally sufficient) for the proper invocation of the concept of privacy. This definition is frankly normative. Its acceptance or rejection carries with it a set of at least preliminary conclusions about rights and wrongs. The definition draws, moreover, on two purportedly shared intuitions — one normative and the other descriptive: first, that we have some common commitment to the *value* of what is private in our lives; and, second, that we have some common conception of what in our lives in fact *is* private.[15] These intuitions suggest the necessary working hypothesis of definition: that privacy, whatever its sources of derivation and protection, is but *one* concept — and is thus definable.[16] If

---

[14] This is a simple point going back to Kant: concepts without intuitions are, as he put it, empty (and intuitions without concepts, blind). *See* I. KANT, THE CRITIQUE OF PURE REASON §§ A51/B75 (N. Kemp-Smith tr. 1933). At some point a concept simply applies, and we recognize that point not by arguments alone but by arguments aided by intuitions, by felt certainties of one kind or another. "At some point one has to pass from explanation to mere description." L. WITTGENSTEIN, ON CERTAINTY § 189 (1969).

The point at which certainty is felt, it might be argued, is subjective, but *shared* certainties are at least intersubjective: if enough people share them — and act on them — we say we *know* them to be so. The definition of privacy given here rests on the persuasiveness of the arguments for its concepts (and against alternative concepts), on the one hand, and, on the other, in the evocativeness, as it were, of its purportedly "shared" intuitions.

[15] These intuitions are necessary to the argument (and perhaps to any argument) in favor of a general set of rights to privacy, but cannot be *proven* here — or perhaps anywhere. Ordinary language, like ordinary adjudication, is replete with privacy claims which, if often exaggerated, are nonetheless founded on a consensus in these matters. The consensus is no doubt imperfect: our intuitions surely vary; but were there no such consensus, the claims themselves would be senseless.

[16] Following sociological and philosophical usage, as well as ordinary usage, I will assume that there *is* an interesting and valid general concept of privacy in the welter of diverse claims and practices that we speak of as privacy rights. The "proof" of this assumption must remain in the "pudding" of the pages to follow. Some lawyers will bridle at the joint treatment of constitutional and tort matters. The only answer is to ask whether the definition *works* in both areas. If it does not, the fault lies either in this attempt at definition *or* else in the assumption underlying it of one general concept of privacy. Obviously various institutions in various cultures implement this concept of privacy — which often carries great moral authority — in various ways. Sociologists and philosophers have made too little of the different styles of implementation among the different institutions of our own legal culture. *See, e.g.,* Simmel, *Privacy,* in THE INTERNATIONAL

indeed we *can* define privacy, we may hope to effect a sufficient retrenchment in its applications — particularly in constitutional settings —
to argue once again for its legal viability and even necessity.

## I. DEFINITION AND INTUITION

Until very recently, discussions of privacy did not often indulge in
the typically humbling and menial task of definition.[17] Warren and Brandeis made only the most discursive gestures in the direction of a definition of the relatively narrow interests to which they proposed to attach
limited legal rights and remedies.[18] Their casual neglect of definition,
coupled with their enormous success in persuasion, led to a situation in
which the moral basis for the right to privacy seemed everywhere to
exceed its legal basis — which was then, as now, quite narrow. Perhaps
they confused the two bases from the start. If so, it was a confusion not
easily dispelled in the midst of a campaign of advocacy,[19] for the Warren

---

ENCYCLOPEDIA OF THE SOCIAL SCIENCES 480-87 (D. Sills, ed. 1968). But we want to
bridge here both the legal-institutional and the conceptual-definitional embarassments
of privacy rights. A better general definition of the concept of privacy makes for
better specific judgments of the rights to privacy — who has them and when and how and
why. All along an attempt is made to keep in mind the varying institutional constraints on
the implementation of a general right to privacy.

[17] For a canvass of the recent definitions see note 106 *infra*. The older discussions,
prior to that of Sir James Fitzjames Stephen, *see* p. 238 *infra*, were placed in terms of
the conflict between the private and the public realms felt so deeply by the post-classical
Greeks and Romans. To the earlier Greeks, what was private was often suspect as limited,
peculiar, or inferior: the private person was the *idiotes* who takes no part in public life — or
sanity. By the time of Cicero it was a matter of dispute whether the public life was superior
to the private. Nonetheless, the confident affirmation of privacy as a value — or at least as
the condition of other values — seems a distinctly modern phenomenon, dating perhaps
from as late as the Enlightenment and the Romantic movement. *See* H. ARENDT, THE
HUMAN CONDITION 23-73 (1958).

[18] Warren and Brandeis said that their guiding principle was the protection of the right
to "an inviolate personality." Warren & Brandeis, *supra* note 1, at 205. But they discussed
only cases of a newspaper's mass disclosure of "private" facts. *See* pp. 266-96 *infra*.
Surely the right of "inviolate personality" must protect us from more than this. In fact, we
(and they) would be hard put to say what legal protections it does not include. To be sure,
they do discuss, *id.* at 214-20, "what are the limitations of this right to privacy, and what
remedies may be granted for the enforcement of the right." However, they set out their
"limitations" as exceptions to their rule rather than as boundaries to it — or as conditions to
its valid application. And so they fail to define it.

[19] An analogous confusion still persists on the constitutional border between privacy
and a free press. *See* Note, *The Right of Privacy: Normative-Descriptive Confusion in the
Defense of Newsworthiness*, 30 U. CHI. L. REV. 722 (1963) [hereinafter cited as *Defense
of Newsworthiness*].

and Brandeis article, almost of its own force, launched such a campaign as continues even now.[20]

As the debate has moved, however, from tort law to the Constitution, the convenience of confusing the two bases has less and less outweighed the vulnerability to analytic attack to which it subjects privacy rights generally. It is one thing to say that we should defend privacy here, there, and perhaps everywhere. It is another to admit that privacy, legally defensible privacy, cannot be absolutely ubiquitous.[21] Our laws can never enforce *all* of our values to their logical limits. Any balanced advocacy must take into account both the felt moral urgency of the right and the legal and conceptual economies necessary to its enforcement, and must respect conflicting rights of equal moral urgency.

Will the *definition* of privacy really help us to achieve such a balance? There is good reason to doubt it. Sir James Fitzjames Stephen, who, two decades before Warren and Brandeis, was the first modern lawyer or philosopher to discuss the concept explicitly, remarked that "to define the province of privacy distinctly is impossible."[22] Impossible, that is, because we cannot escape from the bias of our own times and places, our own historical situations. Privacy is largely a matter of shared expectations and sensibilities, Stephen seems to have thought: it is too concrete, too close to experience and history, to give way to precise and abstract analysis.

Nevertheless, Stephen conceded that privacy, if beyond definition, was not beyond description "in general terms."[23] He had in mind, one suspects, some middle ground between abstract (and ahistorical)

---

[20] Harry H. Wellington summarizes the classic law review article as "an attempt to fashion a legal principle from changes in moral perception." *See* Wellington, *Common Law Rules and Constitutional Double Standards: Some Notes on Adjudication,* 83 YALE L.J. 221, 249-51 (1973). Wellington remarks, *id.* at 251, that "apart from pace, that article does model better than anything in the literature the emergence of a common law principle." Similarly, Ronald Dworkin noted that the Warren and Brandeis essay "is a paradigm of argument in the constructive model." Dworkin, *The Original Position,* 40 U. CHI. L. REV. 500, 511 n.6 (1973).

[21] Warren and Brandeis never said that privacy was *legally* ubiquitous. The problem was an overpowering moral ubiquity that neither of the two — witness Brandeis' rhetoric in his dissent in Olmstead v. United States, 277 U.S. 438, 471 (1925) (Brandeis, J., dissenting) — questioned at all rigorously: a right of "inviolate personality" would seem to require a thousand-and-one remedies each as urgent as the next.

[22] J.F. STEPHEN, LIBERTY, EQUALITY, FRATERNITY 160 (1967; 1st ed. 1873). Stephen wrote to answer the younger Mill, whose ON LIBERTY argued for an expansive and overriding "right" of personal autonomy that surely included and implied a right to privacy — under almost any definition or description. *See* J.S. MILL, ON LIBERTY (1st ed. 1859).

[23] *Id.*

philosophical definitions and concrete (all-too-historical) legal applications. Inhabiting the middle ground are the "principles of law" that, as Paul Freund and others have noted,[24] mediate between the legal rules of decision for any case and the political concepts — of liberty, fairness, and so on — undergirding the legal system as a whole. In our reflections on any right, this middle ground, while not the highest, is perhaps the most advantageous. It alone promises to bring together perspectives upon both the normative and descriptive contents of a right such as privacy. While never so ultimate in its pretenses as a more abstract and general definition, nor so determinate in its effects as the simple rule of past applications and precedents, the middle ground of principles may well command both. For with time, definitions must yield to realities just as precedents must yield to ideals. Yet this leaves unresolved the question of how to occupy this middle conceptual ground between pure law and pure philosophy.

Perhaps the simplest strategy is that of "strictly" interpreting a given text. With any textually based right, a form of literalism seems to provide an easy and sure criterion for the application of a rule — so long, that is, as ambiguities in the text itself are averted or disguised. But privacy has no textual basis in the Constitution[25] or even in the landmark

---

[24] Freund, *supra* note 10, at 193-98. *See also* Dworkin, *Judicial Discretion*, 60 J. PHIL. 624, 634-35 (1963); Dworkin, *The Model of Rules*, 35 U. CHI. L. REV. 14, 22-23 (1967); Dworkin, *Social Rules and Legal Theory*, 81 YALE L.J. 855 (1972).

[25] Its implicit textual basis, on the other hand, is arguably quite significant, albeit unsettled and obscure. The fourth amendment (and also the third) confers special protections on "persons, houses, papers, and effects" that only a right to privacy seems adequately to explain. *See* Katz v. United States, 389 U.S. 347, 360-62 (1967) (Harlan, J., concurring). *See also* Beaney, *The Constitutional Right to Privacy in the Supreme Court*, 1962 SUP. CT. REV. 212. More tenuously, the fifth amendment, while perhaps more easily understood as bottomed on other policies and principles, affords the protection of fundamental right to what we may call the privacy of incriminating self-knowledge. *See* Griswold, *The Right to be Let Alone*, 55 N.W.U.L. REV. 216 (1960). A similar (and similarly tenuous) argument has been made as to the first amendment. *See* Note, *Privacy in the First Amendment*, 82 YALE L.J. 1402 (1973). No doubt the most important constitutional support for privacy rights is not to be found implicit in any textual provision, but rather is derived from general constitutional theory. The ninth amendment was often cited in the *Griswold* litigation and indeed was the basis of Justice Goldberg's concurrence joined by Justice Brennan and Chief Justice Warren. 381 U.S. at 486 (Goldberg, J., concurring). *See* Redlich, *Are There "Certain Rights . . . Retained by the People"?*, 37 N.Y.U.L. REV. 787 (1972). But as Redlich conceded, "the textual standard should be the entire Constitution," *id.* at 810, and thus the basis of the ninth amendment argument is not so much "textual" as "structural" or "relational." *See* C. BLACK, STRUCTURE AND RELATIONSHIP IN CONSTITUTIONAL LAW (1965). And, at this level of argument, the due process clause of the fourteenth amendment may provide the surest constitutional basis for the right

common law precedents studied by Warren and Brandeis.[26] Moreover,
even if it *did* have an explicit textual basis,[27] it would not have even the
much controverted precision of reference that leads some of our Justices
some of the time to take all such phrases to "mean what they say," and
so to bar any and all official abridgment of the right in question.[28]

---

to privacy. The Douglas opinion in *Griswold* seemed to shy away from the due process
clause, however, fearing a revival of that most terrifying of all constitutional hobgoblins:
Lochner v. New York, 198 U.S. 45 (1904), *cited in* Griswold v. Connecticut, 381 U.S.
479, 482 (1965). Fear of an overly discretionary "substantive due process" seems to have
forced Douglas, in his *Griswold* opinion, to recur to the notorious notion of "penumbras"
of "specific guarantees in the Bill of Rights . . . formed by emanations from those guarantees that help give them life and substance." 381 U.S. at 484. Privacy was thus made a
penumbral — or half-shadowed — right in constitutional law. Justice Harlan argued against
this obscure and cautious interpretation of the due process clause: "In my view, the proper
constitutional inquiry in this case is whether the Connecticut statute infringes the Due
Process Clause of the Fourteenth Amendment because the enactment violates basic values
'implicit in the concept of ordered liberty. . . . I believe that it does. While the relevant
inquiry may be aided by resort to one or more of the provisions of the Bill of Rights, it is not
dependent on them or any of their radiations. The Due Process Clause of the Fourteenth
Amendment stands, in my opinion, on its own bottom." 381 U.S. at 500 (Harlan, J.,
concurring). More recent privacy cases have not settled this question of constitutional
derivation. *See, e.g.,* Paul v. Davis, 424 U.S. 693, 712-14 (1976); Roe v. Wade, 410 U.S.
113, 152-55 (1973). *See also* Henkin, *Privacy and Autonomy,* 74 COLUM. L. REV. 1410
(1974).

[26] I mean, of course, the common law precedents that *preceded* Warren and Brandeis'
identification of a distinct and independent right to damages in tort for the invasion of
privacy. *See* Warren & Brandeis, *supra* note 1. The early cases were decided under the law
of defamation, trespass, or implied contract. Perhaps the most celebrated of these cases is
Prince Albert v. Strange, 1 Mac. & G. 25, 41 Eng. Rep. 1171 (1849), *aff'd* 2 De G. &
Sm. 652, 64 Eng. Rep. 293 (1849). In that case Strange had exhibited private etchings and
published a catalogue of them. But since the etchings came from the hand of a member of
the royal family, the court showed extraordinary solicitude for the as yet unarticulated right
to privacy and enjoined further publication or exhibition of them.

[27] If, for instance, the first amendment read "the privacy of the individual" where it
now reads "the freedom of the press."

[28] Consider Justice Black's fairly consistent position in first amendment cases. *See,
e.g.,* New York Times Co. v. Sullivan, 376 U.S. 254, 293 (1964) (Black, J., concurring);
Black, *The Bill of Rights,* 35 N.Y.U.L. REV. 865 (1960). He drew the lessons of this
position for privacy rights in his *Griswold* dissent. "The Court talks about a constitutional
'right of privacy' as though there is some constitutional provision or provisions forbidding
any law ever to be passed which might abridge the 'privacy' of individuals. But there is not
. . . . I like my privacy as well as the next one, but I am nevertheless compelled to admit
that the government has a right to invade it unless prohibited by some specific constitutional
provision . . . ." Griswold v. Connecticut, 381 U.S. 479, 508-10 (Black, J., dissenting).
This Article follows another line of interpretation. The intellectual and practical embar-
rassments of "strict construction," even of the first amendment or the contract clause, are
now more or less notorious. The problem is that most legal and constitutional concepts are

Of privacy, much more than of freedom of the press, one must ask to what exactly it refers. Privacy lacks both precise historical antecedents and precise conceptual limits. Stephen himself acknowledged that the concept was vague, perhaps too vague for definition or description.[29] He saw, however, another alternative, for he took privacy to be a concept of sufficient moral urgency and, what is more, of sufficient moral *plainness* for lawyers, judges, and legislators to give it legal force within relatively precise limits. "Legislation and public opinion," he wrote, "ought in all cases whatever scrupulously to respect privacy."[30] But how can privacy be respected if it remains undefined?

Stephen's answer was intuition,[31] a venerable, if controversial, alternative in both law and philosophy to literalism[32] on one side or rationalism[33] on the other. The difficulty here is that, in the application of a general law or principle to a specific set of facts, intuitionism has neither the texts of literalism nor the arguments of rationalism to defend

---

subject to widely divergent interpretations *despite* explicit textual declarations. Nonetheless the temptation of "strict construction" remains always powerful in its illusion of simplicity and directness. *See* Grey, *Do We Have An Unwritten Constitution?*, 29 STAN L. REV. 703 (1975).

[29] *See* STEPHEN, *supra* note 22, at 162. ("[T]here is a sphere, none the less real because it is impossible to define its limits. . .")

[30] *Id.* at 160.

[31] Intuition is my word, not Stephen's. Stephen has neither a text, referring to some concept, nor even a concept alone, somehow interpreted or defined. Stephen nonetheless identified privacy with decency and decency with itself, as felt and as evinced in the English language of his time. Of course the intuition embodies, for Stephen, shared values which are "definite enough" in any "given age and nation." STEPHEN, *supra* note 22, at 150. Intuitionism must validate its results by prompting people to say, "Yes, I feel the same way — that *is* privacy." One appeals from one's own intuitions to another's (just as, in rationalism, from one's own reasons to another's). It is thus indispensable that others agree — that intuitions be shared in fact and acknowledged as such.

[32] Literalism is simply the strict construction of a text *without more* — without any appeal to shared intuitions or shared principles (giving rise to cogent rational argument) from without.

[33] Rationalism, for our purposes, may be said to involve only the appeal to independent rational arguments about independent rational principles. In contrast to literalism, the principles of rationalism may come from outside a text. Indeed, even when we lack any text we may appeal to principles either generally agreed upon or else plainly needed to make sense of other lesser principles that we agree upon or even intuitions that we share. In this sense rationalism is not an independent strategy or an exclusive alternative. To get our reasoning going we must end with intuitions of some sort. And so too, a test will often be the beginning of reasoned arguments about its interpretation and application. One celebrated instance of the rationalist turn in applied jurisprudence is the widespread but ambiguous insistence on the "reasoned elaboration of neutral principles of constitutional law." *See* Wechsler, *Toward Neutral Principles of Constitutional Law*, 73 HARV. L. REV. 1 (1959).

its exercise of judgment against charges of arbitrariness and caprice. It will be conceded that intuition spans the gap between the general and the specific as quickly and as efficiently as the other methods.[34] But unlike them it is a magic box, a machine whose working parts are hidden and silent. What is to prevent its operator from slipping in, like a magician, his purely personal scarves and rabbits of conviction, and then pulling them out again as applications of principle? This question adds only a metaphor to the celebrated dissents of Justice Black from what he regarded as judicial intuitionism.[35] But Stephen had an answer to the charges of imprecision and idiosyncracy.

Intuition need not be a purely personal and variable affair; on some questions it may yield a consensus within definite limits. Our intuitions, after all, respond to shared values and shared conditions of life.Thus in his own translation of the concept of privacy from the sphere of moral to that of legal rights Stephen propounded "a practical test which is almost perfect upon the subject."[36] He found the needed standard in an unpretentious bit of ordinary English usage: "Conduct which can be described as indecent is always in one way or another a violation of privacy."[37]

Of course Stephen's precise rule for the guidance of our intuitions will hardly suffice now, after a century and more of concern — and reason for concern — with the right to privacy. For all its quaintness and

---

[34] Intuition, like the other methods, allocates roles in the processes of legislative and judicial decision-making. Thus, general intuitions about privacy arrived at by particular judges or particular juries will control their decisions as to whether specific facts proven in court show a wrongful intrusion upon a particular someone's privacy. Should the legislature effectively define its concept of privacy in advance and in more applicable detail, the judges and juries will presumably have that much less power of discretion in making their decisions. Notice, however, that both definition *and* intuition come into play at different levels: a legislature may say "Follow your own intuitions about privacy," *cf.* MASS. GEN. LAWS ANN. ch. 214, § iB (1974) ("A person shall have a right against unreasonable, substantial, or serious interference with his privacy.") or, what is different, "To find privacy, follow your own intuitions about *decency*." So with definition: a legislature may say, for instance, that due process is that process which is due in any given situation. Such a circular definition is perhaps no definition at all, but it *does* serve to leave the decision to a judge or jury — while reasserting, somehow, the fundamental values at issue. Whatever the strategy, legal principles are likely to remain more general, at least, than the particular applications of them required to adjudicate a given case. And there will always be details of fact and value presented in a case but unforeseen when the purportedly governing principle was declared binding. For this reason, intuition may be an indispensable aid in the judicial process of deriving specific rules from general principles.

[35] *See, e.g.,* Adamson v. California, 332 U.S. 46, 90-92 (1947) (Black, J., dissenting).

[36] STEPHEN, *supra* note 22, at 160.

[37] *Id.*

curiosity, however, his rule tells us something we may miss at first. A rule from ordinary usage has two distinct advantages that we have more often sought than found in later definitions of privacy: it is clear and it is relevant to a given state of society, culture, and law. Without the literalist's text, remember, the rationalist's definition provides the only alternative to the intuitionist's rule of thumb.

Stephen's rule is, moreover, just that: a rule of thumb, a rule ready for application in everyday decisions without recourse to elaborate scruple and argument. This means that in courts of law either judges or juries may easily apply it to evidence brought and argued before them.[38] It has the simplicity required of all such ready standards of judgment by ordinary or "reasonable" people. With simplicity, however, goes inscrutability: those called upon to apply the standard do so, by definition, on the basis of their own intuitions and convictions. These may be confined, both by instructions and by review on appeal, within certain limits of reasonableness that judges will impose. But the particular intuitions and convictions at work in the particular judgment as to the particular facts need not be buttressed with reasons — and in a jury verdict they never are. There is thus a heightened possibility of caprice, of inconsistency, of "irrationality."

A rule like Stepnen's answers to the felt needs of most of those it protects and restrains. To make privacy coterminous with decency is after all to make it definite, concrete, and identifiable — so long, that is, as we share a more or less generalized and stabilized intuition of decency; but of course we do not.

There is more than quaintness, indeed there is almost poignancy, in this failing of Stephen's rule to yield certain results from our own changed sensibilities and judgments. Such a rule can only work where the moral quality in question is as certain as, say, the color red. However it may in fact have been with the Victorian sense of decency, it is not so with our own. Somewhere along the way we seem to have lost all the once generally available certainty for moral — and hence legal — intuition. And thus the quandary of definition arises.

While our intuitions have lagged our definitions have not gained by much. At present there is no widely accepted general rule for the iden-

---

[38] "Ideally, a definition of privacy should meet the following . . . criteria. First, it should fit the data. Data, for purposes of this article, means our shared intuitions when privacy is or is not gained or lost. . . . [Another] criterion . . . is applicability by lawyers and courts . . . in instructions to jurors, in complaints, and in court opinions. . . ." Parker, *A Definition of Privacy*, 27 RUT. L. REV. 275, 276-77 (1974).

244    Harvard Civil Rights-Civil Liberties Law Review    [Vol. 12

tification of justiciable privacy rights.[39] In this sense Stephen is much closer to us than we might imagine.

We have only recently caught up with him in our intuitions or judgments of the *value* of privacy in our lives. Now, more than a decade after the *Griswold* decision, the moral urgency and even the legal viability of *some* such right is no longer in much doubt. The problem with the right to privacy is not its uncertainty or invalidity generally but its lack of a specific identity in the foreground of legal rights and remedies, particularly under the Constitution. We now know full well that we have a right to privacy in some such broad sense as Justice Brandeis argued in his *Olmstead* dissent, but what that right comes to in conflict with other rights and interests we cannot easily say — any better than the Supreme Court itself.

What else is this, then, but Stephen's dilemma? We share a common intuition of right but are without any adequate and agreed upon definition or delineation of it. We have no way to know it when we see it.[40] And in this posture, as recent decisions have demonstrated,[41] the right to privacy is inevitably infirm. Thus Stephen's attempt to devise a litmus test for privacy rights teaches us something even as it fails. He recognized that what we need is not so much a philosophical definition as a legal one — answering at one and the same time to the imperatives of moral intuition and legal application. In such a definition we want essentially what he wanted from his rule: a yardstick as accurate as we can make it to tell what is legally private — that is, protectible as a legal right with remedies and sanctions — from what is and must be left legally public — that is, beyond such protections.

---

[39] Let me emphasize the phrase "general rule." There are, of course, specific rulings in constitutional and common law upholding a right to privacy in particular situations, notably the home, *see, e.g.,* Stanley v. Georgia, 394 U.S. 557, 564-66 (1969); Walker v. Whittle, 83 Ga. App. 445, 64 S.E.2d 87 (1951); the "bedroom," *see, e.g.,* Griswold v. Connecticut, 381 U.S. 479 (1965); the body, *see, e.g.,* Rochin v. California, 342 U.S. 165 (1952); York v. Story, 324 F.2d 450 (9th Cir. 1963), *cert. denied,* 376 U.S. 939 (1964).

[40] *Cf.* Justice Stewart's "I-know-it-when-I-see-it" rule for hard-core pornography in Jacobellis v. Ohio, 378 U.S. 184, 197 (1964) (Stewart, J., concurring). This sort of literal *intuitio* falls far short of Stephen's, however, for it seems to base judgment on sight alone whereas Stephen's rule of decency bases judgment on a complex of perceptions and of descriptions of these in ordinary language. One need not follow Wittgenstein or 20th century analytic philosophy to recognize the relatively more stable and accountable nature of a linguistic convention. We may argue endlessly about what counts as indecent, citing evidence of usage from this or that group or region, but, if you know obscenity when you *see* it, and you *say* you see it, I have no way at all to gainsay your judgment.

[41] *See, e.g.,* Doe v. Commonwealth's Att'y, 403 F. Supp. 1199 (E.D. Va. 1975), *aff'd mem.,* 425 U.S. 901 (1976). *See also* pp. 278-81 *infra.*

The "truth" of such a definition is to be found in the uses it has. For our purposes, privacy is not a metaphysical entity but an ethical and legal boundary that we prescribe for others and ourselves. In defining it we define, as Stephen suggested, a province. Within the bounds of that province other values and activities may or may not thrive in the lives of different individuals. But privacy is the necessary, limiting condition of much or all that we value in our intimate lives. It may well be that as an ethical and philosophical matter, privacy derives rather than creates its own significance. Its value is then a derivative of the value we attach to the *possibility* of the conditions and activities it protects.[42]

This is why privacy occupies a middle ground between ultimate background rights and immediate foreground remedies.[43] Like the rights to due process or a fair trial, the right to privacy requires both institutional delineation and conceptual definition. In a society like our own, intuitions by themselves are simply too inconsistent to provide an adequate basis for delineation. We must have recourse to defining concepts such as intimacy, identity, and autonomy, concepts that, despite abstractness, may be formulated into rules for application to such findings and judgments as courts must come to in adjudicating claimed violations of privacy rights. These concepts, too, will be in a sense derivative, for like privacy itself they bear an important relation to less derivative, but also less readily applicable, concepts such as liberty.

There will still be an irreducible looseness in the application of such middle ground concepts as these. No concept, legal or not, is self-executory. Arguments may go this way or that on questions of intimacy or identity — and so on a question of privacy — in particular situations of fact. To that extent we will not have escaped Stephen's rule of intuition: there are perhaps many privacy cases where some appeal to common standards of decency (or conversely, indecency) will have to be made. It is probably true, moreover, that the necessary community of intuitions is not so much lost as diminished, whether in force or scope. But at the

---

[42] If we care about our privacy chiefly or only because of what we do — or can or might do — within it, we may still care about it mightily all the same. One may say as much of any of the "negative" liberties: freedom of speech, for example, allows us to say what we like or to say nothing at all. *See generally* I. BERLIN, TWO CONCEPTS OF LIBERTY (1963). Charles Fried has argued that privacy is derivative in this sense, but is nonetheless indispensable. Fried, *Privacy*, 77 YALE L.J. 475 (1968). *But see* Reiman, *Privacy, Intimacy, and Personhood*, 6 PHIL. & PUB. AFF. 26 (1976). Davis argues, on the other hand, that privacy is unnecessary in law, particularly tort law, given the law of trespass, defamation, and perhaps mental injury. Davis, *What Do We Mean By "Right to Privacy"?*, 4 S.D. L. REV. 1, 18-20 (1957). *See also* Thomson, *supra* note 7.

[43] *See* pp. 238-39 *supra*.

same time much of the reach and force of the right to privacy will, with adequate conceptualization, come plain. Given an adequate definition and even such constitutional precedents as we now have, one need not appeal to shared intuitions of decency — at least not much — to argue for the right to privacy in most personal choices about sexuality and procreation.[44] Consistency with principle and precedent will take us much of the way. Then again publications of intimate matters of fact may force some such recourse: to intuitions, to expectations, to judgments in the broadest sense. Without conceptual delineation, however, even these will prove uncertain and unpredictable in ways that Stephen cannot have foreseen.

## II. THE VARIEGATE TORT

Nowhere is the lesson about the need for definition plainer than in the development of the tort law of invasion of privacy. Many of the tort cases, however we read them, simply cannot be explained by one concept of privacy. They present us, rather, with at least three divergent principles of tort recovery, only one of which is truly privacy. The other two are extensions of and improvements on the sometimes inadequate common law remedies available in suits for misappropriation, defamation, and fraud where the injury was to some feature of one's specifically public — as opposed to private — identity. An analytic survey of this case law will provide us with the basic conceptual tools and materials for working out our definition of privacy.[45] Not the least useful of these tools is the simple logical device of invoking a concept only where we have need and reason to do so.[46]

---

[44] In part this is because, like Warren and Brandeis, we are not arguing in a vacuum. And even more than they, we have in constitutional law explicit precedents in the application of the concept of privacy. *See, e.g.,* Roe v. Wade, 410 U.S. 113 (1973); Griswold v. Connecticut, 381 U.S. 479 (1965). From these we can draw analogies, of course, but more than analogize we can generalize — or argue for generalization.

[45] What we most need, of course, is a definition of privacy suitable for constitutional argument and adjudication. But use of the concept of privacy in tort law has been much less constrained — almost profligate, in fact. This means that case law in torts gives us a much broader field of trial-and-error applications of the concept itself. As a preliminary study, then, privacy in tort law is much more instructive — negatively *and* positively — than privacy under the Constitution.

[46] This is, of course, a weak statement of Ockham's razor: the maxim that the concepts introduced to explain something ought never to be multiplied beyond what is absolutely necessary. In law, at least, we would probably do best never to try for quite so close an intellectual shave — since given the rough texture of available legal principles we would probably take away as much skin as beard. But we do want to maintain some fairly sharp

Some three quarters of a century after Warren and Brandeis wrote, William Prosser made two gargantuan efforts of scholarship in categorizing first 300 and later 400 "privacy" decisions harking back more or less self-consciously to the right advocated by Warren and Brandeis.[47] In the interlude, the tort right itself had spilled up and over the sides of the cup in which it was originally offered. Prosser found himself beset with issues of several sorts "which are tied together by the common name, but otherwise have almost nothing in common except that each represents an interference with the right of the plaintiff, in the phrase coined by Judge Cooley, 'to be let alone.'"[48] To bring order to this "haystack in a hurricane,"[49] Prosser organized the decisions under four headings "without any attempt to exact definition."[50] These in turn have exerted a great and moderating influence on the ensuing case law.[51] For that reason, and because they open to view the vast field that any definition ought to bound and mark, Prosser's headings bear some analysis.

There are four of them: 1) intrusion upon the plaintiff's seclusion or solitude, or into his private affairs; 2) public disclosure of embarrassing private facts about the plaintiff; 3) publicity which places the plaintiff in a false light in the public eye; and 4) appropriation, for the defendant's advantage, of the plaintiff's name or likeness. In the exercise of a quiet discretion, Prosser first organized and analyzed the four torts in a descending order of what, to beg the question, I will call privateness. Since I have in mind a process of elimination of two of these in the reverse ascending order, I will begin with the last of them.

## A. Appropriation

While not much advocated by Warren and Brandeis, the tort of appropriation of identity was the favorite of all in privacy's early suc-

---

distinctions. If we give them up altogether our legal concepts will perform no useful functions at all: they will all apply everywhere — and nowhere. The point is to achieve, if not the luxuriously austere logical parsimony of a philosopher, at least the logical economy of a lawyer.

[47] Prosser, *Privacy*, 48 CAL. L. REV. 383 (1960) [hereinafter cited as Prosser, *Privacy*]; W. PROSSER, HANDBOOK OF THE LAW OF TORTS § 117 (Privacy) (4th ed. 1971) [hereinafter cited as PROSSER, TORTS].

[48] PROSSER, TORTS, *supra* note 47, at 804. Judge Cooley's phrase, from his T. COOLEY, TORTS 29 (2d ed. 1888), was the one taken up by Warren and Brandeis as a kind of summary definition. Warren & Brandeis, *supra* note 1, at 193, 195.

[49] Ettore v. Philco Tel. Broadcasting Corp., 229 F.2d 481, 485 (3d Cir. 1956) (Biggs, J.).

[50] Prosser, *Privacy*, *supra* note 47, at 389.

[51] This influence is also evident in the RESTATEMENT (SECOND) OF TORTS (Tent. Draft 22, May 19, 1976), which adopted Prosser's categories.

cesses in litigation. The first noted privacy decision was handed down by the Court of Appeals of New York in a suit brought by an Abigail Roberson whose likeness, much against her will, adorned advertising for a certain "Flour of the Family" packaged and distributed by the Rochester Folding Box Company.[52] Relying, somewhat vaguely, on the Warren and Brandeis right, Roberson nonetheless lost in a close (4 to 3) and controverted[53] decision; the court found no precedent that granted relief without a showing of a specific property right in the plaintiff or a breach of trust by the defendant. The failure to find an adequate property right upon which to grant relief was then, as now, dubious.[54] Of course it was not *her* portrait in the sense that she owned the paper, lines, and colors that made it up; but it was hers in the only important sense, in context, that it was at once *of* her and *of commercial value* to Rochester Folding Box. In this light, the question was whether she lent them the service of her likeness for some consideration. The Court of Appeals held that she was entitled to no recovery. The New York legislature disagreed, however, and the following year enacted the first "privacy" statute criminalizing, if only mildly, the wrong done to Abigail Roberson.[55]

Was it a wrong to anything we want to call privacy? We do well to exercise some caution here. The first of the many cases to permit recovery on this basis was *Pavesich v. New England Life Insurance Co.*[56] Pavesich succeeded upon facts showing not only the use of his picture in an advertising campaign, but also, unlike Roberson, explicit falsifica-

---

[52] Roberson v. Rochester Folding Box Co., 171 N.Y. 538, 64 N.E. 442 (1902).

[53] *See* PROSSER, TORTS, *supra* note 47, at 803.

[54] *See, e.g.,* Cepeda v. Swift & Co., 415 F.2d 1205, 1206 (8th Cir. 1969) (baseball player held to have a property right to name and likeness); Price v. Hal Roach Studios, Inc., 400 F. Supp. 836 (S.D.N.Y. 1975) (there is a property right in one's name and likeness). *But see* Eick v. Perk Dog Food Co., 347 Ill. App. 293, 106 N.E.2d 742 (1952) (no recovery on property theory, but recovery allowed for mental distress). The *Roberson* result may in part be attributable to the plaintiff's narrowly gauged pleadings. Some commentators at the time thought Roberson should have stressed more fully the property theory. *See* the source cited in Davis, *supra* note 42, at 4. *See also* D. PECK, DECISION AT LAW 70-96 (1961).

[55] 1903 N.Y. Laws ch. 132 §§ 1, 2 (presently N.Y. CIV. RIGHTS LAW §§ 50-51 (McKinney 1948)). *But see* Galella v. Onassis, 353 F. Supp. 196 (S.D.N.Y. 1972), *aff'd and modified on other grounds,* 487 F.2d 986 (2d Cir. 1973), for a discussion indicating that *Roberson* would not be followed today, the court finding a common law right to privacy beyond the statute. *See generally* S. HOFSTADTER, THE DEVELOPMENT OF THE RIGHT TO PRIVACY IN NEW YORK (1954). The New York statute is limited to unconsented appropriations "for advertising purposes or purposes of trade." The statute, headed "Right to Privacy," makes no mention in its text of the word privacy or its cognates.

[56] 122 Ga. 190, 50 S.E. 68 (1905).

tion. Pavesich's picture was shown with a purely fabricated statement attributed to him in behalf of the defendant insurance corporation.

However, in the bulk of the cases since *Pavesich*, plaintiffs have shown both falsification of testimony and identification by name or likeness.[57] This persistent conjunction in the complaints suggests that the defendants typically seek to portray their products as preferred by the plaintiffs. The tort, then, seems to be another's commercial exploitation of one's identity without one's consent — and, presumably, one's compensation. This suggests, to quote Prosser, that

> the interest protected truly is a proprietary one in the exclusive use of the plaintiff's name and likeness as an aspect of his identity. It seems quite pointless to dispute over whether such a right is to be classified as property. If it is not, it is at least, once it is protected by law, a right of value upon which the plaintiff can capitalize by selling licenses.[58]

If this is so, the privacy analysis in these cases begins to look like an overlay, a gild, because a simpler "property" analysis fully explains the cases.

Still there remains an important objection to this conceptual severance of some of the "privacy" torts into a category closer to copyright or trade infringement. Edward Bloustein, who has fought long and hard for

---

[57] *See* PROSSER, TORTS, *supra* note 47, at 805 n.24 (name) and nn.25-26 (likeness); *see also id.* at 805 nn.27-29.

[58] Prosser, *Privacy, supra* note 47, at 406. *Cf.* PROSSER, TORTS, *supra* note 47 at 805. Judge Jerome Frank, in a 1953 opinion, went so far as to recognize a new right in this form of property that he called "the right of publicity." Haelan Laboratories, Inc. v. Topps Chewing Gum, Inc., 202 F. 2d 866, 868 (2d Cir. 1953), *reversing* Bowman Gum Inc. v. Topps Chewing Gum, Inc., 103 F. Supp. 944 (E.D.N.Y. 1952), *cert. denied*, 346 U.S. 816 (1953). Melville Nimmer made much of the distinction between this exclusive license to publicize or commercialize one's identity — operative only in the context of a market demand — and the right to privacy. *See* Nimmer, *The Right of Publicity*, 19 LAW & CONTEMP. PROB. 203 (1954). As opposed to privacy, publicity would be an assignable property right and not a personal right. An action for its appropriation would recover the value appropriated but not compensate for injury to the plaintiff's sensibilities. Moreover, any waiver or consent to commercial publicity must be far more explicit and precise than for general publicity or news. Despite all of this, however, Judge Frank's opinion and Nimmer's article seem to have languished somewhat of late, and perhaps for good reasons of conceptual economy: the right is easily vindicated under the more traditional notion of an exclusive license, if here in a more or less untraditional property, one's identity.

a unified concept of privacy,[59] has argued that we should not so lightly assimilate our interests in our identities to our interests in other intangible properties over which we exercise exclusive control. We would thus wrongly assume that our interest in identity is proprietary simply because courts in fact have permitted recovery for the use of a name or likeness for trade purposes. "Such a conclusion is mistaken," he writes,

> because in the first place . . . the name or likeness which is used in most instances has no true commercial value, or it has a value which is only nominal and hardly worth the lawsuit. . . .
>
> In the second place, the conclusion that the plaintiff seeks to vindicate a proprietary right in these cases overlooks the true role of the allegation that the plaintiff's name or picture was used commercially. The reason that the commercial use of a personal photograph is actionable . . . is that it is the very commercialization of a name or photograph which does injury to the sense of personal dignity.[60]

Now the first argument simply misjudges the relevant economic facts. The very use of a name or likeness for advertising purposes proves its market value. For reasons that need no explanation, advertisers look with eagerness to the ersatz authenticity of testimony from representatives of the uncelebrated masses of consumers. On a showing that the person in question consented to nothing of the kind, courts have allowed damages. Why?

A blanket privacy rationale will not settle such doubts as skeptics raise because the rationale is itself ambiguous. Certainly the cases show little or no inquiry into the relative secrecy, seclusion, or "privateness" of the particular aspect of identity appropriated.[61] Rather, the courts have looked first to see if an identification was made, and second to find out if some advantage accrued, or was meant to accrue, to the defendant.[62]

---

[59] Bloustein, *Privacy as an Aspect of Human Dignity: An Answer to Dean Prosser*, 39 N.Y.U.L. REV. 962 (1964) [hereinafter cited as *An Answer*]; Bloustein, *Privacy, Tort Law, and the Constitution: Is Warren and Brandeis's Tort Petty and Unconstitutional As Well?*, 46 TEX. L. REV. 611 (1968) (in answer to Kalven, *supra* note 6); Bloustein, *The First Amendment and Privacy: The Supreme Court Justice and the Philosopher*, 28 RUT. L. REV. 41 (1974) [hereinafter cited as *The Justice and The Philosopher*].

[60] Bloustein, *An Answer, supra* note 59, at 987-88.

[61] *See* PROSSER, TORTS, *supra* note 47, at 814.

[62] *See* PROSSER, TORTS, supra note 47, at 804-07. All of the state statutes Prosser mentions *require* such commercial or financial advantage, although Prosser raises the interesting question of whether the constitutional status of the right to privacy will not in the end defeat that restriction. *See id.* at 817.

To some extent, then, the alternative property analysis necessarily applies: when the defendants make some measurable gain at the expense of a measurable loss — or risk of loss — to the plaintiffs, that amounts to unjust enrichment.[63] Confounding this analysis, however, are two items of evidence: first, the remedies available in appropriation suits include both general damages[64] and injunctions; and, second, appropriation suits themselves, as the *Restatement* recognizes, need not conform to the commercial pattern.[65]

---

[63] "The rationale . . . is the straightforward one of preventing unjust enrichment by the theft of goodwill. No social purpose is served by having the defendant get for free some aspect of the plaintiff that would have a market value and for which he would normally pay." Kalven, *supra* note 6, at 331.

[64] Bloustein, *An Answer, supra* note 59, at 987, puts this somewhat obscurely: "it has been held that general rather than special damages are recoverable. . . ." *But cf.* Prosser, *Privacy, supra* note 47, at 509: "So far as damages are concerned, there is general agreement that the plaintiff need not plead or prove special damages. . . . Substantial damages may be awarded for the presumed mental distress inflicted, and other probable harm, without proof. If there is evidence of special damage, such as resulting illness, or unjust enrichment of the defendant, or harm to plaintiff's own commercial interests, it can be recovered. Punitive damages can be awarded upon the same basis as in other torts, where a motive or state of mind appears. . . ." *See, e.g.,* Fairfield v. American Photocopy Equip. Co., 138 Cal. App. 2d 82, 291 P.2d 194, 198 (1955): "While special damages may be recovered if sustained, general damages may be recovered without a showing of specific loss." For cases in which actual damages were found, *see, e.g.,* Pagan v. New York Herald Tribune, 32 App. Div. 2d 341, 301 N.Y.S.2d 120 (1969); Bunnell v. Keystone Varnish Co., 254 App. Div. 885, 5 N.Y.S.2d 415 (1938).

[65] *See* RESTATEMENT (SECOND) OF TORTS § 652c (Tent. Draft 22, May 19, 1976): "One who appropriates to his own use or benefit the name or likeness of another is subject to liability to the other for invasion of his privacy." The "use or benefit" in question is quite general in nature. Thus Comment (b) reads in relevant part: "Apart from statute, however, the rule is not limited to . . . commercial appropriations. It applies also where the defendant makes use of the plaintiff's name or likeness for his own purposes and benefit, even though the benefit sought to be obtained is not a pecuniary one."

Prosser remarks, in citing the commercial limitations in the state statutes, that while "the common law of other states [i.e., without statutes] may therefore be somewhat broader . . . in general . . . there has been no very significant difference in the cases." PROSSER, TORTS, *supra* note 47, at 805. Prosser did find seven reported cases of successful privacy actions for appropriation of plaintiff's identity by name or by other identifying symbols or characteristics arguably *without direct financial or commercial advantage* to the defendant. These cases will be treated here as exceptions to commercialization but not to exploitation — which is the best general concept for the assignment of liability in the appropriation of identity cases. Exploitation may involve either unjust enrichment or, as in these exceptions, outright fraud. In neither situation do we need to refer to privacy analysis; but neither will property analysis explain all the cases. With few exceptions, then, the reported appropriation cases *are* commercialization cases. *But cf.* Hamilton v. Lumbermen's Mut. Cas. Co., 82 So.2d 61 (La. App. 1955) (use of plaintiff's name in advertisement for witnesses of accident is actionable); Cardy v. Maxwell, 9 Misc. 2d 329, 169 N.Y.S.2d 547 (1957) (the use of a name to extort money is *not* commercial use within the statute).

252      Harvard Civil Rights-Civil Liberties Law Review      [Vol. 12

With this first piece of evidence Bloustein bolsters the inference from his first to his second argument: the commercial appropriation of identity is actionable because, and only because, it degrades and abuses human dignity — the purportedly more adequate and general rationale for these cases, and one taken to include and imply privacy. No doubt the failure of the first argument — that most identifications are more or less worthless commercially — weakens the second. Since market value often gives us an alternative ground, on the rationale of unjust enrichment, human dignity is, strictly speaking, superfluous, at least to the decision of most of the cases.[66] But will not the award of general damages (and even occasionally of injunctions)[67] overcome this weakness in the arguments? Bloustein's point seems to be that property interests generally call for the narrower and lesser protections of special damages, measured by the extent of the actual loss only *after* it actually takes place. Were this the rule for misappropriation, it would work an obvious hardship and even an injustice on plaintiffs who, above all else, want their identities let alone.

To treat these plaintiffs as though they sued, say, for trademark infringements, confining their relief to either an accounting for profits or else actual commercial losses, is to mistake the basis of their complaints. Their profits and losses, in the strict commercial sense, have much less significance — and perhaps much less certainty — than their overriding loss of control over an aspect of their identities. But this is not to say, with Bloustein, that these aspects of identity must therefore be "private" or non-proprietary.

There are two fallacies in Bloustein's arguments from the concededly broad range of remedies available in the misappropriation cases. The first is the simple one of assuming violations of property interests cannot generally be remedied except by special damages at law. This is not so: equity will of course enforce many a contract for the sale of land.[68] To give a better example, common law copyright will be protected by injunction and, once infringed, remedied by general, special, or even punitive damages.[69]

---

[66] At a much higher level of abstraction, human dignity is, of course, not at all superfluous to the *explanation* of these cases, along with almost all other presumably fair or just cases in torts and every other department of law. The point is that the concept serves no indispensable purpose in these cases. Moreover, even if human dignity *were* a needed conceptual tool in the decision of these cases, *that* proves nothing as to personal privacy, which is another concept altogether.

[67] *See, e.g.,* Bowman Gum, Inc. v. Topps Chewing Gum, Inc., 103 F. Supp. 944 (E.D.N.Y. 1952).

[68] S. WILLISTON, WILLISTON ON CONTRACTS § 1418A (3d ed. 1968).

[69] *See* M. NIMMER, NIMMER ON COPYRIGHT § 150 (1976).

Copyright, moreover, shows us the second fallacy in Bloustein's analysis. In our own ideas or books or paintings (as in our own name and likenesses) we have property rights uniquely linked to our personal identities. These rights protect our enjoyment of such properties as much as, if not more than, our trade in them. Where enjoyment, as opposed to trade, is threatened or injured, the legal remedies are equitable or at least general. The rights at issue are nonetheless proprietary. Surely we cannot infer that our rights are to "privacy" whenever we find that our remedies are "general".

This counter-analysis may help to explain the somewhat anomalous, and surely not at all "commercial," appropriation cases noted in the *Restatement*. What are we to say, for instance, of a suit for appropriation of identity where the plaintiff's name was against his wishes used in a new political party's name,[70] or signed to a public published petition[71] or to a telegram to a public official?[72] Or of cases in which a woman, for whatever reasons, held herself out to be a man's common-law wife,[73] or put his name down as the father on her child's birth certificate?[74] Dated and few as these cases may be, they press the strict property analysis of the appropriation of identity cases to what may be its limits.

But surely we may be said to retain some property rights in our names and likenesses, and in our identities generally, even where we have no right to sell or lease them for the uses to which these defendants put them. After all, these are cases of outright and perhaps criminal fraud, some of them involving forgery and others misrepresentation or impersonation. The injury to the plaintiffs is again to their right to the secure and exclusive enjoyment of something commonly understood as uniquely *theirs* and no one else's.

Generalizing, then, from both the commercial and non-commercial cases, we can break down the appropriation tort into three elements: 1) wrongful or fraudulent taking 2) of another's identity 3) for one's own advantage.[75] The important conceptual question is then, whether "identity" in the relevant sense ought to be treated as some kind of property or, if not, presumptively as privacy.[76]

---

[70] State *ex rel.* La Follette v. Hinkle, 131 Wash. 86, 229 P. 317 (1924).

[71] Schwartz v. Edrington, 133 La. 235, 62 So. 660 (1913).

[72] Hinish v. Meier & Frank Co., 166 Or. 482, 113 P.2d 438 (1941).

[73] Burns v. Stevens, 236 Mich. 443, 210 N.W. 482 (1926).

[74] Vanderbilt v. Mitchell, 72 N.J. Eq. 910, 67 A. 97 (1907).

[75] "Advantage" now understood as being proprietary or quasi-proprietary but not necessarily commercial.

[76] Bloustein would treat "identity" "as an aspect of human dignity." But the rub is, *which* aspect of human dignity? His answer is implicitly and obviously the *privacy* aspect of human dignity. *See* Bloustein, *An Answer, supra* note 59.

It will help to look back again at the forked roads of the case law: *Roberson* and *Pavesich*.[77] In both cases the plaintiffs seem to have cast their allegations not in terms of wages due for the hire of their identities but rather in terms of the harm done to them by the sheer indignity of it all. Abigail Roberson was said by the dissenting judge to have been "greatly humiliate[d] by the scoffs and jeers of persons who have recognized her face. . . ."[78] (Of the cheers of recognition, if any, we hear nothing.) The *Pavesich* court saw in the poor man's case the much g eater injuries of deprivation of that liberty granted by the law of nature and guaranteed by the federal and state constitutions.[79] The *Pavesich* opinion and the *Roberson* dissent, then, come to this: the plaintiffs were harmed not merely to the degree that their identities were exploited for another's profit but, beyond that, to the degree that their identities, otherwise obscure, were made public at the whim of another — taken from them and displayed in places and ways offensive to them.

The courts' suggestion here is that control over the use of identity belongs, as an aspect of liberty or human dignity, to the individual. But, so put, this right includes too much and must fall of its own weight. We never control many of the uses to which our names, likenesses, and even histories are put, nor can we hope to. These aspects of our identities, in particular, face outward and are in some sense in the public domain. But still they are not public property for others to use as they will.

We draw the line at exploitation, and in drawing it we create a set of exclusive but limited rights of enjoyment (or non-enjoyment) in public identity. Thus we are entitled, where possible and permissible, to give out licenses for the use of our likenesses or opinions. We are, moreover, protected quite generally against most fraudulent uses of our names and likenesses. Call these interests proprietary or not, the legal protections of them safeguard our public and not our private identities. Personal dignity *is* at stake in all of this, as Bloustein thought, but personal privacy is not.

To say that "privacy" is at risk in these cases is to extend the boundaries of that concept not only beyond our legal needs, which are more or less satisfied with familiar concepts from the law of property and of frauds, but also beyond the possibility of relevant legal distinction and definition. Privacy and identity collapse into one another with the result that we have no concept left with which to distinguish, descriptively or

---

[77] Forked because *Roberson* denied the right that *Pavesich* granted. One scarcely need ask at this point "which is the one less traveled by?"

[78] Roberson v. Rochester Folding Box Co., 171 N.Y. 538, 542-43, 64 N.E. 442, 448 (1902) (dissent).

[79] Pavesich v. New England Life Ins. Co., 122 Ga. 190, 197, 50 S.E. 68, 80.

prescriptively, our private from our public identities. In this posture, the right to privacy must become largely meaningless, for it throws its protections over all that we ever are or do.

## B. False Light

Prosser calls his next tort "false light in the public eye."[80] It is an aptly confused metaphor, for indeed the light shines not so much on the private personality (which in fact falls behind a shadow) but on the public eye — blinding it in a sense. By definition, the wrong done in such cases must be at least twofold: first, there is the falsification, whether negligent or intentional, of some matter of fact or opinion attributed to an identified individual. In this respect he or she has simply been misrepresented, for whatever purpose. Second, however, there is the light itself, the illumination, as it were, of the identified individual before the public at large.

We concede to public attention at least some part of our identities simply by being alive. The hermit in this respect is, ironically, the most noteworthy of all.[81] By conceding the least, he may well stimulate our curiousity and so concede the most. Inescapably, we all have an identity of one kind or another by which the public knows us. Loosely, this comes to much the same thing as reputation. Within "reasonable" bounds, established by shared expectations hardened around legal precedents, we remain always subject to the minor false shadows and lights that accompany public curiosity and attention.

This is not simply a matter of "newsworthiness" in the sense that word has in first amendment litigation.[82] Any writer in, say, an article on

---

[80] *See* PROSSER, TORTS, *supra* note 47, at 812.

[81] One thinks, of course, of Emily Dickinson, whose reclusiveness was itself a public identity of some note in the small world of nineteenth-century Amherst. The self, as she wrote, finds its only true concealment behind "the self." *See* Moore, Ourself Behind Ourself Concealed: The Personal and Poetic Expression of Emily Dickinson 1830-1886 (unpublished thesis, Harvard University Library, 1972).

[82] Theoretically the exception is limited to those who are in one way or another "newsworthy". Public officials and "public figures" obviously are; but courts, including the United States Supreme Court, have found it hard to draw a line between "public" and "private" persons (as distinguished from public and private aspects of personalities). One case, in which in fact fictionalization was not at issue, tells more or less the whole tale. *See* Sidis v. F-R Publishing Co., 113 F. 2d 806 (2d Cir. 1940) (holding past, vast publicity as to a uniquely precocious and ingenious child to justify present inquiry and publicity about the uniquely reclusive and eccentric man into whom that child had grown, and note 204 *infra*. The problem with defining the exception is that there are two bases of definition: one focused upon the individual, presuming a waiver on his part; the other upon the public, seeking some justification in its real, if dormant, curiosity. Waiver presents a clear enough

*Privacy I*

people walking to work, may single out someone he recognizes as among those taking a particular path. Were he in error about that person, either because he was not there or because he was there but on another errand, the writer might owe him no more than a retraction or correction in the following days — and more likely not even that.[83] In the United States we tend to thank the first amendment for such liberties or, if you will, such inconveniences. A less parochial view is that there is no felt or acknowledged right infringed by these slight and "reasonable" attentions from the media, the institutionalized eyes and ears of the modern public.

A distinction must be drawn, then, between the private and the public aspects of our identities. In part, this distinction must be descriptive, corresponding to our felt sense of privacy; but in part, too, it must be normative, assigning rights and remedies according to where the line is drawn. The great difficulty in defining privacy comes of just this divided function that any legal definition, at least of a right, must perform.

The false light cases in particular seem to array themselves across a spectrum of exposures of the public self. In part, it is the variable of falsification that skews them so eccentrically.[84] Mr. Pavesich was put in

question, if not an easy one. *See* note 204 *infra*. But curiosity about persons, like desirability in commodities, may be created by those who later point to it in justification of their actions. *See Defense of Newsworthiness, supra* note 19. Warren and Brandeis at least insisted upon the priority, and presumably the immediate priority, of the newsworthiness: "[T]o whatever degree and in whatever connection a man's life has ceased to be private, *before the publication under consideration has been made,* to that extent the protection is to be withdrawn." Warren & Brandeis, *supra* note 1, at 215 (emphasis added).

[83] *See* Miami Herald Publishing Co. v. Tornillo, 418 U.S. 241 (1974).

[84] The best illustration of this comes from a fortuitously "controlled" sample of litigation consisting of two decisions on two suits brought for two separate publications of the same photograph of a husband and wife in full embrace. By itself, without adverse or inappropriate text, the publication of the photograph was held to be privileged. Gill v. Hearst Publishing Co., 40 Cal. 2d 224, 253 P.2d 441 (1953). Accompanied by a text on "the wrong kind of love," however, it was held to be actionable. Gill v. Curtis Publishing Co., 38 Cal. 2d 273, 239 P.2d 630 (1952). Taken in public in the Farmers' Market of downtown Los Angeles, the picture itself made an unlikely submission in a privacy suit, for the plaintiffs embraced without any attempt to conceal either their affection or their identities from the public — or the photographer, who happened to be Henri Cartier-Bresson. All that made the publication of this photograph actionable was the accompanying text allegedly implying that these two people — in fact a well-known man and wife business partnership — were involved in a tawdry and short-lived exercise in sexual attraction.

To limit the application of the New York Privacy statute, and "to avoid any conflict with the free dissemination of thoughts, ideas, newsworthy events, and matters of public interest," Spahn v. Julian Messner, Inc., 18 N.Y.2d 324, 328, 274 N.Y.S.2d 877, 879, 221 N.E.2d 543, 544-45 (1966), the New York courts have gone so far as to require "fictionalization" (as well as "commercialization") in many suits brought for violation of

a false light quite explicitly, as was Ms. Roberson, if only implicitly. With or without falsification, these two classic plaintiffs were able to make out colorable claims on the basis of appropriation for gain. The aspect of identity appropriated — and whether it was in any significant sense private — mattered little if at all. Are the false-light cases, then, on the same footing as the appropriation cases? Do they fall outside privacy analysis proper?

Prosser found his first false light rationale in the case of *Lord Byron v. Johnston*,[85] in which it was held the defendant had taken the sure expedient, in the interests of wider circulation, of affixing Byron's name to a poem that the poet never wrote and even in his stupors never could have written. Wigmore once called this ''the right against false attribution of belief or utterance.''[86] In Byron's case, however, and probably in most others, there was some gain to be gotten by the false attribution. The right at issue is the obverse of that of copyright: the right to keep one's own name for one's own works or faiths. It, too, may be given away for whatever consideration induces consent. Warren and Brandeis, when they studied the copyright analogies,[87] found nothing in such torts to require privacy analysis. It may be that the right to be let alone encompasses the right to have one's name or likeness let alone, if only so that one may use it for one's own purposes. But the same is true of one's home or yard. No doubt in all such cases privacy interests and rights are implicated along with others. These other rights, particularly in the secure enjoyment of intangible forms of property, including reputation, should do as well or better to secure the remedies needed.

Commercial exploitation of some aspect of a person's identity may or may not be the same wrong as results from the negligent or intentional

privacy. This requirement has itself imported a good deal of legal fiction, and confusion, into the decision of such cases. Three separate and divergent questions must be answered as one: Was the plaintiff's privacy invaded by the publication? Was the publication fictionalized? And, often, was the fictionalization for purposes of commercial (or other) exploitation? Whatever a legislature chooses to call its statutes, these are different things with different interests and rights attached to them. Time, Inc. v. Hill, 385 U.S. 374 (1967), the first case in which the Supreme Court explicitly addressed the question of a conflict between claims of privacy and claims of first amendment protection for publication, was inconclusive in its result precisely because the ''falsification'' or ''fictionalization'' issue under the New York rule obscured the underlying question, namely: was there an invasion of privacy?

[85] 2 Mer. 29, 35 Eng. Rep. 851 (1816). *See* Prosser, *Privacy, supra* note 47, at 398 and n.127.

[86] Wigmore, *The Right Against False Attribution of Belief or Utterance*, 4 KY. L.J. 3 (1916).

[87] Warren & Brandeis, *supra* note 1, at 199-205.

falsification of facts about a person. What is more, either or both of these harms may take place without an invasion of some peculiarly or distinctly *private* aspect of personality. More typically, as for Byron, the false light cases involve the actionable misuses of one's *public* identity. The grievance is not injury to privacy but to reputation[88] — if, that is, we measure reputation much more finely than in the usual defamation suit. This is a large "if."

Indeed, the issue of a more sensitive judicial measure for recovery in defamation explains all too well much of the development of the false light rationale within the variegate tort. Defamation is not easy to plead, to prove, or, it seems, to remedy.[89] Its concept of "reputation" (and so of injury) is full of well-entrenched quirks, gaps, and inconsistencies.[90] Thus arises the hidden but potent judicial bias, noted by Prosser and Wade,[91] towards allowing recovery in false light actions even where the injuries proven fall under one or another of "the numerous restrictions which have hedged defamation about for so many years. . . ."[92]

There is no denying the quandary of remedies here, or even the equity in the results often obtained under false light. The injuries pleaded are nonetheless to the public and not the private self. Only the confusion of the two permits the courts to defer in good conscience needed reforms in the law of defamation. Public identity stands in need of legal protections that defamation will not allow and privacy will not justify; but to allow a remedy in privacy bottomed on a justification in defamation is not the answer. False light, in both its remedies and its rationale, belongs with defamation as its unacknowledged but not illegitimate offspring.

Recognition of all of this will help to narrow the range of plausibility and significance in the false light claims themselves. Too often these look

---

[88] "Reputation" and "public identity" come to much the same thing, at least in these cases. There *are* distinctions between them, but none, as I see it, operative in this context, *except* insofar as courts are more stinting of remedies in cases denominated "reputation."

[89] This is, of course, a relative point: compared to false light — which is apparently always available as an alternative ground — defamation is beset with enormous difficulties. "[I]n part as a matter of historical survival and in part in the interest of freedom of the press and the discouragement of trivial and extortionate claims, [there are restrictions on defamation that] can be by-passed by bringing the [false light] action. Certainly this is possible as to the requirement of proof of special damages in cases of libel *per quod* and most kinds of slander, and apparently as to such matters as the applicable statute of limitations, survival of the action, and a statute requiring the plaintiff to file a bond for costs." PROSSER, TORTS, *supra* note 47, at 814.

[90] *Cf.* PROSSER, TORTS, *supra* note 47, at 737: "It must be confessed at the beginning that there is a great deal of the law of defamation which makes no sense. . . ."

[91] PROSSER, TORTS, *supra* note 47, at 813-14; Wade, *Defamation and the Right of Privacy*, 15 VAND. L. REV. 1093 (1962).

[92] Prosser, *Privacy, supra* note 47, at 401.

to an obscure concept of privacy to bolster weak and even jesting suits for defamation by newspapers and the like. Aside from any erosion of the first amendment, these cases present us with often trivialized and even, as Prosser and Kalven suggest,[93] extortionate claims for recovery in cases where little or no harm was done.

This is not to disparage the many serious and substantial cases in the reports of such "privacy" actions brought on disguised defamation grounds. An example of a non-trivial tort of this kind was the illustration of a newspaper article on dishonest cabbies with a photograph of an honest one.[94] Even assuming that his professional reputation survived unscathed — because, say, no customer or employer noticed, or because the news report came out in another city — this cabbie still has a grievance based upon the public affront to his public, and professional, identity. It is a general grievance no doubt best allayed with an award of general damages (since, as we assume, his reputation suffers only *generally* rather than *specifically* in the opinions of named persons). The point is, after all, to give him some remedy in law for outrageous mistreatment of his professional integrity. But in such cases one must still ask why the alternative and underlying ground of defamation was not pleaded. To this question there is only one fair answer: cramped and hedged as it is, defamation gave less promise of success. False light vastly improved the odds. Surely lawyers cannot be expected to blind themselves to the propensities of some judges to espouse the obscurities of a new tort in preference to dispelling those of an old one.[95]

Nor is it enough to say, with Bloustein, that above and beyond injury to reputation "these cases involve . . . the assault on individual personality and dignity which is characteristic of all other privacy cases."[96] Our personalities and our dignities are no doubt most surely and tightly enmeshed in the private world over which we exercise, at times, considerable sway. But whether we like it or not, our selves also extend outside of that world into another in which most of us have very little power or expectation of power over the opinions and impressions others may form of us. Every affront to our dignity in that outer world,

---

[93] Prosser, Torts, *supra* note 47, at 814; Kalven, *supra* note 6, at 338-39.

[94] Peay v. Curtis Publishing Co., 78 F. Supp. 305 (D.D.C. 1948). *See also* F & J Enterprises v. Columbia Broadcasting Sys., 373 F. Supp. 292 (N.D. Ohio 1974).

[95] There is, I admit, another answer: that defamation provides an inadequate basis of recovery for the more inward injuries of what is, after all, a form of defamation. It is a bad answer because it applies to all defamations and because the exception here makes no sense. "Mental distress" may well justify damages in defamation cases — but by itself it does not justify recourse to privacy analysis.

[96] Bloustein, *An Answer, supra* note 59, at 991.

while felt, even keenly, in our inner world, is not a legally cognizable
assault upon our private selves. Much of the time we must take counsel
from the old saw that sticks and stones will break my bones but names —
and pictures — will never hurt me. Where they do hurt sufficiently,
another, publicly focused, legal concept comes to bear: that of injury to
reputation.[97]

The type of control we can expect to exercise over the public fate of
our public identities must of necessity differ sharply from that which we
can expect to exercise over the public fate of our private identities. The
exact line between these two sides of what is, after all, one self must
always remain somewhat uncertain. But the line of legal protection of
privacy surely excludes many or most of the false light cases.

It will help to note now the results obtained from this somewhat
surgical analysis of the variegate tort. Misappropriation is the outer circle, the farthest reach, of Prosser's concentric analysis of the various
legal remedies afforded in the case law to "privacy" rights. It provides a
mantle of protection for identity in even its most public aspects. So, too,
does "false light": unless the suggestion is made that the false juxtaposition of my name or likeness with another's products, ideas, or behaviors
entails some commitment of my inmost soul, there is nothing in the
decisions of these cases to indicate that the courts require a showing of
actual invasion of anything plausibly called the private self. There are
invasions to be found in these cases of certain of the rights and interests of
individual identity, of the self, broadly understood, by exploitation of one
kind or another as well as by implicit or explicit falsification; usually
both. But to say that this makes out an invasion of *privacy* is to bar any
later distinctions between what is private and what is public in our iden-

---

[97] My argument here is *not* that there is *no* mental or inward injury in these cases;
obviously there is; names do in fact hurt. There are different categories of legally cognizable
injury. And while artificial and perhaps forced as to the quantities and qualities of pain,
these legal categories are probably indispensable, as an institutional matter, to judicial
consistency, economy, and, in the end, fairness.

A recent instance of what Prosser calls "the rogues gallery cases" aptly illustrates
these distinctions. In Paul v. Davis, 424 U.S. 643 (1976), the Supreme Court held, in a
majority opinion by Justice Rehnquist, that the damage to the respondent's reputation which
resulted from the inclusion of his name and photograph on a widely-circulated police
department list of "active shoplifters," did not infringe any interest that was protected by
the fourteenth amendment or 42 U.S.C. § 1983. The underlying wrong was, of course,
*official* defamation. Privacy is not in any strict sense implicated in such defamations.
Nonetheless, the retrenchment as to privacy seems much less welcome in a case in which
reputation, as an aspect of liberty or property, or both, is given so little protection from
official abuse — and in which, moreover, such abuse is put beyond all remedy.

tities. In first amendment cases, among others, the failure to make these distinctions leads to absurdity.[98]

Purely as a matter of the logic of our concepts, then, to include misappropriation and "false light" within the bounds of privacy analysis is to commit oneself to variances and waivers of those bounds for the other, less inclusive, wrongs in the variegate tort. What is more, it is to commit oneself to a definition of privacy with two unrestricted terms: identity and control. The difficulty is not with the terms themselves — they must underpin any understanding of privacy rights — but with the failure to restrict them.

## III. INTIMACY AND AUTONOMY

In the inevitable muddle of adjudication, privacy may still look, as it did to Paul Freund,[99] like "too greedy a concept" to let into the storehouse of legal rules and principles. We have to find some way, in our definition of the concept, to keep it from swallowing itself.[100] Legal concepts, if they are to have any application at all, must be kept distinct from one another. Once they fall into a jumble of their own, they cannot help us where they are needed, in sorting out facts and values and policies for judgments of law. Restriction is a necessity in our legal as in our logical economy. An unrestricted concept is perhaps no concept at all.[101]

Failures of restriction beset not only many tort claims in privacy but also many attempts to define the concept itself. Take as an example Alan Westin's influential definition: "Privacy is the claim of individuals, groups, or institutions to determine for themselves when, how and to what extent information about them is communicated to others."[102] Westin has in mind a definition by collection, as Plato might say,[103] inclusive of all the instances of a phenomenon in different settings and even different cultures. "Viewed in terms of the relation of the individual to social participation," he writes, "privacy is the voluntary and temporary

---

[98] This is because, as a logical matter, all varieties of the "newsworthiness" test require the division of the social world into a public (or "newsworthy") realm on the one hand, and a private (or "unfit to print") realm, on the other. *See Defense of Newsworthiness, supra* note 19.

[99] *See* Freund, *supra* note 10, at 192.

[100] Perhaps a better metaphor comes from Aesop's frog who puffed himself so big that he exploded into many little bits and pieces.

[101] There may seem to be exceptions, or at least one: the concept of everything. But, as Hegel wondered and Parmenides asked, what, then, of nothing? Where does *it* fit?

[102] WESTIN, *supra* note 3, at 7.

[103] *See* PLATO, SOPHIST* 226a.

withdrawal of a person from the general society. . . ."[104] But Westin's characterization provides no restricting term of analysis except the "desire" for "participation in society." In the legal context, this simply includes too much.[105]

Lawyers long familiar with the concept of overbreadth need no help from philosophers to understand the failings, both logical and legal, of the definitions of privacy with which we now work.[106] Westin's is surely the most cited and studied of them all,[107] yet when taken as the delineation of a legal concept, it confounds every attempt to cabin the right to privacy with prudent and plausible remedies. Imagine for a moment, the reverse Big Brotherism necessary to implement with sanctions and damages a right to privacy as vast as his definition. One would inquire about one's fellows only at great peril to their rights and one's own. In this extreme view, then, Westin may be said to engage in a kind of logical synecdoche, defining the part by the whole: privacy is only a part of that vast conceptual whole adumbrated in his definition, for it is a definition that on its face includes *all* control over *all* information about oneself,

---

[104] WESTIN, *supra* note 3, at 7.

[105] Prosser, too, gives us a collection of sorts, and it is an excellent one even without any organizing or unifying principle — since to Prosser the decisions were often divergent and inconsistent in concept. *See* PROSSER, TORTS, *supra* note 47.

[106] The two best sources of conceptual, if not necessarily definitional, discussions of privacy are the privacy symposia in XIII NOMOS (1971) and 31 LAW AND CONTEMP. PROB. 251-435 (1966). Among the few who hazard an out-and-out definition are Ernest van den Haag, *On Privacy*, XIII NOMOS 149 ("Privacy is the exclusive access of a person (or other legal entity) to a realm of his own."), and Hyman Gross, *Privacy and Autonomy*, XIII NOMOS 169 ("Privacy [is] considered as the condition under which there is *control* over acquaintance with one's personal affairs by the one enjoying it. . . ."). Edward Shils, in his *Privacy: Its Constitution and Vicissitudes*, 31 LAW AND CONTEMP. PROB. 281, 282 (1966), writes that "privacy exists where the persons whose actions engender or become the objects of information retain possession of that information. . . ." Shils later limits this to "events that occur in the private sphere." *Id.* at 283. Similarly, THE OFFICE OF SCIENCE AND TECHNOLOGY, REPORT: PRIVACY AND BEHAVIORAL RESEARCH 2 (1967), says that "the right to privacy is the right of the individual to decide for himself how much he will share with others his thoughts, feelings, and the facts of his personal life." None of these definitions adds anything by way of restriction to the one given by Westin. And while Westin has been criticized, *see, e.g.*, Lusky, *Invasion of Privacy: A Clarification of Concepts*, 72 COLUM. L. REV. 693 (1972), only Parker, *supra* note 38, has attempted to provide the restrictions necessary to make the concept of privacy legally applicable. *See* pp. 267-68 *infra*.

[107] *See* A. BRECKENRIDGE, THE RIGHT TO PRIVACY (1970); A. MILLER, THE ASSAULT ON PRIVACY (1971); M. SLOUGH, PRIVACY, FREEDOM, AND RESPONSIBILITY (1969). *But see*, criticizing Westin, Greenawalt, *Privacy and Its Legal Protections*, 2 HASTINGS CENTER STUDIES 45, 45-49 (1974); Lusky, *supra* note 106, at 695-700; and Parker, *supra* note 38, at 275-76.

one's group, one's institutions. Surely privacy should come, in law as in life, to much less than this.

It is true that Westin's definition, like Bloustein's characterization, lays down two of the essential predicates for the analysis of privacy: control ("to determine for themselves") and identity ("information about them"). Even more than Bloustein, however, Westin permits himself no restrictions — except perhaps the very ambiguous term "claim" for something that is itself the basis for a variety of claims. Warren and Brandeis began all this by singling out for favor Cooley's "right to be let alone." But any such evocation leaves us with an all-embracing and all-elusive background concept related to, and indeed inclusive of, all that we mean by privacy, but of little or no help in excluding other related concepts at the important juncture of finding rights and remedies.

Intimacy is the chief restricting concept in the definition of privacy given here — intimacy both in its relation to identity and, what is more subtle and complex, to autonomy. To make the argument plain, however, we must turn to the part of the case law that leads straight from torts to the Constitution. Without much question, we now come upon the indispensable border of the right to privacy. It is crossed by both of Prosser's remaining torts: intentional physical intrusion upon seclusion or solitude, on the one hand, and, on the other, that intentional psychological intrusion that takes place when publicity is given to such intimate and secluded details of our lives as to embarrass or humiliate us.

The common law cases of intrusion need little in the way of separate exposition or explanation. They involve intrusions plain and simple, much like those of property law. They are, however, as further analysis will show, trespasses on privacies rather than on lands or chattels. They include deliberate and unauthorized entries into rooms or homes, unjustified searches, illicit eavesdropping and voyeurism, as well as mutations and hybrids of these.[108] At its pith, this is curiosity's tort, providing a remedy for outrageous peering and prying into private lives and things. All of the cases may be taken to illustrate the very basic connections in our concept of privacy between the restricting pull of intimacy on the one hand, and the broadening or deepening pull of autonomy on the other.

From two of the strongest instances in the case law we can construct a paradigm of sorts. In *De May v. Roberts*,[109] a Michigan case decided some years before Warren and Brandeis wrote, a layman by the inauspicious name of Scattergood accompanied a physician into the room

---

[108] *See* PROSSER. TORTS. *supra* note 47, at 807-09 & nn. 53-73.

[109] 46 Mich. 160, 9 N.W. 146 (1881).

where a woman lay in labor about to be delivered of a child. The court held that Scattergood entered under fraudulent pretenses. The fraud was imputed to Dr. DeMay in that he failed to tell Mr. and Mrs. Roberts that Scattergood was not, as they assumed, medically trained. Their tacit consent to his presence was thus "uninformed" and inoperative.[110] Beyond that, however, the court specified no legal ground for its decision. What it did say was that "the occasion [of childbirth] was a most sacred one. . . ."[111] Mrs. Roberts, moreover, had "a legal right to the privacy of her apartment at such a time."[112]

In *York v. Story*,[113] a federal civil rights case decided the year before *Griswold*, a policeman fraudulently obtained the consent of a young woman to take photographs of her in the nude and in various indiscreet poses. The victim of recent crime, she had come to the stationhouse to report it. There the defendant policeman told her that he was obliged to photograph her bruises so as "to attempt to preserve evidence" of the crime.[114] The photographs were later reproduced and distributed among the defendant's colleagues. All of them, his lawyer argued, were entitled as policemen to examine the "evidence" thus "preserved."

Both of these cases were in different ways unprecedented: *DeMay* was perhaps the earliest (and certainly the least self-conscious) common law case explicitly upholding the right to privacy. *York* cited no federal precedents for the remedy sought and no language about privacy in the 1871 Civil Rights Act[115] under which suit was brought. In both cases, understandably enough, the judges seemed surer of their legal intuitions than of their legal concepts. And one may wonder why they felt the need to lodge these intuitions in the novel concepts of a common law or a federal civil right to privacy.

Surely both decisions illustrate the interstitial nature of the remedies in tort, or even constitutional law, for such physical intrusions upon the private self. Other tort and property concepts could no doubt have supported the decision in *DeMay*: there was a trespass and even a battery, since Scattergood at one point touched Mrs. Roberts. In *York*, the plain-

---

[110] The prescience of Michigan's Chief Justice Marston is no less evident here in the area of informed consent than in that of privacy proper. *See* note 117 *infra*.

[111] 46 Mich. at 163, 9 N.W. at 149.

[112] *Id. See also* Feeney v. Young, 191 App. Div. 501, 181 N.Y.S. 481 (1920) (public showing of films of caesarian birth).

[113] York v. Story, 324 F. 2d 450 (9th Cir. 1963), *cert. denied*, 376 U.S. 939 (1964).

[114] 324 F. 2d at 454 n.6.

[115] 42 U.S.C. § 1983 (1970).

tiff argued in part on the strength of the fourth amendment.[116] Should not the overlap in remedies and concepts bar talk of privacy?

Not in these cases: physical intrusion, however much in the interstices of other torts, brings us to the core of our expectations and intuitions about privacy and hence of our rights to it.[117] By the other available standards of tort, property, or constitutional wrongs, the harm done in these cases will be minimal, if not mistaken altogether. No fair measure of damages — general or specific — can be arrived at until we acknowledge that it was not the unexcused touching or the unwarranted search as such that caused the injury. What was injured, rather, was that peculiar aspect of dignity and freedom invested in reasonable expectations of privacy. And this injury, with its accompanying humiliation, seems, in these cases at least, not at all trifling.

By and large, of course, our system of defenses against intrusions of this kind, whether from within or without government, relies upon rights secured in other branches of common and statutory law. Nonetheless, privacy is an indispensable concept in the decision of these cases of physical intrusion. Read in aid of definition, these cases set bounds to the

---

[116] Few will dispute the conceptual necessity of privacy analysis to an understanding of the policies and principles of the fourth amendment. *See* note 25 *supra*. But nonetheless, the fourth amendment states a rule that may be read and applied without recourse to any independent right to privacy. *See* Griswold v. Connecticut, 381 U.S. 479, 508-09 (1965) (Black, J., dissenting).

[117] Some will balk at the notion that *DeMay* brings us to the core of our privacy intuitions or expectations. Childbirth nowadays, in large maternity wards in any case, may seem an almost public occasion, with a variety of more or less helpful or needful medical personnel in attendance. Even among those women who choose to deliver at home, invitations to friends and relatives to witness the birth are no longer unheard of. Nonetheless, it is a confusion of some very subtle and complicated norms and practices in our society to say that childbirth is no longer an intimate, "sacred," or private occasion. In a hospital, the many uninvited witnesses by regulation will all be medical personnel. In this as in other situations nowadays, ordinary hospital practice seems to presume the patient's consent to *unnecessary* medical personnel such as students and interns, and so on. Whether the consent is informed and actual — and the practice justified — is a delicate question of medical ethics. But surely any patient has a right to treatment *without* such witnesses or observers. And if so, that right is a privacy right. (Why we should waive it in the face of surplus expertise is an interesting question that we cannot take the time to answer here.) The witness at a home-birth, make no mistake, stands on a very different ground: he or she is specifically *invited* to witness something taken to be, if not sacred, at least wondrous and intimate. No doubt some people for reasons of their own will choose to give birth before a television public — as others will choose to make love similarly situated. Of course, you cannot have it both ways. Still, for most women — and men — in our culture, childbirth remains a highly intimate and private occasion — if one to which hospitals usually do not afford an adequate respect.

*Privacy I*

core expectations of privacy in our society, expectations chiefly, and not coincidentally, of control over who, if anyone, will share in the intimacies of our bodies. Others have more than adequately discussed the manifold values safeguarded by this control over our most intimate physical identities.[118] Without such control, much that we take as distinctively human — love, reflection, choice — cannot flourish or perhaps even survive in our society.

All of this comes in the end to a control over the most basic vehicle of selfhood: the body. For control over the body is the first form of autonomy and the necessary condition, for those who are not saints or stoics, of all later forms.[119] Any plausible definition of privacy, then, whatever the sources of its normative commitments, must take the body as its first and most basic reference for control over personal identity.

Stephen's rule of a shared intuition of decency[120] is not inconsistent with this: surely decency begins with such mutual respect between persons as to allow any given self the control over its own bodily intimacies. A less consensual, but no less intuitional, normative standard such as natural law or fundamental right[121] stands in no lesser need of some such

---

[118] *See* Fried, *supra* note 42. Fried argues "the necessity of privacy as a context for respect, love, friendship and trust. . . ." Id. at 477. For a derivative and largely indiscernible restatement of Fried's thesis, see Rachels, *Why Privacy Is Important*, 4 PHIL. & PUB. AFF. 295 (1975). A more critical but no less derivative argument is made in Reiman, *supra* note 42.

[119] For most of us this will be self-evident: if we don't control our bodies, what *do* we control? — and indeed who are we? The body is the necessary condition of both identity and autonomy. Nonetheless, philosophers and theologians have disputed the necessity of a body — for these and other purposes — at least since Tertullian and perhaps since Socrates. Most recent discussion begins with the counter-hypothesis in P. STRAWSON, INDIVIDUALS 101-26 (1959). Perhaps the best recent work is in a series of articles by Bernard Williams collected in B. WILLIAMS, PROBLEMS OF THE SELF: PHILOSOPHICAL PAPERS 1956-72 (1973). He argues persuasively that we can give no sense to the concept of a particular personality without reference to a body. *But see* Coburn, *Bodily Continuity and Personal Identity*, 20 ANALYSIS 117 (1960). The body is an indispensable reference for the concept of privacy. *See* Benn, *Privacy, Freedom and Respect for Persons*, XIII NOMOS 1 (1971). The source of the privacy concept may well be tied to concepts of the self which themselves cannot be *reduced*, even though they may need to be *referred*, to the body. *See, e.g.*, Craven, *Personhood: The Right To Be Let Alone*, 1976 DUKE L.J. 699. The problem with personhood is that it, too, for legal application as well as for philosophical analysis, must be reduced to its component parts. Privacy, in our moral and legal universe, is surely among these parts.

[120] *See* p. 238 *supra*.

[121] The question whether *in fact* standards purportedly taken from "natural law" or "fundamental right" are less consensual than those taken from, say, the ordinary language or everyday expectations of a given culture is beyond the scope of this Article. *That* question begs another, namely, is there such a thing as a non-consensual natural law or an

concrete point of reference. Otherwise, it will not effectively translate into claims, judgments, or remedies.

This insight has not been altogether neglected in discussions of privacy. Richard Parker has attempted a definition of privacy confined to the body and its parts. "Privacy," he writes, "is control over when and by whom the various parts of us can be sensed by others."[122] Flatly normative, this definition was meant to gain in applicability what it lost, when compared to, say, Westin's, in flexibility. Parker expressly holds it out as fit "to appear in instructions to jurors, in complaints, and in court opinions."[123]

Nonetheless, when pressed into service, Parker's definition yields to absurdities of both over *and* under-extension. None of my thoughts is private because none of them is, in Parker's sense, a part of my body. In fact, under his definition, no information at all can be directly secluded as private.[124] Only when information escapes our control by way of others' "sensing the various parts of us" is there an implication of privacy rights.

The overextension is even more blatant. Sensing our bodies comes to much the same thing as knowing our identities; certainly the sensing Parker has in mind is a form of *knowing, i.e.,* conscious, intelligent, and so on. Either way, our right to privacy must surely encompass some "sensing" and some "knowing" by others. At issue in litigation over privacy rights is always the question of how much sensing and how much knowing is too much. In Parker's definition *all* sensing (as in Westin's *all* knowing) of us by others becomes subject to our claims of privacy. No two people can pass in the street without invading each other's privacy. And, more to the point, every legal wrong that involves a bodily sensation of another — a punch in the jaw, a knee in the groin, or even a false arrest — becomes now, by Parker's criteria, an invasion of privacy. Surely another concept must restrict and perhaps replace knowledge (or sense perception) even when referred to the body, in order to limit further the control over identity, and thus the autonomy, required by the right to privacy. Otherwise Parker's definition of privacy, like Westin's, would

absolute set of fundamental rights? So long as there is a difference of opinions on this question, it seems fair to say that ultimately rival intuitions underlie the rival arguments. In any case, the argument here hangs on neither of these pegs of derivation. The point is that once you say there *is* some right to privacy, however derived, you have to identify it, *i.e.,* to show when, where, how, and in whom it vests.

[122] Parker, *supra* note 38, at 281.

[123] *Id.* at 277.

[124] *See* pp. 283-90 *infra.*

have us forego much freedom to achieve absolute privacy, and ultimately, absolute isolation.

What is needed is the concept of intimacy. Invasions of privacy take
place whenever we are deprived of control over such intimacies of our
bodies and minds as to offend what are ultimately shared standards of
autonomy.[125] Intimacy itself is always the consciousness of the mind in
its access to its own and other bodies and minds, insofar, at least, as these
are generally or specifically secluded from the access of the uninvited.
Intimacy, while a kind of knowledge, is not at all theoretical, but direct
— personal, immediate, and consented to — and, of course, private. We
should be able to share our intimacy with others only as we choose. It is
the value of sharing such knowledge that is at stake in the right to
privacy.[126] Whenever intimacy is made indirect — that is, impersonal,
second-hand, and involuntary — and public, its value is lost or
diminished.

The distinction between physical and psychological intrusions has
less to do with the right to *control* over intimacy than with the various
intrusions on it.[127] The concept of intimacy is the same in either case,

---

[125] The shared standards for identification may well be only "ultimately," and not
"immediately," shared by the culture at large, or even by the legal culture at large. This is
why the Supreme Court is "counter-majoritarian." *See* note 160 *infra.* Typically, the
moral standards of right most widely and immediately shared are fairly distinct — both to
those in the majority who agree with them and uphold them *and* (perhaps even more) to
those in the minority who disagree.

It is against the deviations of members of this latter group, of course, that these widely
shared standards come into force. In either case, the concept of autonomy rarely enters into
consideration. It is simply too abstract, too far removed, at the levels of immediacy at which
people come to agree on shared moral standards. In this sense, Stephen's "decency"
remains still a more sensitive measuring device than any number of abstract concepts. When
we try to make legal and logical *sense* of the felt moral standards of the majority, however,
we cannot stay on the same plane of immediacy. "Ultimately" we are forced into abstractions. We have need of just such concepts as autonomy or identity. These alone make sense
of the welter of more immediate and less abstract concepts at work in our shared intuitions.
This is why the *immediately* shared standards of privacy are *ultimately* shared standards of
autonomy: the ultimacy is the product of reflection and argument on the actual extent and
the logical implications of the standards we can point to as already in force.

[126] *See* Fried, *supra* note 42.

[127] Psychological invasions will always be harder to make actionable than physical
invasions. This difference corresponds, roughly, to the relatively greater difficulty courts
experience in adjudicating first amendment claims when they cannot make out a clear line
between action and speech. Privacy, like speech, has its blurred edges where our only
recourse is not to our concepts, by themselves, but to these aided by certain intuitions.

Will this throw us back on Stephen's rule? In a sense it will, for we never escape
altogether from the rule of intuition in such difficult legal questions. Concepts, and arguments from them, will always be too abstract for mechanical application. But certainly in

and bears as important a relation to the mind as to the body. All the many invasions of privacy, whether or not by directly physical means, expose us to more than wrongful intrusion; for with wrongful intrusion goes wrongful observation and thus wrongful knowledge — all in relation to an intimate identity as much mental as physical.

The concept of an intimate body, from which that of an intimate mind must derive,[128] remains sufficiently plain in its applications to give limited content to the legal protection of privacy. There must be intuition here, as in any value judgment, but a limiting and necessary intuition: at some point we have to say just what parts of our physical and mental lives *are* intimate and so private. The *Griswold* case is perhaps the best example in the case law of such an application.[129] And, in bringing us back to the Constitution, it gives us added insight into the conceptual relations of privacy, intimacy, and autonomy.

Even the bare bones of the *Griswold* opinion — for Justice Douglas filled them out with little of the flesh of argument — show that the Court accepted an important, if unarticulated, relation between privacy and autonomy. The Supreme Court reviewed convictions under Connecticut statutes forbidding the use of contraceptives by married persons, as well as any aiding or abetting of such use.[130] The Court, in a 7–2 decision,

most cases of *physical* intrusion, whether by entry, observation, or even regulation, the concepts of autonomy and intimacy will leave any intuition of decency very much in the background. Only where the conceptual lines attenuate, as in the mass disclosure cases, will decency come into play in finding rights and remedies.

[128] *See* pp. 288-94 *infra*, for a discussion of the relation of intimacy to informational privacy.

[129] For another excellent example in tort law see Nader v. General Motors Corp., 25 N.Y.2d 560, 255 N.E.2d 765 (1970). There, Chief Justice Fuld of the New York Court of Appeals implicitly relied on a concept such as intimacy to distinguish between well-founded claims in privacy and claims in related torts under Washington, D.C. law.

[130] Griswold and Buxton, the two appellants, were arrested in November, 1961, as the founding and operating directors of a Planned Parenthood Center in New Haven. Usually charging fees to defray expenses, the non-profit Center provided birth control information and instruction, along with medical advice and prescriptions to *married persons only*. Found guilty as accessories to the violation of Connecticut's prohibition against the use of contraceptive drugs or devices, CONN. GEN. STAT. § 53-32 (1958), they had claimed in the state courts that the accessory statute, CONN. GEN. STAT. § 54-196 (1958), as applied to them violated the fourteenth amendment. The Appellants' Brief before the Supreme Court, however, advocated an independent constitutional right to privacy — pleaded as *jus tertii* by Buxton and Griswold — derived from various sources. Appellants' Brief at 90, Griswold v. Connecticut, 381 U.S. 479 (1965). The third party privacy rights in question were not directly and immediately threatened by tortious intrusion on the part of the state. Connecticut did not prosecute the recipients of the information, instruction, or prescriptions. Its prosecution here only cut off the normal channels of professional help available to

held such regulation to invade "the area of protected freedoms"[131] that includes "a relationship [*i.e.* marriage] lying within the zone of privacy created by several fundamental constitutional guarantees."[132] Much of the controversy generated by the *Griswold* opinion, both on and off the Court, was directed to the wisdom of extrapolating a right to privacy either from the first, third, and fifth amendments, or from the ninth, or from the fourteenth only.[133] What bears upon our problem, however, is not the source of the extrapolation, but its result.

---

married persons contemplating birth control or family planning. Nonetheless, Justice Douglas laid great emphasis on the intrusions necessary to enforce the underlying prohibition. These hypothetical intrusions, if carried out pursuant to statute and with warrants, presumably would be immune to any tort claims — not only because of the fortuities of sovereign immunity but also because the state *can* intrude to uphold its criminal laws. Thus the question becomes whether this particular criminal law, sanctioning intrusion, violates the constitutional right to privacy.

[131] 381 U.S. 479, 485 (1965), *citing* NAACP v. Alabama *ex rel.* Flowers, 377 U.S. 288, 307 (1964).

[132] 381 U.S. 479, 485 (1965).

[133] *Id.* at 509-10 (Black, J., dissenting). *See generally Comments on the Griswold Case.* a collection of articles at 64 MICH. L. REV. 197 (1965). Of course privacy was implicitly and indirectly acknowledged as a fundamental right in two important series of cases prior to *Griswold:* 1) In Meyer v. Nebraska, 262 U.S. 390 (1923), and Pierce v. Society of Sisters, 268 U.S. 510 (1925), the Supreme Court, in opinions by Justice McReynolds, held that the substantive liberties protected against state action by the fourteenth amendment's due process clause included the rights of parents to send their children to private schools, including religious, military, and foreign-language schools. In neither case was the term "privacy" employed. But the opinions spoke of "the right of the individual . . . to marry, establish a home and bring up children," 262 U.S. at 399, and of the rights of "those who nurture [a child] and direct his destiny. . . ." 268 U.S. at 53. In Prince v. Massachusetts, 321 U.S. 158 (1944), Justice Rutledge's opinion construed *Meyer* and *Pierce* in dicta as "respect[ing] the private realm of family life which the state cannot enter. . . ." 321 U.S. at 166. Finally, Justice Harlan, in Poe v. Ullman, 367 U.S. 497, 534-55 (1961) (Harlan, J., dissenting), suggested that the due process clause of the fourteenth amendment, in light of the fourth amendment's protections of "the privacy of the home," protects "the life which characteristically has its place in the home," namely, "a husband and wife's marital relations." This concept of "familial" or "marital" privacy was at least arguably all there was (or should have been) to the *Griswold* opinion. *See* 381 U.S. at 500 (Harlan, J., concurring). Later opinions have relied, at least in part, on this interpretation of the concept of privacy. *See, e.g.,* Paul v. Davis, 424 U.S. 693 (1976) Paris Adult Theatre I v. Slaton, 413 U.S. 49 (1973); Roe v. Wade, 410 U.S. 113 (1973) *See also* Wellington, *supra* note 15, at 288-94. But the decisions on contraception and abortion strained to the breaking point both the rationale and the rule of purely "familial privacy. 2) Another derivative strand of "unextrapolated" privacy analysis rested not on substantive due process but on equal protection. *See, e.g.,* Loving v. Virginia, 388 U.S. 1 (1967) (right to marry a person of another race); Skinner v. Oklahoma *ex rel.* Williamson, 316 U.S. 535 (1942) (right to have offspring). Even Eisenstadt v. Baird, 405 U.S. 438 (1972), purported to rest on equal protection grounds. *See also* note 144 *infra.*

Privacy is described in *Griswold* as a zone into which the government may not intrude without either obtaining consent from its occupants or having, in the circumstances, some special and compelling justification. Thus, for example, the fourth amendment bars "unreasonable searches and seizures" of "persons, houses, papers, and effects." But searches, and thus intrusions, of this kind may be consented to[134] or specially justified, as they are in the investigation of crimes, whether upon a warrant issued beforehand or upon probable cause found afterwards to have arisen from circumstances of urgency.[135] Raising this to a higher level of abstraction, we may characterize the zone of privacy as a legal island of personal autonomy in the midst of a sea of public regulation and interaction. Coming ashore, to push this metaphor, is normally forbidden without invitation or good reason. But here the difficulty with the metaphor, and with its concept of autonomy, becomes apparent: for what besides actual physical intrusion by agents of the state is to constitute a "coming ashore"?

In *Griswold* the Court held that a state criminal regulation violated the privacy of the defendants; but why and how? The answer cannot be that the law must cease at the imaginary or artificial borders we lay down around the private person, his home, and effects. By inviting someone to share your home or bed, you do not place him or her beyond the protection of, for instance, the homicide statutes, nor even beyond the police power as to health conditions. The agents of the state cannot use such laws as an excuse to intrude generally and at will upon our zones of privacy, for we may still hold them to account for their intrusions.[136] Rather, they have an adequate justification for such intrusions whenever they have good reason to seek out violations, albeit "in private," of criminal or other legislation that applies to the prohibited conduct wherever it takes place.

This means that to save the relation between privacy and autonomy we will have to qualify the latter concept: it cannot require a grant of general immunity to the application of all or most laws within the asserted zone of privacy; that asks too much of the legal system — leaving us with no legal system[137] at all but only rules of catch-as-catch-can applicability

---

[134] *See, e.g.*, Schneckloth v. Bustamonte, 412 U.S. 218 (1973).

[135] *See, e.g.*, Coolidge v. New Hampshire, 403 U.S. 443 (1971).

[136] *See, e.g.*, Bivens v. Six Unknown Named Agents of the Fed. Bureau of Narcotics, 403 U.S. 388 (1971) (holding that violation of the fourth amendment by a federal agent acting under color of law gives rise to a cause of action for damages).

[137] *See, e.g.*, H. L. A. HART, THE CONCEPT OF LAW (1961); J. RAZ, THE CONCEPT OF A LEGAL SYSTEM (1970).

and generality. Neither privacy nor legality will survive as mutually exclusive concepts; they must coexist and overlap. Again the need is for narrower conceptual bounds — this time in our account of autonomy.

Literally, autonomy means a condition in which a person or a state lays down its own law — its *autos nomos* — but this, taken absolutely, goes too far. Kant,[138] and before him Rousseau,[139] gave a rationalistic turn to autonomy, seeing in all whimsy or desire a threat to reason and so to freedom. Whatever we make of this, it will not take us far enough, or even in the right direction. In its political and ethical uses autonomy implies at a minimum some kind of independence from outside control or authority — from other cities in the case of the Greek city-states, from other impulses in the case of Kant's rationalist ethics.

In what sense is the zone of privacy asserted in *Griswold*, then, a zone of independence? At first glance, and in its last result, the independence seems to be from state regulation. But that reading of the case provides us no valid principle of interpretation, since state regulation must often reach into the zone of privacy, if only to remain generally applicable and effective. Admittedly when it does so by means of search, seizure, or arrest, there must be some account made and special justification given, because, among other things, there is an otherwise illegitimate intrusion upon our privacy. "Would we allow the police," asks Justice Douglas rhetorically, "to search the sacred precincts of marital bedrooms for tell-tale signs of the use of contraceptives?"[140] But just such searches are allowed where there are well-founded suspicions of other prohibited conduct.[141]

Why will autonomy and privacy give way before other prohibitions but not before this one? The only answer lies in a further restriction of that autonomy implicated in privacy by reference to those bodily and mental intimacies over which no one wishes to grant the state the right of regulation.[142] The idea that Justice Douglas found "repulsive" in *Gris-*

---

[138] *See* I. KANT, GROUNDWORK OF THE METAPHYSIC OF MORALS 98 (1961 ed.). *See also* Dworkin, *Autonomy and Behavior Control*. 6 HASTINGS CENTER REPORT 23 (1976).

[139] *See* J.J. ROUSSEAU, THE SOCIAL CONTRACT 169-307 (E. Barker ed. 1969).

[140] 381 U.S. 479, 485 (1965).

[141] And, in fact, lawful investigation of one putative crime itself justifies further, though limited, investigation of other putative crimes. Thus, a legitimate search for illegally possessed drugs may turn up admissible evidence of illegally possessed arms. *See, e.g.,* Coolidge v. New Hampshire, 403 U.S. 443, 464-73 (1971) (discussion of the "plain view" doctrine).

[142] The legislative or judicial selection of these intimacies is not easy. Inevitably one must "find" the particular and evolving shared intuitions of intimacy that underpin privacy rights.

*wold* was not that of the search of the bedrooms of married persons (any more than of unmarried persons) but of such a search conducted in furtherance of state regulation of "the marriage relationship,"[143] by which he can only have meant the intimacies of such a relationship.[144] As Justice Brennan said for the Court in *Eisenstadt v. Baird*,[145] "[i]f the right of privacy means anything, it is the right of the *individual*, married or single, to be free from unwanted governmental intrusions into matters so fundamentally affecting a person as the decision whether to bear or beget a child."[146]

From this language in *Eisenstadt* to the abortion decisions is neither so far-fetched nor so unwarranted a step as some commentators have suggested.[147] *Roe v. Wade*[148] left many questions unanswered and even unasked. Not least among these was that of the scope and force of the

---

[143] 381 U.S. 479, 485 (1965).

[144] Some have tried to restrict the relationship between privacy and autonomy by suggesting that the right to privacy prohibits the state from regulating *only* in areas that affect marriage, the family, childbearing, procreativity, etc. *See, e.g.*, Epstein, *Substantive Due Process By Any Other Name: The Abortion Cases*, 1973 SUP. CT. REV. 159, 169; *Comment, Roe and Paris: Does Privacy Have A Principle?*, 26 STAN. L. REV. 1161, 1174-77 (1974). No doubt a succession of "privacy" decisions may be arranged to conform to that theory. *See, e.g.*, Roe v. Wade, 410 U.S. 113 (1973); Eisenstadt v. Baird, 405 U.S. 438 (1972) (contraception for unmarried people); Loving v. Virginia, 388 U.S. 1 (1967) (striking down antimiscegnation statute); Griswold v. Connecticut, 381 U.S. 479 (1965) (contraception for married people); Skinner v. Oklahoma, 316 U.S. 535 (1942) (striking down sterilization requirement); Pierce v. Society of Sisters, 268 U.S. 510 (1925) (education of children); Meyer v. Nebraska, 262 U.S. 390 (1923) (same). And the Supreme Court itself has now articulated it more than once. *See, e.g.*, Whalen v. Roe, 45 U.S.L.W. 4166, 4168 n.26 (U.S. Feb. 22, 1977); Paul v. Davis, 424 U.S. 693, 713 (1976); Roe v. Wade, 410 U.S. 113, 152-53 (1973). But, perhaps wisely, the Court has never endorsed it. States can (and do) regulate extensively in these areas without much challenge to their substantive powers. Thus you have to take out licenses and undergo blood tests if you wish to marry. You must go to court for a divorce, alleging and proving an often fictional dispute in need of resolution. And your children must attend *some* school. In short, "marriage, procreation, contraception, family relationships and child rearing and education," in themselves, hardly confer a general immunity from state regulation.

But the right to privacy *will* protect the intimacies of marriage and family — as of sexuality and personality more generally. Nonetheless, recent privacy precedents — if we include *Eisenstadt* and *Roe* with *Griswold* — scarcely uphold the "traditional" theory, harking back to *Pierce* and *Meyer* and confining privacy rights to marital and familial relations.

[145] 405 U.S. 438 (1972).

[146] *Id.* at 453.

[147] *See* Ely, *The Wages of Crying Wolf: A Comment on* Roe v. Wade, 82 YALE L.J. 920 (1973).

[148] 410 U.S. 113 (1973).

274     Harvard Civil Rights-Civil Liberties Law Review     [Vol. 12

individual's right to privacy that was there finally and explicitly held binding upon the states under the fourteenth amendment. That right "is broad enough," wrote Justice Blackmun, in a sentence at once stinting and prodigal, "to encompass a woman's decision whether or not to terminate her pregnancy."[149] But why so? The opinion recites no reasons but only the uncertain precedents, including *Griswold* and *Eisenstadt*, and the no doubt certain but still inconclusive "detriments" imposed on the woman forced to carry a fetus to term.

Nonetheless, the reasons for invoking privacy in defense of abortion are plain to see. A woman's decision to have or forego an abortion is perhaps more than any other she makes an intimate one, expressive of both her identity and her autonomy. This is true insofar, at least, as that decision affects only (or chiefly) herself, in her sexuality and procreativity.[150] Granted that an ethical line may be drawn between contraception and abortion — drawn by "deep and seemingly absolute convictions"[151] about the beginnings of human life — that line must be conceded to be a boundary to the right to privacy and the autonomy it assures.[152] It is an autonomy vouchsafed to such personal decisions not simply because they are fundamental, but because they are at once fundamental, intimate, and, as the Court of Appeals emphasized in *Eisenstadt* (and the Supreme Court apparently concluded in *Roe*), innocent "of demonstrated harm."[153]

---

[149] *Id*. at 153.

[150] The only question, then, is the tragic and perhaps futile one: is the fetus in the womb to be considered simply as an expendable part of its bearer's anatomy or as more, as a person — or almost a person? The Supreme Court majority in *Roe* took it upon itself to answer that question. There were perhaps pressing reasons to do so. *See* Tribe, *The Supreme Court, 1972 Term — Foreword: Toward a Model of Roles in the Due Process of Life and Law*, 87 HARV. L. REV. 1 (1973). Nonetheless, the wisdom of attempting an inevitably summary answer — for the Justices are neither philosophers nor, more to the point, prophets — may be doubted. In any event, once the question is answered, the applicability *vel non* of privacy rights follows mechanically.

[151] Roe v. Wade, 410 U.S. 113 (1973).

[152] The line between *Eisenstadt* and *Roe* is well within the bounds of both intimacy and identity, and so, in a sense, well within the bounds of privacy. But how much autonomy does privacy comport with it, and how much is needed to justify abortion? Obviously, the protection of one person's autonomy is not a sufficient justification for the destruction of another's. Is the pregnant woman alone in her autonomy and privacy? Or is there, and at what point is there, an "other" whose autonomy — and life — will be destroyed by an abortion? Obviously, wherever that point is placed, you have, as it were, put the pencil-end of your compass of privacy down at its outer limit.

[153] Baird v. Eisenstadt, 429 F.2d 1398, 1402 (1st Cir. 1970) (emphasis added), *aff'd*, 405 U.S. 438 (1972). It should be emphasized that Chief Judge Aldrich's opinion speaks of "*demonstrated* harm." This qualification is of the utmost constitutional and even moral significance. We may assume that the government must stand ready to justify its infringe-

The Supreme Court opinion in _Eisenstadt_ explicitly left aside this last qualification. It was admittedly unnecessary to the narrow holding on equal protection grounds that was more or less fully warranted by the inconsistency between a state prohibition on the use of contraceptives by the unmarried and the _Griswold_ precedent. Nonetheless an emergent

---

ments of personal liberty as at least (a) in rational furtherance of (b) some legitimate public purpose. Not only the fourteenth amendment but also the Constitution as a whole, with behind it much moral and political philosophy, requires this much. _See, e.g._, Henkin, _Morals and the Constitution: The Sin of Obscenity_, 63 COLUM. L. REV. 391, 401-11 (1963). But to justify such infringements as necessary to the prevention of harm, you must at least be able to show that the particular harm results from the particular liberty exercised. That demonstration will never be satisfactory if it is self-validating, _i.e._, requires no more than that those who say they are harmed _say they are harmed_. A harm in that sense is not even interpersonally or objectively demonstrable — never mind demonstrated.

The question of demonstrability also cuts across the distinction between self-regarding and other-regarding crimes. So long as there is some victim, even a self-victim, suffering demonstrable harm, the constitutionality and morality of infringement will at least be arguable. This is one reason why suicide, addictions of various kinds, severe self-mutilations, and self-denials present somewhat different considerations for the morality and constitutionality of governmental action than, say, obscenity or adultery or homosexuality. _See_ Louch, _Sins and Crimes_, and Dworkin, _Paternalism_, in MORALITY AND THE LAW 73-85, 107-26 (R. Wasserstrom ed. 1971).

Surely the right to privacy casts some doubt on the various prohibitions upon self-inflicted injuries. But as Justice Blackmun noted in his majority opinion in Roe v. Wade, 410 U.S. 113, 154 (1973), the right to privacy and the "unlimited right to do with one's body as one pleases" are not synonymous. Surely we may concede to individuals _some_ bodily autonomy without thereby conceding to them _all_ bodily autonomy. It is true but probably trivial that in disposing of your body at your pleasure you create problems — "harms" — for others. What is important is that privacy, while it must have its first reference in the body, is limited to _intimacy_, bodily _or_ mental. One has still to explain why, say, suicide is a wholly _intimate_ matter, while murder is not. _See_ J. FEINBERG, SOCIAL PHILOSOPHY 25-54 (1973). _See generally_ P. DEVLIN, THE ENFORCEMENT OF MORALS (1965); H. L. A. HART, LAW, LIBERTY AND MORALITY (1963).

This analysis of bodily autonomy saves us, as well, from the absurdities of calling _all_ bodily compulsion — including, say, military conscription — an invasion of privacy. _See_ Henkin, _Privacy and Autonomy_, 74 COLUM. L. REV. 1410, 1429 (1974). To give an even simpler example, compulsory medical procedures such as vaccinations and blood tests, however discomfiting, need not always involve the invasion of privacy: a forced needle in the arm, while undoubtedly requiring some public justification, may interfere with my autonomy, but it hardly offends the intimacy of my personal identity. _See, e.g._, Jacobson v. Massachusetts, 197 U.S. 11 (1905) (upholding compulsory vaccination). _See also_ Schmerber v. California, 384 U.S. 757 (1966) (forced blood test admissible as evidence in criminal prosecution); Breithaupt v. Abram, 352 U.S. 432 (1957) (same). Lesser public "compulsions," amounting to no more than irritations, surely require lesser justifications. _See, e.g._, Public Utilities Comm'n v. Pollak, 343 U.S. 451 (1952) (radio broadcasting on private mass transit bus line was not a violation of right to privacy). _Cf._ Lister, _The Right to Control the Use of One's Body_, in THE RIGHTS OF AMERICANS 348 (N. Dorsen ed. 1971) (right to control body must protect at least the right to control sexuality).

understanding of the relation between privacy and autonomy seemed to require just such a qualification. It brought the Justices to the edge of an intellectual precipice, one they have since shied away from with silent fierceness: over it had to topple either the right to privacy, in any strong sense, or else the freedom of the state and federal governments to impose criminal sanctions upon activities which, however abhorrent to conventional morality, cannot be shown to do harm.

Harm is itself at issue here: our definition of it — and our *demonstration* of it once defined — will condition most of the significant constitutional applications we seek for the concept of privacy.[154] Surely, privacy should not, in justice, allow us to do harm to others with impunity.[155] The difficulty begins only when others, particularly in a majority,[156] feel themselves harmed even by those "private actions done privately" which have only private or trivially public consequences.[157] For

---

[154] The right to indulge privately in intimate but deviant sexual activities is still uncertain. *See, e.g.,* Doe v. Commonwealth's Att'y, 403 F. Supp. 1199 (E.D. Va. 1975), *aff'd mem.,* 425 U.S. 901 (1976) (upholding a state anti-sodomy statute against attack by homosexuals engaging in such activity privately and as consenting adults). *Cf.* Lovisi v. Slayton, 539 F.2d 349 (4th Cir. 1976) (upholding enforcement of the same statute against a married couple who concededly engaged in such activity in the presence of a third party). The claim to private or intimate indulgence, *see* Stanley v. Georgia, 394 U.S. 557 (1969), is not on the same footing as the claim to public or notorious indulgence. *See, e.g.,* Singer v. United States Civ. Serv. Comm'n, 530 F.2d 247 (9th Cir. 1976) *judgement vacated,* 45 U.S.L.W. 3453 (U.S. Jan. 11, 1977) (upholding the dismissal of a homosexual government employee found to have "flaunted his homosexual way of life" on the job). Public indulgence raises separate questions about the balance between the "public peace" and individual rights to public association and expression. *Compare* Gay Students v. Bonner, 509 F.2d 652 (1st Cir. 1974) (striking down the denial of access to facilities by a public university to a group of homosexual students), *with* Acanfora v. Board of Educ., 491 F.2d 498 (4th Cir. 1974), *cert. denied,* 419 U.S. 836 (1974) (upholding transfer of homosexual teacher to non-teaching duties on the basis of a deliberate withholding of information about sexual preferences, but *not* on the basis of his public discussion of homosexual rights and problems).

[155] This has been recognized at least since Sir James Fitzjames Stephen, *supra* note 22, responded to John Stuart Mill's ON LIBERTY, *supra* note 22. Their argument — over Mill's principle that the only justification for interfering with the liberty of any individual is self-protection — underlies much of the controversy over the extent of the right to privacy.

[156] It need not be a numerical or enduring majority, so long as, on a particular vote, it is an effective one. *See generally* R. DAHL, A PREFACE TO DEMOCRATIC THEORY (1956).

[157] A distinction of course may be drawn between direct and indirect public consequences, either of which will justify legislation. Thus, prohibitions against obscenity, prostitution, and gambling are often justified on the basis of indirect but predictable and tangible consequences — for example, the probable takeover by organized crime, or the probable deterioration of a neighborhood. The argument here goes to those cases in which neither sort of consequence can be shown as probable; and since we are talking about intimacy and privacy, things done in secret, such consequences are dubious in any case.

some of these others may still find our private conduct offensive, if only on aesthetic, religious, or "moral" grounds.[158] The harm done is then doubly "moral," since it contravenes the majority in its morale as well as its morality. But in a working democracy popular morale and morality must sooner or later obtain a fair measure of authority in legislation.[159] What if that authority is exercised in criminal legislation governing our intimate, and otherwise private and autonomous, lives? Any court sitting in review of the constitutionality of such legislation sits uncomfortably astride the two stools of American judicial, and indeed constitutional, policy: majority rule and minority rights. The plain fact is that the right to privacy as we seek to apply it — with generality and consistency — must often be "counter-majoritarian."[160] Nor do we lack a recent example of

---

[158] "Moral" in a very limited sense: meaning that which, while without direct or indirect "harmful" consequences, is nonetheless seen as wrong, as bad, as evil. Now, of course, "harm" itself is objectionable because we take it to be wrong, bad, or evil. It, too, rests on a shared moral intuition. But nearly everyone shares *that* intuition and, what is more, no one can consistently deny it without licensing others to harm him or her at will. This most basic intuition is, in other words, indispensable to legal and moral prohibitions generally. *See* Dworkin, *Lord Devlin and the Enforcement of Morals,* 75 YALE L.J. 986 (1966).

[159] "Every opinion tends to become a law. I think that the word liberty in the Fourteenth Amendment is perverted when it is held to prevent the natural outcome of a dominant opinion, unless it can be said that a rational and fair man necessarily would admit that the statute proposed would infringe fundamental principles as they have been understood by the traditions of our people and our law." Lochner v. New York, 198 U.S. 45, 76 (1905) (Holmes, J., dissenting).

[160] Here one can only refer to the familiar analyses and convictions of Alexander Bickel. *See generally* A. BICKEL, THE MORALITY OF CONSENT (1975); A. BICKEL, THE LEAST DANGEROUS BRANCH (1962). Despite his more and more trenchant skepticism in the last years of his life, Bickel himself embraced judicial "minoritarianism," as it were, and even judicial activism. *See* Purcell, *Alexander M. Bickel and the Post-Realist Constitution,* 11 HARV. C.R.-C.L.L. REV. 521 (1976). The right to privacy generates a considerable tension between what Bickel called principle and expediency — the expediency of consent, that is. The tension may be stated thus: the *principle* of a right to privacy is now, after *Griswold, Eisenstadt,* and *Roe,* a majoritarian principle, at least in the minimal sense that it is formally and legally binding. As such, privacy is a fair subject for further consistent legal and philosophical analysis and for further consistent legal application. But the further consistent application of the majority's principle offends the majority's *actual* will. Still, privacy remains a majoritarian principle, and one of the utmost importance and significance. Now, there are unexplored subtleties here as to the level of abstraction at which the principle is stated. This effort in restriction of the principle, however, has gone to make it as concrete as, in all coherence, it can be made. (Wellington, *supra* note 20, at 285-311, in making it yet more concrete, would have us do without it altogether.) The issue of "harm" is of course much more general, and raises the question of whether some other and superior majoritarian principle — here, that of doing no unnecessary harm to others — overcomes the principle of personal privacy. And while Bickel might have disagreed with

the acute and even paralyzing discomfort our judges and Justices may feel at such junctures — or precipices — in the adjudication of privacy rights.

Take the Supreme Court's recent action in summarily affirming a lower court holding that homosexuals may constitutionally be subjected to criminal prosecutions for sexual practices carried on in privacy between consenting adults. At least three Justices on the present Court overcame their discomfort to vote, without the needed fourth, to note probable jurisdiction and set down for oral argument and full hearing the case of *Doe v. Commonwealth's Attorney*.[161] Six other Justices voted without opinion simply to affirm the lower court decision as it stood. They slighted thereby the relevance and importance, or perhaps even the validity, of the right to privacy as a constitutional limit to the reach, through the criminal law, of majority public opinion and its professed morality.

*Doe* was a suit brought by several male homosexuals for declaratory and injunctive relief from the enforcement or threat of enforcement of the Virginia sodomy statute.[162] The law they challenged had been on the books in Virginia, in one form or another, since 1792, and went back to Leviticus and other ancient authorities.[163] It made the usual sexual practices of these men a crime punishable by from one to three years imprisonment. In no sense in desuetude, either in conventional morality or in the legislative will, the statute put the threat of an occasional and discreet prosecution into the hands of local police officers and prosecutors. To the plaintiffs this threat was all the more intimidating because it was directed against any possibility, for them as they were and chose to be, of enjoying the most basic of interpersonal intimacies.

In his opinion, Judge Bryan stated their complaint in these terms: "Virginia's statute making sodomy a crime is unconstitutional, each of the male plaintiffs aver, when it is applied to his active and regular homosexual relations with another *adult male, consensually* and *in private*."[164] The words "regular" and "active," so strangely out of place, as it may seem, in a claim made under an asserted constitutional right to privacy, come straight out of some lawyer's close reading of *Griswold*

---

what is said here, he himself at times espoused equally counter-majoritarian applications of implicit majoritarian principles. Integration of public schools is perhaps the best example. *See* Bickel, *The Original Understanding and the Segregation Decision*, 69 HARV. L. REV. 1 (1955).

[161] 403 F. Supp. 1199 (E.D. Va. 1975), *aff'd mem.*, 425 U.S. 901 (1976) (Justices Brennan, Marshall, and Stevens voting to grant *certiorari*).

[162] VA. CODE § 18.1-212 (1950)

[163] 403 F. Supp. 1199, 1202 n.2.

[164] *Id.* at 1200.

and its commentary. In *Griswold* Justice Douglas had spoken of "the marriage relation"; and his opinion, narrowly applied to the facts, brought only that relation within the zone of privacy protected by the Constitution. *Eisenstadt*'s inclusion within this zone of the unmarried in their sexual relationships has been criticized as, among other things, unnecessary to the holding that equal protection required that a state, in banning contraception purely on moral grounds, ban it to one and all.[165] But will not the *Griswold* right to privacy, in any case, protect every intimacy whose only plausible harm lies purely in the eyes of its necessarily intrusive beholders?[166]

Justice Harlan, in his dissenting opinion in *Poe v. Ullman*,[167] had suggested that Connecticut's anti-contraceptive statutes infringed a fundamental liberty protected by the due process guarantee of the fourteenth amendment. It was not, however, the liberty (or, as we have called it, the autonomy) of sexual intimacies generally. Rather, it was confined to the intimacies of marriage, "an institution which the State not only must allow, but which always and in every age it has fostered and protected."[168]

Following Justice Harlan, Harry H. Wellington rationalized *Griswold* on the basis of a social compact made between the state and any two of its citizens who marry, conceding at least to them some limited sexual autonomy.[169] On this reasoning, *Eisenstadt* implies no more than that single persons may have equal access to contraceptive devices with married persons for purposes of a *quasi-marital* intimacy. So in *Doe*, the plaintiffs sought to portray their relationships as tantamount to marriage.

It may well be, as a matter of either ethics or conduct, that homosexuals form bonds of sexual and personal loyalty as strong and lasting as those of heterosexuals. And if so, perhaps homosexuals ought to be allowed to marry.[170] But need they or anyone else marry — or all but marry — to make good their rights to privacy? To say "yes" here is to grant far too much to the state by way of a power to make compacts for liberties with some persons and purposes, but not with others. Surely the

[165] *See* Wellington, *supra* note 20, at 296-98. *See also* P. BATOR, P. MISHKIN, D. SHAPIRO, & H. WECHSLER, THE FEDERAL COURTS AND THE FEDERAL SYSTEM 189-91 (2d ed. 1973).

[166] In other words, those who are offended — and so "harmed" — by the knowledge of deviant sexual or other practices carried on in private among consenting adults bring the harm on themselves by their excessive vigilance.

[167] 367 U.S. 497, 539-45 (1960) (Harlan, J., dissenting).

[168] *Id.* at 553.

[169] Wellington, *supra* note 20, at 285-311.

[170] *See* Note, *The Legality of Homosexual Marriage*, 82 YALE L.J. 573 (1973).

liberties of adult intimacy in our society are more fundamental than this implies. Equal protection alone requires a more even-handed dispensation.

Wellington called the zone of privacy "an unfortunate invention."[171] Ultimately, as he saw, the Harlan analysis in *Poe* and *Griswold* dispenses altogether with any general right to privacy. What privacy it leaves, some will have and others will not; some intimacies will be protected by it and some will not. Apparently the sole differentiating variable will be the state's acknowledgement *vel non* of a certain civil status: marriage or its equivalent.

The Supreme Court majority that affirmed[172] *Doe* may well have understood that there can be no constitutional right to privacy of equal and consistent application where such a restricted and intimate autonomy as the plaintiffs sought to vindicate is denied. This is the conceptual minimum of any notion of privacy: an autonomy sufficient to bar state intrusion, observation, or regulation of the harmless intimacies of personal identity. By any standard of intuition or analysis, those intimacies begin with the body and its sexuality.[173]

---

[171] Wellington, *supra* note 20, at 294.

[172] Summary affirmances, while precedents, "are not of the same precedential value as an opinion of this Court treating the question on the merits." Edelman v. Jordan, 415 U.S. 651, 671 (1974). Thus principles of *stare decisis*, which are never absolute in constitutional adjudication, constrain the Court even less than usual when it returns to a case such as *Doe*. "Indeed, upon fuller consideration of an issue under plenary review, the Court has not hesitated to discard a rule which a line of summary affirmances may appear to have established." Fusari v. Steinberg, 419 U.S. 379, 392 (1975) (Burger, C.J., concurring). It may well be argued, in future discussions of *Doe*, that the plaintiffs' relatively weak showing of ripeness and standing — none of the plaintiffs was indicted or convicted — prompted the Supreme Court majority to affirm without hearing arguments or handing down an opinion.

[173] Wellington might well object here that unless one takes an absolutistic position as to autonomy — namely that autonomy *in its very nature* must include the harmless and hidden sexual intimacies of consenting adults — one cannot force the state and the effective majority it must be presumed to represent to concede any greater autonomy than that stated or implied in the basic constitutional compact. And, of course, even the added margin provided by a changing "conventional morality," however measured, is unlikely today to allow for the generalized autonomy as to intimacy for which I argue. But our evolving conventional and constitutional morality require us to yield to ideals of consistency and generality in any concession of right. These comport awkwardly at best with the sort of particularized "social compacts" that Wellington finds necessary to distinguish *Griswold* from *Eisenstadt*. For if privacy is after all a constitutional right to some form of "liberty" (as opposed to property), how are we to justify its very selective application to the married (or all-but-married) and not to the unmarried, to the heterosexual and not to the homosexual? Conventional morality makes distinctions of this sort, and perhaps constitutional morality makes them too; but in either case is there a moral or constitutional justification for

The *Doe* plaintiffs offended no one who did not seek offense. Harmless and consensual, their conduct in their own homes and bedrooms deserved all the protections of a constitutionally guaranteed right to privacy. But the decision in *Doe* was wrong not only because it mistook the force and scope of the right to privacy. It was wrong as well because it failed to uphold the constitutional rights of the politically weak and isolated to work out their own lives in their own ways.[174] One may only be thankful, in a case like *Doe*, that neither this Supreme Court nor any state legislature can ever altogether deprive people of such an elementary personal freedom.

## IV. PRIVACY IN INFORMATION

Privacy is, then, the control over or the autonomy of the intimacies of personal identity. These three concepts — intimacy, identity, and autonomy — limit and focus the valid applications of the concept of privacy. When applied to cases of physical intrusion and state regulation, this definition of the concept yields what we have wanted all along: a right to privacy at once strong — in the sense that it will take some strong argument of policy or urgency to justify us in overriding it — and limited in scope.[175] The correlation between the strength of this right and its limitations is more or less direct.

---

them that we can accept as well-founded and well-reasoned? In other words, do these past conventions, with their limitations in scope and generality, hold up under moral and constitutional scrutiny?

On the question of whether or not privacy is reducible to a kind of property, and therefore to a right dependent upon prior state acknowledgement or "civil status," see Davis, *supra* note 42, at 20-24 (arguing that invasion of privacy in tort law comes to no more than expropriation of property and/or intentional infliction of mental anguish); and Thomson, *supra* note 7 (arguing that a right to privacy is otiose as either (a) reducible to other other rights such as property or (b) no right at all). *But see* Scanlon, *Thomson on Privacy*, 4 PHIL. & PUB. AFF. 315 (1975), and Rachels, *Why Privacy is Important*, 4 PHIL. & PUB. AFF. 323 (1975), for rejoinders to Thomson.

[174] *See* Justice Stone's celebrated footnote 4, in United States v. Carolene Prod. Co., 304 U.S. 144, 152 n.4 (1938). For a problematic extension of this argument to minors in their sexual intimacies, see Carey v. Population Serv. Int'l. 398 F. Supp. 821 (S.D.N.Y. 1975) (3-judge court), (No. 75-443), 45 U.S.L.W. 3481 (U.S. Jan. 18, 1977) (oral argument before the United States Supreme Court). In that case several plaintiffs (none of them minors) are attacking the constitutionality of a New York law limiting the access of minors to contraceptives. People over 16 may obtain them from pharmacists; those under 16, only from physicians.

[175] Intimacy gives us a concept to confine the scope of our intuitions by argument and analysis. But the content of the intimacies of identity remains to be worked out case-by-case and application-by-application. Certainly it is possible to magnify that content in such a

282     Harvard Civil Rights-Civil Liberties Law Review     [Vol. 12

Is it, however, too limited a definition, yielding too limited a right? There may be over-definition as well as under-definition in discussions of this sort, too much concreteness as well as too much abstraction. Applicability depends, after all, upon flexibility. The most telling test of any legal definition of privacy is its application to several different *sorts* of cases. So far we have dealt chiefly with intrusion and regulation. A harder sort of case, conceptually and constitutionally, is that of an assertedly violated privacy right in information or in knowledge.

We will have to draw a distinction here between the concepts of privacy and confidentiality. Almost any information not generally available may be kept in confidence: an implicit or explicit mutual agreement suffices for that. Contrast with this specifically *private* information. Privacy itself is a narrow and more or less fixed category. The information included within it must be in some plain sense private, either in its content or in its use. By definition this excludes all but such information as is necessary to the intimacies of our personal identities, for standards of intimacy, unlike standards of confidentiality, cannot be created simply by mutual agreement. Moreover, it takes only one person to make information private; it takes two at least to make information, even originally private information, confidential.[176]

Private information and confidential information require legal protection, but in varying degrees and from different quarters. Private information needs only a very few legal protections, but including, at times,

---

way as to make the concept — as a *limiting* concept — useless. But "intimacy" lends itself less easily than the allied concepts of privacy, identity, and autonomy to this sort of magnification. In fact, its scope may seem *too* constricted, as, for instance, where we take all of intimacy as reducible to what may be its paradigm, sexual intimacy. That it *has* such a paradigm at all is an important count in its favor: it is at least the beginning, and an immediately felt and almost unanimously shared beginning, for our reasoning towards consistent and general standards for application of the concept of privacy. Decency failed precisely because it no longer elicited sufficiently shared and distinct responses of this kind. Intimacy has a quite certain and quite exact core of meaning or application. One finds it with little difficulty in the case law, not only in *Griswold, Eisenstadt,* or *Roe,* but even in such a negative landmark as Sidis v. F-R Publishing Co., 113 F.2d 806 (2d Cir.), *cert. denied,* 311 U.S. 711 (1940). *See* note 82 *supra. See also* Paris Adult Theatre I v. Slaton, 413 U.S. 49, 65-69 & n.13 (1973). No concept will make it a simple mechanical operation for litigators and adjudicators. Nonetheless the concept of intimacy, together with those of identity and autonomy, makes the task manageable.

[176] Thus when you apply for a job you still have a right to privacy — vis-a-vis your prospective employer in much intimate information — *e.g.,* your medical records — that he might request. To get the job, however, you will probably have to waive that right with respect to the employer. Your only protection is, then, the *confidence* that you explicitly or implicitly impose on the employer in his handling of the information. Whether his duty of confidentiality is a *legal* one depends of course on the relevant facts, and statutes.

the protection of enforced confidentiality.[177] What few protections private information obtains must be able to withstand many forceful arguments of constitutional principle and policy available to a free press, but also to a free people. And if one implication of the supremacy clause[178] is that only a federal constitutional principle may limit another federal constitutional principle, then the right to privacy in information, in its contest with the right of access to information, gives us a final test of the constitutional status of our concept of privacy.

To make it a fair test, we will have to "purify" our case law somewhat artificially. Nearly always, informational and physical privacy are violated at the same time.[179] What constitutes a purely informational violation turns not so much on how the information is obtained but rather on how it is used. For the significant intrusiveness here must be "purely" psychological[180]: perhaps the paradigm is for us, as for Warren and Brandeis, the publication by a newspaper or magazine of some otherwise private fact that embarrasses or humiliates us.

But such private information may well have been obtained without any tort or illegality at all; we may even have given it out inadvertently ourselves.[181] And, leaving aside for a moment the first amendment, judges and juries will encounter nearly insurmountable difficulties in finding an invasion of privacy without any physical or objective correlative and in fashioning an adequate remedy for that invasion after it has occurred and the information is out.

In any claim to autonomy in information, we seem inevitably to be caught between too little and too much: we seek to extend our control over our identities to some part of the knowledge[182] that others may have

---

[177] *See* pp. 285-86 *infra*.

[178] "This Constitution and the Laws of the United States which shall be made in Pursuance thereof; and all Treaties made, or which shall be made, under the Authority of the United States, shall be supreme Law of the Land . . . ." U.S. CONST. art. VI.

[179] *See, e.g.,* York v. Story, 324 F.2d 450 (9th Cir. 1963).

[180] Abstractly, it is true, any invasion of our privacy, no matter how direct or physical, is a psychological invasion, for it takes away some of our control over the intimacy of our identities. This is something that cannot be reduced to a purely physical reference or category. Perhaps only a false dualism leads us to distinguish sharply between the invaded intimacies of the body and the mind. We are prompted to do so, however, because we *can* readily distinguish between classes of injuries; some are felt purely mentally and some are felt both mentally and physically.

[181] This is in fact the pattern in the case reports. *See, e.g.,* Sidis v. F-R Publishing Co., 113 F. 2d 806 (2d Cir.), *cert. denied,* 311 U.S. 711 (1940).

[182] By knowledge I mean information in the broad and extended sense, perceptions or judgments of us that may be transmitted by some concrete reproduction, as in a photo or on a tape, or some more abstract report, as in spoken or written words.

of us, but knowledge of one another is simply too shapeless a category to divide neatly in two, one part labeled private rights and the other public uses. When we attempt the division on the basis of the contents of the knowledge in question, we enter a legal and philosophical morass, involving ourselves in possibly endless inquiries and disputes over the classification of this or that "item" of personal information. What we need is an analogue, in informational privacy, to trespass or regulation in the cases of intrusion. Use — or the threat of it — is all that we can look to.

Not *all* uses of such information are on the same legal footing. Take the case of gossip. Why, after all, is it left to go its often pernicious way? Gossip may deal in the most intimate and even humiliating truths and mistruths about us. We may tolerate it merely because we cannot effectively suppress it; but that is hardly an analytically dispositive reason. Were we able to put a stop to gossip of the same quality as, say, the worst newspaper or broadcast publicity, we would not do so; why not?[183] Part of the difference is perhaps quantity, for by its very quantitive limitations in transmission gossip remains compatible with privacy — and autonomy. We suffer less, or differently, from private than from public (or what Warren and Brandeis called quasi-public) speculation about our intimacies and secrets. Sheer numbers make a difference. No one can make privacy absolute; few ever try. We may in fact have some need for others to find out at least some of our secrets. There is, in any case, reason enough to tolerate the more or less constant seepage of information, and often intimate information, about ourselves that comes with living in society. Our privacy, and with it our autonomy, will not be at an end, even as to these very details of information, simply because someone else has found them out and passed them on without our consent or even without our knowledge: privacy is thus diminished but not destroyed. We maintain our autonomy to the extent that we retain some measure of control over further significant disclosures, and thus further significant uses, of such information. Others will continue to talk without our consent, but the power and even the life-span of such talk is likely to be limited, for memories are short and curiosity is inconstant.

A striking illustration of the decisive importance of the use of information may be found in the right of a defendant to criminal charges to suppress evidence against him gained by the intrusion of eavesdropping without warrant or sufficient cause. In the line of cases from *Olmstead v.*

---

[183] This disregards perhaps our pre-eminent lack of hypocrisy. Most of us gossip and enjoy gossip: we are, as Ogden Nash had it, both gossipers and gossipees. And, in a leaden (as opposed to golden) rule of consistency, we would not ban what we would not forego.

*United States*[184] to *Katz v. United States*[185] evaluating, with less and less sympathy, the various techniques of electronic or mechanical surveillance used by police and prosecutors, the Supreme Court has returned again and again to privacy analyses of the interests protected by the fourth amendment.[186] In *Silverman v. United States*,[187] the Court for the first time applied the exclusionary rule[188] to evidence obtained by "an actual intrusion in a constitutionally protected area."[189]

Since *Katz*, at least, that area has been understood as bounded, if somewhat vaguely, by the "reasonable expectation of privacy" the individuals have in the various life-situations that typically shelter the intimacies of both the mind and body.[190] In all of the criminal cases, the relief sought was suppression of the evidence in court, a prohibition, in

---

[184] 277 U.S. 438 (1928).

[185] 389 U.S. 347 (1967). For citation and discussion of the intervening cases on mechanical and electronic surveillance, *see, e.g.,* J. VORENBERG, CRIMINAL LAW AND PROCEDURE: CASES AND MATERIALS 628-45 (1975); Parker, *supra* note 38, at 288-91.

[186] *See* Amsterdam, *Perspectives on the Fourth Amendment*. 58 MINN. L. REV. 349 (1974).

[187] 365 U.S. 505, 512 (1961).

[188] *See* Mapp v. Ohio, 367 U.S. 643 (1961); Weeks v. United States, 232 U.S. 383 (1914). *Weeks* held that in federal prosecutions the fourth amendment barred the use of evidence secured through an illegal search and seizure. *Mapp*, which overruled Wolf v. Colorado, 338 U.S. 25 (1949), held that the fourth amendment exclusionary rule was applicable to state prosecutions as well.

[189] 365 U.S. 505, 512 (1961).

[190] This formula, first stated in Terry v. Ohio, 392 U.S. 1 (1968), derives from Justice Harlan's concurring opinion in *Katz*, 389 U.S. 347, 360-62 (1967) (Harlan, J., concurring). "My understanding of the rule. . ." he wrote, "is that there is a twofold requirement, first that a person have exhibited an actual (subjective) expectation of privacy and, second, that the expectation be one that society is prepared to recognize as 'reasonable'." *Id.* at 361. But "subjective expectation" is a poor phrase for actual or constructive waiver and, short of that, one wonders why *particular* subjective expectations, which may be biased towards too much or too little, should matter. The emphasis should surely fall on *shared* expectations, as Justice Harlan himself indicated in dissent in United States v. White, 401 U.S. 745, 787 (1971) (Harlan, J., dissenting). *See* Amsterdam, *supra* note 186. "The constitutionally protected area" must be seen as private and intimate *per se* in order to extend to it my privacy analysis. These are places or situations wherein the intimacies of life — physical *and* mental — most often are conducted. Without general protection, these places and situations will not afford the security necessary for this to remain true. *See* Fried, *supra* note 42, at 477-84. But what goes on in such protected areas need not be intimate in any further sense: our private conversations by telephone are no less protected when we talk politics — or sports — than when we talk sex. *But see* Belle Terre v. Boraas, 416 U.S. 1 (1974). This analysis applies to the analogous private torts as well. *See, e.g.,* LeCrone v. Ohio Bell Tel. Co., 114 Ohio App. 299, 182 N.E.2d 15 (1961) (private wiretapping an intrusion on privacy); Rhodes v. Graham, 238 Ky. 225, 37 S.W.2d 46 (1931) (same).

other words, of its later use in a limited context decisive of the autonomy of the accused. By itself, that remedy sufficed, by restoring control, to protect an already intruded upon but not yet destroyed privacy. Curiously, the right to *privacy* thus imposed on its violator, at least in the courtroom, a duty of *confidentiality*.[191]

We have a needed clue in this to the application of the concept of autonomy to the pervasive and disquieting misuses of personal information about us kept in permanent files by the institutions that tax, police, employ, finance, educate, or even heal us. Such information, or misinformation, as they possess seems often to be not so much *private* — in the strict sense of intimate, personal knowledge with little or no bearing on public conduct — as *confidential*, that is, held in trust and in secret for certain limited and specified purposes *usually more or less definite and temporary.* Sometimes we will have consented, implicitly or explicitly, to

---

[191] Whether that duty is *constitutionally* mandated is at present a vexed question at the Supreme Court. *See* Stone v. Powell, 96 S.Ct. 3037 (1976); United States v. Janis, 96 S.Ct. 3021 (1976). In *Stone* the Court denied federal habeas corpus relief sought on the ground that evidence obtained in an unconstitutional search and seizure was introduced in a state trial leading to conviction and imprisonment. In *Janis* the Court refused to extend the exclusionary rule to civil proceedings brought by the Internal Revenue Service on the basis of "evidence seized by a state criminal law enforcement officer in good faith, but nonetheless unconstitutionally." *Id.* at 3023. Justice Powell's majority opinion in *Stone* argued that the exclusionary rule — which for half a century applied to the federal government but not to the states — was fashioned by the courts to deter police conduct in violation of the fourth amendment. Deterrence was thus its "primary justification." *Id.* at 3048. Other interests, including judicial integrity, were in his view at best secondary. *Id.* at 3047. Moreover, his opinion, along with Chief Justice Burger's concurrence and Justice White's dissent, expressed misgivings about the actual deterrent efficacy of the exclusionary rule. *Id.* at 3050. Justice Blackmun's opinion in *Janis* raised further questions about the propriety of the judiciary exercising "a supervisory role that is properly the duty of the Executive and Legislative Branches." *Id.* at 3034-35. In both cases Justice Brennan, joined by Justice Marshall, dissented, *id.* at 3055, and *id.* at 3035, arguing that the fourth amendment *requires* redress of such privacy violations by means of the exclusionary rule. *See* Linde, *Judges, Critics, and the Realist Tradition,* 82 YALE L.J. 227, 240-42 (1972): "To hold that a process in which public officers ignore a defendant's constitutionally guaranteed rights is not the 'due process' of the Constitution asserts that the due process clause is concerned with the individual immediately jeopardized by the process, not merely with optimizing the system's efficiency or protecting the government's moral reputation." *Id.* at 242.

Surely some remedy ought to be provided, if only to keep federal judges above the appearance of tacit acquiescence in violations of the fourth amendment and the right to privacy. Exclusion, whether it deters or not, seems to be the only remedy available. Obviously no court can restore the intruded-upon privacy itself; money damages are awarded too infrequently to be an effective deterrent. The imposition of a limited and assured duty of confidentiality is all that judges can do. Is this a *constitutional* mandate? The answer is "yes", but subject to alternative possibilities that courts or legislatures may devise.

give this information, as when we apply for a job or even for a phone. Sometimes, however, as when we are under some general (but non-intrusive)[192] surveillance, we will have given no consent at all.

In either case, no invasion of privacy need occur. But there are two significant vices latent in the very collection of this information: first, there is the possibility, virtually a certainty in many cases, that its life as information will be prolonged beyond necessity or justification; and second, there is the possiblity that its contents will be divulged without our consent or knowledge and so without our corrections. When this happens, the information is not usually made public but simply passed on in violation either of the original confidence, if any, or else of the original purpose for which it was gathered and stored.[193] This comes, trivially, to a kind of institutionalized gossip, and its vice is its tendency to distortion and incompleteness, tempting others to make decisions about us, as gossips will, behind our backs and on uncertain grounds.

What is not at all trivial about this is that the gossip and the decisions based upon it are institutionalized at such a level and to such an extent as to deprive us of autonomy in information at just those points where autonomy in other important life-choices is at stake. We are often forced to present ourselves for judgments by others occupying decisive institutional positions in our society and in our lives: they will make judgments about a job, a mortgage, or even a sentence or parole. These others may well have in their possession such stale, partial, or false information about us as may be found in permanent, easily reproducible and transmittable files. Far from consenting to this, we will often have no knowledge of it, and of course no way to prevent or correct it.

What hurts us is not that we lose control over the decisions themselves, for *ex hypothesi* we never had such control. It is rather that we suffer a behind-the-scenes depreciation of the value of our own input into such decisions, since whatever we say or do is discounted without our

---

[192] Non-intrusive surveillance includes all manner of legally and constitutionally permissible observations of our comings and goings in and out of the public world — all the places, that is, where people pass more or less freely as they go about their business or pleasure. Privacy obviously imposes fairly strict — and no doubt unwelcome — limits on those who engage in such surveillance. *See, e.g.,* Galella v. Onassis, 353 F. Supp. 196 (S.D.N.Y. 1972), *aff'd and modified on other grounds,* 487 F.2d 986 (2d Cir. 1973) (free lance photographer of celebrities); Nader v. General Motors Corp., 25 N.Y.2d 560, 307 N.Y.S.2d 647, 255 N.E.2d 765 (1970) (private detectives and their "operatives" hired by automobile manufacturer to discredit consumer advocate).

[193] Obviously wiretaps and the like violate *privacy* rather than confidentiality. The latter comes into play only as a judicially (and perhaps constitutionally) imposed remedy for privacy violations. *See* note 191 *supra*.

knowing how or why. Even if we do know that our autonomy is undercut by such a transmission of information, we often cannot stop it without such legislative remedies as are only now slowly and fitfully being made available.[194] But in all of this, however objectionable, there is no loss of privacy. Autonomy is impaired, more or less grievously, but beyond that, what intimacy has been intruded upon or invaded?

The very possiblity of divulging information stored in files depends, as noted above, upon another and more intrinsic vice: the life of the information is radically and artificially prolonged. Records are mechanical memories not subject to the erosions of forgetfulness and the promise of eventual obliteration. The threat of misuse becomes as permanent as the records themselves. The risks to autonomy multiply not simply because of the heightened possibilities of unconsented reproduction and distribution at any given time, but also because those possibilities, however reduced by regulation, now extend indefinitely through time. Such a chronic and enduring risk must count as itself an injury.

In all of this there is a curious and elusive twist for the limited concept of privacy advocated here. The intimacy of the body depends upon the exercise of a de facto control over others' access to it: the stripper in her work restricts her own bodily intimacy to the vanishing point, and *pro tanto* she waives her right to privacy; yet her intimacy, if diminished in value, remains more or less within her control. When she leaves the stage, she, as much as anyone, can re-assert the usual bounds of physical intimacy and privacy simply by clothing herself in the conventional manner.[195]

In matters of information, of purported mental privacy, however, this simple analysis of autonomy proves too much. In a sense all of our mental (as opposed to physical)[196] life is autonomous, since we control,

---

[194] There are specific provisions of federal statutes which identify various "rights" to privacy. *See, e.g.,* the Federal Privacy Act of 1974, 5 U.S.C. § 552a (1974) (providing for disclosure of agency records to individuals); the Fair Credit Reporting Act, 15 U.S.C. § 1601 (1974) (establishing citizens' rights regarding information held regarding them); the Bank Secrecy Act, 12 U.S.C. § 1829b (1970) (providing for the retention of records by banks). Various states have enacted provisions providing penalties for unauthorized use of likenesses. *See, e.g.,* CAL. CIV. CODE § 3344 (West 1971). In Washington, Chapter 9.73 of the Revised Code, "Violating Right of Privacy," makes it a misdemeanor to divulge the contents of a telegram, or to open or read any sealed message or letter. WASH. REV. CODE ANN. §§ 9.73.010, 9.73.020 (1961).

[195] She has, however, no doubt lost the privacy of the very chaste and very modest who never under any circumstances have allowed themselves to be seen by strangers. After all, the members of the stripper's audience remember something of her naked body.

[196] The lapse into dualism in this paragraph is deliberate, provisional, and perhaps inescapable. None of the concepts discussed here fit very well what Ryle called "the

or like to think we control, its every expression; and to that extent all of it is perhaps intimate. How, then, to qualify the forms of intimacy and autonomy at issue? Institutionally and legally, there are two questions here — one as to the misuse of records and the other as to the abuses of the press.

Once what we know becomes known to others, whether or not they record or remember it, our de facto autonomy is at an end. Information can never be so easily re-clothed or re-possessed as the body. This much is perhaps obvious, and in the case of records poses only the problems of a procedural and remedial kind already touched on. The extent of autonomy here will depend on a variety of issues that legislatures will have to weigh one against the other: should we, for instance, expunge the criminal records of juveniles in order to help them on their way, or should we keep those records in order to maintain a watchful eye on their later conduct? The underlying question, beyond that of waivers of various sorts, will remain always how much personal information the various institutions of a society need to perform their functions and how much they need to record or divulge. Our present legislative usage insists that this is the measure of at least one aspect of the right to privacy.[197]

More often than not, however, the question of the intimacy or privateness of such information is never raised, much less settled. Confidential information need not be intimate information: it may involve such scarcely "intimate" matters as social security numbers, tax returns, or business records.[198] The interests or rights at stake are important, but

official doctrine" of our dual and coincidental existence as disembodied minds and lobotomized bodies. G. RYLE, THE CONCEPT OF MIND 11 (1949). Nonetheless, both ordinary and legal conventions often presuppose such a dualism: "mental distress" or "bodily injury" are examples. We probably cannot escape them since we have used them for so long and since they do answer to a need to simplify and concretize "concepts" in order to apply them to "facts" — another example of a provisional and necessary dualism. Because most of us think in these categories, moreover, they are much more than legal fictions. And of course the legitimacy of our conceptual fictions, like our monetary ones, depends more on their common currency than anything else. The non-dualist positions, which are philosophically more adequate, must bide their time until they become the popularly more acceptable vision of the relation of the "mind" and "body" — at which point their philosophical adequacy may be threatened by yet other views. *See, e.g.,* G. RYLE, *supra,* at 11-24; S. HAMPSHIRE, THOUGHT AND ACTION 80-89 (1959).

[197] *See* note 194 *supra.*

[198] *See, e.g.,* United States v. Miller, 425 U.S. 435 (1976); Fisher v. United States, 425 U.S. 391 (1976). Miller was convicted for trafficking in "moonshine" liquor. Part of the evidence against him came from records of his signed checks and deposit slips maintained by local banks pursuant to the Bank Secrecy Act, 12 U.S.C. § 1829b(d) (1970). Justice Powell's majority opinion affirming Miller's conviction insisted that the checks, in particular, were "not *confidential* communications but negotiable instruments to be used in

we should not mistake their singularity and distinctness: they have to do with the implied or express trusts that ought to be established in our favor by those who feel they must record information about us. Such information is vulnerable to abuse in part because it is not private, because it is taken not from our "persons, houses, papers, or effects," but from other sources which, while perhaps not exactly public, are at least far from intimate.[199]

commercial transactions. All of the documents obtained," the opinion went on, "contain only information voluntarily conveyed to the banks and exposed to their employees in the ordinary course of business." 425 U.S. at 442 (emphasis added).

In *Fisher*, the Supreme Court upheld summonses compelling attorneys to provide to the Internal Revenue Service business records belonging to their clients but prepared by their clients' accountants. The Court held that the taxpayers had no fifth amendment privilege to withhold such records, despite their incriminating tendency, since the records were not private papers in the taxpayers' possession. Justice Brennan concurred in the judgment but not in the opinion. He disagreed with the majority opinion's failure to distinguish plainly between "private papers and effects" and "business records." In *Fisher*, Justice Brennan agreed, the papers were not private. But he objected to "the implication that the privilege might not protect against compelled production of tax records that are [the taxpayer's] 'private papers'. . . ." 425 U.S. at 415 (Brennan, J., concurring).

Neither Fisher nor Miller suffered the slightest intrusion upon personal intimacy, mental or physical, and only a slight intrusion upon personal identity. Given the constitutionality of statutorily enforced record-keeping, as in the Bank Secrecy Act, 12 U.S.C. § 1829b (1970), *see* California Bankers Assn. v. Schultz, 416 U.S. 21 (1974), the holdings in *Miller* and *Fisher* are not surprising. *See* 425 U.S. at 455 (Marshall, J., dissenting). Once the records are kept, the game is up whenever the government umpire blows his whistle — and perhaps before. Surely the banks themselves had a right to make and keep such records, if only to settle disputes with their customers. The issue is, then, what will justify their breach of the implied confidence? As a legal matter, only well-drawn statutes and regulations can squarely settle this.

[199] The obvious examples are one's name, address, and telephone number, all of which are obtainable in most instances from local telephone directories. Driver's licenses and social security numbers are more confidential, but still are not intimate, and few non-lawyers hesitate to give them out. Nonetheless, we may hesitate over even such "routine" information in the context of special relationships touching on mental or physical intimacy. Professional relationships, which almost always require records, may sometimes require the protections of privacy as well as confidentiality. A psychiatrist, a priest, a physician, or even perhaps a lawyer (but likely not an accountant) learn much that is intimate about their clients. Disregarding evidentiary privileges, one may still ask how much of the information they obtain is *private* and so doubly confidential. Judgments of intimacy must control here. *See, e.g.*, Whalen v. Roe, 45 U.S.L.W. 4166 (U.S. Feb. 22, 1977), in which the Supreme Court unanimously upheld a New York statute requiring that records of medical prescriptions for certain dangerous drugs be made, and kept for five years. The records included only the name of the drug prescribed, and the names and addresses of the users and prescribing physicians. Prescription users attacked the statute as an invasion of the "zone of privacy" that includes the physician-patient relationship. Without determining whether

In these matters privacy affords us a convenient rhetoric of advocacy and legitimacy. Nonetheless, it is not the issue; at bottom, the issue is another form of autonomy: an immunity from institutionalized gossip. For it is above all the confidentiality of such information that needs safeguarding. Only so long as institutions keep this confidence can we trust them enough to provide them what information they do need. Certainly, most individuals cannot police this trust or this need. And it will take much legislation and perhaps much regulation to enforce our rights in confidential information. Many of our constitutional values pull with us in this. But even as they do, they need not draw us into the conceptual trap of so attenuating the bounds of privacy as to make them weak and uncertain.

This Article has put off until last what is arguably all that Warren and Brandeis had in mind: the tort of public disclosure, as Prosser describes it, of private truths (or, as in some few false light cases, half-truths) that embarrass or humiliate us.[200] Because of the face-off with the first amendment, this tort gives us the clearest test yet of our definition of the right to privacy: is it sufficiently narrow and plain to justify us in cutting off by the application of its rules and concepts the counter-application of the rules and concepts of freedom of expression? As Thomas Emerson has pointed out, there are two systems of rules here, one of privacy and the other of free expression, and they are, or ought to be, mutually and conceptually exclusive.[201]

The polar terms "public" and "private" must here be taken strictly: disclosure must be effectively and perhaps intentionally to the public at large. Warren and Brandeis saw the press as the villain of their piece, "overstepping in every direction the obvious bounds of propriety and decency."[202] Leaving aside for now these no longer so obvious

---

such a zone exists, the Supreme Court held that "New York's statutory scheme, and its implementing procedures, evidence a proper concern with, and protection of, the individual's interest in privacy," *id.* at 4170, and also said that "this record does not establish an invasion of any right or liberty protected by the Fourteenth Amendment." *Id.*

No doubt such a zone exists because the relationship touches upon the intimacy of the patient. Surely, clinical photographs or detailed case histories should not be divulged short of some compelling public interest. On the other hand, not everything in the relationship is intimate and beyond regulation: the complained-of disclosure in *Whalen* was only of the names and addresses of legitimate users of a given drug. Moreover, given the state's elaborate procedures to protect the confidentiality of the information, it may be doubted that the regulation actually burdens or invades the privacy of the physcian-patient relationship.

[200] Prosser, Torts, *supra* note 47, at 809-14.

[201] *See* Emerson, *supra* note 3, at 549.

[202] Warren & Brandeis. *supra* note 1, at 196.

bounds,[203] the institutional focus remains indispensable. Only mass media can make such disclosures effectively public in a mass society; anything less is likely to go unnoticed by the public and so remain to that extent private. When effective, however, such disclosures wrench what was private out of its context with an abruptness and force indeed massive. The psychological injury will at times, as in the sadly celebrated case of William Sidis,[204] be irreparable.

Information kept in data banks, in contrast, will almost never pass beyond retrieval and out of all control; it can be destroyed, as evidence can be suppressed, and so control restored or at least remedied. Not so with mass public disclosures; massive publicity destroys privacy once and for all by transforming it into its opposite, leaving no control over later use or misuses.

As to the disclosed information — which may be a picture, a story, a report — neither privacy, nor autonomy, nor intimacy is any longer possible. This is another injury of expression for which "more speech" is not the remedy,[205] since neither retraction nor correction is of any help at all. The question is, then, whether there is any remedy compatible with first amendment protections. For these not only guard the press in its right to publish what it will, but also the public in its right to know.[206]

The implicit strategy of these pages has been to give to the concept of privacy sufficient precision and restriction to make feasible and justifiable its exclusive application to limited categories of choice, conduct, and expression. Even as against the right to know, there is a right,

---

[203] *See* pp. 255-56 *supra*.

[204] Sidis v. F-R Publishing Co., 113 F.2d 806 (2d Cir.), *cert. denied*, 311 U.S. 711 (1940). William Sidis was, as a child and adolescent, a mathematical prodigy of some note. Newspapers followed his graduation from Harvard and his lectures on the fourth dimension. Shortly afterwards, however, a troubled Sidis gave up mathematics to become a recluse in various cities and various nondescript occupations. The *New Yorker* published a feature article on Sidis in his late thirties. Accurate to a fault, and not without kindly condescension, the article "merciless[ly] dissect[ed]" its subject. One can never know, but it seems the article (and perhaps the unsuccessful litigation over it) contributed to Sidis' later suicide. *See also* note 212 *infra*.

[205] Whitney v. California, 274 U.S. 357, 377 (1927) (Brandeis, J., concurring). "If there be time to expose through discussion the falsehood and fallacies, to avert the evil by the processes of education, the remedy to be applied is more speech, not enforced silence." In *Whitney*, this principle was applied to criminal speech. For an application of it to a defamation case, *see* Gertz v. Robert Welch, Inc., 418 U.S. 323, 344 (1974).

[206] *See* New York Times Co. v. Sullivan, 376 U.S. 254 (1964). *See also* Rosenbloom v. Metromedia, Inc., 403 U.S. 29 (1971); Curtis Publishing Co. v. Butts, 388 U.S. 130 (1967); Time, Inc. v. Hill, 385 U.S. 374 (1967).

as Emerson calls it, *not* to be known.[207] But it must be a right of the most residual and limited sort, strictly confined to intimate matters and always subject, as intimacies are, to the actual or constructive waivers of those who make their private lives of public interest.[208]

Consider two little discussed and painful examples from the case reports. In *Barber v. Time, Inc.*,[209] the plaintiff was afflicted with a disorder that gave her an insatiable appetite. Above her protests, two photographers took pictures of her in her hospital bed. These were later published, along with a short news story about her, giving her name and other details of her identity, in a regular weekly edition of *Time* Magazine. In another case, *Briscoe v. Reader's Digest*,[210] a reformed convict first learned from his young daughter that some of her schoolmates had read about his crime, already eleven years behind him, in an article about hijacking. Both claims were upheld, if in no great amounts; and on moral grounds — of wrong done to persons without justification — both deserved to be upheld.

---

[207] *See* Emerson, *Legal Foundations of the Right to Know*, 1976 WASH.U.L.Q. 1.

[208] Plainly the right to privacy will share some stretch of contested borderland with the right to know. An obvious example is the sexual intimacies of political figures, particularly presidents, their secretaries, and advisers. To some extent, their intimate lives are inevitably matters "of public interest." Legally speaking, then, to the degree that the public interest is legitimate, the public figure in question has *no* privacy. Various contexts of power and so on will govern various degrees of legal exposure. But the personal intimacy of the public figure is always, in some degree and in some contexts, vulnerable. Thus, a president may be said to have almost no personal intimacy because he has almost no private identity. In most cases, an implied waiver explains this loss of the legal protections of privacy; but in some cases — of accidental or incidental publicity, for instance — the implied waiver is actually a risk imposed after the fact.

[209] 348 Mo. 1199, 159 S.W.2d 291 (1942). *See also* Banks v. King Features Syndicate, 30 F. Supp. 352 (S.D.N.Y. 1939) (publication of X-rays of woman's pelvic region); Cason v. Baskin, 155 Fla. 198, 20 So.2d 243 (1944) (publication of embarrassing details of a woman's masculine characteristics and eccentric behavior); Feeney v. Young, 191 App. Div. 501, 181 N.Y.S. 481 (1920) (public exhibition of films of caesarian operation).

[210] 4 Cal. 3d 529, 93 Cal. Rptr. 866, 483 P.2d 34 (1971). *See also* Melvin v. Reid, 112 Cal. App. 285, 297 P. 91 (1931). In *Melvin* the plaintiff, once a notorious prostitute and homicide defendant, had, after her trial and acquittal, changed her name — and her life. Newly married and settled, she enjoyed for a time the luxury of having no known past. After seven years, however, the defendant and his associates produced a motion picture film linking by name the past prostitute and the present housewife. Citing Art. 1, § 1, of the California constitution (with its right of "pursuing and obtaining happiness"), the court held that there was an actionable invasion of the plaintiff's right to privacy. No adequate argument was made in terms of the intimacy of the plaintiff, however, and perhaps none was possible. The problem is that most of the facts, as in *Briscoe*, appeared in court records open to the public. From there to the plaintiff's present identity was not far to search.

Nonetheless, the concept of privacy elaborated here cannot be applied to the *Briscoe* case, perhaps the more poignant of the two, since no narrowly conceived intimacy was intruded upon and since, moreover, the information was a matter of public record.[211] Were it not for the physical intrusion into a hospital room, even the *Barber* case would fall short of any strict conception of intimacy. To make this all the more concrete, had the photographers, knowing of her ailment, taken her picture as she entered the hospital and then published it, they would have been immune to suit.

In this summary paragraph of analysis no reference is made to the familiar but indistinct exceptions to the first amendment's right to know doctrine, namely, Judge Clark's formulation in *Sidis v. F.R. Publishing Co.*[212] of what is "newsworthy," and the older formulation, going back to Warren and Brandeis but revived in *Time, Inc. v. Hill,*[213] of what is "of public interest." There has been much telling criticism of those standards,[214] but the best criticism of all is that except in the cases of implied waivers by politicians and the like,[215] the standards are unneces-

---

[211] In the recent case of Cox Broadcasting Corp. v. Cohn, 420 U.S. 469 (1975), the Supreme Court, in a rare gesture towards definition, held that the accurate publication of the publicly recorded name of the victim — and *a fortiori* of the accused or convicted perpetrator — of a crime cannot in any circumstances be made actionable.

[212] 113 F.2d 806, 807 ( 2d Cir. 1940). Judge Clark's opinion in the case reserved the question of whether Sidis could have recovered for "[r]evelations . . . so intimate and so unwarranted in view of the victim's position as to outrage the community's notions of decency." *Id.* at 809. As to Sidis, he found no such revelations. Sidis' present privacy, moreover, was offset by his past publicity. Judge Clark's premise was that "at some point the public interest in obtaining information becomes dominant over the individual's desire for privacy." *Id.* He noted the RESTATEMENT OF TORTS' concept of a public figure. From this he reasoned that Sidis' "subsequent history, containing as it did the answer to the question of whether or not he had fulfilled his early promise, was still a matter of public concern." *Id.* The rule thus arrived at says, in effect, once a public figure, always a public figure. This unfortunately seems to be true, at least as a descriptive matter. *But see* Bloustein, *The Justice and the Philosopher, supra* note 59. Applying Meiklejohn's theory of the legitimate scope of free inquiry and expression, Bloustein argues that the public had no need to know — and the press no right to publish — at least Sidis' name. Under the definition of privacy proposed here, however, the invasion of Sidis' personal intimacy, while arguable, was not plain.

[213] 385 U.S. 374 (1967).

[214] *See, e.g.,* Bloustein, *The Justice and the Philosopher, supra* note 59; Nimmer, *The Right to Speak From Times to Time: First Amendment Theory Applied to Libel and Misapplied to Privacy,* 56 CAL. L. REV. 935 (1968).

[215] Despite the tendency of the decisions from New York Times Co. v. Sullivan, 376 U.S. 254 (1964), onwards, the requirement of an actual waiver of privacy rights by people who seek publicity — perhaps as an incident of a career in politics, sports, theater, or what have you — has of late taken on new life at the Supreme Court. In Time, Inc. v. Firestone,

sary. A close analysis of the negative right of privacy makes it what the more affirmative right of free expression can never be: self-limiting. There is an uncertain and uneasy "balance" between the first amendment and the right to privacy in these cases because the quantities themselves, to which weights are to be assigned by judges, remain uncertain. This uncertainty is probably salutary and even necessary in the case of the first amendment. As perhaps the most fundamental constitutional principle, it should be bounded only by other fundamental constitutional principles — like privacy or perhaps national security — and even then only when these are themselves as narrowly defined as possible.

---

424 U.S. 448 (1976), the wife of an heir to the Firestone fortune sued the publisher of *Time* magazine for its allegedly false and defamatory report of the results of her prolonged and notorious domestic relations litigation with her husband.

A divided Supreme Court refused to apply the "actual malice" test from *New York Times*. Relying on Gertz v. Robert Welch, Inc., 418 U.S. 323 (1974), the plurality opinion of Justice Rehnquist remarked that, despite "a few press conferences" called by Mrs. Firestone and despite the notoriety of the litigation, the respondent "did not assume any role of special prominence in the affairs of society, other than perhaps Palm Beach society, and she did not thrust herself to the forefront of any particular public controversy in order to influence the resolution of the issues involved in it." 424 U.S. at 453. The Court held that the extension of the *New York Times* rule "to falsehoods defamatory of private persons whenever the statements concern matters of general public interest," as in Rosenbloom v. Metromedia, Inc., 403 U.S. 29 (1971), was an improper and invalid abridgment of the powers of the states to devise their own rules of liability with fault in defamation cases. By the same token, then, the respondent's resort to legal action was not chargeable to her as a waiver of privacy rights since "[s]he was compelled to go to court by the State in order to obtain legal release from the bonds of matrimony." 424 U.S. at 454. See Boddie v. Connecticut, 401 U.S. 371, 376 (1971).

The *Firestone* case points up the inevitable entanglement of defamation and invasion of privacy issues where the publication is of intimate and identified facts or fictions. Reputation and intimacy are both at stake, and each implicates separate aspects of personal autonomy. The charge of adultery touches on one's sexual intimacies. Resort to the courts, however, involves a risk of publication. In the case of the Firestones, the risk was assured: they were certainly prominent enough locally for the local media to cover the story and prominent enough nationally, by name and fortune, for the national media to pick it up from there. *See* 424 U.S. at 454 (Marshall, J., dissenting). The news conferences called by Mrs. Firestone were the strongest evidence of her own recognition and acquiescence in this degree of prominence or celebrity. Nevertheless, the Rehnquist opinion overcomes all of these indications of "constructive" waiver. The reluctance here derives from the legitimate concern that *as to sexual intimacy at least* none of the parties in fact intended to waive their rights to privacy. The problem is that to insist upon such a high standard of voluntariness is to create a fiction that legal proceedings, or at least those touching on sexuality and marriage, are not in the "public realm" — even when you have to go to the press to clarify your own views of such proceedings. This relies on an unduly expansive concept of privacy as to sexual intimacies. This is objectionable not only because it imposes complicated canons of restraint on the press but also because it suggests an inconsistent and patchwork pattern of constitutional rules and exceptions for the various privacy rights.

*Privacy I*

## CONCLUSION

Privacy, then, as a concept and a right, stands in great need of the few certainties and limitations that definition affords us. But however artful or ingenious, definition will never go the whole way towards the ideal of the unambiguous application of legal rules to situations of fact. The concepts of identity, autonomy, and intimacy are meant only to focus litigation within a narrower range of possible invocations of a right to privacy.

As we move from the paradigm of an actual invasion of sexual intimacy to the subtle analogies of the intrusions of regulation or observation or publication upon the intimacies of conversation or association, we are inevitably less sure of our claims of legal right. Privacy has become the over-burdened camel of much individual rights (and wrongs) litigation. The public disclosure tort gives us example after example of the sort of straw that lawyers have sometimes sought to throw on privacy's back.

Much of the case law of this last tort is, as Harry Kalven so puckishly remarked, "unbeatably trivial."[216] In the realm of information, one is hard put to unearth cases so strong as *York*,[217] *Griswold*,[218] or *Doe*.[219] In all of these there was outright and outrageous invasion of the intimacies of sexuality and personality that we customarily and intuitively recognize as such. This is not to say there have not been other sorts of invasions, and morally wrongful ones, of personal sensibilities; there have often been and will continue to be. *Briscoe*[220] and *Sidis*[221] are examples of them. But like so much else that matters in our lives, most of these are beyond the reach or help of law.

---

[216] Kalven, *supra* note 6, at 337. And sometimes the cases are unbeatably comical. *See, e.g.,* Virgil v. Sports Illustrated, Inc., 424 F. Supp. 1286 (S.D. Cal. 1976). The plaintiff there sued a nationally distributed sports magazine for invasion of privacy by the disclosure, in a feature article, of embarrassing personal facts. They included reports of such feats as eating spiders as snacks, putting out lit cigarettes in his mouth, and diving headlong down stairs. Nonetheless these were held to be insufficiently *private* facts to overcome a first amendment "newsworthiness" test. They showed him as a reckless and eccentric anti-hero, a body-surfer of some public grandeur, surely worthy of public interest and even knowledge. More to the point, the published facts hardly touched on the intimacies of Virgil's personal identity.

[217] York v. Story, 324 F.2d 450 (9th Cir. 1963).

[218] Griswold v. Connecticut, 381 U.S. 479 (1965).

[219] Doe v. Commonwealth's Att'y, 403 F. Supp. 1199 (E.D. Va. 1975), *aff'd mem.,* 425 U.S. 901 (1976).

[220] Briscoe v. Reader's Digest Ass'n, 4 Cal. 3d 529, 93 Cal. Rptr. 866, 483 P.2d 34 (1971).

[221] Sidis v. F-R Publishing Co., 113 F.2d 806 (2d Cir.), *cert. denied,* 311 U.S. 711 (1940).

# [9]

## PRIVACY: ITS ORIGIN, FUNCTION, AND FUTURE

*JACK HIRSHLEIFER**

> The first man who, having enclosed a piece of ground, bethought himself of saying "This is mine," and found people simple enough to believe him, was the real founder of civil society.
> — Rousseau, *Discourse on the Origin of Inequality*

Explorers must accept the bad with the good. In the new-found lands gold may lie on the ground for the taking, but pioneers are likely to encounter rattlers and desperadoes. Recently a new territory has been discovered by economists, the intellectual continent we call "privacy." The pioneers are our peerless leaders Posner and Stigler whose golden findings have already dazzled the world. It is high time for rattlers and desperadoes—that's the rest of us—to put in an appearance. Of course, I ought to add parenthetically, "new" is relative to one's point of view. Our pioneering economists, like explorers in other places and other times, found aborigines already inhabiting the territory—in this case intellectual primitives, Supreme Court justices and such. Quite properly, our explorers have brushed the natives aside, and I shall follow in that honorable tradition.

### I. WHAT IS PRIVACY?

So much for flowery introduction. The first issue I shall address is whether our pioneers have correctly mapped the major features of the "privacy" continent. Have they possibly mistaken a peninsula for the mainland, foothills for a grand sierra, or perhaps even misread their compass so as to reverse north and south? Well, not quite so bad as the last, but I will be contending that the mainland of "privacy" is not the idea of *secrecy* as our pioneers appear to believe—secrecy is only an outlying peninsula. The central domain of what we mean by "privacy" is, rather, a concept that might be described as *autonomy within society*. Privacy thus signifies something much broader than secrecy; it suggests, as I shall be maintaining in detail below, a particular kind of social structure together with its supporting social ethic.

In his 1978 article Posner deals *only* with aspects of privacy as secrecy, as ability to control dissemination and use of information about (or possessed

* Professor of Economics, University of California, Los Angeles.

by) oneself.[1] Stigler's recent paper has much the same narrow orientation.[2] This limited angle of view perhaps explains why our pioneers' attitude toward privacy is—occasional qualifications aside—on the whole hostile. Their tone suggests that we have more privacy than ever before—probably more than is actually good for us or, at any rate, good for economic efficiency—and, furthermore, that any person displaying a special desire for privacy is probably just out to hoodwink the rest of us.

In his later paper Posner does however glimpse the central massif of the privacy continent.[3] He there considers a category of privacy he calls *seclusion*. The desire for seclusion is regarded by Posner as a more or less inexplicable "taste"—and one that is not, probably, very widely shared. "Seclusion" approaches but does not yet arrive at what I take to be the heart meaning of privacy; seclusion denotes *withdrawal from* society, whereas I am speaking of privacy as a *way of organizing society*. Still, seclusion does suggest one of the major aspects of the situation, the human desire for autonomy—for independence from control by others. Among the group of us assembled here today, due respect for this desire should not be difficult to find. Autonomy of the individual is the bedrock value of that classical liberalism still popular hereabouts.

The etymology of the word "privacy" is suggestive. The basic Latin form is the adjective *privus,* the original archaic meaning being "single." Standard later use signified that which is particular, peculiar, or one's own—the implied context being not the solitary human being but rather the individual facing the potential claims of other persons. Clearly, this root idea is what the word "private" still means when we speak of *private property.* Secrecy, which is an information preserve maintained about oneself, is but one aspect of (or is perhaps an instrumentality of) privacy in this more fundamental sense. Being rung up on the telephone only to hear a recorded message hawking some product would be regarded as an invasion of our privacy, even though no secret information about ourselves is thereby elicited.

The desire for privacy in the sense of private property is most intense insofar as it concerns control of one's own person and one's own time. The felt urgency gradually diminishes in moving outward to embrace family, home, and possessions. But even in the case of material objects, I would argue, our desire to have and to hold them transcends the merely physical benefits derivable therefrom. Possessions are not just things. They are guarantors or at least symbols of our autonomy from others, of our status as self-sustaining individuals.

[1] Richard A. Posner, The Right of Privacy, 12 Georgia L. Rev. 393 (1978).

[2] George J. Stigler, An Introduction to Privacy in Economics and Politics, 9 J. Legal Stud. 623 (1980).

[3] Richard A. Posner, Privacy, Secrecy, and Reputation, 28 Buffalo L. Rev. 1 (1979).

PRIVACY: ITS ORIGIN, FUNCTION, AND FUTURE 651

So far I have addressed the privacy of an individual as against other members of society. A special case of enormous importance concerns individual autonomy as against those other members of society who constitute the "government." This is the privacy meant in the line we draw distinguishing the *private sphere* from the public sphere. In this connection, failure to perceive the centrality of the autonomy conception of privacy leads Posner to decry the Supreme Court's recent constitutional doctrine of "sexual privacy," as applied for example in striking down antiabortion statutes.[4] I would be among the last to defend the usual thought processes of the present occupants of the Supreme Court bench. But their judgment setting sexual matters outside the reach of government control, whether or not soundly based in law or morals, is surely a declaration of a *privacy right* in the most essential meaning of that term.

Autonomy as against the *state* is more than the leading special case of the general problem of privacy. Privacy can be attained, to some *de facto* degree, simply by individual patrolling and self-defense. Nor is this an unimportant phenomenon even today; a person who remains passive in the face of invasions of his rights is unlikely to retain them. But for defending privacy we rely, for the most part, upon the support of *law,* a system of impersonal third-party definition and enforcement of private property rights. Laws can be enacted by a general town meeting and enforced by a general hue and cry as need arises. But society long ago arrived at (or had imposed upon it) the alternative system of *specialized coercion* that is government. A dangerous solution, evidently. How to defend autonomous private rights against the organized professional guardians of those rights is the key problem of liberal political philosophy. But I am not going to solve that problem today. Instead, my purpose is to look both into the sources and the social consequences of what our pioneers regard as the somewhat peculiar "taste" for privacy.

## II. ON THE EVOLUTION OF "TASTES"

Economics has not done a good job on "tastes." The use of this trivializing word, suggestive of the choice of French dressing versus Thousand Island, is itself an evasion. If we spoke of human drives or aims, of ingrained ethics, or of value systems or goals for living, we would be inclined to treat the subject with more respect. One hardly need emphasize that *what* we want is often of greater significance for personal and social life than how precisely we manage to balance marginal cost against marginal benefit in achieving our desires. Even if preferences were arbitrary brute facts, independent of economic forces, simply mapping them should have aroused more interest than

---

[4] *Id.*

it has. But what we call tastes are *not* completely arbitrary. On the most elementary level, it is not difficult to understand why ice water is more desired in July than in December. In what has been called "the new theory of consumption,"[5] economists have begun to interpret preferences for observable market goods as derived from and dependent upon more fundamental desires. But lacking an analytical explanation of these latter, our theories have only pushed the underlying arbitrariness back a notch.

Starting with Alchian,[6] a number of economists have analyzed how the market environment selects for commercial survival only those firms choosing the "best" decisions—even though those decisions were very likely made via a process of at best limited rationality.[7] Thus, the blind forces of environmental selection lead to a *simulation* of conscious rationality. The solutions we see in the world about us tend to be well-adapted *because* they have survived, however arrived at.

Curiously, and undoubtedly because of the tunnel vision that enables us not to see "tastes" as an economic problem, economists have never attempted to apply the idea of evolutionary selection to the essential makeup of the human fabric itself. Even in the "new theory of consumption," the provenance of our underlying deeper desires remains an unanalyzed mystery. But the biologists, in a long tradition starting with Darwin's *Descent of Man* and recently flowering as a topic under the heading of sociobiology, have been better economists than we. They have shown that not only our physical but our psychic constitution—what we desire, what "tastes sweet" to us—[8]is what has been found by natural selection to work as a genetically implanted motivator. I hasten to interpolate a word of warning, however: our implanted structures and orientations represent successful evolutionary solutions *in the past,* and there is no implication that they will continue to succeed in the future. Nor is there any implication that these solutions are "right" by any standard other than success—for example, by the standard of ethics.

We do not usually dignify the implanted tropisms of primitive organisms, to seek or avoid light or heat or water, by calling them desires. They are "hard-wired" controls on behavior. Higher organisms have genetic controls that tend to be increasingly "soft-wired" as we approach the human level. Such controls permit the organism to choose, to some degree, among the implanted ends—for example, by deferring gratification. More important for our purposes, the controls are subject to social influence. Man is, preemi-

[5] Kelvin J. Lancaster, A New Approach to Consumer Theory, 74 J. Pol. Econ. 132 (1966).

[6] Armen A. Alchian, Uncertainty, Evolution, and Economic Theory, 58 J. Pol. Econ. 211 (1950).

[7] Herbert A. Simon, A Behavioral Model of Rational Choice, 69 Q. J. Econ. 99 (1955).

[8] David P. Barash, The Whisperings Within (1979).

PRIVACY: ITS ORIGIN, FUNCTION, AND FUTURE          653

nently, the *indoctrinable*—the teachable—animal.[9] Western man does not munch grass, like the cows, because his genetic constitution forbids it; he does not drink animal blood, like the Masai, because his cultural constitution forbids it.

Culture is evidently important, exceptionally so on the human level, but it does not abolish biology. For one thing, the genetic foundation sets a limit upon the cultural superstructure: human beings cannot even be taught to digest grass. For another, the human capacity for culture—the fact that our innate instructions *are* soft-wired—is itself a biological adaptation. Finally and most important of all, cultural and genetic factors are simultaneously under the sway of natural selection. Within economics this idea has played a notable role in the thinking of the Austrian school, which emphasizes that human social structures typically emerge without rational planning on anyone's part.[10] Nor need they be any the worse for that lack; there is not only a "wisdom of Nature" but a "wisdom of culture." Of particular relevance for us is the *law* as one of the social structures that follows an evolutionary course,[11] possibly doing better the less the purportedly "rational" element in its unfolding development. Again, however, a word of caution. Nature is not always wise,[12] and cultures (including our own) are also likely to have evolved seriously dysfunctional characteristics. Natural selection selects for survivability pure and simple, and a trait *may* survive that is bad for the ecology or for the species or even for its individual bearer.

Having made these general points about tastes, it is time to become more specific about privacy. Has the genetic origin of mankind or, alternatively, have successful cultures like our own implanted within us as individuals a "taste for privacy"? In this context, the word *ethic* is a more accurate term than "taste." We are dealing with a two-sided situation, a balancing of autonomy and sociality. The privacy ethic, whether internalized as Adam Smith's Impartial Spectator or some analogous metaphor, would urge the individual to insist on his own claims to inviolability of persons and property *while being prepared to concede corresponding rights to others*. The question is whether we are, as individuals, driven internally (at least to some degree) by this ethic.

Consider "economic man." This intellectual creation, acting dispassionately yet ruthlessly in pursuit of self-interest, is free of implanted social controls. If he concedes rights to others, it is only as a means of self-gratification: honesty *may* be the best policy. But actual man as we know

[9] Edward O. Wilson, Sociobiology: The New Synthesis 562 (1975).

[10] Friedrich A. Hayek, The Three Sources of Human Values (1978).

[11] Paul H. Rubin, Why Is the Common Law Efficient?, 6 J. Legal Stud. 51 (1977).

[12] Michael T. Ghiselin, The Economy of the Body, 68 Am. Econ. Rev. 233 (1978).

him does sometimes sacrifice his interests for others in a way not purely instrumental to his own goals. The biological explanation is interesting. There *is* ultimate relentless selfishness in Nature, but on a level deeper than the individual—on the level of the gene.[13] Organisms are just survival machines designed to carry packets of genes over from generation to generation. Most obviously when it concerns one's offspring, therefore, a selfish gene might instruct the *individual* to be unselfish. Generalizing from this, the biologists have shown that shared genetic endowments among kin lead to natural selection in favor of the trait of helping one's relatives.[14] And even beyond the kinship tie, *group selection* may lead to the genetic implanting of an ethic of loyalty to neighbors and allies,[15] as will be discussed below. And finally, building upon this genetic base, natural selection operating on cultures undoubtedly has promoted ethics of self-sacrifice for larger groups identified by language or ethnicity or ideology.

## III.   THREE STRUCTURES OF SOCIALITY AND THEIR SUPPORTING ETHICS

There are some animal species whose members are social isolates, whose biologically driven coming together is limited to the sexual act. Jean-Jacques Rousseau put natural man in this category:

. . . wandering up and down the forests, without industry, without speech, without home, an equal stranger to war and to all ties, neither standing in need of his fellow-creatures nor having any desire to hurt them, and perhaps even not distinguishing them one from another; let us conclude that, being self-sufficient and subject to so few passions, he could have no feelings or knowledge but such as befitted his situation.[16]

This passage sounds rather like "economic man." Egoistic economic man might, in view of the material advantages of cooperation (in production, in trade, or in defense), associate with others—but only on a quid pro quo basis as expressed in the famous *social contract*. This is not quite the line of

---

[13] Richard Dawkins, The Selfish Gene (1976). I should not imply that there is unanimity on this point among biologists; various strands of opinion have their supporters. For example, some detect a deep cooperative or sympathetic urge in the life principle. See Lewis Thomas, The Lives of a Cell: Notes of a Biology Watcher (1974). Others question the saliency of the acting-gene metaphor, as genes do not act alone nor are they entirely distinct particles.

[14] W. D. Hamilton, The Genetical Evolution of Social Behavior, 7 J. Theoretical Biology 1 (1964).

[15] "When two tribes of primeval man, living in the same country, came into competition, the tribe including the greater number of courageous, sympathetic, and faithful members would succeed better and would conquer the other." Charles Darwin, The Descent of Man, in The Origin of Species and the Descent of Man 498 (Modern Library ed., n.d.).

[16] Jean-Jacques Rousseau, A Discourse on the Origin of Inequality, in The Social Contract and Discourses 230 (Everyman's Library 1950).

Rousseau's thinking, which is rather more complex (not to say confused); Rousseau also postulated a certain natural goodness and sense of compassion in primitive man. The early Sophists were more consistent in their view that our basic nature is entirely selfish, that the social contract is only of instrumental significance for mankind.[17]

Theories of a social contract among truly economic men have difficulty with the problem of enforcement. In the absence of a social ethic, individuals carry out their shares of the social bargain only as they can be forced to do so. But enforcement services are a public good in many respects; punishing a malefactor tends to benefit the community, whether or not the agent who punishes gains thereby. Hence we would expect enforcement services to be undersupplied by economic men. There is no doubt that, from the most primitive to the most advanced stages of society, a higher degree of cooperative interaction (including "moralistic aggression"[18] against malefactors) takes place than can be explained simply as a pragmatic option for totally egoistic man.

But the mere fact of natural association does not tell us enough. The often-bruited idea of a generalized "social instinct" omits essential distinctions. There are many different kinds of natural societies. While still leaving matters seriously oversimplified, since none of these are probably ever observed as pure forms, as a first approximation it seems possible to classify the main structures of sociality in animals and men on the basis of their reliance on the principles of: (1) communal sharing, (2) private rights, or (3) dominance. It may be easiest to remember these in terms of their underlying ethics. If sharing is the Golden Rule, mutual recognition of private rights is the Silver Rule, while the struggle for dominance is the Iron Rule of social interaction.[19] These structures and ethics have evolved, each only in particular ecological contexts, because individuals so organized turned out to have a survival advantage (through group selection) over those expressing different behavioral traits.

Dominance in social groups, the Iron Rule, does not require any very roundabout explanation. In the evolutionary competition for survival and reproduction, no particular subtlety is involved when selfish genes instruct their bearers to attempt to subordinate other organisms in a continuing

---

[17] Roger D. Masters, Of Marmots and Men: Animal Behavior and Human Altruism, in Altruism, Sympathy, and Helping: Psychological and Sociological Principles 59 (Lauren Wispé ed. 1978).

[18] Robert L. Trivers, The Evolution of Reciprocal Altruism, 46 Q. Rev. Biology 35 (1971).

[19] In another context I distinguished behaviors in accordance with the golden, the silver, and the brass rules. The last of these represented "economic man," free of implanted constraints. I shall not need the brass metaphor here. See Jack Hirshleifer, Natural Economy versus Political Economy, 1. J. Soc. & Biological Structures 319 (1978).

656                          THE JOURNAL OF LEGAL STUDIES

pattern of association. The only problem is why the dominated individuals, having lost the struggle for the alpha position, submit rather than secede. And, in fact, defeated contenders or other dissatisfied group members sometimes do secede. But there are advantages to group affiliation even in a subordinate position; as Hobbes contended, isolation may be worse. There are lone baboons, but they do not survive the leopard long. Furthermore, in an uncertain world there always remain possibilities of promotion; today's subordinate may become tomorrow's alpha.

Is there an ingrained ethic associated with the Iron Rule of dominance? Yes, and this can be seen in various ways. In the combat for top position, animals typically fight by limited conventional means, often not using their most lethal weapons.[20] The defeated animal thus does not fight to the death, and his submission is accepted. More generally a degree of *noblesse oblige* constrains the leader—for example, he might have to protect weaker group members against predators. And followers must do more than prudently know their place. If the group is to survive severe competition, they must act with a measure of loyal enthusiasm.[21] That the dominance pattern is indeed two-sided is also revealed by the fact that the alpha animal does not always monopolize the male reproductive role.

What of the Golden Rule of sharing? That this might be viable (to some degree) in a world of selfish genes is only superficially paradoxical. As an obvious example, all mammals are tied to a way of life requiring maternal unselfishness toward infants. More generally, kin selection leads to many types of mutual helping among nuclear or extended families in Nature. The extent to which unselfish sharing among *unrelated* individuals may be favored by group selection is a much debated matter among biologists, but is clearly operative to some degree.[22] In any case, most natural groupings do involve an important kinship element as well.

The underlying ethic of sharing is not all hearts and flowers. The kin-selection process may have implanted the supportive emotion of love, as in the instance of maternal care, so that no external pressure is required.[23] Beyond this case, there may be two sides to the story. At least on the human level the less attractive emotions of *envy* and *fear of envy* (the latter perhaps internalized as conscience or guilt) may serve as enforcers of the noble Golden Rule.[24] And, as is well known, Adam Smith emphasized *self-esteem* as a

[20] Konrad Lorenz, On Aggression (Marjorie Kerr Wilson trans. 1966).

[21] An instructive instance of a two-sided dominance ethic, implanted not by natural but by artificial selection over many generations, is the relation between the dog and his human master. This example shows that a "society" may cut across the species barrier.

[22] W. D. Hamilton, Innate Social Aptitudes of Man, in Biosocial Anthropology (R. Fox ed. 1975).

[23] Gary S. Becker, Altruism, Egoism, and Genetic Fitness: Economics and Sociobiology, 14 J. Econ. Lit. 817 (1976).

[24] See Helmut Schoeck, Envy: A Theory of Social Behavior (1970); and F. H. Willhoite, Jr.,

PRIVACY: ITS ORIGIN, FUNCTION, AND FUTURE 657

major motivator of unselfish action.[25] So sharing behavior is supported by a complex mixture of internal drives. Nevertheless, imposed societal sanctions may always be required to help repress egoistic self-interest.

The really interesting problems for our purposes concern the Silver Rule. Can Nature actually evolve a social system of private rights with its supporting ethic? It has in fact done so in the social structure known as *territoriality*. Members of many animal species, humans among them, carry about them a bubble of personal space, invasion of which is resisted. How human cultural differences modify the detailed expression of this kind of "taste for privacy" is entertainingly described by Hall.[26] Many animals also defend geographically fixed territories, defined on the level of the family or of larger bands or troops.

But *de facto* possession of space is not enough. The supporting ethic is still needed, namely, a complementary *reluctance to intrude*. In Nature, this does occur. Among many, possibly all territorial species (man excluded, perhaps) it has been found that "proprietors" defending their territories are almost always able to fight off incursions. Such intrusions as do take place tend to be exploratory rather than determinedly invasive.[27] Internalized respect for property is what permits autonomy to persist within society.

More than one mechanism for the evolution of this social pattern can be imagined. It has been contended that Nature has somehow gotten the individuals to so behave "for the good of the species,"[28] an explanation which fails to cope with the free-rider problem. That is, even if reluctance to intrude is bad for the species on average, it may be good for the genes carried by the intruder. A more plausible argument starts from the observation that, other things equal, a territory is *worth more* to its proprietor than to the intruder. The proprietor will have a more accurate knowledge of its resources, and indeed may have to a degree adapted them to his own personal requirements (or himself to them). It therefore pays the proprietor to fight harder and longer. This being the case, evolution might have "hard-wired" defensive belligerence into proprietors together with the complementary traits of reluctance to intrude and willingness to retreat on the part of potential challengers—the two together comprising what I have called the privacy ethic. And Maynard Smith has shown that such a "bourgeois" strategy can

Rank and Reciprocity: Speculations on Human Emotions and Political Life, in Human Sociobiology and Politics (Elliot White ed. 1980).

[25] R. H. Coase, Adam Smith's View of Man, 19 J. Law & Econ. 529 (1976).

[26] Edward T. Hall, The Hidden Dimension (1966).

[27] See Robert Ardrey, The Territorial Imperative (1966). A wolf pack will even respect a human being's territorial claims, if asserted in proper wolf language. (If you're interested, correct wolf etiquette requires urinary marking of the boundary of your claim. See Farley Mowat, Never Cry Wolf (1963).)

[28] V. C. Wynne-Edwards, Animal Dispersion in Relation to Social Behavior (1962); and Ardrey, *supra* note 27.

be viable in evolutionary terms even if proprietorship is founded upon no more than a convention like "first come, first served."[29]

As indicated above, social structures and their supporting ethics tend to evolve where they are adaptive in particular ecological contexts. The unselfish sharing represented by maternal care is adaptive where high "quality" of offspring[30] pays off more than large numbers. Selfless sharing in mated pairs is typically observed where severe environments make close teamwork essential to survival.[31] Territoriality, by eliminating duplication of effort in exploiting the resource field, is a kind of minimal teamwork; it tends to emerge where resources are fixed in place and more or less uniformly distributed.[32] Territories may be held at individual, family, or group levels, depending mainly upon returns to scale. Under severe ecological pressure, individual territoriality has been observed to break down in favor of a group dominance structure.

To summarize, all three main social principles—dominance, sharing, and private rights—have evolved in Nature, each as an adaptation to a particular type of social niche. Each principle also tends to be associated with an ingrained supporting ethic, since a mere "social contract" entered into by purely egoistic individuals is unlikely to survive the free-rider problem. Typically, strands of all three may be woven together in the behavioral pattern of each species. And of course the merely egoistic element probably never totally disappears. Indeed, sometimes what seems superficially to represent an organized social unit may be only a "selfish herd" lacking any real cooperative element.[33]

## IV.  ON THE NATURAL HISTORY OF PRIVATE RIGHTS

Hayek has argued that the transition from the small human band to settled communities and civilized life resulted from man's learning to obey the abstract rules of an emergent market order.[34] The alternative to this cultural constraint, Hayek supposed, was for man to remain under the guidance of "innate instincts to pursue common perceived goals" (our Golden Rule). The way of face-to-face communal sharing, probably adaptive to the primitive hunter-gatherer economy in which man may have lived for 50,000 generations, allegedly had to be bypassed if progress was to be made.

There are curious parallels and divergences between Hayek's ideas and

[29] John Maynard Smith, The Evolution of Behavior, Sci. Am., Sept. 1978, at 176.

[30] Gary S. Becker, A Theory of Social Interactions, 82 J. Pol. Econ. 1063 (1974).

[31] Wilson, *supra* note 9, at ch. 15.

[32] *Id.* at ch. 12.

[33] W. D. Hamilton, Geometry for the Selfish Herd, 31 J. Theoretical Biology 295 (1971).

[34] Hayek, *supra* note 10.

those of the Marxist anthropologist Sahlins.[35] For Sahlins also, human social development required overcoming innate instincts. But in his view the innate instincts are those of "animality"—selfishness, indiscriminate sexuality, dominance, and brute competition. Sahlins agrees with Hayek once again, as to the sharing ethic of the primitive human band.[36] But for Sahlins the shift to the Silver Rule ethic—associated with the transition from a hunting to an agricultural way of life—represented moral degeneration rather than progress.[37]

As indicated earlier, the degree to which alternative social ethics may have been *genetically* implanted rather than *culturally* renewed in each human generation will not be emphasized here. Both genetic and cultural inheritances are subject to natural selection; both track environmental change. However, genetic adaptation has much more inertia. It is therefore reasonable to believe that the untold aeons of man's primate heritage laid down a foundation of behavioral as well as structural traits that still remain with us; that the 50,000 generations of hunter-gatherer life have also left their mark; that man has partially yet probably only incompletely adapted genetically to the life of regular labor that began with agriculture; and, finally, that modern urban patterns in some ways clash considerably with our deeper ingrained attitudes.[38]

Turning to the historical question, primeval communism and sharing, as an Eden-like stage of early human societal evolution[39] is a myth.[40] Essentially all known primitive communities have been found to possess relatively elaborate structures of property rights. Though these private rights are defined in ways that vary from society to society, invasions of them are always strongly resented. Golden-Rule motivations were probably present in early man, as they may still be today. But only as one element, probably the smallest element, in the human mixed brew of motivations: sheer egoism

[35] Marshall D. Sahlins, The Origin of Society, Sci. Am., Sept. 1960, at 76; and his, Stone Age Economics (1972).

[36] A contradiction leaps to the eye here. Suppression of "indiscriminate sexuality" sounds rather like a move from group sharing to private rights, which Sahlins ought (in the interests of consistency) to deplore rather than approve.

[37] Sahlins, Stone Age Economics, *supra* note 35. A fascinating strand to this argument, which unfortunately cannot be pursued here, is the claim that even in material terms—leisure, health, protein consumption, etc.—the tiller of the soil was far worse off than had been the cooperative hunters of the earlier era. See also Marvin Harris, Cannibals and Kings: The Origins of Culture (1977).

[38] See Desmond Morris, The Naked Ape (1967): A Zoologist's Study of the Human Animal and his, The Human Zoo (1969). Wilson, *supra* note 9, at 569, is somewhat unusual in the degree of lability he assigns to genetic traits; he would be inclined therefore to minimize their possible current maladaptedness.

[39] Frederick Engels, The Origin of the Family, Private Property, and the State (1902).

[40] See Ernest Beaglehole, Property, in 12 Int'l Encyclopaedia of the Soc. Sci. 359 (1968).

competing with overlapping (partially conflicting, partially reinforcing) elements of dominance, privacy, and sharing ethics.

I shall be following Hayek and Sahlins in going back to the origins of these social ethics. But in contrast with their views, to me it seems clear that the first and deepest layer of human sociality was the Iron Rule of dominance.[41] It is generally agreed that man evolved from a primate line that left the forest to live in the African savannah. In this highly dangerous environment, primates lacking biological weaponry could initially survive only by banding in groups. Sharing is essentially unknown in the primate heritage, and territoriality was not a viable principle in the savannah ecology. In consequence, dominance had to be the governing rule holding the band together. (The baboons, a currently successful savannah-dwelling species, are at this stage today.) That all human history testifies to the importance of the struggle for power and status is too obvious to require underlining. I shall add only two points: (1) the instinctive drive for leadership could only succeed in tandem with the complementary quality of willing *followership*,[42] and (2) dominance need not be the result of strictly individual force but may involve also the ability to form effective coalitions.

The crucial step toward moderation of the Iron Rule was, it seems, the shift to a largely carnivorous diet. Hunting of big game probably placed a greater premium upon a more egalitarian form of cooperation, requiring distributed individual enterprise and cleverness. The consequence was a reduction in the steepness of the dominance gradient. Something approaching monogamous sexual pairing—private rights in mating—may have been the result of the sexual division of labor associated with hunting.[43] At some point the development of tools and weapons opened up another dimension of the division of labor, between hunter and specialized craftsman. It seems likely that the first systematic pattern of exchange of material goods was between tools and weapons on the one side and meat on the other.[44] The possibility of such exchange required prior mutual recognition of private rights. Already at the primate level, the beginnings of private sexual rights as well as material property rights (in meat) have been observed. *Exchange* of material goods seems uniquely human, however.[45]

---

[41] Lionel Tiger & Robin Fox, The Imperial Animal (1971); Fred H. Willhoite, Jr., Primates and Political Authority: A Biobehavioral Perspective, 70 Am. Pol. Sci. Rev. 1110 (1976).

[42] Willhoite, *supra* note 41.

[43] Morris, *supra* note 38.

[44] The exchange of interpersonal cooperative *services* (sex, grooming, mutual aid) long anteceded this, of course.

[45] On sexual rights among baboons, see Willhoite, *supra* note 41. An economic analysis of rights in meat, maintained even against dominant animals among chimpanzees, appears in Melvin C. Fredlund, Wolves, Chimps, and Demsetz, 14 Econ. Inquiry 279 (1976). For "the propensity to truck, barter, and exchange" as an exclusively human trait, see Adam Smith, The Wealth of Nations, bk. 1, ch. 2, at 13 (Modern Library ed. 1937).

PRIVACY: ITS ORIGIN, FUNCTION, AND FUTURE          661

Parallel with the evolution of the privacy ethic, we need not exclude a tendency to broaden the Golden Rule of sharing beyond immediate kin. Successful "begging," a normal behavior pattern between offspring and parent, is found to some extent between unrelated adults among the higher primates, once again in connection with meat.[46] In primitive human societies, anthropologists have emphasized, *patterns of redistribution* are nearly universal as limitations upon property rights. However, it would be misleading to place excessive emphasis upon the Golden-Rule aspects of redistributive sharing; among primitive peoples, reciprocation of "gifts" is almost always expected.[47] Under conditions of resource variability, sharing may also serve a mutual insurance function.[48] And, finally, in some cases where resources are held in common rather than privately partitioned, productive efficiency may provide a satisfactory explanation.[49]

The uniquely human development of language led to an open-ended increase in the complexity and subtlety of behavior patterns. One point of great interest concerns interband relations. When primate bands split up, for demographic or other reasons, they shortly become strangers. But human bands could retain recognition of kinship ties, could form clan and tribe alliances. The widening field of interaction opened up further possibilities of specialization and exchange, both on the group and on the individual level.

The ecological shift to pastoralism and to agriculture was not, if this argument is correct, the origin of private rights. But pastoralism requires private ownership of flocks, and agriculture private ownership of crops. The two systems tend to develop rather different human types. Pastoralism is typically associated with extended-family or clan units, relatively strong dominance, and polygyny (as in the patriarchical period pictured in *Genesis*). Agriculture tends to be associated with the monogamous peasant homestead, unmatchable in efficiency terms by any form of group farming. On the other hand, the military helplessness of a dispersed farming population tends to lead to their subjection or enslavement by dominant overlords or invaders.

In fact, the role of war in selection of human types and social structures has been enormous. From the most primitive times, it seems impossible to

---

[46] Wilson, *supra* note 9, at ch. 26.

[47] The "norm of reciprocity" seems to be universal in the human species. And, so far as we can tell, it is uniquely human (see Adam Smith citation, *supra* note 45). The need to form and to manage reciprocal ties is likely to have played a critical role in the evolution of man's individual intelligence as well as his social repertory. See Willhoite, *supra* note 24.

[48] Richard A. Posner, A Theory of Primitive Society, with Special Reference to Law, 23 J. Law & Econ. 1 (1980).

[49] Harold Demsetz, Toward a Theory of Property Rights, 57 Am. Econ. Rev. 347 (Papers & Proceedings, May 1967). Even though what appears to be sharing *may* often represent disguised egoistic or private-right motivations, economists ought not be too hasty in excluding the possibility that Golden-Rule sharing is actually taking place.

doubt that man as superpredator also preyed on his own kind,[50] particularly in times of resource stress. Warfare as an economic activity is characterized by an overwhelming economy of scale leading to larger group size: "God is on the side of the bigger battalions." Against this, however, has to be balanced diminishing returns to scale in exploiting game or crops or other localized resources. Warfare has undoubtedly had complex and multidirectional effects upon the human makeup itself. On the one hand, it selects for selfless loyalty and dedication—Golden Rule properties within the group. It also selects for the strong charismatic leadership typical of dominance structures. Yet the more individualistic virtues associated with private rights may also play an important role in war, for a variety of reasons: private men are more likely to have developed habits of ingenuity and enterprise, they may fight more strongly for what they regard as their own, and the commercial societies organized on the principle of private rights will have become richer and more innovative. Thus, while Adam Smith along with other philosophers[51] deplored the loss of heroic qualities due to the spread of affluence and commerce, the outcome of the contest between Athens and Sparta is not in general predictable. (It was "a nation of shopkeepers" that defeated Napoleon.) And, finally, reinforcing the fact that each separate individual represents a mixture of motivations, the large scale of modern societies makes it possible to combine many *different human types* into a mutually supportive alliance.

## V.  SOME CONCLUDING POINTS

I will finish by setting down, not in any very systematic order, some points that may reinforce the key ideas and perhaps provide hints as to where they might lead.

1. To distinguish, as is common, between "selfish" and "unselfish" behavior, between pursuit of private goals and public goals, is a very serious oversimplification. Man does have egoistic, purely selfish drives. But his social instincts are more complex, involving (at least) the three principles of *dominance, sharing,* and *private rights.* Each of these is not a simple one-sided urge, but a two-sided ethic.

2. These ethics have evolved and have become ingrained in the human makeup in association with various forms of social organization over the history of mankind. Each ethic and associated social structure has been

---

[50] Richard D. Alexander, The Search for a General Theory of Behavior, 20 Behavioral Sci. 77 (1975); Harris, *supra* note 37.

[51] Edward C. Banfield, The Contradictions of Commercial Society: Adam Smith as a Political Sociologist (Mont Pelerin Society Lecture, 1976).

adaptive to certain of the ecological contexts and constraints in which humanity has lived.

3. The "taste for privacy" is a misleading term. It *may* represent nothing more than a selfish claim, of which we may appropriately be suspicious. But insistence on one's own rights is also part of a two-sided ethic involving willingness to concede corresponding rights to others, and even willingness to participate as a disinterested third-party enforcer against violators.

4. Like the privacy ethic, each of the other two-sided ethics has a "selfish" aspect. This is obvious for the dominance drive, but even sharing involves the supportive emotions of envy and fear of envy.

5. Economic study of market interactions may yield satisfactory results while postulating purely egoistic men, acting within an unexplained social environment of regulatory law. But as the power of economic analysis comes to be employed outside the traditional market context, for example in the area of public choice, the egoistic model of man (as in "social contract" theories) will not suffice.[52]

6. The privacy ethic is an enormously powerful device for creating wealth, but beyond a certain point affluence creates great social dangers in permitting or perhaps even promoting a relaxation of social discipline together with the spread of disruptive ideologies.[53] Pursuit of affluence may be self-defeating, not only on the individual level as moralists have always contended, but in terms of social survival as well. This ought to raise doubts in our minds about too-ready use of "efficiency" (which is essentially maximization of aggregate wealth) as the criterion of social policy.[54]

7. The conflict between the privacy ethic and its competitors (alternative social ethics on the one hand and sheer egoism on the other) takes place partly within social groups, partly between them. Man has ingrained within him elements favoring each of these social tendencies, "soft-wired" so as to leave a range of ideological choice. So the future of the privacy ethic rests in part upon its ability to capture the hearts and minds of men. At least

---

[52] Note Stigler's inability to satisfactorily explain privacy (secrecy) legislation without bringing in an element he calls "social altruism." Stigler, *supra* note 2. See also H. Margolis, Selfishness, Altruism, and Rationality (1979) (unpublished paper at Center for Int'l Studies, Mass. Inst. of Technology).

[53] J. A. Schumpeter, Capitalism, Socialism, and Democracy (1942).

[54] At this point my analysis diverges from that of Harold Demsetz, Ethics and Efficiency in Property Rights Systems, in Time, Uncertainty, and Disequilibrium (Mario J. Rizzo ed. 1979), with which it otherwise has many points of agreement. I will note here one other significant divergence. Demsetz, concerned to counter certain naive ethical views held by ideological defenders of private property as a "natural" right of man, strongly emphasizes the socially conventional (not to say arbitrary) aspects of how rights are actually defined. In contrast, it seems to follow from my approach that there is, indeed, some "natural" element in property rights, that there are intrinsic limits constraining what is merely contingent and artificial. I cannot develop this idea further here, however.

equally important is the competition between groups, primarily military competition. While it is conventional to deplore merely "commercial" ethics, societies organized on this principle have given a good account of themselves historically—not only militarily, but in terms of the values we consider civilized. I shall not attempt here to forecast the future prospects of privacy as a social structure balancing individual autonomy with communal responsibility except to say: They don't look very good!

# Part II
# The Value of 'Privacy'

# [10]

# 1

## PRIVACY, FREEDOM, AND RESPECT FOR PERSONS

STANLEY I. BENN

When your mind is set on mating
It is highly irritating
To see an ornithologist below:
Though it may be nature-study,
To a bird it's merely bloody
Awful manners. Can't he see that he's *de trop!**

## INTRODUCTION

If two people retire to the privacy of the bushes, they
go where they expect to be unobserved. What they do is done

I wish to acknowledge my indebtedness to my colleague Geoffrey Mortimore
for his many helpful suggestions and no less for his trenchant criticism of this
paper.
* From "Bird-watching—The Song of the Redstart," in A. N. L. Munby,
*Lyra Catenata* (printed privately 1948). Quoted in John Buxton, *The Redstart* (London: Collins, 1950).

1

2                                                    STANLEY I. BENN

*privately,* or *in private,* if they are not actually seen doing it. Should they later advertise or publish what they were about, what *was* private would then become public knowledge. Or they may have been mistaken in thinking their retreat private—they may have been in full view of passersby all the time. One's *private affairs,* however, are private in a different sense. It is not that they are kept out of sight or from the knowledge of others that makes them private. Rather, they are matters that it would be inappropriate for others to try to find out about, much less report on, without one's consent; one complains if they are publicized precisely because they are private. Similarly, a private room remains private in spite of uninvited intruders, for, unlike the case of the couple in the bushes, falsifying the expectation that no one will intrude is not a logically sufficient ground for saying that something private in this sense is not private after all.

"Private" used in this second, immunity-claiming[1] way is both norm-dependent and norm-invoking. It is norm-dependent because *private affairs* and *private rooms* cannot be identified without some reference to norms. So any definition of the concept "private affairs" must presuppose the existence of *some* norms restricting unlicensed observation, reporting, or entry, even though no norm in particular is necessary to the concept. It is norm-invoking in that one need say no more than "This is a private matter" to claim that anyone not invited to concern himself with it ought to stay out of it. That is why the normative implications of "Private" on a letter or a notice board do not need to be spelled out.[2]

The norms invoked by the concept are not necessarily immunity-conferring, however; one can imagine cultures, for instance, in which they would be prohibitive, where to say that

---

[1] I do not use "immunity" in this paper in the technical Hohfeldian sense. Where it is not used in a simple descriptive sense, I intend that a person shall be understood to be immune from observation if he has grounds for complaint should anyone watch him; an activity is immune if it is not appropriate for unauthorized persons to watch it.

[2] Of course, though "Someone has been reading my private letters" is enough to state a protest, it need not be well founded; the letters may not really qualify as private, or even if they are, there may be other conditions overriding the implicit claim to immunity.

someone had done something in private would be to accuse him of acting inappropriately—perhaps cutting himself off from a collective experience and cheating others of their right to share in it. Or again, "privacy" might apply mandatorily; that is, anything private *ought* to be kept from the knowledge of others. This is rather the sense of the somewhat old-fashioned phrase "private parts," referring not to parts of the body that one might keep unseen if one chose, but to parts that one had a duty to keep out of sight. In our culture, sexual and excretory acts are private not merely in the sense that performers are immune from observation but also in the sense that some care ought to be taken that they are not generally observed. Thus, liberty to publicize, that is, to license scrutiny and publicity, whether generally or to a select public, is commonly but by no means necessarily associated with the right to immunity from observation.

The norms invoked by the concept of privacy are diverse, therefore, not only in substance but also in logical form; some grant immunities, some are prohibitive, some are mandatory. There may be cultures, indeed, with no norm-invoking concept of privacy at all, where *nothing* is thought properly immune from observation and anything may be generally displayed. It might still be possible, of course, to seek out private situations where one would not be observed, but it would never be a ground of grievance either that an action was or was not open for all to see or that someone was watching. But whatever the possible diversity, some privacy claims seem to rest on something a bit more solid than mere cultural contingency. The first objective of this paper is to explore the possibility that some minimal right to immunity from uninvited observation and reporting is required by certain basic features of our conception of a person.

## THE GENERAL PRINCIPLE OF PRIVACY AND RESPECT FOR PERSONS

The umbrella "right to privacy" extends, no doubt, to other claims besides the claims not to be watched, listened to, or reported upon without leave, and not to have public attention focused upon one uninvited. It is these particular claims, however, that I have primarily in mind in this paper. It deals, therefore, with a cluster of immunities which, if acknowledged, curb the freedom of others to do things that are generally quite innocent if done to objects other than persons, and even to persons, if done with their permission. There is nothing intrinsically objectionable in observing the world, including its inhabitants, and in sharing one's discoveries with anyone who finds them interesting; and this is not on account of any special claims, for instance, for scientific curiosity, or for a public interest in the discovery of truth. For I take as a fundamental principle in morals a general liberty to do whatever one chooses unless someone else has good reasons for interfering to prevent it, reasons grounded either on the freedom of others or on some other moral principle such as justice or respect for persons or the avoidance of needless pain. The onus of justification, in brief, lies on the advocate of restraint, not on the person restrained. The present question, then, is whether any moral principle will provide a quite general ground for a prima facie claim that B should not observe and report on A unless A agrees to it. Is there a principle of privacy extending immunity to inquiry to all human activities, to be overridden only by special considerations, like those suggested? Or is it rather that there is a general freedom to inquire, observe, and report on human affairs as on other things, unless a special case can be made out for denying it with respect to certain activities that are *specifically* private?

My strategy, then, is to inquire, first, whether anyone is entitled, prima facie, to be private if he chooses, irrespective of what he is about: would the couple in the bushes have grounds for complaint if they discovered someone eavesdropping on their discussion of, say, relativity theory? Second, whether or not such grounds exist, can any rational account be given (that is, an account not wholly dependent on conventional norms) of "private affairs," the area in which uninvited intrusions are judged *particularly* inappropriate?

The former, more sweeping claim may appear at first sight extravagant, even as only a prima facie claim. Anyone who wants to remain unobserved and unidentified, it might be

*Privacy, Freedom, and Respect for Persons* 5

said, should stay at home or go out only in disguise. Yet there is a difference between happening to be seen and having someone closely observe, and perhaps record, what one is doing, even in a public place. Nor is the resentment that some people feel at being watched necessarily connected with fears of damaging disclosures in the Sunday papers or in a graduate thesis in social science. How reasonable is it, then, for a person to resent being treated much in the way that a birdwatcher might treat a redstart?

Putting the case initially at this rather trivial level has the advantage of excluding two complicating considerations. In the first place, I have postulated a kind of intrusion (if that is what it is) which does no obvious damage. It is not like publishing details of someone's sex life and ruining his career. Furthermore, what is resented is not being watched *tout court,* but being watched without leave. If observation as such were intrinsically or even consequentially damaging, it might be objectionable even if done with consent. In the present instance, consent removes all ground for objection. In the second place, by concentrating on simple unlicensed observation, I can leave aside the kind of interference with which Mill was mainly concerned in the essay *On Liberty,* namely, anything that prevents people doing, in their private lives, something they want to do, or that requires them to do what they do not want to do.[3] Threatening a man with penalties, or taking away his stick, are ways of preventing his beating his donkey; but if he stops simply because he is watched, the interference is of a different kind. He could continue if he chose; being observed affects his action only by changing his perception of it. The observer makes the act impossible only in the sense that the actor now sees it in a different light. The intrusion is not therefore obviously objectionable as an interference with freedom of action. It is true that there are special kinds of action—any that depend upon surprise, for example—that could be made objectively impossible merely by watching and reporting on them; but my present purpose is to ask whether a *general* case

[3] W. L. Weinstein's illuminating contribution to this volume, "The Private and the Free: A Conceptual Inquiry," is mainly concerned with Mill's questions; I shall touch on them only indirectly.

6                                                    STANLEY I. BENN

can be made out, not one that depends on special conditions
of that kind.

Of course, there is always a danger that information may be
used to harm a man in some way. The usual arguments against
wiretapping, bugging, a National Data Center, and private in-
vestigators rest heavily on the contingent possibility that a
tyrannical government or unscrupulous individuals might misuse them for blackmail or victimization. The more one knows
about a person, the greater one's power to damage him. Now
it may be that fears like this are the only reasonable ground
for objecting *in general* to being watched. I might suspect a
man who watches my house of "casing the joint." But if he
can show me he intends no such thing, and if there is no
possibility of his observations being used against me in any
other way, it would seem to follow that I could have no further
reasonable ground for objecting. Eliza Doolittle resents Professor Higgins's recording her speech in Covent Garden because
she believes that a girl of her class subject to so close a scrutiny
is in danger of police persecution: "You dunno what it means
to me. Theyll take away my character and drive me on the
streets for speaking to gentlemen."[4] But the resentment of the
bystanders is excited by something else, something intrinsic in
Higgins's performance, not merely some possible consequence of
his ability to spot their origins by their accents: "See here:
what call have you to know about people what never offered
to meddle with you? . . . You take us for dirt under your
feet, dont you? Catch you taking liberties with a gentleman!"
What this man resents is surely that Higgins fails to show a
proper respect for persons; he is treating people as objects
or specimens—like "dirt"—and not as subjects with sensibilities,
ends, and aspirations of their own, morally responsible for
their own decisions, and capable, as mere specimens are not,
of reciprocal relations with the observer. This failure is, of
course, precisely what Eliza, in her later incarnation as Higgins's
Galatea, complains of too. These resentments suggest a possible
ground for a prima facie claim not to be watched, at any
rate in the same manner as one watches a thing or an animal.

---

[4] G. B. Shaw, *Pygmalion*, Act I.

*Privacy, Freedom, and Respect for Persons*　　　　　　7

For this is "to take liberties," to act impudently, to show less than a proper regard for human dignity.

Finding oneself an object of scrutiny, as the focus of another's attention, brings one to a new consciousness of oneself, as something seen through another's eyes. According to Sartre, indeed, it is a necessary condition for knowing oneself *as* anything at all that one should conceive oneself as an object of scrutiny.[5] It is only through the regard of the other that the observed becomes aware of himself as an object, knowable, having a determinate character, in principle predictable. His consciousness of pure freedom as subject, as originator and chooser, is at once assailed by it; he is fixed *as something*—with limited probabilities rather than infinite, indeterminate possibilities. Sartre's account of human relations is of an obsessional need to master an unbearable alien freedom that undermines one's belief in one's own; for Ego is aware of Alter not only as a fact, an object in his world, but also as the subject of a quite independent world of Alter's own, wherein Ego himself is mere object. The relationship between the two is essentially hostile. Each, doubting his own freedom, is driven to assert the primacy of his own subjectivity. But the struggle for mastery, as Sartre readily admits, is a self-frustrating response; Alter's reassurance would be worthless to Ego unless it were freely given, yet the freedom to give it would at once refute it.

What Sartre conceived as a phenomenologically necessary dilemma, however, reappears in R. D. Laing's *The Divided Self*[6] as a characteristically schizoid perception of the world, the response of a personality denied free development, trying to preserve itself from domination by hiding away a "real self" where it cannot be absorbed or overwhelmed. The schizoid's problem arises because he cannot believe fully in his own existence as a person. He may *need* to be observed in order to be convinced that he exists, if only in the world of another; yet, resenting the necessity to be what the other perceives him as, he may try at the same time to hide. His predicament, like Sartre's, may seem to him to arise not from the *manner* of his being observed, but to be implicit in the very relation of observer and observed.

[5] See J.-P. Sartre: *L'être et le néant* (Paris, 1953), Part 3, "Le pour-autrui."
[6] Harmondsworth, England, 1965.

Sartre, however, does not show why the awareness of others as subjects must evoke so hostile a response. Even if it were true that my consciousness of my own infinite freedom is shaken by my being made aware that in the eyes of another I have only limited possibilities, still if I am not free, it is not his regard that confines me; it only draws my attention to what I was able formerly to disregard. And if I *am* free, then his regard makes no real difference. And if there is a dilemma here, may I not infer from it that the Other sees me too as a subject, and has the same problem? Could this not be a bond between us rather than a source of resentment, each according the other the same dignity as subject?

It is because the schizoid cannot believe in himself as a person, that he cannot form such a bond, or accept the respectful regard of another. So every look is a threat or an insult. Still, without question, there are ways of looking at a man that do diminish him, that provide cause for offense as real as any physical assault. But, of course, that cannot be a reason either for hiding or for going around with one's eyes shut. Yet it does suggest that if, like a doctor, one has occasion to make someone an object of scrutiny and study, or like a clinician the topic for a lecture, the patient will have grounds for resentment if the examiner appears insensible to the fact that it is a person he is examining, a subject to whom it makes a difference that he is observed, who will also have a view about what is discovered or demonstrated, and will put his own value upon it.

It would be a mistake to think that the only objection to such examination is that an incautious observer could cause damage to a sensitive person's mental state, for that could be avoided by watching him secretly. To treat a man without respect is not to injure him—at least, not in *that* sense; it is more like insulting him. Nor is it the fact of scrutiny as such that is offensive, but only unlicensed scrutiny, which may in fact do no damage at all, yet still be properly resented as an impertinence.

I am suggesting that a general principle of privacy might be grounded on the more general principle of respect for persons. By a *person* I understand a subject with a consciousness of himself as agent, one who is capable of having projects, and assessing his achievements in relation to them. To *conceive* someone as a person is to see him as actually or potentially a chooser, as one attempting to steer his own course through the world, adjusting his behavior as his apperception of the world changes, and correcting course as he perceives his errors. It is to understand that his life is for him a kind of enterprise like one's own, not merely a succession of more or less fortunate happenings, but a record of achievements and failures; and just as one cannot describe one's own life in these terms without claiming that what happens is important, so to see another's in the same light is to see that for him at least this must be important. Professor Higgins's offense was to be insensitive to this fact about other people. Of course, one may have a clinical interest in people as project-makers without oneself attaching any importance to their projects. Still, if one fails to see how their aims and activities could be important for them, one has not properly understood what they are about. Even so, it requires a further step to see that recognizing another as engaged on such an enterprise makes a claim on oneself. To *respect* someone as a person is to concede that one ought to take account of the way in which his enterprise might be affected by one's own decisions. By the principle of respect for persons, then, I mean the principle that every human being, insofar as he is qualified as a person, is entitled to this minimal degree of consideration.

I do not mean, of course, that someone's having some attitude toward *anything* I propose to do is alone sufficient for his wishes to be a relevant consideration, for he will certainly have attitudes and wishes about actions of mine that do not affect his enterprise at all. B's dislike of cruelty to animals is not in itself a reason why A should stop beating his donkey. It is not enough that B will be gratified if he can approve A's action, and disappointed if not; it is the conception of B as a chooser, as engaged in an active, creative enterprise, that lays an obligation of respect upon A, not the conception of him as *suffering* gratifications and disappointments. This can be a ground for sympathetic joy or pity, but not respect. B's attitudes are considerations relevant for A's decisions only if what A does will make a difference to the conditions under which B makes *his* choices, either denying him an otherwise available option (which would be to interfere with his freedom of action) or changing the sig-

nificance or meaning for B of acts still open to him. B may dis-
approve of A's watching C or listening to his conversation with
D, but B's own conditions of action—what I have called B's
enterprise—remain unaffected. On the other hand, if C knows
that A is listening, A's intrusion alters C's consciousness of himself, and his experienced relation to his world. Formerly self-
forgetful, perhaps, he may now be conscious of his opinions as
candidates for A's approval or contempt. But even without self-
consciousness of this kind, his immediate enterprise—the conversation with D—may be changed for him merely by the fact
of A's presence. I am not postulating a private conversation in
the sense of one about personal matters; what is at issue is the
change in the way C apprehends his own performance—the topic
makes no difference to this argument. A's uninvited intrusion is
an impertinence because he treats it as of no consequence that
he may have effected an alteration in C's perception of himself
and of the nature of his performance.[7] Of course, no *damage*
may have been done; C may actually enjoy performing before
an enlarged audience. But C's wishes in the matter must surely
be a relevant consideration (as B's are not), and in the absence
of some overriding reason to the contrary, if C were inclined to
complain, he has legitimate grounds.

The underpinning of a claim not to be watched without leave
will be more general if it can be grounded in this way on the
principle of respect for persons than on a utilitarian duty to
avoid inflicting suffering. That duty may, of course, reinforce
the claim in particular instances. But respect for persons will
sustain an objection even to secret watching, which may do no
actual harm at all. Covert observation—spying—is objectionable
because it deliberately deceives a person about his world, thwarting, for reasons that *cannot* be his reasons, his attempts to make
a rational choice. One cannot be said to respect a man as engaged on an enterprise worthy of consideration if one knowingly
and deliberately alters his conditions of action, concealing the

---

[7] Of course, there are situations, such as in university common rooms,
where there is a kind of conventional general license to join an ongoing
conversation. A railway compartment confers a similar license in Italy, but
not in England. In such situations, if one does not wish to be listened to,
one stays silent.

fact from him. The offense is different in this instance, of course, from A's open intrusion on C's conversation. In that case, A's attentions were liable to affect C's enterprise by changing C's perception of it; he may have felt differently about his conversation with D, even to the extent of not being able to see it as any longer the same activity, knowing that A was now listening. In the present instance, C is unaware of A. Nevertheless, he is wronged because the significance to him of his enterprise, assumed unobserved, is deliberately falsified by A. He may be in a fool's paradise or a fool's hell; either way, A is making a fool of him. Suppose that in a situation in which he might be observed, there is no reason why he should not choose to act privately (for instance, he is doing nothing wrong); then for anyone to watch without his knowledge is to show disrespect not only for the privacy that may have been his choice, but, by implication, for him, as a chooser. I can well imagine myself freely consenting to someone's watching me at work, but deeply resenting anyone's doing so without my knowledge—as though it didn't matter whether I liked it or not. So a policeman may treat suspected criminals like this only if there are good grounds for believing that there is an overriding need to frustrate what they are about, not because they have no rights as persons to privacy. Psychiatrists may be entitled to treat lunatics like this —but only to the extent that being incapable of rational choice, they are defective as persons. (Even so, their interests, if not their wishes, will be limiting considerations.)

The close connection between the general principle of privacy and respect for persons may account for much of the resentment evoked by the idea of a National Data Center, collating all that is known about an individual from his past contacts with government agencies. Much has been made, of course—and no doubt rightly—of the dangers of computerized data banks, governmental or otherwise. The information supplied to and by them may be false; or if true, may still put a man in a false light, by drawing attention, say, to delinquencies in his distant past that he has now lived down. And even the most conforming of citizens would have reason for dread if officials came to regard their computers as both omniscient and infallible. A good deal of legislative invention has been exercised, accordingly, in seek-

ing safeguards against the abuse of information power. Yet for
some objectors at least it altogether misses the point. It is not
just a matter of a fear to be allayed by reassurances, but of a
resentment that anyone—even a thoroughly trustworthy official—
should be able at will to satisfy any curiosity, without the knowledge let alone the consent of the subject. For since what others
know about him can radically affect a man's view of himself, to
treat the collation of personal information about him as if it
raised purely technical problems of safeguards against abuse is
to disregard his claim to consideration and respect as a person.

I have argued so far as though the principle of respect for persons clearly indicated what a man might reasonably resent. This
needs some qualification. If someone stares at my face, I cannot
help seeing his gaze as focused on me. I am no less self-conscious
if I catch him scrutinizing the clothes I am wearing. But would
it be reasonable to resent scrutiny of a suit I am not wearing—
one I have just given, perhaps, to an old folks' home? Or of my
car outside my home? Or in the service station? Granted that
I can reasonably claim immunity from the uninvited attentions
of observers and reporters, what is to count for this purpose as
*me?* As I suggested above, it cannot be sufficient that I do not
*want* you to observe something; for the principle of respect to
be relevant, it must be something about my own person that is
in question, otherwise the principle would be so wide that a
mere wish of mine would be a prima facie reason for everyone
to refrain from observing and reporting on anything at all. I
do not make something a part of me merely by having feelings
about it. The principle of privacy proposed here is, rather, that
any man who desires that he *himself* should not be an object
of scrutiny has a reasonable prima facie claim to immunity. But
the ground is not in the mere fact of his desiring, but in the
relation between himself as an object of scrutiny and as a conscious and experiencing subject. And it is clearly not enough for
a man to *say* that something pertains to him as a person and
therefore shares his immunity; there must be reasons for saying
so.

What could count as a reason? The very intimate connection
between the concepts of *oneself* and *one's body* (about which
philosophers have written at length) would seem to put that

*Privacy, Freedom, and Respect for Persons* 13

much beyond question (though some schizoids' perception of the world would suggest that dissociation even of these concepts is possible). Beyond that point, however, cultural norms cannot be ignored. In a possessive individualist culture, in which a man's property is seen as an extension of his personality, as an index to his social standing, a measure of his achievements, or an expression of his taste, to look critically on his clothes or his car is to look critically on him. In other cultures, the standards might well be different. The notion we have of our own extension, of the outer limits of our personalities—those events or situations in respect of which we feel pride or shame—is unquestionably culture-variant; consequently, the application even of a quite general principle of privacy will be affected by culturally variant norms—those regarding family, say, or property.

## APPLYING THE GENERAL PRINCIPLE

Allow that the principle of respect for persons will underpin a general principle of privacy; even so, it would amount only to a prima facie ground for limiting the freedom of others to observe and report at will. It would place on them a burden of justification but it would not override any special justification. The principle might be thought quite inadequate, for instance, to sustain on its own a case for legal restraints; the protection of privacy is less important, perhaps, than the danger to political freedom from legal restrictions on reporting. It might be argued that in every case it is for the press to show what reasonable public interest publicity would serve. But so uncertain a criterion could result in an overtimorous press. The courts have been properly wary of recognizing rights that might discourage if not disable the press from publicizing what *ought* to be exposed.

General principles do not *determine* solutions to moral problems of this kind. They indicate what needs to be justified, where the onus of justification lies, and what can count as a justification. So to count as an overriding consideration, an argument must refer to some further principle. Consider the difficult case of the privacy of celebrities. According to a learned American judge, the law "recognizes a legitimate public curiosity about the personalities of celebrities, and about a great deal of otherwise private and personal information about them."[8] But is all curiosity equally legitimate, or must there be something about the kind of celebrity that legitimizes special kinds of curiosity? Is there no difference between, say, a serious historian's curiosity about what (and who) prompted President Johnson's decision not to run a second time and that to which the Sunday gossip columnists appeal? If a person is in the public eye for some performance that he intends to be public or that is in its nature public—like conducting an orchestra—this may, as a matter of fact, make "human interest stories" about him more entertaining and exciting than similar stories about an unknown. But the fact that many people enjoy that kind of entertainment is no reason at all for overriding the principle of privacy; for though there is a presumptive liberty to do whatever there is no reason for not doing, there is no general claim to have whatever one enjoys. To treat even an entertainer's life simply as material for entertainment is to pay no more regard to him as a person than to an animal in a menagerie. Of course, anyone who indiscriminately courts publicity, as some entertainers do, can hardly complain if they are understood to be offering a general license. But merely to be a celebrity—even a willing celebrity—does not disable someone from claiming the consideration due to a person. Admittedly, it opens up a range of special claims to information about him, to override his general claim to privacy. Candidates for appointment to the Supreme Court must expect some public concern with their business integrity. Or—a rather different case—because an eminent conductor participates in a public activity with a public tradition, anyone choosing conducting as a profession must expect that his musical experience, where he was trained, who has influenced his interpretations, will be matters of legitimate interest to others concerned as he is with music. But this is not a warrant for prying into other facts about him that have nothing to do with his music: his taste in wines, perhaps, or women. The principle of privacy would properly give way in one area, but it would stand

[8] See W. L. Prosser, "Privacy," *California Law Review*, 48 (1960), 416–417.

in any other to which the special overriding grounds were irrelevant. For the principle itself is not limited in its application; it constitutes a prima facie claim in respect to *anything* a man does.

## "PRIVATE AFFAIRS" AND PERSONAL IDEALS

To claim immunity on the ground that an inquiry is an intrusion into one's *private affairs* is to make an argumentative move of a quite different kind. For this concept entrenches the privacy of certain special areas far more strongly than the mere presumptive immunity of the general principle. To justify such an intrusion, one has to have not merely a reason, but one strong enough to override special reasons for *not* intruding. So while the interests of phonetic science might justify Professor Higgins's impertinence in Covent Garden, they would not be good enough reasons for bugging Eliza's bedroom.

The activities and experiences commonly thought to fall within this special private area are diverse and largely culture-dependent. Some seem to have no rational grounds at all. For instance, why should the bodily functions that in our culture are appropriately performed in solitude include defecation but not eating? Of course, so long as certain acts are assigned to this category anyone who has internalized the social norms will experience a painful embarrassment if seen doing them; embarrassment, indeed, is the culturally appropriate response in a society with the concept of *pudenda,* and anyone not showing it may be censured as brazen or insensitive. But though this furnishes a kind of rational interest in privacy of this kind, its rationale depends on a conventional norm that may itself be wholly irrational.

Not all areas of privacy are like this, however; others are closely related to ideals of life and character which would be difficult, perhaps impossible, to achieve were privacy not safeguarded. The liberal individualist tradition has stressed, in particular, three personal ideals, to each of which corresponds a range of "private affairs." The first is the ideal of personal relations; the second, the Lockian ideal of the politically free man

16

in a minimally regulated society; the third, the Kantian ideal of the morally autonomous man, acting on principles that he accepts as rational.

### The Privacy of Personal Relations

By personal relations, I mean relations between persons that are considered valuable and important at least as much because of the quality of each person's attitude to another as for what each does to, or for, another.

All characteristically human relations—I mean relations of a kind that could not exist between stones or wombats—involve some element, however small, of role-expectancy. We structure our relations with others according to an understanding of *what* they are and what accordingly is due to them and from them. That may exhaust some relations: if the railway booking clerk gives me the correct ticket in exchange for my fare, he has fulfilled his function. Moreover, the point of the relationship calls for no more than this; the grating that separates us, with just space enough to push through a ticket or a coin, appropriately symbolizes it. One cannot be indifferent to his performance, but one need not attend to his personality.

The relation between father and son, or husband and wife, is necessarily more than this, or if in a given instance it is not, then that instance is defective. Here, too, there are role-expectancies, but each particular set of related persons will fulfill them in a different way. There is room for being a father in this or in that manner. Moreover, only a part of what it is to be a father has been met when the specified duties of the role have been fulfilled. Beyond that, the value of the relation depends on a personal understanding between the parties, and on whether, and how, they care about one another. Father and son might be meticulous in the performance of the formal duties of their roles, but if they are quite indifferent to each other, the relationship is missing its point. The relationship between friends or lovers is still less role-structured than family relations, though even here there are conventional patterns and rituals—gifts on ritual occasions, forms of wooing, etc. But they are primarily symbols: their main point is to communicate a feeling or an

*Privacy, Freedom, and Respect for Persons*                    17

attitude, to reassure, perhaps, or make a proposal. And though they could be gone through even if the feeling did not really exist, such a performance would surely be a pretense or a deception, and therefore parasitic on the primary point.

Personal relations can of course be of public concern; children may need to be protected, for instance, from certain kinds of corrupting relations with adults. But while it may be possible and desirable to prevent such relations altogether, there is little that third parties can do to regulate or reshape them. By inducing the booking clerk to do his job more efficiently, or passengers to state their destinations more clearly, the railway staff controller can improve the relation between them. But this is because he can keep them up to the mark—they are all interested exclusively in role-performance, and each can have a clear notion of the standard that the other's performance should reach. But friends can be kept up to the mark only by one another. There is no "mark" that anyone outside could use to assess them, for friendship is not confined by role requirements.[9]

To intrude on personal relations of this kind may be very much worse than useless. Of course, people do take their troubles to others, to friends or marriage counselors for guidance and advice. But this is to invite the counselor to become, in a small way perhaps, a party to the relationship—or rather, to enter into a relationship with him, the success of which depends on his resolve to keep it a purely second-order relationship, demanding of him a sensitive and reticent understanding of the first. Personal relations are exploratory and creative; they survive and develop if they are given care and attention; they require continuous adjustment as the personalities of the parties are modified by experience, both of one another and of their external environment. Such relationships are, in their nature, private. They could not exist if it were not possible to create excluding conditions. One cannot have a personal relation with

---

[9] "According to the newspaper *Szabad Nép*, some members of the Communist Party in Hungary have not a single working man among their friends, and they are censured in a way that implies that they had better quickly make a friend of a worker or it will be the worse for them" (*The Times* [London], July 20, 1949, quoted by P. Halmos, *Solitude and Privacy* [London, 1952], p. 167).

18                                                          STANLEY I. BENN

all comers, nor carry on personal conversations under the same
conditions as an open seminar.[10]

If we value personal relations, then, we must recognize these
at least as specifically private areas. And since the family and
the family home are the focal points of important and very
generally significant personal relations, these must be immune
from intrusion, at least beyond the point at which minimal public role requirements are satisfied. A father who regularly beats
the children insensible cannot claim, of course, that intrusion
could only spoil his personal relations. But while the public is
properly concerned that there should be no cruelty, exploitation,
or neglect, these are only the minimal conditions for personal
relations. The rest are the private business of the parties.

Preoccupation with privacy—in particular with the privacy of
family relations—has been criticized by some writers, however,
as an unhealthy feature of post-Renaissance bourgeois society.
Consider Edmund Leach's strictures:

> In the past, kinsfolk and neighbors gave the individual
> continuous moral support throughout his life. Today the
> domestic household is isolated. The family looks inward
> upon itself; there is an intensification of emotional stress
> between husband and wife, and parents and children. The
> strain is greater than most of us can bear. Far from being
> the basis of the good society, the family, with its narrow
> privacy and tawdry secrets, is the source of all our dis-
> contents.[11]

Paul Halmos, too, speaks of "a hypertrophied family devotion
and family insularity," arising from the attempt by contemporary
man "to transcend his solitude. . . ."

> [He] may finally negate his apartness in an obsessional

[10] Charles Fried has argued that privacy is logically prior to love and
friendship, since a necessary feature of these concepts is a "sharing of information about one's actions, beliefs, or emotions which one does not share
with all, and which one has the right not to share with anyone. By conferring this right, privacy creates the moral capital which we spend in
friendship and love" ("Privacy," in G. Hughes, ed., *Law, Reason, and Justice*
[New York, 1969], p. 56).

[11] E. Leach, *A Runaway World,* The 1967 Reith Lectures (London, 1968),
p. 44.

affirmation of family ties. . . . Friendship and companion-
ship, when manifestly present in the marital couple, is regarded as an instance of great virtue even when it is equally
manifestly absent in all other relationships. Furthermore,
the nepotistic solidarity of the family is another symptom
of the contemporary attitude according to which the world
is hostile and dangerous and the family is the only solid
rock which is to be protected against all comers.[12]

The insistence on the private area is, in this view, either a
symptom or a contributory cause of a pathological condition.
But to concede this diagnosis need not weaken the argument I
am advancing for the right of exclusion, for it may imply only
that in modern society we seek personal relations with too few
people, the ones we succeed in forming being overtaxed in consequence by the emotional weight they are forced to bear.

Halmos concedes the value and importance of the personal
relations between lovers and "the composed intimacy and com-
panionship of man and wife," admitting these as properly and
necessarily exclusive: "Such retreat and privacy may vary according to cultural standards but they are on the whole universal
among mankind and not infrequent among animals."[13] It is not
clear, however, how much value Halmos attaches to personal
relations in general. It may be that men suffer least from neurotic
maladjustments in communities like the kibbutz, where everyone
feels the security and comfortable warmth of acceptance by a
peer group, without the tensions of too-personalized individual
attachments. But the children of the kibbutz have been found
by some observers defective as persons, precisely because their
emotional stability has been purchased at the cost of an incapacity to establish deep personal relations. Perhaps we have to
choose between the sensitive, human understanding that we
achieve only by the cultivation of our relations within a con-

[12] P. Halmos; *Solitude and Privacy* (London, 1952), pp. 121–122.
[13] Halmos, *Solitude and Privacy*, p. 121. The standpoint Halmos adopts
may be inferred from the following passage: "While . . . the material needs
of man . . . have been increasingly satisfied, since the Industrial Revolution,
the bio-social needs have been more and more neglected. Culture, a fortuitous
expression of the basic principia of life, rarely favoured man's pacific, creative
gregariousness . . ." p. 51.

fined circle and the extrovert assurance and adjustment that a *Gemeinschaft* can confer. However this may be, to the extent that we value the former, we shall be committed to valuing the right of privacy.

Though personal relations need some freedom from interference, different kinds of interference would affect them differently. An extreme kind is to attempt to participate—to turn, for instance, a relation *à deux* into one *à trois*. It is not evident, however, that the attentions of the observer and reporter are necessarily so objectionable. A strong-minded couple might pursue their own course undisturbed under the eyes of a reasonably tactful and self-effacing paying guest. Of course, the uncommitted observer makes most of us self-conscious and inhibited —we do not find it as easy to express our feelings for one another spontaneously, to produce the same kind of mutually sensitive and responsive relations, in full view of a nonparticipant third party, as we do in private. I do not know, however, whether this is a psychologically necessary fact about human beings, or only a culturally conditioned one. Certainly, personal relations are not impossible in places where people live perforce on top of one another. But they call for a good deal of tact and goodwill from the bystanders; there is some evidence that in such conditions, people develop psychological avoidance arrangements— a capacity for not noticing, and a corresponding confidence in not being noticed—that substitute for physical seclusion.[14]

The importance of personal relations suggests a limit to what can be done by antidiscrimination laws. Whatever the justification for interfering with the freedom to discriminate in, say, hiring workers, there are some kinds of choice where a man's reasons for his preferences and antipathies are less important than that he has them. If the personal relations of a home are valued, its constituent members must be left free to decide who can be accepted into it, for example, as a lodger. Club membership might be different. True, we join clubs to cultivate personal relations, like friendships; but we do not expect to enter into such relations with every member. The mere presence in the clubroom of people whom one would not invite to join one's

---

[14] See A. F. Westin; *Privacy and Freedom* (New York, 1967), p. 18, for references to evidence of this point.

circle of intimates need not endanger the relations within that circle. Nevertheless, if the club's members are, in general, antipathetic to a particular group, to deny them the right of exclusion may create tensions defeating the end for which the club exists.

Of course, merely having prejudices gives no man a right to discriminate unfairly and irrationally in all his relations at whatever cost to the personal dignity of the outsider; insofar as the relations can be specified in terms of role-performances, it is reasonable to demand that discriminations be based only on relevant differences. But to the degree that the point of the relationship has built into it a quality of life depending on reciprocal caring, it qualifies as an area of privacy, and therefore as immune from regulation. (There may be overriding reasons, in times of racial tension and hostility, for discouraging the formation of exclusive clubs, whose rules can only appear inflammatory. But this is to adduce further special reasons against privacy, overriding reasons for it based on the value of personal relations.)

### The Privacy of the Free Citizen

The second personal ideal to which privacy is closely related is that of the free man in a minimally regulated society, a way of life where, first, the average individual is subject only within reasonable and legally safeguarded limits to the power of others, and, second, where the requirements of his social roles still leave him considerable breadth of choice in the way he lives. The first of these considerations, the one that has received most attention in the polemical literature on privacy, I have referred to already. The dossier and the computer bank threaten us with victimization and persecution by unscrupulous, intolerant, or merely misunderstanding officials. But these misgivings might be set at rest, at least in principle, by institutional safeguards and assurances. More fundamental is the second consideration, which depends on a conceptual distinction between the private and the official.

The judge's pronouncements on the bench have public significance; though he may not be easily called to account, still there is an important sense in which he has a public respon-

sibility. What he says in his home or in his club—even on matters
of law—is another matter; it has no official standing and no
official consequences. Of course, if he happens also to be club
secretary, what he says about other members in *this* official
capacity is not "his own private affair"; but conversely, the members might resist a police inquiry into its secretary's statements
as an interference with the club's private affairs. What is official
and what is private depends, therefore, on the frame of reference. But for there to be privacy of this kind at all the distinction
between official and nonofficial must be intelligible. Admittedly,
we may all have some public (that is, official) roles as voters,
taxpayers, jurymen, and so on. But we distinguish what we do
as family men, shopkeepers, and club treasurers from such public
functions. A private citizen, unlike a public official, has no *special*
official roles, just as a private member of parliament, not being a
minister, has no special official function in Parliament.

This conception of privacy is closely bound up with the liberal
ideal. The totalitarian claims that everything a man is and does
has significance for society at large. He sees the state as the self-
conscious organization of society for the well-being of society;
the social significance of our actions and relations overrides any
other. Consequently, the public or political universe is all inclusive, *all* roles are public, and every function, whether political,
economic, or artistic, can be interpreted as involving a public
responsibility.

The liberal, on the other hand, claims not merely a private
capacity—an area of action in which he is not responsible to the
state for what he does so long as he respects certain minimal
rights of others; he claims further that this is the residual category, that the onus is on anyone who claims he is accountable.
How he does his job may affect the gross national product, and
not only his own slice of it. But he will grant that this is socially
significant only in the same way that a drought is, for that too
can have serious economic consequences. He may consent to
public manipulation of the environment of private choices, by
subsidies or customs duties, for instance, as he may agree to
cloud-seeding to break a drought, but he resists the suggestion
that every citizen should be held publicly responsible for his

economic choices as though he were a public servant or the governor of the central bank.

This ideal of the private citizen provides no very precise criteria for distinguishing the private realm; it is rather that no citizen other than actual employees of the administration can be held culpable—even morally culpable—for any action as a failure in public duty unless special grounds can be shown why this is a matter in which he may not merely please himself. Of course, there will be duties associated with roles he has voluntarily assumed—as husband, employee, and so on—but such responsibilities are of his own choosing, not thrust upon him, like his public roles of juror, or taxpayer.

Just as the privacy of personal relations may be invoked to rationalize an obsessive preoccupation with the restricted family, to the exclusion of all other human concern, so the privacy of the free citizen may be invoked to rationalize a selfish economic individualism. One critic, H. W. Arndt, has written that

> The cult of privacy seems specifically designed as a defence mechanism for the protection of anti-social behaviour. . . . The cult of privacy rests on an individualist conception of society, not merely in the innocent and beneficial sense of a society in which the welfare of individuals is conceived as the end of all social organisation, but in the more sepecific sense of "each for himself and the devil take the hindmost." . . . An individualist of this sort sees "the Government" where we might see "the public interest," and this Government will appear to him often as no more than one antagonist in the battle of wits which is life—or business.[15]

There is room for a good deal of disagreement about the extent to which considerations like those of general economic well-being, social equality, or national security justify pressing back the frontiers of the private, to hold men responsible for the way they conduct their daily business. For the liberal, however, every step he is forced to take in that direction counts as a retreat from

[15] H. W. Arndt, "The Cult of Privacy," *Australian Quarterly*, XXI: 3 (September 1949), 69, 70–71.

an otherwise desirable state of affairs, in which because men may please themselves what they are about is no one's business but their own.

### Privacy and Personal Autonomy

The third personal ideal is that of the independently minded individual, whose actions are governed by principles that are his own. This does not mean, of course, that he has concocted them out of nothing, but that he subjects his principles to critical review, rather than taking them over unexamined from his social environment. He is the man who resists social pressures to conform if he has grounds for uneasiness in doing the conformist thing.

Much has been made of the need for privacy, as a safeguard against conformism. Hubert Humphrey has written:

> We act differently if we believe we are being observed. If we can never be sure whether or not we are being watched and listened to, all our actions will be altered and our very character will change.[16]

Senator Edward V. Long deplores the decline in spontaneity attendant on a situation where "because of this diligent accumulation of facts about each of us, it is difficult to speak or act today without wondering if the words or actions will reappear 'on the record.' "[17]

It is not only the authorities we fear. We are all under strong pressure from our friends and neighbors to live up to the roles in which they cast us. If we disappoint them, we risk their disapproval, and what may be worse, their ridicule. For many of us, we are free to be ourselves only within that area from which observers can legitimately be excluded. We need a sanctuary or retreat, in which we can drop the mask, desist for a while from projecting on the world the image we want to be accepted as ourselves, an image that may reflect the values of our peers

[16] Foreword to Edward V. Long, *The Intruders* (New York, 1967), p. viii.
[17] *Ibid.*, p. 55.

rather than the realities of our natures. To remain sane, we need a closed environment, open only to those we trust, with whom we have an unspoken understanding that whatever is revealed goes no farther.

Put in this way, however, the case for privacy begins to look like a claim to the conditions of life necessary only for second-grade men in a second-grade society. For the man who is truly independent—the autonomous man—is the one who has the strength of mind to resist the pressure to believe with the rest, and has the courage to act on his convictions. He is the man who despises bad faith, and refuses to be anything or to pretend to be anything merely because the world casts him for the part. He is the man who does not hesitate to stand and be counted. That sort of man can be greatly inconvenienced by the world's clamor—but he *does* what lesser men claim that they are not free to do. "There is no reason," writes Senator Long, "why conformity must be made an inescapable part of the American dream. Excessive pressures can and must be prevented: there must be preserved in each individual a sphere of privacy that will allow his personality to bloom and thrive."[18] One wonders, however, whether the Senator has drawn the right moral. Excessive pressures can be prevented not merely by allowing an individual to hide, but by tolerating the heresy he is not afraid to publish. Socrates did not ask to be allowed to teach philosophy in private. Senator Long quotes a speech of Judge Learned Hand, with apparent approval: "I believe that community is already in process of dissolution . . . when faith in the eventual supremacy of reason has become so timid that we dare not enter our convictions in the open lists to win or lose."[19] But the moral of that sentiment is that preoccupation with the need for a private retreat is a symptom of social sickness.

Of course, there are not many like Socrates in any society; not many have the knowledge of what they are, the virtue to be content with what they know, and the courage to pretend to be nothing else. For the rest of us, the freedom we need is the freedom to be something else—to be ourselves, to do what we

[18] *Ibid.*, p. 62.
[19] *Ibid.*, p. 63.

think best, in a small, protected sea, where the winds of opinion cannot blow us off course. We cannot learn to be autonomous save by practicing independent judgment. It is important for the moral education of children that at a certain stage they should find the rules porous—that sometimes they should be left to decide what is best to do. Not many of us perhaps have gone so far along the road to moral maturity that we can bear unrelenting exposure to criticism without flinching.

This last stage of my argument brings me back to the grounds for the general principle of privacy, to which I devoted the first half of this paper. I argued that respect for someone as a person, as a chooser, implied respect for him as one engaged on a kind of self-creative enterprise, which could be disrupted, distorted, or frustrated even by so limited an intrusion as watching. A man's view of what he does may be radically altered by having to see it, as it were, through another man's eyes. Now a man has attained a measure of success in his enterprise to the degree that he has achieved autonomy. To the same degree, the importance to him of protection from eavesdropping and Peeping Toms diminishes as he becomes less vulnerable to the judgments of others, more reliant on his own (though he will still need privacy for personal relations, and protection from the grosser kinds of persecution).

This does not weaken the ground for the general principle, however, for this was not a consequentialist ground. It was not that allowing men privacy would give them a better chance to be autonomous. It was rather that a person—anyone potentially autonomous—was worthy of respect on that account; and that if such a person wanted to pursue his enterprise unobserved, he was entitled, unless there were overriding reasons against it, to do as he wished. The argument there was in terms of respect for the enterprise as such, irrespective of the chances of success or failure in any particular instance. In this last section, I have suggested a further, reinforcing argument for privacy as a condition necessary, though to a progressively diminishing degree, if that enterprise is to succeed.

# [11]

## THE POLITICAL IDEAL OF PRIVACY

### By H. J. McCloskey

Privacy is a value or ideal in our society, in the Western World, and in liberal thought generally. By this I mean at least, and perhaps only, that *ceteris paribus* we think much more highly of a society which respects privacy and much less highly of one in which privacy is exposed to invasions. Privacy is therefore in some sense a basic contemporary liberal value. We liberals abhor the thought of a society in which there is censorship of letters, un-restricted phone tapping, bugging of private homes and of offices, searching, compulsory questionnaires by the government, employers, etc. Indeed, much of the force of novels such as *Brave New World* and *1984* rests on the total loss of privacy portrayed in the imagined new society. We value privacy, and we believe ourselves to have a right to privacy ; and the right is thought of as not simply a negative right, the basis of which consists in the lack of rights in others to invade our privacy, but as a positive right in the enjoyment of which we may, by virtue of it, demand the help of the state, society, and other persons. The right to privacy, like all other rights, is of course seen to be a *prima facie* right. It may legitimately be over-ridden and is so overridden in situations such as those of national emergency. However, it is generally believed that there must be very good reasons for overriding this right, for invading privacy. This too is part of what I mean by saying that privacy is a value or ideal of our society, namely, that it is generally believed that there must be positive, powerful, justificatory reasons for invading a person's privacy. The U.N. acknowledged this. In its declara-tion concerning human rights it noted in its *International Covenants of Human Rights*, Article 17, that :

" 1. No one shall be subjected to arbitrary or unlawful interference with his privacy, family, home or correspondence, nor to unlawful attacks on his honour or reputation.

" 2. Everyone has the right to the protection of the law against such interference or attacks."[1]

This, unfortunately, has the customary equivocation of U.N. statements about rights. Of course individuals are entitled to protection by the law from unlawful interference. The problem is, as this statement brings out, that of defining and determining what ought to be made to be unlawful interferences with privacy. This involves discussing three distinct issues, namely : (i) How is privacy to be characterised, defined, or explained ?

---

[1]Quoted by S. H. Hofstadter and G. Horowitz in *The Right to Privacy* (New York, 1964), p. 3.

304                          H. J. McCLOSKEY

What properly counts as protecting and what as losing one's privacy ? What relates to privacy and what to other ideals and rights, ideals such as liberty, rights such as property rights ? To say that privacy relates to that which is of private concern to the person, and which is no business of any one else, circumscribes the area of privacy too narrowly, whilst at the same time leaving unresolved the different but equally difficult problem concerning what is and what is not of purely private concern to the individual. (ii) There is also the issue concerning how privacy as an ideal, or the right to privacy as a right, is to be defended, i.e., there is the question concerning what are the grounds upon which the ideal or right is based. The obvious line of defence in the terms of the lack of right of others to invade my privacy may prove to be the only line of defence available. However, judging by the role played by the demand for protection of privacy in our society, a more positive, stronger line of defence would seem generally to be assumed to be available. (iii) Another distinct issue concerns what constitute legitimate and what illegitimate losses or invasions of privacy. Clearly, there are occasions on which a person may legitimately be deprived of some or all of his privacy. The right to privacy is not an absolute, inviolable right, but one which may legitimately be overridden and even lost for long periods of time. It is important that consideration be given to the general principles relevant to determining when the right is overridden, forfeited, or yielded up.

WHAT IS PRIVACY ?

What relates to privacy, and what to other ideals and rights ? Although privacy has been an important liberal value for a considerable time now, few political philosophers have addressed themselves to this question. Indeed, the only discussion of privacy prior to 1950 known to me as being by a philosopher is that of James Fitzjames Stephen who was a lawyer *cum* philosopher. Stephen wrote :

" Legislation and public opinion ought in all cases whatever scrupulously to respect privacy. To define the province of privacy distinctly is impossible, but it can be described in general terms. All the more intimate and delicate relations of life are of such a nature that to submit them to unsympathetic observation, or to observation which is sympathetic in the wrong way, inflicts great pain, and may inflict lasting moral injury. Privacy may be violated not only by the intrusion of a stranger, but by compelling or persuading a person to direct too much attention to his own feelings and to attach too much importance to their analysis. The common usage of language affords a practical test which is almost perfect upon this subject. Conduct which can be described as indecent is always in one way or another a violation of privacy."[2]

The absence of serious discussion of privacy is one of the most remarkable features of the writings of such British liberals as J. S. Mill, Spencer, Hob-

[2]*Liberty, Equality, Fraternity* (Cambridge, 1967), p. 160 (1st ed., 1873).

THE POLITICAL IDEAL OF PRIVACY                305

house, and Tawney. It has been suggested in the writings of lawyers that the relatively recent emergence of recognition of privacy in the law has in a large measure been due to the development of such threats to privacy as the camera and the many electronic bugging devices. This may well be true in respect of the development of laws restricting invasions of privacy, but it would seem not to be the explanation of the absence of philosophical discussion of the ideal. The latter appears rather to have resulted from a confusion of thought, privacy and negative liberty being identified as one and the same thing. Both have been explained and characterized as consisting in " being let alone ", and a notable legal work on privacy, that by M. L. Ernst and A. U. Schwartz, is entitled *Privacy : The Right To Be Let Alone*.[3] Although the two things are closely related, they are nonetheless distinct.

Two considerations are available which provide clear grounds for distinguishing negative liberty and privacy as separate notions, and hence, as relating to separate, distinct, political ideals. First, the greater the extent of the interference with a person's liberty, the more inclined we are to think of him as being rendered incapable of being a full person ; complete interference in the form of complete control over his decisions and actions during the whole of his life is incompatible with his remaining a full *person*, in the Kantian sense of ' person '. Further, usually although not necessarily, such lengthy, extensive interference or control would be known to the person concerned. By contrast, a person's privacy can be totally invaded during the whole of his life without his knowledge, and without his freedom being in any way restricted or curtailed, and without his being any less a person, qua *person*. Here I need only invite you to enter the world of philosophy-science-fiction, and to imagine the materialist theory of mind to be proven philosophically and scientifically true, and that science so advances that bugging devices not merely for bugging private homes but for bugging minds are invented (Brain-Mind-Bugs as they may come to be called) which can publish the contents of their victims' minds without their knowledge. In this case, there *need* be no interference with the individual's freedom of action, nor with his freedom of thought and expression ; yet there would be a total loss of privacy. Secondly, there may be a conflict between the right of privacy and the right to liberty, even where liberty is conceived of as negative liberty. Part of the right to liberty is the right to observe, to know, to report, and to publish. The ideal society from the point of view of the exponent of negative liberty, the kind of society one finds commended as such, as in the writings of Humboldt and Spencer, is that in which there is as little interference by way of coercion as possible, where the only coercion which is justified, is coercion directed against coercive interference. Nonetheless, privacy can be invaded by members of such a community, who at the same time respect the liberty of their fellows by not interfering with

[3] New York, 1962.

306                                    H. J. McCLOSKEY

them. Privacy would be invaded by the person who eavesdrops on her neighbour, by someone who used his binoculars to watch a distant person working in his garden, or hanging out her washing, etc. Yet these are not forms of interference in the sense relevant to negative or other kinds of liberty. To seek to justify coercion of the eavesdropper and the spy as coercion directed against coercion would be utterly implausible, and would involve gross distortion of the concept of interference. The contrast with privacy is publicity. Privacy is something which is to be respected, which may be forgone, lost, forfeited, or invaded. The contrasts with negative liberty are interference and coercion ; negative liberty may be lost by interference and coercion. With positive liberty, the contrasts are more various —coercion, interference, and lack of facilities are the more obvious contrasts. Positive liberty is something which may have to be brought into being ; privacy, on the other hand, typically needs only to be protected.

It has been the lawyers, particularly the lawyers of the U.S.A., rather than the philosophers, who have engaged in useful discussions of privacy, and to such good effect that there are laws defining the right to privacy in the U.S.A., although not in Great Britain and Australia (unless such laws have been introduced in the immediate past few years). In Britain and in Australia attempts are made to deal with grosser invasions of privacy under property-type laws such as those relating to trespass, breach of contract, copyright, defamation, or libel. However, useful though the U.S. legal discussions are, they are of less value philosophically than might be hoped, and this for two reasons. The legal concept is distinct from the political concept as most of us conceive it. It is in some respects broader, covering such things as using a person's photo without his consent, and in some states, even the writing about a relative who is now dead. It is in other respects narrower, allowing as not invasions of privacy " accidental " or non-deliberate photographs of individuals in the private pursuit of their pleasures, as in newscasts. The legal approach has, by and large, been by way of making invasion of privacy a civil offence (in some cases, and in important areas, a criminal offence), and the concern of lawyers and legislators has been to define what are illegitimate invasions of privacy for which damages can reasonably be sought and awarded, rather than to define what constitute losses and invasions of privacy. The legal discussions are nonetheless worthy of very serious consideration. The most famous is the article, " The Right to Privacy ", by Samuel D. Warren and Louis D. Brandeis in the *Harvard Law Review*, IV, 1890. A key passage runs :

" These considerations lead to the conclusion that the protection afforded to thoughts, sentiments, and emotions, expressed through the medium of writing or of the arts, so far as it consists in preventing publication, is merely an instance of the enforcement of the more general right to be let alone. . . . The principle which protects personal writings and all other personal productions, not against theft and physical appropriation, but against publica-

### THE POLITICAL IDEAL OF PRIVACY 307

tion in any form, is in reality not the principle of private property, but that of an inviolate personality." (p. 206)

They then go on to list applications and exceptions, namely :

" 1. The right of privacy does not prohibit any publication of matter which is of public or general interest." (p. 215)

" 2. The right to privacy does not prohibit the communication of any matter, though in its nature private, when the publication is made under circumstances which would render it a privileged communication according to the law of slander and libel." (p. 217)

" 3. The law would probably not grant any redress for the invasion of privacy by oral publication in the absence of special damage." (p. 218)

" 4. The right to privacy ceases upon the publication of the facts by the individual, or with his consent." (p. 219)

" 5. The truth of the matter does not afford a defence." (p. 219)

" 6. The absence of ' malice ' in the publisher does not afford a defence." (p. 219)

The Warren-Brandeis article was a key step in the development of the law relating to the right to privacy in the U.S.A. Since then the law has so developed that it can be briefly summed up, as by S. H. Hofstadter and G. Horowitz in *The Right to Privacy* thus :

" The diversity of the situations and of the cases in which the right of privacy may be involved precludes precise delimitation. It may be described broadly as the right against the unwarranted appropriation or exploitation of one's personality ; or the publicizing of one's private affairs with which the public has no legitimate concern ; or the wrongful intrusion into one's private activities in such manner as to outrage a person of ordinary sensibilities or cause him mental suffering, shame or humiliation."

The authors then represent Prosser's classification of the four broad groups of acts against which the right offers protection in the following way :

" 1. Intrusion upon the plaintiff's seclusion or solitude, or into his private affairs.

2. Public disclosure of embarrassing private facts about the plaintiff.

3. Publicity which places the plaintiff in a false light in the public eye.

4. Appropriation for the defendant's advantage, of the plaintiff's name or likeness."[4]

Such accounts are no doubt very useful in law ; they are less useful as philosophical elucidations of the concept of privacy, and this chiefly because they are concerned with marking off illegitimate invasions of privacy rather than with what in general counts as an invasion and what as a loss of privacy. However, the initial, general formula has important considerations to offer which bear on this, in particular the suggestion that one suffers a loss or an invasion of privacy if one's private activities and concerns are intruded

[4]*Op. cit.*, pp. 7, 8. See W. L. Prosser, *The Law of Torts* (St. Paul, 1964).

308                    H. J. McCLOSKEY

into in such a manner as to outrage a person of ordinary sensibilities or
cause him mental suffering, shame or humiliation. A modification has been
suggested along the lines of writing in the clause ' cause or may reasonably
cause '.

Such an account, modified in the suggested way, might seem to accommodate most types of losses and invasions of privacy—phone-tapping, eavesdropping, peeping, spying, prying, bugging, etc. In fact, it does not come
near to doing so, and this for two reasons. First, as noted above, the key
notion of " private " has to be explained further ; and secondly, the section
of the formula relating to outraging, paining, shaming, or humiliating,
actually or potentially, a person of ordinary sensibilities, needs modification
to guard against the dangerous degree of relativity of which it admits.

It is of course true that we suffer a loss of privacy if our private activities
are intruded upon, but the major problem with privacy is that of determining what activities and concerns may properly be deemed to be purely
private activities and concerns. Attempts to explain this by contrast with
what is of public or general concern, that is, in terms of their relation to the
general interest, will not do. Something may still be in the area of privacy
and yet relate to the general interest, for example, whether one has venereal
disease. Here the general interest provides a justification for invading a
person's privacy. Other private acts, for example a planned suicide by the
country's leading scientist, may be relevant to the general interest, and yet
not justify invading his privacy as by spying on him to see how advanced
his plans are before acting to interfere with his liberty by thwarting the
suicide. Further, others, besides the state, society, or the community, may
have genuine interests in what otherwise would be private acts or concerns
of the individual. People are thought to have a right to privacy in respect
of the *affaires* they have, unless one or other party to the *affaire* is married.
Yet, I suggest that if the girl involved in the *affaire* is a minor, a father who
spied on the pair could not be charged with an improper invasion of their
privacy ; and if the man involved knew that she was a minor, he could not
complain that he had suffered a loss of privacy as a result of the father's
spying, because, by his actions he had put that area of his life outside the
area of privacy. A better case illustrating the latter might be that of a
single woman who is supporting her illegitimate child and who is seeking
marriage with a man who suspects this but who has not been told the facts.
The woman's intentions here would render it no invasion of her privacy for
the man to check up on her. (His doing so may make his approach to marriage less romantic than romanticists would like approaches to marriage to
be.) Another case would be that of a divorcee who is seeking to marry a
devout Roman Catholic, and from whom she is seeking to conceal the fact
that she has been married and divorced. The man would not be invading
her privacy if he made the relevant inquiries. The test here would seem to
consist in whether the person has a right to know, i.e., whether the individual

whose privacy is said to be involved has, by her actions, rendered this aspect of her life public for the person with a right to know. If, as I suggest is the case in respect of the father of the minor, the prospective husband, and the Roman Catholic, those concerning whom they obtained information had not suffered a loss of privacy thereby, then the right to know would seem to be very relevant to determining the area which relates to privacy.

Unfortunately, things are not as simple and straightforward as that. There is an element of arbitrariness in our usage here, for there can be cases in which others possess the right to know facts about us (for example, the taxation department) and yet we suffer a loss and an invasion of privacy in their gaining this knowledge, albeit a justifiable loss or invasion. Here the fact that we have no choice but to enter into the situation seems relevant —the mother of the illegitimate child, the divorcee, and the seducer of the minor freely put themselves into the position of making certain areas of their lives properly knowable by certain other people. This is why we should deem it a lack of respect for privacy for those who have a right to know, to pass on what they learn to those who lack the right to know. The persons have freely chosen to act in such a way that *for some*, their lives are less in the area of the right to privacy than for others. With respect to matters relating to taxation, for most of us in respect of most such matters, we have no choice. An interesting, in-between kind of case which suggests that the element of arbitrariness in our usage is slighter than first appearances suggest, is that of the news film of a race, which at the same time takes in the spectators, these including malingerers, men with their mistresses, and the like, and a criminal in the pursuit of his calling, picking pockets. It is certainly a loss, and I should suggest, an invasion of privacy for the malingerers, and others who wish not to be observed, to have the film shown on the TV ; often it would be a loss or invasion which could be justified in terms of the general interest, and the fact that those concerned knew the risks they were running. However, I suggest that the criminal pickpocket, who is filmed whilst actually picking pockets, cannot reasonably object that the film ought not to be shown publicly on the grounds that such publicity involved a loss or even an invasion of his privacy. It would involve neither an illegitimate invasion of his privacy, nor even an invasion of it ; indeed, I suggest that we should be disinclined to say even that he had suffered a loss of privacy as a result of the showing of the film.

Thus, in so far as both the right to know and freely entering into activities in ways and under conditions which confer the right to know on others are relevant to privacy, our problem resolves itself, to that extent, into determining who have rights to know, and on what occasions, as a result of the individual's free actions. No doubt many people would dispute certain of my examples, but I suggest that other examples could easily be produced which would be acceptable as illustrations that there are personal " private " acts and concerns which are such that other individuals, or society, or the state have the right to knowledge of them, and in such a way that we should not describe their taking steps to obtain this knowledge as depriving the individual of his privacy. This being so, it would follow that it is impossible to mark off certain areas or certain concerns as those which are the peculiar concern of privacy. Any concern, any activity, no matter how personal, may fall outside the area of privacy. Further, it is impossible to mark out the area of privacy in terms of those areas concerning which others lack the right to knowledge, for many non-personal matters are of such a character, for example, such trivial matters as concern the brand of soap I use, the grade of oil I use in my car, the barber I use, and the like. No one has the right to obtain this knowledge *from me, ceteris paribus*, yet it is knowledge which does not relate to privacy although in certain circumstances it, like almost any other knowledge relating to me, could do so.

The second important issue here relates to the clause concerning invasions which may actually or reasonably outrage, hurt, shame, or humiliate a person of ordinary sensibilities. This clause results from an attempt to take note of the relativity between societies and within societies concerning what are judged to be losses and invasions of privacy. Different societies judge different things to be or to involve losses and invasions of privacy. Subject to certain qualifications, one's sexual arrangements other than *via* marriage are matters appertaining to privacy in our society. One may voluntarily consent to a loss of privacy by making one's arrangements publicly known, but this is nonetheless seen as a forgoing of one's right to privacy. It is unlikely that this would in the eighteenth and nineteenth centuries have been seen to be so in Tahiti and the Trobriand Islands even if the natives could have grasped the concept of privacy ; and it would seem to be much less the case in Moslem than in Christian countries today. On the other hand, whether one drinks alcoholic beverages may well be a matter relating to privacy in Moslem countries but less so in ours. Within any one society there are changing standards. Matters such as the nature of the work done by one's forebears, one's salary, one's wealth and possessions, the diseases one has or has had, used formerly to be considered matters of purely private concern, but now are not generally regarded as such. The formula goes a long way towards accommodating this relativity by making the effect or emotional reaction a vital part of the characterization of privacy being lost. However, it does this at the cost of denying to be losses or invasions of privacy what are the grossest and most objectionable ones.

Part of our objection to totalitarian regimes is that they render persons of ordinary sensibilities no longer outraged, hurt, shamed, or humiliated by invasions of privacy. The invasions become so frequent, so commonplace, the emotional reactions and hurts cease to follow. This is true even of the losses and invasions of privacy experienced in the armed services, for example, during a war. Persons of ordinary sensibilities become used to all their affairs being common knowledge, to their letters being read by prying

THE POLITICAL IDEAL OF PRIVACY 311

censors, and the like, so that, before very long, only the hypersensitive are outraged, hurt, shamed, or humiliated. (Those involved in the last world war would confirm this.) Yet any account of privacy, more especially of what constitute losses and invasions of privacy, must be such as to explain life under Nazism and life in the armed services as life with little privacy. To attempt to save the formula by adding some such clause as ' under normal circumstances ', or ' for the natural rather than normal man ' will not do. Cultural relativity does need to be accommodated at least to some extent. Further, privacy is not tied to some vague philosophical concept of a natural man, but relates to men as they are, and hence to a concept of a normal rather than of a natural man. There are obvious difficulties in the way of elucidating satisfactorily and relevantly the concept of normality here.

I suggest, therefore, that there are two types of problems in characterizing the concept or notion of privacy, namely, the basic one of cutting off that which is the individual's private concern or activity from that which is legitimately the concern of others. That an individual may so act as to give another or others a right to know is relevant here, but seems to fall short of being the complete story. In any case, much work needs to be done on what does and what does not give another a right to know, and in this context, what kinds of freely chosen conduct give rise to such a right. Secondly, there is the problem of characterizing the losses and invasions of privacy in such a way that relativity is acknowledged in the right ways and only in the right ways.

## PRIVACY AS AN IDEAL : ITS GROUNDS

Privacy is so very highly valued in our society that we are prepared to render some invaders of privacy criminals, with all that that involves, in order to protect the individual's privacy. Individuals such as Peeping-Toms, those who phone-tap, listen-in on crossed lines, those who bug private homes, and the like, where they are prosecuted may not always be prosecuted under the label or crime of being violators of privacy. However, support for such laws as exist and under which they are prosecuted, and the demand for laws banning such activities, spring in a large measure from a concern for privacy as a value in this society. My concern now is to consider why privacy is so valued, and whether it is rightly so valued.

There are obvious reasons for looking upon such invasions of privacy as undesirable, dangerous activities which ought to be discouraged as such. The information obtained by those who act in these ways may be used to harm the individuals whose privacy is invaded. Private individuals may use the information to blackmail, intimidate, hurt, or interfere with others ; the police and/or others may harrass and persecute individuals on the basis of their prying and thereby make the lives of the legally blameless, miserable. Invasions of privacy may also lead to thefts and other losses of property

312                    H. J. McCLOSKEY

rights, or of rights closely associated with property rights. The Peeping-Tom may photograph the girl and sell her photo ; the business spy may learn his competitor's plans and thwart them, or use discoveries not yet patented, and the like. Further, there will often be the loss of private pleasures. Most people in our society enjoy freedom from involuntary loss of privacy. They prefer to converse and act in contexts where the only privacy they have lost is that to which they have voluntarily consented.

Yet there remains the problem of explaining the very great stress attached to the value of privacy. The loss of pleasure and private enjoyment which comes with a sudden loss of privacy seems not to be the explanation, for we soon adjust and adapt to such losses, and the loss of pleasure and contentment is only temporary. Indeed, slum dwellers who, against their wishes, are given good housing which affords them a degree of privacy they never formerly enjoyed, frequently loathe the privacy which is forced upon them. It has often been suggested that privacy is an essential context for the emergence and development of sensitive feelings, that gross invasions of privacy as in prying in love-making, reading love letters, observing the intimacies of private life, are inimical to the development, and even the survival of such delicate, valuable human feelings.[5] This seems to be empirically untrue. Human beings seem to have an unlimited capacity to adapt to publicity, provided that the publicity is not connected with interference. It is of course true in our society that publicity is commonly associated with interference by way of social, legal, or simply personal pressures. Where it is not so associated, it seems not to be the case that these civilized emotions and relations wither ; on the contrary, they appear to thrive.

It has been argued by S. I. Benn in a paper, " Privacy, Freedom, and Respect for Persons ",[6] that the duty of respect for persons entails respect for privacy. This is associated with the view that invasions of privacy consist in knowing what is desired by the individual concerned not to be known. (All knowledge of facts about another person, it would seem on this view, involve a loss, although not necessarily an invasion of privacy.) The suggestion seems to be that invading privacy is a kind of forcing of or opposing the will of another, and that the right to privacy is a right to secrecy. Privacy and secrecy are related but distinct concepts.

In reply to this kind of argument, I suggest that respect for persons may dictate repudiating privacy so construed. The relation of lover to lover is similar to that of the respecters of persons. Yet love, and like it respect for persons, may dictate invasions of privacy. The lover, because of his love, wants to know all about his loved one, because he loves her, and he wants to know her more fully as the person she is. Indeed, love involves knowledge, extensive, ideally, complete knowledge of the loved one. So too, real

[5]C. Fried in " Privacy ", *Yale Law Journal* 77, 1967-8, pp. 475-493 so argues in respect of trust, love and friendship as requiring privacy.

[6]Forthcoming in *Nomos*.

THE POLITICAL IDEAL OF PRIVACY 313

respect for persons must be for real persons, persons as they really are, as concrete individuals with certain traits, weaknesses, vices. Love, and equally respect for persons, may dictate the seeking of knowledge against the wishes of the person concerned. The lover may be distressed at the unhappiness of his loved one, and rightly and reasonably seek, without her permission, to learn the cause ; or he may suspect that she has a serious disease and is afraid to have it diagnosed and treated, and know that if it is diagnosed and treated soon it will not be fatal. Love, and respect for persons, lead to attempts to obtain the knowledge relevant to such situations. They would also lead to attempts to persuade the diseased person to accept the treatment. Love, and respect for persons, involve an attitude of concern for others or another ; concern involves knowledge, even undesired, unwanted knowledge.

Nonetheless, there are considerations which suggest that the duty of respect for persons is relevant to the ideal of privacy. Consider the individual who takes pleasure in encouraging girls to reveal details of their intimate, private lives (usually but not only sexual aspects). If both parties take pleasure in the exercise and thereby knowingly debase themselves, then I suggest that the individual is showing lack of respect for the girl as a person, and he and she for themselves as persons. Respect for persons involves living up to certain standards as persons, a treating of oneself and of others not merely as animals in a scientific experiment but as persons. Needlessly and deliberately to reveal certain aspects of one's intimate, personal life would seem to offend against this principle.

Further, to invade privacy is often to show lack of respect for persons. Without good reason, to ignore a person's wishes to conceal, pretend, or hide facts about himself, is to show lack of respect.[7] Nonetheless, the duty need not, and often does not, give rise to a corresponding right. Rights and duties are not correlative in this sense.[8]

Nevertheless, I wish to suggest that the case for privacy is basically an ideal utilitarian one, grounded on values such as human happiness, justice, and, to an extent, liberty. (Elsewhere I have argued that the case for liberty is, in turn, founded on goods such as happiness, knowledge, justice and fraternity.) Hence, to answer the third question noted in the introductory discussion concerning what constitute legitimate and what illegitimate invasions and losses of privacy, it may here be argued that a serious case could be made out for accepting invasions of privacy where these goods are not jeopardized, and where no great evils result, for example, in the cases of Peeping-Toms who are proven to be simply harmless observers.

It is relevant here to compare harmless invasions of privacy, and the hurt, outrage, shame, and humiliation they may cause, with offensive and

---

[7]For this and the preceding point I am in large measure indebted to Miss Christina Bell.

[8]See my discussion in " Rights ", this journal, Vol. 15, 1965.

314                              H. J. McCLOSKEY

indecent behaviour which may shock, offend, or hurt the bystander. I
suggest that the truly liberal response to offensive and indecent persons
(and behaviour) is not that of attempting to curtail the liberty of all who
would be offensive and indecent, by making offenders criminals, but that
of tolerating the offences and putting up with the temporary inconvenience
of a readjustment of one's feeling reactions. This is because, on the one
hand, it is important that we avoid curtailing liberty and rendering individuals criminals when we can do so without any hardship to anyone, and,
on the other hand, because of the adaptability of human beings and human
feelings. (Also some account must be taken of good manners—most people
most of the time are reluctant needlessly to shock or hurt others.) So much
that would have shocked, outraged, offended, and hurt people fifty years
ago, clothing such as bikinis, mini-skirts, see-through clothing, and activities
such as extensive public sexual conduct, talks concerning whether Christ
was a homosexual, and the like, arouse, at the time of writing this paper,
no unfavourable reaction. Many members of the community have found
the period of adjustment difficult and unpleasant, but this is a small price
to pay for the liberty enjoyed, and the absence of the harm done in rendering
some individuals criminals. I hope the time will come when there will be
no such crimes as those of offensive and indecent behaviour. I suggest
that, if and when we can be sure that the ideal utilitarian considerations
for restricting invasions of privacy do not apply, it is a better and a more
liberal position to adopt to accept the loss of privacy or, alternatively, to
make private arrangements to prevent this, rather than to curtail the freedom of many and to render some persons criminals and many more exposed
to costly legal actions. Our feelings soon adapt themselves as they have in
respect of so-called offensive and indecent behaviour.

*La Trobe University.*

# 2

## THE PRIVATE AND THE FREE:
## A CONCEPTUAL INQUIRY

W. L. WEINSTEIN

Without assuming there is a definitive answer, let alone a simple one, I pose the question: What may be the main presuppositions of a belief in a private sphere of action or human relations?

Granted that the line dividing the private and the public can be shifting and uncertain, different in different times and places, as well as subject to both reconcilable and intractable disagreements, my immediate concern is not with a recipe for drawing the line in a particular way, important as this can be, but with an issue which is at least implied in any such line-drawing enterprise, namely: What must I believe (or correspondingly reject) if I assert (or deny) that there is a private sphere? I hope here to present a brief exposé of some of the essentials at stake in arguments in the private versus public territory, for example, factors on which shifts in the dividing line may depend. But the fundamental issues here, involving nothing less than our ways, often messy and ill-defined, of con-

27

ceiving of human actions and their social contexts, are so complex that in the end I may succeed in showing no more than that general accounts, such as mine, of the nature of controversies in this territory are themselves as subject to controversy as particular ways of distinguishing between the private and the public. In fact the two types of controversy may well be closely connected.

The importance of the questions posed above may be explained in at least two preliminary ways. First, our thinking that there ought to be a sphere of private actions and relations is a necessary, though not sufficient, condition of the existence of such a sphere, that is, something constituted by recognition and observance in actual social behavior.[1] Thus spheres of the private exist when they do as parts of the community's ways of thought—its recognized ways of claiming to be immune from intrusion or control. In this sense part of social reality itself, for example, the reality of counting on being protected against interference or intrusion by others in what is seen by the agents as a private concern, is constituted by the beliefs of the agents who are involved; that is, by individuals in sufficient number or of sufficient importance, or some combination of the two, claiming and respecting claims to a certain sphere roughly marked, "Not your business: keep out." By the same token a sphere of the private, such as may exist at a given time, may be extinguished by not respecting the rules required to preserve it; it may of course be sufficient to police it out of existence even when there are beliefs hostile to such repression, and easier still never to constitute it by not developing the beliefs that are essential to its existence. However, to see spheres of the private as typically depending on generally accepted beliefs in a community is not to see all the possibilities. It is equally important to understand the sense in which individuals who systematically opt out of the roles, relations, and activities their

---

[1] Taken without qualification this statement would best apply to societies like our own, in which recognition of the private in several specific forms is explicit and there are highly articulated general conceptions of the private and the public. In some societies the relevant distinctions may be made, if at all, only implicitly, and it may be difficult for an anthropologist or historian to decide whether, for instance, a given limit on authority counts as recognition of the claims of the private.

community makes available to them, or imposes on them, may thereby create a private sphere for themselves in opposition to prevailing conceptions of the private (certain Stoics, for example).

Second, an answer to "What belongs in the private sphere?" admitting of several overlapping answers, and perhaps some different or even mutually opposed ones, can be much affected by the presuppositions that underlie claims to such a sphere. That is, what I claim to be properly a private matter—whom I befriend or love or marry, or what religion (if any) I profess—may be determined by why I claim it as such. Thus a relation can be so conceived that its point is to give effect to my likes, or a conviction can be held whose very nature is seen as a matter for the individual freely to accept or reject.

## I

There is in our own culture alone an extensive range of diverse views, which may not even share a common moral footing, about what matters are properly private; from this range a few examples may be selected in outlining some familiar views. No doubt these examples are historically determinate ones. For example, it may well be true, as Arendt among others has argued, that the importance ascribed to "intimacy" is distinctively modern; and that modern liberals' ways of marking off some forms of private life (including those extending beyond personal and family relations) as freedoms of the individual stand in contrast to the ancient Greeks' equations of freedom with participation in public activities, and of privacy (in the household, the realm of women, children, and slaves) with deprivation of the highest human status.[2]

One might best begin with ways in which we often think of privacy as intimacy. Where there is recognition of intimate aspects of life on one's own or in relation to others, there are conventions, of morality or etiquette, specifying the circum-

[2] Hannah Arendt, *The Human Condition* (Chicago: University of Chicago Press, 1958), chaps. 4–9; Isaiah Berlin, *Four Essays on Liberty* (London: Oxford University Press, 1969), pp. xl–xlii; Benjamin Constant, *De l'esprit de Conquête* (1814), Part II, chap. 6 (excerpt translated by John Plamenatz, ed., *Readings from Liberal Writers* [London: George Allen & Unwin, 1965], pp. 60–62).

stances in which persons should not be observed, counseled,
talked about, or physically intruded upon. For example, a
stranger's tendering uncalled-for advice to parents about how
their children should be reared may count as an invasion of a
sphere that is of intimate concern to them. Such an intrusion
may cause offense or embarrassment, or be merely a distraction;
it is therefore a nuisance, though not an interference with the
parents' freedom. For the giving of advice, even if unwanted or
without entitlement, does not make the choice of an action less
available to the agent who is intruded upon.[3] To insist on one's
privacy in these circumstances is not to stake a claim to freedom.

Similarly, observing people when they are off-guard or unaware, as in voyeurism, counts as an intrusion upon privacy,
but not as an interference with the freedom of the observed
agent so long as his behavior remains uninhibited (because of
his being unaware). If the agent knew he was being observed
and did not care, one might be inclined to say that, for him at
any rate, privacy was not violated, although it might still be
thought that observing him was improper and that he should
care. Again, prying into a person's innermost feelings and
thoughts, even when he is a willing subject (such as a volunteer
for psychological testing), may be felt to be an invasion of
privacy, especially if his everyday defenses and inhibitions are
overcome. Furthermore, many of us feel embarrassed or disturbed by others eagerly baring their souls, though reactions
to certain kinds of personal revelation do vary with individuals,
groups, and nationalities, some taking them as steps toward
honesty in social relationships, others as improper attempts to
impose one's private life on other people's private lives.

It is hardly possible here to analyze the very complex beliefs
that may account for the feeling that revelations of the intimate,
whether extracted from or willingly provided by the agent, are
somehow wrong or unpleasant, at any rate in certain circumstances. Perhaps a particular range of such taboos, against
physical and, as it were, psychological, nudity, is connected with
beliefs about the maintenance of a certain personal identity or
integrity in social relations, or about treating people as agents

---

[3] This point is argued more fully in S. I. Benn and W. L. Weinstein,
"Being Free to Act, and Being a Free Man," to be published in *Mind*.

## The Private and the Free 31

rather than as objects, or possibly about the risk of changing profoundly important human phenomena into trivial or vulgar ones through overexposure. The nature of these and other relevant types of belief is far from clear. Moreover, nowadays one has to reckon with conflicting theories, some of which call for the preservation of the intimate in the name of a civilized way of life as well as freedom, whereas others see human liberation and happiness in some therapeutic process that involves stripping away at least some privacy conventions which have hitherto counted as the bases of correctly restrained social behavior. There are important variations in how the bounds of the intimate aspects of personality and behavior are drawn, and correspondingly, in opinions about who, and in what circumstances, may legitimately acquire what sort of knowledge or experience of which other people. For example, Mumford remarks on a shift in attitudes toward nudity and sexual intercourse in the presence of others even when they occur between spouses.[4]

The two examples mentioned so far, unsolicited advice-giving and voyeurism, seem not to raise doubts about the freedom of the agent whose privacy is held to be invaded; in fact, successful voyeurism, unlike advice-giving, does not even imply an intention to change the agent's behavior.[5] But such doubts may begin to arise in other cases: gate-crashing a wedding reception, disturbing a widow in her grief to find out more about it, or persisting in talking to people on airplanes who want to get on with their sleep or reading. It is arguable that the agents intruded upon remain free to continue what they had been doing, or experiencing, before, and that at least in the first two examples in this trio it might be supposed that the intruder does not intend to affect the mood or action of those he intrudes upon. Yet there is perhaps a real enough sense in which they are disturbed directly, and possibly seriously, by what is done to them. They may reasonably, if not convincingly to all, claim that they are not free to do, or experience, what they had been

[4] Lewis Mumford, *The Culture of Cities* (London: Secker & Warburg, 1940), p. 41.

[5] However, this is not to suggest that intentionality is always a necessary condition for counting an interference as an interference with freedom. The impersonal operation of social forces, once seen as in principle subject to human control, may be identified as a source of unfreedom.

doing, or experiencing, before the intrusion occurred, though the strength of their claim may depend on the particular description, among the several that could be available, of what they claim is interfered with, as well as the importance ascribed to it.

However, cases on the borderline of intrusions upon privacy that either do or do not count as interferences with freedom fall outside the scope of this paper, which may be more clearly defined with the aid of further distinctions. First, the claims of privacy as intimacy may be at odds with other claims, such as those made on behalf of what is held to be the interests of other persons or the wider community, of some worthwhile activity or the very person whose private life is intruded upon. Such counterclaims may extend to knowledge only, or beyond to advice-giving or open discussion, or further to interference.[6] I shall be concerned with privacy as intimacy only to the extent that claims for and against it touch on its freedom, and even more so with those claims to privacy which identify it as intrinsically free in a sense which will be explained in due course.

Second, privacy as intimacy refers to certain aspects of the single person or his relations with only one other or a few. Privacy in this sense is what is of intimate concern to me or us; how strongly or extensively others are excluded varies with the

[6] The intimate is not always thought to be improperly revealed or investigated; and even when unspecified individuals belonging to the public at large have no title to go beyond a particular conventional boundary, the state or some other agency may justifiably claim it. Thus, the police or a coroner may properly disturb a widow in her grief; a private party may properly be the subject of a public inquiry; a judge in a divorce case may have to go into intimate details. Probing the intimate may be justified in the interests of knowledge and general human welfare; one notes the controversy over the use of a sex laboratory divulged in W. H. Masters and V. E. Johnson, *Human Sexual Response* (Boston: Little, Brown, 1964). Revelations in psychiatric treatment or the confessional, though equally the strict observance of confidentiality, may be held to be for the good of the person; furthermore, outsiders' attempts to break an intimate relation between persons, one of whom is dominant and the other submissive, may arguably promote the latter's autonomy. Treating certain forms of sexual behavior as inherently sinful may go with unreadiness to vouchsafe to them protective conventions of secrecy and freedom, which may surround other forms of such behavior on grounds of their intimate nature: to turn a blind eye to the works of the Devil is not easily condoned by those who are determined to fight him.

*The Private and the Free*                                            33

example. On the other hand, there is a wide range of instances where to speak of something as private is not to imply intimacy. Individuals not intimately related may nevertheless assert that their relation or activity is a private one in the sense that it is not the proper concern of the community or some institution, such as the state, a church, or a business firm; and a church or firm may in turn claim that it is itself private vis-à-vis the wider community or the state.[7] This second range of uses occurs in, for example, private enterprise, private medical care, and private school. What goes on in a private meeting, or an institution placing itself in a private sphere, may be widely known within it, but attempts by outsiders to obtain information or exert control may be resisted. Indeed, private enterprise or private property, when allied with ideals of free competition, implies that the state may not do what competitors may attempt against each other; to drive the other out of business.

As this analysis proceeds we shall see that examples of the two types of the private distinguished here may count as freedoms, for the individual, and where appropriate for a group or an institution, when the involvement, whether it is friendship or philosophical inquiry, is seen as crucially requiring freedom. However, all this begins to suggest that there are multiple applications of the notion of "public" as well, and therefore perhaps immediate hazards in its use. But once it is assumed that "public" and "private" are contrast-concepts jointly exhausting the full range of *social* phenomena and that they typically have a normative basis and function in moral and political discourse, it is possible to make good use of their variability. If by "public" one loosely means what counts as being of proper concern to some community which is identified as the *wider* social context of an action or relation, then it is possible to see why it is no more helpful to restrict "private" to a formula such as "the atomic individual," or "the person when unrelated to others," or "being alone" than it is strictly to conceive of "public" as "the widest possible relevant community," for example, the

[7] In principle, though not normally in choice of words, a state's claim to manage its internal affairs without outside interference, or even help, involves a similar claim to a private sphere.

state.[8] For my purposes the two notions are probably best seen
as layers of onion skin, any given layer potentially counting
as private in relation to one or more outer layers, that is, various
publics. This would help to explain why the solitary individual
is not necessarily implied when we refer to private enterprise,
but why on the other hand within a firm so characterized we
may identify both officially required types of privacy (confidentiality, for example) and informal, discretionary types (friendship); and equally, how forms of group life (religious
organizations or much less institutional units such as neighbors
on a street) may sensibly be seen as part of a wider community
or more inclusive group, and thus be counted as private for at
least certain purposes.

In what is to follow I shall examine forms of the private,
some of them seen as having aspects of intimacy and others not,
in human involvements which tend to be assimilated to the
concept of freedom typically developed within a liberal perspective, though similar views have found a place in other
perspectives. Briefly, freedom in this perspective is understood
in terms of the range of options available to an agent who is
seen, at least potentially, as a chooser.[9] Furthermore, the focus
will be on that area of private actions, relations, and beliefs
marked off because the element of freedom in them is often
thought to carry a special value, either instrumentally or, more
interestingly, noninstrumentally. What is at stake in this narrowed area of inquiry is the possibility of seeing some human
involvements as opportunities to exercise choices and not (or
not merely) in terms of the individual's sensibility and the need
to respect, that is, not intrude upon, what is considered his

[8] This is not to imply rejection of such formulae. Privacy as intimacy
includes, among other things, individual solitude as well as certain innermost thoughts and feelings; and it may be morally relevant to know the
location of an action, for example, whether nudity or the loud crinkling of
a popcorn wrapper occurs in seclusion or in a classroom. The special sense
of "public" cited above, as "an indefinite number of nonassignable individuals," familiar to readers of Bentham, has a special range of uses: see Brian
Barry, *Political Argument* (London: Routledge & Kegan Paul, 1965), pp. 190–
192. (For several points in this analysis I am indebted to my colleague, Alan
Montefiore.)

[9] An interpretation explained in Benn and Weinstein, "Being Free to Act,
and Being a Free Man."

intimate feelings and relations.[10] This distinction, often difficult and sometimes impossible to apply, may be illustrated as follows. Members of a small group practicing free love may see themselves as exercising their freedom of choice in sexual relations in ways not made available by the strict observance of "bourgeois" morality, but consistently with this could complain of a concomitant lack of sheer privacy—not having enough moments of solitude, for example, or for easily cooking and eating occasionally apart from others.

## II

Beliefs in the private sphere as a sphere of freedom seem to require at least two types of presupposition. First, freedom is a principle. Interferences with it require justification, though they may be justifiable; and it is in place to ask for a justification for restrictions if we can suppose that things could be otherwise than they are.[11] Second, there ought to be an area of human involvements which is not the normal province of a wider community, of public policy, though not of course in the sense that the freedom of such involvements should not be publicly endorsed and protected.

However, more than this is required. Although the first presupposition explains why certain intrusions upon the private may be condemned as more than an uncivilized nuisance or disrespectful behavior, there can be important variations in belief as to the value of freedom—that is, why it is claimed in given cases. And why it is claimed is relevant when assessing the relative strength of attempts to justify interferences with freedom. This consideration applies equally to the second presupposition, which requires content, namely, accounts of particular human involvements.

Two main types of belief in the value of freedom, instrumental and noninstrumental, will be compared briefly, and the

[10] But this is not to exclude the possibility that freedom may be seen as necessary to the creation and fulfillment of an intimate relation. (Many issues not focused upon in this paper are, however, clarified in Mr. Benn's contribution, "Privacy, Freedom, and Respect for Persons.")

[11] The complex arguments needed to defend this view are developed in Benn and Weinstein, "Being Free to Act, and Being a Free Man."

latter will provide the peg on which the rest of this paper will hang.

First, it has been believed that interference with the choices of individuals is not required in certain circumstances to achieve a particular result, for example, when interference would be inefficient or too easily evaded, or if effective nevertheless too costly. Thus there could be left to the individual some area of choice, allowing him to achieve the good, typically his own, that may be involved. A kind of Hobbesian residue of freedom may exist by virtue of the absence of legal and social restrictions. But it is not more than a residue, its extent depending on the existing, and possibly changing, distribution of the relevant knowledge and resources as between individual agents on the one hand and the authorities, even if beneficently disposed, on the other. This defense of freedom from a purely instrumental, or, more narrowly utilitarian, point of view[12] has troubled liberals at least since Bentham's rejection of natural rights theory, in spite of the possibility of taking utilitarianism as a blank check for the pursuit of any possible object of human desire, so long as it increases the agent's happiness. How, then, might the special preserve of "private" freedoms be explained in more positive terms, creating a stronger presumption in its favor?

One answer had been sought by some utilitarians themselves by postulating that each individual is more likely than anyone else to know what would promote his interests, adding that even if he made mistakes on particular occasions it is more likely that he would learn from such experience if he were left free.[13] The difficulties in this view have been pointed out too often to call for repetition here,[14] though it is not one which is unworthy of further salvage efforts; nor has it ceased to be argued with political success.

[12] Exemplified by Bentham, *Introduction to the Principles of Morals and Legislation*, chap. 17.

[13] This was usually held to be valid for sane adults. See J. S. Mill, *On Liberty*, chap. 4, para. 4; chap. 5, paras. 18, 19 (women were pointedly included in this category in some of Mill's other writings); Henry Sidgwick, *Elements of Politics*, 3rd ed. (London: MacMillan, 1908), chaps. 4, 6, 9.

[14] See John Plamenatz, *The English Utilitarians* (Oxford: Basil Blackwell, 1958), chap. 8.

*The Private and the Free* 37

There is, however, a second type of claim to freedom not so directly (though it may nevertheless be) limited by considerations of efficiency and the distribution of knowledge in reaching some good, such as happiness or welfare. This claim consists in the belief that the individual has a right to exercise a choice as to whether, and possibly how or on what terms, he shall become involved in certain activities and relations because *their nature* is such that other people's or the state's legitimate concern with them, if they have any at all, has a definite limit.

This belief does not imply that all claims to freedom are necessarily claims to "private" freedom in the special sense intended here, which would normally exclude, for example, voting rights. Nor is its hard-core sense derived strictly from the notion of negative freedom, of being left alone by others, though perhaps that phrase has been used to express it.[15] It is more than this; it is the notion that certain human involvements are defective, lose all or much of their value or special quality, when the agent concerned is not free to act on his own preferences or in his own way.[16]

For example, when I claim that I am not answerable, not obliged to give reasons, to anyone for the making up of my invitations list for a dinner in my home, and still less that anyone has a right to interfere, I may be implying that this is the sort of thing in which to be deprived of the choice of my own guests would defeat the enterprise, involving, as it may be seen to do, the choice of my friends, or more widely, of company I expect to be congenial. Seen in these terms, my preferences for certain people may be accepted as sufficient reasons for inviting

---

[15] See Isaiah Berlin, *Two Concepts of Liberty* (Inaugural Lecture, Oxford: The Clarendon Press, 1958), pp. 7–16, reprinted in Berlin, *Four Essays* on *Liberty*, pp. 122–131; but see H. J. McCloskey, "A Critique of the Ideals of Liberty," *Mind*, LXXIV (Oct. 1965), especially pp. 486–494.

[16] No doubt this thesis contains possibilities for divergent interpretations, not least about what is to count as a person's preference or the conditions in which his preference is properly his own (and not, say, vicarious or determined by antecedent social or psychological factors); and such divergencies may have important political implications. But, holding these issues in reserve, my immediate aim is to make clear how a noninstrumental view of freedom's value may be presupposed when a special domain of freedom is marked off as private, as I take Mill to have attempted in *On Liberty*.

them. It is preeminently in such a sphere that one finds apposite Hart's claim that if one believes that an agent's disapproval or disgust may override another agent's preference, one can hardly begin to regard oneself as a believer in freedom.[17]

It is worth adding at once that actions and relations conceived in such terms may nevertheless affect others: Jones's hope of receiving an invitation may be disappointed, as may Smith's of avoiding the embarrassment of refusing one. The essence of the claim that choice is integral to the value of a certain range of social relations is not that the exercise of choice has no effect on others or is of no interest to them.[18] Nor does it amount to, or strictly depend on, the view (which may well be complementary) that there are some aspects of social relations which could *safely* be left to individual choice when no harm would be caused to others. It is rather that, even when others may be

---

[17] H. L. A. Hart, *Law, Liberty and Morality* (London: Oxford University Press, 1963), pp. 46–47. See also J. R. Lucas, "Against Equality," *Philosophy*, XL: 154 (October 1965), 307.

[18] As J. C. Rees rightly argued when attempting to tidy up Mill's distinction between "self-regarding" and "other-regarding" actions, in "A Re-reading of Mill on Liberty," *Political Studies*, VIII:2 (June 1960), 113–129. Rees usefully moves the argument one stage further, to a consideration of interests that might be prejudicially affected, but only one stage.

However, many liberals of a later day, such as Hobhouse, have argued against Mill that *in principle* there is nothing done by the individual which may not be the proper concern of the community. It seems reasonable to interpret this, not as support for a kind of totalitarianism, but as a readiness to appreciate that there may be, but are not always, public causes sufficiently weighty to justify interferences with what may be counted as a private freedom, and that claims for the latter, often implying inalienability, exist instead in a continuously changing balance against rival claims. Nevertheless, it is one thing to criticize Mill for assuming a priori that there are certain private freedoms which could not justifiably be interfered with by the community, but quite another to reject the thesis that choices are integral to a certain range of relations, activities, and beliefs. Perhaps Mill's liberal critics have also been tempted to reject his thesis that all choosing as such is good, because it is argued with very little awareness of the difficulties. On the other hand, I doubt whether they could have rejected a more limited thesis, depending on certain characterizations of selected human involvements, which is sketched in this paper. See L. T. Hobhouse, *Liberalism* (London: Oxford University Press, 1911), pp. 120, 142; A. D. Lindsay, Introduction to *J. S. Mill, Utilitarianism, Liberty, & Representative Government* (New York: E. P. Dutton, 1951), p. xxvii; Isaiah Berlin, *Two Concepts of Liberty*, p. 40; *Four Essays on Liberty*, p. 155.

*The Private and the Free*                                39

affected prejudicially or in ways they merely dislike,[19] the agent's choice is a necessary value in the involvement in some specified activity or relation. The value is conceived noninstrumentally, though endorsement of choices on particular occasions may be qualified or withdrawn because of the agent's ignorance or imprudence, his illusions or malevolent motives, and the like.[20] Nevertheless, in this view, even assuming choices of certain types and in certain circumstances to be genuine and untainted, there may be justifications for interfering with them, based on considerations of, say, justice or the prevention of harm to others; and, as will be explained more fully below, the introduction of such principles may involve reclassifying as "public" what had been understood as something "private."

How there may be ways of picking out a private freedom may be explained through a more detailed example. The mutual exercise of choice of marriage partners in one type of society, given the importance ascribed to mutual love in the making of a match, counts as an item in the modern catalog of private freedom.[21] Were a computer employing a science of compat-

[19] "Merely dislike": added to cover cases where others have no legitimate counterclaim, for example, I have no duty to invite Jones to dinner or to marry one person rather than another, although one might freely create such obligations.

[20] But this is no easy line of argument to sustain while continuing to adhere to the general value of choice-making. Mill says that we abdicate our freedom when we, presumably, choose slavery (*On Liberty*, chap. 5, para. 11). If this were the only case where it was arguable that the agent's freedom could be interfered with for the sake of preserving or improving his capacity as a chooser, the liberal's position would be much easier than it is in fact. See McCloskey, "A Critique of the Ideals of Liberty," pp. 498–503; S. I. Benn, "Freedom and Persuasion," *Australasian Journal of Philosophy*, 45 (1967), 259–275; Benn and Weinstein, "Being Free to Act, and Being a Free Man." The thesis that choices have a special value, *when* made by men with the capacity to choose, remains, however, something worth defending.

[21] For the sake of simplicity only the choices of whether to marry and, if so, whom, are picked out here. There are, however, many other relevant points of potentially large implications. For instance, taking into account subjective factors that may affect the formation of the marriage partners' choice of spouse, were the choices they made really free? If only monogamous marriage makes available certain kinds of satisfaction in a society, in what sense is the choice between marrying and not marrying effectively free? Or again, if the marriage role itself is seen as severely circumscribed by pressures to conform to a social pattern, what importance in the catalog of private freedoms

ibility profiles able to arrange marriages with a given aim,
durable happiness, say, in the view under analysis here, even if
people were prepared to acknowledge the computer's superiority
and that mutual love at the outset is no guarantee of lasting
happiness, they would justifiably prefer it as an adviser, like a
confidant or premarriage guidance counselor, whose advice need
not be sought at all, or if sought not taken, rather than as an
agent to whom one's choice may be derogated. What can be
properly resisted, then, is pressure to accept the computer's
advice, even if it is good advice.[22]

From this perspective one may see how in another society a
similar human involvement may be classified as public in some
sense that it is not in our own, though it remains private vis-à-vis
many other institutions in that society, with the possible consequence that the role or relation into which people enter may
not be seen by them as crucially requiring an element of individual choice. The institution of marriage, even when implying
some form of consent by the parties concerned, can operate in
a community in which marriages are arranged by relations, the
purpose being to maintain the social position, the traditions,
and reputation of the family or kin-group. Within their perspective such interests may not be seen as hostile to the desires
or preferences of marriageable individuals, who are seen as
representatives acting in the family's interest, which is their
interest. The practice of interdynastic marriages in a' monarchy-
ridden Europe was on a similar footing, marked, however, by a
close conjunction of family and state interests.

---

could then be attached to the freedom to choose or reject a partner? In general, classical liberalism tended to focus on the option to *enter* certain roles
and relations (freedom of contract, the career open to talents) and commitments (religious belief or disbelief), making certain assumptions about the
conditions and consequences of choices, social and psychological, which, for
example, Marxism and Freudian analysis called into question. Some implications of these remarks are briefly followed up at the end of Section IV.

[22] Nowadays there are more commonly corresponding ways of conceiving
the nature and value of the whole sphere of sexual relations such as to
bring it under the banner of private freedom. In the terms thus far used
here, these represent, at least in part, attempts to reject, or possibly to
expand, the type of private relations hitherto officially (or at any rate in
some social groups, conventionally) reserved to only male and female in the
role of marriage partner.

Although such marriages, once contracted (possibly under duress), might carry a bonus of conjugal affection and devotion, and possibly on that account a crumb of comfort to the critical liberal by providing a ground for arguing that the same couple might have wished to marry had they both had freedom of choice and sufficient knowledge of the future, plainly the main point was not to give effect to the preferences of the individuals —preferences conceived, of course, in abstraction from their family responsibilities and in terms of what the liberal takes to be the centrally relevant reason for marrying.

The liberal critic may be prepared to concede, should the facts justify it, that the intimacy which, at least in part, makes marriage informally what it is, could well be respected as properly private even in a community which gave people no choice as to whom they married. But he would hardly endorse the thesis that the legitimacy of choice depends on a kind of knowledge of the future of a marriage that could not reasonably be expected of the normal person, though he assumes some minimum of experienced judgment and prudence when he draws the line at minors' right to marry. On the other hand, his defense of individual choice is understood to include cases of people who, without dictation, might dutifully marry for *raison d'état* or *raison de la famille;* although such cases, like some others, may provoke doubts, perhaps founded on evidence as to how choices may be determined by some process of socialization, about whether individuals have chosen "for themselves" or as autonomous agents. Furthermore, resisting the implication of "illusory choices" that one might try to extract from a strong correlation between choice of marriage partner and similarity of social background in the liberal's own society, which he tends to see as one of individually mobile people freed from the yoke of the kin group, the liberal would emphasize that within such socially determined limits there remains a vital element of non-assignability of potential spouses in a marriage free market: this, for him, gives sufficient reality to the choices that are made.[23]

[23] Another dimension to the claim to private freedom in this sphere is that, by an analogy with free economic competition limited by the criminal law and duties arising from the law of tort and specific contracts between individuals, the orthodox liberal associates mutual love as the centrally

It is evident through the thick and thin of these complexities that the liberal sees the invasion of freedom stemming from the way in which the marrying individual is deprived of a choice; instead, his family, or some authority within it, makes the choice. The area of private freedom in relation to some wider community is seen as coextensive with the family unit, and though it is not natural for us to do so, one may speak of the choice of spouse by the family as a decision on a "public" level vis-à-vis the individual. If he had his own preference, based on love, the onus of justifying his claim to choose would be on him in such circumstances. Just how a liberal may characterize marriage, as well as some other relations, activities, and beliefs, as specially relevant to individual fulfillment, conceived in particular ways, and how he sees the making of choices as deeply imbedded in such phenomena, are points on which further comments will be made in Section IV.

### III

It is now appropriate to consider examples in our own type of society of conflict between the claims of private freedom, its value conceived noninstrumentally, and those of public policy, such as the promotion of justice, or welfare, or social solidarity.

Suppose that I will not invite black men into my home, but that in the wider community the choice of employees by employers, of house-buyers by house-vendors, of pupils by schools, is restricted for the sake of preventing deprivation to blacks of options normally available to whites. In other words, these latter types of choice are seen as partly belonging to the public (and in one of our usual senses, political) sphere. Furthermore, assuming there are no calls, à la Sorel, for the preservation of the life style and group solidarity of blacks, but on the contrary there are demands in the name of fraternity for fuller social

---

relevant reason for marrying with open competition, at any rate among as yet unmarried individuals, the hazards of which may be balanced against the benefit of noninterference by family, church, and state.

integration, my preference may then become exposed to criticism and possibly demands for interference.

It would still make sense, however, to hold that whom I choose to invite into my home is not a matter with which the community could properly be concerned.[24] It is not "political" because no evidence suggests that such choices are systematically connected with ways in which blacks are deprived economically and politically. Yet such a view, while implying that it is groundless to complain that I, as a white, am depriving blacks of an intimate relationship with me, also implies that I would have to change my mind should the weight of evidence be balanced differently. Nor might I be content to argue, even if I thought it true, that any attempt to enforce fraternity on this level would in fact fail or be too costly. What might seem the strongest argument is that the very notion of issuing an invitation incorporates a right, which in turn implies choice. But lest this argument should appear to depend directly on property rights (especially the right to exclude others), which would in their turn require justification, I may fall back on another rationale. This would consist in the claim that in this sphere of human relations what is paramount is the kind of satisfaction that depends crucially on personal preference and inclination. To attempt to enforce fraternity, or more strongly, friendship, is to mistake its essential nature. True, invitations may be issued for many different purposes; they may be instrumentally useful, as when I call in the plumber to mend a broken pipe or invite the boss to dinner with the hope of promotion, but they are not useful merely in this way when it comes to friendship or similar personal relations, which are in part constituted by the disposition to issue invitations. In other words, the disposition normally counts, in our society at any rate, as part of what is friendship. Whether or not friendship is valuable intrinsically (or functionally, as part of, though not literally a means to, the individual's health or wellbeing), in this view not to see the decisive importance of the exercise of personal preference and the scope for choice this

[24] Assuming of course that no criminal actions are committed or plotted in my home, and that what is done there is not a serious nuisance or an injury to my neighbors.

44                                                   W. L. WEINSTEIN

normally implies is not to have a grasp of this human relationship. It would follow that I am not obliged to give reasons for
my choice of invitees for friendship's sake; indeed my likes are
sufficient reasons.[25]

I have in effect been restating part of the classic liberal distinction between society and the state, by noting the way in
which political arguments for classifying something as public
may be resisted by the claim that it is, by its nature, essentially
private and free. Of course, governments have been known to
move the line dividing public and private, though not often for
the sake of fraternity; notoriously the South African government,
for instance, seeks to prevent racially mixed company and sexual relations.[26] There is, however, another important dimension
to arguments about the politicization of the private which has
been no more than implied thus far. It may be picked out more
clearly by transposing the example of invitations to a slightly
more institutional level.

A golf club, all white, may insist that its own affairs are private
vis-à-vis the rest of the community, regarding its main purpose,
besides golf itself, as extending relations of friendship and sociability that at the same time depend on a network controlled
by individual choices. These choices, by whites of whites for
membership, may be seen as political in character; and equally,
club members, rebutting such a view, may see outside (or, if they
exist, inside) agitators as "bringing politics into" a situation
normally seen from the inside as nonpolitical. Yet the agitators
may reasonably deny that they are arbitrarily introducing a
political ingredient into the situation, for it is already there:
the social reality they describe is one seen as created not by their
agitation but by the club's policy. Each side, one may say, has
a theory of social life, which, because it determines the way in

---

[25] It is a further issue, arguably relevant in this context, whether I
must have reasons for liking and disliking people, and on what criteria
certain reasons are actually irrelevant or bad. Thus, the blackness of a man's
skin may be held to be no more relevant to liking or disliking him as a
person than for treating him differently from whites on issues of equality
and justice. This issue is not faced by Lucas, who claims that liberty implies
unfairness when the exercise of a personal preference is legitimate, as in
love, friendship, and the like ("Against Equality").

[26] Immorality Act, 1950.

which reality is depicted, can lead to a conflict as to how human actions and their contexts should be classified. In one view the club rests on a rationale of sport and friendship; in the other, it is seen as a microcosm of a larger community which in other spheres similarly deprives blacks of opportunities. However, the conflict need not be total. The agitators need not be blind to the special points of golf or friendship, but only prepared to override them in this case for the sake of some greater good in their view, and not prepared to accept as a sufficient defense the argument that black men as such are not excluded but merely that, as the criteria of choice are golfing ability and sociability, they are contingently ineligible. Nevertheless, the way in which men on opposite sides, the club members and the agitators, may hold their opponents responsible for creating "the situation," itself given a different account within their own respective terms, suggests that there can be a wider range of normative implications to such accounts of social reality. Such implications may be extracted in the following way.

Although I have tried to be objective and detached in describing this conflict, it may be a real question as to whether it is possible for me or others to remain neutral observers. For even if I saw no interest of mine prejudiced or promoted by the victory of one side or the other, it may well appear that I am taking sides if I suppose that the golf club, all things considered, is essentially private. If I then hedge about this, I may be seen by club members and their supporters as giving theoretical aid and comfort to the other side. Although it may then be argued that my neutrality is based precisely on my becoming caught in the middle—exposed to hostility from each side to the degree that I adopt the account used by one side or the other—this may only presuppose that neutrality consists in being thought by each side to be unfavorable to itself. Yet, even accepting this (for how, logically, could both sides be right?), the possibilities of my remaining uninvolved with both sides may be distinctly limited. If, for example, I were to retreat into a "private" position of indifference, the views held by either side may nevertheless imply, somewhat paradoxically perhaps but sensibly, that such a retreat was itself a political act; and thus a third corner of the argument over the public and the private may develop.

Indeed, in such circumstances, even if it were possible to dispel all reasonable doubt as to whether a neutral position as among all relevant perspectives its attainable, it would still be possible to ask whether it is desirable.[27]

These questions open very large and difficult areas of philosophical inquiry lying beyond the scope of this paper, though not in principle that of its subject. However, the foregoing discussion may have been sufficient to suggest that positions taken in disputes (and even when there are no disputes) about what is public and private depend on the terms for explaining social phenomena, including the nature of the individual, for example, his characteristic involvements and their associated satisfactions or achievements, as well as their wider social context. Since there is not, or at any rate seems not to be, a definitive way of settling the terms (a view which, like its contrary, requires philosophical argument), no analysis of the nature, scope, or importance of private freedom can expect to be definitive: no more than, and for the same reasons as, corresponding accounts of the proper ends and scope of politics.

With these remarks in mind I shall now examine more fully the terms in which liberals have understood some human involvements, by covering a wider range of phenomena that have been characterized in terms implying their necessary independence and therefore their status as private freedoms. Some problems raised by such characterizations will also be identified. In consequence the functions in political discourse of such concepts as the private and the public may emerge more clearly.

[27] Cf. W. H. Morris Jones, "In Defense of Apathy," *Political Studies*, II: 2 (1954), 25–37, where it is argued that citizens have a right to opt out of politics, such a private freedom standing against the politicization tendencies of a totalitarian regime, in which anyone seen as failing in his duty to contribute to a 100-percent voters' turnout counts as a political enemy. It is true that modern democratic theories normally imply a right not to become involved politically, but by legitimating conflicts, at any rate within certain limits, over the public and the private, such theories in principle underwrite attempts by groups that are in conflict to involve a wider public on one side or the other. Although groups in conflict are given no right to compel others to take sides, there can nevertheless be strong politicization tendencies in democratic theories, potentially putting them at odds with liberal theories.

## IV

We have seen how a certain rationale of a human involvement, such as marriage or friendship, explains the anti-interference, and specifically antipoliticization, position of liberalism. Stated more generally, this position requires us to see human fulfillment not in terms of one achievement (such as man qua citizen in a perfect community) but of diverse achievements appropriate to man's different powers. He is seen as capable of achievements and satisfactions in a variety of directions. Such involvements may also be seen, as they were by Mill, as constituting some, or several different types of, harmonious whole.[28] But it is by giving an account of the special point of each involvement, each according a satisfaction or achievement not necessarily afforded by any or some others, that the liberal seeks to explain the plurality of values in his perspective.[29] However, it is also important to consider just how the special point

[28] Mill, *On Liberty,* chap. 3, paras. 2, 4, 5, 9.

[29] It will be obvious by now that the ideas here ascribed to liberals, for the sake of bringing out presuppositions and problems in their theories, have had wide currency and a long history. They exist in some minimal form in any society with a division of functions and a system of beliefs which has both instrumental and noninstrumental justifications of activities. Marx, in the *German Ideology,* depicts a "communist society, where no one has one exclusive sphere of activity but each can become accomplished in any branch he wishes." Hegel, in the *Philosophy of Right,* Part III, depicts a community containing diverse values in a diversity of involvements, bringing out the separate value of family life on the one hand, and philosophy, religion, and art on the other. Hegel's importance as a critic of classical liberalism partly consists in his systematic attempt to extract the moral implications of seeing human involvements from a "public" point of view, arguing that such involvements collectively constitute a community's way of life, and that men's understanding of the value of any one involvement, because connected conceptually and in practice with the value of others, is revisable and subject to increasing complexity. In Hegel's view such an understanding requires a fully consistent and coherent philosophy of politics. But this understanding, like social harmony, he seems to argue, is unattainable unless men learn by experience to modify the radical claims made on behalf of the ideals they attach to each of their involvements; they learn this as they see their ideals given institutional or practical form in an actual community. My later remarks on "internal" and "external" characterizations of human involvements bear some resemblance to this Hegelian view of the interplay between the ideal and the real.

of an involvement is characterized. To see it as an essentially free and private thing in a particular social milieu requires an account whose features may be illustrated, if not exhaustively summarized, by the following types of example.

The pursuit of knowledge, the creation or appreciation of works of art, and religious belief are, it is often claimed, understood as containing considerations intrinsic to each. Similar claims have, by extension, been made for loosely formed groups or highly formal organizations, such as universities and churches, which may be seen as promoting their respective values, even if not exclusively by themselves or successfully. The rationale of each is immanent within the structure of thinking and acting which characterizes it. Knowledge, art, and religion are not to be seen as good or bad in terms of phenomena that, *ex hypothesi,* lie outside them, for they are to be appraised by standards immanent in them.[30] To seek the value of art in its political or economic utility is thus to subvert its autonomy,[31] just as to see the family as only a unit for the making of good citizens, or to abolish it for failing in this respect (as Plato advocated), is to destroy a distinctive form of fulfillment and private freedom.[32] On the contrary, to grasp the independent identity of these things implies a readiness to demand control over social conditions or limitations on authorities which threaten their autonomy or internal qualities.[33]

However, the task of explaining the special character and status of each form of human activity and relationship involves making distinctions which may have to cover (or by implication would cover) the full range of human phenomena. It also in-

[30] See R. S. Peters, *Ethics and Education* (London: George Allen & Unwin, 1966), pp. 154–155.

[31] See Stuart Hampshire, "The Conflict between Art and Politics," *The Listener* (October 13, 1960), 629.

[32] As the earlier analysis of "public" implies, the "political" is only one level of public contrasted by liberals to the private. Thus to disavow Plato is not fully to establish the family as a sphere of private freedom in modern terms. At any rate historically in Europe the family's close control by the Church suggests that a secular characterization of the internal nature of family life, no doubt derived from the Church's own teachings, was required before the family could be seen in such terms.

[33] Thus claims made on behalf of certain human involvements to be free of political control may in certain contexts lead proponents into active politics; to limit the jurisdiction of "politics" is a moral-political decision.

volves seeing how given activities and relations answer, instrumentally or expressively, to given needs, or how the needs imply
the activities and relations; and marking off spheres of excellence
and achievement implies corresponding accounts of what is understood as the essential human capacities, their limits and po-
tentialities. For example, to grasp the intrinsic worth of the
pursuit of knowledge requires understanding how and with what
difficulties it is acquired, which is connected with theses as to
what properly counts as knowledge. In this way political theories
depend on theories of human nature, which in their turn presuppose philosophies of mind and knowledge.

In fact it is just in such philosophies that certain possibilities
of choice are often defined, and at times the nature of some
human involvements has been explained in terms that call for
choice. For example, the nature of religious belief or experience
may be explained as the acceptance of a body of true knowledge,
expounded by God's chosen intermediaries. But if, while upholding the truth of a doctrine, what is seen as inherent in such
beliefs is that they must be those of the believer, that it is for
him to come to terms with God as best he can, then the way is
opened to diversity of conviction, even though commitment is
still required. It is to invite men to interpret the truth as each
of them sees it. Furthermore, to be allowed (or by virtue of some
theory of knowledge to demand) to challenge the whole body
of belief as untrue, or as neither true nor false, is to open
further possibilities for the individual: either to believe in his
own way or not to believe at all.[34]

Similarly, to see artistic creation as essentially the outpouring
of the active individual's imagination, of his capacity to conjure
up what is novel and striking, and as a necessary way of com-

[34] The suspicion may be well founded that this is a potted version of
transitions from Catholicism to Lutheranism to the rationalism of the
eighteenth and nineteenth centuries, seen through liberal- or Hegelian-
tinted spectacles. Be that as it may, it is only an account of how religious
beliefs, and perhaps associated moral and political ones, may come to be
seen as matters of private freedom vis-à-vis religious (and allied secular)
authorities. Long before Luther and on many occasions since, churches have
claimed special immunity against political authority; their claim to be treated
as a private enterprise has depended on a particular view of their internal
character, namely, their other worldly concerns or their constitution as a community of Christian brothers seeking salvation.

plementing his life as a creature of reason by bringing forth his gifts as a sensuous being, is to imply that dictation is at odds with its nature as an essentially individually fulfilling involvement. In this sense such experience is conceived as "private," in potential opposition to claims made on behalf of some relevant wider community (possibly by virtue of a different view of art, such as Socialist Realism), but not as something occurring in absolute isolation, any more than mathematics would be in an account of its special nature.[35]

Thus accounts of the intrinsic nature of some involvements have far-reaching implications for the manner in which they are classified as either essentially free and private in relation to some wider community or as public. The foregoing analysis has suggested the kind of theory which forms the basis for the belief in areas of private freedom—a belief which functions in political discourse to deflect "public" claims, or to make claims on the wider community, in the name of intrinsically fulfilling involvements requiring scope for individual choice. Of course identifying the "essential" nature of any such phenomenon is a moral activity itself; and to claim that some involvement is "essentially free" is often to make the point that it ought to be free when in fact it is not, while conversely involvements not so classified may

[35] See Hampshire, "The Conflict between Art and Politics." However, these are only examples, as were friendship and marriage earlier in this paper. Although men have at times sought to understand a particular human involvement in terms modeled on some other, my argument implies that one reasonable way of proceeding is to take each phenomenon in turn, explaining how a given way of characterizing its distinctive properties may imply that it is inherently valuable or fulfilling, and that it requires certain choices, such as initially to opt in or out, or subsequently in the course of the involvement itself. Nevertheless, how one characterization is presented may have logical implications for others. Yet not all human involvements have always been described in terms suggestive of their intrinsic value (contracts, for example), though perhaps aspects of them may have been. Typically we tend not to see involvements in trade and industry in such terms (though ways have been tried), but instrumentally. Of course labor in production has its defining characteristics; it has its rules, standards of performance, and appropriate objects. But beyond this labor may be seen, as Marx saw it, as an activity fundamentally marked by its noninstrumental importance. To see it as a species of art, and thus as potentially fulfilling in the way that the creation of works of art can be, is to see it also as inherently "free activity." To deprive men of choices in their labor is thus to deny them both freedom and fulfillment. In this context, see Arendt, *The Human Condition.*

in fact be free. Philosophies create the possibility of not taking a certain human phenomenon on its own terms, as these may be commonly represented at a given time, but of seeing it, as Marx, for example, saw religion, as a social activity without independent validity, the need for which would some day disappear (or would, as in the Soviet Union, be helped to disappear), or of seeing another, as Marx saw labor, as understood and treated merely instrumentally by a society that inescapably does violence to its intrinsic nature as a free, creative activity.

However, in addition to the possibility of conflict over the internal nature of a human involvement and whether it is essentially free in the sense explained above, there are important problems that arise from representing it in such terms. How these problems are contended with may affect, or be affected by, the ways in which agents identify and value the particular freedoms of choice associated with a private freedom. The problems that arise do so because the involvement is not an isolated phenomenon in any actual social world.

Activities, relations, and beliefs, as well as theories about them, exist in social contexts. The pursuit of knowledge, for example, has a history of its own development which cannot be separated from the history of other social phenomena. In general the connections between social phenomena in the same historical context are often so close, even without conscious efforts to bring them still closer,[36] that the liberal pluralist may have real difficulties in preserving the distinctions necessary to his arguments for the independent identity and value of a range of involvements; or the validity of such arguments may be questioned because of the position of such involvements in an actual society. When such involvements are seen in institutions and practices, and therefore as having certain necessary relations with other items in a social structure, it may be difficult to distinguish be-

---

[36] On an individual level we are often aware of the fact that behavior in one sphere may be relevant to performance in another, and this could become a source of tension. If I drink for fun it may affect my competence as a teacher. Moreover new standards set in one sphere may require instrumental interpretations of what occurs in another; the efficient running of business firms may change the internal qualities of family life for the sake of the breadwinner's career (see Margaret L. Helfrich, *The Social Role of the Executive's Wife* [Athens, Ohio: Ohio State University Press, 1965]).

tween a given phenomenon's "internal," that is, "essential," nature (for example, labor as a species of art, or a university as a community of scholars) and its "external" relations, that is, how its own nature is in fact affected by such other items, and what effects it has on them (labor as assembly-line production, or universities as parts of the job market). At the very least, when such distinctions are made, there remains the problem of deciding whether "internal" or "external" considerations are to carry more weight in a given policy argument.

Adherence to such "internal" descriptions in the face of supplementary or rival "external" descriptions, or acceptance of the validity of the latter (with or without continuing allegiance to some version of the former), has important moral and political implications.[37] Policies and tactics may depend on whether an institution is seen as corrupted, according to a standard determined by its "internal" nature. To assert its status as essentially free and private may involve internal reform or rejection of the institution; or it may involve political, public action, such as rejection of controls exerted by, or disengagement from commitments to, the wider community. And that community, or the state, instead of responding to demands for changes in its own structure designed to meet the needs of the institution, may claim that it is in the public interest to maintain the existing internal identity and social position of the institution.

Thus, for example, a university may claim academic freedom vis-à-vis the wider community by virtue of ideals of objective, politically uninvolved scholarship and free inquiry. There may, however, be disputes as to how far it has fulfilled itself and which factors in the wider social context are compatible with or hostile to its "internal" nature. Such choices as it had made in the past may be seen to have undermined its pretensions to, or possibilities for, academic freedom. Furthermore, the types of option effectively available in a given situation may be in dispute. Some may hold that the situation is such that no relevant option represents an escape from political involvement, others that no real options exist. The differences between Paris and Prague in 1968 over the role of universities in the wider com-

---

[37] As the example of the golf club began to show.

munity suggest that in different circumstances, as well as within each set of circumstances, there can be different assessments of "internal" and "external" identities, their relations and relative priority, and of the possibilities and significance of choice. The tensions between accounts of social phenomena in terms of their "internal," independent (ideal and abstract) nature on the one hand and, on the other, their positions, achievements, and possibilities in a given social context provide some of the stuff of ideological conflict.

The liberal pluralist may face similar difficulties in distinguishing between what properly counts as the individual (conceived in terms of essential needs and purposes) and what is the social context which makes him what he is and his involvements what they are. Here, too, there are tensions between the ideal value set on something seen as essentially private and free and what is understood to be its actual nature in social reality.

Societies may be seen as both making a range of choices available and limiting them by rules, the types of its activities and relations, and the structure of its prevailing beliefs. Thus, for example, as part of a general picture, liberal in inspiration, of a society affording diverse opportunities for individuals to enter relations at their option (and often with scope to negotiate at entry, or to interpret subsequently), to choose a spouse without dictation may count as one kind of private freedom. That freedom may also be seen as partially extending to the scope for development of an intimate relation in marriage.

However, it is possible to see that the relation, once entered, involves duties and other restrictions that form part of a common social pattern to which couples are expected, and become disposed, to conform. It may become a real issue as to how much an individual can modify the role, which he did not create, or on what conditions he can withdraw from it. Furthermore, the sense in which individuals in a system of marriage by free contract may be effectively choosing (either whether to marry, or if so, whom), may be questioned by analysis of the social and subjective conditions of choice. For example, if preferences are seen as decisively shaped by a socialization process, it may be argued that the freedom of choice commonly assumed to exist is in fact illusory.

By such arguments as these, existing provisions for a human involvement, commonly represented as private and free, may have their value called into question. The involvement may be held to require types and conditions of choice which an existing community excludes or diminishes the chance of having. Hence the contrast between "bourgeois" marriage and ideals of free love as a perfect (if not in some versions of free love a wholly obligation-free) expression of a private freedom. Against the background of such ideals, even if modified, it is possible to see more clearly that justifications of freedom of choice on entering "bourgeois" marriage presuppose that, all things considered, there is sufficient scope for choice and for fulfillment of its general rationale. Recognition of its inadequacies may give rise to reformist demands to modify "external" factors working against fulfillment in it, or to grant individuals greater freedom of choice, or to a plea for acceptance of those seeking the same fulfillment without marriage or to radical rejection of the arrangement itself.

It is worth noticing, however, that up to this last point most examples have represented a conflict between some claim that might be made by a wider community and that which might be made on behalf of a private freedom, presumably to expand or protect its domain. Another possibility is suggested by the clash between ideal characterizations of an involvement and what is taken to be its identity in reality. If we see society as providing unfulfilling or illusory options, and conceive of fulfilling and authentic alternatives, we may be led to reject what is available, as Marx rejected wage labor. To see himself properly as free, in one view of freedom, man must be capable of choosing and therefore rejecting the forms of private freedom made available to him, and of seeing other forms as more faithful to his appreciation of his necessary involvements.

At this point to speak of private freedom may well imply not what is generally meant in a given society, nor even action to establish a new boundary line around a private freedom, but in fact opting out of society. Indeed, at times men may see themselves as having a choice between a quietist withdrawal and radical political action to change society. Although Marx drew very different conclusions from those of Hegel, we may let Hegel,

*The Private and the Free* 55

who saw more deeply into many issues reviewed in this paper than any other modern theorist, have the last word on this last point:

> When the existing world of freedom has become faithless to the will of better men, that will fails to find itself in the duties there recognized and must try to find in the ideal world of the inner life alone the harmony which actuality has lost. . . . It is only in times when the world of actuality is hollow, spiritless, and unstable, that an individual may be allowed to take refuge from actuality in his inner life.[38]

[38] *Philosophy of Right* (Oxford: The Clarendon Press, 1942), translated by T. M. Knox, pp. 92, 255. Of course, the particular words quoted, from Part II, were hardly his last on this subject.

# [13]

# 5

# THE USES OF PRIVACY
# IN THE GOOD LIFE

## MICHAEL A. WEINSTEIN

Privacy, like alienation, loneliness, ostracism, and isolation, is a condition of being-apart-from-others. However, alienation is suffered, loneliness is dreaded, ostracism and isolation are borne with resignation or panic, while privacy is sought after. Frieda Fromm-Reichmann has written of the descriptive interpretations of loneliness that "various different experiences which are descriptive and dynamically as different from one another as culturally determined loneliness, self-imposed aloneness, compulsory solitude, isolation, and real loneliness are all thrown into the one terminological basket of 'loneliness.' "[1] The same criticism can be made of the various phenomenological accounts of privacy which may equate this condition with hysteric neurosis, anonymity, unbridled individualism, or alienation and loneliness. In each case the fact that privacy is highly regarded by the conscious person seeking it is either ignored

[1] Frieda Fromm-Reichmann, "Loneliness," *Psychiatry*, 22 (February 1959), 1.

*The Uses of Privacy in the Good Life*                                89

or introduced as evidence of false consciousness and rationalization. The case for reducing privacy to some other less desired
or actually averted condition is apt to be especially compelling
in a social order which grounds self-definition in human relationships and interactions. In such a society the quest for
privacy is likely to be distrusted and the way from distrust to
abhorrence is quickly traversed. In general, the critics of privacy
argue that a careful analysis of this condition reveals that it has
no redeeming qualities because privacy represents a severance
of social relationships, albeit a temporary detachment. Are there
good reasons for defending this position or are different phenomena being confused?

Typical of the scholars who reduce privacy to some other condition is Edmund Leach, who argues that ". . . most of us are so
deeply committed to being alone in a crowded world that we
turn the whole problem back to front: we worry about privacy
rather than loneliness."[2] Anthropologists who do field work in
a "primitive society" complain about their lack of privacy, but
this is a case of false consciousness. Privacy is "the source of fear
and violence" and is defined as the creation of "artificial boundaries between men who are like us and men who are not like
us."[3] Once the human universe has been sundered by the arbitrary institution of in-groups and out-groups, selves and others,
fear of the other appears and the person is ". . . isolated, lonely
and afraid because [his] neighbor is [his] enemy."[4] Privacy, on
analysis, is really the condition of unwanted isolation accompanied by the emotion of fear and the latent desire for communion. As a phenomenological description this argument is
weak. First of all, Leach presumes that privacy appears as an
invidious and conventional distinction that a conscious person
draws in order to separate himself from the natural condition
of communion. The operation is carried out for no apparent
reason and it inevitably ends in unhappiness supervening on
consciousness. Further, when the distinction is made the person
believes that he is proceeding toward a good. Why self-defeating

[2] Edmund Leach, *A Runaway World?* (New York: Oxford University Press,
1968), p. 46.
[3] *Ibid.*
[4] *Ibid.*

activity of this sort is such a prevalent phenomenon is left un-explained. Perhaps being-in-the-world involves an interplay be-tween the poles of communion and separation rather than a dichotomy. If this is the case, privacy may be a condition of ambiguity and productivity instead of a fall from the perfection of tribal wholeness.

Bruno Bettelheim takes a similar approach, maintaining that privacy arises socially through the demands of a propertied elite for separation from others. As the ideology of bourgeois indi-vidualism becomes predominant, people begin to perform their bodily functions in seclusion and experience shame about their bodies. Shame breeds alienation from one's body, which results in discomfort in the presence of others. Even more privacy is desired as a futile palliative for the ills of alienation. In the end, bourgeois society leaves people with two selves: a private self with interests that cannot be pursued in public and a social mask for the conduct of human relations. When the conflict between covert and overt demands becomes too sharp, neurosis and hysteria appear.[5] While false consciousness in Leach re-ferred to a departure from the healthy condition of communion, in Bettelheim this phenomenon is connected with a split between mind and body. Instead of fear, shame accompanies privacy and the latent desire is for a reunion of mind and body. Again the argument depends upon the claim that there is a primal ex-perience of fullness which is not available in contemporary society. From a phenomenological point of view this position is difficult, because any demand for privacy will be interpreted as a self-defeating defense mechanism which can only cause more shame. The motives of the conscious person seeking privacy have no standing. However, both Leach and Bettelheim do pro-pose tests in experience. Fear or shame should accompany the condition of privacy. That either of these emotions necessarily supervenes on the condition of privacy is doubtful.

Another attempt to reduce privacy to some other condition is made by Margaret Mead, who asserts that privacy and anonymity are frequently confused. At present many demands for privacy

[5] Bruno Bettelheim, "The Right to Privacy Is a Myth," *Saturday Evening Post* (July 27, 1968), 9.

are rationalizations for a refusal to fulfill one's responsibilities to his fellow man. People do not call the police or give aid and comfort when they see a fellow human being under attack by a criminal. They prefer to remain anonymous in such cases, demonstrating by their behavior that they are immature and too incompletely socialized to accept the duties of urban life. Privacy is sacrificed in favor of social control and solidarity in rural societies, and this normal condition should also prevail in urban societies.[6] Mead, then, equates the condition of privacy with the condition of being uninvolved in the concerns of one's neighbors. Since the natural and healthy life is one of relatedness and solidarity, the demand for privacy is an example of false consciousness about the human situation. While privacy should be accompanied by the feeling of guilt for one's parasitic tendencies, it appears in consciousness as associated with self-righteousness. Unlike Leach and Bettelheim, Mead does not posit a latent desire functioning beneath the wish for privacy. It is not that man must return to an original perfection, but that he must be socialized into acceptance of his proper estate. Thus, false consciousness for Mead is defined in terms of a sociological standard instead of a norm which supposedly operates in the state of nature. In view of this distinction she cannot be criticized for explaining away every demand for privacy as an example of self-defeating activity. It is in the interest of the individualist to shirk his social responsibilities, but what is comfort for the man in the short run is chaos for the society over the long term. Perhaps the most effective response to Mead's argument is the claim that often privacy is sought as a means for deepening one's involvement with others. If being-in-the-world involves polarity between withdrawal and participation, a life of unbroken solidarity with others is as partial as an existence of irresponsible autonomy.

The same critique applies to the arguments of Granville Hicks, who maintains that "complete privacy means complete irresponsibility, which in turn can mean extinction of the personality."[7] Hicks makes the useful point that limitations on privacy are

[6] Margaret Mead, "Our Right to Privacy," *Redbook*, 124 (April 1965), 16.
[7] Granville Hicks, "The Limits of Privacy," *American Scholar*, 28 (Spring 1959), 192.

probably less resented in tightly knit communities than they are in urban settings because restrictions on privacy in urban societies are enforced impersonally: ". . . intimate details of your life are fed into a business machine; the investigator who may get you fired hasn't the slightest interest in you as an individual; the photographer who infuriates you with his persistence is merely doing a job."[8] Simply, the necessity for limitations on privacy is easier to understand in a *Gemeinschaft* setting than it is in the context of a *Gesellschaft,* even though restrictions are equally needed in both situations. It would be foolish to argue that when people perceive that their social relations are constituted in such a way that they minimize personal concern, they will not tend to diminish their involvement in public responsibilities. Hicks at least provides a reason why the conscious person may seek anonymity. However, all demands for privacy are not demands for anonymity in disguise. The activities that occur while the person is in the condition of privacy are at least as important as the bare fact of being-apart-from-others.

The case for reducing privacy to some other condition has been argued along two lines. First, privacy may be interpreted as a fall from the primal condition of social communion or personal wholeness. If the argument proceeds in this way, privacy is itself evil and the demand for privacy is an expression of false consciousness. The claim is advanced that the condition of privacy is accompanied by such unpleasant feelings as alienation, loneliness, shame, and unhappiness. Phenomenologically, this approach is weak because conscious persons actively seek privacy and report satisfaction while in the condition. Second, privacy may be interpreted as an anonymity which allows a person to escape from his social responsibilities. Again privacy is evil and its pursuit as a good a rationalization. There is no claim, however, that privacy is unpleasant; it is immoral. The weakness of this argument lies in its neglect of the full range of reasons why conscious persons seek privacy.

The most striking aspect of the two arguments for depreciating privacy is the fact that they conceal theoretical interpre-

[8] *Ibid.*

tations of human nature. In short, Leach and Bettelheim argue
from the position of a moral idealism usually associated with
liberalism and radicalism, while Mead and Hicks proceed from
a standpoint of moral realism that frequently accompanies conservatism. For Leach and Bettelheim there is a human essence,
which is good, and its attainment has been thwarted by social
contrivances. Privacy is the unfortunate result of ethnocentrism
or class exploitation that breed alienation from self and alienation from others. The condition of privacy is essentially unnatural and would disappear with the discontinuance of ethnic
or class distinctions. At best privacy is a flight from exploitation,
conflict, and censure, in which the person trades suffering for
loneliness. It may sometimes be the lesser of two evils. The
human essence, which is defined as either communion or personal wholeness, perhaps has a reference point in a golden age.
However, it is certainly not realized in the modern age and
awaits fulfillment in the next stage of social development. Both
Leach and Bettelheim look favorably upon a younger generation
which seems to be less interested in privacy than its predecessors.
On the contrary, Mead and Hicks are wary of privacy because
they distrust human nature. Man is not so much deprived as
he is depraved. In the absence of efficient socialization he will
follow his narrow self-interest to the point at which public life
becomes chaotic. To allow him satisfaction in his search for
privacy means to grant him the right to behave in a socially
irresponsible manner. Since the human essence is to be selfish,
social policy demands that men be civilized to the degree that
they do not destroy the means to life and health. Privacy, therefore, must be restricted, if not abolished.

It is not surprising that moral idealists and moral realists
should agree in concluding that privacy should be reduced to
some other condition. The one strives for the realization of a
human essence which is not yet of this world and regards with
suspicion the satisfactions which people claim to attain at the
moment, while the other views with distrust the notion that a
person may fulfill part of his moral being on his own. More significant is the fact that the claims of both moral idealists and
moral realists are contrary to the position of existential phenom-
enologists because they involve affixing a determinate essence to

the human being. If the human being is defined neither as a good soul corrupted by perverted institutions nor a depraved soul who must be kept in line, there may be no reason to scorn privacy in all cases.

Shorn of theoretical interpretation, privacy appears in consciousness as a condition of voluntary limitation of communication to or from certain others, in a situation, with respect to specified information, for the purpose of conducting an activity in pursuit of a perceived good. The variables of choice, limited communication, relevant others, a situational context, activity, and a good to be attained must all be present in the full construction of privacy. Any addition or subtraction of variables will define another phenomenon. For example, if the condition is entered involuntarily, it is isolation when a matter of circumstance and ostracism when a result of the choice of others. Either isolation or ostracism may become loneliness when accompanied by a desire for communication. In the condition of privacy there is no such unsatisfied longing for communication. Since privacy is a condition of being-apart-from-others, limitation of communication is required. However, when communication is restricted because the person believes that the other will misunderstand him because they do not hold common symbols, meanings, or values, there is a condition of alienation from other. While isolation, ostracism, and loneliness may be clearly distinguished from privacy, alienation is closely related to it. Often people seek privacy to perfect their communication with others, to understand why communication has failed. When such efforts to resolve misunderstandings are consistently ineffective, privacy fades into alienation. Privacy demands that there are relevant others with whom communication is possible. If there are no relevant others and communication is limited voluntarily, the condition is one of hermitic isolation. If limitation is involuntary, the condition is one of simple isolation. Privacy must be a function of certain defined situations rather than a condition which persists over all situations. Communication in some situations must be anticipated and even desired or else the condition of withdrawal appears. If no particular activity is contemplated in the condition of privacy, there is a state of mere se-

*The Uses of Privacy in the Good Life*                    95

clusion. If no good is sought in or as a result of the condition of privacy, there is a state of irresponsible anonymity when an evil is contemplated and simple anonymity when neither good nor evil is contemplated. On the other hand, that type of privacy in which communication to certain others is limited may be called secrecy, while the kind of privacy in which communication is limited from certain others may be called solitude. The situation in which a group of people limits communication to others may be called by the old word "privity."

By no means is this a full phenomenological description of the different kinds of being-apart-from-others. Such a description would include the feelings which accompany each condition and the desires expressed in each condition. However, enough distinctions have been made to proceed with a discussion of the uses of privacy and a defense of this condition as a necessary aspect of the good life. It should be clear that privacy must not be confused with isolation, ostracism, loneliness, alienation, withdrawal, seclusion, or anonymity. It is a phenomenon with its own peculiar structure.

The essential structure of privacy described above is generally consistent with other treatments in the literature. The phenomenological description rendered by Alan P. Bates defines privacy as a structure of a "psychological region"; "Privacy . . . is a structured portion of a person's total phenomenological field. It is differentiated from the total field by the fact that the self is in some degree involved in excluding in some (or possibly all) circumstances, some (or possibly all) other persons from knowledge in the person's possession."[9] While this description really identifies secrecy and does not fully account for solitude, it does distinguish privacy from alienation and loneliness. However, the definition allows for hermitic isolation and withdrawal to be classed as types of privacy. This diminishes the precision of privacy as a condition of temporary and contextual being-apart-from-others. The significant aspect of privacy as a limitation of communication which is also voluntary is maintained,

---

[9] Alan P. Bates, "Privacy—A Useful Concept?" *Social Forces*, 42 (May 1964), 430.

96                                    MICHAEL A. WEINSTEIN

although even here privacy may be confused with anonymity
and seclusion because Bates does not discuss the purposes of
private states.

Edward Shils also proposes a similar definition: "We may say
that privacy exists where the persons whose actions engender or
become the objects of information retain possession of that information, and any flow outward of that information from the
persons to whom it refers (and who share it where more than one
person is involved) occurs on the initiative of its possessors."[10]
Again, solitude is not recognized and the uses of privacy are
slighted. However, the situational character of privacy is ac-
counted for.

Once privacy has been phenomenologically described, it remains to identify the activities and purposes which render this
condition valuable in the realization of the good life. Just as
was the case for commentators who depreciated privacy, there
are at least two major kinds of argument present in the essays
of writers who think privacy is desirable. On the one hand,
privacy may be considered as essential for the maintenance of
personality systems and social systems, while on the other this
condition may be considered necessary for their improvement.
Proponents of the first approach usually find some weakness
which they claim is inherent in social relations and then argue
that only personal privacy can prevent the dissolution of these
relations. For example, Anthony West contends that human
beings have both a social self and an actual self. The social self
is constituted by activity and attitudes which are consonant with
social norms, while the actual self is constituted by personal
activities and inclinations. Although the two selves may overlap,
it is impossible for the human being consistently to fulfill the
social standards because they are too demanding and perhaps
inconsistent. People recognize this situation and grant privacy
to one another so that each can pretend he is better than he is.
Social relations are, thus, maintained and the individual has a
sphere of being-for-himself. Such pretense is functional for the
maintenance of the social system because it gives people an in-

[10] Edward Shils, "Privacy: Its Constitution and Vicissitudes," *Law and
Contemporary Problems,* 31 (Spring 1966), 282.

*The Uses of Privacy in the Good Life*                        97

centive to realize social norms which would not be present if they were continuously confronted with the weak actual selves of their fellows.[11]

Similar to West's treatment is that of Bates, who argues that human beings need privacy for protection against the disclosure of damaging mistakes, for restoring self-esteem after "bruising" social contact, for evaluating strategies in the conduct of social relations, and for rationalizing disapproved conduct and inclinations.[12]

Barry Schwartz has presented the most complete exposition of the position that privacy is a necessary means to system maintenance. He remarks: "The very act of placing a barrier between oneself and others is self-defining, for withdrawal entails a separation from a role and, tacitly, from an identity imposed upon oneself by others via that role."[13] This type of separation between social self and actual self is functional because the person can invisibly transgress social norms and thereby keep up appearances in his social relations, undertake consumption which is disapproved, enact unorthodox postures, and, most important, relax after encounters with unbearable people with whom relations are necessary. In fact, excessive contact with anyone is dysfunctional to the relationship because it is ". . . the condition under which Freud's principle of ambivalence most clearly exercises itself, when intimacy is most likely to produce open hostility as well as affection."[14]

In brief, to the functionalist writers the condition of privacy is valuable because it is a means to lessening the personal tensions which are built into the conduct of social relations. Is the functionalist case phenomenologically sound?

Functionalism can be considered conservatism brought up-to-date. While being-apart-from-others is no longer described as base self-seeking, it is defined as inferior to states of relatedness. The condition of privacy is merely a palliative to relieve the

[11] Anthony West, "Secrets: Why You Need Them," *Vogue* (August 15, 1967), 127.

[12] Alan P. Bates, "Privacy—A Useful Concept?" pp. 432–433.

[13] Barry Schwartz, "The Social Psychology of Privacy," *American Journal of Sociology*, 73 (May 1968), 747.

[14] *Ibid.*, p. 741.

strains associated with social relations. Human existence is an interplay between the poles of publicity and privacy, both of which are unsatisfactory. As social self, the human being shows his best and is yet unsatisfied with it, while as actual self he enacts his weaknesses and must inevitably feel guilty for it. That is, he must feel guilty unless he adopts false consciousness by declaring that the condition of being-apart-from-others is somehow superior to being-with-others. In other words, the condition of privacy serves the latent functions of pattern maintenance and tension management and is justified by the manifest function of providing the individual with a sphere of being-for-himself. The functionalist position, then, describes human existence as tragic. The person must strive to fulfill social norms which are inconsistent and severe. Inevitable failure must be rationalized. The other person is hell because he is known only as role and knows me only as role. However, to know him in any other way would be to know his inferior actual self. Existence, thus, becomes a game of pretending that the actual self is really better than the social self, while everyone recognizes that the condition of privacy is at best a state of rest and relaxation and at worst a stage for the enactment of shameful deeds.

While it is true that in states of despondency and despair this view frequently appears, it is not a compelling description of the uses of privacy. First, the functionalists are ambiguous about the nature of pretense. Does the person really deceive himself that the condition of privacy is superior to states of relatedness? Does he falsify his weak actual self and contrive yet a new ideology or self-image which attributes to him desirable qualities? Is the extreme form of daydreaming in which the person loses consciousness that he is elaborating a fiction the main use of privacy? If all this is so, then the person actually will find privacy preferable to publicity and he will attempt to be rid of social relationships whenever possible. In this case, the condition of privacy would no longer be a means to pattern maintenance and tension management. Instead, it would be disruptive of social solidarity. On the other hand, if the person recognizes the disparity between social self and weak actual self, and perceives that justifications of privacy are merely excuses for letting oneself go, he will resent both the social norms and his own self. He will have consciousness of the absurd and lose commitment to irrational social relations. Again the latent functions will not be performed. In short, the fact that people often do seek privacy as a condition of rest, relaxation, and escape from social norms does not imply that these are the major uses of privacy and certainly does not imply that they are the only uses.

The functionalist approach can be questioned in the same way in which the arguments from moral idealism and moral realism were criticized. An essence is still attributed to the human being. In this case he is a soul divided between natural desires and social norms which restrict these desires. The social norms provide . the conditions under which any life at all is possible, so the person must be tricked into fulfilling them. Since he cannot fulfill them consistently, he is granted a sphere of being-apart-from-others in which he can enact socially undesirable behavior without destroying the relational pattern. Of course, the wisdom of the social norms is never questioned. They are the invariant rules under which the tragedy is played out. As in Mead and Hicks, the human being is an individualist who must be tamed. However, he is tamed here by granting him well-defined states of privacy. Discretion is the better part of valor. Functionalism, then, contains a theoretical interpretation which is phenomenologically inadmissible. The conscious person seeking privacy cannot be seen as a tool of latent social functions. To look at him that way is, in the end, to claim that he would seek privacy in all contexts (if he turns pretense into belief) or that he would never seek privacy (if he perceives existence as pretense).

While the functionalist writers develop a defense of privacy in terms of an essentially conservative interpretation of the human being and an organic theory of society, humanist and religious commentators who look favorably upon privacy carry forward the notion of communion. Essentially, they argue that the highest goods in human relations can only be attained if individuals are granted privacy. One group contends that privacy is essential for realizing the creation of worthwhile cultural objects—aesthetic, scientific, and utilitarian. Thus, Frieda Fromm-Reichmann speaks of states of "creative loneliness" which are "self-induced, and may be voluntarily and alternately sought out and rejected."[15] Such conditions of privacy are prerequisites for the conception of "nearly all works of creative originality," and "only the creative person who is not afraid of this constructive aloneness will have free command over his creativity."[16] Another point of view is held by Georg Simmel, who argues that privacy is necessary for devising plans to alter social relations: ". . . secrecy procures enormous extension of life, because with publicity many sorts of purposes could never arrive at realization. Secrecy secures, so to speak, the possibility of a second world alongside of the obvious world, and the latter is most strenuously affected by the former."[17] A third use of privacy is suggested by Howard B. White, who asserts that privacy is a requirement for the perfection of political understanding: "The greatest and most difficult duty of the private life must be to undermine the assumptions of civil society, provided that they are merely assumptions, that they are undermined in the interest of something better than assumptions, and that the undermining is done in such a way as to appeal only to reasonable men."[18] Finally, it can be argued that the condition of privacy provides an opportunity for experiences which are goods in themselves rather than means to the realization of social goods. Sidney Jourard speaks of "consciousness-expansion" which "illumines a man's being-for-himself, changes his being-for-others, and potentiates desirable growth of his personality."[19] Such development, borne of reflection and experimentation, can only occur in the condition of privacy. From a religious standpoint, privacy may be considered a necessary condition for spiritual growth and experience, both of which demand "a spirit of recollection and contemplation."[20] In either the secular or the religious argument

[15] Frieda Fromm-Reichmann, "Loneliness," pp. 22, 2.

[16] *Ibid.*

[17] Georg Simmel, "The Sociology of Secrecy and of Secret Societies," *American Journal of Sociology*, 11 (January 1906), 462.

[18] Howard B. White, "The Right to Privacy," *Social Research*, 18 (June 1951), 202.

[19] Sidney M. Jourard, "Some Psychological Aspects of Privacy," *Law and Contemporary Problems*, 31 (Spring 1966), 312.

[20] "Technology and Contemplation," *America*, 100 (November 15, 1958), 189.

an "interior man" who must be granted "concentric corridors of protective privacy" is identified.[21]

In all, the writers who defend the condition of privacy as essential to the realization of goods may define desirable private activities as the creation of valuable cultural objects, the contrivance of plans for better forms of social relations, the perfection of political understanding, and the experiencing of significant modes of consciousness. Two questions arise from this discussion. Do these activities have anything in common, and why is the condition of privacy necessary if the goods in which they are supposed to issue may be realized?

All of the activities cited by the commentators who defend privacy are, in Justus Buchler's terms, kinds of query. Query appears when human contrivance "assumes more purposive and elaborate proportions, when the qualitative aspect of the potential product grows in importance. . . ."[22] The consequences of concern with definite purpose and quality are a larger role for contrivance within "the total economy of effort," greater risk that activities will fail to realize objectives, an increased importance for human resourcefulness, more alternatives within the process of contrivance, and greater "rigor of selection and choice."[23] In short, query is the improvement of human judgment, through which life becomes art. As maker is succeeded by artist, "the process of making becomes crucial": "The materials of nature are no longer ready at hand but need as it were to be quarried. The greater the project of contrivance, the less adequate is the surface of nature."[24]

There are several types of query, each of which corresponds to a mode of human judgment. Assertive query aims at compelling assent, through evidence, to judgments of true and false; exhibitive query has as its purpose the creation of "a qualitative whole which needs no alteration"; and active query takes its object as a tenable social relationship.[25] Each of the activities which have privacy as one of their conditions exemplifies a type of

---

[21] "Let Me Alone!" *Christian Century*, 83 (September 21, 1966), 135.

[22] Justus Buchler, *Nature and Judgment* (New York: Columbia University Press, 1955), p. 60.

[23] *Ibid.*

[24] *Ibid.*

[25] *Ibid.*, p. 80.

query. Frieda Fromm-Reichmann's condition of creative loneliness is essentially a prerequisite for certain kinds of exhibitive query which issue in objects of the fine arts. Howard B. White defends privacy as necessary for the elaboration of assertive judgments concerning politics. Georg Simmel contends that secrecy is essential for the active query which devises new patterns of social relations. Finally, Sidney Jourard and the religious theorists hold that privacy is a necessary condition for query into the modes of human judgment themselves—the most comprehensive sort of philosophical or theological query, which Buchler does not discuss, but which is implied in his analysis of the other modes of judgment.

Thus, it is the category of query which unites the proposed uses of privacy. Most generally, one may seek privacy to increase his understanding of nature, culture, and society, to appreciate or create objects of beauty, to devise or experiment with modes of social relations, or to quest for apprehension of his existence. In each of these cases the claim is not made that all uses of privacy are necessarily moral. One may become an aesthete and renounce his responsibilities, seek understanding of how to construct better gas chambers, attempt to contrive effective propaganda, or become intoxicated with Being. The notion of query does, however, provide a reason why people regard highly the condition of privacy. They believe that it is essential if certain goods are to be realized through query. Further, the notion of query is helpful in understanding why privity, secrecy, and solitude are often treated in a similar fashion. Some kinds of query may be most effectively carried on by a small group, while others may be most suitably effected by a single person. Are people correct in believing that some kinds of query demand privacy for their proper conduct?

Part of the relationship between satisfying query and the condition of privacy can be explained simply by the consideration that most query demands undisturbed concentration. At least some kinds of information must be screened out if the person is to keep his mind on the task he has set for himself. All sorts of activities, from reflection on the consequences of a sales report to criticism of a philosophical argument, require that the person does not have other interests aroused by signals impinging from the outside. Thus, the condition of solitude is essential for the conduct of much query. More interesting are the reasons why secrecy or privity may be prerequisites for carrying on query. All of the components of query—contrivance, risk, a wide range of alternatives, and rigor of selection and choice—define this process as indefinite. Until the person is satisfied that query has resulted in an object which he wants to reveal to others, he will have good reasons to desire secrecy. First of all, if his product is incomplete he will not want others to waste their time judging it. Further, he will not want others to misjudge his capabilities and thereby prejudice them against his final product. The process of query issues in mistaken assertive judgments, ugly exhibitive judgments, and inharmonious active judgments, along the way. If these are allowed to die in secrecy or privity, social communion will be all the more probable. For example, a discussion is much more satisfying when the participants have thought out the problems beforehand than when they come unprepared and rehearse easily resolved difficulties before others. Also, the moral man presumably seeks to minimize the exposure of others to misunderstanding, ugliness, and conflict. Insofar as it is possible he will not burden his fellows with his inferior products. Of course, this does not mean that he will not call upon others for aid when they might help him in his query. Rather, he will recognize that others also have their projects and should not be disturbed without good reason. If, however, others seek to learn about his process of query, he may still have good reasons for maintaining secrecy. The dignity of the human being requires that he be judged only on the basis of those products he decides to make public so long as he is fulfilling his moral obligations. Of course, the person is obligated to maintain secrecy when the other desires information for immoral purposes.

In summary, query necessitates privacy because query demands concentration and implies incompletion and indefinition which may be remedied by the person or the small group. Query itself is justified so long as compelling assertive judgments, beautiful exhibitive judgments, tenable active judgments, and spiritual growth are part of the good life. The experimental nature of query demands that the burden of proof be placed on the person who would deny privacy to an individual who is ful-

     MICHAEL A. WEINSTEIN

filling his other moral obligations. Some minimum grant of privacy for each person is morally necessary if only because contemplation is a part of the good life. The human being who understands the full range of his consciousness will be more fit to participate as a full person in his social relations than one who does not have such knowledge. William Ernest Hocking stated the position best when he identified privacy with adventure: ". . . suppose a community which admits privacy for every member, thus adding to the prior common property the now-common property of privacy. In that case there is also added the possibility of making common the experience of the private adventure. The total scope of community is by so much the greater; without the common privacy, no one would have a good story to add to the common experience!"[26]

Phenomenologically, privacy is a condition of being-apart-from-others. It is voluntary limitation of communication to or from others for the purpose of undertaking activity in pursuit of a perceived good. Perhaps it is because privacy is a condition of being that so much of the discussion about it has been confused. A condition is not moral or valuable in itself. Rather, a condition is an opportunity for conducting an activity which may realize value in process or issue in a moral outcome. The two primal conditions of man are being-with-others and being-apart-from-others. Certain activities are possible in each; some activities are excluded in one or the other. There is no guarantee that being in the condition of privacy will result in valuable query. It is maintained that only in the condition of privacy can certain types of query, which may be valuable, go on. To say this, however, is to strictly distinguish privacy from alienation, loneliness, ostracism, isolation, and anonymity. In the interplay between public and private, private states may provide the preparation for communion just as public states may provide the means to spiritual experience.

[26] William Ernest Hocking, "Response to Professor Krikorian's Discussion," *Journal of Philosophy*, 55 (March 1958), 278.

# [14]

# California Law Review

VOL. 77            OCTOBER 1989            No. 5

## The Social Foundations of Privacy: Community and Self in the Common Law Tort

### Robert C. Post†

*In this Article Professor Post argues that the common law tort of inva-sion of privacy safeguards social norms, which he calls "rules of civility," that in significant measure constitute both individual and community identity. The tort is predicated upon the assumption that personality, as well as human dignity, are injured by the violation of these norms. Civility rules also create a "ritual idiom" that allows individuals to recognize and differentiate between respect and intimacy; fluency in this idiom enables individuals to become autonomous persons. In protecting civility rules, however, the law must transform social norms into workable legal doctrine, and it must determine the nature of the community whose norms it will preserve. Civility rules that control the dissemination of information con-flict with the prerequisites of the "public," which is a social formation cre-ated when persons, otherwise unrelated, are united by access to common social stimuli. Within the "public," communication is driven by a logic of accountability that is largely indifferent to norms of civility. The values of privacy, and the identity of persons and communities predicated upon those values, are thus endangered by the vast contemporary expansion of the public created by the mass media.*

---

Copyright © 1989 by Robert C. Post. All rights reserved.

   †   Professor of Law, Boalt Hall School of Law, University of California, Berkeley. A.B. 1969, Harvard College; J.D. 1977, Yale Law School; Ph.D. 1980, Harvard University. Many of the issues addressed in this manuscript stem from a seminar on the sociology of privacy that I was privileged to teach with Jerome Skolnick. His assistance and inspiration have been invaluable. I also want to acknowledge my profound debt to the advice and insights of Bruce Ackerman, Ed Baker, Melvin Eisenberg, Kristin Luker, Sheldon Messinger, Paul Mishkin, Hanna Pitkin, and Philip Selznick.

958                    CALIFORNIA LAW REVIEW                    [Vol. 77:957

## INTRODUCTION

Privacy is commonly understood as a value asserted by individuals against the demands of a curious and intrusive society.[1] Thus it is remarked that "[p]rivacy rests upon an individualist concept of society,"[2] and that one of "the main enemies of privacy in our own time" is "Community."[3] Consistent with this understanding, the function of the common law tort of invasion of privacy is usually said to be protecting the "subjective" interests of individuals against "injury to the inner person."[4] The stated purpose of the tort is to provide redress for "injury to [a] plaintiff's emotions and his mental suffering."[5]

The origins of the tort of invasion of privacy lie in a famous article on *The Right to Privacy* published in 1890 by Samuel Warren and Louis Brandeis.[6] Arguing powerfully for legal recognition of "the right to privacy, as a part of the more general right to the immunity of the person,— the right to one's personality,"[7] the article sparked the development of the modern tort,[8] which has now evolved into four distinct branches: unreasonable intrusion upon the seclusion of another,[9] unreasonable publicity given to another's private life,[10] appropriation of another's name or likeness,[11] and publicity that unreasonably places another in a false light

---

1. *See* T. EMERSON, THE SYSTEM OF FREEDOM OF EXPRESSION 549 (1970). For an excellent discussion and critique of this understanding, see Boone, *Privacy and Community,* 9 SOC. THEORY & PRAC. 1, 1-3, 14-21 (1983).

2. R. HIXSON, PRIVACY IN A PUBLIC SOCIETY: HUMAN RIGHTS IN CONFLICT at xv (1987); *see also* A. WESTIN, PRIVACY AND FREEDOM 27 (1967); Andre, *Privacy as an Aspect of the First Amendment: The Place of Privacy in a Society Dedicated to Individual Liberty,* 20 U. WEST L.A. L. REV. 87, 89 (1988-89).

3. B. MOORE, PRIVACY: STUDIES IN SOCIAL AND CULTURAL HISTORY 267 (1984). Or, conversely, it is said that "[p]rivacy means alienation" and hence impedes the attainment of "authentic community." Freeman & Mensch, *The Public-Private Distinction in American Law and Life,* 36 BUFFALO L. REV. 237, 238-39 (1987).

4. Emerson, *The Right of Privacy and Freedom of the Press,* 14 HARV. C.R.-C.L. L. REV. 329, 333 (1979).

5. Froelich v. Adair, 213 Kan. 357, 360, 516 P.2d 993, 997 (1973); *see also* Hazlitt v. Fawcett Publications, Inc., 116 F. Supp. 538, 544 (D. Conn. 1953).

6. Warren & Brandeis, *The Right to Privacy,* 4 HARV. L. REV. 193 (1890). The article "is perhaps the most famous and certainly the most influential law review article ever written." Nimmer, *The Right of Publicity,* 19 LAW & CONTEMP. PROBS. 203, 203 (1954). For a discussion of the historical circumstances surrounding the Warren and Brandeis article, see D. PEMBER, PRIVACY AND THE PRESS: THE LAW, THE MASS MEDIA, AND THE FIRST AMENDMENT 20-57 (1972).

7. Warren & Brandeis, *supra* note 6, at 207.

8. The tort is today recognized in one form or another in almost every jurisdiction in the nation. For a state-by-state overview, see LIBEL DEFENSE RESOURCE CENTER, 50-STATE SURVEY 1988: CURRENT DEVELOPMENTS IN MEDIA LIBEL AND INVASION OF PRIVACY LAW 924-67 (1988). The tort is still not recognized by English courts. J. FLEMING, THE LAW OF TORTS 572 (7th ed. 1987); *see also* W. PRATT, PRIVACY IN BRITAIN 16-17 (1979).

9. RESTATEMENT (SECOND) OF TORTS § 652B (1977).

10. *Id.* § 652D.

11. *Id.* § 652C.

before the public.[12]  In this essay I shall analyze the first two of these branches,[13] and attempt to demonstrate that the tort does not simply uphold the interests of individuals against the demands of community, but instead safeguards rules of civility that in some significant measure constitute both individuals and community.  The tort rests not upon a perceived opposition between persons and social life, but rather upon their interdependence.  Paradoxically, that very interdependence makes possible a certain kind of human dignity and autonomy which can exist only within the embrace of community norms.

Interpreted in this way, the common law tort of invasion of privacy offers a rich and complex apprehension of the texture of social life in America.  That apprehension is sensitive not merely to the prerogatives of social norms in defining persons and communities, but also to the limitations of those prerogatives when faced with competing demands from, for example, the requirements of public governance and accountability.

I

THE TORT OF INTRUSION: PRIVACY, CIVILITY,
AND THE SELF

The conceptual structure that underlies the branch of the tort which regulates unreasonable intrusion can be illuminated by consideration of an elementary case, *Hamberger v. Eastman.*[14]  *Eastman* was decided by the New Hampshire Supreme Court in 1964, and constituted the state's first official recognition of the tort of invasion of privacy.  I choose the case because it is so entirely unexceptional and representative in its reasoning and conclusions.  The plaintiffs were a husband and wife who alleged that the defendant, their landlord and neighbor, had installed an eavesdropping device in their bedroom.  The New Hampshire Supreme Court, adopting William Prosser's novel proposal that the tort of invasion of privacy be divided into four distinct branches,[15] characterized the plaintiffs' complaint as "the tort of intrusion upon the plaintiffs' solitude or seclusion."[16]

The plaintiffs alleged that as a result of the discovery of the eavesdropping device they were "greatly distressed, humiliated, and embarrassed," that they sustained "intense and severe mental suffering and

---

12.  *Id.* § 652E.

13.  I defer analysis of the "false light" branch because of its close affiliation with the tort of defamation; I similarly defer analysis of the appropriation branch because of its subtle and complex relationship with concepts of property rights in personal image.

14.  106 N.H. 107, 206 A.2d 239 (1964).

15.  *See* Prosser, *Privacy,* 48 CALIF. L. REV. 383, 389 (1960); *compare id. with* RESTATEMENT OF TORTS § 867 (1939).

16.  *Eastman,* 106 N.H. at 110, 206 A.2d at 241.

distress, and ha[d] been rendered extremely nervous and upset."[17] The New Hampshire Supreme Court had little difficulty in finding that, "by way of understatement," the type of intrusion suffered by the plaintiffs "would be offensive to any person of ordinary sensibilities."[18] It did not matter, said the court, that the plaintiffs could not establish that anyone ever "listened or overheard any sounds or voices originating from the plaintiffs' bedroom,"[19] since the gravamen of the plaintiffs' cause of action rested solely on the intrusive installation of the offensive device.

At first glance *Eastman* tells a rather simple story. "Marital bed-rooms," as the United States Supreme Court has had occasion to observe in the first of its modern constitutional right to privacy cases, are "sacred precincts,"[20] in which we expect privacy and into which it is plainly highly offensive to intrude.[21] An invasion of privacy is "an injury to personality. It impairs the mental peace and comfort of the individual and may produce suffering more acute than that produced by a mere bodily injury."[22] The plaintiffs in *Eastman* experienced just such "mental suffering," and the function of the tort is to provide redress for that injury.[23]

In all probability this story accurately reflects how the vast majority of judges and lawyers understand the tort of invasion of privacy. It is a story, however, that places an intense and narrow focus on the actual mental suffering of specific individuals. The limitations of this focus become apparent once it is understood that the eavesdropping device in *Eastman* was not defined as an invasion of privacy merely because the plaintiffs were in fact discomforted, but rather because the installation of the device was "offensive to any person of ordinary sensibilities."[24] In the later language of the second *Restatement of Torts*, the placement of the eavesdropping device was actionable because it "would be highly offensive to a reasonable person."[25]

---

17.  *Id.* at 109, 206 A.2d at 240.

18.  *Id.* at 111, 206 A.2d at 242.

19.  *Id.* at 112, 206 A.2d at 242.

20.  Griswold v. Connecticut, 381 U.S. 479, 485 (1965).

21.  For an historical account of the origins of these expectations, see W. RYBCZYNSKI, HOME: A SHORT HISTORY OF AN IDEA 15-49 (1986).

22.  *Eastman*, 106 N.H. at 112, 206 A.2d at 242 (quoting 3 R. POUND, JURISPRUDENCE 58 (1959)); *see also* Emerson, *supra* note 4, at 333; Wade, *The Communicative Torts and the First Amendment*, 47 MISS. L.J. 671, 707-08 (1977).

23.  "The action sounds in tort and when authorized is primarily to recover for a hurt to the feelings of the individual." Wheeler v. P. Sorensen Mfg. Co., 415 S.W.2d 582, 584 (Ky. 1967); *see also* Goodrich v. Waterbury Republican-Am., Inc., 188 Conn. 107, 128 n.19, 448 A.2d 1317, 1329 n.19 (1982); Froelich v. Adair, 213 Kan. 357, 362, 516 P.2d 993, 998 (1973); Billings v. Atkinson, 489 S.W.2d 858, 861 (Tex. 1973); Crump v. Beckley Newspapers, Inc., 320 S.E.2d 70, 87 (W. Va. 1984).

24.  *Eastman*, 106 N.H. at 111, 206 A.2d at 242.

25.  RESTATEMENT (SECOND) OF TORTS § 652B (1977). The *Restatement* provides that "[o]ne

The "reasonable person" is of course a figure who continually reappears in American common law, most especially in the law of torts. The important point about the reasonable person is that he is no one in particular; "[h]e is not to be identified with any real person."[26] He is rather, as a standard text would have it, "an abstraction," a representative of "the normal standard of community behavior," who embodies "the general level of moral judgment of the community, what it feels ought ordinarily to be done."[27] Thus in *Eastman* the installation of the eavesdropping device is transformed into an actionable invasion of privacy because the general level of moral judgment in the community finds it highly offensive for landlords and neighbors to spy on marital bedrooms. The *Eastman* court states that "[i]t is only where [an] intrusion has gone beyond the limits of decency that liability accrues."[28] The tort of invasion of privacy, we may thus conclude, is at least as concerned with policing these "limits of decency" as with redressing the mental distress of particular plaintiffs.

The *Restatement* characterizes these limits as those whose transgression would be "highly offensive." At first blush this notion of "offense" appears to describe the actual mental distress alleged to have been suffered by the *Eastman* plaintiffs. *Webster's Third New International Dictionary*, for example, defines "offensive" as that which gives "painful or unpleasant sensations" or causes "displeasure or resentment."[29] But the "displeasure" or "painful sensations" at issue in the *Eastman* case cannot be those of the plaintiffs, for their particular mental condition is not determinative of whether the installation of the eavesdropping device is an actionable invasion of privacy. So it must be the "reasonable person" who suffers. But that leaves us with something of an enigma, for the reasonable person is only a generic construct without real emotions.

For this reason, the pain or displeasure at issue cannot be understood as actual sensations or emotions. Because the reasonable person is not simply an empirical or statistical "average" of what most people in the community believe, the mental distress at issue also cannot be understood as a mere empirical or statistical prediction about what the majority of persons in a community would be likely to experience. Instead, because the reasonable person is a genuine instantiation of community norms, the concept of offensiveness at issue in *Eastman* must be understood as predicated upon a quality that inheres in such norms.

---

who intentionally intrudes, physically or otherwise, upon the solitude or seclusion of another or his private affairs or concerns, is subject to liability to the other for invasion of his privacy, if the intrusion would be highly offensive to a reasonable person." *Id.*

26. *Id.* § 283 comment c.

27. 2 F. HARPER & F. JAMES, THE LAW OF TORTS § 16.2 (1956).

28. *Eastman,* 106 N.H. at 111, 206 A.2d at 242.

29. WEBSTER'S THIRD NEW INTERNATIONAL DICTIONARY 1556 (unabr. 1986).

The dictionary suggests the nature of that quality when it states that the adjective 'offensive' "describes what is disagreeable or nauseating or painful because of outrage to taste and sensibilities or affronting insultingness."[30] The pain or displeasure associated with the offensive can be understood as flowing from this "outrage" or "affront." Outrage or affront, however, are ways of describing how it is appropriate to feel when certain social norms have been transgressed. Hence when the law asks whether the reasonable person would find certain invasions of privacy "highly offensive," it is not seeking merely to predict actual emotions, but rather to characterize those social norms whose violation would appropriately cause affront or outrage.

Thus a more precise characterization of the conceptual structure underlying *Eastman* is that a plaintiff is entitled to relief if it can be demonstrated that a defendant has transgressed the kind of social norms whose violation would properly be viewed with outrage or affront, and that the function of this relief is to redress "injury to personality." This legal structure typifies the tort of intrusion. It rests on the premise that the integrity of individual personality is dependent upon the observance of certain kinds of social norms.

This premise, of course, also underlies much of sociological thought. For purposes of analyzing the privacy tort, the most systematic and helpful explication of the premise may be found in the work of Erving Goffman. He most explicitly states the premise in his early article on *The Nature of Deference and Demeanor,* where he offers an image of social interactions as founded on rules of "deference and demeanor."[31] Rules of deference define conduct by which a person conveys appreciation "*to* a recipient or *of* this recipient, or of something of which this recipient is taken as a symbol, extension, or agent."[32] Rules of demeanor define conduct by which a person expresses "to those in his immediate presence that he is a person of certain desirable or undesirable qualities."[33]

Taken together, rules of deference and demeanor constitute "rules of conduct which bind the actor and the recipient together" and "are the bindings of society."[34] By following these rules, individuals not only confirm the social order in which they live, but they also establish and affirm "ritual" and "sacred" aspects of their own and others' identities.[35] Thus Goffman states that each "individual must rely on others to com-

---

30. *Id.*
31. E. GOFFMAN, *The Nature of Deference and Demeanor,* in INTERACTION RITUAL: ESSAYS ON FACE-TO-FACE BEHAVIOR 47, 47 (1967).
32. *Id.* at 56 (emphasis in original).
33. *Id.* at 77.
34. *Id.* at 90.
35. *Id.* at 91.

plete the picture of him of which he himself is allowed to paint only certain parts":

> Each individual is responsible for the demeanor image of himself and the deference image of others, so that for a complete man to be expressed, individuals must hold hands in a chain of ceremony, each giving deferentially with proper demeanor to the one on the right what will be received deferentially from the one on the left. While it may be true that the individual has a unique self all his own, evidence of this possession is thoroughly a product of joint ceremonial labor, the part expressed through the individual's demeanor being no more significant than the part conveyed by others through their deferential behavior toward him.[36]

According to Goffman, then, we must understand individual personality as *constituted* in significant aspects by the observance of rules of deference and demeanor; or, to return to the more prosaic language of *Eastman,* by the rules of decency recognized by the reasonable man.[37] Violation of these rules can thus damage a person by discrediting his identity and injuring his personality. Breaking "the chain of ceremony" can deny an individual the capacity to become "a complete man" and hence "disconfirm" his very "self."[38]

It is for this reason that the law regards the privacy tort as simultaneously upholding social norms and redressing "injury to personality." We must be clear, however, that in any particular case individuals may or may not have internalized pertinent rules of deference and demeanor, and hence may or may not suffer actual injury to personality. But the device of the reasonable person focuses the law not on actual injury to the personality of specific individuals, but rather on the protection of that personality which would be constituted by full observance of the relevant rules of deference and demeanor, those whose violation would appropriately cause outrage or affront. I shall call such rules "civility rules," and I shall call the personality that would be upheld by these civility rules "social personality."

The concept of social personality points simultaneously in two distinct directions. On the one hand, the actual personalities of well-socialized individuals should substantially conform to social personality, for such individuals have internalized the civility rules by which social personality is defined. It is for this reason that the tort of intrusion, even though formally defined in terms of the expectations of the "reasonable person," can in practice be expected to offer protection to the emotional

---

36. *Id.* at 84-85.

37. George Herbert Mead similarly argues that "[w]hat goes to make up the organized self is the organization of the attitudes which are common to the group. A person is a personality because he belongs to a community, because he takes over the institutions of that community into his own conduct." G.H. MEAD, MIND, SELF AND SOCIETY 162 (1934).

38. E. GOFFMAN, *supra* note 31, at 51.

well-being of real plaintiffs. But, on the other hand, social personality also subsists in a set of civility rules that, when taken together, give normative shape and substance to the society that shares them. In fact these rules can be said to define the very "community" which the "reasonable person" inhabits. They constitute the "special claims which members [of a community] have on each other, as distinct from others,"[39] and hence which create for a community "its distinctive shape, its unique identity."[40] Thus even if particular plaintiffs are not well-socialized and hence have not suffered actual injury because of a defendant's violation of civility rules, the law nevertheless endows such plaintiffs with the capacity to bring suit, thereby upholding the normative identity of the community inherent in the concept of social personality.

This interpretation of the tort explains what would otherwise be a puzzling aspect of its legal structure. Most torts require, as distinct elements of a prima facie case, allegation and proof that the violation of a relevant social norm has actually caused some form of harm or damage. For example, if you drive your car carelessly and have an accident, a lawsuit against you for negligence can succeed only if it establishes that your negligent behavior has actually caused some demonstrable injury.[41] The basic idea is "no harm, no foul." But the tort of invasion of privacy is qualitatively different because the injury at issue is logically entailed by, rather than merely contingently caused by, the improper conduct. An intrusion on privacy is *intrinsically* harmful because it is defined as that which injures social personality.

The profile of the invasion of privacy tort reflects this logical structure. In contrast to the usual cause of action for negligence, the privacy tort enables a plaintiff to make out his case without alleging or proving any actual or contingent injury, such as emotional suffering or embarrassment. The privacy tort shares this profile with other torts which redress "dignitary harms."[42] In the area of defamation, for example, where the law also seeks to uphold civility rules,[43] a plaintiff could at common law successfully prosecute a suit, and even receive substantial

---

39. J. GUSFIELD, COMMUNITY: A CRITICAL RESPONSE 29 (1975).

40. K. ERIKSON, WAYWARD PURITANS· A STUDY IN THE SOCIOLOGY OF DEVIANCE 11 (1966).

41. *See* RESTATEMENT (SECOND) OF TORTS § 328A (1977).

42. The phrase comes from Kalven, *Privacy in Tort Law—Were Warren and Brandeis Wrong?*, 31 LAW & CONTEMP. PROBS. 326, 341 (1966). Torts that redress dignitary harms share this structure with the larger category of "traditional intentional torts." *See* Givelber, *The Right to Minimum Social Decency and the Limits of Evenhandedness: Infliction of Emotional Distress by Outrageous Conduct,* 82 COLUM. L. REV. 42, 49-50 (1982). For a roughly analogous distinction between "damage" torts and "interference" torts, see F.H. LAWSON, *"Das subjektive Recht" in the English Law of Torts,* in 1 MANY LAWS: SELECTED ESSAYS 176-92 (1977).

43. Post, *The Social Foundations of Defamation Law: Reputation and the Constitution,* 74 CALIF. L. REV. 691, 707-19 (1986).

sums in "general damages," despite a defendant's credible proof that the plaintiff had suffered no actual or contingent injury whatever.[44] In their 1890 article, Warren and Brandeis conceived of the "remedies for an invasion of the right of privacy" as analogous to "those administered in the law of defamation."[45] In 1939 the first *Restatement of Torts* stated flatly that damages in a privacy action "can be awarded in the same way in which general damages are given for defamation."[46] In its second edition the *Restatement* was somewhat more circumspect,[47] stating:

> One who has established a cause of action for invasion of his privacy is entitled to recover damages for
>
> > (a) the harm to his interest in privacy resulting from the invasion;
> >
> > (b) his mental distress proved to have been suffered if it is of a kind that normally results from such an invasion; and
> >
> > (c) special damage of which the invasion is a legal cause.[48]

The *Restatement* thus enables a plaintiff to maintain a suit, and even to receive damages, because of harm to an "interest in privacy," notwithstanding the absence of allegations or proof of actual injury, such as mental distress. This in effect renders the invasion of privacy tort theoretically independent of any merely empirical or contingent consequences of the violation of the underlying civility rule.[49] The most plausible interpretation of this legal structure is that the *Restatement* has empowered plaintiffs to use the tort to uphold the interests of social personality, which are *necessarily* impaired by a defendant's breach of a civility rule.

The strength of this conclusion, however, should be qualified somewhat because of the paucity of reported decisions on point. I have been able to locate only a very few decisions where plaintiffs have been unable or unwilling to present any evidence of actual injury. But in those few cases courts have followed the implications of the *Restatement's* analysis

---

44. *See id.* at 697-98. In 1974 in Gertz v. Robert Welch, Inc., 418 U.S. 323, 348-50 (1974), the United States Supreme Court held that the first amendment sharply limits awards of such general damages, although in a recent decision the Court has somewhat loosened these constitutional restrictions. *See* Dun & Bradstreet, Inc. v. Greenmoss Builders, Inc., 472 U.S. 749, 753-61 (1985).

45. Warren & Brandeis, *supra* note 6, at 219.

46. RESTATEMENT OF TORTS § 867 comment d (1939).

47. The circumspection was no doubt due to the Supreme Court's recent constitutional decision in *Gertz, discussed at supra* note 44; *see also* RESTATEMENT (SECOND) OF TORTS § 652H comment c (1977). (Query, however, the impact of the Court's subsequent decision in *Dun & Bradstreet.*) Because the tort of intrusion does not involve speech, it is not subject to the kind of first amendment limitations imposed by *Gertz.*

48. RESTATEMENT (SECOND) OF TORTS § 652H (1977).

49. Thus in the tort of intrusion the *Restatement* provides that a plaintiff can recover damages for the violation of his "interest in privacy," which means "the deprivation of his seclusion." *Id.* § 652H comment a.

966 *CALIFORNIA LAW REVIEW* [Vol. 77:957

and awarded damages,[50] even if only nominal.[51]

The minuscule number of such decisions is itself instructive, however, for it indicates that as a practical matter virtually every plaintiff will allege and be able to produce some credible evidence of contingent and actual injury in the form of emotional suffering. The very credibility of this evidence suggests how dependent our personalities in fact are upon the observance of civility rules, and hence confirms the close congruence between social personality and the actual individual personalities of those who use the legal system. The strength of this congruence is illustrated by the confidence with which we instinctively feel the plausibility of the emotional suffering alleged by plaintiffs in the *Eastman* case, even though we have absolutely no empirical knowledge of who those plaintiffs really are. This confidence can be grounded only on the almost irresistible assumption that the personalities of those plaintiffs have been forged by the same rules of civility as have shaped our own personalities.

The privacy tort thus represents a complex pattern in which legal interventions supportive of general rules of civility occur at the behest of specific aggrieved individuals. This pattern can be viewed as an attempt to disperse enforcement authority. In contrast to the criminal law, in which all power to prosecute infractions of important legal norms is concentrated in the hands of accountable public officials, the privacy tort devolves the authority of enforcement into the hands of private litigants. But concomitant with this decentralization—or perhaps because of it— the privacy tort is also concerned with the specific interests of those plaintiffs who take the trouble to bring violators of civility rules before adjudicative tribunals. This concern is particularly visible in how the tort is structured to redress the claims of those who have suffered actionable injuries.

We may roughly distinguish between two kinds of plaintiff interests. The first arises because of contingent psychological injuries that plaintiffs may suffer as a result of the violation of civility rules. Mental anguish and humiliation are examples of such injuries that are common and routine. But so are more exotic forms of damage. In *Eastman,* for example, the husband alleged that the discovery of the eavesdropping device in his bedroom had rendered him impotent; his wife alleged that she had been

---

50. *See, e.g.,* Socialist Workers Party v. Attorney General, 642 F. Supp. 1357, 1417-23 (S.D.N.Y. 1986).

51. *See, e.g.,* Manville v. Borg-Warner Corp., 418 F.2d 434, 437 (10th Cir. 1969); Cason v. Baskin, 159 Fla. 31, 41, 30 So. 2d 635, 640 (1947); S. HOFSTADTER & G. HOROWITZ, THE RIGHT OF PRIVACY 265-68 (1964). *But see* Brents v. Morgan, 221 Ky. 765, 774-75, 299 S.W. 967, 971-72 (1927); Hazlitt v. Fawcett Publications, Inc., 116 F. Supp. 538, 544 (D. Conn. 1953). In negligence actions, by way of contrast, awards of nominal damages are not permitted, because a plaintiff can succeed only if he demonstrates actual injury. RESTATEMENT (SECOND) OF TORTS § 907 comment a (1977).

made frigid. Although these injuries are idiosyncratic, they nevertheless deserve redress, and the tort is structured to provide that redress.[52]

The second kind of interest arises from the dignitary harm which plaintiffs suffer as a result of having been treated disrespectfully. Violations of civility rules are intrinsically demeaning, even if not experienced as such by a particular plaintiff.[53] This is because dignitary harm does not depend on the psychological condition of an individual plaintiff, but rather on the forms of respect that a plaintiff is entitled to receive from others.[54] We need to ask how the law can provide redress for the dignitary harm which results when these forms of respect are, in important ways, violated.

The answer can perhaps be found in those not infrequent cases where juries use the pretext of "psychic and emotional harm" to return "large verdicts, although little objective evidence is available"[55] to support them.[56] The *Restatement* shrewdly characterizes such damages as "vindicating" a plaintiff:

> [F]or certain types of dignitary torts, the law serves the purpose of vindicating the injured party. Thus, in suits for defamation [or] invasion of privacy . . . the major purpose of the suit may be to obtain a public declaration that the plaintiff is right and was improperly treated. This is more than a simple determination of legal rights for which nominal damages may be sufficient, and will normally require compensatory or punitive damages.[57]

The *Restatement's* conclusion that large damage awards which are

---

52. There is, however, a limit to the idiosyncrasies that the law will recognize. The *Restatement* notes, for example, that a plaintiff may "recover damages for emotional distress or personal humiliation that he proves to have been actually suffered by him, *if it is of a kind that normally results from such an invasion and it is normal and reasonable in its extent.*" RESTATEMENT (SECOND) OF TORTS § 652H comment b (1977) (emphasis added). Apparently the law will not tolerate too great a divergence between social and individual personality.

53. The formulation of this point is a bit tricky, because often the question of whether a civility rule has been violated depends upon the subjective attitude of a plaintiff. For example, if the eavesdropping device in *Eastman* had been placed with the consent of the plaintiffs, we would not understand the defendant as having transgressed a civility rule, but rather as having entered into some mutual, erotic relationship with the plaintiffs. The point in the text, however, is that if the placement of the device has broken a civility rule—if, for example, the plaintiffs in *Eastman* had been unaware of its installation—then the plaintiffs would have been demeaned regardless of their subjective apprehension.

54. *Cf.* Feinberg, *The Nature and Value of Rights,* 4 J. VALUE INQUIRY 243, 252 (1970):
> [R]espect for persons . . . may simply be respect for their rights, so that there cannot be the one without the other; and what is called 'human dignity' may simply be the recognizable capacity to assert claims. To respect a person, then, or to think of him as possessed of human dignity, simply *is* to think of him as a potential maker of claims.

55. Vassiliades v. Garfinckel's, Brooks Bros., 492 A.2d 580, 594 (D.C. 1985).

56. On the issue of "excessive" damage awards, see, for example, LIBEL DEF. RESOURCE BULL., No. 11, Summer-Fall 1984, at 12-18; *Socking It to the Press,* EDITOR & PUBLISHER, Apr. 7, 1984, at 31.

57. RESTATEMENT (SECOND) OF TORTS § 901 comment c (1977).

968                    *CALIFORNIA LAW REVIEW*                    [Vol. 77:957

seemingly unrelated to any contingent harm represent a form of vindication is an informed and convincing interpretation.[58] To say that the plaintiff in an invasion of privacy suit requires vindication, however, is to imply that he is somehow in need of exoneration. But this implication is puzzling, for the plaintiff has been the victim, not the perpetrator, of a transgression. The shame of the victim, however, is made explicable by the fact that he has been denied respect, and consequently his status as a person to whom respect is due has been called into question.

The victim of the breach of a civility rule, in other words, suffers a special kind of injury: He is "threatened" with being "discredited"[59] because he has been excluded from the "chain of ceremony" which establishes the respect normally accorded to full-fledged members of the community. Since the boundaries of a community are marked by the "special claims which members have on each other, as distinct from others,"[60] the defendant's disregard of the plaintiff's claim to be treated with respect potentially places the plaintiff outside of the bounds of the shared community. The plaintiff can accordingly be vindicated only by being reaffirmed as a member of the community. It is plausible to interpret the seemingly excessive damages that sometimes characterize invasion of privacy actions as such an affirmation, which occurs through the simultaneous enrichment of the plaintiff and the punishment of the defendant.[61] The privacy tort, in other words, functions not merely to uphold the chain of ceremony, but also, in appropriate cases, to reforge it when it has been fractured.

## II
### PRIVACY AND CIVILITY: SOME THEORETICAL IMPLICATIONS

We have come a long way, then, from the first simple story we were able to tell about the *Eastman* case. The underlying structure of the privacy tort is as much oriented toward safeguarding rules of civility and the chain of ceremony they establish, as it is toward protecting the emotional well-being of individuals. This understanding of the tort has several important theoretical implications, both for the concept of privacy and for the functioning of the law.

---

58. In the area of defamation, for example, the punishment of a defendant through the exaction of high civil damages can be interpreted as the law's attempt to "vindicate" a plaintiff's honor. *See* Post, *supra* note 43, at 703-06.

59. E. GOFFMAN, *supra* note 31, at 51.

60. J. GUSFIELD, *supra* note 39, at 29.

61. On the relationship between punishment and vindication, see Post, *supra* note 43, at 704-05.

A.  *The Normative Nature of Privacy: The Reconciliation of
    Community and Autonomy*

Consider first the concept of privacy that underlies the tort. It is obviously quite different from the "neutral concept of privacy"[62] which some commentators have proposed, and which attempts to define privacy in purely descriptive and value-free terms. Ruth Gavison, for example, has defined privacy as a gradient that varies in three dimensions: secrecy, anonymity, and solitude. She believes that an individual's loss of privacy can be objectively measured "as others obtain information" about him, "pay attention to him, or gain access to him."[63] The presence or absence of privacy is thus a fact capable of ascertainment without regard to normative social conventions.

A "neutral" concept of privacy has certain obvious advantages and uses. It is useful, for example, in the cross-cultural analysis of privacy, because it creates an object of analysis that is independent of the various perceptions of the cultures at issue. It is also useful for efforts to create a functional account of privacy. The hypothesis that "privacy" is necessary to cause certain consequences will be cleaner and more easily verifiable if the "privacy" at issue is conceived as a measurable fact. Thus Robert Merton rests his claim that privacy "is an important functional requirement for the effective operation of social structure" on the neutral definition of privacy as "insulation from observability."[64] Privacy is necessary, argues Merton, because without it "the pressure to live up to the details of all (and often conflicting) social norms would become literally unbearable; in a complex society, schizophrenic behavior would become the rule rather than the formidable exception it already is."[65]

Whatever the virtue of such neutral definitions of privacy, they are most certainly not at the foundation of the common law, which rests instead upon a concept of privacy that is inherently normative. The privacy protected by the common law tort cannot be reduced to objective facts like spatial distance or information or observability; it can only be understood by reference to norms of behavior. A defendant who stands very close to a plaintiff in a crowded elevator will not be perceived to have committed a highly offensive intrusion; but the case will be very different if the defendant stands the same distance away from a plaintiff in an open field. In the common law, as in everyday life, issues of privacy refer to the characterization of human action, not to the neutral and objective measurement of the world.

Thus the sphere of privacy protected by the tort can only be per-

---

62.  Gavison, *Privacy and the Limits of Law,* 89 YALE L.J. 421, 425-40 (1980).

63.  *Id.* at 428.

64.  R. MERTON, SOCIAL THEORY AND SOCIAL STRUCTURE 429 (1968).

65.  *Id.*

ceived through the exercise of what Simmel calls "moral tact."[66] Gavison argues that privacy defined in terms of social norms "is simply a conclusion, not a tool to analyze whether a certain invasion should be considered wrong in the first place."[67] But in the end this objection simply highlights that the common law attempts not to search out and articulate first ethical principles, as would a certain kind of moral philosopher, but instead to discover and refresh the social norms by which we live, the very norms that to Gavison provide only the starting point for respectable critique.

Civility rules of course protect dignitary interests other than those of privacy. But because the common law has not attempted to define "privacy" in the neutral manner advocated by Gavison, it has on the whole been almost indifferent to any systematic effort to distinguish between those civility rules which protect privacy and those which safeguard other dignitary interests. For this reason the single act of a defendant will often be the basis for a lawsuit alleging various kinds of dignitary harms, ranging from invasion of privacy, to defamation, and to the intentional infliction of emotional distress.[68]

The common law attempts to distinguish privacy from other forms of social respect primarily through the specification of the formal elements of the privacy tort. The formal elements of the branch of privacy law known as "intrusion," the precise privacy law tort at issue in *Eastman,* require a plaintiff to allege that a defendant has intentionally intruded upon the plaintiff's solitude or seclusion in a manner that would be highly offensive to a reasonable person.[69] The formal elements of the tort of intentional infliction of emotional distress, on the other hand, require a plaintiff to allege that a defendant has, by means of extreme and outrageous conduct, intentionally caused the plaintiff severe emotional distress.[70]

Obviously these elements overlap substantially, and it is not surprising that plaintiffs will frequently allege both intrusion and intentional infliction of emotional distress.[71] But the elements of the two torts are

---

66. G. SIMMEL, THE SOCIOLOGY OF GEORG SIMMEL 324 (K. Wolff trans. & ed. 1950).

67. Gavison, *supra* note 62, at 426 n.18.

68. For a recent and notorious example in which all three torts were alleged, see Hustler Magazine v. Falwell, 108 S. Ct. 876, 878 (1988). For a more typical case, see Sawabini v. Desenberg, 143 Mich. App. 373, 372 N.W.2d 559 (Ct. App. 1985). For a statistical study of pleading practices with respect to dignitary torts, see Mead, *Suing Media for Emotional Distress: A Multi-Method Analysis of Tort Law Evolution,* 23 WASHBURN L.J. 24, 36-44 (1983).

69. RESTATEMENT (SECOND) OF TORTS § 652B (1977), *quoted at supra* note 25.

70. *Id.* § 46. Although the tort of intentional infliction of emotional distress requires, as a formal matter, allegation and proof of contingent emotional injury, "the tort . . . in practice tends to reduce to a single element—the outrageousness of the defendant's conduct." Givelber, *supra* note 42, at 42-43.

71. *See, e.g.,* Galella v. Onassis, 353 F. Supp. 196 (S.D.N.Y. 1972), *aff'd in part and rev'd in*

logically distinct, for the intrusion tort focuses narrowly on policing what Simmel calls that "ideal sphere [which] lies around every human being" and which "cannot be penetrated, unless the personality value of the individual is thereby destroyed,"[72] whereas the tort of intentional infliction of emotional distress focuses upon preventing the intentional violation of civility rules for the purpose of causing harm to the personality. Thus the latter tort prohibits evil intentions, while the former guards against the penetration of private space. But this formal distinction is less helpful than it might appear, for the penetration of private space is often not "highly offensive" unless perpetrated with improper intent,[73] and so the boundary between the two torts is obscured.

That the common law lives comfortably with such ambiguity is evidence that it is primarily interested in maintaining the forms of respect deemed essential for social life, and relatively indifferent to whether particular forms of respect should be denominated as "privacy." Certain kinds of respect are in ordinary discourse understood to be concerned with privacy, and the common law roughly incorporates this understanding into the formal elements of the privacy tort. But the common law makes no great effort systematically to analyze that understanding so as to isolate the "private" as a distinct object of protection.

The intrusion branch of the privacy tort has intuitively obvious connections to ordinary understandings of privacy. Certainly in common usage a basic meaning of privacy is that of a private space, like a bathroom or a home, from which others may be excluded.[74] The forms of respect that underlie such spaces are well displayed by Erving Goffman in his essay on *The Territories of the Self.*[75] Goffman defines a territory as a "field of things" or a "preserve" to which an individual can claim "entitlement to possess, control, use, or dispose of."[76] Territories are defined not by neutral, objective factors, like feet or inches, but instead

---

part, 487 F.2d 986 (2d Cir. 1973); Fletcher v. Florida Publishing Co., 319 So. 2d 100 (Fla. Dist. Ct. App. 1975), rev'd, 340 So. 2d 914 (Fla. 1976), cert. denied, 431 U.S. 930 (1977); Pemberton v. Bethlehem Steel Corp., 66 Md. App. 133, 502 A.2d 1101 (Ct. Spec. App.), cert. denied, 306 Md. 289, 508 A.2d 488, cert. denied, 479 U.S. 984 (1986); Nader v. General Motors Corp., 25 N.Y.2d 560, 255 N.E.2d 765, 307 N.Y.S.2d 647 (1970); Mead, supra note 68, at 49.

72. G. SIMMEL, supra note 66, at 321.

73. See, e.g., Housh v. Peth, 165 Ohio St. 35, 40-41, 133 N.E.2d 340, 343 (1956) (violation of right to privacy where defendant acted "willfully or intentionally for the purpose of producing mental anguish and pain").

74. As Joel Feinberg notes:

The root idea in the generic concept of privacy is that of a privileged territory or domain in which an individual person has the exclusive authority of determining whether another may enter, and if so, when and for how long, and under what conditions. Within this area, the individual person is—pick your metaphor—boss, sovereign, owner.

J. FEINBERG, OFFENSE TO OTHERS 24 (1985) (citation omitted).

75. E. GOFFMAN, *The Territories of the Self,* in RELATIONS IN PUBLIC: MICROSTUDIES OF THE PUBLIC ORDER 28 (1971).

76. *Id.* at 28-29.

are contextual. Their boundaries have a "socially determined variability" and depend upon such "factors as local population density, purpose of the approacher, . . . character of the social occasion, and so forth."[77]

That territories are defined by normative and social factors, as opposed to "neutral" or "objective" criteria, is well illustrated by the recent case of *Huskey v. National Broadcasting Co.,*[78] in which Arnold Huskey, a prisoner at the United States Penitentiary at Marion, Illinois, sued NBC because its cameras had filmed him while in the prison's "exercise cage," a room roughly twenty-five feet by thirty feet with a concrete floor and surrounding fence. Huskey was wearing only gym shorts, leaving several distinctive tattoos exposed. Huskey claimed that NBC had intruded on his seclusion, because he had expected that "the only ones able to see him would be persons 'to whom he might be exposed as a necessary result of his incarceration': the guard assigned to watch him, other prison personnel and other inmates."[79] NBC argued that it could not "be held liable for intrusion upon Huskey's seclusion because he was not secluded"; the exercise cage was " 'open to view and used by other prisoners.' "[80]

The court refused to accept the "neutral" fact of Huskey's visibility as determinative of the territory from which he could rightfully exclude others:

> Huskey's visibility to some people does not strip him of the right to remain secluded from others. Persons are exposed to family members and invited guests in their own homes, but that does not mean they have opened the door to television cameras. Prisons are largely closed systems, within which prisoners may become understandably inured to the gaze of staff and other prisoners, while at the same time feeling justifiably secluded from the outside world (at least in certain areas not normally visited by outsiders).[81]

The court concluded that the success of Huskey's claim would have to await further development of the factual record regarding the actual customs and usages of the exercise cage. These customs and usages, not the "objective" facts of visibility, secrecy, anonymity, and solitude, defined the territory in which Huskey could legally claim the right to undisturbed "seclusion."

Goffman's central and profound point is that territories, defined in this normative way, are a vehicle for the exchange of meaning; they serve

---

77. *Id.* at 31, 40. Goffman makes clear that the conduct of the individual claiming the territory is also relevant to the social recognition of the territory. *Id.* at 41-44.

78. 632 F. Supp. 1282 (N.D. Ill. 1986).

79. *Id.* at 1285 (quoting the Complaint at ¶ 9).

80. *Id.* at 1287 (quoting Respondent NBC's Memorandum at 8).

81. *Id.* at 1288.

as a kind of language, a "ritual idiom,"[82] through which persons communicate with one another. We indicate respect for a person by acknowledging his territory; conversely, we invite intimacy by waiving our claims to a territory and allowing others to draw close. An embrace, for example, can signify human compassion or desire, but if it is unwelcome it can instead be experienced as a demeaning indignity.[83] The identical physical action can have these two very different meanings only because its significance is constituted by the norms of respect which define personal space. It is characteristic of "territories of the self" to be used in this "dual way, with comings-into-touch avoided as a means of maintaining respect and engaged in as a means of establishing regard."[84]

Goffman's analysis suggests that by lending authoritative sanction to the territories of the self, the tort of intrusion performs at least three distinct functions. First, it safeguards the respect due individuals by virtue of their territorial claims.[85] Second, it maintains the language or "ritual idiom" constituted by territories, thus conserving the particular meanings carried by that language. Third, the tort preserves the ability of individuals to speak through the idiom of territories, and this ability, as Goffman notes,

> is somehow central to the subjective sense that the individual has concerning his selfhood, his ego, the part of himself with which he identifies his positive feelings. And here the issue is not whether a preserve is exclusively maintained, or shared, or given up entirely, but rather the role the individual is allowed in determining what happens to his claim.[86]

An individual's ability to press or to waive territorial claims, his ability to choose respect or intimacy, is deeply empowering for his sense of himself as an independent or autonomous person. As Jeffrey Reiman has noted, "[p]rivacy is an essential part of the complex social practice by means of which the social group recognizes—and communicates to the individ-

---

82. E. GOFFMAN, *supra* note 75, at 60.

83. *See* Craker v. Chicago & N.W. Ry., 36 Wis. 657, 660 (1875) (railroad company liable for the "indignity" of the unsolicited advances of conductor).

84. E. GOFFMAN, *supra* note 75, at 60-61. For commentators making a similar point, see C. FRIED, AN ANATOMY OF VALUES: PROBLEMS OF PERSONAL AND SOCIAL CHOICE 142 (1970); Rachels, *Why Privacy is Important,* 4 PHIL. & PUB. AFF. 323, 327-29 (1975).

85. Since such respect is constitutive of the self, it is not surprising to find the early cases describing privacy norms in the language of "natural law":

> The right of privacy has its foundation in the instincts of nature. It is recognized intuitively, consciousness being the witness that can be called to establish its existence. Any person whose intellect is in a normal condition recognizes at once that as to each individual member of society there are matters private and there are matters public so far as the individual is concerned. Each individual as instinctively resents any encroachment by the public upon his rights which are of a private nature as he does the withdrawal of those of his rights which are of a public nature. A right of privacy in matters purely private is therefore derived from natural law.

Pavesich v. New England Life Ins. Co., 122 Ga. 190, 194, 50 S.E. 68, 69-70 (1905).

86. E. GOFFMAN, *supra* note 75, at 60.

ual—that his existence is his own. And this is a precondition of personhood."[87]

There is now a fierce debate in law and political philosophy between, speaking roughly, liberals and communitarians.[88] The former stress those aspects of the self which are independent and autonomous, the latter emphasize those aspects which are embedded in social norms and values. In the intrusion tort, however, this debate is miraculously transcended, for the tort presides over precisely those social norms which enable an autonomous self to emerge.

Some norms, like those prohibiting murder, cannot be waived by the consent of individuals. But the norms policed by the intrusion tort are different. They mark the boundaries that distinguish respect from intimacy, and their very ability to serve this function depends upon their capacity for being enforced or waived in appropriate circumstances. In the power to make such personal choices inheres the very essence of the independent self. This mysterious fusion of civility and autonomy lies at the heart of the intrusion tort.[89]

### B. The Legal Enforcement of Civility Rules: Hegemony and Community

Our analysis so far has assumed that the common law incorporates civility rules from society in some relatively unproblematic way. The assumption reflects the common law's understanding of its own project. The elements of intrusion require it to enforce rules of civility as perceived by the "reasonable person," who is meant to embody "the general level of moral judgment of the community." The discernment and application of these civility rules is in general entrusted to a jury, which is a randomly selected group of persons designed to be representative of the community.[90] The prevailing image is that of a legal system transpar-

---

87. Reiman, *Privacy, Intimacy, and Personhood,* 6 PHIL. & PUB. AFF. 26, 39 (1976).

88. For an overview of this debate, see Gutmann, *Communitarian Critics of Liberalism,* 14 PHIL. & PUB. AFF. 308 (1985); Thigpen & Downing, *Liberalism and the Communitarian Critique,* 31 AM. J. POL. SCI. 637 (1987); Wallach, *Liberals, Communitarians, and the Tasks of Political Theory,* 15 POL. THEORY 581 (1987); Note, *A Communitarian Defense of Group Libel Laws,* 101 HARV. L. REV. 682, 689-92 (1988).

89. That fusion has been well captured by Edward Shils:

Intrusions on privacy are baneful because they interfere with an individual in his disposition of what belongs to him. The "social space" around an individual . . . *belong[s]* to him. He does not acquire [it] through purchase or inheritance. He possesses [it] and is entitled to possess [it] by virtue of the charisma which is inherent in his existence as an individual soul—as we say nowadays, in his individuality—and which is inherent in his membership in the civil community. [It] belong[s] to him by virtue of his humanity and civility. A society that claims to be both humane and civil is committed to [its] respect. When its practice departs from that respect, it also departs to that degree from humanity and civility.

Shils, *Privacy: Its Constitution and Vicissitudes,* 31 LAW & CONTEMP. PROBS. 281, 306 (1966) (emphasis in original).

90. On the distinction between judge and jury with respect to the discernment and application

ently reflecting community norms.

This image, however, requires three important qualifications. First, social life is thick with territorial norms that contribute substantially to "the concrete density and vitality of interaction."[91] For obvious reasons, however, the common law can maintain only a small subset of these norms. The law itself claims to enforce only the most important of them, only those whose breach would be "highly offensive." This selection criterion serves the interest of legal institutions, which otherwise would be inundated with trivial lawsuits. It also, and somewhat less obviously, preserves the flexibility and vitality of social life, which undoubtedly would be hardened and otherwise altered for the worse if every indiscretion could be transformed into formal legal action.

Second, the legal system must translate civility rules into workable legal doctrine. The complex, tacit, and contextual territorial principles described by Goffman must be stiffened into the relatively clear, explicit, and precise elements of a formal cause of action. This transmutation is captured by Paul Bohannan's notion of "*double* institutionalization," which means that the law must domesticate general social norms so that they are compatible with the needs and functioning of the legal system.[92] Civility rules must thus assume the character of legal doctrine; they must be formulated according to the logic of the rule of law, which means that they must be articulated in such a way "that people will be able to be guided by [them]."[93] They must be capable of generating rules of precedent to constrain future judicial decisions. These transformations imply that legal doctrine is often, as Bohannan puts it, "out of phase with society."[94] If the objective of the law is to shape and alter social norms, this

---

of community norms, see Post, *Defaming Public Officials: On Doctrine and Legal History,* 1987 AM. B. FOUND. RES. J. 539, 552-54.

91. G. SIMMEL, *supra* note 66, at 323.

92. Bohannan states:

Customs are norms or rules . . . about the ways in which people must behave if social institutions are to perform their tasks and society is to endure. All institutions (including legal institutions) develop customs. Some customs, in some societies, are *re*institutionalized at another level: they are restated for the more precise purposes of legal institutions. When this happens, therefore, law may be regarded as a custom that has been restated in order to make it amenable to the activities of the legal institutions.

Bohannan, *The Differing Realms of the Law,* 67 AM. ANTHROPOLOGIST 33, 35-36 (1965) (emphasis in original).

93. J. RAZ, *The Rule of Law and Its Virtue,* in THE AUTHORITY OF LAW 210, 213 (1979).

94. Bohannan, *supra* note 92, at 37. Bohannan notes:

Indeed, the more highly developed the legal institutions, the greater the lack of phase, which not only results from the constant reorientation of the primary institutions, but also is magnified by the very dynamic of the legal institutions themselves.

Thus, it is the very nature of law, and its capacity to 'do something about' the primary social institutions, that creates the lack of phase. . . . It is the fertile dilemma of law that it must always be out of step with society, but that people must always (because they work better with fewer contradictions, if for no other reason) attempt to reduce the lack of phase. Custom must either grow to fit the law or it must actively reject it; law must either

tension between law and custom is desirable. But if the law's purpose is to maintain social norms, as is manifestly the case for the common law tort of intrusion, this dissonance works against the very rationale of the law.

Third, and most important, it is something of a fiction to speak of a single, homogeneous community within a nation as large and diverse as the United States. There is every reason to expect that civility rules regarding privacy will differ "among communities, between generations, and among ethnic, religious, or other social groups, as well as among individuals."[95] It is said, for example, that Warren and Brandeis wrote their famous article because Warren, a genuine Boston Brahmin, was outraged that common newspapers had had the effrontery to report on his private entertainments.[96] As such the class content of the privacy norms advanced by the article is plain.[97] That content is also explicit in the writings of E. L. Godkin, which Warren and Brandeis cite with approval. Godkin characterized privacy as "one of the luxuries of civilization, which is not only unsought for but unknown in primitive or barbarous societies."[98] He illustrated the social consequences of the point by reciting the

> story of the traveller in the hotel in the Western mining town, who pinned a shirt across his open window to screen himself from the loafers on the piazza while performing his toilet; after a few minutes he saw it drawn aside roughly by a hand from without, and on asking what it meant, a voice answered, 'We want to know what there is so darned private going on in there?' The loafers resented his attempts at seclusion in

---

> grow to fit the custom, or it must ignore or suppress it. It is in these very interstices that social growth and social decay take place.

*Id.* (citation omitted).

95. Anderson v. Fisher Broadcasting Co., 300 Or. 452, 461, 712 P.2d 803, 809 (1986). " '"Class, occupation, education, and status within various communities and organizations may significantly affect the way in which an individual thinks of himself as a 'private' individual and what he understands by 'the moral right to privacy.' "' " *Id.* at 461 n.8, 712 P.2d at 809 n.8 (quoting Zimmerman, *Requiem for a Heavyweight: A Farewell to Warren and Brandeis's Privacy Tort,* 68 Cornell L. Rev. 291, 349 n.304 (1983), quoting Velecky, *The Concept of Privacy,* in PRIVACY 25 (J. Young ed. 1983)).

96. A. MASON, BRANDEIS: A FREE MAN'S LIFE 70 (1956).

97. "The Warren-Brandeis proposal was essentially a rich man's plea to the press to stop its gossiping and snooping . . . ." D. PEMBER, *supra* note 6, at 23. In the classic tones of the beleaguered aristocrat, Warren and Brandeis complain:

> The press is overstepping in every direction the obvious bounds of propriety and of decency. Gossip is no longer the resource of the idle and of the vicious, but has become a trade, which is pursued with industry as well as effrontery. To satisfy a prurient taste the details of sexual relations are spread broadcast in the columns of the daily papers. To occupy the indolent, column upon column is filled with idle gossip, which can only be procured by intrusion upon the domestic circle.

Warren & Brandeis, *supra* note 6, at 196.

98. Godkin, *The Rights of the Citizen: To His Own Reputation,* SCRIBNER'S MAG., July 1890, at 58, 65.

their own rude way . . . .[99]

Godkin's story is plainly meant to demonstrate the class basis of privacy norms. In a world in which privacy norms are heterogeneous, however, the common law must choose which norms to enforce. It must pick sides in the confrontation between the traveller and the loafers. And this choice cannot be avoided by an appeal to the judgment of the "reasonable person," for it must first be determined to which community the reasonable person belongs.

In defamation law, the question of which community the law will serve is explicitly thematized as a doctrinal issue. Some courts have said that the law will uphold the values of "a considerable and respectable class in the community";[100] others have adopted the perspective of " 'right-thinking persons.' "[101] But this question is not explicitly addressed in the doctrine of the more recent tort of invasion of privacy, which speaks only in the majestic and abstract accents of the "reasonable person." Thus the civility rules recognized by the common law tort of intrusion are presented as "universalist norms, applicable to the society as a whole rather than to a few functional or segmental sectors, highly generalized in terms of principles and standards."[102]

Whether this claim to universalist status is justified, however, cannot be determined from the mere fact of a judicial decision. It could be that the civility rules enforced by a judicial decision genuinely are expressive of generally accepted norms in a society. I doubt, for example, if anyone would seriously question *Eastman*'s assertion that eavesdropping on marital bedrooms constitutes a serious violation of generally accepted civility rules. But the converse could also be true, and it is possible that the civility rules enforced by a particular court may be understood as hegemonically imposed by one dominant cultural group onto others.[103]

This suggests that care must be taken in evaluating the universalist pretensions of the tort of intrusion. Under conditions of cultural heterogeneity, the common law can become a powerful instrument for effacing cultural and normative differences.[104] The significance of this efface-

---

99. *Id.* at 66.

100. Peck v. Tribune Co., 214 U.S. 185, 190 (1909).

101. Kimmerle v. New York Evening Journal, Inc., 262 N.Y. 99, 102, 186 N.E. 217, 218 (1933) (quoting Sydney v. MacFadden Newspaper Publishing Corp., 242 N.Y. 208, 212, 151 N.E. 209, 210 (1926)); *see* Post, *supra* note 43, at 714-15.

102. T. PARSONS, SOCIOLOGICAL THEORY AND MODERN SOCIETY 510 (1967).

103. On the distinction between expressive and hegemonic functions of law, see Post, *Cultural Heterogeneity and Law: Pornography, Blasphemy, and the First Amendment,* 76 CALIF. L. REV. 297, 299-300 (1988).

104. A good illustration of this potential is the case of Bitsie v. Walston, 85 N.M. 655, 658, 515 P.2d 659, 662 (Ct. App.), *cert. denied,* 85 N.M. 639, 515 P.2d 643 (1973), a decision interpreting the "appropriation" branch of the privacy tort, in which the court held that the "traditional" norms of the Navajo tribe could not be equated with the "ordinary sensibilities" of the reasonable person. *See*

ment, however, lies not only in its hegemonic consequences, but also in the commitment that it reveals to the task of constructing a common community through the process of authoritatively articulating rules of civility. The common law tort purports to *speak for* a community. Yet this very ambition authoritatively to forge a community simultaneously requires the common law to displace deviant communities. Under such conditions, community and hegemony necessarily entail each other.

## III
## THE TORT OF PUBLIC DISCLOSURE

The core of the invasion of privacy tort is commonly understood to lie in the branch of the tort that attempts to regulate the publicizing of private life.[105] The elements of that branch are described by the *Restatement* in the following manner:

> One who gives publicity to a matter concerning the private life of another is subject to liability to the other for invasion of privacy, if the matter publicized is of a kind that
>
> (a) would be highly offensive to a reasonable person, and
>
> (b) is not of legitimate concern to the public.[106]

This branch of the tort (which for convenience I shall call simply "public disclosure") differs from intrusion in three fundamental ways. First, intrusion concerns the physical actions of a defendant, whereas public disclosure involves the dissemination of information. The tort in *Eastman* was complete when the defendant placed the eavesdropping device in the plaintiffs' marital bedroom. Liability did not depend upon whether the defendant actually listened to the device or acquired any information from it, or whether he revealed any such information to others. An essential element of the tort of public disclosure, on the other hand, is a defendant's public disclosure of private information. The tort of public disclosure thus regulates forms of communication rather than physical behavior.

Second, whereas both intrusion and public disclosure turn on what a "reasonable person" would find "highly offensive," the tort of public disclosure penalizes only certain kinds of highly offensive revelations of private life; namely, those in which a defendant has given "publicity" to the offensive information. To give "publicity" to information is to make it

---

*also* Benally v. Hundred Arrows Press, Inc., 614 F. Supp. 969, 982 (D.N.M. 1985), *rev'd on other grounds sub nom.* Benally v. Amon Carter Museum of Western Art, 858 F.2d 618 (10th Cir. 1988).

105.  *See, e.g.,* Kalven, *supra* note 42, at 333.

106.  RESTATEMENT (SECOND) OF TORTS § 652D (1977). Once again, it is important to stress that the specific elements of this tort can vary from state to state, but it is fair to conclude that the *Restatement* version contains by far the most common array of elements.

public. This concept of the public has no analogue in the tort of intrusion.

Third, the tort of public disclosure requires a plaintiff to establish that the offensive information "is not of legitimate concern to the public." This concept of "legitimate concern" also has no analogue in the tort of intrusion.

In the following sections of this essay I shall address these three important differences.

### A.  The Offensive Disclosure of Private Facts: Civility and the Protection of Information Preserves

The public disclosure tort regulates forms of communication rather than behavior. To be actionable, a communication must be about "a matter concerning the private life of another" and the matter must be "of a kind that would be highly offensive to a reasonable person."[107] At first glance, these two criteria appear to concern only the content of information contained in a communication. Either the information is about "private life," or it is not; either the information is "highly offensive," or it is not. In fact, however, these two criteria do not concern merely the information that may be contained in a communication. They serve instead as standards for the evaluation of communicative acts, and are used to assess not merely communicative content, but also such varied aspects of these acts as their timing, justification, addressees, form, and general context.

This distinction between the regulation of information and the regulation of communicative acts is illustrated by the facts of a venerable case, *Brents v. Morgan*,[108] which was the first decision to recognize the invasion of privacy tort in the state of Kentucky. It appears that in 1926 in the town of Lebanon, Kentucky, W.R. Morgan, a veterinarian, owed a debt of $49.67 to George Brents, a garage mechanic. Brents made several unsuccessful efforts to collect the debt, and in frustration finally put up a sign, five feet by eight feet, in the window of his garage facing one of the principal streets of the town. The sign stated:

> *Notice.*
>
> *Dr. W. R. Morgan owes an account here of $49.67. And if promises would pay an account this account would have been settled long ago. This account will be advertised as long as it remains unpaid.*[109]

Dr. Morgan sued Brents for damages, alleging that the sign had "caused him great mental pain, humiliation, and mortification," that it exposed "him to public contempt, ridicule, aversion, and disgrace," and that it

---

107.  *Id.*
108.  221 Ky. 765, 299 S.W. 967 (1927).
109.  *Id.* at 766, 229 S.W. at 968 (emphasis in original).

had caused "an evil opinion of him in the minds of tradesmen and the public generally."[110] Morgan's complaint was styled in the language of a typical libel or defamation suit. But in Kentucky, as elsewhere, truth was a complete defense to an action for defamation, and Dr. Morgan did in fact owe Brents $49.67.

The Kentucky Supreme Court, however, held that although truth may be a defense against an action for defamation, it does not constitute a defense against the "new branch of the law [which] has been developed in the last few years [and] which is denominated the right of privacy."[111] The right of privacy concerned "the right of a person to be free from unwarranted publicity, or the right to live without unwarranted interference by the public about matters with which the public is not necessarily concerned."[112] The court concluded that Brents' posting of the sign violated Morgan's right of privacy. The facts of the case have been cited ever since as a paradigmatic illustration of invasion of privacy.[113]

The *Restatement* would have us ask two questions about the content of Brents' notice. First, we are instructed to inquire whether the information on the sign concerns "the private life" of Dr. Morgan. This inquiry, however, is somewhat puzzling, for it is not certain in what sense Dr. Morgan's debt, and his refusal to pay it, are "private" facts. Certainly these facts were known to Brents and were not viewed as "secret" by either party. And surely Brents would have been within his rights to discuss them with his wife or his banker or his accountant. We would even feel nothing improper about his relating them to a perfect stranger who was attempting to determine the worth of Brents' garage in the expectation of purchasing the business.

This suggests that we cannot determine whether the information on the sign concerns "private" facts simply by examining the content of the information; we must instead have some notion of the circumstances surrounding the revelation of that information. The same information can be viewed as "private" with respect to some kinds of communications, but not with respect to others. To say that the information on Brents' sign concerns "private life," therefore, is really to say that he should not have revealed it in the manner in which he did.

This conclusion is dramatically illustrated by the line of cases hold-

---

110.  *Id.*

111.  *Id.* at 770, 299 S.W. at 969.

112.  *Id.* at 770, 299 S.W. at 970. The court quoted language to the effect that the foundation of the right of privacy

"is in the conception of an inviolate personality and personal immunity. It is considered as a natural and an absolute or pure right springing from the instincts of nature. It is of that class of rights which every human being had in his natural state and which he did not surrender by becoming a member of organized society."

*Id.* at 773, 299 S.W. at 971 (quoting 21 Ruling Case Law § 3, at 1197-98 (1929)).

113.  *See, e.g.*, RESTATEMENT (SECOND) OF TORTS § 652D comment a, illustration 2 (1977).

ing that a defendant who reveals the past crimes of a rehabilitated felon can be liable for invasion of privacy. The California Supreme Court, for example, has held in *Briscoe v. Reader's Digest Association*[114] that a plaintiff who is leading an exemplary and respectable life can bring an action for public disclosure on the basis of a story in a national magazine revealing that he has been convicted of hijacking a truck eleven years earlier.[115] The Court distinguished between publishing "the facts of past crimes," and publishing the identity "of the *actor* in reports of long past crimes."[116] Liability could be predicated on the latter communication, but not on the former.

It is obvious, however, that the identity of the plaintiff was, at the time of his conviction, as "public" a fact as the events of his crime. The characterization of the information as "private," therefore, cannot possibly turn solely upon either its content or the extent to which it has previously been disseminated. It must instead depend upon an assessment of the total context of the communicative act by which that information is revealed. The court's conclusion makes sense only if it is read as resting on the perception that it was somehow deeply inappropriate for the defendant to have revealed the plaintiff's identity in that way, or at that time, or to that audience.

---

114. 4 Cal. 3d 529, 483 P.2d 34, 93 Cal. Rptr. 866 (1971).

115. In 1975 the United States Supreme Court held in Cox Broadcasting Corp. v. Cohn, 420 U.S. 469 (1975), that the first amendment prohibited a plaintiff from suing for damages for invasion of privacy on the basis of "the publication of truthful information contained in official court records open to public inspection." *Id.* at 495. Subsequent cases, however, as well as the 1977 edition of the *Restatement,* have continued to view liability as appropriate if the publication of such information occurs after a sufficient lapse of time. *See, e.g.,* Conklin v. Sloss, 86 Cal. App. 3d 241, 247-48, 150 Cal. Rptr. 121, 125 (Ct. App. 1978); Roshto v. Hebert, 439 So. 2d 428, 431 (La. 1983); RESTATEMENT (SECOND) OF TORTS § 652D comment k (1977); *cf.* Capra v. Thoroughbred Racing Ass'n, 787 F.2d 463 (9th Cir.), *cert. denied,* 479 U.S. 1017 (1986). The *Restatement* provides that if publicity is given to a public event after a sufficient lapse of time, it must be determined

whether the publicity goes to unreasonable lengths in revealing facts about one who has resumed the private, lawful and unexciting life led by the great bulk of the community. This may be true, for example, when there is a disclosure of the present name and identity of a reformed criminal and his new life is utterly ruined by revelation of a past that he has put behind him. . . . [T]he question is to be determined upon the basis of community standards and mores.

RESTATEMENT (SECOND) OF TORTS § 652D comment k (1977).

The Supreme Court has itself recently signalled that the holding of *Cox* is to be narrowly parsed. In Florida Star v. B.J.F., 109 S. Ct. 2603 (1989), the Court emphasized that *Cox* did not "exhaustively" resolve the "tension between the right which the First Amendment accords to a free press, on the one hand, and the protections which various statutes and common-law doctrines accord to personal privacy against the publication of truthful information, on the other." *Id.* at 2607. The Court specifically refused to hold that "truthful publication is automatically constitutionally protected, or that there is no zone of personal privacy within which the State may protect the individual from intrusion by the press, or even that a State may never punish publication of the name of a victim of a sexual offense." *Id.* at 2613. It held only that "where a newspaper publishes truthful information which it has lawfully obtained, punishment may lawfully be imposed, if at all, only when narrowly tailored to a state interest of the highest order . . . ." *Id.*

116. *Briscoe,* 4 Cal. 3d at 537, 483 P.2d at 39-40, 93 Cal. Rptr. at 871-72 (emphasis in original).

The California Supreme Court had in fact explicitly articulated this sense of inappropriateness in *Melvin v. Reid*,[117] the precedent relied upon by *Briscoe. Melvin* upheld a plaintiff's claim of invasion of privacy against a defendant who had made a movie about the plaintiff's past life that accurately identified her as a notorious prostitute and an accused felon.[118] The court branded the movie as one made in "willful and wanton disregard of that charity which should actuate us in our social intercourse and which should keep us from unnecessarily holding another up to the scorn and contempt of upright members of society."[119]

If the conclusion that a communicative act reveals the "private life" of a plaintiff ultimately turns on whether, under the circumstances, the communication wantonly disregards social norms of appropriateness, so also, and in a more obvious way, does the second question propounded by the *Restatement*. In assessing whether Brents' sign is an actionable invasion of privacy, the *Restatement* would have us ask whether the information contained in the sign "is of a kind that would be highly offensive to a reasonable person."[120]

The *Restatement's* formulation of the question invites us to focus on the content of the sign and to assess it according to community norms. We might say, for example, that community norms view the commission of a crime as inherently stigmatic, and hence that the communication of such information would be highly offensive. But the facts of *Brents* do not fit easily within this understanding of the question. Dr. Morgan's debt and his delinquency on that debt are not "inherently" offensive in the same way as would be his commission of a crime. Information about the debt, for example, would not be highly offensive as between Morgan and his banker, or as between Brents and Morgan, or as between Morgan and his wife or children. Indeed, twenty-four years after *Brents* the Kentucky Supreme Court held in *Voneye v. Turner*[121] that it was neither offensive nor an invasion of privacy to communicate the fact of a debt and the debtor's refusal to pay it to the debtor's employer.[122] As one

---

117.   112 Cal. App. 285, 297 P. 91 (Ct. App. 1931).

118.   *Id.* at 292, 297 P. at 93-94.

119.   *Id.* at 291, 297 P. at 93.

120.   RESTATEMENT (SECOND) OF TORTS § 652D (1977).

121.   240 S.W.2d 588 (Ky. 1951).

122.   The court stated that conveying such information would not impair " 'the standing of an individual and bring him into disrepute with right thinking people in the community.' " The court explained:

> A debtor when he creates an obligation must know that his creditor expects to collect it, and the ordinary man realizes that most employers expect their employees to meet their obligations and that when they fall behind in so doing the employer may be asked to take the matter up with them. Indeed, most debtors would prefer to have their delinquencies referred to their employers in a courteous and inconspicuous manner rather than to have a suit filed against them and their wages garnished.

*Id.* at 591, 593 (quoting in part Neaton v. Lewis Apparel Stores, 267 A.D. 728, 48 N.Y.S.2d 492, 494

court put it, "An employer 'is not in a category with the general public which cannot have any legitimate interest in a purely private matter between a creditor and a debtor,' "[123] in large part because

> when one accepts credit, he impliedly consents for the creditor to take reasonable steps 'to pursue his debtor and persuade payment . . . .' It is only when the creditor's actions constitute oppressive treatment of a debtor, including the unreasonable giving of undue publicity to private debts, that such actions have been held to be an actionable invasion of a debtor's right of privacy.[124]

The offensiveness of the sign in *Brents,* therefore, is not merely a matter of the content of the information which it contains, but also of the "oppressive" manner in which it disseminates that information. This distinction is illustrated by the recent case of *Vassiliades v. Garfinckel's, Brooks Bros.,* [125] in which a woman sued her surgeon for public disclosure because he had shown "before" and "after" pictures of her cosmetic surgery on a television program. The trial court had directed a verdict for the defendant, in part on the theory that "the photographs were not highly offensive because there was nothing 'uncomplimentary or unsavory' about them."[126] The appellate court reversed, stating that the trial court had misconceived the issue. The question was not whether the content of the photographs was offensive, but rather "whether the publicity of Mrs. Vassiliades' surgery was highly offensive to a reasonable person."[127]

This formulation of the offensiveness requirement, however, essentially asks whether the communicative act at issue, considered in its full context, is "highly offensive."[128] But this inquiry is virtually identical to that which underlies the "private facts" requirement. Both focus broadly on the appropriateness of the communicative act in question, rather than narrowly on the specific content of that communication. The distinct contribution of the "offensiveness" requirement is primarily that it makes

---

(App. Div. 1944)). The holding of the Kentucky court is typical of decisions dealing with this issue. *See* S. HOFSTADTER & G. HOROWITZ, *supra* note 51, at 173-76.

123.   Harrison v. Humble Oil & Refining Co., 264 F. Supp. 89, 92 (D.S.C. 1967) (quoting Patton v. Jacobs, 118 Ind. App. 358, 78 N.E.2d 789 (App. 1948)).

124.   *Id.* (quoting Cunningham v. Securities Investment Co. of St. Louis, 278 F.2d 600, 604 (5th Cir. 1960)).

125.   492 A.2d 580 (D.C. 1985).

126.   *Id.* at 588.

127.   *Id.*

128.   Consider, in this light, the ambiguity of the *Restatement's* own gloss on the "offensiveness" requirement:

> The rule stated in this Section gives protection only against unreasonable publicity, of a kind highly offensive to the ordinary reasonable man. The protection afforded to the plaintiff's interest in his privacy must be relative to the customs of the time and place, to the occupation of the plaintiff and to the habits of his neighbors and fellow citizens.

RESTATEMENT (SECOND) OF TORTS § 652D comment c (1977).

explicit the notion that the law will not regulate every inappropriate reve-lation, but only those which are "highly offensive." Thus the public dis-closure tort, like the intrusion tort, penalizes only serious transgressions.

As with intrusion, the elements of the public disclosure branch of the tort roughly approximate an everyday understanding of privacy. When we speak in ordinary language about violations of privacy, we often have in mind inappropriate revelations of intimate facts that ought not to be disclosed.[129] The twin requirements of "private facts" and "offensiveness" are a rough attempt to specify when such revelations are inappropriate. But, as with intrusion, the public disclosure tort does not depend upon a neutral or objective measure of when disclosures should be subject to legal liability. Instead the tort draws upon the social norms that govern the flow of information in modern society. And these norms, like those that define private space, have a "socially determined variabil-ity," and so are sensitive to such "factors" as the "character of the social occasion,"[130] the purpose, timing, and status of the person who makes the disclosure, the status and purposes of the addressee of the disclosure, and so on. Information about a debtor, which may be perfectly appropri-ate to disclose to his employer or banker or wife, would be inappropriate to disclose to his neighbors. Information that may be widely known in some circles, may be inappropriate to reveal in others.

We can understand information, then, as confined within "bounda-ries"[131] that are normatively determined. These boundaries function analogously to those which define the spatial territories analyzed by Goffman. And indeed, Goffman specifically notes that one kind of terri-tory is an "information preserve," which contains the "set of facts about himself to which an individual expects to control access," and which is "[t]raditionally treated under the heading of 'privacy.' "[132] Goffman's point is that just as individuals expect to control certain spatial territo-ries, so they expect to control certain informational territories. The almost physical apprehension of this informational space is evident, for example, in Warren and Brandeis' famous complaint that "[t]he press is overstepping in every direction the obvious bounds of propriety and of decency."[133] Because the boundaries of an individual's informational

---

129. Such revelations violate what Elizabeth Beardsley has termed "the right of selective disclosure"; in Beardsley's view, "selective disclosure constitutes the conceptual core of the norm of privacy." Beardsley, *Privacy: Autonomy and Selective Disclosure,* in PRIVACY 56, 70 (J. Pennock & J. Chapman eds. 1971) (NOMOS XIII).

130. E. GOFFMAN, *supra* note 75, at 31, 40.

131. Seipp, *English Judicial Recognition of a Right to Privacy,* 3 OXF. J. LEGAL STUD. 325, 333 (1983).

132. E. GOFFMAN, *supra* note 75, at 38-39.

133. Warren & Brandeis, *supra* note 6, at 196. For another example of this almost physical apprehension, see Brents v. Morgan, 221 Ky. 765, 774, 299 S.W. 967, 971 (1927) (defining a

space are "relative to the customs of the time and place, and . . . determined by the norm of the ordinary man,"[134] the public disclosure branch of the tort can be said to maintain those civility rules which establish information preserves, in the same way that the intrusion branch upholds the civility rules which define spatial territories.

Information preserves, like spatial territories, provide a normative framework for the development of individual personality. Just as we feel violated when our bedrooms are invaded, so we experience the inappropriate disclosure of private information "as *pollutions* or *defilements*."[135] Although the social norms that define information territories concern communications between defendants and third parties, we nevertheless depend upon those norms, and experience their breach to be "just as violent and morally inadmissible as listening behind closed doors."[136] Thus courts enforcing the public disclosure tort see themselves as protecting persons from "indecent and vulgar" communications that would "outrage or cause mental suffering, shame or humiliation to a person of ordinary sensibilities,"[137] or that would have the effect of "degrading a person by laying his life open to public view,"[138] or that would threaten plaintiffs with a "literal loss of self-identity."[139]

The civility rules which delineate information preserves must therefore be understood as forms of respect that are integral to both individual and social personality. They comprise an important part of the obligations that members of a community owe to each other. This perspective helps to clarify a perplexing feature of the public disclosure tort. The tort has always seemed somewhat strange because a plaintiff can recover damages for the public disclosure of "private" facts only by definitively and widely re-broadcasting those same "private" facts through an official adjudicative process. Thus while few may have heard of Mrs. Vassiliades' plastic surgery as a result of her doctor's announcements over the television—in fact Mrs. Vassiliades could identify only two persons who had seen the broadcast—her surgical alteration is now forever imprinted in the law books, and the very process of her trial no doubt made the fact of her surgery known to many of her acquaintances who

---

violation of the right to privacy as "interference with another's seclusion by subjecting him to unwarranted and undesired publicity").

134. Wheeler v. P. Sorensen Mfg. Co., 415 S.W.2d 582, 585 (Ky. 1967).

135. Schoeman, *Privacy and Intimate Information,* in PHILOSOPHICAL DIMENSIONS OF PRIVACY: AN ANTHOLOGY 403, 406 (F. Schoeman ed. 1984) (emphasis in original).

136. G. SIMMEL, *supra* note 66, at 323.

137. Daily Times Democrat v. Graham, 276 Ala. 380, 382, 162 So. 2d 474, 476 (1964).

138. Diaz v. Oakland Tribune, Inc., 139 Cal. App. 3d 118, 126, 188 Cal. Rptr. 762, 767 (Ct. App. 1983) (quoting Nimmer, *The Right to Speak From* Times *to* Time: *First Amendment Theory Applied to Libel and Misapplied to Privacy,* 56 CALIF. L. REV. 935, 959 (1968)) (emphasis omitted).

139. Briscoe v. Reader's Digest Ass'n, 4 Cal. 3d 529, 534, 483 P.2d 34, 37, 93 Cal. Rptr. 866, 869 (1971).

986              *CALIFORNIA LAW REVIEW*              [Vol. 77:957

otherwise would not have been aware of it. If the public disclosure tort is understood simply as a mechanism for protecting the secrecy of private facts, it would seem to be entirely self-defeating.[140] But if the tort is instead understood as a means of obtaining vindication for the infringement of information preserves, the disclosure of information in the course of a judicial action may be of only secondary importance so long as the plaintiff is ultimately reintegrated into that chain of ceremony which defines and embraces members of the community.

This suggests that the public disclosure tort fulfills the first two of the three functions we previously identified for the intrusion tort—safeguarding the respect due individuals by virtue of their territorial claims, and protecting the "ritual idiom" through which such respect finds social expression.[141] The idiom at issue in the context of public disclosure, however, appears somewhat different than that at issue in intrusion. This is because intrusion regulates dyadic relationships, which involve the appropriateness of direct interactions between plaintiffs and defendants, whereas public disclosure regulates triadic relationships, which involve the appropriateness of defendants' disclosures of private information about plaintiffs to third party addressees.

This difference has significant consequences. The intrusion tort regulates situations in which a plaintiff's direct control over whether to assert or to waive pertinent civility rules is constitutive of the most intimate aspects of his social existence. In public disclosure, on the other hand, the pertinent civility rules specifically control only the relationship between a defendant and his audience. It is therefore awkward to speak of these rules as norms that intrinsically establish the intimate life of a plaintiff. For this reason the idiom at issue in public disclosure is chiefly expressive of respect, and does not characteristically function in the "dual way" of the civility norms protected by intrusion, which mark the

---

140. *See, e.g.*, Anderson v. Fisher Broadcasting Co., 300 Or. 452, 462, 712 P.2d 803, 809 (1986); Gavison, *supra* note 62, at 458.

141. *See supra* text accompanying notes 85-86. This conclusion implies that it is a great mistake to view the tort, as some have proposed, as simply a device for protecting secrecy. *See, e.g.*, Posner, *The Right of Privacy*, 12 GA. L. REV. 393, 393 (1978); Stigler, *An Introduction to Privacy in Economics and Politics*, 9 J. LEGAL STUD. 623 (1980). Secrecy depends upon a purely descriptive concept of privacy, which is quite different from the normative concept that actually underlies the tort. The difference is most apparent in the fact that the tort deems the right of privacy to be a "personal" right that "can be maintained only by a living individual whose privacy is invaded." RESTATEMENT (SECOND) OF TORTS § 652I (1977). Thus corporations, which have secrets to protect but which are not entitled to claims of social respect, have "no personal right of privacy" and cannot bring a "cause of action" to enforce any such right. *Id.* at comment c. For this reason, as Jack Hirshleifer has argued, privacy in the common law must be interpreted as signifying "something much broader than secrecy; it suggests . . . a particular kind of social structure together with its supporting social ethic." Hirshleifer, *Privacy: Its Origin, Function, and Future*, 9 J. LEGAL STUD. 649, 649 (1980). By preserving the civility rules that define a community, the tort constitutes nothing less than "a *way of organizing society.*" *Id.* at 650 (emphasis in original).

boundary between respect and intimacy. It follows from this that the public disclosure tort cannot systematically be linked to the third function that we attributed to the intrusion tort, that of preserving the ability of individuals to use the language of territories to develop a sense of their own autonomy. Viewed in this light, limitations on the tort of public disclosure carry somewhat less profound social implications than do limitations on the tort of intrusion.

### B.  The Requirement of "Publicity": The Tension Between Civility and Intimacy

The *Restatement* contains two explicit limitations on the tort of public disclosure that have no counterparts in the tort of intrusion. The first of these limitations is the requirement that a defendant give "publicity" to the information at issue. The *Restatement* defines giving "publicity" as communicating information "to the public at large, or to so many persons that the matter must be regarded as substantially certain to become one of public knowledge":

> Thus it is not an invasion of the right of privacy, within the rule stated in this Section, to communicate a fact concerning the plaintiff's private life to a single person or even to a small group of persons. On the other hand, any publication in a newspaper or a magazine, even of small circulation, or in a handbill distributed to a large number of persons, or any broadcast over the radio, or statement made in an address to a large audience, is sufficient to give publicity within the meaning of the term as it is used in this Section. The distinction, in other words, is one between private and public communication.[142]

The effect of this rather stringent requirement is that the public disclosure tort differs from intrusion in that it will not offer redress for every highly offensive infringement of a territory. Although it would be highly offensive for Mrs. Vassiliades' surgeon to display her "before" and "after" pictures at a private dinner party, the surgeon would not be subject to liability under the public disclosure tort as defined by the *Restatement*, because he would not have given adequate "publicity" to the pictures.

These consequences are undoubtedly harsh. Perhaps because the purpose of the publicity requirement is unclear, courts have been uncertain about whether to follow the *Restatement* by enforcing a strict publicity requirement. Although the common law is still evolving, two distinct approaches can be identified. The first, a minority approach, is exemplified by the case of *Beaumont v. Brown*,[143] in which the plaintiff, a labor safety supervisor for the Michigan Department of Labor, had been

---

142.  RESTATEMENT (SECOND) OF TORTS § 652D comment a (1977).
143.  401 Mich. 80, 257 N.W.2d 522 (1977).

fired for leaving his job for a month of military duty without informing his supervisor or arranging for someone to take over his duties. The plaintiff appealed his discharge, and his supervisors wrote a long and very nasty letter to the Army Reserve, ostensibly seeking to verify the plaintiff's military duties. The plaintiff alleged that the letter constituted a tortious invasion of privacy. The Michigan Court of Appeals ruled for the defendants on the grounds that they had not given "publicity" to the contents of the letter: "Supportive personnel of the sender and receiver of a letter do not constitute the 'general public' or a 'large number of persons.' "[144] But the Michigan Supreme Court reversed, stating that the publicity requirement should not degenerate into a "numbers game": "An invasion of a plaintiff's right to privacy is important if it exposes private facts to a public whose knowledge of those facts would be embarrassing to the plaintiff. Such a public might be . . . fellow employees, club members, church members, family, or neighbors."[145] The court even suggested that "publication of the embarrassing facts to only one person alone" might meet the test.[146] The issue, therefore, was not the amount of publicity, but rather whether the publicity was "unnecessary" or "unreasonable."[147]

The approach in *Beaumont* collapses the publicity test into the "private" facts and "offensiveness" requirements. These requirements, as we have seen, concern not merely the content of a communication, but also the appropriateness of its manner, addressees, and timing. To characterize publicity as unnecessary or unreasonable disclosure is simply another way of saying that the addressees of a communication are inappropriate. The publicity requirement is thus rendered superfluous; it ceases to interpose any independent barrier to the protection of informational territories. Hence it is not surprising that those courts which have followed the *Beaumont* approach have stressed the "need for flexibility" in interpreting the publicity requirement so that "[e]gregious conduct" may be "found actionable."[148]

The second understanding of the publicity requirement found in contemporary cases can be labelled the *Restatement* approach, for it attempts to follow the prescriptions of the *Restatement* and interpret the publicity requirement in a stringent way. Most jurisdictions have taken this path.[149] The contrast between the two approaches is well illustrated

---

144.  Beaumont v. Brown, 65 Mich. App. 455, 464, 237 N.W.2d 501, 506 (Ct. App. 1975), *rev'd*, 401 Mich. 80, 257 N.W.2d 522 (1977).

145.  *Beaumont*, 401 Mich. at 105, 257 N.W.2d at 531.

146.  *Id.* at 100, 257 N.W.2d at 529.

147.  *Id.* at 102-06, 257 N.W.2d at 530-32.

148.  McSurely v. McClellan, 753 F.2d 88, 112 (D.C. Cir.), *cert. denied*, 474 U.S. 1005 (1985).

149.  *See, e.g.*, Tureen v. Equifax, Inc., 571 F.2d 411, 419 (8th Cir. 1978); Beard v. Akzona, Inc., 517 F. Supp. 128, 132-33 (E.D. Tenn. 1981); Vogel v. W. T. Grant Co., 458 Pa. 124, 130-33, 327

by a comparison of *McSurely v. McClellan*[150] and *Pemberton v. Bethlehem Steel Corp.*[151] The court in *McSurely* followed the *Beaumont* approach and held that the disclosure to a husband of his wife's private premarital love letters constituted an actionable invasion of privacy, despite the fact that the communication was addressed to only one person.[152] The court in *Pemberton* held that the disclosure to a wife of her husband's extramarital affair was not an actionable invasion of privacy, because there had been no publicity.[153] *Pemberton* is a particularly striking case because of the egregious character of the disclosure, which formed part of the Bethlehem Steel Corporation's effort to discredit and harass a labor organizer.[154] Some of the evidence of the extra-marital affair anonymously sent to the organizer's wife was gathered by an eavesdropping device secretly placed in the plaintiff's motel room.[155]

*Pemberton* illustrates the powerful implications of the publicity requirement as codified in the *Restatement*. It underscores the need to inquire into the purposes served by that requirement. One hypothesis is that the requirement is meant to restrict the availability of legal redress so that not every social indiscretion will carry the potential of formal legal adjudication. Such a restriction would serve both the interests of the legal system in not being flooded with suits, and the interests of society in maintaining the spontaneity and informality of social life. This hypothesis, however, lacks explanatory power, for it is not clear why these anticipated effects should justify the publicity requirement. Those courts which follow the *Beaumont* approach are apparently willing to risk the potential "flood" of litigation and the possible formalization of social life. In the area of defamation courts have for centuries also been willing to risk these effects in order to regulate defamatory communications, even those published only to a single addressee.[156] Why then would these effects be determinative for those courts which follow the *Restatement* approach?

A second hypothesis to explain the publicity requirement is that the damage to a plaintiff becomes large enough to justify legal intervention only when disclosure is made to "the public at large, or to so many persons that the matter must be regarded as substantially certain to become

---

A.2d 133, 136-38 (1974); Lemnah v. American Breeders Serv., 144 Vt. 568, 575-76, 482 A.2d 700, 704-05 (1984).

150. 753 F.2d 88 (D.C. Cir.), *cert. denied*, 474 U.S. 1005 (1985).

151. 66 Md. App. 133, 502 A.2d 1101 (Ct. Spec. App.), *cert. denied*, 306 Md. 289, 508 A.2d 488, *cert. denied*, 479 U.S. 984 (1986).

152. *McSurely*, 753 F.2d at 113.

153. *Pemberton*, 66 Md. App. at 166, 502 A.2d at 1118.

154. *Id.* at 156, 502 A.2d at 1106.

155. *Id.* at 164-65, 502 A.2d at 1116-17.

156. RESTATEMENT (SECOND) OF TORTS § 577 (1977).

one of public knowledge."[157] The fallacy of this reasoning, however, is illustrated by the facts of *Pemberton*. It is often more important to a plaintiff to keep information from a few specific people than from an anonymous public.[158] In addition, the logic of the common law ordinarily dictates that considerations of the extent of a plaintiff's injuries go to the remedy aspect of a tort, to the amount of damages that a plaintiff might be entitled to receive, rather than to the liability aspect of a tort, to whether or not a plaintiff can even bring an action.

The most plausible justification for the publicity requirement is yet a third hypothesis, implied by the *Restatement's* suggestion that the requirement rests on a distinction in kind rather than of degree. The "distinction," the *Restatement* tells us, "is one between private and public communication."[159] The difference between these two forms of communication may be illustrated by the following example. Suppose a defendant, in the course of an address to a large audience, speaks truthfully about a plaintiff's adultery. The *Restatement* explicitly provides that a "statement made in an address to a large audience . . . is sufficient to give publicity within the meaning of the term as it is used in this Section."[160] Ordinarily, in other words, a statement made in such an address would be viewed as communicating "to the public at large." But suppose that the defendant is a minister, the audience is his church, and the statement is made in the course of a proceeding to administer church discipline to the plaintiff. Although the statement is made in an address to a large audience, we are likely to view the statement as qualitatively different from one made in the course of a lecture to a large audience of strangers. If the lecture to strangers feels unambiguously like a "public" communication, the church proceeding feels considerably less so.[161] Thus the publicity requirement cannot coherently turn merely on the number of persons in an audience; it must instead depend upon some qualitative judgment about the context of the relevant communication.

What is the nature of that judgment? How can we distinguish, for example, between addressing an audience that consists of a plaintiff's

---

157. *Id.* § 652D comment a.

158. As the Michigan Supreme Court said in *Beaumont*:

Communication of embarrassing facts about an individual to a public not concerned with that individual and with whom the individual is not concerned obviously is not a "serious interference" with plaintiff's right to privacy, although it might be "unnecessary" or "unreasonable." An invasion of a plaintiff's right to privacy is important if it exposes private facts to a public whose knowledge of those facts would be embarrassing to the plaintiff.

Beaumont v. Brown, 401 Mich. 80, 104-05, 257 N.W.2d 522, 531 (1977).

159. RESTATEMENT (SECOND) OF TORTS § 652D comment a (1977).

160. *Id.*

161. *See* Buzzard, *Scarlet Letter Lawsuits: Private Affairs and Public Judgments,* 10 CAMPBELL L. REV. 1, 41-42 (1987); *cf.* Landis v. Campbell, 79 Mo. 433, 439-41 (1883); Shurtleff v. Stevens, 51 Vt. 501, 514-15 (1879).

church and an audience that consists of the general public? One obvious difference is that members of a plaintiff's church are united with the plaintiff in an explicit and recognized commitment to communal norms and forms of interaction. Members of the general public, however, need not share any such connections with a plaintiff. Thus Alvin Gouldner has observed that

> [a] "public" emerges when there is an attenuation between culture, on the one side, and patterns of social interaction, on the other. Traditional "groups" are characterized by the association and mutual support of both elements; by the fact that their members have patterned social interactions with one another which, in turn, fosters among them common understandings and shared interests, which, again in turn, facilitates their mutual interaction, and so on. A "public" "refers to a number of people exposed to the same social stimuli," and having something in common even without being in persisting interaction with one another. . . . "Publics" are persons who need not be "co-present," in the "sight and hearing of one another."
>
> . . . .
>
> . . . To make matters "public" means to open them even to those who are not known personally, to those who do not ordinarily come into one's sight and hearing. On the paradigmatic level, to make things public is to take them (or to allow them to go) beyond the *family,* where all is in the sight and hearing of others, and which constructs a context for communication that may, in consequence, be cryptic, allusive, seemingly vague.[162]

Gouldner's observations suggest that the publicity requirement, as defined by the *Restatement,* distinguishes communications which form part of the "allusive," affective, and primary interactions of a traditional group, like a church, from those which form part of the impersonal interactions of strangers who comprise a public. The *Restatement* and most courts require that only communications of the second kind comply with the civility rules enforced by the public disclosure tort. This is consistent with the common sense expectation that public interactions ought to be more formal and restrained, whereas private interactions may be more informal and spontaneous.[163] As Richard Sennett has observed, tradi-

---

162. A. GOULDNER, THE DIALECTIC OF IDEOLOGY AND TECHNOLOGY 95, 101 (1976) (citations omitted); *see also* J. BENNETT & M. TUMIN, SOCIAL LIFE: STRUCTURE AND FUNCTION 140 (1948).

163. Harold Garfinkel once asked his students as an experiment to act at home as if they were in public, as if they were "boarders," and thus "to conduct themselves in a circumspect and polite fashion." H. GARFINKEL, STUDIES IN ETHNOMETHODOLOGY 47 (1967). The results dramatically illustrate the perceived strangeness of acting according to civility rules within the privacy of the family. In eighty percent of the cases,

> family members were stupefied. They vigorously sought to make the strange actions intelligible and to restore the situation to normal appearances. Reports were filled with accounts of astonishment, bewilderment, shock, anxiety, embarrassment, and anger, and with charges by various family members that the student was mean, inconsiderate, selfish, nasty, or impolite. Family members demanded explanations: What's the matter? What's

tionally the "line drawn between public and private was essentially one on which the claims of civility—epitomized by cosmopolitan, public behavior—were balanced against the claims of nature—epitomized by the family."[164]

We can interpret the publicity requirement, then, as an attempt to ensure that public communications comply with minimum standards of civility, while liberating private communications from the threat of legal enforcement of such restraints. The requirement thus safeguards the personal and expressive quality of interactions among individuals who are not strangers. So interpreted, however, the publicity requirement in effect sacrifices the right to extract social respect through the maintenance of an information preserve to the "mutual dependency, affection, and tact"[165] associated with traditional group interactions.

This interpretation of the publicity requirement leads to results that are quite counter-intuitive from an individualist perspective. Precisely because primary group interactions are emotional and personal, they are also volatile and potentially very hurtful. We often care more about what those within our "group" think of us than we do about our reputation among the strangers who comprise the general public. Yet the publicity requirement, as defined by the *Restatement,* would impose sanctions for the disclosure of a husband's marital infidelity to the general public, but not for its disclosure to his wife, on the grounds that the law should not enforce the formal requirements of an information preserve between husbands and wives. The justification of such a requirement obviously cannot be the protection of individuals from mental distress or suffering. Its purpose must instead be understood in specifically *social* terms, as the maintenance of spontaneous and expressive forms of group interaction. The commitment to this purpose fundamentally divides the *Restatement* approach from the *Beaumont* approach.

---

gotten into you? Did you get fired? Are you sick? What are you being so superior about? Why are you mad? Are you out of your mind or are you just stupid? One student acutely embarrassed his mother in front of her friends by asking if she minded if he had a snack from the refrigerator. "Mind if you have a little snack? You've been eating little snacks around here for years without asking me. What's gotten into you?"

*Id.* at 47-48 (1967).

If Garfinkel's experiment illustrates the inappropriateness of acting with civility within the informal and private bounds of the family, David Karp's work demonstrates the converse, that even in situations of extreme public anonymity, "anonymity itself constitutes a norm to be maintained, and there are rules for preserving it, which, if broken, subject the transgressor to negative sanctions." Karp, *Hiding in Pornographic Bookstores: A Reconsideration of the Nature of Urban Anonymity,* 1 URB. LIFE & CULTURE 427, 446 (1973). Even anonymity, in other words, is *"produced* by actors" whose conduct is made meaningful by civility rules. *Id.* (emphasis in original).

164. R. SENNETT, THE FALL OF PUBLIC MAN: ON THE SOCIAL PSYCHOLOGY OF CAPITALISM 18 (1978). Thus Sennett observes: "[W]hile man *made* himself in public, he *realized* his nature in the private realm." *Id.* at 18-19 (emphasis in original).

165. A. GOULDNER, *supra* note 162, at 102.

The difficulty with the *Restatement's* delineation of a publicity requirement, however, is that it attempts to achieve this purpose in a way that obscures the pertinent underlying values. The *Restatement* defines the publicity requirement not merely in terms of the qualitative distinction "between private and public communication," but also in terms of the quantitative distinction between communications "to a single person or even to a small group of persons," and communications "to so many persons that the matter must be regarded as substantially certain to become one of public knowledge."[166] The *Restatement* appears to assume, in other words, that communications to a single person or to a small group of persons are necessarily part of the primary dynamics of group life. But this assumption masks a host of ambiguities.

Consider, first, the possibility that a defendant has communicated private facts to the members of a small group to which the plaintiff, but not the defendant, belongs. In *Pemberton*, for example, the Bethlehem Steel Corporation anonymously sent a detective's report of the plaintiff's marital infidelity to the plaintiff's wife. The plaintiff and the addressee of the communication were in a primary relationship to each other, but the defendant, Bethlehem Steel, was a stranger to that relationship. In this circumstance the publicity requirement might be defended on the grounds that members of a primary group have, so to speak, yielded to each other their claim to enforce their respective information preserves. The law's rejection of the plaintiff's claim could thus be seen to stem from its refusal to check the flow of information between spouses, a refusal calculated to promote the vitality of the very group to which the plaintiff and addressee both belong.

The publicity requirement must be defended on quite different grounds, however, if the defendant and his audience are members of a small and intimate group to which the plaintiff does not belong. If Mrs. Vassiliades' surgeon were to show her "before" and "after" pictures to a private dinner party, for example, the communication forms part of the dynamics of a group from which Mrs. Vassiliades is excluded. While it may make sense to view Mrs. Vassiliades as in some sense having "waived" her claims to an information preserve with respect to those groups in which she claims membership, it does not make sense to view her as having waived those claims with respect to a group consisting of her surgeon's dinner guests. In such circumstances the publicity requirement can be defended only on the grounds that it is more important to foster spontaneous communication among members of a group, than to enforce respect for the information preserves of non-members.

There is, however, yet a third possibility. It is conceivable that

---

166. RESTATEMENT (SECOND) OF TORTS § 652D comment a (1977).

neither the plaintiff, nor the defendant, nor the addressee of the defendant's communication are members of a common group. This situation is illustrated by the facts of *Lemnah v. American Breeders Service*, [167] in which the plaintiff was a local distributor and salesperson for the defendant, which produced and nationally marketed bovine semen. Plaintiff's contract with the defendant was terminated for delinquency in the payment of monies owing. The plaintiff alleged that defendant's employee had stated to a farmer, who was also plaintiff's customer, that the termination was in part due to the "heavy drinking problem" of the plaintiff. [168]

The three parties to this transaction—the plaintiff, the defendant, and the farmer—were in effect strangers to each other, connected only through the arm's-length transactions of the market. No two of them were members of a common group. Assuming that the defendant's communication was a highly offensive disclosure of a private fact, it is hard to understand what possible justification the Vermont Supreme Court could have had in using the publicity requirement to bar recovery. The use of the publicity requirement cannot be justified on the grounds of protecting some special relationship of conversation or good fellowship between the defendant and the farmer, nor can it be explained on the grounds of promoting the plaintiff's intimate relationship with the farmer. The communication to the farmer was, quite simply, a "public" communication, and the farmer can be expected to hold the plaintiff coldly and impersonally accountable for his drinking problem.

This suggests that there are circumstances in which the *Restatement's* rule does not correspond to the underlying sociological point of the publicity requirement. There may, however, be an explanation for this disparity. The accurate differentiation of public from private communications would require courts to develop explicit and workable criteria for distinguishing the exact kinds of intimacies or group dynamics that would preclude enforcement of the public disclosure tort. Thus, for example, we might characterize the communication to the farmer in *Lemnah* as "public" if the farmer were only the plaintiff's customer, but as "private" if he were the plaintiff's intimate friend. The recognition and justification of these distinctions would be difficult enough in the abstract; it would be virtually impossible in the context of the common law system of case-by-case adjudication, with its intense pressure to articulate explicitly the reasons for distinguishing or following pertinent cases. The drafters of the *Restatement* might with good reason have concluded that such a task was beyond the capacity of courts, especially given the subtlety and elusiveness of the sociological concepts at issue.

---

167. 144 Vt. 568, 482 A.2d 700 (1984).

168. *Id.* at 568, 482 A.2d at 700.

Thus they might have settled for a clear and workable rule-of-thumb, roughly associating private group communications with those to a single person or to a small group of persons, with full knowledge that in particular cases the rule would fail to accomplish its underlying purpose.

On this account, then, the *Restatement's* publicity requirement is an example of a social norm transformed by the practical necessities of the legal system. Although this "re-institutionalization" (to use Bohannan's phrase) of the norm obscures the social purposes of the legal rule and consequently leaves its underlying values ambiguous, such obscurity is occasionally the price for a workable system of legal doctrine. It is appropriate to take that price into account in evaluating the controversy between the *Beaumont* and *Restatement* approaches. The more fundamental question, however, is whether we believe it to be more important to promote group life than to require respect for individual claims to information preserves.

## C. The Concept of "Legitimate Public Concern": The Tension Between Civility and Public Accountability

If the concept of the "public" plays a controversial and ambiguous role in the *Restatement's* "publicity" requirement, it takes undisputed center stage in the last element of the public disclosure tort. In order to satisfy this element a plaintiff must demonstrate that a defendant's communication "is not of legitimate concern to the public."[169] This requirement, which is sometimes called the "privilege to report news,"[170] or the "privilege to publicize newsworthy matters,"[171] is acknowledged by all common law courts that have recognized the public disclosure tort. The requirement is the single most important distinction between the intrusion and public disclosure branches of the invasion of privacy tort.[172] If the former seeks to regulate all highly offensive violations of spatial territories, the latter permits information territories to be freely broken if the information at issue is "newsworthy."

The reason for this difference is not obscure: It lies in the distinction between a territory conceived as a physical space, and a territory conceived as an array of information. Preservation of the former requires no more than the regulation of discrete forms of physical conduct; preservation of the latter, however, implies no less than control over the diffusion of information throughout an entire society. The common law long ago came to recognize the importance of that diffusion for maintaining social

---

169. RESTATEMENT (SECOND) OF TORTS § 652D (1977).
170. Kalven, *supra* note 42, at 336.
171. Virgil v. Time, Inc., 527 F.2d 1122, 1128 (9th Cir. 1975), *cert. denied,* 425 U.S. 998 (1976).
172. *See, e.g.,* Fletcher v. Florida Publishing Co., 319 So. 2d 100, 111 (Fla. Dist. Ct. App. 1975), *rev'd on other grounds,* 340 So. 2d 914 (Fla. 1976), *cert. denied,* 431 U.S. 930 (1977).

order and solidarity. In his 1826 *Treatise* on defamation law, for example, Thomas Starkie noted the "difficulties" involved in the regulation of information about persons, because its

> subject matter is more subtle and refined, and does not admit of the broad and plain limits and distinctions which may be established in respect of forcible injuries; for instance, in the case of battery of the person, the law can, without hesitation, pronounce, that any, the least degree of violence shall be deemed illegal, and entitle the complainant to his remedy; but, communications concerning reputation cannot be so prohibited; every day's convenience requires, that men, and their affairs, should be discussed, though frequently at the hazard of individual reputation; and it conduces mainly to the ends of morality and good order, to the safety and security of society, that considerable latitude should be afforded to such communications. The dread of public censure and disgrace is not only the most effectual, and therefore the most important, but in numberless instances the only security which society possesses for the preservation of decency and the performance of the private duties of life.[173]

From the perspective of individuals, respect for information preserves is a matter of common decency. From a more general perspective, however, decency would itself be undermined if individuals could hide immoral acts within the secrecy of information preserves. Moreover, as Starkie observes, legal protection of information territories would have other social costs, including those associated with transactions based upon imperfect information.[174]

Long before the Constitution was relevant to the regulation of the invasion of privacy tort,[175] the common law was sensitive to just such policy concerns regarding the diffusion of information. Warren and Brandeis, for example, flatly asserted that "[t]he right to privacy does not prohibit any publication of matter which is of public or general interest."[176] The first decision to recognize a right of privacy, *Pavesich v. New England Life Insurance Co.*,[177] stated with equal firmness that "[t]he truth may be spoken, written, or printed about all matters of a public nature, as well as matters of a private nature in which the public has a legitimate interest."[178] From the beginning, therefore, the task of the

---

173. T. STARKIE, A TREATISE ON THE LAW OF SLANDER, LIBEL, SCANDALUM MAGNATUM, AND FALSE RUMOURS at xx-xxi (New York 1826).

174. *See* G. SIMMEL, *supra* note 66, at 323.

175. The first amendment did not become applicable to state law until 1925 in the case of Gitlow v. New York, 268 U.S. 652 (1925). It was not until 1964 that the first amendment was deemed to control state defamation law. *See* New York Times Co. v. Sullivan, 376 U.S. 254 (1964). The first decision of the United States Supreme Court to apply the first amendment to state privacy law was Time, Inc. v. Hill, 385 U.S. 374 (1967).

176. Warren & Brandeis, *supra* note 6, at 214.

177. 122 Ga. 190, 50 S.E. 68 (1905).

178. *Id.* at 204, 50 S.E. at 74.

common law has been to balance the importance of maintaining individual information preserves against the public's general interest in information.

In conceptualizing the claims of the public, courts have tended to follow two distinct forms of inquiry. The first is directed toward the social status of the plaintiff; the second toward the social significance of the information at issue.[179] Both inquiries ultimately lead to the same issue, which is the nature of the public and its right to demand information.

The first inquiry is best illustrated by the example of public officials or candidates for public office. The obvious political importance of the dissemination of full information about such individuals has led courts to view them as having only extremely attenuated claims to information preserves.[180] Although the recent flap over the disclosure of Gary Hart's extramarital affair indicates that this view is still somewhat controversial,[181] it is profoundly unlikely that courts will intervene to decide what information may or may not be disclosed about a public official or candidate.[182] The underlying metaphor is that of the expropriation of private property, for "public men, are, as it were, public property."[183] The claims of public officials to a "private" information preserve are simply overridden by the more general demands of the public for political accountability.

Courts have reached a similar conclusion with regard to so-called "voluntary public figures." In the words of the *Restatement*:

> One who voluntarily places himself in the public eye, by engaging in public activities, or by assuming a prominent role in institutions or activities having general economic, cultural, social or similar public interest, or by submitting himself or his work for public judgment, cannot complain when he is given publicity that he has sought, even though it may be unfavorable to him. . . . [T]he legitimate interest of the public in [such an] individual may extend beyond those matters which are themselves made public, and to some reasonable extent may include information as to matters that would otherwise be private.[184]

---

179. This twofold inquiry has also formed the basis for contemporary first amendment regulation of state defamation law. *See* Philadelphia Newspapers, Inc. v. Hepps, 475 U.S. 767, 775 (1986).

180. *See, e.g.,* Kapellas v. Kofman, 1 Cal. 3d 20, 36-38, 459 P.2d 912, 922-24, 81 Cal. Rptr. 360, 370-71 (1969); Stryker v. Republic Pictures Corp., 108 Cal. App. 2d 191, 194, 238 P.2d 670, 672 (Ct. App. 1952).

181. *See, e.g.,* Nelson, *Soul-Searching Press Ethics,* NIEMAN REP., Spring 1988, at 15.

182. *See* Levinson, *Public Lives and the Limits of Privacy,* 21 POL. SCI. & POL. 263 (1988); *cf.* Monitor Patriot Co. v. Roy, 401 U.S. 265, 273-75 (1971).

183. Beauharnais v. Illinois, 343 U.S. 250, 263 n.18 (1952); *see also* Mayrant v. Richardson, 10 S.C.L. (1 Nott & McC.) 347, 350 (S.C. 1818).

184. RESTATEMENT (SECOND) OF TORTS § 652D comment e (1977); *see also* R. SACK, LIBEL, SLANDER, AND RELATED PROBLEMS 410-11 (1980).

Although the reasoning of the *Restatement* is almost entirely in terms of the voluntary public figure's waiver of any right to an information preserve, this logic is ultimately incomplete. For in almost every case a public figure will bring an action for the disclosure of information which he has not voluntarily made public, and it would be patently fictional to assert that in such circumstances he has "waived" his claim to the protection of this information. In such cases, therefore, the law's refusal to protect the public figure's information preserve must be justified in terms of a substantive analysis of the public's "legitimate interest" in the information at issue.

The second line of inquiry that courts have used to interpret the "legitimate public concern" requirement contains just such a substantive analysis. This inquiry focuses not on the social status of the plaintiff, but rather on the nature of the information at issue. As the *Restatement* asserts, "Included within the scope of legitimate public concern are matters of the kind customarily regarded as 'news.' "[185] Gouldner's discussion of the concept of the "public" suggests what is at stake in the common law's emphatic position that the public's interest in "news" overrides individual claims to an information preserve. According to Gouldner, "news is a public (and a public-generating) social phenomenon."[186] In large and diverse modern societies, in which common personal and patterned social interactions are quite limited, news provides precisely those "same social stimuli" that gather together the population into a "public."[187] Thus the "[e]mergence of the mass media and of the 'public' are mutually constructive developments."[188] To restrict the news is therefore simultaneously to restrict the public.

The public, however, has certain overriding claims to resist such restriction. One such claim, raised in the context of public officials, is

---

185. RESTATEMENT (SECOND) OF TORTS § 652D comment g (1977); *see, e.g.,* Campbell v. Seabury Press, 614 F.2d 395, 397 (5th Cir. 1980); Virgil v. Time, Inc., 527 F.2d 1122, 1128-29 (9th Cir. 1975), *cert. denied,* 425 U.S. 998 (1976); Logan v. District of Columbia, 447 F. Supp. 1328, 1333 (D.D.C. 1978); Neff v. Time, Inc., 406 F. Supp. 858, 861 (W.D. Pa. 1976); Kapellas v. Kofman, 1 Cal. 3d 20, 36, 459 P.2d 912, 922, 81 Cal. Rptr. 360, 370 (1969); Jacova v. Southern Radio & Television Co., 83 So. 2d 34, 40 (Fla. 1955); Cape Publications, Inc. v. Bridges, 423 So. 2d 426, 427 (Fla. Dist. Ct. App. 1982), *petition denied,* 431 So. 2d 988 (Fla. 1983), *cert. denied,* 464 U.S. 893 (1983); Bremmer v. Journal-Tribune Publishing Co., 247 Iowa 817, 827-28, 76 N.W.2d 762, 768 (1956); Fry v. Ionia Sentinel-Standard, 101 Mich. App. 725, 729-30, 300 N.W.2d 687, 690 (Ct. App. 1980); B. SANFORD, LIBEL AND PRIVACY: THE PREVENTION AND DEFENSE OF LITIGATION 447 (1987 Supp.).

186. A. GOULDNER, *supra* note 162, at 106.

187. *See* Molotch & Lester, *News as Purposive Behavior: On the Strategic Use of Routine Events, Accidents, and Scandals,* 39 AM. SOC. REV. 101 (1974).

188. A. GOULDNER, *supra* note 162, at 95-96. As de Tocqueville put it: "[T]here is a necessary connection between public associations and newspapers: newspapers make associations, and associations make newspapers . . . ." 2 A. DE TOCQUEVILLE, DEMOCRACY IN AMERICA 112 (P. Bradley ed. 1945) (H. Reeve trans. 1st ed. 1840).

political. Because American law views the public, in its role as the electorate, as ultimately responsible for political decisions, the public is presumptively entitled to all information that is necessary for informed governance. This theory is well canvassed in the first amendment literature,[189] and it is responsible for the frequent reiteration by the Supreme Court that "expression on public issues 'has always rested on the highest rung of the hierarchy of First Amendment values.' "[190]

But although the application of the theory of political governance to the public disclosure tort is uncontroversial, it is far too narrow to explain the broad scope of "legitimate public concern" that courts have felt compelled to protect. An excellent illustration is the classic case of *Sidis v. F-R Publishing Corp.,*[191] which involved William James Sidis, a famous child prodigy who in 1910 at the age of eleven had lectured distinguished mathematicians on the subject of four-dimensional bodies. His graduation from Harvard College at the age of sixteen attracted "considerable public attention."[192] But Sidis unfortunately never lived up to his promise. Soon after his graduation he slipped into a public obscurity from which he was rudely retrieved in 1937 by a biographical sketch in the "Where Are They Now?" section of *The New Yorker.* The sketch was "merciless in its dissection of intimate details of its subject's personal life, and this in company with elaborate accounts of Sidis' passion for privacy and the pitiable lengths to which he has gone in order to avoid public scrutiny."[193] The Second Circuit characterized the article as "a ruthless exposure of a once public character, who has since sought and has now been deprived of the seclusion of private life."[194] The court nevertheless concluded that Sidis could not recover for invasion of privacy, because the "public interest in obtaining information" was "dominant over the individual's desire for privacy."[195]

The court's decision to favor the interests of the public over Sidis' claim to an information preserve cannot be explained by a narrowly political theory of the public. The information contained in the article was not relevant to the governance of the nation. Nor, except in a purely tautological sense, can the court's decision be explained on the grounds that Sidis' present pathetic condition was "news," for by 1937 he had

---

189. *See, e.g.,* BeVier, *The First Amendment and Political Speech: An Inquiry Into the Substance and Limits of Principle,* 30 STAN. L. REV. 299 (1978); Meiklejohn, *The First Amendment Is an Absolute,* 1961 SUP. CT. REV. 245.

190. NAACP v. Claiborne Hardware Co., 458 U.S. 886, 913 (1982) (quoting Carey v. Brown, 447 U.S. 455, 467 (1980)).

191. 113 F.2d 806 (2d Cir.), *cert. denied,* 311 U.S. 711 (1940).

192. *Id.* at 807.

193. *Id.*

194. *Id.* at 807-08.

195. *Id.* at 809.

faded completely from public view. On what grounds, then, could the court conclude that the public was entitled to the information contained in the article?

The court reasoned that Sidis "was once a public figure" who had "excited both admiration and curiosity"; the article was "a matter of public concern" because it contained "the answer to the question of whether or not [Sidis] had fulfilled his early promise."[196] In effect, then, the court equated the notion of legitimate public concern with efforts to answer reasonable questions about public matters. Thus the court's analysis ultimately rested on the assumption that the public has a right to inquire into the significance of public persons and events.

This assumption has deep historical and sociological roots. Gouldner notes, for example, that because relations outside the family lack "affection, emotional dependency, tact, and . . . direct power over one another, there will be far fewer constraints in what may be questioned in public."[197] Thus public actions "are open to a critique by strangers who have fewer inhibitions about demanding justification and reasonable grounds,"[198] and for this reason such action must "routinely have to give an accounting of itself, either by providing information about its conduct or justification for it."[199] "The public," in short, "is a sphere in which one is accountable," and being accountable "means that one can be *constrained* to reveal *what* one has done and *why* one has done it."[200]

Gouldner's claim, of course, is not that public discussion is invariably characterized by a rational inquiry into accountability. Anyone familiar with the "unfair, intemperate, scurrilous and irresponsible"[201] character of much of our public discourse, or with the susceptibility of that discourse to manipulation by what Walter Lippmann called "publicity men,"[202] would know otherwise. Indeed, the discovery of the many irrational elements of our public discourse in the 1920s led to a serious "crisis" of democratic theory.[203] Gouldner's point is rather that the very attempt to assess the meaning of public phenomena implies "a cleared and safe space" in which the value of competing assessments may be "questioned, *negated* and *contradicted*."[204] The public search for

196. *Id.*

197. A. GOULDNER, *supra* note 162, at 102.

198. *Id.*

199. *Id.* at 103.

200. *Id.* at 102 (emphasis in original); *see also* Freeman & Mensch, *supra* note 3, at 243.

201. Desert Sun Publishing Co. v. Superior Court, 97 Cal. App. 3d 49, 51, 158 Cal. Rptr. 519, 521 (Ct. App. 1979).

202. W. LIPPMANN, PUBLIC OPINION 345 (1922).

203. E. PURCELL, THE CRISIS OF DEMOCRATIC THEORY: SCIENTIFIC NATURALISM AND THE PROBLEM OF VALUE 95-114 (1973).

204. A. GOULDNER, *supra* note 162, at 98 (emphasis in original); *see also id.* at 96-97.

accountability, in other words, creates a structure of communication which is inherently "*critical*."[205]

Gouldner's observations suggest that the public, as a collection of strangers united by access to common stimuli, is a social formation that has its own distinctive dynamic. An important aspect of this dynamic is the constant need to evaluate the significance of those stimuli whose "public" dissemination establishes the public's own continued existence. This need generates a critical logic in which no given evaluation can be rendered invulnerable to contradiction. The power of this logic is plainly visible in the reasoning of the *Sidis* opinion. The case in effect creates "a cleared and safe space" in which rival interpretations of the meaning of public persons and events may compete. The *Sidis* court refuses to circumscribe that space by withholding the information necessary for any given interpretation.

Thus *Sidis* ultimately rests on what might be termed a normative theory of public accountability, on the notion that the public *should* be entitled to inquire freely into the significance of public persons and events, and that this entitlement is so powerful that it overrides individual claims to the maintenance of information preserves. The theory is highly influential in modern case law, and it has led courts to interpret the "legitimate public concern" requirement as protecting the disclosure of all information having "a rational and at least arguably close relationship" to public persons or events "to be explained."[206]

The theory of public accountability offers a justification for the *Restatement's* rules regarding "voluntary public figures," for such persons are by definition already public, and hence subject to the free competition of rival interpretive assessments. Thus even if voluntary public figures have not "waived" their right to foreclose inquiry into nonpublic aspects of their lives, the public nevertheless has the right to scrutinize those aspects if they are relevant to its evaluation of the significance of public action.[207]

The theory also accounts for the *Restatement's* treatment of what it calls "involuntary public figures." These are individuals who, without their consent or approval, have become involved in public events like crimes, disasters, or accidents. The *Restatement* concludes that such persons

---

205. *Id.* at 98 (emphasis in original).

206. Virgil v. Sports Illustrated, 424 F. Supp. 1286, 1289 n.2 (S.D. Cal. 1976); *see, e.g.,* Gilbert v. Medical Economics Co., 665 F.2d 305, 308-09 (10th Cir. 1981); Campbell v. Seabury Press, 614 F.2d 395, 397 (5th Cir. 1980); Dresbach v. Doubleday & Co., 518 F. Supp. 1285, 1290-91 (D.D.C. 1981); Vassiliades v. Garfinckel's, Brooks Bros., 492 A.2d 580, 590 (D.C. 1985); Romaine v. Kallinger, 109 N.J. 282, 302, 537 A.2d 284, 294 (1988).

207. *See, e.g.,* Bilney v. Evening Star Newspaper Co., 43 Md. App. 560, 570-73, 406 A.2d 652, 659-60 (Ct. Spec. App. 1979).

are regarded as properly subject to the public interest, and publishers are permitted to satisfy the curiosity of the public . . . . As in the case of the voluntary public figure, the authorized publicity is not limited to the event that itself arouses the public interest, and to some reasonable extent includes publicity given to facts about the individual that would otherwise be purely private.[208]

Because concepts of "consent" and "waiver" are obviously inappropriate, the *Restatement* cannot explain exactly why the information preserves of involuntary public figures should be subject to "authorized publicity." The theory of public accountability, however, would justify the dissemination of information necessary to assess the significance of the public events in which such persons have become embroiled. Publicity would be actionable only when it bears "no discernible relationship" to the public events that require explanation.[209]

The theory of public accountability, with its requirement that the legal system permit public events and persons to be critically assessed, can collide with the aspiration to subject public communications to civility rules, an aspiration embodied in the "publicity" requirement. This conflict can be seen by comparing *Sidis* with *Briscoe*. In *Sidis* a public figure was deemed accountable to the demands of public inquiry despite the passage of time and a successful quest for anonymity; in *Briscoe* the passage of time and the successful achievement of anonymity were deemed to signify that a public figure had "reverted to that 'lawful and unexciting life' led by others," so that "he no longer need 'satisfy the curiosity of the public.' "[210] In *Sidis* public accountability runs roughshod over civility; in *Briscoe* civility forecloses the potential evaluation of a public person and event, and hence impedes the critical process of public accountability.

The reconciliation of this tension is an essential problematic of the public disclosure tort. *Sidis* itself allows for the possibility that the public accountability of public figures may be theoretically limited by the requirements of civility, but it predicts that these limits will be so attenuated as to be practically nonexistent:

We express no comment on whether or not the newsworthiness of

208. RESTATEMENT (SECOND) OF TORTS § 652D comment f (1977); *see, e.g.,* Campbell v. Seabury Press, 614 F.2d 395, 397 (5th Cir. 1980); Virgil v. Time, Inc., 527 F.2d 1122, 1129 (9th Cir. 1975), *cert. denied,* 425 U.S. 998 (1976); Logan v. District of Columbia, 447 F. Supp. 1328, 1333 (D.D.C. 1978); Jacova v. Southern Radio & Television Co., 83 So. 2d 34, 37, 40 (Fla. 1955); Waters v. Fleetwood, 212 Ga. 161, 167, 91 S.E.2d 344, 348 (1956); Bremmer v. Journal-Tribune Publishing Co., 247 Iowa 817, 827-28, 76 N.W.2d 762, 768 (1956); S. HOFSTADTER & G. HOROWITZ, *supra* note 51, at 116.

209. Howard v. Des Moines Register & Tribune Co., 283 N.W.2d 289, 302 (Iowa 1979), *cert. denied,* 445 U.S. 904 (1980); *see also* R. SACK, *supra* note 184, at 411-12.

210. Briscoe v. Reader's Digest Ass'n, 4 Cal. 3d 529, 538, 483 P.2d 34, 40, 93 Cal. Rptr. 866, 872 (1971) (quoting RESTATEMENT OF TORTS § 867 comment c (1939)).

the matter printed will always constitute a complete defense. Revelations may be so intimate and so unwarranted in view of the victim's position as to outrage the community's notions of decency. But when focused upon public characters, truthful comments upon dress, speech, habits, and the ordinary aspects of personality will usually not transgress this line. Regrettably or not, the misfortunes and frailties of neighbors and "public figures" are subjects of considerable interest and discussion to the rest of the population. And when such are the mores of the community, it would be unwise for a court to bar their expression in the newspapers, books, and magazines of the day.[211]

The development of the law has in general supported *Sidis'* prediction. Even the California Supreme Court has come to characterize *Briscoe,* its own precedent, as "an exception to the more general rule that 'once a man has become a public figure, or news, he remains a matter of legitimate recall to the public mind to the end of his days.' "[212] Thus the logic of public accountability has proved virtually overpowering with respect to the discussion of public persons or events. Any information with a "discernible relationship" to such public matters will likely be deemed "of legitimate concern to the public," and hence its dissemination to the public will not be actionable.[213]

That leaves open, however, the question of when information about nonpublic persons or events may also be protected as "of legitimate concern to the public." This question is nicely illustrated by the case of *Meetze v. Associated Press,*[214] in which the South Carolina Supreme Court held that a story reporting the birth of a healthy baby boy to a married twelve-year-old mother was of legitimate public interest, despite the mother's request that there be no "publicity."[215] The birth was not a public event until the Associated Press made it so, and for this reason the court's holding cannot be explained by any theory of public accountability. The publication of the story cannot be justified on the grounds of the public's need to understand public events or persons. Instead the court's protection of the story must depend upon a different theory, one which addresses the question of when events or persons may be made public in the first instance.

---

211. Sidis v. F-R Publishing Corp., 113 F.2d 806, 809 (2d Cir.), *cert. denied,* 311 U.S. 711 (1940).

212. Forsher v. Bugliosi, 26 Cal. 3d 792, 811, 608 P.2d 716, 726, 163 Cal. Rptr. 628, 638 (1980) (quoting Prosser, *Privacy,* 48 CALIF. L. REV. 383, 418 (1960)); *see also* Dresbach v. Doubleday & Co., 518 F. Supp. 1285, 1289 (D.D.C. 1981); Romaine v. Kallinger, 109 N.J. 282, 303-04, 537 A.2d 284, 294-95 (1988); McCormack v. Oklahoma Publishing Co., 6 Media L. Rep. (BNA) 1618, 1622 (Okla. 1980).

213. With regard to such matters, courts have registered their appreciation of the "force" in "the simple contention that whatever is in the news media is by definition newsworthy, that the press must in the nature of things be the final arbiter of newsworthiness." Kalven, *supra* note 42, at 336.

214. 230 S.C. 330, 95 S.E.2d 606 (1956).

215. *Id.* at 334, 95 S.E.2d at 608.

One such theory is that of political governance. Because we understand the public, in its role as the electorate, to be the ultimate source of political authority, it follows that information pertinent to informed governance should be made public. As Walter Lippmann observed at the dawn of the modern first amendment era, "[N]ews is the chief source of the opinion by which government now proceeds."[216] But this theory, although uncontroversial, is too narrow to account for a case like *Meetze,* and the South Carolina Supreme Court made no attempt to use it. Instead the court defended its interpretation of the "legitimate public concern" requirement on the grounds that it "is rather unusual for a twelve-year-old girl to give birth to a child. It is a biological occurrence which would naturally excite public interest."[217]

This notion of "naturally" exciting public interest is puzzling. The precise issue posed by *Meetze* is whether a mother's information preserve should be forced to yield to the curiosity of the public. That the public is in fact curious may well be true, but it merely restates the problem. As the court itself notes, "[T]he phrase 'public or general interest' in this connection does not mean mere curiosity."[218] But this brings us back full circle, for we cannot distinguish between "natural" and "mere" curiosity without some criterion of when it is justifiable to drag nonpublic matters into the light of public scrutiny.

The second *Restatement,* in a widely cited and influential commentary,[219] offers just such a criterion. It suggests that the question of whether giving publicity to nonpublic matters is of legitimate public concern should be decided by reference to "the customs and conventions of the community":

> [I]n the last analysis what is proper becomes a matter of the community mores. The line is to be drawn when the publicity ceases to be the giving of information to which the public is entitled, and becomes a morbid and sensational prying into private lives for its own sake, with which a reasonable member of the public, with decent standards, would say that he had no concern. The limitations, in other words, are those of common decency, having due regard to the freedom of the press and its reasonable leeway to choose what it will tell the public, but also due regard to the feelings of the individual and the harm that will be done to him by the

---

216. W. Lippmann, Liberty and the News 12 (1920).

217. *Meetze,* 230 S.C. at 338, 95 S.E.2d at 610. The court expressed "regret" that it could not "give legal recognition to Mrs. Meetze's desire to avoid publicity but the courts do not sit as censors of the manners of the Press." *Id.* at 339, 95 S.E.2d at 610.

218. *Id.* at 337, 95 S.E.2d at 609 (quoting 41 Am. Jur. *Privacy* § 14 (1942)).

219. *See, e.g.,* Gilbert v. Medical Economics Co., 665 F.2d 305, 307-08 (10th Cir. 1981); Wasser v. San Diego Union, 191 Cal. App. 3d 1455, 1461-62, 236 Cal. Rptr. 772, 776 (Ct. App. 1987); Bilney v. Evening Star Newspaper Co., 43 Md. App. 560, 572-73, 406 A.2d 652, 659-60 (Ct. Spec. App. 1979); Montesano v. Donrey Media Group, 99 Nev. 644, 651, 668 P.2d 1081, 1086 (1983), *cert. denied,* 466 U.S. 959 (1984).

exposure.[220]

At first blush, the *Restatement's* interpretation would appear to explain why, for example, the South Carolina Supreme Court, thirty years after *Meetze,* would in *Hawkins v. Multimedia, Inc.*[221] uphold a finding of liability against a newspaper for publicly disclosing the identity of a teenage father of an illegitimate child in a story about teenage pregnancies. It is plausible to suggest that "community mores" would be more offended by such a story than by a comparatively inoffensive article identifying the married twelve-year-old mother of a baby son.[222]

Upon further reflection, however, the gloss placed upon the *Restatement* by a decision like *Hawkins* is inadequate, for it essentially equates the "customs and conventions of the community" that determine whether nonpublic matters are of legitimate public concern with the social norms that underlie the twin requirements of "offensiveness" and "private facts." It thus collapses the "legitimate public concern" test into the very criteria that define whether disclosures are actionable, thereby rendering the test superfluous. As a result the capacity of the news to make persons and events public would be completely subordinated to the civility rules enforced by the public disclosure tort.

Most courts, however, have refused to subordinate the news in this manner. In *Kelley v. Post Publishing Co.,*[223] for example, a newspaper was sued for publishing the photograph of a hideously deformed body of a child after a fatal automobile accident. While the display of such a photograph might well exceed the bounds of common decency, the court in *Kelley* ruled that it was not actionable for the newspaper to publish the photograph, on the grounds that any contrary conclusion would prevent the publication of pictures "of a train wreck or of an airplane crash if any of the bodies of the victims were recognizable."[224]

*Kelley's* reasoning rests on two widely-shared and important premises. The first is that we want information about events like disasters to be made public; the second is that we want this information disseminated even if doing so would violate the civility rules that would otherwise be

---

220. RESTATEMENT (SECOND) OF TORTS § 652D comment h (1977).

221. 288 S.C. 569, 344 S.E.2d 145, *cert. denied,* 479 U.S. 1012 (1986).

222. Thus in *Meetze* the court had offered

    another reason why the facts do not show a wrongful invasion of the right of privacy. It would be going pretty far to say that the article complained of was reasonably calculated to embarrass or humiliate the plaintiffs or cause mental distress. Although Mrs. Meetze was only eleven years old when she married, the marriage was not void.

    *Meetze,* 230 S.C. at 338, 95 S.E.2d at 610. At first this reason appears to pertain to whether the story at issue is "highly offensive." But a case like *Hawkins* suggests that a lack of such offensiveness is equally pertinent to the judgment that the public's curiosity in Mrs. Meetze's delivery is not unjustified.

223. 327 Mass. 275, 98 N.E.2d 286 (1951).

224. *Id.* at 278, 98 N.E.2d at 287.

enforced by the tort.[225] It is clear that the *Restatement* shares these premises, for it explicitly states that "[a]uthorized publicity includes publications concerning homicide and other crimes, arrests, police raids, suicides, marriages and divorces, accidents, fires, catastrophes of nature . . . and many other similar matters of genuine, even if more or less deplorable, popular appeal."[226]

Thus the *Restatement*, and in fact almost all courts, interpret the "legitimate public concern" requirement as insulating from legal liability news that is uncivil and "deplorable."[227] But this implies that the "community mores" which determine whether the disclosure of nonpublic matters is of legitimate public concern cannot be the same as the civility rules which determine whether communications are "highly offensive" disclosures of "private" facts. The *Restatement* tells us that the community mores at issue in the "legitimate public concern" test are instead those which identify "matters . . . customarily regarded as 'news.' "[228] These mores circumscribe the scope of the press' "reasonable leeway to choose what it will tell the public."[229]

But while this interpretation of the "legitimate public concern" requirement has the virtue of internal coherence, it simultaneously raises a distinct and pressing issue of public policy: Why should the press be confined by the customary definition of "news"? It is true that the mores which define newsgathering define the boundaries of public life as we now know it, but why should the law hinder attempts to enlarge that life, particularly if there is a public desire for the information constitutive of such enlargements?

The answer, of course, is that once persons or events are made public, the logic of public accountability will all but displace rules of civility. In the public sphere all persons and events are subject to an unblinking scrutiny that searches for meaning and significance; in the sphere of com-

---

225. A good example of the expression of these premises may be found in the recent remarks of the Dutch journalist Joop Swart, at an exhibition of the winners of the World Press Photo Competition:

> Some of the pictures you see here might shock you deeply. And some of you might be inclined to denounce them as sensational, distasteful, intruding into the privacy of the individual.
>
> But let me remind you that the photographers who made those pictures chose reality over escapism. . . .
>
> Let us be grateful to them, because they expanded our world.

Morris, *In Press Photos, the World at Its Worst,* Int'l Herald Tribune, May 12, 1989, at 9, col. 3.

226. RESTATEMENT (SECOND) OF TORTS § 652D comment g (1977).

227. *See, e.g.,* Cape Publications, Inc. v. Bridges, 423 So. 2d 426, 427-28 (Fla. Dist. Ct. App. 1982); Waters v. Fleetwood, 212 Ga. 161, 91 S.E.2d 344 (1956); Beresky v. Teschner, 64 Ill. App. 3d 848, 381 N.E.2d 979 (App. Ct. 1978); Bremmer v. Journal-Tribune Publishing Co., 247 Iowa 817, 827-28, 76 N.W.2d 762, 768 (1956); Costlow v. Cusimano, 34 A.D.2d 196, 311 N.Y.S.2d 92 (App. Div. 1970).

228. RESTATEMENT (SECOND) OF TORTS § 652D comment g (1977).

229. *Id.* at comment h.

munity such scrutiny is experienced as demeaning and as utterly destructive of the conventions that give meaning to human dignity.[230] The two spheres are deeply incommensurate and can coexist only in an uneasy tension. The common law therefore resists enlargement of the public sphere because it is inconsistent with the maintenance of social personality. What is ultimately at stake in this resistance is thus the protection of both individual dignity and community identity, as constituted by rules of civility, from the encroachments of the logic of public accountability.

In the modern tort the reach of this logic is as a practical matter determined by the application of the "legitimate public concern" test to nonpublic matters. The test thus bears an enormous social pressure, and it is not surprising to find that the common law is deeply confused and ambivalent about its application.[231] One jurisdiction abandons the field to the public sphere and refuses to enforce communal norms of civility,[232] while another gives full sway to " 'the customs and conventions of the community,' "[233] while yet a third holds that "in borderline cases the benefit of doubt should be cast in favor of protecting the publication."[234] Some courts confine the sphere of legitimate public concern to information that is, in Gouldner's phrase, "*de*contextualized,"[235] so that they "distinguish between fictionalization and dramatization on the one hand and dissemination of news and information on the other."[236] Other courts hold that "it is neither feasible nor desirable for a court to make a distinction between news for information and news for entertainment in determining the extent to which publication is privileged."[237]

In these various and inconsistent interpretations of the "legitimate public concern" test one can trace the wavering line between the insistent demands of public accountability and the expressive claims of communal

---

230. *See* E. GOFFMAN, ASYLUMS 23-32 (1961).

231. *Compare* Zimmerman, *Requiem for a Heavyweight: A Farewell to Warren and Brandeis's Privacy Tort*, 68 CORNELL L. REV. 291, 350-51 (1983) *with* Woito & McNulty, *The Privacy Disclosure Tort and the First Amendment: Should the Community Decide Newsworthiness?*, 64 IOWA L. REV. 185 (1979).

232. Hall v. Post, 323 N.C. 259, 269-70, 372 S.E.2d 711, 717 (1988); Anderson v. Fisher Broadcasting Co., 300 Or. 452, 469, 712 P.2d 803, 814 (1986).

233. Virgil v. Time, Inc., 527 F.2d 1122, 1129 (9th Cir. 1975), *cert. denied*, 425 U.S. 998 (1976) (quoting RESTATEMENT (SECOND) OF TORTS § 652D comment f (Tent. Draft No. 21, 1975)).

234. Cordell v. Detective Publications, Inc., 307 F. Supp. 1212, 1220 (E.D. Tenn. 1968), *aff'd*, 419 F.2d 989 (6th Cir. 1969).

235. A. GOULDNER, *supra* note 162, at 95 (emphasis in original).

236. Garner v. Triangle Publications, Inc., 97 F. Supp. 546, 550 (S.D.N.Y. 1951); *see* Hazlitt v. Fawcett Publications, Inc., 116 F. Supp. 538, 545 (D. Conn. 1953); Diaz v. Oakland Tribune, Inc., 139 Cal. App. 3d 118, 134-35, 188 Cal. Rptr. 762, 773 (Ct. App. 1983); Aquino v. Bulletin Co., 190 Pa. Super. 528, 536-41, 154 A.2d 422, 427-30 (Super. Ct. 1959). On the distinction between newspapers getting "the facts" and getting "the story," see M. SCHUDSON, DISCOVERING THE NEWS: A SOCIAL HISTORY OF AMERICAN NEWSPAPERS 88-120 (1978).

237. Jenkins v. Dell Publishing Co., 251 F.2d 447, 451 (3d Cir.) (footnote omitted), *cert. denied*, 357 U.S. 921 (1958); *cf.* Winters v. New York, 333 U.S. 507, 510 (1948).

life. Common law courts, like the rest of us, are searching for ways to mediate between these two necessary and yet conflicting regimes. We can understand the public disclosure tort, then, as holding a flickering candle to what Max Weber in 1918 called the "fate of our times," which is of course the "rationalization and intellectualization and, above all, . . . the 'disenchantment of the world.' "[238]

## IV
## CONCLUDING THOUGHTS: THE FRAGILITY OF PRIVACY

I hope I have made good on my initial claim that the common law tort of invasion of privacy reflects a complex and fascinating apprehension of the social texture of contemporary society. The tort safeguards the interests of individuals in the maintenance of rules of civility. These rules enable individuals to receive and to express respect, and to that extent are constitutive of human dignity. In the case of intrusion, these rules also enable individuals to receive and to express intimacy, and to that extent are constitutive of human autonomy. In the case of both intrusion and public disclosure, the civility rules maintained by the tort embody the obligations owed by members of a community to each other, and to that extent define the substance and boundaries of community life.

The tort's preservation of civility rules appears in its clearest and least qualified form in the branch of the tort that protects the seclusion of individuals from intrusion. But when civility rules attempt to control communication, as in the branch of the tort that regulates the public disclosure of private information, the common law must confront the tension between such rules and the demands of public accountability. The common law has been torn between maintaining the civility which we expect in public discourse, and giving ample "latitude"[239] to the processes of critical evaluation that are also intrinsic to that discourse.

This interpretation of the tort carries with it several significant implications for the understanding of privacy in contemporary society. First, it suggests that in everyday life we do not experience privacy as a "neutral" or "objective" fact, but rather as an inherently normative set of social practices that constitute a way of life, our way of life. The privacy protected by the common law has no special "function," like the protection of secrecy or the maintenance of role segregation, although it may, to a greater or lesser extent, accomplish each of these purposes. In the tort, "privacy" is simply a label that we use to identify one aspect of the many forms of respect by which we maintain a community. It is less

---

238.  M. WEBER, *Science as a Vocation,* in FROM MAX WEBER: ESSAYS IN SOCIOLOGY 129, 155 (H. Gerth & C. Mills eds. & trans. 1958).

239.  Afro-American Publishing Co. v. Jaffe, 366 F.2d 649, 654 (D.C. Cir. 1966).

important that the purity of the label be maintained, than that the forms of community life of which it is a part be preserved.

Second, privacy understood as subsisting in the ritual idiom of civility rules can exist only where social life has the density and intensity to generate and sustain such rules. It is important to stress, however, that social life does not always have these characteristics. Certain kinds of "total institutions," for example, deliberately violate civility rules so as to degrade and mortify inmates.[240]

A less exotic and more significant example of the loss of civility rules can be found in the writings of James Rule, who has extensively studied large scale surveillance organizations like consumer credit rating agencies. Rule found that attempts to limit the access of such organizations to personal information in the name of privacy were invariably transformed into requirements that such organizations ensure the accuracy and instrumentally appropriate use of such information.[241] This transformation ultimately rested on the unimpeachable assumption that organizations could reach better, more precise decisions with greater information, and on the more questionable assumption that "both organizations and individuals shared an interest in [this] enhanced efficiency."[242] What Rule found striking was the absence of any strong privacy claims that could limit the *absolute* amount of information obtainable by such organizations.

This absence, however, is rendered explicable by Rule's own account of the nature of the "privacy" interest at stake, which in his view amounted to no more than " 'aesthetic' satisfactions in keeping private spheres private."[243] In the instrumental world of large surveillance organizations, in other words, the realm of the private has dwindled to the domain of the "instinctive."[244] This strongly suggests that relationships between individuals and large organizations like credit rating agencies are not sufficiently textured or dense to sustain vital rules of civility, and that as a result privacy has lost its social and communal character. But if the value of privacy can be conceptualized only in personal or subjective terms, it should be no surprise that its value has not proved politically powerful.

Third, the specific areas of social life that are governed by rules of

---

240.  E. GOFFMAN, *supra* note 230, at 14-35.

241.  J. RULE, D. MCADAM, L. STEARNS & D. UGLOW, THE POLITICS OF PRIVACY 70-71 (1980).

242.  *Id.* at 70.

243.  *Id.* at 71.

244.  *Id.* at 22. In an earlier work, Rule characterized the value of privacy as the pre-social good of "autonomy." J. RULE, PRIVATE LIVES AND PUBLIC SURVEILLANCE 349-58 (1973). He expressed his hope that "values of individual autonomy and privacy can prevail in these contexts over those of collective rationality." *Id.* at 354.

civility are vulnerable to displacement by exogenous institutions. The preemption of civility by the rational accountability characteristic of the public sphere is only one example of such exogenous pressure. Another would be the claims of the state to control and regulate communal life. Stanley Diamond has eloquently documented how the modern state has "cannibalized" the "spontaneous, traditional, personal, [and] commonly known" aspects of "custom."[245] This tension between the prerogatives of state power and the norms of communal life is plainly visible in our fourth amendment jurisprudence, which attempts to subordinate the conduct of state law enforcement officials to the community's normatively sanctioned "expectations of privacy," while simultaneously balancing against these expectations "the government's need for effective methods to deal with breaches of public order."[246] In this balance it is not uncommon for the instrumental needs of the state to override community norms.

The ultimate lesson of the tort, then, is the extreme fragility of privacy norms in modern life. That fragility stems not merely from our ravenous appetite for the management of our social environment, but also from the undeniable prerogatives of public accountability. In the attempt to assess the meaning of public phenomena, the way of life that happens to constitute us, and to bestow our privacy with its meaning, appears to be merely arbitrary—a matter of aesthetics or instinct. And we are thus led to attempt to rationalize the value of privacy, to discover its functions and reasons, to dress it up in the philosophical language of autonomy, or to dress it down in the economic language of information costs. But this is to miss the plain fact that privacy is for us a living reality only because we enjoy a certain kind of communal existence. Our very "dignity" inheres in that existence,[247] which, if it is not acknowledged and preserved, will vanish, as will the privacy we cherish.

---

245. Diamond, *The Rule of Law Versus the Order of Custom,* 38 Soc. Res. 42, 44-47 (1971).

246. New Jersey v. T.L.O., 469 U.S. 325, 337 (1985); *see also* United States v. Montoya de Hernandez, 473 U.S. 531, 537 (1985); Skinner v. Railway Labor Executives' Ass'n, 109 S. Ct. 1402, 1414 (1989).

247. Rorty, *Postmodernist Bourgeois Liberalism,* 10 J. Phil. 583, 586-87 (1983).

# Part III
# The Economics of 'Privacy'

# [15]

# GEORGIA LAW REVIEW

VOLUME 12        SPRING 1978        NUMBER 3

## JOHN A. SIBLEY LECTURE

## THE RIGHT OF PRIVACY

*Richard A. Posner**

### INTRODUCTION

The concept of "privacy" is elusive and ill defined. Much ink has been spilled in trying to clarify its meaning.[1] I will avoid the definitional problem by simply noting that one aspect of privacy is the withholding or concealment of information. This aspect is of particular interest to the economist now that the study of information has become an important field of economics.[2]

Heretofore the economics of information has been concerned with topics relating to the dissemination and, to a lesser extent, concealment of information in explicit (mainly labor and consumer-goods) markets: such topics as advertising, fraud, price dispersion, and job search. The present Article attempts an economic analysis of the dissemination and withholding of information primarily in personal rather than business contexts. It is thus concerned with such matters as prying, eavesdropping, "self-advertising," and gossip. The line between personal and commercial is not always clear or useful, and I shall not maintain it unwaveringly; the emphasis, however, is on the personal.

The first part of the Article develops the economic analysis. I

---

* Professor of Law, University of Chicago. This Article is the text of the John A. Sibley Lecture delivered on March 2, 1978, at the University of Georgia School of Law, and is part of a collaborative project with George J. Stigler on the law and economics of privacy, conducted under the auspices of the Center for the Study of Economy and the State at the University of Chicago. I am indebted to (among others) Richard A. Epstein, Charles Fried, Kent Greenawalt, Anthony T. Kronman, William M. Landes, George J. Stigler, Geoffrey R. Stone, James B. White, and participants in the Law and Economics Workshop at the University of Chicago Law School for helpful comments on earlier drafts.

[1] *See, e.g.,* Thomson, *The Right to Privacy,* 4 PHIL. & PUB. AFF. 295 (1975). On the variety of legal contexts of the term "privacy," see Comment, *A Taxonomy of Privacy: Repose, Sanctuary, and Intimate Decision,* 64 CALIF. L. REV. 1447 (1976).

[2] *See* G. STIGLER, *The Economics of Information,* in THE ORGANIZATION OF INDUSTRY 171 (1968).

394        *GEORGIA LAW REVIEW*            [Vol. 12:393

remark in passing the irony that personal privacy seems to be valued more highly than organizational privacy, judging by current public policy trends, although a reverse ordering would be more consistent with the economics of the problem. The second part of the Article examines the principles of tort law that protect a "right of privacy" in both commercial and personal contexts (the former is discussed only briefly, however) and concludes that the judges in tort cases have been sensitive to the economics of privacy.

## I. THE ECONOMICS OF PRIVACY

### A. *Privacy and Curiosity as Intermediate Goods*

People invariably possess information, including facts about themselves and contents of communications, that they will incur costs to conceal. Sometimes such information is of value to others: that is, others will incur costs to discover it. Thus we have two economic goods, "privacy" and "prying." We could regard them purely as consumption goods, the way economic analysis normally regards turnips or beer; and we would then speak of a "taste" for privacy or for prying. But this would bring the economic analysis to a grinding halt because tastes are unanalyzable from an economic standpoint. An alternative is to regard privacy and prying as intermediate rather than final goods, instrumental rather than ultimate values. Under this approach, people are assumed not to desire or value privacy or prying in themselves but to use these goods as inputs into the production of income or some other broad measure of utility or welfare.

The second approach, which views privacy and prying as intermediate goods, is the one taken here, in order to allow the economic analysis to proceed. Obviously, that would be an inadequate reason if privacy and prying did not in fact possess important attributes of intermediate goods. I shall try to show that they do; the reader will have to decide whether this approach captures enough of the relevant reality to be illuminating.

### B. *The Demand for Private Information*

The demand for private information (viewed, as it will be throughout this Article, as an intermediate rather than final good) is readily comprehensible where the existence of an actual or potential relationship, business or personal, creates opportunities for gain by the demander. This is obviously true of the information which the tax collector, fiancé, partner, creditor, and competitor, among others, seek. Less obviously, much of the casual prying (a term used here without any pejorative connotation) into the private lives of friends and colleagues that is so common a feature of social life is also motivated, to a greater extent than we may realize, by rational considerations of self-interest. Prying enables one to form a more accurate picture of a friend or colleague, and the knowledge gained is useful in one's social or professional dealings with him. For example, in choosing a friend one legitimately wants to know whether he will be discreet or indiscreet, selfish or generous, and these qualities are not always apparent on initial acquaintance. Even a pure altruist needs to know the (approximate) wealth of any prospective beneficiary of his altruism in order to be able to gauge the value of a transfer to him.

The other side of the coin is that social, like business, dealings present opportunities for exploitation through misrepresentation. Psychologists and sociologists have pointed out that even in everyday life people try to manipulate by misrepresentation other people's opinion of them.[3] As one psychologist has written, the "wish for privacy expresses a desire . . . to control others' perceptions and beliefs vis-à-vis the self-concealing person."[4] Even the strongest defenders of privacy describe the individual's right to privacy as the right to "control the flow of information about him."[5] A seldom-remarked corollary to a right to misrepresent one's character is that others have a legitimate interest in unmasking the deception.

Yet some of the demand for private information about other people is not self-protection in the foregoing sense but seems mysteriously disinterested—for example, that of the readers of newspaper gossip columns, whose "idle curiosity" Warren and Brandeis deplored,[6] groundlessly in my opinion. Gossip columns recount the

---

[3] Erving Goffman develops this point in an interesting book in which he refers explicitly to "misrepresentation" but uses the term without any pejorative connotation. E. GOFFMAN, THE PRESENTATION OF SELF IN EVERYDAY LIFE 58 (1959).

[4] Jourard, *Some Psychological Aspects of Privacy*, 31 LAW & CONTEMP. PROB. 307, 307 (1966).

[5] Stone, *The Scope of the Fourth Amendment: Privacy and the Police Use of Spies, Secret Agents, and Informers*, 1976 AM. BAR FOUND. RESEARCH J. 1193, 1207.

[6] Even gossip apparently harmless, when widely and persistently circulated, is potent for evil. It both belittles and perverts. It belittles by inverting the relative importance of things, thus dwarfing the thoughts and aspirations of a people. When personal gossip attains the dignity of print, and crowds the space available for matters of real interest to the community, what wonder that the ignorant and thoughtless mistake its relative importance. Easy of comprehension, appealing to that weak side of human nature which is never wholly cast down by the misfortunes and frailties of our neighbors, no one can be surprised that it usurps the place of interest in brains capable of

396          *GEORGIA LAW REVIEW*          [Vol. 12:393

personal lives of wealthy and successful people whose tastes and
habits offer models—that is, yield information—to the ordinary person in making consumption, career, and other decisions. The models
are not always positive. The story of Howard Hughes, for example,
is usually told as a morality play, warning of the pitfalls of success.
Tales of the notorious and the criminal—of Profumo and of Leo-
pold—have a similar function. Gossip columns open people's eyes
to opportunities and dangers; they are genuinely informational.

The expression "idle curiosity" is misleading. People are not
given to random, undifferentiated curiosity. Why is there less curiosity about the lives of the poor (as measured, for example, by the
frequency with which poor people figure as central characters in
novels) than about those of the rich?[7] The reason is that the lives of
the poor do not provide as much useful information in patterning
our own lives. What interest there is in the poor is focused on people
who are (or were) like us but who became poor rather than on those
who were always poor; again the cautionary function of such information should be evident.

Warren and Brandeis attributed the rise of curiosity about people's lives to the excesses of the press.[8] The economist does not
believe, however, that supply creates demand.[9] A more persuasive
explanation for the rise of the gossip column is the secular increase
in personal incomes. There is apparently very little privacy in poor
societies,[10] where, consequently, people can easily observe at first

---

other things. Triviality destroys at once robustness of thought and delicacy of feeling.
No enthusiasm can flourish, no generous impulse can survive under its blighting influ-
ence.
Warren & Brandeis, *The Right of Privacy*, 4 HARV. L. REV. 193, 196 (1890).

[7] Surely not because writers know the lives of the rich more intimately than those of the
poor: Shakespeare's protagonists are kings and nobles, but he was no aristocrat.

[8] The press is overstepping in every direction the obvious bounds of propriety and of
decency. Gossip is no longer the resource of the idle and of the vicious, but has
become a trade, which is pursued with industry as well as effrontery. . . . To occupy
the indolent, column upon column is filled with idle gossip, which can only be procured
by intrusion upon the domestic circle.
Warren & Brandeis, *supra* note 6, at 196.

[9] "In this, as in other branches of commerce, the supply creates the demand." *Id.*

[10] *See* D. FLAHERTY, PRIVACY IN COLONIAL NEW ENGLAND 83 (1972); T. GREGOR, MEHINAKU:
THE DRAMA OF DAILY LIFE IN A BRAZILIAN INDIAN VILLAGE 89-90, 360-61 (1977); and anthropological data reported in the first chapter of A. WESTIN, PRIVACY AND FREEDOM (1967). Gregor's
findings on privacy are summarized in M. HARRIS, CANNIBALS AND KINGS: THE ORIGINS OF
CULTURES 12 (1977):
[T]he search for personal privacy is a pervasive theme in the daily life of people who
live in small villages. The Mehinacu apparently know too much about each other's
business for their own good. They can tell from the print of a heel or a buttock where

hand the intimate lives of others. Personal surveillance is costlier in wealthier societies both because people live in conditions that give them greater privacy from such observation and because the value (and hence opportunity cost) of time is greater[11]—too great to make a generous allotment of time to watching neighbors worthwhile. People in the wealthier societies sought an alternative method of informing themselves about how others live and the press provided it. A legitimate and important function of the press is to provide specialization in prying in societies where the costs of obtaining information have become too great for the Nosey Parker.

## C. *Property Rights in Private Information*

That disclosure of personal information is resisted by, *i.e.*, is costly to, the person to whom the information pertains yet is valuable to others may seem to argue for giving people property rights in information about themselves and letting them sell those rights freely. The process of voluntary exchange would then assure that the information was put to its most valuable use. The attractiveness of this solution depends, however, on (1) the nature and provenance of the information and (2) transaction costs.

The interest in encouraging investment in the production of socially valuable information presents the strongest case for granting property rights in secrets. This is the economic rationale for according legal protection to the variety of commercial ideas, plans, and information encompassed by the term "trade secret." It also explains why the law does not require the "shrewd bargainer" to disclose to the other party to the bargain the bargainer's true opinion of its value. What we mean by shrewd bargainer is (in part) someone who invests resources in acquiring information about the true values of things. Were he forced to share this information with potential sellers he would obtain no return on his investment, and the process—basic to a market economy—by which people transfer goods through voluntary exchange into successively more valuable uses would be impaired. This is true even though the lack of candor in the bargaining process deprives it of some of its "voluntary" character.

---

a couple stopped and had sexual relations off the path. Lost arrows give away the owner's prize fishing spot; an ax resting against a tree tells a story of interrupted work. No one leaves or enters the village without being noticed. One must whisper to secure privacy—with walls of thatch there are no closed doors.

[11] *See* S. LINDER, THE HARRIED LEISURE CLASS ch. VII (1970).

At some point nondisclosure becomes fraud. One consideration relevant to deciding whether a transacting party has crossed the line is whether the information that he seeks to conceal is a product of significant investment.[12] If not, the social costs of disclosure, which, to repeat, arise from the effect of disclosure in dampening the incentive to invest in information gathering, will be low. This consideration may be decisive on the question, for example, whether the law should require the owner of a house to disclose latent, *i.e.*, nonobvious, defects to a purchaser. The ownership and maintenance of a house are, of course, productive activities in which it is costly to engage. But the owner acquires knowledge of the defects of his house costlessly (or nearly so); hence forcing him to disclose those defects will not reduce his incentive to invest in discovering them.

Transaction-cost considerations may also militate against the assignment of a property right to the possessor of a secret. Consider, for example, (1) whether the law should require the Bureau of the Census to buy the information that it seeks from the firms or households it interviews and (2) whether the law should allow a magazine to sell its subscriber list to another magazine without obtaining the subscribers' consent. Requiring the Bureau of the Census to pay (that is, assigning the property right in the information sought to the interviewee) would yield a skewed sample were the price uniform. To get a representative sample despite the different costs of disclosure (and hence price for cooperating) to the firms and households sampled, the Bureau would have to use a highly complicated, differential price schedule. In the magazine case the costs of obtaining subscriber approval would be high relative to the value of the list.[13] If, therefore, we believe that these lists are generally worth more to the purchasers than being shielded from possible unwanted solicitations is worth to the subscribers, we should assign the property right to the magazine; and the law does this.[14]

The decision to assign the property right away from the individual is supported in both the census and subscription-list cases by the fact that the costs of disclosure to the individual are small. They are small in the census case because of the precautions the government takes against disclosure of the information collected to creditors, tax

---

[12] *See* Kronman, *Mistake, Disclosure, Information, and the Law of Contracts*, 7 J. LEGAL STUD. 1 (1978).

[13] A few magazines offer the subscriber the option of having his name removed from the list of subscribers that is sold to other magazines. But this solution is unsatisfactory to the subscribers (presumably the vast majority) who are not averse to *all* magazine solicitations.

[14] *See* Shibley v. Time, Inc., 45 Ohio App. 2d 69, 341 N.E.2d 337 (1975).

collectors, or others who might have transactions with the individual in which they could use the information to gain an advantage over him. They are small in the subscription-list case because the information about the subscribers that is disclosed to the purchaser of the list is trivial; the purchaser cannot use it to impose substantial costs on the subscribers.[15]

The type of private information discussed thus far is not, in general, discreditable to the individual to whom it pertains. Yet we have seen that there may still be good reasons to assign the property right away from him. Much of the demand for privacy, however, concerns discreditable information, often information concerning past or present criminal activity or moral conduct at variance with a person's professed moral standards. And often the motive for concealment is, as suggested earlier, to mislead those with whom he transacts. Other private information that people wish to conceal, while not strictly discreditable, would if revealed correct misapprehensions that the individual is trying to exploit, as when a worker conceals a serious health problem from his employer or a prospective husband conceals his sterility from his fiancée. It is not clear why society should assign the property right in such information to the individual to whom it pertains; and the common law, as we shall see, generally does not. A separate question, to which we return later, is whether the decision to assign the property right away from the possessor of guilty secrets implies that the law should countenance any and all methods of uncovering those secrets.

An analogy to the world of commerce may help to explain why people should not—on economic grounds, in any event—have a right to conceal material facts about themselves. We think it wrong (and inefficient) that the law should permit a seller in hawking his wares to make false or incomplete representations as to their quality. But people "sell" themselves as well as their goods. They profess high standards of behavior in order to induce others to engage in social or business dealings with them from which they derive an advantage but at the same time they conceal some of the facts that these acquaintances would find useful in forming an accurate picture of their character. There are practical reasons for not imposing a general legal duty of full and frank disclosure of one's material

---

[15] No doubt many subscribers to *Christian Motherhood* would be offended to be solicited by *Playboy*, but it is unlikely that *Playboy*'s publisher would consider the subscribers to *Christian Motherhood* a sufficiently promising source of new *Playboy* subscribers to want to buy the subscription list.

personal shortcomings—a duty not to be a hypocrite. But everyone should be allowed to protect himself from disadvantageous transactions by ferreting out concealed facts about individuals which are material to the representations (implicit or explicit) that those individuals make concerning their moral qualities.

It is no answer that such individuals have "the right to be let alone."[16] Very few people want to be let alone. They want to manipulate the world around them by selective disclosure of facts about themselves.[17] Why should others be asked to take their self-serving claims at face value and be prevented from obtaining the information necessary to verify or disprove these claims?

Some private information that people desire to conceal is not discreditable. In our culture, for example, most people do not like to be seen naked, quite apart from any discreditable fact that such observation might reveal. Since this reticence, unlike concealment of discreditable information, is not a source of social costs, and since transaction costs are low, there is an economic case for assigning the property right in this area of private information to the individual; and this, as we shall see, is what the law does. I do not think, however, that many people have a *general* reticence that makes them wish to conceal nondiscrediting personal information. Anyone who has ever sat next to a stranger on an airplane or a ski lift knows the delight that people take in talking about themselves to complete strangers. Reticence comes into play when one is speaking to people—friends, relatives, acquaintances, business associates—who might use information about him to gain an advantage in some business or social transaction with him. Reticence is generally a means rather than an end.

The reluctance of many people to reveal their income is sometimes offered as an example of a desire for privacy that cannot be explained in purely instrumental terms. But I suggest that people conceal an unexpectedly low income because being thought to have a high income has value in credit markets and elsewhere, and that they conceal an unexpectedly high income in order (1) to avoid the attention of tax collectors, kidnappers, and thieves, (2) to fend off

---

[16] Olmstead v. United States, 277 U.S. 438, 478 (1928) (Brandeis, J., dissenting). It is a good answer if the question is whether people should have a right to be free from unwanted solicitations, noisy sound trucks, obscene telephone calls, etc. These invade a privacy interest different from the one discussed in this paper, since they involve no effort to obtain information.

[17] *See* text at note 3 *supra*.

solicitations from charities and family members, and (3) to preserve a reputation for generosity that might be demolished if others knew the precise fraction of their income that they give away. Points (1) and (2) may explain anonymous gifts to charity.

D. *Privacy of Communications*

To the extent that people conceal personal information in order to mislead, the economic case for according legal protection to such information is no better than that for permitting fraud in the sale of goods. However, it is also necessary to consider the *means* by which others obtain personal information. Prying by means of casual interrogation of acquaintances of the object of the prying must be distinguished from eavesdropping, electronically or otherwise, on a person's conversations. A in conversation with B disparages C. If C has a right to hear this conversation, A, in choosing the words he uses to B, will have to consider the possible reactions of C. Conversation will be more costly because of the external effects, and the increased costs will result in less, and less effective, communication. After people adjust to this new world of public conversation, even the C's of the world will cease to derive much benefit in the way of greater information from conversational publicity, for people will be more guarded in their speech. The principal effect of publicity will be to make conversation more formal and communication less effective rather than to increase the knowledge of interested third parties.

Stated differently, the costs of defamatory utterances and hence the cost-justified level of expenditures in avoiding defamation are greater the more publicity that is given the utterance. If every conversation were public, the time and other resources devoted to assuring that one's speech was free from false or unintended slanders would rise.[18] Society can avoid the additional costs by the simple and relatively inexpensive expedient of providing legal sanctions against infringement of conversational privacy.

Some evidence in support of this analysis is the experience, well-known to every academic administrator, under the Buckley Amendment.[19] That law gives students access to letters of recommendation written about them, unless they waive in advance their right of

---

[18] To be sure, the elimination of the false slander is a social gain, as it might mislead the individual hearing it (*B* in the example in text). But the elimination of the true slander is a social loss.

[19] Family Educational Rights and Privacy Act of 1974, § 513, 20 U.S.C. § 1232g (1974).

access. Almost all students execute such waivers because they know
that the information value of a letter of recommendation to which
the subject of the letter has access is much less than that of a private
letter of recommendation.

As additional evidence, notice that language becomes less formal
as society evolves. The languages of primitive peoples are more
elaborate, more ceremonious, and more courteous than that of
twentieth-century Americans. One reason may be that primitive
people have little privacy. Relatively few private conversations take
place because third parties are normally present and the effects of
the conversation on them must be taken into account. Even today,
one observes that people speak more formally the greater the number of people present. The rise of privacy has facilitated private
conversation and thereby enabled us to economize on communication—to speak with a brevity and informality apparently rare
among primitive peoples.[20] Allowing eavesdropping would undermine this valuable economy of communication.

In some cases, to be sure, communication is not related to socially
productive activity. Communication among criminal conspirators is
an example. In these cases, where limited eavesdropping is indeed

---

[20] There is some anthropological evidence supporting this analysis in a paper by Clifford
Geertz, who writes:

> In Java people live in small, bamboo-walled houses, each of which almost always
> contains a single nuclear family. . . . There are no walls or fences around them, the
> house walls are thinly and loosely woven, and there are commonly not even doors.
> Within the house people wander freely just about any place any time, and even outsi-
> ders wander in fairly freely almost any time during the day and early evening. In brief,
> privacy in our terms is about as close to nonexistent as it can get. . . . Relationships
> even within the household are very restrained; people speak softly, hide their feelings
> and even in the bosom of a Javanese family you have the feeling that you are in the
> public square and must behave with appropriate decorum. Javanese shut people out
> with a wall of etiquette (patterns of politeness are very highly developed), with emo-
> tional restraint, and with a general lack of candor in both speech and behavior. . . .
> Thus, there is really no sharp break between public and private in Java: people behave
> more or less the same in private as they do in public—in a manner we would call stuffy
> at best. . . .

Unpublished paper *quoted in* A. WESTIN, *supra* note 10, at 16-17.

An additional bit of evidence concerning the relationship between linguistic formality and
publicity is that written speech is usually more decorous, grammatical, and formal than
spoken. In part this is because spoken speech involves additional levels of meaning—gesture
and intonation—which allow the speaker to achieve the same clarity with less semantic and
grammatical precision. But in part it is because the audience for spoken speech is typically
smaller and more intimate than that for written speech. This makes the costs of ambiguity
lower and hence the cost-justified investment in achieving precision through the various
formal resources of language smaller. This potential for ambiguity is the reason why people
who speak to large audiences normally do so from a previously prepared text.

permitted, its effect in reducing communication is not an objection to but an advantage of it.

The analysis in this section can readily be extended to efforts to obtain people's notes, letters, and other private papers; the efforts would inhibit communication. Photographic surveillance—for example, of the interior of a person's home—presents a slightly more complex question. Privacy enables a person to dress and otherwise disport himself in his home without regard to the effect on third parties. This informality, which is resource-conserving, would be lost were the interior of the home in the public domain. People dress not merely because of the effect on others but also because of the reticence, remarked earlier, concerning nudity and other sensitive states; that reticence is another reason for giving people a privacy right with regard to places in which these sensitive states occur.

## E.  *Summary of the Economic Approach*

The two main strands of the argument—related to personal facts and to communications—can be joined by remarking the difference in this context between ends and means. With regard to ends there is a prima facie case for assigning the property right in a secret that is a byproduct of socially productive activity to the individual if its compelled disclosure would impair the incentives to engage in that activity; but there is a prima facie case for assigning the property right away from the individual where secrecy would reduce the social product by misleading the people with whom he deals.[21] However, merely because under this analysis most facts about people belong in the public domain does not imply that the law should generally permit intrusion on private communications, given the effects of such intrusions on the costs of legitimate communications.

I admit that the suggested dichotomy between facts and communications is too stark. If you are allowed to interrogate my acquaintances about my income, I may take steps to conceal it that are analogous to the increased formality of conversation that would ensue from abolition of the right to conversational privacy, and the costs of these steps are a social loss. The difference is one of degree. Partly because eavesdropping and related modes of intrusive surveillance are such powerful methods of eliciting private information and partly because they are relatively easy to protect against, we can expect that people would undertake evasive maneuvers, costly

---

[21] The concept of "dealings" is to be broadly understood: we all have dealings in a non-trivial sense with the President of the United States, for example.

in the aggregate, if surveillance compromised conversational privacy. It is more difficult to imagine that people would take effective measures against casual prying. One is unlikely to alter his income or style of living drastically in order to assure better concealment of his income or of other private information from casual or journalistic inquiry. (Howard Hughes, however, was a notable exception to this generalization.)

I have now sketched the essential elements of a legal right of privacy based on economic efficiency: (1) the protection of trade and business secrets by which businessmen exploit their superior knowledge or skills (applied to the personal level, as it should be, the principle would, for example, entitle the social host or hostess to conceal the recipe of a successful dinner); (2) generally no protection for facts about people—my ill health, evil temper, even my income would not be facts over which I had property rights although I might be able to prevent their discovery by methods unduly intrusive;[22] (3) the limitation, so far as possible, of eavesdropping and other forms of intrusive surveillance to surveillance of illegal activities.

## F.  *Application to Legislative Trends in the Privacy Area*

Some implications of the analysis are perhaps startling in light of current legislative trends in the privacy field. As noted, the law should in general accord private business information greater protection than it accords personal information. Secrecy is an important method of appropriating social benefits to the entrepreneur who creates them while in private life it is more likely to conceal discreditable facts. Communications within organizations, whether public or private, should receive the same protection as communications among individuals, for in either case the effect of publicity would be to encumber and retard communication.

Yet, contrary to this analysis, the legislative trend is toward giving individuals more and more privacy protection respecting both facts and communications and giving business firms and other organizations, including government agencies, universities and hospitals, less. The Freedom of Information Act, sunshine laws opening the deliberations of administrative agencies to the public, and the erosion of effective sanctions against breach of government confidences have greatly reduced the privacy of communications within the government. Similar forces, for example the Buckley Amend-

---

[22] A conclusion also reached, though on different grounds, in Thomson, *supra* note 1.

ment and the opening of faculty meetings to student observers, are at work in private institutions such as business firms and private universities. Increasingly, moreover, the facts pertaining to individuals—arrest record, health, credit-worthiness, marital status, sexual proclivities—are secured from involuntary disclosure, while the facts concerning business corporations are thrust into public view by the expansive disclosure requirements of the federal securities laws (to the point where some firms are "going private" in order to secure greater confidentiality for their plans and operations), the civil rights laws, line of business reporting, and other regulations. A related trend is the erosion of the privacy of government officials through increasingly stringent ethical standards requiring disclosure of income.

The trend toward elevating personal and downgrading organizational privacy is mysterious to the economist. To repeat, the economic case for privacy of *communications* seems unrelated to the nature of the communicator, whether a private individual or the employee of a university, corporation, or government agency, while so far as *facts* about people or organizations are concerned the case for protecting business privacy actually seems stronger, in general, than that for individual privacy.

Greenawalt and Noam appear to reach the opposite conclusion in a recent paper.[23] Since they base their analysis, in part anyway, on economics, it requires attention here. They offer two distinctions between a business's or other organization's interest in privacy and an individual's interest. First, they argue that the latter is a matter of rights while the former is based merely on instrumental, utilitarian considerations. However, their reasons for recognizing a right of personal privacy seem utilitarian—that people should have an opportunity to "make a new start" by concealing embarrassing or discreditable facts about their past, and that people cannot preserve their sanity without some privacy. Inconsistently, Greenawalt and Noam disregard the utilitarian justification for secrecy as an incentive to investment in productive activity—a justification mainly relevant, as I have argued, in business contexts.

The second distinction they suggest between business and personal claims to privacy is a strangely distorted mirror of my argument for entrepreneurial or productive secrecy. They argue that it is difficult to establish property rights in information and even re-

---

[23] K. GREENAWALT & E. NOAM, *Confidentiality Claims of Business Organization* (forthcoming in Columbia University conference volume).

mark that secrecy is one way of doing so. But they do not draw the obvious conclusion that secrecy can promote productive activity by creating property rights in information. Instead they use the existence of imperfections in the market for information as a justification for the government's coercively extracting private information from business firms. They do not explain how the government could, let alone demonstrate that it would, use this information more productively than firms, and they do not consider the impact of this form of public prying on the incentive to produce the information in the first place.

## G. *Noneconomic Theories of Privacy*

By way of contrast to the economic theory of privacy, I shall examine briefly some of the other theories of privacy that have been proposed, beginning with that of Warren and Brandeis. They wrote:

> The press is overstepping in every direction the obvious bounds of propriety and of decency. Gossip is no longer the resource of the idle and of the vicious, but has become a trade, which is pursued with industry as well as effrontery. To satisfy a prurient taste the details of sexual relations are spread broadcast in the columns of the daily papers. To occupy the indolent, column upon column is filled with idle gossip, which can only be procured by intrusion upon the domestic circle. The intensity and complexity of life, attendant upon advancing civilization, have rendered necessary some retreat from the world, and man, under the refining influence of culture, has become more sensitive to publicity, so that solitude and privacy have become more essential to the individual; but modern enterprise and invention have, through invasions upon his privacy, subjected him to mental pain and distress, far greater than could be inflicted by mere bodily injury. Nor is the harm wrought by such invasions confined to the suffering of those who may be made the subjects of journalistic or other enterprise. In this, as in other branches of commerce, the supply creates the demand. Each crop of unseemly gossip, thus harvested, becomes the seed of more, and, in direct proportion to its circulation, results in a lowering of social standards and of morality.[24]

This analysis of privacy is wholly unsatisfactory. Narrowly directed

---

[24] Warren & Brandeis, *supra* note 6, at 196. *See also* quotation in that footnote.

to providing a justification for a right not to be talked about in a newspaper gossip column, the analysis is based on a series of unsupported and implausible empirical propositions: (1) newspapers deliberately try to debase their readers' tastes; (2) the gossip they print harms the people gossiped about far more seriously than bodily injury could; (3) the more gossip the press supplies, the more the readers will demand; (4) reading gossip columns impairs intelligence and morality.

Professor Edward Bloustein is representative of those theorists who relate privacy to individuality:

> The man who is compelled to live every minute of his life among others and whose every need, thought, desire, fancy or gratification is subject to public scrutiny, has been deprived of his individuality and human dignity. Such an individual merges with the mass. His opinions, being public, tend never to be different; his aspirations, being known, tend always to be conventionally accepted ones; his feelings, being openly exhibited, tend to lose their quality of unique personal warmth and to become the feelings of every man. Such a being, although sentient, is fungible; he is not an individual.[25]

At one level, Bloustein is saying merely that if people were forced to conform their private to their public behavior there would be more uniformity in private behavior across people—that is to say, people would be better behaved if they had less privacy. This result he considers objectionable apparently because greater conformity to socially accepted patterns of behavior would produce (by definition) more conformists, a type he dislikes for reasons he must consider self-evident since he does not attempt to explain them.

To be sure, Bloustein is suggesting that publicity reduces not only deviations from accepted moral standards but also creative departures from conventional thought and behavior. However, history does *not* teach that privacy is a precondition to creativity or individuality. These qualities have flourished in societies, including ancient Greece, Renaissance Italy, and Elizabethan England, that had much less privacy than we in the United States have today.

Professor Charles Fried argues that privacy is indispensable to the fundamental values of love, friendship, and trust. Love and friendship, he argues, are inconceivable "without the intimacy of shared

---

[25] Bloustein, *Privacy as an Aspect of Human Dignity: An Answer to Dean Prosser*, 39 N.Y.U. L. Rev. 962, 1003 (1964).

private information,"[26] and trust presupposes an element of ignorance about what the trusted one is up to: if all is known, there is nothing to take on trust. But trust, rather than being something valued for itself and therefore missed where full information makes it unnecessary, is, I should think, merely an imperfect substitute for information. As for love and friendship, they, of course, exist and flourish in societies where there is little privacy. The privacy theories of both Bloustein and Fried are ethnocentric.

Even within our own culture, it may be questioned whether privacy is more supportive than destructive of treasured values. If ignorance is the prerequisite of trust, equally knowledge, which privacy conceals, is the prerequisite of forgiveness. The anomie, impersonality, and lack of communal or altruistic feeling that some observers find in modern society can be viewed as aspects of the high level of privacy our society has achieved. The relationship of privacy to social values seems, in short, highly complex.

Fried is explicit in not wanting to ground the right of privacy on utilitarian considerations, the sort congenial to economic analysis. But the quest for nonutilitarian grounds has thus far failed. It may be doubted whether the kind of analysis that seeks to establish rights not derived from a calculation of costs and benefits is even applicable to the privacy area. As Walter Block has pointed out, it makes no sense to treat reputation as a "right." Reputation is what others think of us, and we have no right to control other people's thoughts.[27] Equally we have no right, by controlling the information that is known about us to manipulate the opinions that other people hold of us. Yet this control is the essence of what most students of the subject mean by privacy.

Greenawalt and Noam mention additional, though utilitarian, grounds for valuing privacy besides those emphasized in economic analysis—the "fresh start" ground and the "mental health" ground.[28] The first holds that people who have committed crimes or otherwise transgressed the moral standards of society have a right to a "fresh start" which the inability to conceal their past misdeeds would deny them; the second states as a fact of human psychology that people cannot function effectively unless they have some private area where they can behave very differently, often scandalously differently, from their public self, *e.g.*, the waiters who curse in the

---

[26] C. FRIED, AN ANATOMY OF VALUES: PROBLEMS OF PERSONAL AND SOCIAL CHOICE 142 (1970).

[27] W. BLOCK, DEFENDING THE UNDEFENDABLE 60 (1976).

[28] *See* note 23 *supra*.

kitchen the patrons they treat so obsequiously in the dining room. The first point rests on the popular though implausible and, to my knowledge at least, unsubstantiated assumption that people do not evaluate past criminal acts rationally, for only if they irrationally refused to accept evidence of rehabilitation could one argue that society had unfairly denied the former miscreant a fresh start.[29] The second point has some intuitive appeal but seems exaggerated and ethnocentric and, to my knowledge, is offered as pure assertion without any empirical or theoretical support.

The foregoing review of noneconomic theories of privacy is incomplete. But if I have not done full justice to the previous literature on privacy, I may at least have indicated sufficient difficulties with the noneconomic approaches to suggest the value of an economic analysis. To recapitulate, that analysis simply asks (1) why people, in the rational pursuit of their self-interest, attempt on the one hand to conceal certain facts about themselves and on the other hand to discover certain facts about other people, and (2) in what circumstances such activities will increase rather than diminish the wealth of the society.

## II. THE TORT LAW OF PRIVACY

It is well known that, although the Warren-Brandeis article stimulated the development of the tort law of privacy, the law has evolved very differently from the pattern they suggested; and Bloustein offered his theory of privacy by way of criticism of Prosser's authoritative article describing the privacy tort.[30] Perhaps, then, the tort law is closer to economic than to noneconomic thinking about privacy. This possibility raises an interesting question in the positive analysis of law. Another advantage of focusing on the tort law of privacy is that since it involves mainly private rather than governmental intrusions, we can consider the privacy issue free of the complexities which the quite proper concern with privacy as a safeguard against political oppression injects.[31]

---

[29] I return to this point *infra* at note 46.

[30] Prosser, *Privacy*, 48 CALIF. L. REV. 383 (1960).

[31] With regard to the political dimension of the privacy question, I shall digress only long enough to register disagreement with the widespread view that technological advances have increased the power of government vis-à-vis the citizens. The increase in governmental surveillance and the refinement of surveillance techniques are better viewed as responses to the growth in urbanization, income, and mobility—developments that have weakened governmental control by reducing the information that government has about people: by, in short, increasing privacy.

410          *GEORGIA LAW REVIEW*              [Vol. 12:393

## A. *Commercial Privacy*

The broad features of the tort law are those described earlier in the discussion of what an economically based privacy right would look like: (1) substantial protection of the confidentiality of business dealings; (2) public entitlement to obtain by prying most private facts about individuals; but (3) strict limitation on *intrusion* to obtain those facts. The first of these areas is the domain of trade-secrets law, a branch of the tort law of unfair competition. Although the best known kind of trade secret is the secret formula or process, the legal protection is much broader—"almost any knowledge or information used in the conduct of one's business may be held by its possessor in secret."[32] In a well-known case, the court held that aerial photography of a competitor's plant under construction was tortious and used the term "commercial privacy" to describe the interest protected.[33] This decision illustrates the judicial willingness to protect those secrets that enable firms to appropriate the lawful benefits that their activities create.

The appropriate outer bounds of the commercial-privacy tort are somewhat difficult to discern. It is accepted, for example, that a firm may buy its competitor's product and take it apart with a view to discovering how it was made even though "reverse engineering" may reveal secrets of a competitor's production process. How is this type of prying to be distinguished from aerial photography? One difference is that if the law permitted aerial photography of a competitor's plant under construction, the principal effect would not be to generate information; it would be to induce the competitor to expend resources on trying to conceal the interior of the plant. These resources, as well as those devoted to the aerial photography itself which they offset, would be socially wasted. In contrast, the possibility of reverse engineering is unlikely to lead a manufacturer to alter his product in costly ways. Another difference is that aerial photography might disclose secrets that would be more difficult to protect alternatively through the patent system than the kinds of secrets that reverse engineering is likely to reveal.

My analysis of commercial privacy is incomplete. It merely suggests that economic principles may be at work in this field, a field worthy of independent attention.

---

[32] Smith v. Dravo Corp., 203 F.2d 369, 373 (7th Cir. 1953).

[33] E. I. du Pont de Nemours & Co. v. Christopher, 431 F.2d 1012, 1016 (5th Cir. 1970). *See also* Smith v. Dravo Corp., 203 F.2d at 377 (7th Cir. 1953).

B. *Personal Privacy*

The tort of invasion of personal privacy has four aspects: (1) appropriation, (2) publicity, (3) false light, and (4) intrusion.[34]

1. *Appropriation.*—In the earliest cases involving a distinct right of privacy, an advertiser uses someone's name or photograph without his or her consent.[35] The classification of these as "privacy" cases is sometimes criticized because often what the law protects is an aversion not to publicity but to not being remunerated for it: many of the cases involve celebrities avid for publicity. But this characteristic of the cases is an embarrassment only to a tort theory that seeks to base the right to privacy on a social interest in concealment of personal information—an unattractive approach, for reasons explored in Part I. There is a perfectly good economic reason for assigning the property right in a photograph used for advertising purposes to the photographed individual: this assignment assures that the advertiser to whom the photograph is most valuable will purchase it. Making the photograph the communal property of advertisers would not achieve this goal.

The subscription-list question discussed earlier may seem to involve the identical "right to publicity."[36] However, transaction costs preclude a magazine from purchasing from another magazine's subscriber the right to solicit him. Furthermore, the multiple use of the identical photograph to advertise different products would reduce its advertising value, perhaps to zero. This cost makes it important to have a method for assigning the photograph to one of a few very valuable uses. But the multiple use of a subscription list has little or no negative impact on the list's value.

Professor Bloustein, as one might expect, does not want to recognize an economic basis for the "right of publicity" and tries to make this branch of privacy law a criticism rather than vindication of the market place. He writes: "Use of a photograph for trade purposes turns a man into a commodity and makes him serve the economic needs and interests of others."[37] But this cannot be the theory of the tort law. The law does not forbid a man to use his photograph "for trade purposes"; it merely gives him a property right in such use.

---

[34] For a good summary of the legal principles in this area, see W. PROSSER, HANDBOOK OF THE LAW OF TORTS ch. 20 (4th ed. 1971).

[35] *See, e.g.,* Pavesich v. New England Life Ins. Co., 122 Ga. 190, 50 S.E. 68 (1905).

[36] *See* Note, *The Right of Publicity—Protection for Public Figures and Celebrities,* 42 BROOKLYN L. REV. 527 (1976).

[37] Bloustein, *supra* note 25, at 988.

Nor is the theory of the tort protection against a subtle form of misrepresentation which may occur when an advertiser uses another person's name in conjunction with an advertising message. Although this is an element in some of the cases, the legal right is much broader. The decision in *Haelan Laboratories v. Topps Chewing Gum* shows this to be so. The court held that when a baseball player had licensed the exclusive right to the use of his likeness in advertising to one manufacturer of bubble gum, no other bubble gum manufacturer could use the player's photograph in advertising without the licensee's permission.[38] The court expressly stated that "a man has a right in the publicity value of his photograph, *i.e.,* the right to grant the exclusive privilege of publishing his picture."[39] A misrepresentation rationale cannot explain the result in cases such as *Haelan.*

2. *Publicity.*—If an advertiser uses an individual's picture without his consent, that individual's legal rights are, as we have just seen, infringed. But if the same picture appears in the news section of the newspaper there is no infringement (at least if the picture is not embarrassing and does not portray the person in a false light—separate tort grounds discussed later). The difference in treatment seems at first glance arbitrary. If a particular publication of an individual's photograph would represent the most valuable use of his likeness, why cannot the newspaper purchase the property right from him?

A superficial answer is that the news photograph has public-good aspects that are absent when an advertiser uses the same photograph. A newspaper that invests resources in discovering news of broad interest to the public may not be able to appropriate the social benefits of the discovery and hence recoup its investment because a competitor can pick up and disseminate the news with only a slight time lag, without having to compensate the first newspaper. In other words, the first newspaper's research creates external benefits, and one method of compensating the newspaper for conferring these benefits is to allow it to externalize some of its costs as well (whether it is the best method is a separate question). But while external benefits conceivably may explain (as we shall see) why a newspaper does not have to pay the newsworthy people about whom it writes, they do not explain the newspaper's right to print

---

[38] Haelan Laboratories v. Topps Chewing Gum, 202 F.2d 866 (2d Cir.), *cert. denied,* 346 U.S. 816 (1953).

[39] *Id.* at 868. For similar cases see Note, *supra* note 36, at 534-41.

*photographs* without payment. The newspaper can copyright the photograph and then no competing medium can republish it without the newspaper's permission.[40]

Two other reasons may, however, explain the difference in legal treatment between the photograph used in advertising and the same photograph used in the news column. First, the social cost of dispensing with property rights is greater in the advertising than in the news case. As suggested earlier, if any advertiser can use a celebrity's picture, its advertising value may be impaired; if Brand *X* beer successfully utilized Celebrity *A*'s picture in its advertising, competing brands might run the same picture in their advertising until the picture ceased to have any advertising value at all. In contrast, the multiple use of a celebrity's photograph by competing newspapers is unlikely to reduce the value of the photograph to the newspaper-reading public. Second, in the news case the celebrity might use the property right in his likeness, if he had such a right, to misrepresent his appearance to the public—he might permit the newspaper to publish only a particularly flattering picture. This form of false advertising is difficult to prevent except by communalizing the property right.

The case for giving the individual a property right may seem even more attenuated where the publicity is of offensive or embarrassing characteristics of the individual, for here publicity would appear to serve that institutionalized prying function which, as noted above, is important in a society in which there is a great deal of privacy facilitating the concealment of discrediting facts from one's fellows. This conclusion is both correct, in general, and the result reached, in general, in the cases; but there is a class of facts which the individual strongly desires to conceal and of which the social value of disclosure is also quite limited. Suppose a person has a deformed nose. The deformity is of course well known to the people who have dealings with him. A newspaper photographer snaps a picture of the nose and publishes it in a story on human ugliness. Since the deformity is not concealable or concealed from people who have dealings with the individual in question, publication of the photograph does not serve to correct a false impression that he might exploit.

---

[40] This is so even after Time, Inc. v. Bernard Geis Assoc., 293 F. Supp. 130 (S.D.N.Y. 1968), held that the "fair use" exception to copyright encompassed the publication of detailed, accurate charcoal sketches of the Zapruder film of the assassination of President Kennedy in a book about the assassination. The court emphasized the absence of competition between plaintiff and defendants, who did not publish a magazine. Also, the book did not reproduce the photograph itself.

To be sure, readers of the newspaper derive value from being able to see the photograph; otherwise the newspaper would not publish it. However, because the individual's desire to suppress the photograph is not related to misrepresentation in any business or social market place, there is no basis for a presumption that the social value of disclosure exceeds that of concealment. In these circumstances the appropriate social response is to give the individual the property right in his likeness and let the newspaper buy it from him if it wishes to publish a photograph of his nose.[41]

*Daily Times Democrat v. Graham*[42] is a similar case. A woman was photographed in a fun house at the moment when a jet of air had blown her dress up around her waist. The local newspaper later published the photograph without her consent. In holding that the newspaper had invaded her right of privacy, the court stressed that it was undisputed that she had entered the fun house solely to accompany her children and had not known about the jets of air. In these circumstances the photograph could convey no information enabling her friends and acquaintances to correct misapprehensions about her character which she might have engendered. If anything, the photograph misrepresented her character.

The foregoing analysis may seem to support recognition of a property right in privacy wherever (1) no element of misrepresentation is involved and (2) the information is contained in a photograph which a purchaser of the property right could copyright, thereby eliminating any externality. However, an exception to this rule is necessary for the frequent case where the nature of the event photographed makes transaction costs prohibitive. It would be inefficient to assign the property right in his likeness to an individual photographed as part of a crowd watching a parade, and unidentified to the photographer; or, perhaps, to the accident victim with whom negotiations would be infeasible given the time limit within which the photograph must be published if it is not to lose its newsworthiness. In the former case, the property right is plainly more valuable, as a general matter, to the photographer than to the subject of the photograph; but this conclusion is less clear in the latter case, so that, putting aside first amendment considerations, which will not

[41] This hypothetical case was suggested by the facts of Griffin v. Medical Society, 11 N.Y.S.2d 109 (Sup. Ct. 1939), where, however, publication was in a medical journal rather than a newspaper and the suit was based on alleged appropriation of the photograph for advertising purposes. Lambert v. Dow Chem. Co., 215 So. 2d 673 (La. App. 1968), is closer to the hypothetical case.

[42] 162 So. 2d 474 (Ala. 1964).

be discussed here, some type of balancing of costs and benefits is required. I shall have something to say a bit later on about how this balancing is done.

The cases discussed above are sharply distinguishable in terms of the economic analysis developed in this Article from those where, for example, a newspaper reveals past illegal or immoral activity that an individual has sedulously endeavored to conceal from his friends and acquaintances. Since such information is undeniably material in evaluating an individual's claim to friendship, respect, and trust, affording legal protection to its concealment would be inconsistent with the treatment of false advertising in the market for goods. Nevertheless, an early California case, *Melvin v. Reid*, held that the right of privacy extended to such information.[43] The case was rather special because its posture on appeal required the court to accept as true the plaintiff's allegations which implied that disclosure of her unsavory past could convey no useful information to anybody.[44] And a later California case, *Briscoe v. Reader's Digest Association*, held that the right of privacy does not extend to information concerning recent, as distinct from remote, past criminal activity.[45] This distinction moves the law in the right direction but, from an economic standpoint, not far enough. Remote past criminal activity is less relevant to a prediction of future misconduct than recent—and those who learn of it will discount it accordingly—but such information is hardly *irrelevant* to people considering whether to enter into or continue social or business relations with the individual; and if it were irrelevant, publicizing it would not injure the individual.[46] People conceal past criminal acts not out of bashful-

---

[43] 112 Cal. App. 285, 297 P. 91 (1931).

[44] Among the facts alleged were that "after her acquittal, she abandoned her life of shame and became entirely rehabilitated; that during the year 1919, she married Bernard Melvin and commenced the duties of caring for their home, and thereafter at all times lived an exemplary, virtuous, honorable and righteous life . . . ." 112 Cal. App. at 286, 297 P. at 91.

[45] 4 Cal. 3d 529, 483 P.2d 34, 93 Cal. Rptr. 866 (1971).

[46] It is arguable that the privacy of past criminal acts is based on a social policy of encouraging the rehabilitation of criminals. This argument raises complex issues. Rehabilitation may reduce recidivism, but it also reduces expected punishment costs; hence, whether there is more or less crime in a system that emphasizes rehabilitation is unclear. And there is a question whether concealment is a "fair" method of rehabilitation, since it places potentially significant costs on those who deal in ignorance with the former criminal. It remains, however, possible that rehabilitative goals have been a factor in judicial protection of the former criminal's privacy.

Another factor may be a belief, very uncongenial to economic analysis, that people react irrationally to information concerning past criminal acts. The Restatement gives the example of a former criminal, Valjean, who, though completely rehabilitated, is ruined when news of

ness but precisely because potential acquaintances quite sensibly regard a criminal past as negative evidence of the value of cultivating an acquaintance with a person.

In light of this analysis, one is not surprised to find that, outside of California, the principle of *Melvin v. Reid* is rejected.[47] This result has been reached under the tort law, but it has been reinforced by the recent decision of the Supreme Court in *Cox Broadcasting Co. v. Cohn,* which suggests that the first amendment may privilege the publication (or, as in that case, the broadcast) of any matter, however remote, contained in public records.[48] This privilege would seem to erase the distinction between recent and remote past criminal activity and to eliminate any right of privacy with respect to either. However, it should be noted that *Cox* itself did not involve past criminal activity. The fact publicized was the name of a dead rape victim. The publicity caused distress to the victim's family while providing no information useful to people contemplating transactions with her (since she was dead) or with her family. Nor was her name critical to the information value of the broadcast in which it appeared. As a matter of tort law (my only concern in this Article), it would seem that the state court acted properly in holding that the broadcast invaded the family's right of privacy.

Another, but I think more defensible, case in which a court refused to recognize an invasion of the right of privacy despite the absence of potential misrepresentation is *Sidis v. F-R Publishing Corp.*[49] The *New Yorker* magazine published a "where is he now" article about a child-prodigy mathematician who had as an adult become an eccentric recluse. One could argue that the *New Yorker*'s exposé had produced information useful to people contemplating dealing with Sidis, but the argument would be rather forced because his craving for privacy was so extreme as to reduce to a very low level

---

his past comes to light. RESTATEMENT (SECOND) OF TORTS §652D, Illustration 26 (Tent. Draft No. 22, 1976). On the assumption of complete rehabilitation, the suggestion that the information would ruin Valjean's career imputes irrationality to the people dealing with him.

Perhaps the Restatement's draftsmen were referring not to irrationality, but to the rational basing of judgments on partial information. To attach adverse significance to past criminal acts without conducting the kind of thorough investigation that would, in a few cases, dispel their significance is not irrational or malevolent; it is a method of economizing on information costs. *See also* Phelps, *The Statistical Theory of Racism and Sexism,* 62 AM. ECON. REV. 659 (1972).

[47] *See* Rawlins v. Hutchinson Publishing Co., 318 Kan. 295, 543 P.2d 988 (1975); Pember & Teeter, *Privacy and the Press Since* Time, Inc. v. Hill, 50 WASH. L. REV. 57, 81-82 (1974).

[48] 420 U.S. 469 (1975).

[49] 113 F.2d 806 (2d Cir. 1940).

his dealings with other people. And, given that craving, it is not at all certain that the *New Yorker* would have been willing to pay the price Sidis would have demanded from the magazine to sell his life story to it. But a distinct economic reason, alluded to earlier, provides some support for the court's conclusion that the publication did not invade Sidis' legal rights. The story was newsworthy in the sense that it catered to a widespread public interest in child prodigies. But once the *New Yorker* published its story any other magazine or newspaper could, without compensating it, publish the facts that the *New Yorker* had gathered (perhaps by costly research), so long as the republication did not contain the actual language of the *New Yorker* story. Given the number of potential republishers, there was no market mechanism by which the full social value of the information that the *New Yorker* had gathered could be brought to bear in negotiations with Sidis over the purchase of the right to his life story. In these circumstances there is an argument for not giving him that right—in other words, for allowing the *New Yorker* to externalize some of the social costs of its research, *i.e.*, the costs imposed on Sidis, since it must perforce externalize some of the benefits.

This discussion may seem to overlook a simple way of reducing the costs of disclosure to Sidis without substantially impairing the value of publication to the readers of the *New Yorker*'s story or to readers of other magazines that had picked up the story—not use his real name in the story. But the magazine would also have to change other details in order to conceal his identity effectively, and the changes would substantially reduce the information value of the story: readers would not be certain whether they were reading fact or fiction. In *Barber v. Time, Inc.*,[50] however, the court held that a magazine had invaded an individual's right of privacy by naming her in a story about a disagreeable disease she had, because the news value of the story was independent of the use of her true name. The same was true, I have suggested, in *Cox*.

All this is not to say that the result in *Sidis* was necessarily correct, especially in a global economic sense. Merely because the *New Yorker*'s story may have generated external benefits, it does not follow that that the sum total of the benefits of the story exceeded the sum of the costs, including the costs to Sidis. Obviously this is a difficult comparison for courts to make. They do, however, try: in

---

[50] 348 Mo. 1199, 159 S.W.2d 291 (1942).

deciding whether newspaper publicity is unlawful they look to the offensiveness of the details publicized and the newsworthiness of the publication, and offensiveness and newsworthiness serve as proxies for the costs and benefits, respectively, of publication.[51]

These proxies are, however, extremely crude, raising the question why, rather than eliminate property rights in one area (privacy) in order to offset the inefficient consequences of failing to recognize property rights in another area (news), the law has not recognized a property right in news. Then there would be no objection to allowing Sidis to block publication of his story. The existence of property rights in both news and privacy would enable the market to function effectively and courts would no longer have to estimate values.

To answer this question, and thus decide whether decisions like *Sidis* are appropriate second-best solutions to intractable problems of economic optimization or simply wrong, would carry us too far away from the privacy area and entangle us in difficult questions of copyright law and policy. Nor could one stop there. If practical difficulties preclude extending copyright protection to ideas, there is still to be considered the possibility that Sidis might be given a property right in (certain) facts about himself, which the *New Yorker*, once having purchased it from him, could enforce against any newspaper or magazine that published its own version of Sidis' story. This solution would assimilate Sidis' case to that of the man with the deformed nose, but would also involve serious practical difficulties that cannot be adequately addressed here. Nor is this the place to evaluate the other privileges the law grants to newspapers in order (perhaps) to offset their lack of property rights in the news. Clearly, however, an adequate theory of the legal rights and liabilities of the news media would consider the extent to which news gathering confers external benefits and whether the recognition of property rights in the news might not be more efficient than the many immunities society has extended to the press—at some cost to the Sidises of this world—in order to compensate it for not having property rights in the fruits of its efforts.

To summarize a rather untidy discussion of the most interesting branch of the tort law of privacy, the law distinguishes in a rough way between discreditable and nondiscreditable private information and accords much less protection to the former, as it

---

[51] In the language of the Restatement, the matter publicized, to be actionable, must be "of a kind which (a) would be highly offensive to a reasonable person, and (b) is not of legitimate concern to the public." RESTATEMENT, *supra* note 46, at 21.

should—though, in California, still too much from an economic standpoint. Where privacy is not a form of misrepresentation, the protection is broader but is limited by problems of externalities and transaction costs that argue against complete privacy protection even with regard to nondiscrediting facts. In a rough way, the Restatement's test, which involves a balance between offensiveness and newsworthiness, captures the essential economic elements of the problem; but it would be a better economic test if it were limited to the class of cases in which publicity serves no unmasking purpose. If what is revealed is something the individual has concealed for purposes of misrepresenting himself to others, the fact that disclosure is offensive to him and of limited interest to the public at large is no better reason for protecting his privacy than if a seller advanced such arguments for being allowed to continue to engage in false advertising of his goods.

3.  *False Light.*—Sometimes the privacy plaintiff seeks damages because the newspaper or other news medium has distorted the facts about him. The existence of a tort of defamation which, as the commentators have noted, covers much of the same ground as the false-light privacy tort may seem to compel the conclusion that portraying someone in a false light should be actionable. There is, however, an economic argument that no legal remedy is either necessary or appropriate. The argument is that the law can and should leave the determination of truth to competition in the market place of ideas. What this argument overlooks, however, is that competition among the news media may not take into account the full costs of being placed in a false light. Suppose *Life* magazine runs an article about a family held hostage which inaccurately shows the captors subjecting the family to beatings, verbal sexual assaults, and other indignities. The article imposes private and social costs by conveying misinformation about the family that may deter others from engaging in certain social or other relationships with its members. If there is a public demand for the accurate portrayal of the family's characteristics, a competing magazine *may* run a story that will correct the false impression created by *Life*'s story, but this is not certain. For in considering whether to publish such an article, the competitor will not consider the benefits of correction to the family and the people who might transact with its members; it will consider only its readers' interest in reading such an article.[52]

---

[52] *See, e.g.,* Time, Inc. v. Hill, 385 U.S. 374, 407-08 (1967) (separate opinion of Harlan, J.). To be sure, the family could, in principle at least, pay *Life* to run a correction, but this

This argument may not seem decisive in light of the earlier point that the publication of newsworthy articles generates external benefits which might justify allowing the newspaper or magazine to externalize some of its costs as well. However, encouraging cost externalization to take the form of distorting the truth would be inefficient since distortion would reduce the social benefits as well as costs of publication.

The analysis in this section suggests, incidentally, an economic reason why the law limits the rights of public officials and other "public figures" to seek legal redress for defamation. The status of a public figure increases an individual's access to the media by making his denials newsworthy, thus facilitating a market, as distinct from a legal, determination of the truth of the defamatory allegations. The analysis may also explain, on similar grounds, the traditional refusal of the common law to recognize a right to recover damages from a competitor for false disparagement of his goods:[53] the disparaged competitor can rebut untruthful charges in the same advertising medium the disparager used.

4. *Intrusion.*—Eavesdropping, photographic surveillance of the interior of a home, ransacking private records to discover information about an individual, and similarly intrusive methods of penetrating the wall of privacy with which people surround themselves are tortious.[54] This result is consistent with the economic analysis in Part I, but cases involving "ostentatious surveillance," as by a detective who follows someone about everywhere, present a more difficult question. The common thread running through the cases in which the courts have held that ostentatious surveillance was tortious is that the surveillance exceeded what was reasonably necessary to uncover private information and became a method of intimidation, embarrassment, or distraction. An example is the famous case of Mrs. Onassis and the aggressive photographer, Ron Gallela.[55] The court affirmed Gallela's right to photograph Mrs. Onassis but required him quite literally to keep his distance, since the methods he was using to obtain the photographs impaired her freedom of movement to a degree impossible to justify in terms of the additional information he could obtain thereby. It is no answer to say

---

solution has the unfortunate characteristic, compared with tort liability, of encouraging inaccurate reporting.

[53] *See* American Washboard Co. v. Saginaw Mfg. Co., 103 F. 281 (6th Cir. 1900).

[54] *See, e.g.,* Roach v. Harper, 143 W. Va. 869, 105 S.E.2d 564 (1958); Dietemann v. Times, Inc., 449 F.2d 245 (9th Cir. 1971).

[55] Galella v. Onassis, 487 F.2d 986 (2d Cir. 1973).

that she could have paid him to keep his distancc; if she had no property right, paying him to desist would simply invite others to harass her in the hope of being similarly paid off.

Consistent with the analysis in this Article, the common law does not limit the right to pry through means not involving interference with the subject's freedom of movement. Thus in Ralph Nader's suit against General Motors the court affirmed the latter's right to hire someone to follow Nader about, question his acquaintances, and, in short, pertinaciously ferret out personal information about Nader which General Motors might have used to undermine his public credibility.[56] Yet I would expect a court to enjoin any attempt through such methods to find out what Nader was about to say on some subject in order to be able to plagiarize his ideas.

## CONCLUSION

The analysis in Part II of this Article suggests that the common law response to the problem of privacy has been broadly consistent with the economics of the problem as developed in Part I.[57] I have

---

[56] Nader v. General Motors Corp., 25 N.Y.2d 560, 255 N.E.2d 765, 307 N.Y.S.2d 647 (1970).

[57] There is a danger that by examining as narrow a branch of the common law as the privacy tort, one will overlook other common law principles related to privacy but perhaps inconsistent with the privacy tort. Blackmail may appear to be such a principle. If I am correct that the facts about a person (as distinct from his communications) should be in the public domain so that those who have to decide whether to initiate (or continue) social or business relations with the person will be able to do so on full information, does it not follow that the Nosey Parker should be allowed to sell back the information he obtains to the individual?

Imagine that a person has a criminal record which he is anxious to conceal. Newspaper publication would be privileged because the crimes were committed in the recent rather than the remote past, although having served his sentence the person is not subject to further criminal liability in respect of them. Someone who made it his business to conduct research into people's pasts and sell the results to the newspaper would thus be subject to no sanction, but if he tried to sell his research to the object of it he would be guilty of the crime of blackmail.

The difference of treatment is all the more puzzling because in the analogous area of false advertising of goods there seems to be no difference. If a customer sues a seller for false advertising, his objective is more likely to be to obtain a financial settlement than to publicize the falsehood, but this is not considered an improper objective, and settlement is freely permitted. Blackmail would seem to serve a function similar to that of the false advertising suit by creating a deterrent to acquiring or concealing characteristics that are undesirable in the eyes of people having social or business dealings with the person blackmailed.

The cases are not, however, precisely analogous. A closer analogy to the customer's suit for false advertising might be a wife's divorce action based on her husband's concealment from her of his homosexuality. Here, too, settlement is permitted. The counterpart to the blackmail case in the false advertising area would be a suit, which is not permitted, by someone, neither customer nor competitor, who is simply in the business of bringing enforcement actions. The policy against such suits, as against blackmail, is founded on considera-

not discussed all of the privacy cases nor are all those I have discussed consistent with economic theory. Nonetheless, especially given the absence of a well-developed competing positive theory of the privacy tort, the economic approach holds promise of increasing our understanding of this puzzling branch of law.

No one has argued that most *legislation* has an implicit economic logic, so it is not surprising that recent legislative trends in the privacy field have not conformed to the economics of the privacy problem. Broadly stated, the trend has been toward expanding the privacy protections of the individual while contracting those of organizations, including business firms. This trend is the opposite of what one would expect if efficiency considerations were motivating privacy legislation.

---

tions—based on the economics of private law enforcement—that have nothing to do with a judgment that false advertising is a less serious offense in the personal than in the commercial sphere. These considerations are expounded in Landes & Posner, *The Private Enforcement of Law*, 4 J. LEGAL STUD. 1, 42-43 (1975).

# [16]

# A TASTE FOR PRIVACY?
# EVOLUTION AND THE EMERGENCE OF A
# NATURALISTIC ETHIC

*RICHARD A. EPSTEIN\**

## I. INTRODUCTION

IN his paper "Privacy: Its Origin, Function, and Future," Jack Hirshleifer has attempted to link the modern theories of sociobiology to the legal rules governing privacy.[1] Stated in its most general form, the subject of his inquiry is whether a theory of natural selection can explain an inborn preference for privacy and a collective impulse for its legal protection. His work rests in large part upon the biological theory of natural selection—developed by Darwin in the nineteenth century and enriched by modern evolutionary theory—as it relates to both kin selection and sociobiology. The basic precepts of the modern view towards evolutionary principle are in essence two.[2] The first is that individual patterns of behavior are subject to the same sorts of selection pressures as anatomical structures or biochemical processes. The second is that the principle of *inclusive,* not individual, fitness functions as the test for natural selection. Inclusive fitness concentrates not upon the survival of the individual organism as such, but upon the propagation of its genes over future generations. The shift in focus from the individual to the gene has enormous consequences, because it introduces a limited and specialized altruism, as individual behavior, in addition to individual self-interest, must take into account the effect of behavior an organism has upon all its biological relations, discounted by the remoteness of the relationship.[3]

---

* Professor of Law, University of Chicago Law School.

[1] Jack Hirshleifer, Privacy: Its Origin, Function, and Future, 9 J. Legal Stud. 649 (1980).

[2] For a lucid exposition and defense of these basic principles, see David P. Barash, Sociobiology and Behavior (1977), esp. at ch. 4.

[3] The classical exposition of the principle of inclusive fitness is found in W. D. Hamilton, The Genetical Evolution of Social Behaviour, 7 J. Theoretical Biology 1 (1964). In formal terms, the key ratio for inclusive fitness is $k = 1/r$, where $k$ represents the ratio of the benefits to others to the costs to the organism itself, and $r$ represents the degree of genetic relatedness between the two organisms. What the formula says is that the fewer the common genes between the two organisms, the greater the benefit to another from the expenditure of any given degree of labor. In the common case of parent and offspring, each unit of cost to the parent must generate two units of benefits to the offspring. Given the great abilities of the parent, especially the mother,

The consequences of the shift of orientation are, as should be plain, of especial importance in matters of sexual reproduction and parenting.

In this essay I do not question the soundness of these two basic assumptions, but instead use them to explore, in somewhat speculative fashion, a question that lies on the borderland between biology and law. To what extent can an evolutionary theory of behavior account for the emergence of a generalized human willingness to regard certain interests, in particular individual privacy, as legitimate? The inquiry is not about the normative question of how claims of right are legitimated, but about the descriptive question of whether, and if so how, human beings come to regard certain claims as legitimate, irrespective of their ultimate ethical status. The inquiry can be made not only about privacy but about many substantive legal issues.

## II. THE DOMAIN OF PRIVACY

It is important to identify at the outset the nature of the privacy interest in question. In his paper, Hirshleifer assumes that the interest in privacy should be equated with the interest in *personal autonomy*.[4] As a matter of legal theory, this equation is too simple.[5] Personal autonomy may account for the right of privacy in the narrow sense of that term, but it also accounts for much, if not all, of the legal protection that goes beyond privacy. Respect for the physical integrity of the individual and his material possessions, and their protection from external aggression, is fundamentally attributable to a concern with autonomy. The same can be said about the protection of reputation, or the right to dispose of one's person and property as he chooses, or even the right to speak one's mind on the political issues of the day. Whereas each of these interests might have some connection with privacy, it would be wrong to insist that privacy interests lie at, or close to, their root. Since a theory about the evolution of tastes depends upon the proper identification of likes and dislikes, it is imperative to establish the proper place of privacy

---

and the great needs of the offspring, this condition will frequently be satisfied early in the development cycle. As the offspring grow more self-sufficient, the ratio begins to shift. Weaning, for example, becomes in the interest of the mother when that two to one benefit-cost ratio is not satisfied. Matters are not quite the same from the point of view of the offspring who (even with the interests of future unborn siblings taken into account) normally wants parental protection somewhat longer than the parent wishes to provide it, as it measures the benefits provided against its own loss of acquisition. For a discussion of this and other implications of the inclusive fitness principle, see Robert L. Trivers, Parent-Offspring Conflict, 14 Am. Zoologist 249 (1974).

[4] Hirshleifer, *supra* note 1, at 649-51.

[5] This equation is also found in the seminal article on the right to privacy, Samuel D. Warren & Louis D. Brandeis, The Right to Privacy, 4 Harv. L. Rev. 193, 205 (1890). "The principle which protects personal writings and all other personal productions, not against theft and physical appropriation, but against publication in any form is in reality not the principle of private property, but that of inviolate personality."

upon the legal map before speculating about the evolutionary forces that might have led to a psychological disposition to regard that interest as legitimate.

Fortunately, the taxonomy of privacy has been much clarified by a four-fold classification proposed by Prosser in 1960.[6] To Prosser, a close examination of the decided cases shows that the privacy cases could, with tolerable accuracy, be broken down into four separate classes:

1. Intrusion upon the plaintiff's seclusion or solitude, or into his private affairs.
2. Public disclosure of embarrassing private facts about the plaintiff.
3. Publicity which places the plaintiff in a false light in the public eye.
4. Appropriation, for the defendant's advantage, of the plaintiff's name or likeness.[7]

While this scheme is of great organizational use, it highlights the difficulty of equating the privacy interest with individual autonomy, as many of the wrongs catalogued under privacy are covered elsewhere in the law of torts. The first class of wrongs, the intrusion upon the plaintiff's seclusion or solitude, may be and often is the consequence of some immediate invasion of the plaintiff's land. As such it is compensable as an element of consequential damages in an action for trespass to land.[8] Even where the defendant does not enter the plaintiff's premises, disturbances of seclusion and solitude— say, by noises and odors—have long been remedied by the action of nuisance, which deals with substantial interferences with the plaintiff's use and enjoyment of property that fall short of physical entrance.[9] Lastly, situations in which the defendant harasses or bothers the plaintiff, be it over the telephone or on a public street, are typically actionable as intentional infliction of emotional distress.

The pure case of invasion of privacy under this heading therefore must begin only where the traditional protections for personal freedom and real property leave off. In essence, therefore, the case that *defines* invasion of seclusion or solitude is the situation in which the defendant, while off the plaintiff's premises, observes (or overhears) the plaintiff, especially while on his own premises. Yet the moment that we are forced to characterize the privacy right in this manner, its marginal importance to personal autonomy becomes apparent. As a practical matter, the interest is not very important to those who might wish to claim it. If, moreover, it is thought important, it

[6] William L. Prosser, Privacy, 48 Calif. L. Rev. 383 (1960).

[7] *Id.* at 389.

[8] See, e.g., Bouillon v. Laclede Gaslight Co., 143 Mo. App. 462, 129 S.W. 401 (1910).

[9] See, e.g., Morgan v. High Penn Oil Co., 238 N.C. 185, 193, 77 S.E.2d 682, 689 (1953). "[A]ny substantial non-trespassory invasion of another's interest in the private use and enjoyment of land by any type of liability forming conduct is a private nuisance. . . ."

can usually be protected by simple actions of evasion or self-defense that do not depend upon the assistance of the state. Second, as a theoretical matter the insistence upon the right to this form of privacy is most problematic because of the correlative duty that it necessarily entails. Most individuals think that they are entitled to look around and observe, yet these activities become wrongful under any expansive interpretation of this privacy interest. This is not to say that eavesdropping over a private (can we use the word?) conversation need not be regarded as a good thing. Yet any protection afforded against such practices is trivial in importance when set against the much more important protections afforded by the legal system against bodily injury and property damage. Trespass and nuisance are matters of great moment. The pure case of invasion of seclusion and solitude is not.

Putting aside for the moment the second class of wrongs, disclosure of embarrassing facts, a similar assessment is proper for the "false light" cases. Although the tort of false light is not covered by trespass and nuisance actions, it is covered by the traditional tort of defamation. Defamation involves false statements about the plaintiff made to third parties that induce them not to engage in (or not remain in) mutually advantageous relationships with the plaintiff.[10] The law of defamation could not well serve its central mission of protecting reputation if it extended only to explicit written or verbal statements about the plaintiff's conduct. Protection against improper portrayal of the plaintiff's character or personality—even a subtle portrayal by innuendo and implication—is necessary as well.[11] Yet that concern with reputation is precisely what is involved in all false light cases. So understood, false light is but a small corner of the tort of defamation that in no sense needs its own niche in the law of privacy.

The same charge of redundancy cannot be leveled against Prosser's second class of privacy torts, the disclosure of *true* embarrassing facts about the plaintiff. Here no action could rest on a defamation theory, because the truth of the defendant's assertions necessarily denies the misstatements essential to defamation. The new ground broken by this tort underscores the serious difficulties with its own intellectual foundations: the tort places enormous restrictions upon the freedom of speech that most individuals ordinarily enjoy. For that reason it has received but limited acceptance, largely with revelations about events long past where the *identification* of the particular plaintiff by name is thought to serve no important social value.[12] It may well

[10] See, e.g., George v. Jordan Marsh Company, 359 Mass. 244, 268 N.E.2d 915 (1971).

[11] See, e.g., Restatement (Second) of Torts § 559 (1977). "A communication is defamatory if it tends so to harm the reputation of another as to lower him in the estimation of the community or to deter third persons from associating or dealing with him."

[12] See, e.g., Youssoupoff v. Metro-Goldwyn-Mayer Pictures, Ltd., 50 T.L.R. 581 (Ct. App. 1934); Burton v. Crowell Publishing Co., 82 F.2d 154 (2d Cir. 1936).

be that even this modest survival of the tort is unwise because it does not allow third parties to assess *for themselves* the weight and significance of true information about the plaintiff. Even supposing such criticism is misplaced, this third form of privacy must be consigned to a fringe role, wholly dwarfed in importance by the law of defamation.

The last of the identified privacy torts involves protection against the appropriation by the defendant of the plaintiff's name or likeness. Without doubt, the interest protected here is both substantial and important. The plaintiff's interest is not protected by any other common law action, and recognition of the tort has never given rise to the nagging questions of uniqueness or soundness that occur in discussions of other forms of invasions of privacy. It is not therefore surprising that the early cases of privacy were concerned with this particular tort.[13] Ironically enough, the asserted right does not usually involve "the right to be let alone" thought to lie at the root of the action. Instead the basic issue is whether the name or likeness of a given person should be subject to the use and exploitation by its natural holder, or whether it should be placed in the public domain where all can use it without fear of legal reprisal. Of course no one can reduce to exclusive physical possession the name or likeness of any person. Intangible form, however, has not prevented the institutional creation of patents and copyrights which can be acquired, abandoned, sold, licensed, and protected against infringement by others. Analogous rules can be, and have been, developed for name and likeness, if only because of the general deep-seated conviction that they are almost as much a part of a person as an arm or a leg. The tort of improper appropriation is thus perceived as an outer bulwark for the protection of self. The comparison between slavery and appropriation of name or likeness was made with great conviction in the leading cases.[14] It should not be dismissed as an idle or ignorant sentiment.

## III. THE EVOLUTION OF TASTES FOR LEGAL RULES

What then can be said about the relationship between a right of privacy, as defined above, and the emergence of an inclination for that right? Here the question is descriptive and one of evolutionary theory. The short answer seems to be that it is most unlikely any set of selection pressures have fostered the development of a widespread, persistent, and strong preference for the right of privacy. The gene-environment interactions that drive

---

[13] See, e.g., Briscoe v. Reader's Digest Association, 93 Cal. Rptr. 866 (1971); Cox Broadcasting Corp. v. Cohn, 420 U.S. 469 (1975).

[14] See Roberson v. Rochester Folding Box Co., 171 N.Y., 538, 64 N.E. 442 (1902), where the cause of action was rejected; and Pavesich v. New England Life Insurance Co., 122 Ga. 190, 50 S.E. 68 (1904). See Barash, *supra* note 2.

*Privacy I*

natural selection are strongest in matters that day in and day out come closest to the raw nerve of survival and propagation. The questions of privacy are simply too far removed from these dominating concerns to have much imprint upon the development of tastes for any given normative orders. Such is not to say that all matters of desires for legal rules are necessarily beyond the influences of selection pressures. To the contrary, these pressures are apt to play a powerful role in the formation of dispositions and tastes in the individual organism. As attitudes influence behavior, so they influence the probabilities of survival. Surely no one doubts this truism with respect to basic sexual drives or the emotion of fright in response to danger. The simple thesis here is that similar pressures can be exerted with respect to tastes for legal rules, and for the same evolutionary reasons. These include: (a) the prohibition of the use of force against strangers in the same species except in self-defense; (b) the rule of first possession of an unowned thing as the root of title; (c) the status obligations of parents to their offspring; and (d) promissory obligations. We turn first to these questions and leave the matter of privacy until last.

## A.  *Traditional Areas*

1.  *The Use of Force.* The use of force is one characteristic way in which disputes are resolved between any two organisms that assert (by appropriate behavior) claims over themselves or over some external things. Force is of course a most common means of doing business between members of different species, as predator-prey relationships are among the most recurrent in nature. It is highly doubtful that there is any survival advantage in self-restraint in these situations, and we should predict, as is the case, that concern with the welfare of other species—fish, poultry, livestock—is, if anything, strongly selected against in nature. Conflict between conspecifics is, however, a very different matter. Aggression against conspecifics promises certain advantages to the organism that uses it, but it holds out certain perils as well: force in attack is apt to be met by force in defense. Whatever the differences between conspecifics, the rivals will likely be closely matched,[15] such that in a fight to the finish the costs of *winning*—not to mention those of losing—are, correspondingly, likely to be quite high. The vanquished organism may inflict wounds upon its conqueror that will hinder its ability to use force against third parties, be they conspecifics or not. Given

---

[15] Such is not of course the case when the rivals are at different stages of development, as in conflicts between the very young and fully mature members of a given species. Yet even here there are devices designed to forestall conflict. Thus it is thought that the delay of puberty in young males promotes fitness because it prevents young males from entering into conflict with fully mature males.

## A TASTE FOR PRIVACY 671

the perils associated with the unrestrained use of force, it is not too difficult to envision the selection pressures that work to control the desire to commit unrestrained aggression against conspecifics—as evidenced by the forms of ritual combat that have evolved to facilitate ordering dominance relations without resorting to all-out force.[16]

By the same token it becomes possible to predict the emergence among conspecifics of a stronger willingness to use force in self-defense than as a means of attack. The gains for aggression are in general apt to be less than the gains from defense; that is, the survival of the attacked organism counts for more than the conquest of a rival. Gains from defense are likely to be very great, for example, in the case of a mother protecting her young. If, and it is a big if, such is indeed the case, there is reason to expect an instinctive receptiveness to a general rule prohibiting all from using force against all, when measured against an alternative rule countenancing the unbridled use of force. Organisms that learn *not* to attack but to defend their conspecifics should have greater survival capacity than those that do not. To be sure, the depth (or direction) of the preference must vary. Yet the everyday fact of confrontation, especially in primitive conditions of scarcity, makes it unlikely that a tendency against the unrestricted use of force could long escape the pressures of natural selection.

Here one vital caveat must be observed. It is most unlikely under any set of environmental conditions that *all* organisms will develop a natural or uniform inclination against aggression. To the contrary, any unanimous preference in that direction, even if achieved, should prove unstable over time. Suppose, *ex hypothesi,* that every member of a given society is willing to abjure the use of force. Enormous opportunities are thereby created for the single member of that society that breaks with the general rule by engaging in acts of aggression against his fellows. Such an individual is likely to find that his fellows are themselves lax in defense against force (from one of their own kind), given that typical defensive efforts are geared towards attacks by outsiders. Also, an evident want of competition by others willing to use agressive force gives ample opportunity for the successful exploitation of force. So long as genetic variation can exist in the inclination to use force,

---

[16] For a mathematical illustration of much of this point, with extensive reliance upon models of expected values, see John Maynard Smith, The Evolution of Behavior, Scientific American, September, 1978, at 176, 184-89.

It is easy to envision situations in which there will be a fight to the death between rough equals, as when there is a single resource necessary to the survival of both but which is capable of possession only by one. See, e.g., B. Heinrich, Bumblebee Economics 18 (1979), where it is observed that rival queen bees will fight to the death for the occupation of a single nest. Such behavior is less likely to emerge among large animals where the ability to control a single resource is less likely to be a life or death matter. The large animal that loses a ritual conflict is free to engage in a similar conflict at some later time.

some members of the group will develop a strategy that relies in some degree upon the use of force against other members.

The increased use of force cannot, however, continue without limit. As other individuals seek to imitate the aggression of the first, the suitable targets for aggression will diminish. As individual organisms become the object of more frequent attack, selection pressures should tend to favor the individuals who are better able to take defensive measures. In the end some sort of equilibrium should emerge in which some members of society prefer to use force, while most remain inclined to resist its use. The preference against the unrestrained use of force will not be unanimous, but it will in most cases be widespread enough to create a predisposition to regard its use as wrongful. That murder, rape, and pillage (especially between individuals of different genetic groupings) *do* occur in human societies is, as a descriptive matter, consistent with the theory, as is the intense and widespread desire to curb their spread. The case for controlling force rests not only on intellect but also on the instinct borne of evolutionary pressures that antedate the organization of any modern society. Early writers who spoke of self-defense as being justified by "natural" reason,[17] who thought vengeance to be the "natural" desire of mankind may not have thought in explicit biological, let alone evolutionary, terms. But they did understand something about the common instinctive responses to crime and punishment—an understanding that is lost in some modern economic and sociological treatments of the same subjects.

2.  *First Possession.* A similar account can be given of the wide acceptance of the rule that possession is the root of title, again as between conspecifics.[18] In any primitive setting an organism must expend resources to obtain control over some bit of territory or some material thing. Any other organism that wants the same land or the same thing must expend energy in order to take it away from the first, as the benevolence of the first possessor towards a stranger is the one behavioral pattern that cannot emerge in a system dominated by inclusive fitness. To acquire the first possession of another therefore necessarily entails aggression or stealth against a fellow organism. If force is used, the attacker is apt to labor under systematic disadvantages in the battle that follows.[19] His attack will normally endanger the life or health of his rival and thus provoke very strong defensive measures. The territorial conflict is apt to occur at a place where the party in possession can call upon his superior knowledge of his environment. Given these natural disadvantages the organism that develops a respect for the claims of a first possessor is

---

[17] Such is the sentiment expressed in the Lex Aquilia, Digest, IX 2.4 pr.

[18] I have already written on some of the normative difficulties with this legal proposition in, Richard A. Epstein, Possession as the Root of Title, 13 Ga. L. Rev. 1221 (1979).

[19] A point made by Hirshleifer, *supra* note 1, at 657-58.

in general likely to have a better survival rate than the organism that does not. There is indeed empirical evidence that the rule of first possession has been adopted in nature. For the speckled wood butterfly an important territory is an area of sunlit space in a forest. Where there are two male contestants for any such space, both the owner and the interloper commonly follow what has been termed a "bourgeois" strategy, whereby the owner adopts hawkish behavior and the interloper dovish behavior. The net effect of the combined strategies is that the party in possession can best the very rival to whom it would submit if their roles were reversed. First possession, as it were, lends a sense of legitimacy to the claim. And as the theory suggests, sustained and closely fought conflicts occur only in cases where (through the manipulation of an experimenter) both of the butterflies believe themselves to be the first possessor of the territory in question. Although the principles of decision followed by the butterflies cannot be known, their disposition to follow the rule of first possession is illustrative of our point. It is immaterial that the butterflies cannot articulate their rules of decision; it is their behavior that matters.

The tendency to respect first possession will not be universal within any group for the same reasons discussed above in connection with the use of force. Yet a collective consensus in favor of the rule is apt to emerge, thus accounting for the broad acceptance that the rule receives in the legal order, usually on instinctive and nonintellectual grounds.

3. *Status Obligations.* Status obligations, requiring the special protection and care of the young by their parents, are easily subject to the same general analysis. At one level it might be argued that the existence of any status obligation is inconsistent with the rule of first possession on the ground that there can be no obligations toward the very children of whom the parents take possession and in fact own. Yet whatever the possible formal contradiction between status obligations and the first possession rule, clearly on biological grounds the first possession rule plays no role whatsoever with children, given the necessity in the evolutionary process for care of the young in advanced species. In light of the evident importance of children, we should expect, as is indeed the case, that the obligations owed them by their parents are far more extensive than those which individuals owe generally to strangers. It will not do for a parent simply to refrain from using force against or lying to their children. Affirmative care is required and, typically, willingly given.

As in the case with aggression and the first possession rule, however, there is no reason to suppose that the tendency to care for the young is uniform across all individuals and all environments. Sex differences, for example, play a very important role; inclusive fitness clearly implies that females typically have a greater interest in the care of their offspring than do males, as they can often provide offspring greater benefits at lower cost. By the

674                    THE JOURNAL OF LEGAL STUDIES

same token environmental circumstances may be important, for parental care—often the care of both parents—will be needed more by infants born in harsh and hostile environments. These differences in intensity are, however, just that. In all advanced species, especially man, there seems to be a strong natural urge for parents to care for their young, an urge that has been fostered and preserved by evolutionary forces operative from the earliest times. Common law lawyers have long spoken of "natural love and affection" as a strong motive for individual generosity in family contexts.[20] Not surprisingly, the distinction between transactions within the family and transactions made at "arm's length" with strangers has proved one of the most durable in the legal system.[21] It simply will not do to treat parents and children as individual actors whose energies are directed solely towards individual utility or wealth maximization. There is a strong evolutionary bias towards the voluntary acceptance of status obligations toward offspring. The task of legitimating social rules is surely easier when those whom they govern are predisposed to accept them, even if for reasons not always fully understood by the individuals so governed.

4. *Promissory Obligations.* There is a similar explanation for acceptance of the well-nigh universal proposition that a promise is, prima facie, the source of an obligation to a party. The key biological analogy is the misnamed practice of "reciprocal altruism" that can exist both between members of the same species and members of different species.[22] Long-term alliances can be to the benefit of both parties, even in the absence of a system of formal remedies that governs in the event of breach.[23] The principle is not

[20] See Smith, *supra* note 16, at 190-91. The original observations were made by N.D. Davies of Oxford University.

[21] For an illustration of the rights of children to enforce promises made for their benefit by their parents, see Dutton v. Pool, 1 Ventris 318 (K.B. 1677). Note that modern American law will generally allow any intended beneficiary *C* to enforce against *B* a promise exacted for *C*'s benefit by *A*. See for the early important case, Lawrence v. Fox, 20 N.Y. 268 (1859).

[22] See Robert L. Trivers, The Evolution of Reciprocal Altruism, 46 Q. Rev. Biology 35 (1971). The problem is also discussed in Edward O. Wilson, Sociobiology: The Abridged Edition 58 (1980). One of the examples discussed by both Trivers and Wilson concerns the evolution of a taste to be a Good Samaritan, which they think can be fostered if each person knows he will be saved by others when in imminent peril. If rescuing has but a one-in-two chance of failure and being saved has a 90 percent chance of success, there is no question everyone would be better off with universal rescue instead of universal indifference. (Wilson, *supra* at 58.) But in the absence of a mechanism that guarantees a substantial probability of a rescue, it is doubtful a taste for such efforts will solidly emerge. For reasons against imposing such duties of rescue as a matter of private common law, see Richard A. Epstein, A Theory of Strict Liability, 2 J. Legal Stud. 151, 189-204 (1973); Richard A. Epstein, Causation and Corrective Justice: A Reply to Two Critics 8 J. Legal Stud. 477, 490-93 (1979).

[23] Thus pure gratuitous promises receive special treatment in the law that separates them from standard commercial engagements. Note that it is important to distinguish in the legal context between those legal promises that are gratuitous only in the sense that they are not supported by consideration—as with firm offers—but which are but the first steps in matured

at all different from that of long-term business relationships that operate without legal protection, as is often the case in an international setting. The party wishing to violate the basic understanding in order to reap some short-term advantage risks detection and the enormous costs of losing repeated future interactions that would otherwise be available. If the future gains that are sacrificed are greater than the short-term gains from violation, an organism will be worse off by breaking an implicit understanding than by abiding by it. It therefore follows that to the extent stable long-term interactions offer continued mutual advantage, the development of an inclination for keeping promises will advance the fitness of the organism that has it. In the human context these pressures make individuals receptive to a legal or moral norm that requires such conduct. The self-interested tendency to respect promissory arrangements, especially in the long term, will not of course be universal, even in human beings, for reasons already discussed in connection with the use of force and the first possession rule. Let any stable arrangement of perfect respect emerge and it will be in the interests of some individuals to evolve cheating mechanisms that exploit the good will created by other honor-bound organisms. The tendency to cheat, however, is itself subject to limitations, for if (or when) the cheaters become too numerous they disrupt long-term mutual arrangements for everyone. Clearly reciprocal altruism does work in some cases, and its effectiveness is enhanced by the ability of some individuals to detect, avoid, and possibly punish cheaters. In the end therefore there may well be some intermediate equilibrium position in which a small number of cheaters coexist with a larger number of individuals prepared to honor the long-term expectations (or, differently put, where the probability of expected cheating is not uniform across all individuals, with some being more willing than others). In this environment the moral sentiment to respect promises may well dominate, but not displace, the tendency to disregard them.

## B.  *Privacy Interests*

There is then good reason to believe that strong evolutionary pressures favor the emergence of the dominant legal rules of tort, property, family, and contract. The question is whether these same evolutionary forces can account as well for the emergence of a legal right for privacy. The question is an important one, but it cannot be answered in the round. It is first necessary to retrace our earlier steps and note the distinctions of Prosser's fourfold classification.

---

bargain transactions, and gratuitous promises that are meant to be preludes to gifts and not to bargain between the parties. See, on the point, Friedrich Kessler & Grant Gilmore, Contracts: Cases and Materials 409-10 (2d ed. 1970).

1. *Solitude and Seclusion.* To the extent that protection of solitude and seclusion involves restricting the use of the threat of force by others, we should expect the same results reached earlier. The general, but not unanimous, social preference should support the emergence of legal restraints. Matters are however much more clouded when we turn to the "pure" privacy interest, represented, for example, by the right not to have other people observe what you do, especially when on your own property. To recognize this right generally, all persons would have to give up the right of observation. Yet, unlike the case with force, it is a hard task to write a convincing script that explains why one constellation of legal rights—such as that favoring privacy—will advance inclusive fitness better than an alternative legal regime—such as that favoring dissemination of information. Indeed the entire question seems so far removed from the central questions of survival and reproduction that the intensity of the evolutionary pressures are apt to be very low, even as their direction is largely undetermined. There is little reason therefore to think that a strong taste for or against the "pure" privacy interest will emerge over time, a point that is well borne out by the spotty and belated recognition the interest receives in virtually all legal systems. It is an area in which we have not been programmed and in which our intuitions do not function well.

2. *False Light.* The analysis is much more complicated in the case of false light. False light is a species of defamation; and defamation is a species of misrepresentation, but misrepresentation of a third party. To determine whether a natural taste for a false light rule could emerge, the particular wrong must be placed in its larger tort context of misrepresentations. As regards misrepresentations made by one party *to* another, the arguments will, in some measure at least, parallel those raised in the context of force. Many individuals stand to gain from the ability to deceive another; instances of misrepresentation are widespread in nature. Nonetheless there are enormous costs to deception, given that disastrous steps may be taken by relying upon it. Therefore, although the gains that derive from deception may well be great, the losses to others might be greater. Those who persistently engage in deceitful conduct will find themselves cut off from gainful associations with their fellows and will perhaps be exposed to the use of force by others who come to justify their own aggression as self-defense. The costs of engaging in misrepresentation are apt to be high, and I expect, therefore, the equilibrium would be pushed in the direction of honest behavior. The pressure will not, however, lead to the adoption of the corner solution of perfect honesty in all affairs, for the reasons noted in connection with the force case. My guess is that fraud would survive in more substantial proportions than naked aggression, if only because it does not pose in general as great a threat to other persons, who have, after all, the option of simply not relying upon what they have been told.

The taste for misrepresentation is more puzzling with defamation, where misrepresentions are made to third parties who deal, or might deal, with the plaintiff. At the outset there is a real question about the effectiveness of the misrepresentations. The third party, especially in closed primitive societies, may have easy access to information about the party who is subject to defamation; he is, moreover, interested in having reliable information if only to preserve his own options. In addition, the defamed party may well have opportunities to speak on his own behalf; he will often discover the substance of the charge against him, even if he cannot discover its original source. Defamation then differs in two major respects from fraud. First, it is apt to be less devastating to an individual because the defamation will be diluted by the true information available about the injured party. Second, defamation is, if anything, more difficult to defend against than fraud, precisely because it works through third parties, some of whom the defamation itself keeps from dealing with the defamed party. It is difficult to know whether the taste against defamation will be greater or less than that which develops with respect to fraud. Perhaps the best first approximation is that fraud and defamation are about the same level of importance.

What is true of defamation in general is especially true in false light cases, which involve the misrepresentation of the general character or personality of the injured party. False light cases do not normally arise out of specific charges of individual wrongdoing by the aggrieved party. Rather, they involve situations in which a person, against his own will, is thrust into the public eye because of some event that befell him, such as being taken hostage or being victimized by natural disasters, such as hurricanes and earthquakes. Even in primitive societies, where charges of specific wrongdoing are apt to have severe consequences for the accused parties, false light cases seem to be of little importance. At the very least, false light requires a sophisticated use of language and communication; and it will not be effective when directed at individuals who are generally well known within a particular group. The modern false light cases typically involve magazine or other media portrayals of otherwise anonymous individuals thrust into prominence by events beyond their control. It is possible to see the link between these cases and the general law of defamation as an intellectual matter. It is difficult to believe that concern with this asserted wrong could have been significant at a time it would have had any evolutionary impact whatsoever.

3. *Embarrassing Past Facts.* The treatment of this class of privacy interests follows closely from what has gone before. As with the false light cases, it is doubtful that any strong taste with regard to the action could emerge in primitive close-knit societies, if only because it is difficult if not impossible for one person to keep such sensitive information away from the others in the tribe or group. If, moreover, any such taste did emerge, it would probably cut slightly against the recognition of the cause of action, for, unlike the false

light cases, the true information is of considerable benefit to those who receive it. All of this is not to say that it is impossible to advance modern social justifications for the protection against revelation of past embarrassing facts. Indeed the modern concern with rehabilitation is arguably one such policy. It does indicate, however, that such a cause of action will have little instinctive or intuitive appeal, as indeed seems to be the case today.

4. *Name and Likeness.* The last of the privacy interests in question—that of protection of name and likeness—raises unique problems of its own. On the one hand, the interest closely parallels the false light and embarrassing fact cases in that it is impossible to see how a need for its protection could arise before the onset of a relatively advanced society. Any misappropriation of name and likeness typically presupposes that there is a large society in which the institutions of mass communication are well developed. It therefore seems unlikely that a specific taste against this form of abuse could develop in early human culture and virtually no chance it could develop in prehuman organisms.

There may, however, be other general evolutionary pressures that have impact in this connection. As has already been noted, the tort in question is novel only to the extent that the underlying property interest is not one that can be vindicated by possession alone. Perhaps the native intellectual capacity of human beings includes the ability to extend by analogy tastes first acquired about tangible property to cases of name and likeness, when material conditions emerge that make the protection of such interests both possible and important. The point is not dissimilar to saying that an aptitude for spatial relationships entails an aptitude for chess, even though there is no gene or set of genes for chess playing as such. All that matters is that there be a close connection between the embedded aptitudes that were subject to evolutionary pressures and their modern counterparts. The early judicial opinions in appropriation of name and likeness are marked by the eager willingness to make analogies to slavery, which is the denial of autonomy and self-ownership as we know it. The very fact that such analogies are made and understood suggests that the evolutionary pressures may be strong, even though they manifest themselves only in some indirect way.

## IV.

The central theme of this paper has been to try to develop, in a somewhat speculative way, a positive theory of "natural" rights that explains why certain forms of basic rights and duties tend to emerge in most societies most of the time. In order to achieve that end, the paper began with the accepted sociobiological assumption that questions of preference (including preferences about right and wrong) are not immune from the pressures of natural selection that play such an important part in the evolution of all species, including man. Tastes for certain definable legitimate expectations will help the individual organism that holds them evolve in ways that maximize its own inclusive fitness.

The lessons to be learned from this exercise seem also to extend beyond the substantive conclusions that have been reached. For philosophers the message is that it is difficult, if not impossible, to construct models on an assumption that all human beings share certain uniform tastes in any given dimension. To take but the most famous illustration, John Rawls's effort to create a theory of social justice[24] rests on what evolutionary theory shows to be a necessarily wrong assumption: that all individuals are uniformly risk averse when in fact the principle of inclusive fitness precludes any uniform taste for risk, as much as it does a uniform taste for anything else. No social norm can be based on a presupposition (no matter how abstract) of universal support for, or consent to, that norm. The very possiblity of uniformity creates the reason for an individual to develop tastes that set him apart from the group in order to exploit through specialization the very opportunities that all other persons were hitherto prepared to renounce. Instead we must be satisfied with a procedure that seeks in rough measure to respond to the needs and tastes of *most* members of a society *most* of the time and that recognizes the need to exercise independent moral judgment to convert, for example, a general taste for bodily integrity into the philosophical principle of individual autonomy. The theory of evolutionary biology may well predict the types of rules that are likely to command general consent. Yet they do not, by the same token, state the rules that necessarily *ought* to command that consent. The ghost of Hume still haunts us.

The exercise also has important implications for economists. All too often in economic theory individual tastes are treated either as if they were wholly arbitrary or as not bound by genetic constraints. It is as though tastes on the fundamental normative issues discussed here involved nothing more than picking vanilla instead of chocolate ice cream. Likewise, the fundamental proposition of individual self-interest is often stated as either a necessary methodological assumption or a self-evident truth. Economists' assumptions of individual altruism do not take into account the importance of inclusive fitness, but instead depend on constructs that are, if anything, at variance with biological insights.[25] One central contribution of sociobiology to economics lies in demonstrating that tastes themselves are governed by discernible principles, and that self-interest, far from being merely an economic premise, is in the guise of inclusive fitness a biological conclusion. Undoubtedly, the human powers of individual reflection are sufficient in many cases

---

[24] John Rawls, A Theory of Justice (1971).

[25] See, e.g., Gary S. Becker, A Theory of Social Interactions, 82 J. Pol. Econ. 1063 (1974).

to overcome the inborn tendency to maximize inclusive fitness. But it is quite another matter to say that all expressions of self-interest vanish with an awareness of biological drives and, as with birth control, the means to control them. A full account of human self-interest must take into account conscious ends and purposes, but it must also take into account more basic drives and desires that can be controlled, shaped, and diverted but not wholly eliminated.

Last, there is in this article an important message for lawyers. An inveterate tendency in modern legal circles is to justify virtually all legal rules in terms of the larger social purposes or policies that they might, or should, serve. In some circles this practice translates into efforts to show how a concern with efficiency or wealth maximization is advanced by the adoption of certain types of rules and practices. In others the enterprise adopts the same grand strategy, while appealing to different social principles: protection of minority groups from exploitation, the elimination of poverty, and the like.

Whatever the substantive differences, both enterprises are fraught with the same difficulties if what I have said about the natural evolution for taste is correct. The principles of evolution make but very limited allowance for a notion of group preference or group choice.[26] Instead, all evolution is based upon the effort of individual genes or groups of genes to maximize their own fitness, such that any perceived group end must be a simple aggregation of individual preferences and tendencies of the group members. Within this framework all tastes for rights and duties are doubtless based upon the individual responses of individual organisms to their immediate environment. Therefore rules that have to do with property, with aggression, and with family are intuitively understood and justified for reasons that have nothing to do with some hidden social welfare function. They are intuitively understood and justified in more immediate and elemental terms, because they have worked their way into the mental map of the individuals who hold them. When it is pointed out that utilitarianism as a social philosophy seems deeply counterintuitive, it is precisely because it has no evolutionary analogue. This criticism of social theory is not necessarily negative, as there are reasons to believe that natural sentiments can get in the way of sensible social organization. The first possession rule, for example, might work well in nature where all organisms and things can enter into some form of stable equilibrium. But with human technology the use of the rule leads to a systematic overexploitation of given resources that can be corrected only by a conscious willingness—be it with buffaloes or oil—to limit individual

---

[26] V. C. Wynne-Edwards, Animal Dispersion and Its Relation to Social Behavior (1962). For a statement of the severe limitations of the group approach, see Barash, *supra* note 2, at 70-103.

A TASTE FOR PRIVACY 681

exploitation by some complicated mode of regulation for which there is little intuitive biological appeal.[27] To the extent that attitudes cannot change as rapidly as material conditions, there is, oddly enough, good reason to believe that *inefficient* rules will necessarily emerge at common law. Wild animals and oil again furnish examples, as the taste for the first possession rule could hardly evolve at a pace needed to keep up with the vast technological changes of the last century, if not the last millennium.

Just as we must be alert for the important cases of rapid material changes, we should recognize as well that basic ingrained expectations should not be ignored in explaining or justifying social practices that move at a more glacial pace, as with family, property, and force. To speak of legal rights and duties solely in terms of some grander social function is to speak of them in a way that sets up a persistent dissonance between our natural instincts on the one hand and our political order on the other. There is nothing which says that any system will be morally superior simply because it follows the dominant sentiments of those whom it rules. But I for one think that prospects for both individual and social betterment are apt to be more promising in a society that gives sufficient weight to the general sentiments about rights and duties that have emerged over time, even if it be through natural selection and not conscious design.

---

[27] See, e.g., Hague v. Wheeler, 157 Pa. St. 324 (1893), where the first possession rules were treated as proper at common law even as the court recognized that some legislation to curb waste was appropriate. Only belatedly has the common law recognized that it might be possible, for example, to impose reciprocal duties upon owners of wells to take precautions against "blowouts." See, e.g., Elliff v. Texon Drilling Co., 146 Tex. 575, 210 S.W.2d 558 (1948).

# [17]

## Privacy Is Dear at Any Price: A Response to Professor Posner's Economic Theory

*Edward J. Bloustein\**

The persuasiveness of Professor Posner's Article on the economic theory of privacy[1] hinges on his apparent success in transforming, in classical rationalist fashion, a complex and disorderly jumble of legal rules into a simple and unified scheme of explanation. Unfortunately, in at least one important sense, Posner's theory is simplistic, not simple, because it accomplishes its objective by avoiding, rather than confronting, complexity. He seduces by reduction, rather than convincing by explanation. The simple analytical elements of the scheme do not add up to the complex whole. His Truth about Privacy turns out to be some truth about one aspect of privacy.

I do not mean to suggest that Posner knowingly misleads us into thinking that we will discover in the economic theory of privacy more than is there; nor do I mean that his economic views are not helpful in understanding some aspects of privacy. Indeed, he explicitly disclaims the attempt to provide a complete theory of privacy,[2] and much of what he says about the limited area of privacy with which he deals is significant and true. But despite his explicit disavowals, Posner promises in his Article on privacy much more than he delivers. Moreover, in at least some respects, I believe his theory is wrong, and in others seriously misleading.

The thesis which Posner asserts deserves to be argued at greater length and in greater detail than I shall attempt in this Article. But the form in which this exchange between us takes place—although valuable in its own right—prevents such fullness. Posner's Article provides what he himself recognizes is only an outline of an argument. My response is cut of the same cloth.

### I. THE CONCEPTUAL LIMITATIONS OF THE THEORY

Philosophers and economists have long employed Ockham's razor as a methodological principle of parsimony in explanation. It is em-

---

\* President and Professor of Law and Philsophy, Rutgers, The State University of New Jersey; B.A. 1948, New York University; B. Phil. 1945, Oxford University; Ph.D. 1954, Cornell University; J.D. 1959, Cornell University Law School.
[1] *See* Posner, *The Right of Privacy*, 12 GA. L. REV. 393 (1978).
[2] *Id.* at 409.

bodied in maxims like "plurality is not to be assumed without necessity" and "what can be done with fewer [assumptions] is done in vain with more."[3] Posner violates the principle of Ockham's razor in two important respects. First, in both his economic theory and his analysis of privacy, Posner invites "[p]lurality . . . without necessity." Second, in both his economic theory and his analysis of privacy, even where he seeks to do "what can be done with fewer assumptions," his razor does not cut sharply enough; his explanatory parsimony turns out to be neglect of complexity. Let me illustrate these limitations in both his economics and his law.

## A. *The Economic Theory*

I am not an economist, and I am only barely acquainted with economic theory. I can pretend to significant critical insights into Posner's economics only with respect to its internal logic and only insofar as it departs from other well-established economic theories. Posner succinctly sets forth his economic assumptions in *Economic Analysis of Law.*[4] Although he does not make these assumptions explicit in his Article, Posner obviously relies heavily on them.[5]

1. *General Applicability of Posner's Economics.*—The first of Posner's assumptions is his description of economics as "the science of human choice in a world in which resources are limited in relation to human wants."[6] As a barely literate reader of economics, I am not about to ask whether this is a good description of that "dismal science." As a student of privacy, however, it is fair that I ask how well economics can serve the purposes of legal analysis.

The essential determinant of the applicability of Posner's economics to privacy is whether economics involves, as Posner assumes, choices of "resources" which are "limited in relation to human wants." I believe that much of privacy involves what Posner terms "costless" resources, such as air (Posner's example), which one can use "without depriving anyone" else of all of that resource he might desire.[7] In the alternative, as Posner sees it, privacy involves a "good with only one use," another kind of resource which puts its study beyond economic analysis.[8] My sense of pride and

---

[3] *See* 8 ENCYCLOPEDIA OF PHILOSOPHY 307 (1967).

[4] R. POSNER, ECONOMIC ANALYSIS OF LAW 3 (2d ed. 1977).

[5] *See* Posner, *supra* note 1. The early and incomplete stages of his economic thinking about privacy appear in his book. *See* R. POSNER, *supra* note 4, at 55.

[6] *See* R. POSNER, *supra* note 4, at 3.

[7] *Id.* at 6.

[8] *Id.*

self-esteem in my unique identity and individualism is not a resource that is "limited in relation to human wants." Indeed, it is,
in Posner's terms, "costless" or possibly, "a good with only one use."
To the degree, then, that the "right to be let alone"[9] involves a
person's spiritual nature,[10] self-esteem, and human dignity, "costless" resources, or goods "with only one use," Posner's economics is
irrelevant to understanding the right to privacy.

2. *Disputed Assumptions.*—A second concern about Posner's
economics is that he assumes that a person is "a rational maximizer
of his self-interest"[11] and that the "unseen hand" of the market
insures that "a process of voluntary exchange" will shift resources
"to those uses in which the value to consumers, as measured by their
willingness to pay, is highest."[12] Many economists have gravely criticized these two classical economic concepts as economic theorems,
and their criticisms must a fortiori cause lawyers to be skeptical of
their applicability to law.

Posner acknowledges that these assumptions may appear
"oversimplified and unrealistic as descriptions of human behavior"[13]; he insists, nevertheless, that economic theory "may be judged
a success" in its ability "to predict correctly how people will behave
in response to changes in their environment."[14] Other well-respected
economists dispute Posner, in purely economic terms, on the
"considerable" predictive power of these assumptions.[15] For the lawyer concerned with the applicability to law of the assumptions,
they not only appear "unrealistic" and "oversimplified," but they
also seem to lack substantial predictive power because they incompletely describe the reality involved.

Let us look at one example Posner offers to support the applicability of these classic marketplace principles to criminal law. One
may infer some indication of the insufficiency of Posner's economic

---

[9] Warren & Brandeis, *The Right of Privacy,* 4 HARV. L. REV. 193, 195 (1890) (quoting T.
COOLEY, LAW OF TORTS 29 (2d ed. 1888)).

[10] *Id.* at 197.

[11] R. POSNER, *supra* note 4, at 4.

[12] *Id.* at 10.

[13] *Id.* at 12.

[14] *Id.* at 13.

[15] *See, e.g.,* C. CROSLAND, THE FUTURE OF SOCIALISM 29-35 (1963); J. GALBRAITH, THE NEW
INDUSTRIAL STATE 388-99 (1st ed. 1967); R. HEILBRONER, THE WORLDLY PHILOSOPHERS 56-72 (4th
ed. 1972); F. HIRSCH, SOCIAL LIMITS TO GROWTH 60-64 (1976); J. SCHUMPETER, CAPITALISM,
SOCIALISM, AND DEMOCRACY 61-163 (2d ed. 1947). *Cf.* E. MISHAN, THE ECONOMIC GROWTH
DEBATE: AN ASSESSMENT, 14-15, 29-37 (1977) (economic theories are of little consequence in
social policy analysis since social tendencies have a greater impact on social welfare).

model by changes he made in the example in the second edition of *Economic Analysis of Law.* In the first edition, Posner stated that the criminal sanction offers the "clearest" proof of the "economic content of legal theory."[16] Citing Jeremy Bentham,[17] he boldly and unequivocally asserted that "crime can be prevented by subjecting the criminal offender to a punishment more painful to him than the commission of the crime is pleasurable."[18] Since people are "rational maximizers of satisfaction,"[19] Posner went on to say that as we increase "the severity of the punishment [for crime] or the likelihood of its being imposed," we will reduce its incidence."[20]

In the second edition, Posner no longer asserts that the criminal sanction is the "clearest" vindication of his economic theory.[21] Indeed, he seems to have softened his purist Benthamite convictions considerably and admits that "the notion of the criminal as a rational calculator will strike many readers as highly unrealistic, especially when applied to criminals having little education or to crimes not committed for pecuniary gain."[22] Posner also introduces in the second edition factors in the putative criminal's calculus which he did not even mention in the first edition. He points out that "the benefits of theft, and hence its incidence, might be diminished by a redistribution of wealth . . . [and] by reducing unemployment and thereby increasing the gains from noncriminal income-producing activity."[23] And finally, Posner recognizes "crimes of passion" as an exception to his model, a point which he neglected in the first edition.[24]

Nevertheless, Posner insists in both editions of *Economic Analysis of Law* that "a person commits a crime because the expected benefits . . . to him exceed the expected costs"[25] and that "criminals respond to changes in opportunity costs, in the probability of apprehension, in the severeity of punishment, and in other relevant variables, as if they were indeed the rational calculators of the economic model."[26] And in both editions he argues that "[t]he

---

[16] R. Posner, Economic Analysis of Law 357 (1st ed. 1970).

[17] J. Bentham, Theory of Legislation 325-26 (R. Hildreth ed. 1864).

[18] R. Posner, *supra* note 16, at 357.

[19] *Id.*

[20] *Id.* at 2.

[21] *Compare* R. Posner, *supra* note 16, at 357 *with* R. Posner, *supra* note 4, at 163.

[22] R. Posner, *supra* note 4, at 164-65.

[23] *Id.* at 164.

[24] *Id.*

[25] *Id.*

[26] *Id.* at 165.

function of the criminal law, viewed from an economic standpoint, is to impose additional costs on unlawful conduct . . . [in order] to limit that conduct to the efficient level."[27] Finally, Posner asserts the "predictive power" of his economic analysis.[28]

Even though the second edition of *Economic Analysis of Law* is much more sophisticated than the first, I still find a number of difficulties with Posner's second edition, post-Benthamite, rational calculus theory of the criminal sanction. To begin with, Posner admits that one of the determinants of criminal behavior is passion and that criminals are frequently poorly educated and unable to calculate the "costs" of their behavior. Posner's predictions of criminal behavior, either for any given crime or for many classes of crimes, are, therefore, highly unreliable if possible at all. Taking into account—as Posner admits we must—the impact on criminal behavior of "a redistribution of wealth" and a "[reduction] of unemployment" reenforces this conclusion. Once Posner recognized in his second edition the complexity of criminal behavior, he should have made much more modest claims of the predictive value of his economic model.

In particular, the predictive value of Posner's model with respect to the effect on criminal behavior of the severity and probability of the sanction is also limited.[29] According to Dershowitz, there is evidence to demonstrate that "some punishments deter some crimes by some people."[30] But even where a threat of sanction acts as a deterrent, the effect will vary widely depending upon, among other things, the knowledge available to the would-be criminals, their attitudes toward authority, their perceptions or responses to the same threatened sanction, and their emotional or personality types.[31] At best, one can conclude only that the threatened sanction has a general deterrent effect for some people.[32] But it is far-fetched to use a marketplace analogy to demonstrate a direct relationship, similar to that between cost and demand, between severity of sanc-

---

[27] *Id.* at 163-64.

[28] *Id.* at 165.

[29] I am grateful to my colleages Dean Don M. Gottfredson and Professor Andrew von Hirsch of the School of Criminal Justice of Rutgers, The State University, for discussing the calculus of deterrence with me.

[30] A. DERSHOWITZ, FAIR AND CERTAIN PUNISHMENT 71 (1976). *See also* A. VON HIRSCH, DOING JUSTICE: THE CHOICE OF PUNISHMENTS 37-44 (1976); von Hirsch, *The Aims of Imprisonment,* 71 CURRENT HISTORY 1, 3-4 (1976).

[31] F. ZIMRING, PERSPECTIVES ON DETERRENCE 32-49 (1971).

[32] *Id.* at 32. *See also* Andenaes, *The General Preventive Effects of Punishment,* 114 U. PA. L. REV. 949 (1966).

434            *GEORGIA LAW REVIEW*            [Vol. 12:429

tion and effectiveness of deterrence. In fact, most authorities agree
with Dershowitz that "it is almost impossible to demonstrate the
precise effectiveness of a given punishment on a given crime."[33]

Not only is Posner's post-Benthamite calculus weak as a method
of predicting criminal behavior, it also has severe limitations as a
means of understanding the social and legal system of punishment.
The criminal sanction is not only a deterrent to crime but also an
instrument of social retribution and vindication, as well as a social
symbol and a ritual assertion of moral values.[34] The philosopher
Kant espoused one aspect of this broader view of the penal law:
"The Penal Law is a Categorical Imperative; and woe unto him who
creeps through the serpent-windings of Utilitarianism to discover
some advantage that may discharge him from the Justice of Punishment."[35]

I do not accept Kant's view as the exclusive rationale for punishment. But I agree with Dershowitz that although our system of
criminal justice can and should take into account the objective of
deterrence, it can and should also take into account "the gravity
and culpability of the underlying crime."[36] In other words, our
system of criminal justice balances cost-benefit factors with moral
factors. Posner's use of the criminal sanction as an example of the
economic basis of legal theory is, therefore, at least insufficient and
misleading and may be substantially inaccurate.

3.   *"External" Costs and Benefits.*—A third criticism of Posner's
economic theory relates to his reliance on the concept of "external"
costs and benefits. Although Posner seems to disparage this concept
in *Economic Analysis of Law,*[37] he relies heavily on it in his Article
on privacy.[38] An external cost is one that imposes a burden on someone outside the marketplace, or in other words, on someone outside
the cost structure. An example is the burden an additional car on

---

[33] A. Dershowitz, *supra* note 30, at 72. *See also* Deterrence and Incapacitation: Estimat-
ing the Effects of Criminal Sanctions in Crime Rates 19-63 (A. Bloustein, J. Cohen & D.
Nagin eds. 1977); J. Gibbs, Crime, Punishment and Deterrence 5-11, 115-21 (1975); A. von
Hirsch, *supra* note 30, at 40-44.

[34] *See, e.g.,* J. Feinberg, *The Expressive Function of Punishment,* in Doing and Deserving
95 (1970); Andenaes, *supra* note 32; Cohen, *Moral Aspects of the Criminal Law,* 49 Yale L.J.
987, 1009 (1940).

[35] I. Kant, Philosophy of Law 195-96 (Hastie trans. 1887), *quoted in* A. Dershowitz, *supra*
note 30, at 132.

[36] A. Dershowitz, *supra* note 30, at 73. *See also* A. von Hirsch, *supra* note 30, at 45-55.

[37] R. Posner, *supra* note 4, at 52, 139.

[38] *See, e.g.,* Posner, *supra* note 1, at 412, 417, & 420.

the road imposes on all automobile users. An external benefit is an advantage that is outside the marketplace because it is not translatable into a lower price.

These concepts may have value for economic theory, but they are at best misleading and pretentious when applied to social policy analysis generally,[39] or to legal analysis in particular. As the legal scholar Calabresi, an adherent of one form of the economic analysis of law, stated: "[S]uch terms as external social costs and benefits . . . are not self-defining and are in fact as narrow or as broad as any society cares to make them."[40] In using the concept of "externality," the economist is, in effect, abandoning the marketplace as a determinant of social choice and disguising his abandonment by the use of a term which looks like a term of economics: "external" or "social cost." The real issue, as Calabresi recognizes, is not whether there are "hidden social costs or hidden social savings" but rather "how often a decision for or against an activity should be made outside the market."[41] And the realistic conclusion is, again to quote Calabresi, that "the frequency with which decisions to ignore the market are made tells something about the nature of a society—welfare, laissez-faire, or mixed. It is clear, however, that in virtually all societies such decisions to overrule the market are made, but are made only sometimes."[42] The point, as I see it, is that to the degree that the economist relies on "externalities," he is, in effect, admitting, albeit in a disguised and misleading fashion, the limitations of economic analysis of law.

4. *Limitations in Theory Are Not Recognized in Application.*— The last of the observations I shall offer concerning the purely economic aspects of Posner's theory of privacy is that although he explicitly recognizes the limitation of economic analysis in law he seems to forget these theoretical reservations when he applies his economic theory to specific legal problems. Thus Posner plainly says that "[t]he economist's competence in a discussion of the legal system . . . is strictly limited."[43] He goes on to say that

---

[39] *See, e.g.*, F. HIRSCH, *supra* note 15, at 60-64; E. MISHAN, *supra* note 15, at 14-15, 29-37, 70-71, 203-05.

[40] G. CALABRESI, THE COSTS OF ACCIDENTS 18 (1970) (citing A. PIGOU, THE ECONOMICS OF WELFARE (4th ed. 1932)).

[41] *Id.* at 19. *See also* E. MISHAN, *supra* note 15.

[42] G. CALABRESI, *supra* note 40, at 19. For a similar recognition, although in historical terms, of the limitation of the marketplace as a determinant of social choice, see R. HEILBRONER, *supra* note 15, at 16.

[43] R. POSNER, *supra* note 4, at 10.

436    *GEORGIA LAW REVIEW*    [Vol. 12:429

economists "cannot prescribe social change."[44] Again and again, however, in discussing the application of economics to legal issues, Posner neglects this reservation. His discussion of crime, as I outlined it above, plainly illustrates this neglect. But one need only read any portion of Posner's *Economic Analysis of Law*[45] or *The Right to Privacy*[46] to detect how limited an influence these theoretical restrictions have on his actual analysis.

## B.  *The Legal Theory*

Delivering less than he explicitly promises, thereby violating Ockham's principle that "what can be done with fewer [assumptions] is done in vain with more,"[47] is also a primary weakness of Posner's conceptual analysis of privacy. Some twenty years ago a federal circuit court judge characterized the confusing state of the law of privacy as a "haystack in a hurricane."[48] Shortly afterwards, Dean Prosser attempted to tidy up the haystack by reducing privacy to four categories of interests,[49] and shortly after Prosser's Article, I attempted further to tidy up the haystack by applying Ockham's razor and suggesting a single privacy interest—human dignity.[50] Posner's Article on privacy takes us back to the "haystack in a hurricane" days.

Posner begins his Article by acknowledging that "the concept of 'privacy' is elusive and ill-defined."[51] Does he intend to bring clarity to the "elusive" concept? No, he says he "will *avoid* the definitional problem by simply noting that *one aspect* of privacy is the withholding or concealment of information," and that it is "[t]his aspect [that] is of particular interest to [him]."[52] Posner further limits his theory by dealing with privacy "primarily in personal rather than business contexts."[53]

No one would argue, I am sure, with a writer's desire to limit his

---

[44] *Id. See also* G. CALABRESI, *supra* note 40, at 18-20, where Calabresi expresses the same reservations.

[45] R. POSNER, *supra* note 4.

[46] *Posner, supra* note 1.

[47] *See* note 3 *supra.*

[48] Ettore v. Philco Television Broadcasting Corp., 229 F.2d 481, 485 (3d Cir. 1956) (Biggs, C.J.).

[49] Prosser, *Privacy,* 48 CALIF. L. REV. 383 (1960).

[50] Bloustein, *Privacy as an Aspect of Human Dignity: An Answer to Dean Prosser,* 39 N.Y.U. L. REV. 962 (1964).

[51] Posner, *supra* note 1, at 393.

[52] *Id.* at ___ (emphasis added).

[53] *Id.*

analysis to one aspect of a complex problem if, indeed, he carries out his promise. But as you read Posner's Article, you realize that its sweep (presaged in his title) belies the seeming modesty of its beginnings. In *Economic Analysis of the Law*, Posner also presents a section entitled *The Right of Privacy* in which he does not even mention or discuss privacy problems other than those in which a person desires to withhold information.[54] The problems of privacy, however, go much beyond the desire of individuals to withhold personal information. Posner violates his modest intentions again and again by using a theory that offers some insight into that limited problem to reach much broader conclusions. Thus, in his "sketch" of "the [three] essential elements of a legal right of privacy based on economic efficiency" Posner includes (1) "protection of trade and business secrets"; (2) "facts about people"—not solely facts "withheld" or "concealed," but simply "facts about people," without qualification; and (3) "eavesdropping and other forms of intrusive surveillance," whether or not related to "concealed" or "withheld" personal information.[55]

Posner exhibits this same tendency in discussing legislative trends in the privacy area.[56] I recently argued for stronger protection for group or associational privacy than is presently available, and I am thus sympathetic, to a degree, to Posner's concerns.[57] But his economic analysis of the problem of concealment of personal information hardly supports the breadth of his conclusions on this score.

Posner's conclusions thus reach further than his data; but at the same time his conclusions do not reach far enough. He avoids discussing the problem of "privacy as a safeguard against political oppression."[58] Offering a theory of privacy which does not touch on this vital issue surely invites, in Ockham's terms, "plurality . . . without necessity." And is his thorough neglect of the line of Supreme Court cases from *Griswold v. Connecticut*[59] to *Roe v. Wade*[60] to the recent *Carey v. Population Services International*[61] reasonable under the circumstances? What grasp can a theory of privacy —even one limited in scope to tort law—really have if it neglects

---

[54] R. POSNER, *supra* note 4, at 55.

[55] Posner, *supra* note 1, at 404.

[56] *Id.* at 404-406.

[57] Bloustein, *Group Privacy: The Right to Huddle*, 8 RUT.-CAM. L.J. 219 (1977).

[58] Posner, *supra* note 1, at 409.

[59] 381 U.S. 479 (1965).

[60] 410 U.S. 113 (1973).

[61] 431 U.S. 678 (1977).

the constitutional dimension, a dimension which descends directly from the tort law origins of Warren and Brandeis?[62]

An even more devastating flaw in Posner's analysis is his failure to discuss privacy as a "final good" ("taste" is another term he uses to describe this aspect of privacy) as well as an "intermediate good."[63] He admits that if one considers privacy to be a "taste" or "final good," "this would bring the economic analysis to a grinding halt because tastes [and, I would add, ultimate values] are unanalyzable from an economic standpoint."[64] He then justifies limiting the scope of his inquiry to privacy as an intermediate good by saying that "the reader will have to decide whether this approach captures enough of the relevant reality to be illuminating."[65] Ockham, where is thy razor?

Thus Posner's Article suffers from both saying too much and saying too little. If it was his intention to deal primarily with the limited problem of concealment of personal information, his conclusions go much beyond this intention and much beyond what his economic argument can support. But if Posner intends to use his economic analysis as a powerful tool in analyzing the right to privacy, as *Economic Analysis of Law* and the pervasive intimations of his Article on privacy suggest, his analysis does not go far enough. Posner is either using a cannon to shoot peas or a pea shooter to accomplish the work of a cannon.

## II. The Substantive Strengths and Weakness of the Theory

But let us put aside questions about Posner's conceptual apparatus and look at actual results. Does Posner explain something that needs explaining? Are his explanations sound? And does he capture—as he puts it—"enough of the relevant reality to be enlightening"?

### A. *A Significant Insight Into Privacy as a Species of Concealment*

Posner makes a significant contribution to our understanding of one aspect of privacy by analyzing privacy as a species of conceal-

---

[62] *Cf.* A. Westin, Privacy and Freedom 338-64 (1967) (traces evolution of the constitutional concept of privacy from an ownership analysis to a personal liberty rationale). *See also* Bloustein, *The First Amendment and Privacy: The Supreme Court Justice and the Philosopher,* 28 Rutgers L. Rev. 41, 69-72 (1974); Bloustein, *supra* note 50, at 993-1000.

[63] Posner, *supra* note 1, at 394.

[64] *Id.*

[65] *Id.*

ment and by balancing it as a social good against the demand for private information.[66] People do indeed "possess information, including facts about themselves and contents of communications, that they will incur costs to conceal."[67] Some of this information is "discreditable"; some is "information concerning past or present criminal activity or moral conduct at variance with a person's professed moral standards."[68] Even where the information is not discreditable, some of it "if revealed [would] correct misapprehensions that the individual is trying to exploit."[69] In sum, the desire for privacy is often an attempt to exploit other people by manipulating their opinions through concealment or misrepresentation of private information.

On the other hand, prying or invasions of privacy are sometimes attempts, founded on self-interest, "to form a more accurate picture of a friend or colleague." The knowledge which we gain of someone by prying is often "useful in one's social or professional dealings with him."[70] In other words, we often seek information about people which is "necessary to verify or disprove" impressions about those people which they have created through "selective disclosure of facts about themselves" in order to "manipulate the world around them."[71] Thus prying is an "economic good"; "the tax collector, fiancé, partner, creditor, competitor" all pry because they gain useful personal information as a result. But privacy is an "economic good" too; individuals seek to conceal and withhold information in order to exploit and manipulate other people.

## B.  *Questionable Social Policy Choices*

Up to this point in his argument, Posner is explaining the economic motives which lead some people to pry and other people to seek privacy. Understanding this behavior in terms of marketplace costs and benefits is certainly helpful. But one must ask two important questions. What legal consequences flow from the economic analysis? And is the search for privacy always a form of concealment or misrepresentation?

One might suppose that if the disclosure of personal information

---

[66] *Id.* at 394-397.
[67] *Id.* at 394.
[68] *Id.* at 399.
[69] *Id.*
[70] *Id.* at 395.
[71] *Id.* at 400.

440          *GEORGIA LAW REVIEW*              [Vol. 12:429

involves a cost and if obtaining the information involves a benefit, the law would favor giving a property right in the personal information to its possessor, thereby creating a free market in personal information as commercial goods. According to Posner's economic theory, such a process of voluntary exchange, like the free market in goods generally, would assure that "human satisfaction as measured by aggregate consumer willingness to pay . . . is maximized."[72]

But significantly, Posner rejects this market solution for personal information. He believes it is appropriate "to assign the property right [in personal information] away from the individual";[73] people "should not . . . have a right to conceal material facts about themselves."[74] Why does he reject the free market solution?

Posner's test for creating a property right in a secret is whether the secret "encourag[es] investment in the production of socially valuable information."[75] Thus he favors the protection of trade and commercial secrets.[76] The question is "whether the information that he seeks to conceal is a product of significant investment," and I assume that this means significant *economic* investment.[77] Evidently, most personal information is not "a product of significant [economic] investment." (I note that Posner protects, as a general exception to the rule, the right of a "social host or hostess to conceal the recipe of a successful dinner."[78])

For Posner, personal information does not deserve protection because it does not involve economic investment and because concealment of personal information is, generally, a species of fraud. He says:

> We think it wrong (and inefficient) that the law should permit a seller in hawking his wares to make false or incomplete representations as to their quality. But people "sell" themselves as well as their goods. They profess high standards of behavior in order to induce others to engage in social or business dealings with them from which they derive an advantage but at the same time they conceal some of the facts that these acquaint-

---

[72] R. Posner, *supra* note 4, at 10. *See also* Posner, *supra* note 1, at 397.
[73] Posner, *supra* note 1, at 398.
[74] *Id.* at 399.
[75] *Id.* at 397.
[76] *Id.*
[77] *Id.* at 398
[78] *Id.* at 404.

ances would find useful in forming an accurate picture of their character. . . . [E]veryone should be allowed to protect himself from disadvantageous transactions by ferreting out concealed facts about individuals which are material to the representations (implicit or explicit) that those individuals make concerning their moral qualities.

. . . Why should [we] be asked to take . . . self-serving claims at face value and be prevented from obtaining the information necessary to verify or disprove these claims?[79]

Are these reasons for denying a property right in personal information economic reasons, reasons of public policy, or assessments of moral value? We must remember that Posner stated in *Economic Analysis of Law* that economics "cannot prescribe social change";[80] it can only tell us about the economic costs of managing it one way or another. I believe that when Posner argues that maintaining the privacy of personal information does not involve an investment in "socially valuable information," he is expressing a moral judgment, not an economic judgment. Economists can perhaps tell us the nature and extent of the investment but not whether it is "socially valuable." Posner, in making this judgment, is going "outside the market," "overruling" it, in fact, and telling us "how society should be managed."[81] The same is true of his characterization of the privacy of personal information as a species of commercial fraud. Both of these reasons for concluding that the law generally should not protect "facts about people"[82] are expressions of a social value judgment rather than implications or conclusions of economic theory. (Indeed, as I have already indicated, had Posner relied on his general economic theory he would have reached a contrary conclusion.[83])

Our society, in fact, places a very high value on maintaining individual privacy, even to the extent of concealing "discreditable" information and even though privacy is not the "product of significant [economic] investment." This social value, for instance, is embodied in the fifth amendment protection against self-incrimination. Even though Posner agrees that there are "reasons for not imposing a general legal duty of full and frank disclosure of

---

[79] *Id.* at 399-400.
[80] R. POSNER, *supra* note 4, at 10.
[81] R. POSNER, *supra* note 16, at 4. *See also* G. CALABRESI, *supra* note 40, at 19.
[82] Posner, *supra* note 1, at 404.
[83] R. POSNER, *supra* note 16, at 10. *See also* Posner, *supra* note 1, at ____.

442            *GEORGIA LAW REVIEW*            [Vol. 12:429

one's material personal shortcomings," he characterizes these reasons as "practical" ones.[84] To the contrary, they are fundamental moral reasons and reasons of social and political policy. As I have argued elsewhere, they involve the protection of individuality and human dignity, two of the highest values in the Judeo-Christian culture.[85]

It may be that Posner's fundamental error arises out of his attempt to distinguish privacy as an "instrumental" value from privacy as a "final" value.[86] Even if privacy of personal information sometimes serves the instrumental value of concealment for material advantage and involves little, if any, "significant [economic] investment," privacy is so integrally and inextricably related to the maintenance of personal dignity, an "ultimate" or "final" social value of extraordinary importance, that the law must also protect privacy; private information is indeed "socially valuable."[87] The social value of private information concealed for material gain, even if unimportant in terms of "significant [economic] investment," is so integrally and inextricably related to the social value of preserving our individuality and the integrity of our inner space or spiritual nature that the law cannot sacrifice one without sacrificing the other.

### C.   *Concealment as an Instrument of Individual Gain Is Only a Small Part of the Privacy We Seek*

I now turn to the difference between privacy as an instrumental value and privacy as a final or ultimate value. Posner admits that recognizing privacy as an ultimate value "would bring the economic analysis to a grinding halt."[88] Posner's treatment of privacy as a form of concealment, an instrumental value, does not "[capture] enough of the relevant reality"[89] to be very illuminating because, fundamentally, privacy is an ultimate value. His analysis, however, does not "come to a halt," but it is halting. The marketplace tells us something about social reality but far from everything and, frequently, far from enough.

Let us begin by looking at an incident which is not directly related to privacy. A minister recently published in a newspaper a letter to

---

[84] Posner, *supra* note 1, at 399-400.
[85] *See* Bloustein, *supra* note 50, at 1000-07. *See also* Bloustein, *supra* note 62, at 51-65.
[86] *See* text accompanying note 63 *supra.*
[87] *See* text accompanying note 75 *supra.*
[88] Posner, *supra* note 1, at 394.
[89] *Id.*

a burglar who had stolen antique jewelry belonging to the minister's wife. He told the burglar that the value of the jewelry "in dollars . . . is substantial."[90] But he went on to say that what the burglar had stolen was only a small part of what was there. "You now have the old ring Kristy's grandfather gave her grandmother in Norway before they came to America, with its tender engraved Norwegian message still clear. But you can never have the love, the memories that ring has symbolized for decades." The burglar had taken another engagement ring, but he did not have "the name inherited in the same family with loyalty and affection for generations." Nor could the burglar steal "the exciting experience of discovering" two Georgian rings in London on a spring dawn, or the "cherishing" that went with the tiny cross, or "the love," "the stories," and "the memories" associated with the other heirlooms he had taken. The minister concluded: "You have our finest things. But you can never have our treasures. They remain in our hearts, not locked, not protected, but there to share in love."

What more poignant insight could there be into the poverty of the marketplace as a countinghouse of social value![91] There are values associated with the goods we exchange in the marketplace which the exchange reflects either inadequately or not at all. As Posner recognizes,[92] there are also other values, the enjoyment of which does not deplete the available resource, values which are simply not part of any system of economic exchange.

A review of some privacy cases proves that concealment as an instrumental value is not central to the right of privacy and that the analysis of privacy as an exchangeable or market good is of limited value. In *De May v. Roberts*,[93] a woman sought recovery against a spectator at the birth of her child. In granting recovery, the court characterized the occasion of childbirth as "a most sacred one" upon which the law should allow no one to intrude "unless invited or because of some real and pressing necessity."[94] In the recent case

[90] N.Y. Times, Feb. 14, 1978, § at 35.

[91] I am grateful to my colleague, Dr. Paul Davidson, Chairman of the New Brunswick Department of Economics and Allied Sciences at Rutgers, the State University, for discussing with me some of the economic aspects of this paper, and, in particular, for pointing out Adam Smith's "paradox of value," the difference between value in use and value in exchange. My point here is not that the classical economists neglect this distinction; indeed, as I say in the text above, Posner recognizes it, even if not in express terms. My purpose is rather to examine the legal and social policy consequences of the distinction.

[92] R. POSNER, *supra* note 4, at 7.

[93] 46 Mich. 160, 9 N.W. 146 (1881).

[94] *Id.* at 165, 9 N.W. at 149.

of *Lamont v. United States*,[95] the plaintiff complained that the CIA and the FBI had opened and copied over one hundred pieces of his correspondence to and from various people in Russia and at least two love letters to his wife. The district court judge set damages at $2,000 and required the government to furnish "a suitable letter of regret." "The sums being awarded," said the court, "are in large measure symbolic. They probably substantially underestimate the deep sense of personal affront and psychic loss . . . . Certainly the wound to his sense of freedom and pride in our Constitution is enormous."[96] The general nature of the damage award—there is no suggestion that it rests on "opportunity costs"[97] or pecuniary loss—and, to an even greater degree, the requirement of a "letter of regret" are unique judicial indications that the values involved in *De May* were not marketplace values.

In the classic *Sidis* case,[98] the *New Yorker* published a profile of a man who had fervently wanted to preserve his anonymity. Although the profile was truthful, it was "merciless in its dissection of intimate details of its subject's personal life."[99] The *New Yorker* story had turned a private life into a public spectacle. Although the Second Circuit denied recovery on the ground that the subject was "newsworthy,"[100] Judge Clark remarked that the magazine's "ruthless disclosure" had "deprived [Sidis] of the seclusion of private life."[101]

Finally, in this brief sketch of prototypical cases, I note the case of *Roe v. Wade*,[102] in which the Supreme Court established as a privacy right protected under the Constitution the right of a woman to have an abortion. Citing a long line of decisions, the Court described the right to privacy as an aspect of "the concept of ordered liberty" and declared that it extended to activities relating to mar-

---

[95] ___ F. Supp. ___ (E.D.N.Y. 1978).

[96] *Id.* at ___. *Cf.* United States v. Van Leeuwen, 397 U.S. 249, 251 (1970) (quoting Ex parte Jackson, 96 U.S. 727, 733 (1878)) (fourth amendment guarantee against unreasonable searches and seizures protects letters and sealed packages from warrantless inspections).

[97] R. POSNER, *supra* note 4, at 7.

[98] Sidis v. F-R Publishing Corp., 113 F.2d 806 (2d Cir. 1940).

[99] *Id.* at 807.

[100] *Id.* at 809. Posner notes in passing that the *New Yorker* could have established the "newsworthiness" of the Sidis story without using Sidis's real name although he does not adopt this suggestion. Posner, *supra* note 1, at 417. But I do. *See* Bloustein, *supra* note 62, at 66-68.

[101] 113 F.2d at 808.

[102] 410 U.S. 113 (1973). For a full typology, see Comment, *A Taxonomy of Privacy: Repose, Sanctuary, and Intimate Decision*, 64 CAL. L. REV. 1447 (1976).

riage, procreation, contraception, family relationships, and child rearing and education.[103]

This taxonomy of privacy cases, including intrusion into private space, public spectacle, mass disclosure, and intimate personal choice, establishes two important propositions. First, people do not always conceal information for personal economic benefit. Second, the quest for privacy does not always involve concealment. The woman seeking seclusion from strangers while giving birth and the man writing love letters to his wife are not seeking privacy to gain economic advantage. Nor were the intruders present in the delivery room or examining the letters to gain financial benefit. In both cases the value involved was not a market or exchange value. The birth case involved what the court called a "sacred" occasion; the defendant had defiled the warm, loving, and cherished intimacy of giving birth.[104] No one could buy or sell this value, any more than a thief could steal the emotional, religious, and sentimental values associated with heirlooms. In the case of the Lamont letters, there was "despicable" prying into the "shared intimacies of husband and wife," "personal affront," and "a wound to [Lamont's] sense of freedom and pride in our Constitution."[105] Again, no one can buy or sell these values.

Moreover, it is characteristic of these values that if a party consents, upon receipt of a reward or benefit, to intrusion by others, the consent does not transfer the protected value; it simply destroys it.[106] A mother can sell tickets to others to watch the delivery of her child, and a husband can sell his love letters, but in each case the parties do not exchange what had been the value to the transferor; the sale destroys that value.

It is significant that Posner recognizes that in *Sidis*[107] there was no "potential misrepresentation" because Sidis was a recluse and his "craving for privacy was so extreme as to reduce to a very low level his dealings with other people."[108] In other words, Sidis did not seek to "manipulate the world around [him]" by concealment or misrepresentation. Nor for the same reasons did the *New Yorker* profile produce "information useful to people contemplating dealing

---

[103] 410 U.S. at 152-53.

[104] De May v. Roberts, 46 Mich. 160, 165, 9 N.W. 146, 149 (1881).

[105] Lamont v. United States, ___ F. Supp. ___ (D. ___ 1978).

[106] For an exception in the "commercial appropriation" cases, see text accompanying notes 117-27 *infra*.

[107] 113 F.2d 806 (2d Cir. 1940).

[108] Posner, *supra* note 1, at 416-17.

with Sidis."[109] What then was the value of Sidis's maintaining his anonymity? Posner does not say. But if it was not a marketplace or an instrumental value, it must have been a final or ultimate value, and in Posner's terms, "this [should] bring the economic analysis to a grinding halt."[110]Instead of "halting," however, Posner, without recognizing or admitting it, resorts to a judgment of social value which he disguises as an economic judgment by alluding to it as an assessment of external costs and benefits.[111]

The economic theory suffers a similar embarrassment because of Posner's argument that the law should prevent the publication of a dead rape victim's name[112] and that publishers of a story on human ugliness should pay for the use of a picture of a person whose nose is deformed.[113] In both instances the concealment serves no instrumental purpose. No misrepresentation to gain an advantageous relationship is involved, and the prying or disclosure presents no occasion for a benefit. The concealment or privacy sought must serve some noneconomic interest, just as it does in the childbirth, the love letter, and *Sidis* cases.

The second proposition that my sketch of privacy cases demonstrates is that privacy does not always involve a form of concealment. Posner does not believe that Sidis was concealing or misrepresenting his identity for economic gain.[114] There is thus no economic or instrumental value. I believe that Sidis desired only not to be turned into a public spectacle. It is one thing for a few neighbors and friends to know Sidis as a child prodigy and mathematical genius; it is another for mass publicity to turn him into a public spectacle.

Sidis's few neighbors, rare acquaintances, and employers knew the little bit about him that they needed to know. He did not hide anything from them to their detriment and his benefit. He just did not want to be in the public limelight; he felt that if hundreds of thousands of people knew the details of his life he would be debased and would feel that he was less than the man he wanted to be. The *New Yorker* story threatened ultimate values such as his sense of self-esteem and individuality.

---

[109] *Id.* at 416.

[110] *Id.* at 394.

[111] *See* text accompanying note 40 *supra*.

[112] Posner, *supra* note 1, at 417.

[113] *Id.* at 413.

[114] *See* text accompanying note 107 *supra*.

Similarly, concealment is not the issue in *Roe v. Wade*[115] and other privacy cases in which the courts extended constitutional protection to intimate personal choices. Rather, the issue is personal liberty. These cases are linked to the Warren-Brandeis tradition and to cases involving intrusion into private space and publication of private facts, *not* because they represent an attempt to manipulate people by misrepresentation or concealment, but because they involve protection of the same underlying value—inner space, a person's spiritual nature, and individual liberty. Private choice—what John Stuart Mill called "self-regarding acts,"[116]—keeping others out of your private space—freedom from surveillance or intrusion, and avoiding being turned into a public spectacle assure individualism and self-esteem.

The self-esteem which flows from privacy is a value which is unique to the individual and is not capable of exchange. Indeed, when an intruder invades another's privacy, he does not take away what the victim loses, because self-esteem cannot be transferred. When a person's decision to use contraception is not her own, she loses self-esteem, and no one gains self-esteem as a result. The same loss occurs when an individual intrudes upon another's private space or makes a public spectacle of another's private life. These are instances of an ultimate value quite different from the instrumental value of concealment of facts.

## D. *The Appropriation Cases*

Thus far, I have dealt with two of the four privacy categories which Dean Prosser established[117]—intrusion and publication of private facts—and which Posner treats in his economic analysis of privacy. (I shall not deal with the so-called false light cases here, because they are of relatively little significance to understanding privacy.[118]) I now turn to the appropriation cases which, in my view, provides no more support for Posner's analysis than the intrusion or publicity cases.

In addition to the numerous statutes which protect a person's name or likeness from unauthorized commercial use, many cases uphold the right to prevent appropriation.[119] Many plaintiffs in

---

[115] 410 U.S. 113, 152-53 (1973).

[116] J. MILL, UTILITARIANISM, LIBERTY, AND REPRESENTATIVE GOVERNMENT 176-200 (1968).

[117] Prosser, *supra* note 49.

[118] I dealt with these cases in my article on Prosser. *See* Bloustein, *supra* note 50, at 991-93.

[119] *Id.* at 985-91.

these cases were not adverse to publicity—they are not like the unfortunate Mr. Sidis—but rather avidly sought publicity. They only wanted to be compensated for the commercial use of their name or likeness. Posner argues that the award of damages in these cases rests on "a perfectly good economic reason"; it "assures that the advertiser to whom the photograph is most valuable will purchase it."[120]

There are a number of weaknesses in this argument. First, is a name or likeness a "scarce resource," subject to the laws of the marketplace? In economic terms, the commercial use of a name costs the owner nothing; in Posner's economic terms, there is no "alternative price," no "opportunity cost" to the use of a name.[121] The same is true of the multiple use of a photograph; once a business takes and uses the photograph, its use by other advertisers would not cost the subject of the photograph a penny.

It may be true, as Posner argues, that the multiple use of the identical photograph (or name) "would reduce its advertising value, perhaps to zero."[122] But the creation of this advertising value is not founded on competition among bidders for a scarce resource; rather, it is founded on the law which artificially creates a scarcity by giving the individual a property right in its use. This is very different from the normal marketplace situation involving truly scarce resources.

A second reason for disputing Posner's view of these cases is that the courts apply a theory of damages which bears little or no relationship to the commercial value of the "property" concerned. Thus in *Fairfield v. American Photocopy Equipment Co.*, the court said, "[t]he fact that damages resulting from an invasion of the right of privacy cannot be measured by a pecuniary standard is not

---

[120] Posner, *supra* note 1, at 411.

[121] R. POSNER, *supra* note 4, at 6-8. It is significant that Posner likens the use of a name or likeness for advertising purposes to subscription-list cases, in which the question is whether individuals should have the right to control who uses their names on a subscription list. In purely economic terms, the use of a name on multiple subscription lists does not cost the individual anything, just as the use of his name in advertising does not cost him anything. Yet, Posner gives a property interest in the use of the name on a subscription list to the holder of the list, rather than to the individual, and takes a contrary view of the use of the name in advertising. Posner, *supra* note 1, at 411. The difference, Posner says, is based on the cost to the user of seeking consent ("transaction cost"). He says, "[subscription] lists are generally worth more to the purchasers than being shielded from possible unwanted solicitations is worth to the subscribers." *Id.* at 398. I take this to be a judgment of social policy, not economics. I believe the fundamental basis for the difference in the subscription list and advertising cases is that the injury to self-esteem, a social value, is vastly different in the two cases.

[122] *Id.* at 411.

a bar to recovery."[123] Courts generally allow the plaintiff to recover general rather than special damages reasoning that the injury is to the person and not to property.[124] In *Fairfield* the court characterized the cause of action as "a direct wrong of a personal character."[125] And in *Pavesich v. New England Life Insurance Co.,* the earliest of these cases, upon which courts have relied again and again as precedent in subsequent cases, the Georgia Supreme Court ordered the defendant to compensate the plaintiff for use of his photograph in an advertisement because "his liberty has been taken away from him," "he is no longer free," and "he is in reality a slave without hope of freedom, held to service by a merciless master."[126]

The classification of the interest protected as a personal rather than a property interest explains the award of substantial damages to people whose names and likenesses have little, if any, commercial value. People have a right to protect their dignity and self-esteem from debasement by unauthorized commercial exploitation of their names or likenesses. This does not mean that the law "forbid[s] a man to use his photograph"[127] (an opinion which Posner attributes to me). It means only that a person can consent to the use of his photograph if he wishes to but that no one can use it without his consent. And once he gives his consent, he obviates the injury, what would otherwise be a demeaning blow to dignity.

Finally, I note that once one establishes a personal right to a name and likeness in terms of the values and interests that I have described, a commercial market in the name and likeness can grow and flourish. A name and likeness can only command a commercial price in a society that permits a person to control the conditions under which he may use his name and likeness for commercial purposes.

### E. *Gossip and Newspapers: Posner vs. Warren and Brandeis*

Posner's review of noneconomic theories of privacy is, as he admits, "incomplete."[128] He deals with my views,[129] Fried's,[130] Greena-

---

[123] 138 Cal. App. 2d 82, 88, 291 P.2d 194, 198 (1955).
[124] *See* Bloustein, *supra* note 50.
[125] 138 Cal. App. 2d 82, 86, 291 P.2d 194, 197 (1955).
[126] 122 Ga. 190, 220, 50 S.E. 68, 80 (1905).
[127] Posner, *supra* note 1, at 411.
[128] *Id.* at 409.
[129] *Id.* at 407-08.
[130] *Id.* at 408.

walt's, and Noam's,[131] each in a scant paragraph or two. It would serve no useful function to review these critiques because they are so brief and conclusory. An analysis of Posner's criticism of Warren and Brandeis, however, will result in some appreciation of his method of dealing with those with whom he differs and the character of his understanding and the soundness of his criticism of the noneconomic literature on privacy.

Posner begins by taking Warren and Brandeis to task for making too much of the phenomenon of "idle curiosity."[132] Warren and Brandeis wrote dispairingly and disparagingly about the widespread and growing influence of gossip in our culture.[133] Kalven observed that their attack on gossip had "a curious nineteenth century quaintness" about it which he felt was at odds with "the more robust tastes or mores of today."[134] Whether or not one agrees completely with Kalven that our tastes have changed, it is safe to say that there is a prissiness to the Warren and Brandeis appraisal of gossip that reflects their Boston Brahman culture and, perhaps, the circumstances under which they wrote the article.[135]

But Posner goes far beyond this criticism. He puts forth a novel—bizarre might be a more appropriate description—theory of gossip. He says, "gossip columns recount the personal lives of wealthy and successful people whose tastes and habits offer models—that is, yield information—to the ordinary person in making consumption, career, and other decisions."[136] He then observes that the very notion of "idle curiosity" is "misleading" because "[p]eople are not given to random, undifferentiated curiosity."[137] What proof is there of this? The proof, he says, is that "there [is] less curiosity about the lives of the poor (as measured, for example, by the frequency with which poor people figure as central characters in novels) than about those of the rich . . . . [T]he lives of the poor do not provide as much useful information in patterning our own lives."[138]

Posner makes no reference in the exposition of this theory to a single psychological, sociological, or newspaper study. Indeed, he

---

[131] *Id.* at 408-09.

[132] *Id.* at 395.

[133] Warren & Brandeis, *supra* note 9, at 196.

[134] Kalven, *Privacy in Tort Law—Were Warren and Brandeis Wrong?*, 31 LAW & CONTEMP. PROB. 326, 329 (1966).

[135] A. MASON, BRANDEIS: A FREE MAN'S LIFE 70 (1946).

[136] Posner, *supra* note 1, at 395-96.

[137] *Id.* at 396.

[138] *Id.*

makes no reference to any empirical evidence. Do gossip columns really "recount the personal lives of wealthy and successful people" in any significant sense? Do they really "yield information" useful "in making consumption, career, and other decisions"? Does *all* curiosity serve a useful function? *Is* there less curiosity about the lives of the poor than of the rich? Do poor people "figure as central characters in novels" less frequently than wealthy ones?

I cannot offer well-supported answers to any of these questions. On the basis of my experience with newspapers and literature, however, I strongly doubt the accuracy of Posner's answers. Even if there were no other basis for doubting the answers, the characteristically cavalier mode of Posner's assertions alone causes grave skepticism if not outright rejection.

The same is true with respect to Posner's attack on Warren and Brandeis's view of the press. Warren and Brandeis thought the press was "overstepping . . . the obvious bounds of propriety and of decency," destroying "robustness of thought and delicacy of feeling" and "lowering . . . social standards and . . . morality."[139] They also thought that the supply of this debasing gossip, catering to people's "prurient tastes," created the demand.[140] Posner argues that supply does not create demand and that the newspaper is merely "an alternative method" of prying which is available in less wealthy societies to inform people "about how others live."[141] "A legitimate and important function of the press," he says, "is to provide specialization in prying in societies where the costs of obtaining information have become too great for the Nosey Parker."[142] It would take extended argument and proof to satisfy me that this conclusion about the function of the press in society is correct; Posner offers none.

I readily admit that some courts and commentators have uncritically worshipped the Warren and Brandeis article and that Warren and Brandeis's attack on the press not only reflected a certain personal prissiness but also a lack of detailed and systematic observation of the influence of the press. But Posner's offer of an alternative theory of gossip and the press with such a flimsy analytical basis and his conclusion that the Warren and Brandeis analysis "is based on a series of unsupported and implausible empirical propositions"

---

[139] Warren & Brandeis, *supra* note 9, at 196.
[140] *Id.*
[141] Posner, *supra* note 1, at 397.
[142] *Id.*

452        *GEORGIA LAW REVIEW*        [Vol. 12:429

seems to me at the very least to be a case of the pot calling the kettle black.

### CONCLUSION

My conclusion is not that Posner's economic analysis of the law of privacy is wrong, but that it is pretentious and immodest; he claims to answer more questions than he actually answers, and many of the answers he does provide are not supported by his economic and legal evidence and reasoning. He convincingly argues that there is an economic motive for concealment of personal information, an argument which most, if not all, writers in the field have neglected. People do conceal personal information and seek privacy in order to manipulate those with whom they are socially involved. Other people pry so that those who conceal or misrepresent personal information cannot manipulate them.

Posner also offers a persuasive economic argument for prohibiting certain forms of surveillance.[143] His argument on this ground is not, however, a novel one,[144] and that is why I have not dealt with it in the body of this Article. Nevertheless, I should say that Posner's economic perspective on this aspect of privacy is valuable indeed and adds substantial support to views other commentators have already expressed.

The main weaknesses of Posner's theory are those which, I believe, he suspects but underestimates. Like other economists, he recognizes that the concept of "external" costs and benefits is an invitation to go outside the marketplace, outside the scope of economic analysis and into the arena of public policy and social ethics. There is no intellectual harm in this, especially since Posner acknowledges the conceptual flaw in the concept of "external" costs and benefits. The difficulty, however, is that his analysis runs contrary to his admission. Again and again he assumes the role of social critic without acknowledging that he is changing intellectual hats, and sometimes he assumes the role of a critic while giving every appearance that he is still acting as the objective, mathematically precise, market price-oriented economist.

A second source of error in Posner's analysis of privacy is his overemphasis on concealment or misrepresentation. Admittedly, concealment or misrepresentation is one of the instrumental values

---

[143] *Id.* at 401.

[144] A. WESTIN, *supra* note 62, at 370 (1967).

which privacy serves. But it is *only one* instrumental value; others include the use of privacy as a condition of creativity of thought and artistic creation and its importance as a condition of forthright and effective social and intellectual communication.[145] Moreover, there are important noninstrumental or ultimate values which privacy serves, the most important of which are a sense of individuality and human dignity.[146] Again, although Posner recognizes the distinction between instrumental and ultimate values and that economic analysis cannot cope successfully with ultimate values, his analysis outruns his sense of limitation and fails to take due account of these distinctions. In sum, Posner's economic analysis of privacy bites off more than it can intellectually chew and leaves untouched much of what a comprehensive theory should consummate.

---

[145] *See* Bloustein, *supra* note 57, at 221-22.
[146] *See* Bloustein, *supra* note 50, at 1000-07. *See also* Bloustein, *supra* note 62.

# Name Index